THE SPANISH BACKGROUND OF AMERICAN LITERATURE

Volume One

Sor Juana Inés de la Cruz in her Library,
from the painting by **Miguel** Cabrera, 1750, from a self-portrait.

The Spanish Background

OF AMERICAN LITERATURE

STANLEY T. WILLIAMS, *Sterling Professor*
of American Literature and Fellow of Calhoun College
in Yale University

Volume One

New Haven: YALE UNIVERSITY PRESS, 1955

London: Geoffrey Cumberlege, Oxford University Press

To M.L.R.W.

.   .   . *por quien yo vivo* .   .   .

DON QUIXOTE II, 32.

PREFACE

ALTHOUGH this book includes no formal bibliographies, the detailed references in the notes to Spanish books and to American books and manuscripts dealing with Spanish themes will, I hope, aid further study of the relations between the literatures of Europe and of the Americas. I shall not list here the numerous special studies or bibliographical articles in magazines which I have found helpful. Allusions to these will be found in the notes. I wish merely to acknowledge my general indebtedness, for suggestions and points of departure, to the following bibliographies and literary histories which throw light directly or indirectly on the problem of Spanish influences on American literature:

Fernand Baldensperger and W. P. Friederich, *Bibliography of Comparative Literature* (Chapel Hill, 1950).

Arturo Farinelli, "España y su literatura en el extranjero," *Ensayos y discursos de critica literaria hispano-europea* (Roma [1925]), *1*, 45–108.

J. H. Fisher, "Serial Bibliographies in the Modern Languages and Literatures," *PMLA, 66*, No. 3 (April, 1951), 138–56.

James Fitzmaurice-Kelly, *The Relations between Spanish and English Literature* (Liverpool, 1910).

R. L. Grismer and others, *A Bibliography of Articles on Spanish Literature* (Minneapolis, 1933).

R. L. Grismer, *A Bibliography of Articles and Essays on the Literatures of Spain and Spanish America* (Minneapolis, 1935).

Martin Hume, *Spanish Influence on English Literature* (London, 1905).

S. E. Leavitt, *Hispano-American Literature in the United States* (Cambridge, Mass., 1932).

R. U. Pane, *English Translations from the Spanish, 1484–1943* (New York, 1944).

Miguel Romera-Novarro, *El hispanismo en Norte-América* (Madrid [1917]).

Rudolph Schevill, "Spanish and Portuguese Literature," *The World through Literature,* ed. C. G. Laird (New York [1951]), pp. 295–331.

Coney Sturgis, *The Spanish World in English Fiction* (Boston, 1927).

I believe that the data in these guides combined with the supplementary detail in the present book will provide an extensive bibliographical definition of Spanish and Spanish-American influences on the culture of the United States.

The notes are arranged numerically within each chapter and may be used readily by turning from the chapter headings in the text to the corresponding ones in the notes. For frequently cited books and articles the following short titles have been used:

B. H.   *The Writings of Bret Harte,* Autograph Edition ([Boston, Houghton Mifflin & Co., 1896–1914]).

CHAL   The Cambridge History of American Literature (New York, G. P. Putnam's Sons, 1917–21).

C of M   W. H. Prescott, *History of the Conquest of Mexico* (New York, Harper and Bros., 1843) .

C of P   W. H. Prescott, *History of the Conquest of Peru* (New York, Harper and Bros., 1847).

Charvat   *William Hickling Prescott: Representative Selections,* ed. William Charvat and Michael Kraus (New York, American Book Co. [1943]).

DAB   Dictionary of American Biography (New York, C. Scribner's Sons, 1943–44).

Duyck.   E. A. and G. L. Duyckinck, *Cyclopedia of American Literature,* ed. M. L. Simons (Philadelphia, T. E. Zell, 1875).

F & I   W. H. Prescott, *History of the Reign of Ferdinand and Isabella, the Catholic,* 2d ed. (Boston, American Stationers' Co., 1838).

G. T.   *Life, Letters, and Journals of George Ticknor* (Boston, J. R. Osgood & Co., 1876.

G. T.'s Travels   George Ticknor's Travels in Spain, ed. G. T. Northup ([Toronto, University of Toronto], 1913).

H. M.   *The Works of Herman Melville*, Standard Edition ([London, Constable, 1922–24]).

H. W. B.   H. W. Bentley, *A Dictionary of Spanish Terms in English* (New York, Columbia University Press, 1932).

H. W. L.   *The Works of Henry Wadsworth Longfellow*, ed. Samuel Longfellow ([Boston, Houghton Mifflin & Co., 1886–91]).

Harrison   *Bret Harte: Representative Selections*, ed. J. B. Harrison (New York, American Book Co. [1941]).

Heiser   M. F. Heiser, "Cervantes in the United States," *Hispanic Review, 15* (Oct., 1947), 409–35.

Helman   E. F. Helman, "Early Interest in Spanish in New England (1815–1835)," *Hispania, 29* (Aug., 1946), 329–51.

I. L. W.   I. L. Whitman, *Longfellow and Spain* (New York, Instituto de las Españas en los Estados Unidos, 1927).

J. F.-K.   James Fitzmaurice-Kelly, *The Relations between Spanish and English Literature* (Liverpool, University Press, 1910).

J. R. L.   *The Works of James Russell Lowell*, Standard Library Edition ([Boston, Houghton Mifflin & Co., 1890–92]).

L. T.   Lawrance Thompson, *Young Longfellow (1807–1843)* (New York, Macmillan Co., 1938).

Miscellanies   W. H. Prescott, *Biographical and Critical Miscellanies* (New-York, Harper and Bros., 1845).

NAR   North American Review.

P. M. I.   P. M. Irving, *The Life and Letters of Washington Irving* (New York, G. P. Putnam, 1862–64).

Penney I   *George Ticknor; Letters to Pascual de Gayangos from the Originals in the Collection of the Hispanic Society of America*, ed. C. L. Penney (New York, Printed by Order of the Trustees, 1927).

Penney II   *Prescott; Unpublished Letters to Gayangos in the Library of the Hispanic Society of America*, ed. C. L. Penney (New York, Printed by Order of the Trustees, 1927).

Philip II   W. H. Prescott, *History of the Reign of Philip the Second, King of Spain* (Boston, Phillips, Sampson & Co., 1855–58).

R.-N.   Miguel Romera-Navarro, *El hispanismo en Norte-América* (Madrid, Renacimiento [1917]).

R. W. E.   *The Complete Works of Ralph Waldo Emerson,* ed. E. W. Emerson ([Boston, Houghton Mifflin & Co., 1903–04]).

S. L.   Samuel Longfellow, *Life of Henry Wadsworth Longfellow* (Boston, Ticknor & Co., 1886).

S. T. W.   S. T. Williams, *The Life of Washington Irving* (New York, Oxford University Press, 1935).

Spanish Travels   W. D. Howells, *Familiar Spanish Travels* (New York, Harper & Bros., 1913).

Spiller   *Literary History of the United States,* ed. R. E. Spiller and others (New York, Macmillan Co., 1948).

W. W.   *The Complete Writings of Walt Whitman* (New York, G. P. Putnam's Sons [1902]).

Williams and Edge   S. T. Williams and M. A. Edge, *A Bibliography of the Writings of Washington Irving* (New York, Oxford University Press, 1935).

Wolcott   *The Correspondence of William Hickling Prescott, 1833–1847,* ed. Roger Wolcott (Boston, Houghton Mifflin & Co., 1925).

Other titles, less recurrent but needing citation in the notes more than once, have been reproduced in full detail (author, title, place, date, volume, page, etc.) at their first appearance in the book. In subsequent references to the same work only enough of the author's name and title is repeated to identify the work and to prevent confusion with others by the same person. The form of the notes is based upon the style sheet recently issued by the Modern Language Association of America. For reasons inherent in the book's organization (see Introduction) it has been necessary to discuss in different sections of the book topics which in themselves are interesting to specialists, notably Cervantes in America, Spanish drama in the Southwest, Alhambraism, or translations. Cross references (and the Index) should enable the reader to follow his own particular interests without difficulty.

The large number of magazine articles which have been cited, particularly in the chapter on the writers for the periodicals, has made it inadvisable to include abbreviations for them in the short-title list. Those which have been used are familiar, but in case of doubt they can be identified in Lewis Leary, *Articles on American Literature Appearing in Current Periodicals* (Durham, N. C., 1947), the *American Bibliography* of the Modern Language Association, *Poole's Index to Periodical Literature,* the *Readers' Guide to Periodical Literature,* and the other indexes published by the H. W. Wilson Co.

In addition, the following abbreviations have been used to indicate the location of manuscripts which have been cited in this work:

B. P. L.   Boston Public Library, Boston, Mass.

C.   Columbia University Library, New York City.

D. C.   Ticknor Collection, Dartmouth College Library, Hanover, N. H.

H.   Harvard University Library, Cambridge, Mass.

L. H.   Longfellow House, Cambridge, Mass.

M. H. S.   Massachusetts Historical Society, Boston, Mass.

N. A.   Diplomatic Dispatches, Spain, General Records of the Department of State, National Archives, Washington, D. C.

N. Y. H. S.   New-York Historical Society, New York City.

N. Y. P. L.   New York Public Library, New York City.

O.   Antonio Osborne, Puerto de Santa María, Spain.

S. C.   South Caroliniana Library, University of South Carolina, Columbia, S. C.

T. T. P. L.   T. T. Payne Luquer, Bedford, N. Y.

W. C.   Chapin Library, Williams College, Williamstown, Mass.

Y.   Yale University Library, New Haven, Conn.

Throughout the book, and particularly in Part III, I have relied upon manuscript materials. These are especially rich in the Washington Irving Collection at Yale University, the George Ticknor Collection at Dartmouth College, the Prescott Collection at the Massachusetts Historical Society, and the Goddard-Roslyn Collection of Bryant in the New York Public Library. I have also had access to the letters and journals in the Longfellow House at Cambridge, Massachusetts, and the letters of Lowell and Howells in the Houghton Library of Harvard University. Whenever possible I have used the original manuscript rather than the printed book, and I have drawn on many unpublished documents which illustrate Spanish patterns in American literature, particularly in the writings of individual authors. One example is the remarkable letter of Longfellow to Ticknor describing his experiences in the teaching of Romance languages (see p. 182). In the transcription of these manuscripts I have retained the original spelling and punctuation even when this principle meant occasionally the perpetuation of errors.

The application of this principle of exact transcription has created problems in the use of Spanish written accents. In preference to the normalizing and standardizing of all accents, I have in every case followed meticulously the original. This procedure has resulted in seeming but not actual inconsistencies, as in the spelling of Calderón both with and without an accent, perhaps even in the same paragraph. The reader should remember this principle when he encounters Spanish titles and names without proper accents. The originals of these names and titles may be in an American magazine article which omitted all accents whatsoever or from a story by Bret Harte who accented only two or three words with a peculiar regularity. The reader should bear this principle in mind also when he encounters eccentric accenting, as in passages from books published before the appearance of the *Diccionario* of the Real Academia Española in 1899, or when he notices the overaccenting for phonetic purposes in the texts of Francis Sales. I cannot hope to have avoided all mistakes, but my aim has been fidelity to the work which I quote. I have translated passages from foreign languages when they are quoted in the text, except in a few phrases retained for the special meanings or connotations which they seem to convey ("leyenda negra"). In notes I have kept the originals. Anglicized place names (Cádiz) have not been accented.

The terms "Hispanic" or "Latin-American" (or "Latin America") are seldom used in this book. "Hispanic" is merely an Anglicized form of the old Latin word for Spain. When "Latin-American" occurs, it may refer to any one or to all of the countries in the Western Hemisphere in which one of the Romance tongues is the national language. The term "Spanish-American" has been employed as the standard term of reference for any or all of the countries in which Spanish is the primary language, and it has sometimes been used in referring to certain regions now within the boundaries of the United States (Florida, Texas, New Mexico, Arizona, or California). Occasionally in alluding in general statements to South America the distinction is difficult to make, but ordinarily the substitution of "Latin-American" for "Spanish-American" implies an inclusion of Brazil or of some country in which Spanish is not the dominant language.

I wish to express my indebtedness here to the following publishers and other individuals for permission to quote published material: Richard H. Bassett; B. T. Batsford Ltd.; John Dos Passos; Doubleday & Co., Inc.; Henry Grattan Doyle; Duell, Sloan & Pearce, Inc.; Harper & Bros.; Harvard University Press; William Heinemann, Ltd.; The Hispanic Society of America; Houghton Mifflin & Co.; Miss Mildred Howells; Liveright Publishing Corporation; Orie W. Long; The Macmillan Co.; Princeton University Library; and Miguel Romera-Navarro.

In making my acknowledgments for aid in the preparation of a work which has occupied me at intervals for almost twenty years, I need not summon up from my memory or from my notes the names of every friend and colleague who has stimulated and encouraged me. Their kindnesses come vividly to mind as I review each chapter in this book. Since I cannot record all their names and all their particular services, they will forgive me, I believe, if there are omissions. I have already thanked them by word or letter, but let me mention again: Theodore Andersson; George W. Arms; José J. Arrom; Leonard Bacon; Mrs. Otis A. Bacon; Turpin C. Bannister; Alfred H. Barr Jr.; John I. H. Baur; Richmond C. Beatty; Thomas G. Bergin; Harry Bernstein; Bradford A. Booth; William Cullen Bryant; Edwin H. Cady; Jean Charlot; William Charvat; George P. Clark; Harry H. Clark; Philip B. Daghlian; Eugene A. Davidson; Norman V. Donaldson; Thomas H. de Valcourt; John Dos Passos; Joseph Downs; T. C. Duncan Eaves; John E. Englekirk; Aurelio M. Espinosa Jr.; Waldo Frank; Werner P. Friederich; Edgar S. Furniss; Donald C. Gallup; William M. Gibson; William H. Gilman; Charles I. Glicksberg; Conrad G.

Goddard; George H. Hamilton; Talbot F. Hamlin; George P. Hammond; Lewis U. Hanke; Thomas R. Hart Jr.; Hoffman R. Hays; Wilson L. Heflin; Merrill F. Heiser; Ernest H. Hespelt; Henry R. Hitchcock; J. Leslie Hotson; Leon Howard; William D. Howells II; Harold S. Jantz; Hampton M. Jarrell; Carl L. Johnson; William H. Jordy; Miss Hazel E. Joslyn; Miss Katherine C. Kane; Fiske Kimball; George A. Kubler; Leonard W. Labaree; Clay Lancaster; Jay Leyda; Thomas O. Mabbott; Dumas Malone; Mrs. Joseph T. Marinan; Señorita Enriqueta Martín y Ortiz de la Tabla; Edwin S. Morby; Hugh Morrison; Kenneth B. Murdock; Mrs. Mary C. Simms Oliphant; Thomas M. Pearce; Norman H. Pearson; Henry F. Pommer; Chandler R. Post; Miss Louise Pound; F. Stephen Reckert; Frank J. Roos; Hugh G. Rowell; Leo Schrade; Merton M. Sealts; José Luis Sert; Miss Barbara D. Simison; Bruce Simonds; Robert C. Smith; James T. Soby; Robert E. Spiller; Miss Edna P. Stauffer; Randall Stewart; Frederick S. Stimson; Richard G. Valeriani; Stanley M. Vogel; Russell L. Voisin; Walter M. Whitehill; Julien T. Williams; Samuel Wilson Jr.; James L. Woodress Jr.

In addition to the libraries mentioned on page xi of this Preface, I have received assistance from the following libraries and institutions: the Bowdoin College Library; the Hayes Memorial Library; the Henry E. Huntington Library; the Hispanic Society of America; and the Metropolitan Museum of Fine Arts. I am indebted to the Library of Congress not merely for materials used in this book but for a grant-in-aid which made possible my months of study in Mexico in the year 1947.

I wish to express my appreciation to Miss Dorothy W. Bridgwater, Assistant Reference Librarian in Yale University, for her aid under many difficulties in the preparation of this manuscript. Finally, let me repeat my gratitude to my friend R. Selden Rose for reading the manuscript. I believe that much of his wisdom is in this book, but its errors are entirely mine.

CONTENTS

INTRODUCTION

I REMEMBER, more years ago than I care to specify, looking down from the roof of a house in the little town of Puerto de Santa María, Spain, upon the plain where Roderick the Goth, so said tradition, had fought the Moors. About a century earlier than my visit Washington Irving had meditated day after day on this identical scene, and here in this house he had written parts of his *Conquest of Granada*. At this time and later, as I concluded a biography of this American author, I reflected on the deep, compulsive influence upon Irving of Spanish music, painting, architecture, and, of course, literature. From the moment that he first crossed the border at Irún in 1825, we may perceive a new temper both in his life and in his writing. Although never excited by what are called in the graduate schools literary "influences," I thought this sensitivity of Irving to Leocadia Zamora, Murillo, the Tower of Comares, or Cervantes extremely provocative. In fact, I wondered a little if some day the story of our first man of letters should not be retold in the light of his three long books and his many essays on Spain, a story enriched perhaps by a detailed consideration of his seven and a half years of residence in the Peninsula.

This temptation to write a "Spanish life" of Irving I have not wholly overcome, as the present book (Part III, Chapter 1) demonstrates. Moreover, I have offended still further. I have told the stories of seven other men of letters in their relationships with the culture of Spain, using the word "culture" as meaning, according to Merriam's *Webster*, the enlightenment and refinement of taste acquired by intellectual and aesthetic training. I have done this and I have prefaced these biographies by six definitions of backgrounds or mediums for the transmission of this culture in order to make the special studies of these authors attain their full implications. For as I sensed the vitality of Spain in Irving's literary and artistic life I soon saw that in different ways a similar spell had been laid upon George Ticknor and William Hickling Prescott; upon the poets Bryant, Longfellow, and Lowell; and upon the creators of fiction, Bret Harte and William Dean Howells. All these belonged to the "Golden Day," not merely of American literature itself but of some more or less united group eager to plunder for the young Republic the cultural riches of Spain. Almost before I knew it, I found myself involved in the larger, more puzzling problem of the precise debts to Spain of the entire literature of the United States.

THIS TOTAL debt is less overwhelming than to England, to France, or to Germany, and it is also less significant, at least quantitatively. Nevertheless, for American men of letters the fascination of Spain has in some ways exceeded that of other European countries, hardly excepting England itself. The importance of this Spanish influence is substantial, and I hope that this book may prove to be the *first complete record of one of the great Continental influences upon our literature.* Perhaps also it will offer incidental aid to others exploring the French, Italian, and German backgrounds, for it has been impossible not to poach upon the vaster areas of these other influences. In any case, my aim has been to take a step forward in the analysis of European patterns in a literature which is, after all is said of the frontier, a transplanted literature. No literature stands alone. To understand it we must know related literatures, and this fact is especially true of our own, which is so manifestly a child of Europe. The literary historian who has watched during the second quarter of the present century the astonishing multiplication of our books of self-appraisal (bibliographies, biographies, journals, letters) can hardly believe that we shall not eventually set all these European influences in their proper critical perspective. Toward this end I hope that this book may contribute.

Although I never shared the common belief that Spanish culture has left few traces on our literature, I began this study convinced that, compared with the French and German cultures, it would prove compact, more manageable. The literature of Spain seems slight in scope if placed beside that of France or Germany, and such intensive centers of influence as Irving or Ticknor are not numerous. As the months and years have passed in the investigation of a subject which, since that first day in Spain has for me never lost its charm, I have found these advantages (if such they are) forgotten. Instead there have been imperious demands of another kind, of complications nonexistent in a study of German or French influences upon our literature.

I refer to the diverse channels by which Spanish culture has become part of our own. The influence from the Peninsula is but a fragment of the story. Immigration from Spain to the United States has never been impressive compared with that from Germany or Italy. Within the borders of our nation, however, live almost two million persons who speak Spanish. Some of them are immigrants or the descendants of immigrants from Spain, but another avenue of influence is plain if we remember that more than a million and a half of these Spanish-speaking men and women are in the Southwest,* including California. On statistics of this sort it is idle to linger. The facts indicate that the Spanish influences cross and recross each other and that they are primarily *three:* the direct influence from the Peninsula; the direct influence from Mexico and other countries in this hemisphere; and the indirect influence of these latter regions through the Spanish settlements in our borderlands and the Southwest.

THIS TRIAD of influences has created problems, both structural and historical. Really one influence, the manifestations are nevertheless dramatically different, as in the effect upon James Russell Lowell of Calderón, upon William Cullen Bryant of the Mexican poet José Rosas Moreno, or upon Bret Harte of the legends concerning Father Junípero Serra. Furthermore, from the day of Samuel Sewall's study of Spanish in seventeenth-century New England until the present interest in Rubén Darío of Nicaragua, emphasis on one or another of these channels has changed and is still changing. From the indifference of George Ticknor or Washington Irving toward any Spanish culture save that of the Peninsula we

* For a definition of this term as used in the present work, see pp. 387–8, n. 6.

have come to the present curiosity about Mexican and South American literatures and to the enthusiasms for the other arts of our neighbors, such as the painting of Orozco. This new and more thoughtful comprehension of the culture of the Spanish-speaking peoples in this hemisphere has not meant the renunciation of the cultural life of Spain itself. Presumably there will never again be so cohesive a coterie as Prescott, Ticknor, Lowell, and the other New Englanders. Nevertheless, at the end of the century William Dean Howells became the enlightened interpreter of the novelists Pérez Galdós and Palacio Valdés, and in our time Ernest Hemingway and John Dos Passos communicate vividly the despair and the dreams of modern Spaniards.

To do less than tell the whole story of the three channels would be not to tell it at all. Bryant, for example, and Bret Harte have been devoted to at least two of these mediums. The former, as we shall see, translated Spanish religious poetry and also adapted the verse of the Cuban José María Heredia. I have, therefore, related this history in detail and at such length that I fear only those who love everything connected with Spain, as did Irving and Lowell, or only those who are deeply curious about these foreign ingredients in American literature will follow me to the end. It is a long story, and sometimes repetitious, but I hope that, particularly in the "Spanish biographies," it may reveal our literature and our men of letters in fresh lights and with new meanings. The portrait of William Dean Howells, for instance, seems to me quite different after we know him intimately through his correspondence with Valdés. To understand precisely what the *Coplas* of Jorge Manrique meant to Longfellow is, I think, to know more of the place of this poet in American literature. In a sense, then, this book is a new literary history of these eight writers and also of those, like Herman Melville and Mark Twain, who occasionally looked toward Spain.

During my study of Irving or of other American writers I was never, as already hinted, especially interested in the use by an essayist or a storyteller of particular passages or incidents in Spanish literature, a use well illustrated by Longfellow's reliance upon Cervantes for his poetic drama, "The Spanish Student,"—in short,

xxii

what are called "parallel passages." The Spanish legacy to American literature included far more than such borrowings. I felt certain that these or Ticknor's *History of Spanish Literature* or Prescott's *History of the Conquest of Mexico* were merely parts of the entire story of Hispanism in America. I did not think myself well qualified to relate this story, but I came to the conclusion that I must tell it to make my readers really understand this golden Spanish thread in our prose and poetry.

As for the structural problems inherent in the subject, it is obvious that a definition of Spanish cultural patterns in America in the seventeenth and eighteenth centuries is less difficult than in the nineteenth and twentieth, whose history forms the center of this book. During the century and a half prior to the founding of the Republic, music, painting, architecture, and literature were less generally respected than after 1800, and each of these arts was less conscious of its particular destiny in this strange, new continent. In the earlier century the bareness of our writing would mean an indifference to anything as esoteric as the arts of Spain. Every reference, such as Cotton Mather's brochure in Spanish, becomes precious for the historian. Even in the eighteenth century the "widening consciousness," as I have called it, of Spanish culture demands no breakdown into categories, into libraries, architecture, scholarship, or travel. The importance of Spanish instruments of culture increased, but the story flows on simply and clearly enough. It is the story of Jefferson's and Franklin's interest in the language, of Joel Barlow's use of the ancient chroniclers of South America, or of Philip Freneau's poetry on Columbus. Though varied, the narrative is all of one piece. Not until 1800 or even until the appearance of the New England Hispanophiles do the influences assume a complexity which, defying an over-all chronology, compels a topical approach.

Therefore, in Parts I and II I have tried to tell this general story, even if it seems sometimes too peripheral and too bibliographical. I hope that the student of literature in arriving, after perhaps too long a journey, at the major interpreters in Part III will perceive how natural was the air they breathed and how inevitable was their devotion to Cervantes or Blasco Ibáñez. My aim has been to create a frame of reference for the study of these eight men of letters and to show chronologically and topically what was knowledgeable and available for writers sensitive to Spain or to Spain in America. After the chapters on the seventeenth and eighteenth centuries (Part I), I have studied the later period (Part II) under specific headings. Necessarily these six sections dealing with the nineteenth and twentieth centuries will evoke the criticism of the specialists, but they will also, I hope, win their indulgence in view of my ultimate aim, the interpretation of Spanish influences upon our literature. This last is my goal and *not,* I most earnestly desire to make clear, a survey of the Spanish culture itself, either in Europe or in the Americas. Cervantes or Calderón, Galdós or Blasco Ibáñez, Picasso or Orozco, San Xavier del Bac or San Juan Capistrano, the surviving miracle plays of New Mexico or the modern poet García Lorca—all these diverse Spanish and Spanish-American immortalities find their places in this book insofar as they relate themselves, directly or indirectly, to our belles-lettres.

FOR THESE 150 years (1800–1950) I have adopted this broad approach. I have attempted a survey, always with the literature in mind, of six persistent sources of Spanish influence, namely, "The Travelers"; "The Writers for the Periodicals"; "The Historians"; "The Teachers, Scholars, Translators, and Critics"; "The Novelists, Poets, and Dramatists"; and "The Painters, Sculptors, Musicians, and Architects." The reader will think of other channels, but these six have long seemed to me basic to the world in which our men of letters thought and wrote. I have omitted chapters on science, economics, government, and other subjects less directly connected with the creation of literature as not essential to the purposes of this book, although in it will be found incidental comment on what we have learned in these respects from Spain and Spanish America. Nor have I discussed American regional cultures as entities, such as that of New Mexico, since analysis of this kind would invalidate the topical plan. The contributions of these areas, however, are clearly discernible in the six chapters, as in the sections on

New Mexico in the chapter on the arts. I should like to write other chapters, but my purpose is an interpretation of the Spanish strand in the *literature* of the United States, not the full examination of local cultural and subliterary patterns.

In some of the six chapters the reader will detect three sub-divisions dealing, respectively, with Spain, with Spain in Mexico and in Central and South America, and with Spain in the United States, that is, with her influence, however diluted, in the regions of Florida or California. In others—for instance, in the chapter "Novelists, Poets, and Dramatists"—these subdivisions have seemed impracticable. Within all subdivisions, however, the arrangement is chronological, and there will always be perceived a sustained distinction between the intellectual and the popular levels of influence. I hope that, apart from the specialized studies of the men of letters in Part III, these six chapters, constituting Part II of the book, may have a general interest. They tell the story of Hispanism in the United States and, in this perspective, that of American literature. The contribution, for example, of George Ticknor to this history of Hispanism is outlined (in anticipation of the special chapter on him) in two chapters, "The Travelers" and "The Teachers, Scholars, Translators, and Critics," just as Longfellow's may be estimated from the last-mentioned chapter and from "The Novelists, Poets, and Dramatists." In this connection, for some necessary repetition in the general and special chapters I ask pardon, but not so humbly as for my trespass in Part II into fields, especially the fine arts, in which I am a layman. Yet, here, too, I hope that in my attempts to record a climate for the literature I have not been guilty of any essential untruth.

Some readers will, I trust, after a trek almost as long as Irving's on muleback from Madrid to Granada, come eventually to Part III and study there the Spanish quality in individual men of letters. This is literary history or biography with reference to European and, especially, Spanish elements. At first the selection of these eight may seem capricious. We think of William Gilmore Simms and his Spanish romances, of Herman Melville and his "Benito Cereno," or of Mark Twain, so deeply in debt to Cervantes. Emerson, Hawthorne, Poe, Whitman, Dos Passos—hardly an American author, as Part II reveals, has avoided entirely the impact of this utterly different culture. Nevertheless, to each of these eight varied types the Spanish influence imparted something particular. For Ticknor and Prescott it meant a prolonged consecration; for Irving an enrichment of his imaginative life; for Longfellow a gateway into the world of European romantic * literature; for Bryant an inward solace; for Lowell a spiritual experience in one or two writers; for Howells an invigorated critical life; and for Bret Harte the arresting of a neglected tradition. On the whole, no others (not even Ernest Hemingway today) illustrate so vividly the strength of the Spanish influence and also its wide range of expression in our men of talent. We shall study a literary historian, a historian, an essayist and romancer, three very different poets, a novelist, and a storyteller of the Southwest.

HAVING committed myself for many years to a task which has proved difficult and complicated, and far from popular in its essential character, I have thought it unwise to shrink from completeness in annotation and bibliographical data. I believe that the nature of the book demands these. I am certain that without notes the book would define less effectively the scope of this continued influence on American literature. I am in agreement with Prescott's defense of notes in his review of Bancroft's *History of the United States* in 1841. No one before or since, as far as I know, has ever spoken more wisely on this problem than the historian in the passage of which the following sentence is a fragment: "We want to see," he says of Bancroft, "the grounds of his conclusions, the scaffolding by which he has raised his structure; to estimate the true value of his authorities . . . We want to have a reason for our faith, otherwise we are merely led blindfold."

It is an ungracious deed to bore readers, even if they can readily escape by laying the book aside. But I think the whole story worth their attention. Each time, as I have finished a chapter, in Jacala,

* For a definition of this term as used in the present work, see 2, 278, and n. 10.

Mexico, in Malaga, Spain, or in the Bret Harte country in California, I have wished that I might make my readers feel the dignity and splendor of this Spanish tradition in the literature of the United States.

STANLEY T. WILLIAMS

Hamden, Connecticut
November 1, 1954.

Part One

The Origins

and Beginnings of

Spanish Culture

in America

CHAPTER ONE/SPANISH CULTURE IN THE SEVENTEENTH-CENTURY COLONIES

(1607–1700)

HATRED of Spain and of all her ways burned deep and lasting in the minds of the English colonists of the seventeenth century on the Atlantic seaboard. These pioneers feared the haughty nation whose colonies in America were many times the area of the mother country.[1] They hated her for her Catholic tyrannies, which in not unrelated ways had helped to motivate their exodus from England and Holland,[2] and for her animosity toward the English settlements.[3] They shrank from the legends concerning the terrible Spaniard: his cruelty and craft, his alleged barbarism (embellished by Bartolomé de las Casas) in his colonies, his fanaticism in his dark religion of the Inquisition, and, above all, his firm, prosperous presence in the rich, warm lands of the South. All these boded restraint to the ambitious Englishman. Race, religion, economic rivalry— everything counseled enmity. As Cotton Mather considered the reassuring differences between the English and Spanish colonies, he was moved to a "sudden composure": "Gentlemen!" he cried. *"It is the* War of the Lord *which you are now Engaged in:* and it is the Help of the Lord, *that we are at Home affectionately imploring for you. We have made a fair and just purchase of our Country from the Natives here; not encroaching on them after* the Spanish Fashion, *in any of their* Properties *and* Possessions." [4]

This bitterness endured. It was nourished by actual combat and before 1700 by feverish commercial competition.[5] In 1655, for example, the New Englanders aided the English in an attack on Jamaica, destined to be for many years a center for unlawful trade with Spain and Spanish America,[6] and in 1686 the Spaniards ruthlessly destroyed the Scotch settlement at Port Royal.[7] There ensued sixteen years of peace, during which Spain was nominally an ally against the French, but in 1702 strife was renewed. Meanwhile, inter-American commerce had grown. John Smith, drying

3

his fish on Monhegan Island, dispatched a shipload to Spain and received for each quintal five Spanish dollars.[8] This was just a beginning. Toward the end of the century New England merchants were sending fish and lumber to the Peninsula and logwood from Central America to other regions of Europe [9] despite the tangle of Spanish laws and the watchful Spanish fleet.

This mutual hostility, racial, religious, and economic, was, as we shall see, to beget a strange cultural history. On September 26, 1686, Samuel Sewall, who eagerly followed every Mexican event, noted with approval the comment of a friend that "All America should be converted, Mexico overcome." [10] Neither he nor Cotton Mather, who shared his views, could have dreamed that in the process of time Spain and Spanish America would, conversely, leave an indelible if subtle imprint upon the Anglo-Saxon culture of North America. Out of this rapidly increasing knowledge of the Spanish civilization there developed in the nineteenth century a romantic interpretation of, to cite only two very different instances, Boabdil and Cortés, and in the twentieth her sensitivity to Orozco or Rubén Darío. In the early days, however, with such prejudices in the hearts of the colonists, with the communications between these extended regions still underdeveloped, with little historical perspective, it is not startling that the English remained cool to the magnificence of the Spanish achievement and incurious concerning the colorful Spanish world of the seventeenth century. They were aware of Columbus and of the two centuries of Spanish exploration. Otherwise they would not have been on this side of the Atlantic. Hakluyt, Eden, Purchas, if not Peter Martyr and Las Casas, had told them the splendid story.[11] Spain had unlocked the door of western Atlantic navigation, and this fact Englishmen knew. Nevertheless, admiration for the impressive development of Mexico, if they felt it, was obscured by ignorance of this mysterious realm and of South America.

What did the average English settler care about the heroic expeditions of De Soto or of Coronado far into the interior? [12] Actually, the far-flung outposts of the Spanish conquests, from Saint Augustine to California, already resembled barriers to his own expansion. These subjugators of Florida, these missionaries of an

4

alien faith, pressing ever farther west, south, and north, these
kinsmen of the heathen Cortés, were enemies who had threatened
openly the very existence of Virginia and the Carolinas. What did
the names of Spain and Mexico connote except the Armada, the
Jesuits, the fear of a Catholic England, a profane culture? All were
symbols of the arrogant nation of which the seventeenth-century
poet John Wilson wrote in angry, halting stanzas:

> Our little Fleet in July first,
> their mighty Fleet did view;
> She came but with a softly course,
> though winds behind her blew.
> Her front much like the Moon was crook't,
> (the horns seven miles asunder)
> Her Mastes like stately Towers look't,
> the Ocean groaning under.
> And now behold they were at hand,
> daring our English Borders,
> Making full sure to bring our Land
> Under their Spanish orders:
> But God above, laughing to scorne
> their wicked wile and wealth,
> To his Annointed rais'd an horne
> Of hope and saving health.[13]

Although allusion has been made to an increasing understanding of the Spanish civilization, it would be wrong to pretend that
this distrust did not linger on, propagating for many years these old
prejudices in new dress. Studies by Spaniards of the reputation of
their country abroad discuss it more fully. A recent book, *La
leyenda negra,* in tracing the persistence of this belief, attacks Ticknor, Prescott, Motley, and George Bancroft for perpetuating it.[14]
A modern historian of the growth of Spanish culture in the United
States laments that everywhere thrive the two immortal illusions:
"la crueldad y el fanatismo español." [15] To many Americans Spain
and Mexico still suggest vaguely: troublesome neighbors, the unfortunate wars of 1848 and 1898, and political instability. Our
historians have solidified the myths by letting us forget that even
now the English areas of civilization in the Americas are smaller

than the Spanish and Portuguese. In the past Spain ruled more than one half of the regions now forming the United States.[16]

Only gradually are we arriving at the more civilized conclusion that there were two great simultaneous cultures in the Americas which were destined to endure in full strength, in ways not vouchsafed the French, the Dutch, or the Swedes. Slowly prejudices are fading in the mutual comprehension of the two cultures. This glance ahead is designed to explain, if it be necessary, the indifference of the English colonist three centuries ago to the depth and beauty of the Spanish civilization in Mexico of the seventeenth century. We ourselves are not yet wholly enlightened. Why expect it of this austere New Englander founding his refuge here against the very principles for which Spain stood? Or of the Virginian in constant dread of direct attack from frigate and galleon?

Their ignorance and insensibility were natural, perhaps inevitable, but in retrospect they appear tragic. As we read the thorny lines which represent the best of New England seventeenth-century poetry, we may wish ardently that someone had thrust into the hands of Michael Wigglesworth or of Anne Bradstreet copies of contemporary Peruvian verse.[17] Sor Juana Inés de la Cruz was the Mexican "Tenth Muse." It is an understatement to remark that Calvinism was less favorable to literature and the fine arts than even an exacting Catholicism in Spanish America. Squarely caught between Puritanism and a very special kind of materialism, humanism in New England withered and died [18] whereas in Spanish America the same impulses attained—who can deny it?—a generous fulfillment. In the use of books, although an active censorship existed, the individual could enjoy an astonishingly free intellectual life. In Mexico, between 1572 and 1600, more than five hundred boxes of books were examined by guardians of this Catholic culture. Such figures take no account of separate items, and one historian estimates that during this epoch some thirty thousand titles were being imported into New Spain, quite apart from those admitted behind the censor's back. Printing had begun here about 1535 or 1536,[19] and even at this time the professional booksellers in Mexico City alone numbered some fifty. Such are merely hints

6

of a cultural wealth undreamed of and, for the most part, undesired in the English colonies.

Nor were all the books introduced openly or secretly into New Spain works of devotion or handbooks for practical living, though these, as in New England and Virginia, were numerous. The similarities of purposes (conversion of the natives, exploration, or colonization), crossed by Catholic differences, might be expected. The arresting contrast is in the availability of such Latin and Greek classics as Cicero, Ovid, Virgil, Terence, Homer, and Marcus Aurelius and from Italy and Spain the works of Ariosto, Petrarch, Jorge Manrique, Lope de Vega, Cervantes, Fray Luis de Granada, and many others of similar distinction.[20] Moreover, the dweller in Mexico City, though Mather would have thought him marked for eternal burning, could read his Ariosto or his *Amadis de Gaula*. He could also listen to secular music, look at paintings by contemporary masters, attend poetic festivals and contests, survey noble monuments of Spanish architecture such as his cathedrals, or study medicine and the mathematical sciences.[21] This rich culture is now emphasized not in order to minimize the compensating depth and power of the thought-patterns of New England and Virginia but to place clearly before us the beginnings of this inexhaustible source of Spanish influence, withheld by a niggardly fate from the seventeenth-century English colonists.

THEORETICALLY, then, two great beacons of Spanish culture were visible to the seventeenth-century colonists, the forbears of the citizens of the United States. One was the imperial, already flourishing art of Spanish America. The other was the intricate Spanish element in the thought of the European island, England, whence they had come. Culturally, direct intercourse with Spain hardly existed. Though copies of some of them were hiding in New England and Virginia libraries, it is difficult to imagine a free flow of the books listed in the last paragraph into Jamestown or Boston. Indeed, had there been landed in these colonies shiploads of such books, reflecting some of the deep-grained peculiarities of the Spaniard in creative literature—genial or savage satire, flamboyance, unrestrained individualism, or mysticism—it is not easy to imagine readers among the Bradfords, Winthrops, and Mathers,[22] so alien just now was the Spanish mind from the English. Whatever the seventeenth-century colonists knew of Spain had to come from England or Mexico and essentially from nowhere else. What vibrations, then, were borne over the waters from the mother island? What news came from plains and mountains in the South, from the land of the *conquistadores,* about language, chronicles, poetry, and fiction?

Literally, very few vibrations indeed. The foundations of a Spanish or Mexican culture were now being laid in the regions later known as Texas, New Mexico, Arizona, and California.[23] In the early years of the sixteenth century Alvar Núñez Cabeza de Vaca crossed into these areas and in 1542 published his famous *Relación.* Fifteen years later appeared the *Relaçam verdadeira* of De Soto, whose pilgrimage through Florida and North Carolina ended at the Mississippi. Meanwhile, Francisco Vásquez de Coronado was in search of the "seven cities of Cíbola" in what is now our Southwest.[24] All this had happened before the settlement at Jamestown. As early as 1598 in New Mexico were acted the religious plays which were to live on through the centuries. Here might have been seen *Los moros y los cristianos, Los pastores, Los tres magos,*[25] and all the dramas which form so picturesque a part of our Spanish folklore literature.

Of all such matters New England knew little, even if Hakluyt described John Chilton's journey in 1570 from Mexico City to California.[26] At this time these regions seemed incredibly remote. Strictly speaking, it is more difficult to find Spanish influences in the northern seaboard colonies in the seventeenth century than in England in the fifteenth and sixteenth—a task arduous enough.[27] What is most difficult of all, in contrast to the twentieth century, is to find much importance in these links with Spanish America. A Spanish word, a phrase, a proverb, the title of a book of chronicles, a Spanish dictionary—if these scattered fragments originated in Mexico, they are still of undemonstrable significance.

Bearded Spanish sailors, taken prisoner or landing voluntarily at northern seaports, did not emanate culture.[28] We have no record of any enlightened traveler from Mexico City, learned and humane, with books in his ship's cabin and the wisdom of ancient Spain in his head, talking long and persuasively to our unrelaxed divines. Not until a century afterward have we the fascinating record of the learned Miranda, blessed with "a perf[ect] Acquaint-a[nce] with the policy & Hist[ory] of all Spanish America," discoursing to Ezra Stiles. "He gave me," wrote Stiles, "the manner of Educa[tion] in the Colleges in Mexico & so of all N[ew] Spain . . ." [29] As to language, the infiltration of Spanish words and idioms into American speech, so important eventually for both our scholars and novelists, seems to have occurred soon after the beginnings of inter-American trade.[30] Did not some fine old copy of Antonio de Herrera or of *Don Quixote* find its way from Mexico City into the loving and attentive hands of a Virginia bookman of the seventeenth century? What was the history of the "rare ancient Spanish book" which George Ticknor, some two centuries later, "bought for a mere trifle, at a sale in Richmond"? [31] We cannot say. Spanish literature may have been far better known than we have believed. If so, its influence was too isolated, too weak to overthrow or even to qualify the complacent impression in New England that the culture of Mexico was negligible, doomed, as Samuel Sewall believed, to be absorbed by the Protestant faith. Not until the eighteenth century did commercial and social relationships open wide this channel of influence.

For these reasons the culture whose surviving glories a twentieth-century American, after a few hours' travel, may view with wonder bestowed apparently no color on seventeenth-century New England and Virginia, except in picturesque details. In imagination we see Cotton Mather writing his book for Mexican Catholics in his newly acquired Spanish or Samuel Sewall deep in Bartolomé de las Casas. The primary transmitter of Spanish culture was England; to London Sewall sent for his Spanish books.[32] In England, too, at the turn of the seventeenth century the Spanish cultural influences are not easy to define. Do they stem from the Oxford lectures of Juan Luis Vives in 1523? "Shortly after Vives' visit," says one authority, "Spain began to produce a series of works which attracted the admiration of Western Europe." [33] These were the "works" which in some cases were to precede Shakespeare in the American colonies.

This association may be true, but the precise patterns of the influence in England are still controversial. It is certain that during the Elizabethan era the impact of the Spanish novel was substantial, but it remains doubtful how much that influence found expression directly from the Spanish and how much through English and French translations.[34] Though different in many ways, the nature of this Spanish bias in England in the seventeenth century may be roughly compared to a similar influence exerted direct from the Peninsula to the United States in the nineteenth. Within the respective countries, old England and the young Republic, in the two different centuries, Spanish historians, Spanish novelists, and, to some extent, Spanish poets, especially religious poets, were known in certain intellectual quarters. In seventeenth-century England the *Amadís de Gaula* was read, and we may link more or less accurately Montemayor's *Diana* with the development of the English pastoral, Antonio de Guevara with euphuism, and Cervantes with the popularity of the picaresque story.[35] Although the notion verges on the absurd, the Puritan emigrants to America could have brought across the Atlantic famous works of Spanish literature. In this England of the seventeenth century, however, versions of Spanish poetry were in effect limited to a few of the Spanish mystics. In 1629 Mabbe translated Cristóbal de Fonseca, thus creating the first adequate version in English of one of these poets.[36]

How much of this Spanish influence in England, highly distilled, would actually penetrate into the culture of the colonists? Certainly Puritan thought and writing seem to have been immune to the fashions of the Spanish mystics unless these affected, for instance, Richard Crashaw and unless Crashaw, in turn, affected the New England poet Edward Taylor. These gossamer relationships must remain hypotheses.[37] The greatest novelist, Cervantes, was in the colonists' libraries, but Spanish fiction influenced at first not the English novel but English drama,[38] a form of art at which the colonists, even more than at fiction, looked askance. We have not yet conclusive proof that the plays of Shakespeare were available in America during the seventeenth century. We should, therefore, hardly expect the colonists to carry to America those Spanish novels which from the middle of the sixteenth century until the beginning of the eighteenth were read at home, such as *Lazarillo de Tormes, Guzmán de Alfarache,* or *Don Quixote.*[39]

The difficulty lay less in the vitality of the influence than in certain aesthetic limitations of the New England colonists. Continental cultural influences were presently active in Dutch New York, in German Pennsylvania (architecture and music), or in Swedish Delaware (architecture). Moreover, much has been exhumed and much written to modify our disdain of the accomplishments of the New Englanders in literature and the fine arts.[40] Little, however, has come to light to alter materially our long-standing conviction that their primary loyalties were to religion and to success in this world. A copy of Spenser's poems is one of the recent discoveries.[41] There will be others. Minds which developed beautiful crafts in pewter, silver, and wood carving would be capable of appreciating the arts of Spanish fiction and poetry. Their insensitivity to Spanish literature was essentially a part of their indifference to special forms of Spanish culture. Even more than those of their kinsmen in England the arts of these pioneer Puritans remained basically unaffected by Spanish alloys.

NEVERTHELESS, possible sources for Spanish culture in North America during the seventeenth century have not been introduced merely to scoff at their reality. The very fact that these two potentials were in the background of our country in its youth was important in a way undemonstrable now by a tabulation of libraries, of books, or of physical interrelations. From the moment of their arrival New Spain was the colonists' neighbor; its proximity could not be ignored. About the resultant psychological pattern there was nothing unique. In the nineteenth century the steppes in Russia or frontier in America influenced their respective cultures directly but also indirectly, as in, let us say, Tolstoi and Emerson.[42] Abundant evidence survives that before our active interpretation of Spain began there existed a latent, unconscious sense of these prodigious areas of Central and South America, and of the great nation which was then their lord. Thus Cotton Mather was keenly sensitive not only to stories of imperial Spain's mass cruelty [43] but also to those concerning "the vast Regions of the *Spanish America*." [44] In similar fashion, Samuel Sewall thought frequently of Mexico and of the magnificence of its capital city. It differed appreciably from his own Boston; he marveled greatly that in Mexico City were "1500 Coaches drawn with Mules." [45]

In brief, we are now studying not, as in later chapters, the immediate relationships established by Ticknor, Irving, and Prescott in their planned examinations of Spanish culture but a subtle, powerful, and almost inarticulate influence. For at least two centuries before the flowering of direct interpretation this took root in the American consciousness.[46] We did *not* possess all America; this fact, in one mood or another, was in many minds, particularly in those of our leaders. Although we might keep aloof or simulate superiority or indifference, still, there it was to the south, that mighty and alien civilization. In the seventeenth century these undercurrents stirred in our thinking, not less real because they were not easily definable.

Even by 1650 such stirrings were audible. Were there, for example, no Spanish-speaking colonists in New England, in Virginia, or in the Carolinas, which were so near Florida? [47] If these were less numerous than in the eighteenth century, when the newspapers began to print advertisements of tutors in the language,[48] they must, in the growing contraband trade with Spanish America, have occasionally emerged. Treading the docks and the ships, men spoke Spanish, if only for practical reasons. Other higher causes for the study of the modern languages were still unborn. No one had yet envisaged a professorship in Romance languages or a great novelist whose youth was nurtured on Cervantes.[49] Even those colonists endowed with something like a grammar-school education had never studied systematically the living languages; their superior accomplishments were limited to the mastery of reading, writing, and Latin.[50] Yet some few must have struggled with the language to further trade or to decipher the Spanish charts and maps. We

Cotton Mather, from the painting by Peter Pelham.

know that Cotton Mather could compose tolerable Spanish, and the Spanish dictionaries in the seventeenth-century libraries could hardly have been altogether decorative.

Such dictionaries could be had both in New England and in Virginia,[51] and though Samuel Sewall elected to send to London for his books, he and Cotton Mather seem to have had hardly more difficulty in laying their hands on the necessary linguistic tools than their descendants in New England two centuries later who essayed the study of German.[52] If these eminent men of early New England conquered Spanish and discussed its uses in some detail, it is not preposterous to believe that, there or elsewhere in the Atlantic settlements, others less vocal, men who did not lay bare their lives in portentous diaries, had other purposes. Some may have known the tongue not to trade, not to proselyte in Mexico, but to read Cervantes or Quevedo. For instance, Francis Daniel Pastorius, who arrived in Philadelphia in 1683, mentions in his *Bee-Hive* or *Bee-Stock,* which has been called "the Magna Charta of German culture in colonial America," [53] Diego Saavedra Fajardo's "100 Emblems," Quevedo's *Visions,* and *Lazarillo de Tormes.*[54] That there were dictionaries is not proof that these were read. Yet if such were not infrequent within the thousand private libraries of Virginia [55] or among the ten thousand separate titles of New England [56]—both figures are modern historians' estimates—certain conclusions are arguable. In the light of Sewall's and Mather's zeal, it is possible that the language was studied more generally than has been supposed and that it was sometimes spoken.

Those who did know Spanish could read in the originals the narratives of western exploration which so fascinated the Elizabethans and which were widely translated, usually by merchants who had learned the language while trading in the Peninsula.[57] Or they could turn to Las Casas, who confirmed flatteringly all their prejudices against the Spaniards by his merciless denunciation of his countrymen's excesses in the colonies.[58] We have no proof of the presence here yet of many of these originals. The eighteenth century was to witness the assembling of the first great Spanish and Spanish-American collections. Since the familiarity of Virginia readers with French has probably been exaggerated,[59] it is even more dangerous to surmise that the colonists wrestled with Spanish in order to devour these spacious histories and tough old records of exploration. Were there, for example, books of voyages and travels in the library of William Brocas of Lancaster County, Virginia, which was appraised in 1655 at one hundred pounds and whose books were "Most of them Spanish, Italyan, and Latin"? [60] And if so, were these Spanish books of travel read?

These questions must remain unanswered. It would be a fair guess to say that only the learned men sought out the originals. The reasons of the magistrate Sewall for studying Las Casas were, as we shall see, religious and political,[61] but Mather undoubtedly attained also a scholar's pleasure in the control of another tongue. He once boasted that he could write in seven different languages.[62] For those who desired the story of "the western route" and its destinations, there were the translations, and these at least kept in our colonists' minds Spanish themes and Spanish history. William Bradford's library contained "Lud. Vives Edition of Augustine's De Civitate Dei," and Nathaniel Morton cites Peter Martyr in his *New Englands Memoriall.*[63]

It is conceivable that Ralph Wormeley and his family read his folio copy of a "Gen^{ll} History of Spaine." [64] Possibly Thomas Prince was familiar, page by page, with his curious item, "Journal of the Last Voyage of La Sale to Gulf of Mexico." [65] That these expatriate Elizabethans never read the translations which had so wide a vogue in England is almost unthinkable, and it is tempting to conjecture that a curiosity about history and geography natural to all practical men would lure some bolder intellects to the original Spanish. Of course, the great body of the colonists went on their way, serenely untroubled by either the original narratives or the translations. We can only believe that some few others were more inquisitive, that their imaginations responded to the spectacle of the Spanish conquest, later to be described to their descendants so brilliantly by William Hickling Prescott.

The fascination of such subterranean, forgotten influences is enhanced if we extend them to belles-lettres. Between 1792 and 1809 Cervantes was to stamp his genius upon our two early comic masterpieces.[66] The story of his influence upon American literature,

14

which will be told in detail in the present book,[67] is extraordinary proof of the universal, compulsive power, defying race and language, of this Spaniard's genius. His immediate presence in seventeenth-century America, where we search in vain for editions of Shakespeare,[68] is both surprising and exciting. In Virginia George Wormeley owned a copy of the peerless satire.[69] In New England George Alcock, a Harvard medical student who died in 1676, harbored in his library Shelton's version of the masterpiece and also, apparently, the English translation (1619) of Cervantes' *Travels of Persiles and Sigismunda*.[70]

Unfortunately we cannot know what the Virginian or the young New Englander thought of Sancho and his master, nor can we be sure that they even turned the leaves of these volumes. Nevertheless, the mere ownership of this classic by seventeenth-century libraries has meaning, as has the fact that Cotton Mather could refer to Roger Williams' "quixotism." [71] Had the word already attained its present connotations in everyday speech? [72] I shall not venture to ascribe to Cervantes a secret vogue in seventeenth-century America. Even in England his popularity was still limited.[73] Yet he was read. The relatively humane Alcock also owned copies of Homer, Horace, Plutarch, and Sir Thomas Browne's *Religio Medici*.[74] The Knight of La Mancha had reached these shores, and he had come to stay.

If we dare believe that copies of Shakespeare, Donne, and Dryden, who appear to be unmentioned,[75] were occasionally imported by the booksellers of Boston and other cities, we may guess that Cervantes, since his name occurs in the catalogues of several libraries, was definitely known. Indeed, in his *Magnalia Christi Americana* Cotton Mather speaks of the "romances of '*Don Quixote*' and the '*Seven Champions*.' " [76] Some French novels were brought into the colonies,[77] and it is quite possible that the listed volumes of Cervantes symbolize a substantial number of silent copies as well as the accessibility of other Spanish fiction. The availability in 1683 in Boston of a translation of Quevedo's *Visions* is almost as interesting.[78] Perhaps this author's brilliant and fantastic descriptions of the Day of Judgment delighted the readers of Michael Wigglesworth's *Day of Doom*.[79] Nevertheless, the polished courtier, bitter

15

wit, and satirist is a strange guest at the Puritan table. It should be remembered that these particular books, like the famous dramatic romance in the Harvard College Library, the *Celestina*,[80] happened to be recorded whereas others were not. Compared with the currency in Mexico City of Jorge Manrique, Lope de Vega, Fray Luis de Granada, and other classic writers, these examples of Spanish literature in America appear isolated and anomalous, but we should not be too sure that they were unique or that eventually we shall not learn of the existence of others.

We may even imagine that we hear faint echoes of Spanish literature in our colonial prose and poetry. We are tempted to believe that this slender knowledge of Spain and its culture bore fruit in our early writing.[81] Actually, the precise influence appears to be limited to allusions to the Spaniard at war and to the theme of the Armada; John Wilson's "Song of Deliverance" exults at the annihilation of this baleful fleet. The chance of a dependence upon the Spanish mystics, directly or once removed through such English verse as Crashaw's, cannot be ruled out, for some of the New England poetry is hauntingly suggestive of these origins.[82] Indeed, New England verse, in long stretches drearily uninspired, reaches dignity chiefly in its moments of rapt contemplation of an invisible landscape, as in *The Day of Doom,* or in certain shining metaphors in Edward Taylor's poems.[83] It might have been well if Cotton Mather, knowing the Spanish language, had, instead of extolling Anne Bradstreet, introduced in translation into New England the competent poetry of his learned, and by no means nameless, contemporary in Peru, Señor Don Pedro de Peralta Barnuevo Rocha y Benavides.[84] So civilized a seventeenth-century cross-illumination, however, was for reasons already mentioned pathetically impracticable.

To fancy Cotton Mather reading *Don Quixote* raises in the mind almost comic contrasts, reminding us of Matthew Arnold's whimsical, imaginative picture of Shakespeare (and Virgil) ill at ease on the voyage to New England with the Puritans. No evidence exists that the learned divine enjoyed like all the rest of mankind this great human experience in the realms of gold. The familiarity with the language which made Mather the author of the first book written in Spanish in the northern colonies was not born of a love of literature. Nor was this the origin of Samuel Sewall's knowledge. At about the same time he used his Spanish dictionary and grammar to master Las Casas and Cipriano de Valera, the famous Spanish Protestant.[85] In studying Spanish the purposes of Mather and Sewall, deeming themselves representatives of their Boston colleagues "who make the best Figures in this Place," [86] were complex: religious, political, and economic. Their modest hope was to Protestantize all the Americas, a consummation to be attended by pardonable material gains. What wonders, in this world as well as in the next, might not be comprehended in such hemispheric religious unity? John Eliot's translation of the Bible into the Indian tongues shone forth as a celestial example.[87] The Protestant Bible in Spanish should be the primary step in this mass conversion. To the modern mind this seems an amusing conspiracy, an anticipatory parody on Walt Whitman's spiritual imperialism of about two and a half centuries later.

The episode, which overlaps a little the limits of this chapter, occurred against a complicated historical background which we may ignore. Its frame of reference was the "revolt" in New Spain which both Mather and Sewall so eagerly awaited, in vain, against attempted French domination.[88] These New Englanders zealously fashioned their weapons. We learn of Sewall's determination to use the Spanish Bible for "the bombing of Santa Domingo, the Havana, Porto Rico, and Mexico it self." "I would," he concludes recklessly, "willingly give five pounds towards the charge of it." [89] Sewall's generosity and the rather dubious firepower of this long-range "bombing" we need not discuss. Instead, we may examine the effect of this plan of study and purposeful writing, pursued with characteristic Puritan intensity, upon the intellectual life of Cotton Mather, now, partly by default, the foremost Spanish scholar in New England. Since the project was cooperative, Mather was not, presumably, the only student of Spanish. "They have attempted," wrote Edward Bromfield of the group, "to send the Notices of the True Christian Protestant Religion into the midst of the Spanish nation by a Sheet which one of their Number did in the Spanish language fit for that intent." [90]

17

Whether or not this "one" was Cotton Mather, it is certain that intermittently during several years he was engaged in studying and composing Spanish and in pondering on New England's relations with Mexico. His enthusiasm rivals any devotee's today. On October 2, 1696, he discovered in himself "a strong inclination to learn the *Spanish* language . . ." [91] Since he was a Mather, he prayed fervently over these purposes, and on January 2, 1699, he set down further proof of these beginnings of Spanish influence:

About this Time, understanding that the way for our Communication with the *Spanish Indies,* opens more and more, I sett myself to learn the *Spanish Language.* The Lord wonderfully prospered mee in this Undertaking; a few liesure [*sic*] Minutes in the Evening of every Day, in about a Fortnight, or three weeks Time, so accomplished mee, I could write very good Spanish. Accordingly, I composed a little Body of the *Protestant Religion,* in certain Articles, back'd with irresistible Sentences of Scripture. This I turn'd into the Spanish Tongue; and am now printing it, with a Design to send it by all the wayes that I can, into the several parts of *Spanish America;* as not knowing, *how great a matter a little Fire may kindle,* or whether the Time for our Lord Jesus Christ to have glorious Churches in *America,* bee not at hand.[92]

Later entries confirm Mather's zeal both in the language and in his missionary aims "in irradiating the Dark Recesses of *America,* with the Knowledge of the Glorious Lord." [93] So commenced, in effect, the study by scholars of Spanish in North America.

This episode of Cotton Mather's indenture to the Spanish language for religious ends is characteristic of the man and also of Puritan New England's conception of the instruments of culture, such as music, painting, literature, and language. In everything must be seen the purposes of the "Glorious Lord." Every incident symbolized His busy participation in human affairs: the overturned wineglass, the child drowned in a well, or the bedbugs at an inn. In the same way, the arts, including literature and language, were consecrated to Him. This thought was in the mind of the poet Michael Wigglesworth as he composed each stave of his doggerel. It is more than possible that Mather read *Don Quixote* solely to enrich his vocabulary for his own ulterior Puritan purposes. For the motives of these early scholars for learning Spanish were primarily religious: "I have," remarked Sewall, "long pray'd for Mexico, and of late in those Words, that God would open the Mexican Fountain." [94]

The path to "the Mexican Fountain" was paved with Spanish syntax and Spanish vocabulary, but when finally opened the "Fountain" would show forth the "Glorious Lord." Another kind of Mexican or Spanish fountain, namely the fountain of culture, whose subtle irrigation of our intellectual soil we shall attempt to describe, did not interest the English colonists. Toward it they were as indifferent as to similar springs, like Elizabethan drama, in their own civilization. Mather and Sewall studied Spanish in order to Protestantize Mexico and South America, the very regions which some two and a half centuries later were to convert us to the beauty of their arts and thus truly open "the Mexican Fountain." Mather's objective is clear, but he leaves us with an impression that underneath his experience he felt the grandeur of the Spanish language. Certainly in his version of the tale of Sir William Phips he is aware of the romance of this Spanish story of galleon and buried treasure. Perhaps he enjoyed more than we know his study and writing of the language, for we recall his Spanish-Indian servant with whom he conversed in Spanish. Is there not a note of satisfaction in his boast that he could write "very good Spanish"? We even play with the heretical thought that Cotton Mather may have smiled a little at the Knight astride his Rosinante.

For Spanish influences on the literature of the United States Mather and Sewall unwittingly prepared the way. If in the reports which they constantly craved from Mexico they demanded no enlightenment concerning literature, painting, or architecture, still the fact remains that their communication with Mexico made the dissemination of such knowledge more possible. The divines prefaced their "bombing" by long talks with one John Bant, who had traveled to Yucatan, Havana, and Matanzas. In all these places he had "conversed with the people." [95] Through such liaisons, ever-increasing in scope, distance, and solidity, the "American Spaniards," [96] as Sewall called them, became less remote. Presently there were to be more and more travelers who would tell their tales, travelers more intelligent, talking not to Puritan dreamers but to civilized men of letters. Instead of poor John Bant, sneaking out news of the "Mexican revolt," there would be Alexander Humboldt, Madame Calderón de la Barca (as she was always called in the United States), or John Lloyd Stephens, all speaking eloquently of the cultural riches of New Spain. To such knowledge the Spanish studies by "the best Figures" of Boston were preliminary. Above all, we should observe that out of Mather's laboratory, a by-product of his research for "bombing," appeared his Spanish book, *La Religion Pura, en Doze palabras Fieles, dignas de ser recebidas de Todos.*[97] It is, indeed, "worthy" in its simple, vigorous Spanish, and it is endowed with peculiar interest as an early augury of this great and lasting influence upon American literary culture.

La Fe
del Chriſtiano:
En
Veyntequatro Articulos
de la Inſtitucion de *CHRISTO.*
Embiada
A LOS ESPAÑOLES,

Paraque abran ſus ojos, y paraque ſe
Conviertan de las Tinieblas a la luz,
y de la poteſtad de Satanas a Dios:
Paraque reciban por la Fe que es en
JESV CHRISTO, Remiſſion de
peccados, y Suerte Entre los *Sanctificados.*

Por C. MATHERO,
Siervo del Señor JESV CHRISTO.

II Timoth. 1. 13.
*Reten la Forma de las Sanas palabras, que de mi
oyſte, en la Fe, y Charidad, que es en Chriſto Jeſus.*

BOSTON, 1699.

Title page of *La Fe del Christiano,*
by Cotton Mather, Boston, 1699.

CHAPTER TWO / WIDENING CONSCIOUSNESS OF SPANISH CULTURE IN EIGHTEENTH-CENTURY AMERICA

(1700–1800)

In 1889 Henry Adams alluded to the immense but *intermittent* influence of Spain upon the United States.[1] His judgment seems pertinent if we think of certain great episodes, such as the exploration of the continent, the occupation of Louisiana, the Spanish-American War, or the Spanish Civil War of 1936, with its far-reaching implications concerning democracy. In some other ways the definition is inexact. The historian's remark does not describe accurately on a detailed scale the Spanish influence upon America within the eighteenth century, this next period of our study. During the entire fateful age of the founding of the Republic, the influence of Spain, geographical, political, and economic, was expanding steadily and was to diminish in these ways only as her empire on this continent declined.

As Spanish culture from Mexico, from South America, and, somewhat more distinctly in these years, from the West and Southwest of mesa and pueblo, became more comprehensible to us, this influence came to include intellectual meanings. The ancient hatred of Spain itself continued. She was detested for her alliance with France against England in the Seven Years' War and for her belated, ineffectual part in the War of the Revolution. She was distrusted for her encroachments, after this struggle, in the Mississippi Valley [2] and for her aggrandizements in regions which seemed designed by Providence for American traders and frontiersmen. Nevertheless, the watchful dread and hopeful isolation of the seventeenth-century colonist had ended. He now participated, especially after 1776, in Spain's wars,[3] in her border conflicts, in her foreign intrigues, and gradually, inevitably, in her culture. The epic of Old and New Spain had come to our very doors.

Though ultimately doomed, the Spanish empire in America

21

under the dynamic Bourbons was brilliantly resurgent, balancing its vast losses by gigantic gains. Here was, indeed, a pageant. This was enacted not only in Mexico City but in Florida, from which the Spaniards were expelled in 1763 only to return twenty years later at the close of the Revolution. It was repeated in Texas with its alternate warfare and interlocking with the French and in Louisiana, ceded by France to Spain at the end of the Seven Years' War, seized again by Napoleon in 1800, and sold to us three years later. It was revived in New Mexico, a Spanish domain during the entire century, and in Colorado and the Californias with those vibrant whiplashes of imperial power, the presidios and missions.

The fall of Quebec in 1759 and the conclusion of the Seven Years' War meant to the colonists the destruction of French power in America, but they at once found themselves facing an invigorated Spain along the Mississippi River. Indeed, the flexible talent of the Spaniards for expansion in one region in bold compensation for their shrinkage in another continued to trouble Americans who, far more than their seventeenth-century predecessors, were beginning to regard the entire continent as their own promised land. Even as the Spaniards fought the English in Cuba, the French in Texas and Louisiana, and native peoples everywhere, they still pushed forward, from Mexico toward Ohio and toward upper California, penetrating as far as Nootka, where they shook warning fists at the colonizing Russians.[4]

So the Spanish plants took root in the areas that have become Texas, New Mexico, Arizona, and California, blossoming in language, customs, folkways, and the arts. Spanish towns sprang up, with names now so familiar that we have almost forgotten their origins (Monterey, San Diego, San Francisco),[5] and the missions with their lovely architectural forms from old Spain developed their systems of education. Through travel and through new settlements Spanish words crept into the language.[6] Spanish plays, already mentioned, historical or religious, such as the *pastorelas* (later studied by our nineteenth- and twentieth-century scholars), were woven into the tradition along with ballads and children's songs.[7] Meanwhile the culture of Mexico [8] was deepening. This culture, whose beginnings were described in the previous chapter,

22

lost nothing from the expansion of Mexico's trade with Peru and with other peoples of South America. The aggressive José Gálvez governed the country well, both in the related colonies and in her interior economic life.[9] Simultaneously, Spain herself, now near the Indian summer of her grandeur, played a powerful role in all these affairs of the New World.[10]

This political presence of Spain was the compelling problem. Americans like Franklin, Jefferson, and John Adams were necessarily analysts of Spain's statesmanship, and by now even the everyday citizen had been made uneasy by her persistent prowling on the periphery of his country. After our independence, achieved in 1783, Spanish diplomacy and Spanish greed inspired a hostility rivaling in intensity, especially on the borders of the Mississippi, that felt toward our archenemy, Britain. In contrast to the ignorant fear cherished by the seventeenth-century pioneer, the eighteenth-century American regarded Spain as an urgent, practical threat. "To sell and make us vassals," wrote a gentleman at the Falls of Ohio to his friend in New England, "to the merciless Spaniards is a grievance not to be borne." [11] Naturally, then, by 1800 Americans felt concerning all things Spanish, even Spanish culture, an anxious curiosity.

To THIS intrusive presence of Spain in the destinies of the United States we may ascribe, apart from a more lively popular interest to be discussed presently, the study of Castilian in the high places of government, especially after the formation of the Republic. Franklin had turned to Spanish in 1733, along with Italian, as part of his ordered program for the mastery of modern languages.[12] Until the end of his life he continued to purchase and, presumably, to read Spanish books. John Adams, however, was motivated by an immediate need. He was certain that a knowledge of Spanish, which he boasted of acquiring very rapidly, was essential for his purposes during a sojourn in the Peninsula in 1779.[13] It helped him to probe the Spanish mind which his great-grandson, Henry Adams, is said to have declared no American ever would wholly comprehend. But John Adams learned a good deal, among other things that the Spanish nation in general have been of the opinion that the revolution in America was a bad example to the Spanish Colonies, and dangerous to the interests of Spain, as the United States, if they should become ambitious, and be seized with the spirit of conquest, might aim at Mexico and Peru.[14]

Such temptations even our most violent imperialists have so far resisted; something operatic hovers over the idea of our conquest of Peru. Nevertheless, to our first leaders these questions were not entirely academic.[15] The various national entities, so solid now, had not yet jelled. Spain and the young Republic fenced warily with each other. It was wise to know Spanish, if not perfectly, at least as well as David Humphreys, our minister at Lisbon and Madrid from 1790 to 1802. On February 16, 1791, he communicated a long and meticulous description of Spain to President Washington.[16] Humphreys—soldier, diplomat, and importer of Spanish merino sheep to Derby, Connecticut—showed his continuing interest in Spain by referring to it, sometimes with unconscious humor, in the couplets of his grandiose poetry.[17] The point, however, is the substantial knowledge of the Spanish language acquired by this postwar statesman.

This consciousness among our eighteenth-century leaders of the relevance of Spanish reaches complete and humane illustration in Thomas Jefferson, whose well-known Francophile enthusiasms have obscured for us his interest in Spanish. Arguments for its study occur frequently in his correspondence and especially in his advice to his young nephew Peter Carr.[18] The subject was at times a genuine preoccupation of Jefferson's highly civilized mind. He loved Italian,[19] but he found Spanish more useful. The "most necessary of the modern languages, after the French," [20] it should, he kept saying, be studied zealously. Though disliking novels, he deigned to read *Don Quixote* [21] twice, probably in translation, and it is rumored that he composed in Spanish an essay on the pronunciation of Greek. In particular, he persisted in his exhortations to his countrymen to perfect this instrument of communication that they might, like John and unlike Henry Adams, apprehend the devious Spanish mind.

Jefferson's reasons for such insistence were, of course, practical and underlie this phase of Spanish influence. What, in his judgment, were they? First, in America there were, he believed, really just these two languages. The Spanish and the English covered, so he declared, "nearly the whole face of America." [22] Second, the language was indispensable, not only for our vital present but for the long future of our relations with Spain and Spanish America.[23] Third, "the ancient history of that part of America, too, is written in that language." [24] These were the arguments of our eighteenthcentury statesman, and after 150 years their validity remains unimpaired.

Jefferson's enthusiasm was sincere. He was multilingual, and his Spanish was excellent, surpassing, presumably, his Italian and German. When and how he was initiated is uncertain—perhaps in his school days, though this is unproved.[25] While he was in Congress in 1775 it was generally believed that he spoke Spanish.[26] Though he had quoted readily enough from Ulloa in *Notes on Virginia* (1781),[27] it is possible that his serious study of the language did not begin until his visit to France in 1784.[28] Reading widely in the writings of the historians, he begged David Humphreys to send him from Spain the letters of Cortés and the life of Columbus by his son Fernando.[29] In 1780 he insisted that Spanish be studied at the University of William and Mary, and in a later chapter we shall perceive his application of his principles of education to this language at the University of Virginia.[30]

His interest in Spanish was inherent in a kind of vision of the future of the Americas. Insight into the language and history of Spain and Spanish America aided him in the many national transactions with these regions in which he was a protagonist, but as his letters to Peter Carr repeatedly suggest, he often focused his knowledge of Spanish history into acute speculation about the ultimate destiny of Spanish America. If we glance ahead a few years, we shall see that his delight in the epoch-making book of Alexander Humboldt led him in a letter to the explorer to prophesy, with how much accuracy the reader may judge for himself:

The subject of New Spain . . . I think it most fortunate that your travels in those countries were so timed as to make them known to the world in the moment they were about to become actors on its stage.

That they will throw off their European dependence I have no doubt; but in what kind of government their revolution will end I am not so certain. History, I believe, furnishes no example of a priest-ridden people maintaining a free civil government.[31]

This emphasis upon Spanish as a sesame to a broad historical view of the Americas is arresting. Indeed, it anticipates the theories of some twentieth-century scholars: [32] American history was to include more than the English colonies. How representative was Jefferson's opinion? Perhaps the wider currency of the Spanish historians, both in translation and in the original, indicates that some readers were following his precepts. Moreover, their vogue suggests a higher purpose. During the last quarter of the century other cultivated persons read these annalists with motives less temporal than Jefferson's. Some were enamored of Spanish-American history for its own sake.

The existence of just such an interest is demonstrated by the reception in 1777 of the *History of America* by the Scotch historian William Robertson.[33] One of the great works of eighteenth-century rationalistic historiography, this book made a considerable use of the Spanish chronicles. Different in method and tone from the later romantic histories of Irving and Prescott, it helped to inspire these and to make fashionable for at least a hundred years various types of narratives in prose and poetry concerning South America and Mexico. Despite the misgivings of Robert Southey when he traversed the same ground,[34] it became a landmark in America as well as in England. In both countries it oriented readers in regard to Spanish America. The *History of America* was serialized, discussed, and excerpted for the periodicals,[35] and from it Joel Barlow hewed the beams for his portentous façade of America in *The Vision of Columbus* (1787) and *The Columbiad* (1807).[36]

WE ARE somewhat ahead of our story but not without purpose. The contrast between the leading men of the late eighteenth century and those of the late seventeenth, between, let us say, Jefferson on the one hand and Cotton Mather on the other, was, in respect

to Spanish culture, vivid. The "bombing" of Mexico by Cotton
Mather and Samuel Sewall had ceased; religion was now hardly
a factor. If, however, we return to about the year 1735, we shall
find in humbler areas a parallel growth of influence. In business
as well as in statesmanship Spain was an active personage in our
affairs. The merchant, like the diplomat or the cultivated reader,
might well strive to know more both of the Peninsula and of Spanish America. For since the day when Mather communicated with
his agents in Mexico for religious purposes, inter-American trade,
in defiance of wars and other deterrents, had grown to unexpected
dimensions. By mid-century it involved all the Spanish-speaking
ports of the world.

So to Cuba, to the Caribbean ports, to South America, to Brazil,
or to Barcelona plied the innumerable vessels, back and forth to
Boston, Salem, or New York. To cite only one or two instances,
between 1750 and 1769 ships from Salem, Massachusetts, made the
voyage to every Spanish and Spanish-American harbor, whether
Malaga or Havana, and during 1793 162 craft from the ten-year-old
"United States" came to anchor in the roadstead of gleaming, white
Cadiz.[37] This trade meant a mingling of peoples and of tongues. It
meant also, in the rear guard of this traffic with Spain and her empire, in nearly every seaboard city, the tutors, the grammars, and
the dictionaries. Traders must know the language of this world of
commerce to write bills of sale, to argue with Spanish skippers, to
talk in Mexico City, or to marry Spanish women.[38]

We should not exaggerate the importance of such Spanish backgrounds, for within the multifarious interests of the growing nation
these were minor. Compared with other European countries, Spain
had little to offer America in the development of economics,
science, or philosophy,[39] and its religion still remained an obstacle
to a full understanding. Many thousands of Americans, more or
less fortunate, lived and died without hearing, speaking, or reading
a word of Spanish.[40] During his boyhood in the last decade of the
century, Washington Irving listened to Dutch on the New York
street corners, and as an anodyne in a time of grief he buried himself in German paradigms. Swedish was perhaps as well known in

27

the city as German,[41] and French was still the language of gentility, the acknowledged civilized language for educated Americans.[42] But what of Spanish?

In 1791 the scholarly William Bentley, who may well serve as an example of the cultivated American of his generation, apparently did not yet speak this language. When Spanish officers, leaving their dismasted ship in the harbor, visited him, he was evidently handicapped not only by their lack of "acquaintance with national manners" but by his own ignorance of their speech. One of these officers, he says rather sadly,

left me, at the request of my Frenchman, the only Book he had, which was a translation from the French into Spanish, of the Character of Friendship . . . The Colonel, so called, was able to converse in French, but was no reader, or man of letters from his appearance & his handling books.[43]

The eagerness with which Bentley listened to his friend Bowditch's pedestrian accounts of the cities of Cadiz and Alicante emphasizes American ignorance of Spain in the year 1799.[44] Today these misconceptions concerning its cultural life appear fantastic. Nevertheless, they were widely held. As late as 1817 the *North American Review* could assert that

as a nation, the Spaniards are at present a full century behind every other nation of Europe in the arts of life, the refinements of society, and the modes of education, and intellectual culture. It may be questioned whether they have taken a step in the right road of learning since the days of the Cid.[45]

INSTRUCTION in Spanish was offered in New York as early as 1735,[46] and in 1766 the first college course in the language was available in Philadelphia.[47] The subject now shared the gentle stir at the end of the century [48] over the teaching of modern languages in university curricula. The *New-York Gazette* for July 14–21, 1735, published the advertisement of a tutor in Spanish,[49] and on October 26, 1747, Augustus Vaughan established "a school . . . in New-Street, near the corner of Beaver-Street, where English, Latin,

Spanish, and Italian are correctly and expeditiously taught." [50] Other schools followed promptly,[51] and in 1751 Garrat Noel, at the lower end of Broad Street, issued *A Short Introduction to the Spanish Language*.[52] This was a step forward. Longfellow's Spanish texts were still almost a century distant. Apparently Noel was the first grammarian of the language in America [53]—a distinction worth mentioning even if posterity has viewed it calmly.

We are tempted to record in detail the ramifications during the eighteenth century of these various forms of instruction in Spanish. Statistics would show its continued inferiority to French in popularity and general use [54] but, presumably, an equality with Italian and a currency wider than that enjoyed by German, Dutch, or Swedish. Closer, however, to our purposes is the understanding of objectives, conscious or unconscious. Some of the tutors merely tried to show "the Usefulness of this Language, particularly in these Parts," [55] but others in their advertisements stressed their talents as translators, with aims less utilitarian. We should observe that a few, notably the distinguished Anthony Fiva,[56] "had an academical education, and resided many years in Paris and Madrid." [57] Though these instructors taught what seemed to them "useful to young persons in business," [58] some of them strove to inculcate the language "after the manner of academies, universities, and colleges of the learned world." [59] Evidently not all their pupils were in inter-American trade. Significant in the work of these early drill-masters in the study of Spanish is the intimation of other than vocational purposes. More ambitious uses of the language were at hand.

Imagine, then, a young American of about the year 1790 for whom the study of Spanish meant not the translation of dull letters from Bilbao or "an epistolary correspondence, so useful to young persons in business," [60] but the capacity to read in the originals the historians of Spanish America. Or even imagine him, like young Washington Irving, agog over the adventures of the Knight of La Mancha. Perhaps this hypothetical American reader shared John Locke's opinion that it was important for a gentleman to be well grounded in history, geography, and books of travel.[61] If so, the "academical education" furnished by Anthony Fiva or Garrat Noel might well hasten him not to the busy docks or to the blackened decks of some Jamaica-bound privateer but to the new libraries of which New York and Philadelphia were now so proud. In such a refuge he could have passed happy hours with the historians, the explorers, or better still, with Sancho, the curate, the innkeeper, and Dorothea. Here he could have tested his attainments in the language; here he could have read in science, in travel, in theology (if the young man was a Bostonian!), or in literature. Modest yet aspiring collections of learning! Here in these libraries of our eighteenth-century ancestors is proof enough of the proliferation of research concerning Spain and Spanish America. In the archives of the Philadelphia Library Company, the Loganian Library, the American Philosophical Society, or the New York Society Library, hardened the core of this particular Spanish element in our American culture.

WITH such facts in our minds, the dim, old catalogues of these eighteenth-century libraries make provocative reading. If we pool imaginatively their implements for study, their resources in history, geography, travel, and literature, their treasures seem more than abundant. Anson, Dampier, Ogilby, Garcilaso de la Vega, Herrera, Mariana, Solís, or Acosta was readily accessible in various collections, and in others were Muñoz, Peter Martyr, and Zurita.[62] Some of the rarer items, which Irving was later to inspect in Madrid in the library of Obadiah Rich and which Ticknor and Prescott were to import for their own shelves, could be read by any incipient Hispanophile willing to venture beyond the bounds of his native city. The specialist might examine an ecclesiastical history of Britain in Spanish, the writings of the economist Uztáriz, the scientific volumes of Francisco Hernández, or the learned books on Mexico and Peru.[63] Already these old tomes formed an antiquarian's paradise, and more recent books brought readers closer to the contemporary Spanish-American world.

Bernal Díaz del Castillo must have enjoyed something like a real circulation, for in 1803 Keatinge's London translation of his *Conquest of Mexico* had a reprinting in the little town of Salem.[64]

No scholar need now send, as had Samuel Sewall, to London for a dictionary.[65] Such aids were available in New York to encourage his browsing in Montemayor's *Diana,* Baltasar Gracián, or *Guzmán de Alfarache.*[66] By 1790 in these various collections might be found at least eight copies in Spanish and English of *Don Quixote.* In addition, a considerable number existed in private hands; [67] William Samuel Johnson, the jurist and statesman, began to read the masterpiece at the age of nine.[68] A union list, though tedious, would reveal in these libraries standard Spanish works in history, literature, travel, and even in philosophy, as well as out-of-the-way items now precious to the investigator.

Apart from this aggregate, the riches of particular libraries hint at the beginnings of special bibliographies of Spanish writers. The collection of John Adams contained, for example, a copy of the Spanish humanist Antonio de Nebrija, and that of Harvard College, Pedro Mexía, the historian of Charles V.[69] The New York Society Library now owned a copy of the *Celestina* and of Francisco Clavijero's *History of Mexico,* accompanied by manuscripts and specimens of Aztec and Mexican paintings.[70] We must move from these recondite wonders to the large, workable, and productive collections, such as that of the New-York Historical Society Library, which took form at the turn of the century and which listed, besides history, numerous examples of books on economics.[71] Perhaps no other collection brought Spanish America so close to so many readers. Here, presumably, Irving read of Spain long before he dreamed of writing a life of Columbus, and Ticknor and Prescott searched these shelves for guidance in the creation of their own libraries.

And for the world at large, always diffident toward learning, Smollett's four-volume translation of *Don Quixote,* fairly well known [72] along the Atlantic coast, was purchasable at the shops of booksellers. Some versions of the famous narrative appeared in French (as did *Guzmán de Alfarache*) [73] and fashionable ladies and gentlemen read it and discussed it endlessly in company. Some knowledge of *Don Quixote* was also absorbed through English masterpieces, by way of *Hudibras,* the essays in the *Spectator, A Tale of a Tub,* or *The Dunciad.*[74] During Miranda's historic tour through America in 1787 he was delighted by a South Carolinian judge who was passionately devoted to this classic, and in Providence he talked long with the eminent Doctor Moyes on the merits of Spanish poetry.[75] One amusing instance of eighteenth-century interest in Spanish literature occurs in Dr. Alexander Hamilton's lively account of the "Governour's Club," which assembled nightly at a Philadelphia tavern. On January 8, 1774, the argument was heated as the members discoursed on "some of the foreign writers, particularly Cervantes, author of Don Quixote, whom [they] loaded with eulogiums due to his character." [76]

Doctor Hamilton's excitement concerning Spanish literature was not confined to Cervantes. At Oyster Pond on July 13, 1774, he dined with evident satisfaction on fat pork and green peas, but first of all he read aloud to his friends from the *Visions* of Quevedo,[77] a writer who continued, somewhat surprisingly, to find an audience in America. In November, 1787, the popular *Columbian Magazine,* after printing a version of Cervantes in the previous July, published also a translation from this author.[78] The literary classics of Spain were no longer ignored. We wonder a little whether this passion for Spanish literature in the late eighteenth century was stimulated by the scholars of Germany.[79] Moreover, through travelers or through the English magazines, British translators and critics of Spanish writers were now audible in America.

ALL these eighteenth-century cultural ties with Spain itself were strengthened or qualified by those with the Spanish-American regions. As the study of the language and the growth of the libraries have suggested, Americans became daily more conscious of these countries through trade, travel, reading, and also through the constant menace of Spanish imperialism. They were learning that not only our economic but our intellectual life was to be more and more sensitive to ways of thought in Mexico and South America. No doubt the translations in the magazines of Cervantes and Quevedo were read, but that they competed favorably with the articles on trade in the West Indies is unlikely. In space the Peninsula was far away, and in time Cervantes was distant. Less remote seemed Doctor Gómez de Ortega's use of quinine or the wild hogs of Honduras.[80] Such subjects were really worth an eighteenth-century businessman's attention!

Meanwhile, Robertson's history, which crystallized the latent interest in Spanish America, was serialized in the magazines and, like the installments of Gage's travels,[81] was far closer to popular taste than even Cervantes. Indeed, for the ordinary citizen of the United States during the last quarter of the century Spanish America was far more pleasant to contemplate than old Spain itself. The former, rich, with a future comparable to our own, was already restless under domination while the latter was still terrifying with its splendid, evil past and its aggressive present.[82] Beginning in 1785 the periodicals teemed with bitter, satirical verse on Spain's Mississippi policy.[83] It was natural that in preference to Spanish literature Americans should turn to essays on the mines of Potosí or to articles on the explorations of Hernando de Soto as related by Jeremy Belknap.[84]

THE comparative breadth and depth in the eighteenth century of the two great channels (Spain and New Spain) cannot be precisely measured even when the outlines of such values are sharper than in the nineteenth and twentieth. Despite the distinction just made between the mother country and the colonies, the two sources were essentially inseparable. Yet in the sum total of higher influences (books, magazines, travel, libraries, or collections), the finger already pointed south rather than east. Proximity was a factor; an American businessman was more likely to find himself in Vera Cruz than in Madrid. It might be asserted that the more distinguished intellectual influences came direct from the Peninsula, but this statement can be no more than an argument. On the level of such relations powerful agents were also linking North and South. These were, in particular, the historians who, after the example of Robertson, wrote of the South American civilizations and also the learned men in scientific and philosophical societies in both Americas.[85]

The traveler Miranda, as already observed, educated Ezra Stiles about Mexico,[86] and though such exchanges of thought were at first more frequently concerned with the mother country they were soon paralleled in respect to all Spanish America. In 1784 the Spanish Academy of History elected Benjamin Franklin as its first representative from the United States, and, to mention only one instance, the American Philosophical Society conferred a similar honor on Alejandro Ramírez, the eminent botanist associated with Cuba and Central America.[87] Membership in these societies, letters, documents, proclamations of good will—all these interchanges cemented common interests of the two Americas, in science and in many other phases of a new, hemispheric intellectual life.

At the same time it must be remembered that the Spanish America which interested the eighteenth-century intellectual included vast stretches destined to become integral portions of the United States. He now knew something of Florida, where in 1767 the Minorcans settled; [88] of Texas, whose Spanish heritage was to survive in place names and architecture; of Louisiana, in which the Spanish culture was to be submerged by the French; [89] and of New Mexico, Arizona, and California. In these regions the Spaniard penetrated so enduringly beneath the surface that his characteristics were to flower in the nineteenth century in building, legend, folk song, "riddle," craft, and medieval custom. By 1790 American traders and frontiersmen had become familiar with these picturesque lands. Tales of the natural wonders and of the natives were wafted back to the North and East; [90] river, mountain, and plain were described as parts of Spanish America. Some time after the technical amputation of this "Southwest" from Mexico in 1848, this section of the country began to assert a separate individuality, acknowledged in the distinctions drawn by travelers between Old and New Mexico and between Upper and Lower California. Not, however, until midway in the nineteenth century and in our twentieth did this deeply rooted Spanish culture rise to the surface in the fiction and poetry of Bret Harte, Helen Hunt Jackson, and Willa Cather. In the 1790's there it lay, with all its color, silent, hidden, germinal. Reserved for the future was the gracious art of Santa Fe or San Xavier del Bac.

Francisco de Miranda, from the painting by Georges Rouget.

THE most exciting aspects of the problem still remain to be discussed. Out of all these miscellaneous, scattered cultural contacts of the eighteenth-century colonies with Spain and Spanish America new concepts evolved. Long before Washington Irving had paraphrased Bernal Díaz or Prescott had romanticized Cortés, these concepts began to shape American writing on Spanish themes. The statesman, the merchant, the student in the library, the editor of the magazine or newspaper, the traveler, the secretary of the learned society—all touched in their own ways the rich, intricate mosaic of Spanish culture, and each reproduced a fragment of it in his own microcosm of American thought. All such fragments, separately or in different combinations, reappeared in the somewhat barren American arts of the eighteenth century.

Spanish music, for example, save for a ballad or two, was little known, and Spanish painting was to wait long for the discipleship of Thomas Eakins and John Singer Sargent. Though the exquisite forms of Spanish architecture were visible in Florida and the Southwest, these graceful buildings were to inspire neither recognition nor imitation until the nineteenth century. Only in our historical and literary arts did the results of our curiosity concerning Old and New Spain seem tangible. To be sure, in our literature of the eighteenth century, a literature primarily of state papers, religious tracts, formal essays, and satire, no single figure came forward dedicated, like Prescott later, to Spanish history. There was no ardent admirer of Spanish fiction comparable to William Dean Howells in his esteem of Pérez Galdós and Juan Valera and no lover of Spanish poetry akin to James Russell Lowell in his devotion to Calderón. Nevertheless, our literature already bore the seal of Spain.

For these few underlying, almost instinctive convictions or points of view concerning Spain and Spanish America were causative. In the beginnings of our essay (Joseph Dennie), of our drama (William Dunlap), of our poetry (the "Connecticut Wits" and Philip Freneau), or of our fiction (Hugh Henry Brackenridge and Charles Brockden Brown), we may perceive the subtle operation of these concepts. We have, indeed, in our acceptance of the idea of English literary domination, underestimated the effect upon these eighteenth-century colonists of some of the great Spanish stories, such as Don Quixote and Sancho or the conquest of Mexico, to name only two examples of epical deeds with which England had nothing to do. So our early writers, reading these narratives more easily than they forgot them, introduced them into their fiction or poetry, not enough to reject but sufficiently to modify the basic English qualities. Repeatedly these authors echoed Cervantes and timidly, imitatively, but not ineffectively they used Spanish scenes, characters, and incidents, and as they wrote they expressed the five or six concepts. These we may now discuss, using our literary experimenters, our first men of letters, as illustrations. These attitudes, undeniably present in our eighteenth-century literature, were to be the groundwork for our nineteenth-century belles-lettres on Spain and Spanish America.

THE first of these attitudes was an intense curiosity, revealing itself in the descriptive essay, article, or letter, in regard to all external aspects of Spain or Spanish America. In this expositional prose the mother country is often represented as a sinister, intriguing, mysterious personality.[91] Or, though the era of travel books on Spain was still in the future, the Peninsula with its people, scenery, and customs is discussed with some objectivity.[92] In this latter way it is pictured in much detail and not without justice in the letters of David Humphreys, Thomas Jefferson, John Jay,[93] and John Adams. Sometimes, however, there is a hint of the immortal prejudices of the black legend, as in the lively "Dialogue between Britain, France, Spain, Holland, Saxony, and America" by the shrewd Benjamin Franklin. Side by side with such realistic definitions of Spain and of her future in the Americas and adjacent to the urbane estimates by the historian Jared Sparks occur the petulances of the "American Farmer," St. Jean de Crèvecœur. Although biased and rhetorical, Crèvecœur's portraits of the Spaniard approximate, if we compare these with the writing on this subject in the magazines, a typical evaluation from an eighteenth-century American. He represents Spain as a picturesque but bigoted conqueror, as a treacherous, brutal colonizer. Crèvecœur's vignettes, composed in his own unique French-English idiom, reflect distinctly this point of view.

No evidence exists that Crèvecœur knew Spanish. There is no proof that he had read any extensive sections of Spanish history or, though he may have done so during his prolonged wanderings, that he ever visited South America.[94] Nevertheless, his paragraphs on the colonists' distaste for the Spaniard probably mirror more than his own opinions. His judgments seem to justify the words of a modern historian that for the English-speaking people "the Latin outskirts of their world were a part of their own setting and inevitably affected their thinking." [95] Admiring the simple devotions of the English settlers, Crèvecœur delighted to contrast their religion with the bogy of Spanish Catholicism:

Unassisted [he says of his religious friends] by any ministerial exhortations, prayers, or religious ceremonies, they will quit this world which they have embellished, as peaceably and with more confidence and tranquillity than a Spaniard who receives daily visits from his confessor, and whose room is filled with every vehicle of assistance his church can confer.[96]

In a little-known piece called a "Sketch of a Contrast between the Spanish and the English Colonies," he denounced the "solemn appearance of Religion in South America" and the "Multiplicity of Priests." In our early literature Crèvecœur is now a classic, and he writes sometimes from firsthand knowledge and usually with a simple eloquence. Yet among his descriptions of colonial church life are such sham ornaments as the following:

Compare this congregation, I pray, with the more Gaudy, more Gorgeous Spanish one of *Lima,* coming out of their superb churches glittering with Gold, Irradiated with the combined effects of Diamonds, Rhubis & Topases, ornamented with everything which the art of Man can execute & the delirious Imagination of Voluptuous Devotee can devise or Furnish . . .[97]

The Farmer's exaggeration is ludicrous. Nevertheless, in his attacks on this alien, florid civilization he speaks for a large constituency of his fellow colonists. Rich, imperial, fanatic Spain! Would the legend never fade? Years later Melville's Captain Ahab savagely desecrated in South America the high altar of the "Voluptuous Devotee."

THIS descriptive or expositional literature, often warped by political and religious prejudice, is common enough in the last quarter of the century. It is balanced by another emphasis, most apparent in the poetry and drama of the period. This second type of writing inclines to romanticize Spain the conqueror or to celebrate its rulers as the transmitters of civilization to the New World. Occasionally the sympathy of the author is with the Aztec or with the native Indian and is allied to still another concept to be discussed on a later page, but the splendor of immemorial Spain glows through these narratives in anticipation of our nineteenth-century romantic historians. Even the poetry of Joel Barlow, who detested Spain even more than he loved France, is intermittently under the spell of the conquistadores. Barlow, who died in Poland with the sound of Napoleon's retreating cavalry in his ears, had a flair for the grandiose, in his life and in his poetry. His republicanism painted the Spanish foe as Milton painted Satan—majestic, heroic, and perfidious.

Probably Barlow knew much less about Spain than did his pompous friend David Humphreys or the other tiewig pillars of the Republic. His antipathy to Spain was so violent that he would probably have been unwilling to learn the language, and his use of Spanish materials was secondhand and bent to his own special purposes. He leaned heavily on Robertson,[98] and for his poetic flights on the noble peoples of South America he had read widely in his beloved Voltaire and in the *Araucana* of Don Alonso de Ercilla.[99] At Yale College he had become acquainted with a rare version of Garcilaso de la Vega's *The Royal Commentaries of Peru*,[100] whose availability offers interesting proof of the increase of Spanish collections in our libraries. The central idea of one section of *The Columbiad*, the contrast between the unfortunate heathen and the fortunate English colonist basking in the sun of revelation, is, like Crèvecœur's prose description of the Spanish devotee, ridiculous. Somehow

Joel Barlow, from the engraving by Anker Smith,
after the painting by Robert Fulton.

Barlow contrived to love the native and at the same time to be dazzled by the glamor of the Spanish conquest.[101]

Indeed, in the early days of a national literature, what could be more inviting for an aspiring American writer than these romantic Spanish themes? There is pathos, as in everything connected with his brief and brilliant career, in the story that in his youth Charles Brockden Brown planned no less than three epic poems—on the discovery of America, on the subjugation of Peru, and on the conquest of Mexico.[102] These proved to be mirages of boyhood; no trace of such manuscripts survives. Nevertheless, Brown's first biographer regards the scheme of these epics as a harbinger of Prescott's *Conquest of Mexico* and *Conquest of Peru*. Throughout this period the attraction of Spanish subjects continued. *Don Carlos,* translated from Schiller, was a favorite on the New York stage,[103] and just at the beginning of the nineteenth century William Dunlap produced at least three plays on Spanish and Spanish-American themes.[104] At about this time New York theatergoers saw Susanna Haswell Rowson's *Slaves in Algiers,* whose plot refashioned the tale of the captive in *Don Quixote*.[105] In the same years they applauded the play which so delighted Alexander Hamilton and John Adams, "The Ladies of Castile," with its story of María de Padilla, whose husband led the insurrection against Charles V.[106]

INHERENT in this concept of "romantic Spain" in our early poetry, fiction, and drama is the imaginative reconstruction of the bold and semimythical Columbus and of his voyages. Our present knowledge of the discoverer is so much more abundant and the validity of his achievements, in contrast to those of some other early explorers, is so unassailable that we must remind ourselves how relatively little the eighteenth century knew concerning him. Columbian illumination, if we may call it that, really commenced in the nineteenth century with the appearance of new documents and new historians and new scholars, such as, to mention a few, Navarrete, Irving, Harrisse, or José María Asensio.[107] For the epoch we are studying the sources for knowledge regarding Columbus were, to all practical purposes, the life by his son Fernando and

39

the narratives by Las Casas. The filial biography was made available in Churchill's *Voyages* (1744–46), a book which anyone might then have unearthed in the New York or Philadelphia libraries.[108] These accounts were sufficient to awaken in a people more and more in search of a historical past and a literary future an immense curiosity concerning the dreamer-navigator.

In Las Casas and in Fernando these eighteenth-century readers crossed the ocean with the voyager, heroic, patient, undaunted, and through his eyes they beheld the gentle beings who were to sate—so ran the black legend—the cruelty of the Spaniard. The periodicals now included essays on Columbus.[109] Poetry invoked him, and Barlow imprisoned him in the heroic couplets of his colossal epic. It was not the fault of Columbus but of Barlow that this enormous folio poem aroused laughter in England.[110] Today it is an oddity on the library shelves for oversized books. Whatever faults in the character of Columbus modern research has brought to light,[111] the simple story of these voyages still remains one of the great romantic tales of mankind. Its grandeur almost redeems Barlow's dreary, moralizing poem. In creating his first version, *The Vision of Columbus,* Barlow became, in effect, the father of Columbian poetry. He and Philip Freneau initiated in American literature an endless series of narratives, tales, and verses on Columbus.

Although the sheer size of his gigantic poem threatened to dwarf all rivals, actually Barlow was not the first American poet to celebrate an idealized Columbus. Philip Freneau, whose voyages to the West Indies moved him to write various articles for contemporary periodicals, including one called "Character of Spanish Women," [112] had composed in his youth a lyric, "Columbus to Ferdinand." [113] More important, in 1774, thirteen years before *The Vision of Columbus,* he finished "The Pictures of Columbus, the Genoese." The eighteen scenes of this readable poem, in octosyllabics and five-stress verse, recount episodes, real and fanciful, in the life of the explorer. At its opening Columbus is making maps and speculating upon the "lengthen'd seas" to the west. At its close he is near death at Valladolid:

> The winds blow high: one other world remains;
> Once more without a guide I find the way;
> In the dark tomb to slumber with my chains—
> Prais'd by no poet on my funeral day.[114]

Freneau, however, centuries later, praises Columbus in this sound eighteenth-century verse. The poet describes him in detail, looking into a mirror, at the cell of an enchantress; addressing King Ferdinand or Queen Isabella; at Palos, Cat Island, and Barcelona; and in a tempest at sea. The entire poem is in the orthodox tradition of the legendary Columbus. Although in his literary associations Freneau himself remained far closer to France than to Spain, his pseudoromantic monologue with Spanish backgrounds and Spanish characters was prophetic of many similar poems on Columbus in the nineteenth century [115]—and even in the twentieth.

THUS, descriptions of Spain and Spanish America, narratives in fiction, poetry, and drama with episodes drawn from the South American conquests, and romantic pictures of Columbus in verse became recognizable elements in American literature of the late eighteenth century. Pervading these heterogeneous forms appeared at times a concept with which Spain was associated, though Spain itself was not the exclusive source of this attitude. This concept involved both man's relation to nature and man's relation to man. Without contradicting our assertion that these writers were sensitive to the Spanish arms (which later flash and reverberate through the pages of Irving and Prescott), it was also true that their sympathy was often bestowed upon the conquered, upon the civilizations subdued by the Spaniard. From the first colonization of New Spain the white man had been profoundly interested in the ways of life, in both war and peace, of the Indian.[116] Already many Americans had heard legends not only of the Halls of Montezuma but of puissant princes, gentle races, amiable peoples living in the light of nature, with wise governments and with simple, beautiful cultures of their own.

Perhaps there was a paradox in the popularity of this myth in North America, where the colonists on some frontiers were still locked in warfare with the Indian in implacable race hatred. The fairy tale flourished concerning these other peoples, these beings endowed with true "sensibility," who, as Columbus had said of the Caribs, could "shed tears in abundance." [117] Whether an escape or a compensation or a mere literary vapor, the fancy was widespread. These tales of natural men, of wronged nations, fascinated our eighteenth-century readers, stirring their republican prejudices of liberty and justice as well as their humanitarianism and their romantic feelings. In some ways the concept was contradictory. It glorified both the triumphs of Cortés and the sufferings of oppressed races. Or often the story of the founding of the New World inclined to become a drama in which the Spaniard was the glittering villain and the native the wistful hero, an Arcadian man of "sensibility."

In other words, this drama was one phase of that darling idea of eighteenth-century Europe sometimes called "the noble savage"—this time in Spanish dress. The notion continued to charm western European literature, of which at this time American writing was so imitatively a part.[118] It is impossible to explain fully the complicated origins of this view of man, but Spanish historians as well as French philosophers and French travelers had a hand in the pretty fiction.[119] Acosta, for instance, could be hard upon the Indian but was not unwilling on occasion to idealize him.[120] Garcilaso de la Vega, as we recall from Barlow's benign muse, spread these primitivistic fancies,[121] and above all, in America the humane but biased Las Casas gave it sanction. To Las Casas the Indian was not only good but perfectible.[122] How acceptable to men believing what they wished to believe were this historian's descriptions of Spanish cruelty and bigotry!

Among our sentimental writers, despite the realities of the frontier, the concept of the noble savage held its ground and, in its combination of French and Spanish influences, secured a place in our imaginative literature of the eighteenth century. In this world moved also Rousseau, Montaigne,[123] Chateaubriand—we must not forget the tide of influence from France. Perhaps the noble savage

Title page of *Breuissima relacion de la destruycion de las Indias,*
by Bartolomé de las Casas, Seville, 1552.

was a creation of the Latin race,[124] but encouragement, too, for this beautiful illusion came directly from England. For by 1790 at least a few Americans were familiar with Sir William Davenant's opera, *The Cruelty of the Spaniards in Peru* [125] (1658), or with the speeches of Almanzor in Dryden's *The Conquest of Granada* [126] or, if later literary representations of Spanish tyranny are needed, with Coleridge's eloquent *Osorio*.[127] Who can measure accurately the weight of each ingredient in this curious formula, of the philosopher's dreams, the traveler's records, the love of the primitive, the French revolutionary ideas? No one; critics have agreed to disagree. Perhaps the narratives of Columbus solidified the foundations of the pattern.[128] All that need be said is that the annals of the early Spanish historians, acting upon the American mind when already hospitable to such notions, helped to give this pattern circulation in our eighteenth-century writing.

So, associated vaguely with the timeless cultures of Spanish America, with the future of the native on this continent, with our republican principles, the idea found frequent expression in, among other books, Richard Alsop's translation of a history of Chile, in the verse of Barlow and Freneau, in the plays of Dunlap, and in the imitations in the magazines of the historian Robertson. Alsop took pains to conclude his rendering of the Chilean Abbé Molina's history of his country with an appendix containing extracts from Ercilla's epic, *The Araucana*,[129] with its account of the docile natives. Likewise Barlow, in his pre-Columbian material on Peru, though resistant to the strong colors of the originals, Garcilaso de la Vega or (perhaps) Marmontel, tried to edify his readers by "the unenlightened efforts of human wisdom." [130]

In this temper Freneau's Columbus meets smiling "swarthy kings," who lay their scepters down for Isabella:

> Sweet sylvan scenes of innocence and ease,
> How calm and joyous pass the seasons here!
> No splendid towns or spiry turrets rise,
> No lordly palaces—no tyrant kings
> Enact hard laws to crush fair freedom here;
> No gloomy jails to shut up wretched men;
> All, all are free!—here God and nature reign.[131]

The mood was to linger on, more or less related to the dream of the noble savage, through Irving's half-fanciful biography of Columbus, through Prescott's graphic *History of the Conquest of Mexico,* and through the sentimental novels of William Gilmore Simms and Robert Montgomery Bird. It was, indeed, to expire only in the archaeological and anthropological researches of the nineteenth century.

WITH some relief we may turn, finally, from these rather elusive traceries of influence to a direct, powerful impact of Spain upon our eighteenth-century literature, namely, that of the Spanish classical writers. In the late eighteenth century Quevedo still commanded a small following, and for a few enthusiasts Lope de Vega and other Spanish dramatists took on immortality. We encounter no eagerness, like Irving's a half-century later, to know contemporary Spanish plays. Only one writer enjoyed a numerous audience among cultivated readers, and that writer was the great, the all-conquering Cervantes. He was everywhere, even in this colonial literature. He was known to all readers and writers from Thomas Jefferson and John Adams [132] to our first civilized essayist, Joseph Dennie, author of *The Lay Preacher.* One incident concerning Dennie is typical of this early man of letters: he could never forget his sophomore year in college when he and his friends all "laughed in concert over the pages of Cervantes." [133]

For in this America, in which the satiric mood was strong and deep, Cervantes, and even his imitators, now delighted many a cool mind which could never diet on "the noble savage." There is, for example, likelihood that Charlotte Lennox' *The Female Quixote,*[134] published in England in 1752, was popular here. Dennie, the founder and editor of the *Port Folio,* alludes repeatedly to Don Quixote as a character,[135] and our eighteenth-century scorpions, such as Freneau, Tom Paine, and Mathew Carey, as well as "The Connecticut Wits" [136] were all in debt to his creator, Cervantes. The Knight of the Woeful Countenance, who, as we have seen, seems to have entered our country before Shakespeare, was to be a personality in American literature. Besides our satirists, our

44

scholars and men of learning were devoted. John Witherspoon, president of Princeton College from 1768 to 1794, ranked Cervantes in irony and wit above Homer and Boileau. "None," he declared, "ever exceeded Cervantes, the celebrated author of Don Quixotte." [137] William Bentley, not content with translations, sent to Madrid for his own edition,[138] and William Wirt set out on his road toward the attorney generalship of the United States with "a copy of Blackstone, two volumes of Don Quixote, and a volume of Tristram Shandy." [139] In eighteenth-century America *Don Quixote*'s triumph was complete.

The peak of this influence, affecting educators, scholars, satirists, university students,[140] men of letters, and all manner of literate citizens, seems to have been at the turn of the century or a little later and should be summarized at this point in our story. In 1802 Dennie published in his magazine a pioneer piece which he grandly called "Biography: The Life of Miguel Cervantes de Saavedra":

Perhaps [he remarked of his idol] he had nothing further in view than to write a diverting and instructive satire of the extravagant tales, which, under the title of romances, over-ran the age, and prejudiced the taste, at least, if not the manners, of his country . . . But books of chivalry, with their monstrous fictions and affected sentiments, were fair game for a man of wit and sense; nor could they be more agreeably ridiculed, than by displaying their effects on the imagination of a madman, resolved to put their lessons into practice.[141]

One may find better criticism of Cervantes but hardly better evidence of Dennie's allegiance and so, symbolically, of the loyalty of thousands of other readers. The content and the techniques of the great satire were now so well known in New York—as if Cervantes were some modern Euphues—that in 1809 gay young Washington Irving, not yet the reflective Irving of *The Sketch Book,* capitalized upon Cervantes in a parody of history which set all New York laughing.[142] A background for the laughter and for the success of the book was the city's intimacy with *Don Quixote.*

Irving's "youthful folly," as he later called his *History of New York*,[143] belongs technically to the succeeding century. Apart from certain amateur satirists and except for John Trumbull, whose

M'Fingal probably owes something to *Don Quixote* as well as to *Hudibras*,[144] the true disciple of these years was Hugh Henry Brackenridge, student, teacher, lawyer, and sharp critic of American democracy. For a long time Cervantes was the daily fare of Brackenridge, not so much, he declared, for his "excellent moral sentiment" as to divert and restore his own mind under all the ills of living.[145] *Modern Chivalry*, Brackenridge's picaresque, vital masterpiece, is, like *M'Fingal,* reminiscent of Samuel Butler.[146] This "ludicrous way of thinking and writing," [147] as Brackenridge described his own prose, is apparently a composite of Butler, Swift, and Cervantes. The delightful succession of incidents, the interior narratives, the anecdotes, the characters of the Captain and his man Teague, as well as many minor touches show that Brackenridge was in the secret. He beheld the comedy of the world through the eyes of Cervantes.[148]

THUS we come to the edge of our third century. During the next hundred and fifty years the major Spanish and Spanish-American influences were to develop so rapidly that the period which we have been studying appears in comparison bare indeed. About the eighteenth century one fact is certain: however tenuous these Spanish influences, however subordinate, however interfused with others closer to the heart of political and practical America, however scattered and undistinguished the works of American literature to which they gave origin, this period between the Revolution and the close of the century was important to the growth of Hispanism in our literature. It is difficult to believe that without such preliminary exploration of varied Spanish materials, Las Casas or Cervantes, Prescott twenty-six years later would have reached his momentous decision. He chose for his lifework not a Roman or an English or a strictly American theme but a history of the Catholic monarchs, Ferdinand and Isabella.

The first four decades of the nineteenth century were to witness the real dedication of talented writers to Spanish studies. Throughout this period and later we shall perceive the far-reaching effects of this early work. We shall recall the descriptive essay, the epical

Miguel de Saavedra Cervantes, from the engraving by E. Mackenzie, after the Spanish print engraved by Fernando Selma.

treatment of the Conquest, the idealization of Columbus, the theme of the noble savage, and the colonial versions of Cervantes' indestructible satire. With these in mind we may now study the 150 years, beginning in 1800, through the six mediums: the traveler, the writer for the magazines, the historian, the scholar, the creator of literature, and the artist.

Part Two

Spanish

and Spanish-American Culture

in the United States

during the Nineteenth and

Twentieth Centuries (1800-1950)

FOR the interpretation of Europe to America in the nineteenth century, especially on the level of popular interest, few agents were more vital than the traveler. He is the main concern of the present chapter. If to the everyday American the voices of the historian, the poet, the translator sounded remote, not so those of the wanderers who had beheld with their own eyes London, Paris, or the Italian Campagna. Like the magazines, often used as their medium, the travelers spoke to a vast and eager audience. This was true whether they reminisced on the lecture platform like Bayard Taylor or in society like Washington Irving, who made his travels, said a friend, "go a great way." [1] The influence of such conversation or of the many diaries and letters on travel, circulated among friends according to the custom of the day, cannot, of course, be appraised precisely. Benjamin Silliman, for example, alludes to the interest aroused by the manuscript version of his travel journal. [2] The imaginative consequences of this writing were hidden but profound. It may even be argued that the deep European roots in our culture were strengthened, at least during the early part of this century, by these myriad accounts, oral and written, of foreign lands. With excitement the home-dwelling American devoured not merely Longfellow's *Outre-Mer,* Irving's *Alhambra,* or Hay's *Castilian Days* but those countless travel books blessed with far less distinction. [3] These travelers were rediscovering Europe.

To ascribe the increase of travel books, expanding from a rivulet at the beginning of the century to a gigantic river at its close, to the growing number of travelers and these to the enlarged facilities of transportation is too simple a logic. By the time of our Civil War, a natural knife-edge in this and other chapters, the popularity of travel books rivaled that of history and fiction; all these helped to satisfy the deep craving of nineteenth-century readers for romantic narrative. [4] The fluid, undefined shape of the travel book was an asset in that it made possible encroachments on other types of literature. [5] Sometimes it trespassed on fiction, as in Irving's

Bracebridge Hall, sometimes on the philosophic and cultural essay, as in Emerson's *English Traits.* It could be a professional handbook, such as J. H. B. Latrobe's *Hints for Six Months in Europe* (1869), or, like Mark Twain's *The Innocents Abroad,* which appeared in the very same year, a boisterous satire—the travel book as buffoonery.

Or it overlapped, as in the writings of J. J. Jarves or in Horace Binney Wallace's *Art, Scenery, and Philosophy in Europe,* on aesthetic criticism.[6] In substance the nineteenth-century travel book was protean, tangential, embracing description, exposition, history, moral reflection, literary and social criticism, letters, journals, and narrative—always narrative, even in verse.[7] In the twentieth century we shall see other transgressions of its conventional limits. For our purposes in this chapter the travel book is any book which depends for its content primarily upon the actual travel of its author. After all, its unifying impulse was critical. The differences between Mordecai Noah's crude *Travels in England, France, Spain, and the Barbary States* (1819), G. S. Hillard's popular *Six Months in Italy* (1853), and Henry James' *Transatlantic Sketches* (1875) are infinite. Yet similar purposes animate their pages: those of the reporter, the critic, the student of comparative civilizations. In many ways the travel book was an unveiling of characteristic tastes of the age.

At the same time the practical reasons for the inundation of travel books during the first four decades of the nineteenth century are inescapable. Travel books concerned with America written and sometimes published in England had been popular in the eighteenth century.[8] These continued to appear, intermingling with our own about Europe. We were the children of Europe but, in a way difficult for us in the twentieth century to realize, isolated from her. Irving described in *The Sketch Book* the scenes of which he had first heard at his mother's knee, and Hawthorne lovingly but critically called England "Our Old Home." The breakdown of isolation through the regular packet service after the War of 1812 meant, at last, a partial satisfaction of the popular curiosity; more books on Europe followed fast. For a period the number and quality of these corresponded with the slowly rising curve of sea travel, still in the second decade far from a comfortable business by reason of war and privateering. In 1813, to cite only one example, that bold traveler, Mordecai M. Noah, was captured by the British. Probably Benjamin Silliman's subtitle for his record book has a note of pride: "Two Passages over the Atlantic, in the Years 1805 and 1806."

The travel books owed much to the inventions which before the end of the century made sea travel dependable: the mighty *Mississippi* in 1833 with its staggering capacity of 750 tons; the *Great Western* in 1838; the *Great Eastern* in 1868; and so on.[9] One by one the menaces of war, pirates, and storms diminished; one by one the more distant countries seemed nearer—France, Germany, Italy, and even Spain, formerly visited only by the foolhardy after a stay in England. Gibraltar, Granada, Madrid found in their streets not merely the American merchant and naval officer but also the tourist. Simultaneously, little by little, the attitude in America toward foreign travel altered.[10] Apparently it did not, as often declared, corrupt all young men; on the contrary, it enriched their culture. The experience seemed to make better Americans instead of worse, and though few women essayed travel during these first decades it could be managed safely. Meanwhile, on the long voyages, in the inns, even in the stagecoaches and on horseback were written the letters and the journals.[11] So the travel books were born along with that droll phenomenon of the century, the professional sight-seer. "During the past twenty-two years," wrote Bayard Taylor in his preface to *By-Ways of Europe* (1869), "I have written and published ten volumes of travels." [12]

The motivations behind the travel books were varied, like the reasons which tempted Americans to go abroad. One objective of the American traveler was health. Even in the days of pirates and banditti he sought convalescence in the long sea voyages and recreation in vagabond days in southern France and Italy. Later this vanguard grew into regiments of idlers at the baths and spas and eventually into the army of expatriates known at various times during the century to Hawthorne, George William Curtis, Charles Eliot Norton, and Henry James. While some traveled for health and refreshment of mind, others, robust fellows, such as Alexander

Slidell Mackenzie, author of two popular books on Spain, boldly wooed adventure in the mountain defiles of Castile.

Still others in quest of a gentler experience rejoiced in Irving's "storied association" of castle and cathedral. Thousands of travelers, such as Harriet Trowbridge Allen, fulfilled in far-off scenes their youthful dreams of romantic Europe.[13] This tender sentiment flourished unashamed until the withering laughter of Mark Twain in *The Innocents Abroad* and *A Tramp Abroad*. Mark Twain and other western humorists counseled a more sensible perspective. Admire, they urged, not the Tiber but the Mississippi.[14] Such enlightenment, however, was reserved for the second half of the century. Young Washington Irving's first journey abroad was typical; at the age of twenty-one, in the year 1804, he sailed for Europe in search of both health and adventure. When he returned to New York two years later, his series of little vellum notebooks reflected his renewed energy, his capture by pirates, and his determination to create a travel book dedicated to the shrines of the Old World.

In the prosperity of the Irving brothers (dealers in hardware), which made possible this journey, is implicit another reason for the increasing travel abroad. America was making money. More persons could afford the costs of ship and diligence and of the heavy fees to our consular agents in Europe. More money to spend meant more extensive travel and so more travel books. In addition, sometimes to the surprise of their authors, the travel books themselves proved profitable, turning the dilettante wanderer into the professional, such as the astounding Bayard Taylor. Perhaps Taylor did not merit the current quip that he had traveled more and seen less than any other American, but he was certainly the inspirer of many a profit-seeking travel book. The sequence became distinct, as in the case of John M. Mackie's *Cosas de España,*[15] from pleasant experiences in a foreign land to a pleasant article in a magazine to a pleasant, nerveless travel book, sold widely in America with pleasant royalties to publisher and author and, in due time, dividends to the steamship companies and the innkeepers chronicled in its pages.[16] In this way the immortal commerce of travel books, which is today a commonplace, began. Europe was a fountain of youth, a land of adventure, our lost, ancestral, romantic home, and it was also a cornucopia for the shrewd hack writer.

No doubt something of the young Republic's naïveté, and also much of its materialism, lurks in these origins of the travel books. Yet two other determinants command our respect. After 1825 more and more intelligent Americans traveled, either to deepen their own intellectual lives by serious study and to transmit what they had learned to their own country or to encourage the germinating political liberalisms of Europe by the advice of the free citizens of the United States. Possibly Henry James was right in esteeming the American a bit heavy-footed in his relationships with Europe.[17] There is a hint of the absurd both in Emerson's flight through Italy in 1833 and in Hawthorne's rather shocked exploration of its art some twenty years later while he was writing *The Marble Faun*. Nevertheless, long before Charles Eliot Norton interpreted Italian art, America had already joined the discipleship of nations whose cultural life owed more to Italy than to any other Continental country save Greece.[18] Hence some of the travel books reflected the American's zealous study of art and also his special need in languages. More and more Italian, German, and Spanish (besides the accepted French) entered into the American gentleman's conception of a true education.

James Fenimore Cooper remarks in his own serene way about his sojourn abroad during the third and fourth decades of the century: "My object is my own health and the instruction of my children in the French and Italian languages." [19] His remarkable travel books [20] comment with characteristic frankness on our educational lacunæ. Far indeed from the Philistinism of the popular travel book, these are in essence social and political essays. They mirror the other purpose mentioned: the critical spirit of the American democrat toward the governmental conservatisms of Europe. Many of the early travelers, astute and politically minded, became, like Cooper after long residence abroad, informed critics of both the European and the American civilizations. Conscious of our provincialism, they offered in their travel books correction through the culture of Europe. At the same time they admonished Euro-

55

peans on their oppression of the common man. Side by side with the weak, sentimental travel books appear the writings of Cooper, George William Curtis, and James Russell Lowell, all encouraging the liberals in, respectively, France, Germany, and Spain.

In the travel books, with their multifarious forms and diverse aims, there developed through the century an increasing sophistication. Lowell's discriminating *Impressions of Spain,* published in 1899, is far indeed from Benjamin Silliman's literal journal of travel in England in 1805. Many of the early records adhered to a monotonous formula. We begin with a chapter on the voyage (a fashion so gracefully perfected by Irving in *The Sketch Book*), culminating in the first glimpse of this unfamiliar, alluring Europe. Then follow the descriptions of cities, countryside, and of type characters, with a soufflé of architecture, painting, economics, and the historic past. The gradual dissatisfaction with this childish recipe altered the form to a kind of selective essay with more precise definitions. After 1860 the point of view shifted, under the leadership of William Wetmore Story, Eugene Benson, and Henry James, away from the conventional toward the unusual and the esoteric.[21] The simple joys of the pioneer traveler rediscovering the world of his fathers sharpened into the detachment of the wanderer shunning the haunts of other wanderers. Instead of Big Ben, the bells of the Giralda; instead of York Minster, the red pillars of the Cordovan mosque.

ALTOGETHER, the general story of American travel books during the nineteenth and twentieth centuries is engaging. We should keep it in mind. It will help us to understand the peculiar impression made upon our culture by these volumes born of Spain and of Spanish America. Perhaps the reader has already drawn conclusions about the particular application of some of these conditions to the travel books which celebrated Spain. All the factors, after a lag of time, were relevant, but in the days of Irving and Longfellow, of the pioneer travelers in the Peninsula few indeed hastened there for health or adventure—though one thinks again of the rambunctious Mackenzie. Fewer still went there to study art

Scene in a Spanish Inn, from a print after the painting by Francisco Domingo y Marqués.

"Vista del Escurial, tomada del camino Real de Madrid," from the engraving in Alexandre de Laborde, *Voyage pittoresque et historique de l'Espagne,* Paris, 1806–20.

An ancient Spanish town, Albarracín, from the painting by Ignacio Zuloaga y Zamora.

or to dream of a new liberalism in Europe. France and Italy were nearer, geographically, intellectually, and even in political ideologies. As to the language, if one wished to master the courtly Spanish, why not study it in New York? For a long time Spain remained to the traveler a special experience. This was one of its charms, and it is also the charm of the travel books which describe the country. To comprehend the importance of these as a unique medium for Spanish influence upon our culture we must pause momentarily over the actual conditions of travel in the Peninsula during the first half of the century.

What Dr. Samuel Johnson remarked in the eighteenth century was still true for Americans in the nineteenth: "There is a good deal of Spain that has not been perambulated." [22] For many years the mere physical ordeal of a stay in Spain disheartened the prospective traveler. Instead of the comparative comfort of England, still a kind of ancestral fireside, he encountered in the Peninsula a Biblical simplicity of life. Instead of the brief transit from Dover to a civilized France, he must suffer the long overland push to Bayonne, or to Perpignan, to reach, at last, Barcelona.[23] Uneasy alternatives were the tedious coastal sailings from London to Cadiz, or from London to Marseilles and thence to Catalonia. At any one of these inconclusive terminals the wanderer's troubles really began. For once inside the primitive country he must endure the unspeakable inns, the berlin and the tartana on the dizzy mountain roads, the exhausting days on horse or burro. The dangers of robber and assassin, too, though exaggerated in song and story, were, at first, intimidating. Mackenzie, who found all routes into and through Spain equally trying, cherished few illusions concerning the risks of life and limb. At least once from the window of his diligence he had watched acts of savage violence.[24] His *A Year in Spain* was widely read. Who, knowing it, could enter the Peninsula lightheartedly for a summer's holiday? In the mountain passes the white crosses spoke an eloquent warning.[25]

Possibly, however, such perils deterred travelers less than other specters, some legendary, some authentic. To many an American Spain seemed the gilded incarnation of those evils for which his democratic newspapers rebuked the European countries. If, for example, Britain was sluggish in its social reforms, it might be said that in Spain philanthropy was almost undiscoverable. If poverty was distressing in France and Italy, in the sister country it was harrowing.[26] Whereas the tourist in Rome shuddered at what he regarded as the sinister splendor of the Catholic church, in Spain he was oppressed by the myrmidons of priests. Crossing the border, he found himself surrounded by these frocked symbols of what he had long believed to be the ultimate in religious bigotry.[27] Did the Inquisition still carry on secretly its dread processes? Here, he believed, and did not trouble to validate his prejudices, here in the Alcázar, at Toledo, in the Escorial, and everywhere in beautiful, sordid Spain were the depths of ecclesiastical and political corruption. Charles Dudley Warner, who wrote ten travel books, referred to the country as touched with "decay"; he thought it at best but a "gorgeous ruin." [28]

It was, indeed, a double antithesis in the traveler's mind, rather than the hardships, which kept him on this side of the Pyrenees. First, he sensed the contrast between modern, backward Spain, with its oppressive land system and its precariously held empire, and the ancient, imperial Spain of Ferdinand and Isabella, Charles V, and Philip II. This was the Spain feared but respected by this same traveler's ancestors. Second, he knew from his reading the contrast between this contemporary, reactionary Spain and the progressive, adjacent nations, sensitive to the beginnings of science, to new liberalisms in all ways of thought. Moreover, to the cultivated pilgrim, Spain had less to offer than Italy, whose ancient art and modern revolutionary spirit were imprinting an indelible stamp upon both English and American literature.[29] Even Cervantes, more and more a spiritual possession of American men of letters, could not lure the tourist readily to La Mancha or to the pass of Despeñaperros, and Spanish painting persuaded few to stand, like David Wilkie and Washington Irving in 1828, rapt before the Murillos of Seville. The great artists were better known than in the eighteenth century, but Jarves, in one of the earliest American interpretations of Spanish art, had emphasized the gloom and fierceness of Spanish religious painters.[30] Italian, not Spanish, masterpieces commanded the homage of the young American artist. Quite naturally, then, until mid-century only the unusual tourist visited the Peninsula.[31]

These barriers could not endure. Although in the 1870's or eighties travel in Spain still savored of novelty, the country had, in its proud, leisurely fashion, begun to share the benefits of the industrial revolution. It was now more aware of the outside world. Meanwhile, other causes for American travel in Spain lay in the increased wealth of the United States, in the complicated Spanish-American issues in the Western Hemisphere, such as Cuba, in the enthusiastic study of Spanish culture by scholars, and in the new passion of travelers for the remote and rare. Neither dangers nor fatigues nor priests nor dictators could forever exclude our traveler, with his bulging journal and his letters home.

So during this second half of the century these curious ones made the journey in great numbers, very conscious of our two ambassadors of good will, Irving and Lowell, and aware, too, of our neighbors in the South. Some travelers had, indeed, visited both Spain and Spanish America.[32] In particular, most travelers in Spain knew of Irving's seven years in the Peninsula. It is a rare book on the country which is silent concerning him or Mateo Ximénez, the essayist's celebrated guide in the Alhambra.[33] In the sixties the second volume of Pierre Munro Irving's biography of his uncle, which focused on the latter's life in Spain, may have set a pattern for vagabonds in the country.[34] It is easy to exaggerate. Even in the last quarter of the century Spain still remained less desirable to the traveler than England, France, or Italy. Nevertheless, between 1865 and 1900 thousands returned to America to speak of Spain with firsthand knowledge.

If we survey the century as a whole, the body of American travel literature on Spain, from Mordecai M. Noah to Lowell, is impressive. It includes hundreds of titles and at least a half-dozen major American authors. Among its distinguished items are the classic *Alhambra*, John Hay's *Castilian Days*, and the solid, descriptive letters of George Ticknor. Examining, first of all, the years prior to the Civil War, we find such leadership less stimulating than the many colorful studies of the Peninsula composed by more obscure writers. Some of these have an unexpected tang. Very possibly the salty anecdotes of Alexander Slidell Mackenzie, which for a time kept him out of Spain, regaled Americans more than saner volumes on France and Italy. These sailors, consuls, and intrepid exiles leave us too long in the familiar Spanish scenes, the Puerta del Sol or the Court of the Lions. Nevertheless, they often report the Andalusian peasant or the Galician innkeeper with that intimacy which occurs only when the traveler has penetrated deeply into the life about him. Noah, Mackenzie, and the cultivated S. T. Wallis feel an excitement denied the more relaxed voyager in France. The modern reader who loves Spain will immediately recognize this as akin to his own on Spanish soil. It still vibrates in these now forgotten travel books. In their brief day they "persuaded," as Carlyle would say, American readers. Vital and authentic, they played their part in shaping certain Spanish elements in American culture.

Not always, however, in the ways of truth. For it cannot be too often emphasized that the travel book as a medium for Spanish culture was, unlike the scholarly translations or the histories, essentially popular in character. Even the superior guides to Spain, such as those by the Cushings, were confused in the average reader's mind with cheaper narratives, fulsome reviews, abstracts, and misinformed magazine articles. Why confusion persisted and why prejudices hardened it is easy to see. A few intelligent persons knew what they were talking about. This concession does not, I think, hold concerning that "gifted daughter of the South," [35] as one example, who begins her section on the Peninsula in her *Souvenirs of Travel* with the ubiquitous quotation from Byron:

O lovely Spain! renowned, romantic land!

Miscellaneous and motley many of these travel books were, so captious and so vapid as to be in themselves, cumulatively, almost a valid cause for the war of 1898. In them Spain is traduced, denounced, sentimentalized. Some dispel one kind of ignorance by creating another. Some are fanciful, as in certain passages written by Bryant long before he had crossed the Atlantic,[36] and some are pretentious, like John Guy Vassar's *Twenty Years around the World*. This contains 598 pages, 164 chapters, and a majestic frontispiece of the author.[37] Yet few of these travel books lacked some insight into Spanish life, and all, on this popular level, stirred the American to even greater curiosity when he heard again and again the mysterious word, "Spain!"

IF, AGAINST this background, we take down from the shelves some of these old travelers and dip into them in rough chronological order, we may learn something of American notions of Spain, and we shall certainly enjoy some amusing hours. One of the earliest, in comic contrast to such civilized Continental travelers as Gautier, Ford, and Widdrington,[38] is the brusque, patriotic Noah. His *Travels in England, France, Spain, and the Barbary States*[39] is a jumble of nearly 500 pages spiced with conceit and dissatisfaction. An aggressive traveler with an invincibly closed mind, Noah sailed from Charleston, South Carolina, on May 28, 1813, to fill a consular appointment in the city and kingdom of Tunis. Captured by a British frigate, he completed his voyage on a packet from London to Cadiz via Corunna, skirted the southern coast of Spain, traveled by tartana from Barcelona to Perpignan, and, crossing the border, "took a last view of Spain without regret."[40]

This book was triumphantly American. Noah was able to keep inviolate all his prejudices concerning Spain's tyranny, her hatred of South American independence,[41] and her "feeble" arts. He also maintained his none too modest conviction that his book would "add to the stock of American literature."[42] Perhaps, after all, it does, as a crude example of our early travel literature on Spain. Perhaps it really does add to the whole in its trifling but precise realism. Noah describes a felucca with its single sail like the wing of a sea gull, the captain sweeping out the hold, and the four Spaniards in Algeciras "seated round a low table . . . eating snails, boiled in vinegar; out of an earthen dish. Some they extracted by pins, others by suction."[43]

About a decade after Noah's wooden volumes, between 1831 and 1834, no fewer than eight books appeared, ranging from the anonymous *Scenes in Spain* to Longfellow's *Outre-Mer* and Irving's *Alhambra*. The era of travelers' bulletins from Spain was now

really under way. This happy identification of Irving and Longfellow, those two literary potentates, with travel in Spain was itself
a major directive, but at the moment other writers exerted a
marked influence. Of these lesser books Caleb Cushing's batch of
essays was the most formal, Carolyn Cushing's the most matter-of-
fact, and Mackenzie's two narratives not only the most popular of
this group but the most comprehensive and spirited. His lively *A
Year in Spain*, running at once into three editions, and its sequel,
Spain Revisited, were hardly less famous than *The Alhambra*. On
these rests securely one type of Spanish influence in America before
1840 as conveyed through travel books, and to it we must pay our
respectful attention—after a few moments' delay.

For before we return it to the shelves, we must let our eyes rove
over the enthusiastic pages of a young man already mentioned
named E. C. Wines, author of *Two Years and A Half in the Navy:
or, Journal of a Cruise in the Mediterranean and the Levant*
(1832).[44] Without unusual powers of expression Wines describes
the cities where his frigate, the *Constellation,* paused. He really
saw few towns besides Port Mahon and Barcelona. In its marginal
experience the volume resembles many an early travel book on
Spain, but, unlike the grim Noah, Wines had a light heart and a
sympathetic mind. On shipboard he read *Don Quixote* in the original, and one of his brittle paragraphs amounts to a winning little
essay on Cervantes.[45] Bred to a romantic view of the country
through his reading of Byron and Southey, he does not renounce
Spain for its priests, for the black dresses of its women, or even for
its beggars. His diction is frequently ludicrous. He can speak of
his twofold purpose: "The acquisition of the languages of the South
of Europe, and the sight of those glorious regions, where Genius
wantoned in her young and vernal hour." [46] He was a naïve, flamboyant young man on holiday. Wines' love for Spain is infectious
even now, and it may have seemed more so to his contemporaries.

Leaving Wines, not without regret, we may return to these sub-
stantial books of the decade, notably the works of Carolyn and
Caleb Cushing, with their patient, serious study of all Spanish life.
This is a type of travel book which, as I say, enlists our respect.
Perhaps the narrative of Mrs. Cushing, who arrived in the Alham-

bra only a few months after Irving bade it farewell in 1829,[47] is, in the twenty-seven letters of Volume 2, too unadorned, too impersonal, too unenlivened by anecdote.[48] Certainly it contrasts strongly, almost strangely, with her husband's erudite, elaborate *Reminiscences of Spain*. In reviewing both books Alexander Hill Everett, himself now in love with the country, commented on the beautiful union of two independent minds in a common interest.[49] Caleb Cushing came to his task with an enviable acquaintance with Spain's past in both history and literature. Indeed, the translator of the old ballads should have been, so Pascual de Gayangos once told Prescott, not John Gibson Lockhart but Cushing.[50] More learned than Irving, even if inferior in style, Cushing's poetic feeling flowered into a volume of curious, imaginative, historical reveries.

Twenty-five of these stories, half truth, half legend, such as "Bernardo del Carpio" or "Isabel of Castile, a Legend of Valladolid," revive the Spanish past. Nevertheless, this is a travel book. The framework of the stories is the journey through Spain, and we are always on the road. We climb the hill to the Alhambra; we hear the bronze bell of the cathedral. Pausing, Cushing uses that ancient device of the romantic historian: in a dream he beholds a "moving phantasmagoria of the real fortunes of Granada." [51] Though untouched by the magic of Irving, the formula is effective; Cushing calls these modestly his "detached pictures." [52] The two volumes are for their purpose somewhat too orderly, perhaps even pedantic. In the history of travel books, however, Cushing's knowledge of Spain represents a distinct advance. His cultivation reveals itself in his mastery of other writers on the Peninsula: Southey, Byron, Scott, Lockhart, Irving, or Disraeli, and, in the Spanish language, Mariana, Garcilaso de la Vega, Lope de Vega, Cervantes, Calderón, or Nicolás Fernández de Moratín. We notice, also, his running accompaniment of Spanish ballads.[53] *Reminiscences of Spain*, appearing within a year of Irving's *Alhambra*, spoke to American readers with something like the authority of the scholar and poet.

Reminiscences of Spain, *Outre-Mer*, and *The Alhambra*, which will be discussed later as the crown of Irving's achievement as an interpreter of Spain, are, despite their adornments of essay and poem, basically travel books. They meet our criterion; they originated in travel. Like Cushing, Irving was enamored of Spain's history but less, except for Cervantes (an early love), of its literature. The bedrock of this, the most inimitable in tone of all nineteenth-century travel books dealing with Spain, was his journey from Madrid to Granada in 1828 and his unique residence in the palace of the Alhambra. Substantial portions of *The Alhambra* derived from Irving's antiquarian studies in Obadiah Rich's library in Madrid. Yet his deeper aim, shaped by the counsel of Fernán Caballero,[54] which was to attain an imaginative version of humble Spanish fact, took form during his travel. In its subtle admixture of truth and fiction,[55] both grounded on the pilgrimages in Spain, *The Alhambra* surpassed Cushing's less flexible book. Oriental in coloring, intimate in spirit, it became for at least a generation, besides a garland of distinguished essays, a guidebook for other American travelers.[56]

Two years later appeared its mild, imitative, and inferior companion piece, Longfellow's *Outre-Mer* (1833–34). In 1827, during his eight months in Spain where he paid homage to Irving, Longfellow wrote his long, detailed letter-journals. These became, with some changes,[57] the Spanish portions of the sentimental record of this most sentimental pilgrim. In this tradition of the romantic wanderer Longfellow outstripped all others. He became the amiable, bookish expatriate, dreaming as unaffectedly as later in "The Village Blacksmith" or "The Children's Hour." The close correspondence of the letter-journals and the text of the essays suggest that in composing the former, carefully preserved by his parents, Longfellow had planned *Outre-Mer* as a travel book. Yet, though it describes inns and peasants,[58] it is, in some sections, virtually a reverie on Spain. Without the firmness of *The Alhambra*, this boyish record does show clearly young Longfellow's unconquerable interest, far deeper than the older man's, in the language and literature and especially in the poetry of Spain.[59]

The scholarly and literary qualities in the volumes of Cushing, Irving, and Longfellow undoubtedly pleased readers more discriminating than those carried away by the informal, vigorous narratives of Mackenzie, to whom we now return. Nevertheless, *A Year in Spain* (1829) and *Spain Revisited* (1836), totaling more than fifteen hundred octavo pages and dealing with almost every corner of the Peninsula, were favorites for at least twenty-five years. The oracular Duyckincks, who passed on everything from an American pen, judged *A Year in Spain* the best of all travel books,[60] and Irving, who knew Mackenzie in Spain, not only sponsored this volume but offered his friend advice concerning *Spain Revisited*.[61] All his life Irving eagerly read and reread the four volumes until in his old age his physician forbade him these too exciting pages. In 1831 at the dinner given to Gulian C. Verplanck, Charles Fenno Hoffman, lifting his glass, proposed a toast to "Alexander Slidell, the author of A Year in Spain—his pen has freshened up the colors and quickened into new life the creations of Le Sage and Cervantes." [62]

It was true. Unlike Cushing and Irving, Mackenzie knew little Spanish history except Mariana and Conde, but his eye was always on *Don Quixote,* and, like Cervantes, he could spin a yarn. As a boy on shipboard he had read Florian, and he owned a natural talent for narration; it was good luck that he should tell us tales of Spain. Many magazines praised his "happy" sketches of Spanish life and his descriptions of Spanish scenery,[63] and the *New-Yorker,* somewhat different from today's, declared *A Year in Spain* superb in its panorama of the "institutions, manners, physical, moral and intellectual features of the Spanish Peninsula." [64] While even the critical Poe assented,[65] another reviewer rashly assigned the book to "the permanent literature of the country." [66] In the number of its translations into Continental languages, among them the Swedish, it rivaled *The Alhambra*. One can see why. It is still a brisk and beguiling travel book.

Its power resides, in contrast to Cushing and Irving, in Mackenzie's good-humored energy. This was well illustrated when *A Year in Spain* was banned by royal decree, with orders to dismiss the author at the frontier should he ever attempt to visit Spain again. As an answer to this threat Mackenzie straightway re-entered the country, wrote *Spain Revisited,* and at the close of his first volume printed conspicuously the royal edict against himself.[67] Whatever his faults, these did not include fear or pretense. If he saw the compliment he may have been, like the present reader, amused at the notion that he had contributed to "permanent literature." He was not inquisitive concerning the spiritual or intellectual mysteries of Spain, but he prized a sharp eye and a bold pen: "I do not feel qualified," he remarked, "to speak of a literature with which I am little acquainted; the more so that I am not critically acquainted even with my own." [68] He wrote his books, so he averred, for those "who have not visited Spain, and have no expectation of doing so." [69] Far from being disturbed by the dearth of tourists in Spain, he announced that he had no desire whatever to tempt them thither. He himself was there for two reasons: to acquire a language which—and he glanced toward Mexico—would surely increase in importance in his native land and to enjoy the adventures without which life was not worth living. [70]

The debonair Mackenzie, with a participation in the rougher life of Spain not permitted the gentlemanly Irving, [71] made Americans see not merely the turkeys in the Puerta del Sol but the shaggy Catalans in their waistcoats of green velvet. He described the murder of the Bishop of Vich by the Constitutionalists, the eunuchs, the execution in the Plazuela de la Cebada, or the girls in the coach from Toledo, "the eldest, a close-built, fast-sailing little frigate, with an exquisitely-pointed foot, a brilliant eye, and a pretty arch face, not much the worse for two or three pock-marks." [72] In spite of repetitions, doubtful grammar, [73] and obtuseness to meanings clear to the intellectual Ticknor, Mackenzie's honest zest is refreshing. His sequel, *Spain Revisited,* is inferior, because here, except for the addition of Galicia, he treads the same ground. In it, however, is no diminution of this restless sailor's relish for Spanish life. Together the two books formed an extensive panorama for Americans whose interest in Spain hardly extended beyond robbers, fandangos, and castanets. This statement is unfair, for Mackenzie wrote also of government, politics, and the arts—but with neither scholarship nor unusual acumen.

PERHAPS Mackenzie's cheerful realism was a signal. Between 1836 and the close of our Civil War, a date inviting pause, there appeared a score of travel books on Spain. Each satisfied in some special way American curiosity, now further aroused by the histories of Irving and Prescott, by Longfellow's poetic versions of Spanish themes, and by the bibliographical studies of Ticknor. Even the most commonplace of these travel books has a few scintillas of insight and humor (sometimes unintentional). We recall one statistical medical volume which dwells on the "bilious and nervous" temperament of the Spaniard,[74] and another in which the forty pages on the country are arranged in topical, catalogic order, with such items as "The Fan," "Butter," and "Philip II." [75]

By 1857 Bryant had written so much about Spain that he evidently thought it his duty to see it, and Bayard Taylor, who had learned the language in his childhood, made it a pinpoint in his frantic design for global travel. Taylor showed no particular comprehension of the country; his descriptions of Granada and the Alhambra hardly excel those of the casual tourist. In comparison with the finished studies of Irving, to whom Taylor dedicated one volume [76] besides mentioning him again and again, his sections on the Peninsula are amateurish: "Of the many thousands of landscapes," he remarks in *At Home and Abroad*, "which have delighted my eyes, there are four . . ." [77] Landscapes in Spain, and little more! We need not expect from this hurried tripper an interpretation of the country. "I am led into these wanderings," he remarked solemnly, "without my will; it seems to be my destiny." [78]

In the forties and fifties we must turn again, as in the cases of Cushing and Mackenzie, for perceptive accounts of Spain to writers now forgotten who cared more for the country than for themselves, more for truth than for retinting the old romantic myths. To be sure, Severn Teackle Wallis [79] could begin his chapter on Granada with the sentence: "Since Irving wrote of the Alhambra, nothing has been left to tell." [80] And in childhood he had dreamed of Spain as of a "fairyland." [81] Yet he spoke from knowledge. He visited the country twice; he was at home in the language; he was familiar with portions of its literature; [82] and he dedicated his book, *Glimpses of Spain*, to Don José Antonio Pizarro, the Spanish vice-consul in Baltimore. Wallis was critical of Irving, and he was troubled by the conflicts of opinion about Spain, a confusion which

we may regard as characteristic of the forties, as a natural consequence of the different voices of historian, scholar, poet, and sentimental traveler.

At the same time Wallis did not consider "prejudice and misinformation" [83] relative to Spain an exclusively American state of
mind. France had sent no De Tocqueville there and had derived,
he believed, her preconceptions of the country from *The Barber
of Seville*. The English traveler still carried to Madrid his copy of
Ford's handbook and his memories of the Armada. As to ourselves,
Wallis submits the following amusing observation on the American attitude a century ago:

Seeing but few of the natives of the Peninsula among us—knowing but
little of their language, and still less of their literature—rarely visiting
their country, too—we have a sort of indefinite idea of the Spaniard,
which places him about half-way between a bloody-minded grand-
inquisitor and an "illustrious hidalgo" of Major Monsoon's Portuguese
regiment.[84]

Weary of tales of banditti, Wallis refused to dwell on "stirring
incidents." [85] The melancholy truth was that travel in Spain was
becoming safe enough.[86] He was tired of moonlight on the Tower
of Comares, and though sensitive to the beauty of the Court of
Lindaraxa he saw the exterior of the Alhambra as "square towers,
of dusky red, with pointed roofs of heavy, graceless tiles,—long
somber walls, monotonous and dreary." [87] Admiring Gautier and
Irving, he nevertheless patiently corrected them in points of detail.
Schooled in the writings of such older travelers as Henry Swin-
burne, he was critically familiar also with Ford, Widdrington, and
Mackenzie. His scholarly, judicial book retained the passion for
truth about Spain which he had first expressed in his article in
the *Southern Literary Messenger* for July, 1841: "Spain: Her History, Character and Literature. Vulgar Errors—Their Extent and
Source." [88] Wallis' crusade, however thankless in his own time, is
helpful to us. It lightened the picture which he thought "unduly
darkened by prejudice and misinformation," [89] and it turned his
urbane criticism into what *Brownson's Quarterly Review* called
"an honest and impartial judgment of Spanish character and so-

ciety." [90] It gave us a compact, sound book on Spanish government, on Spanish customs, on the life of the people themselves.

It seems unwise to claim for *Glimpses of Spain* a survival which apparently it did not attain and perhaps did not deserve. Nevertheless, the content of the book is so impressive with its awareness of daily routine, such as dress or cooking, and with its contemplation of the life of the mind, as in its comprehension of Murillo and of the art treasures of Seville, that one wishes it might be better known to twentieth-century travelers. Acquainted with two distinct kinds of public opinion in America regarding the country, Wallis distinguishes unflatteringly between that "in Congress, in 'literary essays,' schoolbooks, and the less cultivated branches of the periodical press" [91] and that represented by the productions of Irving and Prescott. This was his notion of the American cultural dichotomy.

Wallis is free in mind, temperate, ironical, but understanding. Knowing many books on Spain, he nevertheless sturdily creates his own. He can quote a saying from Rioja, a paragraph from Prescott, or a Spanish ballad in the original. In him are reserves of culture and of good sense on cotton or coal mines. Beginning, after a startling omission of the traditional sea voyage, with an able description of Catalonia,[92] he ends with an illuminating study of Spanish government, and he bids farewell to his reader with characteristic simplicity:

If [he says] I have managed to correct some errors in regard to a noble and much-injured country, I have done quite enough . . . Let me, then, commend the Spanish people to the reader. He will like them better, on acquaintance. He may travel, if he will, among them, generally with comfort, always with pleasure. If they rob or murder him on the highways, poison him in the kitchens, or burn him in a Plaza, as a heretic, he will have worse luck, I can assure him, than has befallen any body, lately, out of the pages of a traveler's story.[93]

After the Civil War, in 1867, Bayard Taylor, examining the guest book in the *posada* at Collbató, could discover during the preceding ten years the names of only three Americans.[94] Four years later Henry Coppée deplored the fact that, though since Irving's stay Granada had become "a sort of American property," [95] few travelers from our country actually visited the city. As late as 1897 San Sebastian, frequented by French, Italian, and Russian tourists, seldom saw an American.[96] Was Spain still merely a renowned terra incognita? In 1872 Joseph W. Revere entered the country on horseback as "the best mode of travelling in countries which, like Spain, have a sort of demi-civilization," [97] and in 1880 Catholics expressed bewilderment that few of the faith were attracted to study more closely a land so imbued with the traditions of the Church.[98] No traveler-observer had appeared comparable to the Englishman, George Borrow, whose *Bible in Spain* had won substantial popularity in America.[99]

Well, the mysterious Peninsula was still remote, but travel to its better-known regions had become easier. In the early nineties that seasoned traveler and reporter William H. Bishop made the trip quite casually from New York to Madrid to interview the novelists Juan Valera and Pérez Galdós. His report, somewhat in the twentieth-century manner, published in *Scribner's Magazine*,[100] was but one of hundreds of articles on Spain in the last decades of the century. The year 1883 witnessed the publication of at least five volumes on Spain, among them Edward Everett Hale's *Seven Spanish Cities*.[101] Evidently travel books were more numerous. That they were more provocative is less certain or that they possessed the traits so winning in the writings of Irving, Mackenzie, or Wallis. For these earlier, simple travel books belonged as naturally to the agricultural-commercial era as did the philosophy of Emerson, which, like them, was to be outmoded. One could no longer amaze one's friends by recording a sentimental journal in the Peninsula. Though Harriet Trowbridge Allen was writing in the old vernacular of Spain's "brilliancy, its color, its noble works of art," [102] these travel books were part of a dying tradition. Perhaps it is significant that Miss Allen's book was published privately.

The romantic itineraries, commonplace even in the newspapers, now formed the groundwork for more mature books: thoughtful studies of life in Madrid and Seville or serious examinations of the fabric of ancient and modern Spain. The travel books be-

"Starting of the Coach from the Posada," from the woodcut in
Harper's New Monthly Magazine, volume 41, page 10, June, 1870.

came less jingoistic, more analytical, more cosmopolitan. What of our great international novelist and observer, Henry James? In the eighties Spain was hardly ready for James, nor was he, though curious, ready for Spain. He never touched more than the edges of the country. His words, however, on a great Italian city at the opening of his *Portraits of Places* were soon to be applicable to Madrid:

It is a great pleasure to write the word; but I am not sure there is not a certain impudence in pretending to add anything to it. Venice has been painted and described many thousands of times, and of all the cities in the world it is the easiest to visit without going there.[103]

In this sense Madrid, Seville, and Granada were now easy to visit. If he desired readers, the traveler must talk of the remote corners of Spain, or, if unwilling to sacrifice Madrid, Seville, and Granada for the posadas of Galicia and Estremadura, he must write of these well-known scenes with fresh perception. James could have done this, but the seasoning of the Spanish dish was too pungent for the Jamesian palate. It must also remain a lasting regret that Howells, for several years a dweller in Italy, found no fulfillment for his deep-seated passion for Spain in travel there until he became a septuagenarian.[104] It is not without irony that the first subtle, penetrating book on Spanish manners should come from a Westerner, a politician, from the author of "Pike County Ballads," namely from John Hay of Indiana.

IT MAY be argued that *Castilian Days* (1871) is not really a travel book. It describes no protracted journey in Spain, and it ends with a discussion of politics. A group of essays originating in Hay's travels and in his meditations in Madrid, its very name hints at leisurely reflection. This is no record of a simple-minded traveler amazed by the Spanish kaleidoscope. Instead it chronicles the "days," the thoughtful moods of a contemplative mind in this ancient land. Obviously its escape from the chronology of travel and history into the reflective essay indicates one direction which our travel literature on Spain was now taking. Was Hay thinking of his friend Howells' book, published four years earlier, called *Venetian Life?* Had the notion occurred to him of doing for Spain what his compatriot had done for Italy? *Castilian Days* is in a restricted sense a travel book. Like *The Alhambra* of some forty years earlier, it is a travel book in its careful progression at the side of the reader through museum, plaza, or city. Even Hay's study of Cervantes centers in a devout pilgrimage to the famous house.

Spaniards could hardly have relished *Castilian Days;* it could be too coolly sarcastic.[105] Despite its comprehension of the sensuous side of Spanish life, its criteria seem to be those of the western democrat. The liberal Hay's prejudices against religious bigotry resemble Charles Eliot Norton's in Italy; [106] Howells spoke of "the very hearty tone of [Hay's] democracy." [107] The modern reader is likely to find Hay's wit too deliberate. *Castilian Days* is, indeed, a highly mannered and self-conscious book, often critical to the point of unfairness. Nevertheless, in "Spanish Living and Dying," its author reaches deep down into the national character. In "Tauromachy" his staccato, half-ironic accounts of this immortal Spanish pastime, over which every tourist and amateur journalist had fumbled,[108] best illustrate this particular quality in the book. *Castilian Days* is always pictorial, and even its historical sections are alive with vignettes of a Spain which was changing slowly but inexorably into a modern nation. This precision is not surprising if we recall Hay's poetry, however different in theme; he had the frontiersman's sharpness of observation. Of the bullfights, of the crowds in "Madrid al Fresco," of the portraits in the Prado, he was a vivid reporter. In 1902 Joseph Pennell made a special journey to the Peninsula to illustrate a fresh edition of *Castilian Days.* Today the book is still a poetic and perceptive record of mid-nineteenth-century Spain.[109]

Five years later the case for an intelligent estimate of Spain was fortified by the sixty pages of travel contained in the *Life, Letters, and Journals of George Ticknor* (1876). Apropos of the travel books we are now discussing, these pages seem out of date, for Ticknor held back his manuscript for nearly sixty years. Eager to prepare himself for his professorship in modern languages at Harvard, he had crossed the frontier in 1818, and unlike Hay he described the Spain of the previous generation. Yet so profound a scholar, identified forever with the country by his history of Spanish literature,[110] by his life of Prescott, and by his matchless library, would speak with authority on any age in the Peninsula. The story of this brilliant young man's experiences in Spain, printed separately as a kind of delayed travel book,[111] is so devoted to essentials and is so simply and strongly told as to be easily the most memorable record of an American traveler in Spain during the second decade of the century. Nevertheless, the story of Ticknor's experience did not attain its niche in American travel literature until nearly 1880.[112]

Ticknor's *aperçus* in this backward Spanish world lend some support to the exaggerations of the early travelers. The moment he had crossed the Pyrenees he had a puzzled sense of having passed also beyond the boundaries of time. Was he in seventeenth-century Spain? As a student of history and government, he was shocked. The king was contemptible; the aristocracy was corrupt; and both the libraries and their custodians were muddled. Browsing in the great library of Madrid among books which he had been told were mere wastepaper, he picked up, almost at once, Laplace's *Mécanique céleste*. Each Spanish library was "a mine for future discovery." [113] Of the many differences between Ticknor and the lightweight travelers who rushed so hastily into print the chief one was that of intellect. Ticknor's strictures on society are never prejudices but thoughtful judgments. He has reasons for defining the middle class as mediocre and ineffectual, and he has others for believing in the Spanish peasant. Solid in mind, equable, endowed with social tact, Ticknor moved on through Spain as through other European countries, meeting and knowing well, unlike other American travelers of the period, the most distinguished men of each nation. It is not strange that these sixty pages speak with some finality. Their postponed appearance has not been wholly unfortunate. They complement the poetic *Castilian Days,* and they belong among the later, enlightened books on Spain.

The reviews of *Castilian Days* and of the Spanish section of Ticknor's *Life, Letters, and Journals* confirm the drift in the seventies and eighties toward a more thoughtful interpretation of the life of the Peninsula. The fanciful tales of robbers, enchanted castles, and phantom Moorish caliphs were less alluring. Even Edward Everett Hale, who had loved Spain since childhood, who had mastered its language, and who was attuned to the romance of this fabled land, voiced the general skepticism:

Anybody [he declares] who will read Amicis's amusing account of his visit to Cordova, or Théophile Gautier's will have reason to expect, even from people as unromantic as we are, something entirely out of the range of the nineteenth century now we come into Cordova. But I will not abuse this reader by inventing black-eyed Moorish houris, as I am afraid both these writers do. There ought to be enough in the square truth, if one could only get on paper the impression which the first Moorish city he has ever seen makes upon him.[114]

Fulfilling his own precept, Hale's Seven Spanish Cities (1883) is a blunt, rather matter-of-fact, if sometimes overenthusiastic account of his short stay in Spain. He was delighted with the "admirable" railroad from Burgos to Madrid, and in Seville he announced: "What the inconveniences are of Spanish travel we have yet to discover." [115] We could inform him, even now. On the age-old prejudices concerning Spanish religion or politics, on the proverbial dangers of Spanish travel, or on garlic, he touched lightly with friendly good sense. Everywhere Hale, if not too astute in ascertaining "the square truth," was charitable, finding the courteous Spaniards not unlike "those nice New Englanders you may see at Block Island." [116] Could compliment to the Castilian go further?

Meanwhile, in the seventies James Russell Lowell,[117] from whom Hale had borne letters of introduction, had been sending to his government his informal, witty dispatches. Simultaneously his personal letters, comparable to those of Irving and Longfellow, became, like theirs when assembled, a species of travel book.[118] Edward FitzGerald had pleaded for a volume from Lowell resembling Hawthorne's Our Old Home.[119] For a similar organization of his opinions of Spain Lowell was too busy "in the amiable traditions of Washington Irving," [120] too absorbed in his study of Cervantes and Calderón, or too overcome with indolence, a trait which he shared with these people whom he loved. Unhappily Spain drew from him no writing like "Leaves from My Journal in Italy and Elsewhere (1835)." Indeed, in the pages of this book he had let himself go in a kind of contemptuous renunciation of travel literature. He preferred to dig deep and write of Calderón or of the enigmatic Spanish character. There remained, however, his lively record in letters of his stay, *Impressions of Spain*.

LOWELL's pretty little volume, describing the Spanish court in the seventies and published posthumously one year after the Spanish-American War, now appears both valedictory and ironical. It marked the end of an era in travel books on Spain; those of the twentieth century were to reflect a more complex outlook.[121] At the same time the urbane *Impressions of Spain* seemed oddly out of key with the intense hatred of Americans now kindled in the Peninsula. The war of 1898 was to leave its stamp upon travel literature, not only by discouraging visitors and so reducing the number of travel books but also by unhappy references in these to this disillusionment of the Spaniards.[122] The new travel books allude uneasily to this bitterness; though not enduring, the animosity was strong. Katherine Lee Bates, entering Spain in February, 1899, speaks movingly of what she calls her intrusion upon "this tragic nation" with its "fresh grief and shame": "Sorrow," she writes, "was still fresh for the eighty thousand dead in Cuba, the hapless prisoners in the Philippines, the wretched *repatriados* landed, cargo after cargo, at ports where some were suffered to perish in the streets. Every household had its tale of loss." [123]

This was bad enough, but three other wars were to be agents in altering definitely the character of American travel books on Spain. The first World War virtually stopped travel in the Peninsula. When this was resumed in 1919 Spain was, at least for the adventure-loving American, in competition with Czechoslovakia and the Balkan countries. One lure for the traveler had dulled still more: the Peninsula now seemed surprisingly near. Statistics can be treacherous, but there is meaning in the official publishing records. Between 1918 and 1922 the number of travel books dealing with Spain was cut in half.[124] Another sampling is less convincing but suggestive. Of about one hundred general accounts of European travel (written after 1900) in one of our largest university libraries, fewer than ten contain sections on Spain, and about one half of these are guidebooks.[125] To ascribe this decline to the affair of 1898 or even to the two world wars would be dangerous. Nevertheless, the ruthless struggle of brother against brother from 1936 to 1939, in which no precise fronts existed to permit safety for the traveler, metamorphosed for a time all American travel books on Spain. Instead of the tourist, the war correspondent.

Had there been no wars, had there been no occasion for such contradictory books on Spain as H. R. Knickerbocker's *The Siege of Alcazar* (1936) or Eliot Paul's *The Life and Death of a Spanish Town* (1937), it is certain that in the twentieth century new species of travel books would have appeared, bold variations on such nineteenth-century insipidities as, let us say, John Mackie's *Cosas de España*. The equivalent light reading by modern authors, including Maud Howe Elliott's *Sun and Shadow in Spain* (1908), Philip Sanford Marden's *Travels in Spain* (1909), Mrs. Tryphosa Bates Batcheller's *Royal Spain of Today* (1913), Robert Medill McBride's *Spanish Towns and People* (1925), Arthur Stanley Riggs' *The Spanish Pageant* (1928), or Eleanor Elsner's *Spanish Sunshine* (1925),[126] had acquired a new outward dignity. For many of these travel books were now enhanced by fresh glories of format —binding, printing, photography, etching, and drawing. The sophistications and ingenuities of twentieth-century publishing had transformed the bare nineteenth-century travel book into an exhibition of the designer's art.[127]

In the light of what was happening in Spain, this *décor* was touched with pathos. If the standard travel books wore a richer dress than their ancestors of the preceding century, others, during the three years of Spain's agony, were thrust into the rough garb of the journalist. These desolating records of the late thirties, these contrasts to the pictures of Spain in peaceful days, reported through sharp eyes and often partisan pens the anguish and destruction of the Civil War. Even these dispatches concerning what the traveler now saw in Spain were varied. Francis Theobald Rogers' *Spain: a Tragic Journey* (1937), a transcript in newspaper prose of human suffering, is at one pole while at the other is Paul's *The Life and Death of a Spanish Town*. Paul's book is at once reportorial, imaginative, and compassionate. Rogers' *Spain* is, to quote one of its three prefaces, "the document of a disillusioned journalist . . . the candid document of a Liberal of humane instincts and keen perceptions observing humanity unleashed." [128] This "Liberal" hopes "to disillusion every American who still backwardly believes in the myth of Spanish-democracy as professed and practised in the so-called Loyalist territory." [129]

Whatever the significance of this book in its time, the reader of the present chapter may well compare Longfellow's gentle travel pages on the Catholic church with this author's story and with his preliminary photographs. One of these, which revisits our dreams, bears the caption: "Mummies of Carmelite nuns torn from the tomb and exposed on the steps of a church at Barcelona." [130] The twentieth-century travel book is indeed changed, both in this volume and in that of Paul, who was on the other side in the terrible conflict. *The Life and Death of a Spanish Town,* not unlike a novel, depicts "The Men and Women of Santa Eulalia" so warmly that they become our intimate friends and then, in Part II, relates the brutal extinction of this Majorcan town by the Franquistas.[131] These two types of travel books were born of the war. Between these extremes lie many others, among them *Wind in the Olive Trees* (1946), "a case-history" of Spain under Franco, or *Wartime Mission in Spain* (1945), a story of American diplomacy in Spain, by C. J. H. Hayes, a seasoned historian.[132] All these varied kinds of writing are based upon travel in Spain.

The sophistication of books on Spain, whether dealing with peace or war, represented, even on the popular level we are now discussing, a similar temper in their twentieth-century audience. Though lacking real intellectual distinction, these were not written for the travel-starved Americans who had been content with Noah and Cushing. Many of these readers were seasoned; they themselves had visited Spain and Spanish America, too. Others, like William Dean Howells, author of *Familiar Spanish Travels*, were devotees of Spanish literature. The real cause for the new types resided not in the war or even in the subsidence of the romantic myth. For evidently this was wearing thin: "Fans and *mantillas,*" began a traveler contemptuously in 1925, "color and romance! One finds little enough of them in the Spain of to-day." [133]

Thirty years earlier Miss Bates, apropos of her first caption in *Spanish Highways and Byways,* had remarked: " 'The lazy Spaniard' has passed into a proverb. The round world knows his portrait—that broad *sombrero,* romantic cloak, and tilted cigarette." [134] No, the new types of travel books came into being primarily through the deepening of our own culture. We now knew much more of Spain. The collapse of these legends was a consequence of our mature demand to penetrate, if possible, into the Spanish mind itself. As in Italy we hoped to comprehend

> The hand that rounded Peter's dome
> And groined the aisles of Christian Rome,

so we wished to know more of the Spanish imagination that lay behind the Giralda, the Alhambra, the paintings in the Prado, or the thinker and poet, Ángel Ganivet.

WITHIN these patterns of change we may examine other types of travel books characteristic of the last fifty years. One of these was that written by the intelligent and sometimes learned student-traveler or teacher-traveler. The scholars Ticknor and Longfellow were, after all, exceptional among nineteenth-century travelers; neither had concentrated on the travel book as a specific form. The *Letters* and *Outre-Mer* had other purposes. Now, however, the increasing need of teachers of Spanish, with its corollary of research in Spain, made this kind of traveler far from unusual. Mackenzie's bravado concerning his ignorance of both Spanish and American culture could hardly be theirs. When these scholars wrote travel books, as they often did, they directed them toward an informed public. Books so unlike as Georgiana Goddard King's *Way of Saint James* and Waldo Frank's *Virgin Spain* were similar in their command of cultivated American readers.

The scholar John Driscoll Fitz-Gerald, an expert on Gonzalo de Berceo, gave us his *Rambles in Spain* (1910),[135] a discerning work based upon his letters written in that country. Or Sister Mary Monica, a member of the Brown County Ursulines, having lived in Spain for four years to investigate Peruvian history, contributed her "simple and unaffected personal record of her experiences and impressions," [136] *And Then the Storm* (1937). In the most unexpected places we encounter the strong influence in the twentieth century of Spain upon the scholar, as in E. V. Greenfield's summary of what four months there had meant to him: "I am deeply grateful to the kind fate that directed my little bark Spainward . . . All of which sounds unduly sentimental. But wait, dear reader, until you have lived several months in Madrid." [137]

These travel books, straying off into the domain of scholarship or of social, literary, and art criticism, grew both in number and in insight, but we can notice here only two or three, selecting through the sweep of the half-century those written by two remarkable women. One of these, Katherine Lee Bates, professor of English at Wellesley College, published her first book on Spain at the beginning of the century. The other, Georgiana Goddard King, professor of the history of art at Bryn Mawr College, did not live to see her final book on Spain appear in 1941. Miss Bates, author of a half-dozen books and articles on Spanish topics, a student of Fernán Caballero and of Emilia Pardo Bazán, is unsentimental, judicial, and alive to comparable or contrasting values in Spain and the United States. Early in her book, after heading her chapter with a stanza from Ángel Ganivet's last poem, she reminds us that "the civilization of Spain, streaked as it is with Oriental barbarisms, belated and discouraged as the end of the nineteenth century finds it, is still in many respects finer than our own." [138] What a solid, satisfactory travel book this is with its 438 pages and, as befits a twentieth-century record, its forty photographs! Learned and witty, anecdotal and analytical, with translations of children's songs and with a rich background of various literatures, *Spanish Highways and Byways* is still far from being obsolete.[139]

Miss King's remarkable study, *The Way of Saint James* (1920), wanders farther still from the travel book form into the purlieus of scholarship, literature, and art. This examination of the churches and chapels which line the road to the famous shrine

79

wavers, some critics think, between the erudition of the investigator and the emotion of the poet.[140] It is, indeed, a strangely beautiful travelogue, part guidebook, part poem, in a style personal yet highly intellectualized. It is also a segment in the history of art.[141] It does not, however, like Miss King's *Heart of Spain* (written in 1926), trespass brilliantly upon literary criticism.[142]

This later book, this civilized miscellany, dwells intermittently upon place, history, work of art, or author. It describes Burgos, the *Poema del Cid,* Segovia, Toledo, Madrid, Daroca, and Madrigal de las Altas Torres, and it tells the thrilling story, so dear to Granada, of Ángel Ganivet. Nevertheless, Miss King finds space for Fray Luis de León and for the literary talents of Blasco Ibáñez and of Ricardo León. In particular, she writes in this "travel book" of the Spanish character as it appeared to her in Madrid:

The fathers [she reflects] of these men had faced the tragic crisis of '98, and solved it each for himself in one way or another, as his temper determined him. The profound and unifying trait of the Spanish temper, as Ángel Ganivet had said only a few years before, is stoicism, "the natural and humane stoicism of Seneca . . ."

In the Spanish temper, it would seem, emotion appears quickly, like grass new-sown, or fruit blossoms in a hot spring; then it passes or is transformed into something else. These slender men, with their high heads, their gloved hands, their race consciousness and pride of race, have grown up into a new discipline: they are better-read, more European-minded than their fathers . . . Pride and a nice sense of honor are ingrained in flesh and bone; in the stuff of their minds, dry reason, and disregard of the cost and the personal consequence of action when a great end is to be attained.

Indeed the key of the Spanish character and to a large part of Spanish literature and thought may be found in a fact which has rarely been apprehended in all its consequences, the actual predominance there of the practical reason over the speculative.[143]

Miss King's books are exceptional. We cannot expect such learning or such vision in all students of art who record their experiences in Spain. Yet through these others, too, the dignity of the travel book on Spain deepened. The line between the worst book by these artists and the ornate, standard travel book is often blurred, but in the best of the latter we again detect their authors' awareness of an informed group of scholars and antiquarians. It is difficult to select, but we might turn to Mrs. Mildred Stapley Byne's *Forgotten Shrines of Spain* (1926), intended, says a reviewer, not for the "boorish tourist" but for the "intelligent, unsophisticated wayfarer, in search of ascetic beauty, or the grandeur of the past." [144] This is pompous enough, but it is true that some of these travel books written by and for artists, with their photographs, water colors, or drawings made on the spot, seem to belong to a genre of their own. They are without real counterparts in the nineteenth century.[145]

The underlying aim of these better travel books was to comprehend more clearly the complicated Spanish mentality. As she crossed the border Miss Bates heard the problem stated, perhaps too alphabetically. This country, declared her adviser, "is a contradiction . . . Spanish blood is a strange *mezcla,* whose elements, Gothic, African, Oriental, are at war among themselves. You will find Spaniards tender and cruel, boastful and humble, frank and secretive, and all at once. It will be a journey of surprises." [146] Some of us may be simple minded enough to believe that these paradoxes can be thus listed but never fully explained or integrated, even by the most percipient students of Spain, into a kind of "national soul." In the twentieth century, in every province described in our six chapters of Part II, and not least in these so-called travel books, Americans more and more often fronted this enigma. More and more our writers attempted an interpretation of the Spanish mind.[147] Even travel books became, as has been suggested by the excerpt from Miss King's *Heart of Spain,* more subjective, more philosophical.

Of various examples the most exciting of these approaches to this sphinx was *Virgin Spain; Scenes from the Spiritual Drama of a Great People* (1926) by Waldo Frank, who was to demonstrate further the enlarged office of the travel book by his imaginative interpretations of Spanish America. The author classifies all these books as "history," [148] and in a very real sense they are. Nevertheless, for our purposes *Virgin Spain* belongs in the expansive category of the present chapter; it is directly connected with the writer's experience in this country. It is a travel book with bold techniques

81

and lofty aims. It attempts to solve the spiritual mystery of Spain.

To explain the "complex integer," the wall against which our more daring travelers were now beating their wings, Frank created "a Symphonic History." All the elements forming the "personality" of the country, whether geography or the arts, appear like actors in a play or like themes in a symphony.[149] The book opens with a cadenced prelude on the sky of Spain and ends with a brief drama in which Columbus and Cervantes talk of America: "It is," said William McFee, "a complete organic whole. The parts fit together in a grand design as though foreordained. It is not *about* Spain. It *is* Spain." [150] Abstruse, tense, impressionistic, *Virgin Spain* is an audacious attempt to unveil "the soul of Spain." So far has the American travel book come since its beginnings in the first decades of the nineteenth century, from "facts" to "an image of the living organism." [151]

MEANWHILE what of the travelers to "Spain in America"? To Mexico? To Quito or Lima? To Albuquerque? To "The City of the Angels"? We must return to the year 1800. We noticed the mounting curiosity in the eighteenth century concerning the unknown continent; such a book as Jorge Juan y Santacilia's and Antonio de Ulloa's *A Voyage to South-America* (1758) [152] had many readers. This interest was merely a beginning. As a stimulant in the early years of the next century, it is impossible to exaggerate the importance of the Philadelphia translation in 1815 of Humboldt's *Personal Narrative* or to overestimate the general currency of this traveler's writings.[153] To read Humboldt was to discover New Spain. Who was this giant at our doors in Spanish cape and sword? During the first half of the nineteenth century the political power of Spain and the story of her empire became every American's business.

At the same time the Spanish-speaking individual, whether from Andalusia or Ecuador, remained in the minds of Americans, save those of a few scholars, indistinct. Editorials in the newspapers, histories of the Spanish-American nations, and political reports had addled any clear notion of what was meant by "Spanish." The culture seemed to come direct from across the Atlantic but also to appear from other sources, diluted via Mexico or South America (with an alloy of the Indian), or to be found in our Southwest in a jumble of Indian, Mexican, and American. We should recall Wallis' shrewd remarks on the American's "indefinite idea" of the "Spaniard": "The common opinion of Spain," he said in 1849, "is mostly based upon the English notion . . . We have added to it some trifling improvements of our own, predicated upon our experience of the half-breed Indians and negroes in Mexico and South America whom we call 'Spaniards.' " [154]

This confusion was not lessened by the sustained indifference of the great New England scholars and writers, such as Lowell, to Spanish America. As late as 1889 William Dean Howells, in reviewing books on Mexico and South America, yielded to his instinctive distaste for these peoples, in contrast to the Spaniards whom he loved so devotedly. Bryant's interest in Cuba was not shared by his fellow men of letters. Unlike them, he was fascinated by the Minorcan customs in Florida, and he listened there with curiosity to the preaching of a Frenchman in Spanish.[155] More typical was the ignorance of Longfellow or the vagueness of Whittier, who, in reviewing Bayard Taylor's *Eldorado*, advised this professional wanderer to visit "the vast Territory of New Mexico—the valley of the Del Norte, and its old Castilian and Aztec monuments and associations." [156]

Eldorado is superficial; it shakes together too easily the very different areas of Spanish culture. In his most businesslike style Taylor reports on Cuba, Mexico, New Orleans, and Panama, and in *At Home and Abroad* he glibly compares the beauty of the Valley of Mexico with that of the vega of Granada.[157] We remember, however, one picture in *Eldorado*. For a moment we see the passengers clustered on the bow of their ship, as it sails along the coast of Florida, "talking of Ponce de Leon, De Soto, and the early Spanish adventurers." [158] Taylor was fond of Spanish names and idioms. His use of these is typical of one contribution, accentuated by the Mexican War, of our travelers in Mexico, South America, or the Southwest: the constant borrowing and addition of Spanish words into our speech.

83

For the apathy toward Spanish America before the American Civil War (again a convenient dividing line) among historians, scholars, and men of letters, one basic reason was the obstacles in travel to Mexico, to South America, or even to the Southwest.[159] In effect, Mexico City was not much nearer than Granada, and in the 1840's the service of sailing ships to Vera Cruz or other Mexican ports was inferior to that between New York and Cadiz. Even if Prescott could at this time refer to "parties of gentlemen and ladies [who] go whizzing along in their steam-ships over the route, which cost so many weary days to the Argonauts of old," [160] his description was misleading. It reminds us of Tennyson's complacence in *Locksley Hall* concerning the newly invented railroad. Actually, in 1838 Madame Calderón de la Barca spent three weeks in her voyage from Havana to Vera Cruz. As for movement within the country itself, her *Life in Mexico* (1843), to be described presently, contains many a passage on roads, inns, and robbers strongly suggestive of Mackenzie's discomforts in Castile or Andalusia.

Under these conditions South America had about the proximity of a distant planet, and even California beckoned only to the rash traveler. In point of fact, Valparaiso was some 8,460 miles from New York, and Callao 9,603.[161] In 1817 George Fracker consumed eighty-two days in a ship between New York and Montevideo,[162] only to be shipwrecked later in the La Plata River. Richard J. Cleveland, an American pioneer-traveler in South America, portrays vividly its isolation in the first decades of the century:

When [he recalled in 1842] I first visited the ports of Brazil, of Chili, of Peru, of Mexico, and of California, they had been for ages, and were then, so exclusively used for their own respective flags, that the admittance of one of a foreign nation, was granted only on the most palpable evidence of a necessity, which it would be inhuman not to relieve. When admitted, no individual belonging to the vessel was permitted to land, or to walk the streets of the city, without the disagreeable incumbrance of a soldier following him; hence the difficulty of obtaining information, and consequently the meagre accounts of the manners and customs of those nations.[163]

Despite obvious differences, we think of Russia today. Cleveland, visiting Madrid in 1824, found it easier on the whole to write of

84

Spain than of Mexico and South America.[164] He might have said the same of our far western regions, for as late as 1850 United States government documents showed the journey to California to have been a rough pioneer trek. To avoid the overland trip to the Coast, not yet a few hours' luxury flight by airplane, some travelers preferred the stern weather off the Horn. Dana's classic 150 days in the *Pilgrim* in 1834 was a gentlemanly version of a not uncommon experience.[165] Seventeen years later Edward Rowland Sill, the poet, made the journey, selecting this route as the easiest to California.[166]

So travel was arduous in the first half of the century. Although American trade with these regions increased rapidly after Spain's preoccupation with the Napoleonic Wars and although such a volume as Humboldt's *New Spain* [167] spurred interest, the travel books were on the whole a bleak array. For many years their authors were, with a few exceptions, businessmen, government officials, explorers, scientists, and the widely scattered naval officers.[168] Nineteenth-century Americans, declared Prescott, traveled for business rather than pleasure.[169] These travelers excelled only in their factual descriptions of city or countryside and in their occasional, illuminating anecdotes.[170] We look in vain for travel books on Spanish America comparable to those on Spain by the Cushings, by Mackenzie, or by Wallis; let us expect no Mexican *Alhambra,* no South American *Outre-Mer.* No one resembling Irving or Longfellow ventured into Mexico. We must remember that of all the major men of letters of the nineteenth century responsible for the introduction of Spanish culture into this country, only Bryant ever visited a Spanish-American nation.

Nevertheless, these bare chronicles of Spanish America, some of them not wholly unlike William Bradford's of New England two centuries earlier, have a kind of authority. In them and in the accounts of the borderlands we are often transported to Spanish scenes and to the companionship of Spanish characters. Reading in them, we sometimes perceive more clearly than in the "literary" travel books the firm Spanish design in these simple frontier societies, whether in Venezuela or Arizona.[171] Joel Poinsett, whose *Notes on Mexico* (1824) [172] is a kind of diary based upon personal letters, travels to Mexico City by corvette, mule-drawn litter, and coach and pictures the country under the regime of Iturbide. Or Waddy Thompson, American minister to Mexico, sets down from memory his matter-of-fact *Recollections of Mexico* (1846).[173] John Lloyd Stephens describes his ten months' travel in Central America including Yucatan—a bolder venture. Timothy Flint tells us of Manuel Lisa, the famous fur trader of Missouri, of the Spanish customs in Natchitoches, of the Spanish hamlet of Adayes, and of the "adjoining Spanish province of Texas." [174] These books lacked the sensitivity and craftsmanship of the European *voyageurs* but had the merit of unpremeditated truth.

Among all these pre-Civil War, nonliterary wanderers in Mexico and Central America we are halted for a moment by one who still captivates the imagination. Stephens, by profession a lawyer, was thirty-four years old and the author of books dealing with Russia, Arabia, Petræa, and a dozen other countries [175] when in 1839–40 he made his first journey to Copán and Guatemala City.[176] In the following year he enlarged these bold explorations, and the resultant book is still excellent reading. *Incidents of Travel in Central America, Chiapas and Yucatan* (1841) was thrice fortunate: in its agreeable style, in its astounding revelations concerning the Mayan cities, and in its happy timing.

For it appeared neither too early nor too late but at a moment of real American interest in everything Spanish. Bryant had already written on Spanish themes in the periodicals; Prescott was at work on *The Conquest of Mexico;* and in one way or another Ticknor, Irving, Cooper, Longfellow, Walt Whitman, and Herman Melville were all conscious of the Spanish civilization. Bryant and Prescott became Stephens' friends, and the enthusiasm of the historian was boundless.[177] His respect qualified the captious criticism of this archaeologist and explorer by Madame Calderón de la Barca. In thanking Prescott for a copy of the book, she wrote him:

The Travels are very amusing, and dashed off in a most free and easy style. I hear they are criticized as being very incorrect by those who know the country. One thing is evident—that he could not speak Spanish, which must have caused him many difficulties, but he might have got someone to *spell* it for him. I observe that there is not a word in Spanish spelt right, even by chance.[178]

What of it? Weak Spanish hardly lessens the greatness of Stephens as a reporter of strange lands and forgotten cultures. Within three months his book passed through twelve editions.[179]

After remarking in the passage cited on the exclusion of foreigners (a kind of Spanish-American "curtain"), R. J. Cleveland noted the breakdown in succeeding years of these prohibitions and commented on the appearance of "numerous and elaborate accounts of South America." [180] Indeed, after the first decade there occurs in American writing an accelerated revelation of all these peoples, from Californian to Argentinean. However barren they are in some ways, the historical interest of these travel books is undeniable whether they discuss the primitive hospitality of the Chileans or the Castilian nobility of Bogotá. One of the first Americans to know South America at first hand, William Shaler of New England, lived in California from 1803 to 1805 and later became in Cuba the friend of José Bernardo Gutiérrez de Lara. It is difficult to say which is more remarkable, his *Diary* published in 1808 or his activities as a champion of liberty. He sowed with gusto the seeds of republicanism in these South American nations. Later he published his history of Chile.[181] By the standards of literature these early nineteenth-century travel books are hardly more than respectable, observant, and sensible, but they form a background for two which excel them all in their imaginative re-creation of Spain in America.

OVER these two we may pause. In one of them, in Richard Henry Dana's classic *Two Years before the Mast* (1841), the Spanish fragments enrich the entire book. Although this masterpiece is primarily "a voice from the forecastle," a realistic but dramatic narrative of life at sea a century ago with asides on such marvels as Tierra del Fuego and the Sandwich Islands, Dana's accounts of Spanish California have outlived those of more experienced but less gifted tourists. The body and color of these episodes do not arise from any overwhelming interest like Shaler's in the growth of the Spanish-American civilization. This Harvard undergraduate was not moved by the spectacle of Spain in America; he gave little attention to the subject, save to undergo an intermittent apprenticeship to the language. At Juan Fernández in Chile he was embarrassed by his complete ignorance of Spanish. Later in the voyage he borrowed from the ship's cabin a grammar and dictionary and was soon able to boast humorously: "As I soon knew more Spanish than any of the crew, (who indeed knew none at all,) and had been at college and knew Latin, I got the name of a great linguist, and was always sent by the captain and officers for provisions, or to take letters and messages to different parts of the town." [182]

So Dana felt at Monterey in 1835, and in January, 1836, he was still hard at work on his pronunciation. His industry was the correction by a cultivated man of his own ignorance. Although his acquaintance with the language (with a grammar in his pocket) helped him to converse with the people, he thought of them only as a part of this varied pageant which his amazed New England eyes now beheld: the Horn, Valparaiso, Santa Barbara, Monterey, and San Francisco. Dana never became, like Wallis, Hispanophile. He portrayed the Spaniards but also with equal relish the Italians or the Sandwich Islanders. He became an interpreter of Spanish California by accident.

In a guess at the influence of Dana's descriptions of California we must remind ourselves of the popularity of *Two Years before the Mast*. More than any book hitherto mentioned in the present chapter, except those by Mackenzie or Irving, it engaged instantly the absorbed attention of thousands of readers. Its success in its role as a truthful recital of life at sea is evident in the wide distribution of copies by the English Admiralty to ships in its navy. Meanwhile, the wider, more sedentary audience which cared less for blue water than for tales of things remote hurried the book into numerous editions and into scores of reviews. The latter reprinted excerpts, among them the bright-colored Spanish sections. The point is that these Spanish scenes enjoyed a vogue connected with this exciting tale of rounding the Horn. Those who shuddered at the brutality of Captain Frank Thompson also read of the mission of San Juan Capistrano. Among a dozen proofs of the force of Dana's influence, we may recall that Bret Harte, who was born in the year of Dana's return from California, learned by heart the Spanish chapters [183] in *Two Years before the Mast*. Harte's manipu-

lation of Spanish themes in fiction and poetry is discussed elsewhere, but at the moment there is meaning for us in his arrival in
Boston for his first lecture there. Introduced by Dana, he spoke of
the older man's Monterey and San Diego. In our complicated pattern of influences we must not forget *Two Years before the Mast*.

Dana's descriptions of a funeral or a fandango, of a cockfight, of
Spanish life on the Pacific Coast in 1835 and 1836 are succinct and
vivid. Some of these equal in their simple truth the best-known
passages in the book, for instance, the unforgettable incident of
the flogging by Captain Thompson. We mingle with the elegant
"Spanish Americans" of Juan Fernández, who wear rags with the
air of grandees and who maintain their dignity unruffled in every
mischance of this mortal life. Only when gusts of wind from the
mountains blow off the roof of a house are they moved to mutter
a few Spanish oaths and to gather their cloaks more closely about
them. How beautiful even in Dana's plain prose is Santa Barbara
with its adobe houses and its mission fronting the crescent bay!
Five chapters, "Trading at Monterey," "Liberty-Day on Shore,"
"Easter Sunday," "California and Its Inhabitants," and "A Fandango," are authoritative accounts of backgrounds which before
their author's death were to enter into both our fiction and our
poetry. We owe much to the fact that this magical "parenthesis"
in Dana's New England life occurred in his impressionable youth.
He sensed the beauty of Spanish even on the lips of these ruffianly-
looking Californians. "It was," he recalled, "a pleasure simply to
listen to the sound of the language, before I could attach any
meaning to it." [184] He delighted in the gaiety of the Spanish wedding, in the breaking of the cologne-filled eggs. Not a sentence is
wasted. Through the eyes of the stripling from Massachusetts we
become for a moment dwellers in this Spanish-American world.

Dana's *Two Years before the Mast* with its episodes from Spanish
life on the Pacific shores appeared midway between two of Prescott's monumental books, *Ferdinand and Isabella* (1837) and *The
Conquest of Mexico* (1843). More and more in the 1840's, as we
now see, Spanish influences on American culture were gaining
both in maturity and variety. In addition to many others, writers
as different as Prescott, Ticknor, Bryant, and Longfellow were

engaged with Spanish themes, and Irving, our minister in Madrid from 1842 to 1846, was writing home to Washington and to Sunny-side of public and private life in the capital. So in the very year of his history of the Spanish monarchs Prescott went out of his way to acclaim another remarkable travel book on Mexico. Fascinated by the letters of Fanny Inglis Calderón de la Barca, he insisted that these be made available to American readers in her *Life in Mexico during a Residence of Two Years in That Country* (1843).[185]

Verbose but informative and witty, this book became for years a standard aid to our knowledge of our southern neighbor. Offi-cially endorsed, elaborately reviewed, graced with a preface by Prescott, adopted in 1847 by General Scott as the official guide for his soldiers in this foreign land, reprinted as late as 1931 in an edition sponsored by the Junior League of Mexico, this clever travel book has enjoyed a long career. It has deserved its fame. Unlike Dana's volume it was in the main stream of our growing interest in Spanish-American culture. Though Scottish by birth, Madame Calderón de la Barca, the wife of the Spanish minister to Washington, had shared her enthusiasm for this culture during her thirty years in the United States in friendships with Prescott, Tick-nor, Longfellow, and Lowell.[186] She and her fascinating travel book belonged to the tradition.

In their special ways Dana and Madame Calderón de la Barca were pioneers; both *Two Years before the Mast* and *Life in Mexico* received literary recognition. Both authors were aware of literature and the arts; [187] both were skillful writers. It is, however, difficult to make similar assertions concerning the travel books written about Spanish America between 1865 and 1900. These, blessed with less talent, began to introduce the characters which were to be so familiar in the twentieth century, among them the archaeologist, the journalist, and the holiday maker. Meanwhile, during this period our trade with the Spanish-American countries temporarily declined. Fewer American flags were seen in the La Plata basin, and fewer naval officers wrote of the wonders of these far-off regions.[188]

Whatever was published in these decades reflected a Spanish-

American world in which conditions were still primitive. The ocean trip was easier, but Zabriskie Gray's *Mexico As It Is* (1878), perhaps the first record made by an American of a pleasure trip in this country, in praising the comfort of the railway coaches observed also the presence of a guard of fifty soldiers to protect the passengers against bandits.[189] In many Spanish-American countries train travel was still elementary. Sure-footed mules were a necessity, and on these by day or night were carried the traveler's food and bedding. In 1881 Mary Hallock Foote traveled in an ordinary Concord coach drawn by eight mules from Mexico City to Morelia.[190] Not until the eighties did guidebooks for the tourist in Mexico begin to appear.[191] Here and in South America the traveler had to steel himself continually against a variety of hardships.[192]

These conditions were described in detail in a section called "How to Travel in South America" in the third edition of James Orton's *The Andes and the Amazon; or, Across the Continent of South America* (1876).[193] This well-known book, together with H. M. and P. V. N. Myer's *Life and Nature under the Tropics* (1871), described the Smithsonian Institution's expedition of 1867. The explorers invaded the mysterious country in two divisions. One proceeded to Caracas and thence pressed on by way of the Orinoco and the Rio Negro to the Amazon. The other set out from the west coast and after descending the Andes followed the Napo River to the Amazon and then down the greatest of all these waters to its mouth. Though matter-of-fact in content and style, these travel books must have stirred American imaginations; they anticipate the excited curiosity of the next century. There is a romantic strain in the work of Ephraim George Squier, who in 1849 was appointed a *chargé d'affaires* to the Central American states through the agency of Prescott. To his benefactor's *History of Peru* Squier owed his passionate determination to "visit the land of the children of the Sun." [194] The fulfillment of his dream was his *Peru; Incidents of Travel and Exploration in the Land of the Incas* with its stories of the journey from New York to Lima, of the city itself, of the Incas, and of other prehistoric civilizations.

In South America, hard on the heels of the explorers in the eighties and nineties followed the newspapermen and, slightly later, the sight-seers. The former were often government publicists, the precursors of our "cultural relations" armies of today. We are now wiser in diplomacy; some of these traveler-officials sound naïve. Nevertheless, William Eleroy Curtis' *The Capitals of Spanish America* (1888) or his *Venezuela, a Land Where It's Always Summer* (1896) is informative on such places as nineteenth-century Caracas.[195] Curtis suggests strongly the changes since the days of William Shaler not merely in South America but in the American visitor. These journalists were evidently preparing for the whirlwind narratives of the twentieth century. Without airplane Frank Vincent made his 35,000-mile journey, and in 1895 Richard Harding Davis relates, as might be expected, a lively story of his wanderings.[196] We may date, I think, the first impetuous flow of tourist travel into Mexico and Cuba in the seventies [197] and into South America in the last decade of the century. Of these tourists' confessions there are hundreds.[198] For illustration we may select one published in 1886, Helen J. Sanborn's *A Winter in Central America and Mexico*.

From the pleasant, undistinguished narrative of this coffee-princess on a business trip with her father in 1885 we learn something of American attitudes toward the Spanish-speaking peoples. Miss Sanborn's account was so popular in a trade journal, the *New England Grocer,* that it was reissued as a book. It tells the tale of her journey from New Orleans to Guatemala by steamer, carriage, and mule and of the return by train to San José, by boat to Panama, and back again to New Orleans. With a sigh of relief, "fairly out of Guatemala," Miss Sanborn quoted Mrs. Stowe with enthusiasm: "The pleasure of travelling is to *have* travelled." [199] Yet she continued on to Vera Cruz and to Mexico City. Why? Even more provocative than her comparison of the Guatemaltecans and the Mexicans is her reflection at the end of the volume:

Spanish countries, the Spanish people, and the Spanish language certainly have a fascination for the Americans. It may be because of the diametrically opposite characteristics; for the one is an affectionate, demonstrative, exceedingly polite, slow, and improvident race, while the other is in comparison a cold, undemonstrative, brusque, nervous, and energetic race. There is something about these countries, when

92

you have visited them, that makes you long to go again. Everyone of
our party in Mexico began to talk about going to Spain next year, and
even now with any thought of a journey first comes to our minds, Spain,
or the West Indies, or Mexico, and we verily believe they have, in one
sense, more attractions than all the glories of Europe.[200]

IT WOULD seem so, especially in the twentieth century. In the
long story of the travel books as a stimulus for our men of letters,
the writings describing twentieth-century Spanish America offer a
variety and color undreamed of in the nineteenth century, even
by Bryant, a traveler sensitive to these qualities in the civilizations
of Cuba or Mexico. Recent travel books on these regions have
profited by the misfortunes of Europe. The wars which slowed
travel in Spain transferred it, so to speak, to Central and South
America. Here, in areas still unfamiliar to Americans, travel, even
during the first decades of the century, discovered not one country
but twenty. Each nation turned out to be peculiar to itself, in
climate, ethnology, industrial development, and politics. Except
for the basic Spanish strain (exclusive of Brazil), each was vividly
different from its neighbors in every province of living. Mexico
and Paraguay or Chile and Costa Rica offered the twentieth-
century traveler contrasts more startling than those which enchanted Irving as he rode on horseback around the triangle of
Cordova, Malaga, and Seville.

The multiplicity of Spanish America's resources, dramatically
revealed, from minerals to Maya cities, explains the varying kinds
of travelers it attracted: engineers, businessmen, diplomats, historians, journalists, archaeologists, artists, and routine tourists.
Probably these were more adventurous, more "modern" men and
women than the visitors to the Peninsula during the same period.
In any event, the travel books themselves wear an air of excitement,
natural in their definition of a new continent. They have a glitter
appropriate for our age of speed. Over the peaks soared Hudson
Strode while "on either side chalky pencils of cathedral spires wrote
Andean choruses on the fresh morning's azure slate. And directly
in front of them the youthful sun god, hurling gold-feathered darts

93

of light, rose to meet the thunderbird." [201] That is, the author's airplane. Strode was carrying out his intention, expressed in the preface of *South by Thunderbird* (1937), "to get a bird's-eye view of the whole show." [202] On the other hand, no South American journey, not even those among the antiquities of the Aztecs and Incas, has yet evoked a travel book equal in learning and insight to Miss King's *Way of Saint James* or *Heart of Spain*. For the most part, these travel books, when they come to earth (literally and figuratively), report on the Indian, on primitive living, on struggling political systems, on advances in the techniques of modern civilization, or on beginnings in national arts. They are occupied not with old Europe, but with the *New* World even if this world is rich in ancient Spanish and Indian traditions.

This rather showy apocalypse of the Spanish-American world owed much to man's subversive invention, the airplane. Wings over South America reduced the distance from the United States to Rio de Janeiro from two weeks to four and a half days; to Santiago, from two and a half weeks to four days; and to Buenos Aires, from three weeks to four and a half days. Almost overnight these remote areas became miraculously accessible. Bogotá had long been near geographically, but few travelers before air transportation had cared to face, after the four-day ocean voyage to Barranquilla, the eleven- to fifteen-day pilgrimage from the coast up the Magdalena. On this leg of the trip the saving of time seemed incredible; the flight over the mountains consumed only four hours.[203]

So not only could our up-to-the minute traveler, notebook in hand and not without his luxuries, inspect easily these corners of the earth, but as modern communications developed among the nations themselves he could within a few hours compare civilizations which for centuries had enjoyed only imperfect knowledge of each other. After describing the Andes, an imaginative traveler remarks: "Here is indeed a barrier between nations; it would be hard to conceive a more inevitable, a more permanent. The plane, the radio, the telephone have broken it. But it prevailed for four centuries to fix the individual traits of Argentina and Chile." [204] It was natural, then, that travel books should now be written about every nation south of Texas. It was natural also that many of these

94

should take form not from the saddle of a mule but from the cock-pit of an airplane, with all that this point of vantage implies of adventure, haste, and shallow romance.

Such panoramas from the air of a new world make us think of Walt Whitman dreaming of a single America. Man would annihilate space and nationality,

> As a strong bird on pinions free,
> Joyous, the amplest spaces heavenward cleaving.[205]

They remind us also of the multiracial characteristics of this cosmos which the travelers were now uncovering. This world was not wholly Spanish. In general, those countries in which pure Spanish blood has been least intermingled with foreign strains (Argentina, Uruguay, or Costa Rica) have been the least visited and, in some respects, the least frequently described. We think first of the noble Indian lineage, now prized by thoughtful Mexicans, or of the princely background of the Incas of Peru. In nearly every country the blood and culture of the mother country have suffered alloys. Apart from gigantic Portuguese Brazil, there are the German and the other non-Spanish Europeans in Chile and the Argentine. Or we think of the Negro in Cuba and the unassimilated, non-Spanish-speaking Indians in Mexico.[206] To the hasty traveler these admixtures did not matter. Instead, they added to the zest of his experience and to the opalescence of his writing. Everywhere he found, if sometimes faint, the underlying Spanish essence.

South by Thunderbird! Sky Roaming above Two Continents! Wings over the Americas! [207] The titles suggest the temper of these twentieth-century travel books. For these conventional narratives, despite their breathless glimpses from the clouds of Chapultepec or Valparaiso,[208] were designed for a perennial audience, not too different from that which had dipped into Slidell Mackenzie on Spain a century earlier. It was an easygoing, easily bored audience, not of the quality which read *Highways and Byways of Spain* and less intellectual than that which could delight in the *Way of Saint James*. The fact is that the sky-roamers and the thunderbirds, with their facile prose and their iridescent mosaic of continents seen from the heavens, had merely substituted Spanish America for

95

Spain. Granada from the vega was an old story; La Paz from the
air was new. It is amusing to recognize the same techniques. Some
of the modern travelers are as tiresomely fond in their opening
chapters of the departure or arrival of the plane as were the old
travelers of the sailing voyage from New York to Liverpool. These
are stories primarily for entertainment, though this is an objective
not to be despised in any travel book.

Our chatty, friendly travelers are not always in the air. In train
and motor they hurry us through the twenty nations. They offer
diverting if not profound reporting. Harry Alverson Franck's
Trailing Cortez through Mexico is an agreeable travelogue,[209] and
Hudson Strode, author of *South by Thunderbird,* writes gracefully
of South America and Mexico—and later, with equal enthusiasm,
of Scandinavia. Strode is in some ways the most popular travel
writer of our time.[210] In his vagabond journeys Franck, the "sky-
roamer," has traversed some ninety countries and is the author of
eleven books on Latin America. His roots in these scattered regions
of the globe are hardly deeper than those of the relatively less-
traveled Strode, but in *Rediscovering South America* (1943) he
evaluates changes in the civilizations of the continent since his visit
there three decades earlier. In mere scope the twentieth-century
traveler to Spanish America puts his predecessors to shame; he
makes a girdle round the universe.

These animated travel books discuss every Spanish-American
country, not omitting Salvador, Panama, and the Caribbean Islands. It was inevitable that those celebrating Mexico, that fascinating land which had enthralled Madame Calderón de la Barca
should multiply and become, on the level which we are considering, more original. Since 1928 these accounts of Mexico have increased unbelievably. From this date until 1932 thirteen volumes
appeared; between 1943 and 1948, thirty-six; the total for this span
of twenty years is 131.[211] These range from the early travel book
Viva Mexico! (1908), which begins with the voyage on a Ward
liner from New York to Vera Cruz and ends in the Zócalo, to guidebooks for the Pan-American Highway, to the mannered writing of
Hudson Strode and Harry Franck [212] (who have also been here with
notebook and camera). Or we may turn to the charming, half-

fictionized *Village in the Sun* (1945) and *City in the Sun* (1949) by Dane Chandos. The former book reassures us that

Ajijic is real. The events related in this book are real. They happened. But, as regards the people, name and appearance, character and profession have been changed and interchanged, so that no person is directly portrayed, while certain houses described do not exist, but have been invented from parts of other houses. This is not a book about Mexico. It is a book about Ajijic.[213]

The more thoughtful travelers in Mexico show this intense interest in the country people and the Indians. These two narratives, like Gertrude Diamant's *The Days of Ofelia* (1942) with its version of "The Stupid Otomis," [214] remind us again how full of insights the good travel book can be.

In the perspective of the present chapter we cannot continue the story of what might be inexactly called travel books on our own Southwest.[215] If Mexico, through air travel and the Pan-American Highway, is near, closer still are the now civilized regions of New Mexico, Arizona, and California. Innumerable books describe these regions, as well as Florida and Texas. Many of these, in discussing the Spanish backgrounds, are less interested in the records of travel than in racial, social, or political problems.[216] Carey McWilliams' *North from Mexico* (1949), as one example, after some history of the borderlands and their settlement, studies the warfare of the three types of culture (Mexican, Indian, and Anglo-American) and, in particular, "the Mexican problem." Erna Fergusson applies the craftsmanship of her travel books on Guatemala, Venezuela, Chile, and Cuba to descriptions of her native Albuquerque and New Mexico.[217] Essentially her work is historical and interpretive, as in her first book, *Dancing Gods* (1931), which deals with the customs and ceremonials of the Pueblos and Navajos. What was said of her *Cuba* (1946) is not inapplicable to all her reports on the Southwest: "a zestful and determined traveler, a serious if not profound thinker, a candid and clear-eyed observer, eagerly sharing with a growing number of readers all her discoveries and experiences and thoughts concerning lands she has visited." [218]

97

IN TELLING the story of this fluid form, it has already been hinted that the travel book sometimes infringed on scientific writing. The tendency of the twentieth-century travel book on Spain was, it will be remembered, to foliate into the antiquarian, into the scholarly, into the history of art. In Spanish America (and even in the Southwest) its encroachments have been in archaeology, anthropology, architecture, handicrafts, government, politics, and science. These studies were usually inseparable from the travel experiences of their authors. Many expeditions in the twenties and thirties to the Mayan cities in Guatemala and Yucatan received an official recording in travel books.

If Earle Parker Hanson's *Journey to Manaos* (1938) checks for the Carnegie Institution terrestrial magnetism at various places in South America, it is also packed with economic and philosophic observation and with the hardships of the explorers.[219] Earlier scientific excursions elicited similar travel books, among them Hiram Bingham's *Across South America* (1911) and *Inca Land* (1912). The former, with eighty illustrations, told in simple language of

an exploration of the most historic highway in South America, the old trade route between Lima, Potosí, and Buenos Aires. The more difficult parts of this road were used by the Incas and their conqueror Pizarro; by Spanish viceroys, mine owners, and merchants; by the liberating armies of Argentina; and finally by Bolívar and Sucre, who marched and countermarched over it in the last campaigns of the Wars of Independence.[220]

The latter volume related the story of four journeys into the interior of Peru. Both books are reliable authorities today.

During the forty years which have elapsed since the first scientific expeditions into Spanish America, the stormy political and economic development of these nations has stimulated the talents of American journalists. It was axiomatic that the travel book should become an instrument for such writers. So we must sometimes put up with long itineraries and with the hasty diagnoses of the political health of a dozen nations. Some travel books became elaborate memoranda on government in Spanish America. Nevertheless, the foundation of this writing, too, was actual travel. Carleton Beals, educated in California and the author of sixteen books on Latin

America, built his *Lands of the Dawning Morrow* (1948) on a nine months' journey through South America. John Gunther owed his wealth of knowledge and his air of authority in *Inside Latin America* (1941) to his airplane trip through all the twenty countries south of our own.[221] Perhaps the original form of the travel book now seems strained past recognition, but this brilliant if ephemeral reporting, these bulletins from newspaper travelers also had their part in the revelation of Spain in America.

Presumably the twentieth-century travel books on Spanish America appear to the reader more superficial, more utilitarian than those of the same era on Spain. Rightly so; they are. Yet we must remember the anthropologists and the archaeologists who, even in the travel books, wrote of the Aztecs and Incas, and we must think also of a few imaginative travelers who were now exploring the history and speculating on the future of these peoples. Some of the travelers discovered, over and above the Spanish and Indian heritage, a spirit similar to our own. These nations were, after all, "American," not European. No such intimacy with the mind of the Peninsula was ever pointed out (save by those of Spanish blood), but Mrs. Niles emphasizes the bond with Spanish America in her *Journeys in Time* and in some of her other seven works on these countries.[222] She believed in our "instinctive identification with the Latin-American countries." [223]

Perhaps her vague feeling that everything in Mexico was "oddly familiar as though some how [she] had known it before" [224] has little significance save as an effective introduction to a romantic travel book. Her idea of identity, however, was important. It unified her anthology of "four centuries of man's life in the Latin Lands of the Americas." [225] Renouncing the feverish journey and the hasty report, she read deeply in the writings of these four centuries, not excluding the most recent years. She then put together a sheaf of travel literature, full of "adventure and philosophy, hate and love, mercy and cruelty, wisdom and gossip." [226] This anthology, ranging from Bernal Díaz to Hudson Strode, contains some queer bedfellows, but the plan succeeds. Few travel books are blessed with equal perspective. None tries more sincerely to make us comprehend the spirit of countries so unlike and yet so like our own.[227]

This concept, on which Mrs. Niles trespassed in her romantic anthology, of one hemispheric America was to be developed, as we shall see, by twentieth-century historians. It was stated again with poetic intensity by Waldo Frank in *America Hispana* (1931), a "panorama of Spanish-American ideas, ideals, history and culture," [228] and in *South American Journey* (1943). Frank, whose *Virgin Spain* was already widely known among Spanish-speaking peoples,[229] was now hailed as a lecturer, as a writer, and as an interpreter of their visions. In *America Hispana* the journey itself is expanded into wide prospects, for example, "The Andes," "The Pampa," "The Pacific," "The Forest," or "The Central Sea." *South American Journey*, a direct record of Frank's trip in 1942 during the war, is vitalized by excellent descriptions of places and peoples.[230] Though neither volume is, like *Virgin Spain*, "a symphony," the poetic and imaginative conception of the interrelated roles of all the Americas distinguishes these two among all other travel books:

I encountered [he said in speaking of Spain in America to the Argentine writers] a poor and exiled fragment of that world as long ago as 1917, in the Southwest of my country. I knew nothing of it; I could not speak its language. But I sensed at once that it had something for me; something for my people; something which my world, the proud industrial world, lacked . . .

It was the sense that *we*, specifically of the United States, in a civilization topheavy with machines . . . needed a new capacity of integration . . . an organic knowledge, which the Hispanic and the Indo-Hispanic worlds appeared to possess.

The second stage of my understanding was that *we* had something . . . which *your* America needed. Later, only later, I was to see the symbol of our being one hemisphere, one America.[231]

This idea some of the twentieth-century travel books helped to establish.

ONE hundred and thirty-five years have passed since the publication of Mordecai M. Noah's *Travels in England, France, Spain, and the Barbary States*, 111 since the appearance of Madame Calderón de la Barca's *Life in Mexico*. During this century (and longer) the backgrounds, motivations, purposes, and attainments of travel books written by Americans about Spanish areas and Spanish peoples have changed astonishingly. Poor Noah hoped that his travel book would "add to the stock of American literature." Looking back on the present chapter it may almost be said that this hope was realized. It set a fashion for other travel books. Basically subliterary, the travel book on Spain and on Spain in America has seldom approached literature in quality. It has, however, been the cause of literature. Its real importance has been as a medium of knowledge and suggestion for the creators of literature. Irving read Mackenzie; Longfellow read Irving; Hay read Longfellow; Howells read Hay; Prescott read Madame Calderón de la Barca; and Harte read Dana. To be for a moment more specific, Melville drew upon obscure works of travel for his brilliant stories, "The Encantadas" and "Benito Cereno." [232] The links are innumerable, and though it is impossible to define precisely, in relation to other influences, the scope of the travel book or to ascribe any particular poem or novel to its influence, still there it is, a continuous and stimulating source of knowledge concerning Spain and Spanish America.

THOUGH often more trivial, more ephemeral than the travel books, the magazines were catalysts of Spanish culture in America. In this respect their history was long and complex. Journals and mushroom magazines of the eighteenth century had never omitted news of Spanish commerce or of Spanish political affairs.[1] At the turn of the nineteenth century, when there flourished some 150 newspapers in the United States and when such provincial sheets as Mathew Carey's *Columbian Magazine* or the *Monthly Anthology and Boston Review* were influential, many reports on Spanish life were available. These were skeletal; in them the cultural situation was ignored. Robert Walsh's *American Review of History and Politics,* which survived through 1811 and 1812, gave particular attention to France but slighted Spain altogether.

As to literature, during the first three decades the magazines allotted more space to that of Germany than to that of any other Continental country. In 1829 one editor lamented: "Our periodicals teem with abstracts and reviews of English and German books . . . While we hear so much about English and German literature, we scarcely read now and then a passing notice upon that of France." [2] Among the early nineteenth-century magazines probably Joseph Dennie's urbane *Port Folio* was most hospitable to Spain. Here we may find frequent references to the Spanish world and also denunciation of the ignorance of the other magazines in respect to Spain. Nevertheless, at the beginning of the century, among Continental influences conveyed through the magazines Spain was a weak fourth.

The magazines reflected, more than the travel books, the casual thoughts of everyday Americans about Spain. Exhumed today from the libraries, these periodicals seem oppressive in their dullness, but the fact that they usually served only transient interests makes them particularly accurate records of their times. Few readers or editors wished to substitute nobler purposes for immediate responses, and this the contributors soon learned.[3] They wrote of ideas which were current, of issues which were imminent. To read a book is sometimes arduous; to write one, more so. Anyone, however, may try his hand at an essay, a story, a review. Undistinguished wanderers in Spain or dreamers concerning this romantic land found the columns of the periodicals, especially after 1830, hospitable to a hesitant poem on Columbus or to a feeble tribute to Cervantes. As we shall see repeatedly, the influence of one culture upon another is not always effected through its most eminent writers.

After a slow start these humble pieces connected in some way with Spain or Spanish America became multitudinous. For the dissemination on the popular level of knowledge about the Spanish civilization, the magazine developed into the most versatile of mediums. It embraced all interpretative forms: essay, history, translation, romance, or poem. In the forties, as the tide of interest in Spain rose through the travelers, the historians, and the men of letters, these magazines, whether short-lived like the *Boston Miscellany* or pontifically enduring like the *North American Review,* reached out to all kinds of readers. They kept pace with all these other spokesmen, echoed them, and became powerful instruments of expression for Spanish influence.

For the magazine was friendly to both the weak and the strong contributor. In saying that the specimens of prose and poetry in the magazines were numerous and varied we have sometimes said all. Many of these essays, stories, or poems were insipid beyond belief. To indicate that they were printed is far from proving that they were read or remembered. Whether in the first decade an arid recital of Spanish posadas or in the last years of the century a novelette of Mexico, much of this writing attained an immediate limbo which we need not too rudely disturb. Yet it played its part; there can be no doubt of that. On the popular plane it left in the American mind indelible if often inaccurate impressions of Europe, including Spain. At the same time a higher indoctrination, a subtler interpretation, was taking place through a few magazines with more intellectual aims. Side by side with the shallow biographical sketches of Ferdinand VII or Saint Teresa might be found the scholarship of Ticknor or at the end of the century the research of the professional students of Romance languages. On both levels the magazine was influential, and its interplay with the other agents of interpretation was close and continuous.

Particularly intimate was the relation of the magazine to the travel book, which it reviewed and from which in the early part of the century it eagerly excerpted. For many years its pages were crammed with descriptions of the European scene. At first selections were offered from the books on Europe. Later the process was reversed: books were made from articles already contributed to the magazines. Selections from Mackenzie's *A Year in Spain* were promptly published in the *North American Review,*[4] but before their appearance as a book Lowell's dispatches, the essential portions of his *Impressions of Spain,* were accessible in the *Century* and the *Critic.*[5] Thus the magazine was both nurse and midwife. Into its pages entered also the other interpreters, such as the historian or the novelist; here may be found preliminary studies or by-products of monumental works on the Peninsula. This heterogeneous material in the magazine made its influence intricate. It was a vast department store exhibiting for inspection samples of every type of writing on Spain.

In the magazine Bryant printed anonymously his first experiments in translations of Spanish religious poetry. Here toward the end of his career Irving tossed the final scraps from his Spanish notebooks.[6] Here the churchman denounced the bigotry of Spain or the antiquarian re-created the world of Moorish culture or the student of government and society reflected on the reverberations of the Revolution of 1868 or the young American girl found space for her unutterable emotions in the Alhambra. Here we may read of lodgings in Zaragossa in the 1830's, of Spanish economics, or, examined with academic precision, of Spanish metaphors. Here Longfellow played with the etymology of the language, and here the great Ticknor reviewed the great Prescott. Finally, at the close of the century the magazines published biographies of the recognized historians of Spain. Everything is here *in parvo.* Reading and rereading these hundreds of magazines, one concludes that in them is latent almost the whole labyrinthine story of Spanish influence.

For these reasons there emerge, as said, two strata of interest like those defined by the traveler Wallis, that of the half-literate reader and that of the scholar and man of letters. In the magazine speaks not only the dilettante romancer but also the bibliographer in the magnificent Ticknor library. This distinction is not always clear-cut. A few obscure travel sketches rival those of Longfellow or of Irving, who with his too acute ear for the public pulse sometimes cheapened his talents. Nevertheless, in the magazines is noticeable the same contrast in quality observed in the sharply differing travel books. As John Hay's *Castilian Days* is superior to the narrative of Mordecai M. Noah, so does Longfellow's "Spanish Devotional and Moral Poetry" in the *North American Review* dwarf Cheever's "Grenada and the Alhambra" in the *Knickerbocker*. With characteristic flamboyance Cheever remarks that

the fiery, generous, industrious Moor is succeeded by the bigoted, lazy, priest-ridden Spaniard . . . Alas! alas! for the melancholy change!

But oh! how bright will be the dawning of christianity upon this lovely region.[7]

These passages alternate in the periodicals with the solid studies of the ancient institutions of Spain by historians like Coppée and Henry Charles Lea.

Often the high area of interpretation reflects accurately the high character of the magazine in which it appears. Ticknor's articles were published in the *North American Review* and toward the end of the century Howells' criticism of the Spanish novelists in the *Atlantic Monthly*. On the other hand, we may expect less from *Godey's Lady's Book* in 1836 or from the *Cosmopolitan* in 1890. In nearly all of these periodicals during the last three quarters of the century, the period which we are now studying, we stumble on uninformed statements concerning Spain's history, government, literature, or ways of life. At the same time in almost all of them we find also an awareness of such scholarly writers as Ticknor or Lea. During the first half-century special preferences for Spain existed in certain quarters. The Catholic magazines urged persistently a better understanding of Spain's religious fabric [8] and tried to direct American readers toward its literature. The *Southern Review* showed early a devotion to Spanish poetry, and on the staff of the *Southern Literary Messenger,* of which the ardent Wallis was a pillar, were intelligent critics of Spanish thought. In later years Howells carried on his battle for realism in *Harper's Monthly,* and percipient writing on the art of Spain appeared in the *Century.* Other predilections might be mentioned, but for illustration we may well limit ourselves to one magazine, the Olympian *North American Review.*

IN INTELLIGENT curiosity all magazines fell short of this periodical, which in a variety of articles consistently encouraged until well past the middle of the century a knowledge of Spain from the highest possible points of view. The establishment in 1815 of this benign oracle, comparable to the renowned quarterlies of England, regularized and articulated the interest of discerning American minds in affairs European, and in this fertilization of our readers Spain had inevitably its share.[9] From its beginnings this magazine was to remain a vital artery from both Spain and Spanish America. It commanded the most eminent of Hispanophiles, among them Ticknor and Prescott, and for its pages it drafted them all. In it appeared in rapid succession the reviews of Irving's Spanish books: in 1829 Alexander H. Everett's of the *Life of Columbus* and Prescott's of *The Conquest of Granada,* and in 1832 Everett's of *The Alhambra.*[10] Ignorance of Spain could hardly survive such aggressive enlightenment. We may regard Jared Sparks' elevation in 1824 to full editorship [11] as the official inaugural of this superior Spanish influence in the periodicals.

The strength of this type of influence lay in its range. Before we arrive at the essential concern of the present chapter, namely the types of writing in the magazines (whether poem or political essay), we may well pause over the scope of this mighty engine of opinion, the *North American Review.* For it contained such antitheses as Longfellow's essay, "Spanish Devotional and Moral Poetry," [12] and a review of J. M. Salazar's *Observaciones sobre las reformas políticas de Colombia.*[13] The magazine's awareness of South America was natural; its founder, William Tudor, became our first consul

Jared Sparks, from the engraving by Stephen Alonzo Schopf,
after the painting by Thomas Sully.

in Peru.[14] This attitude was derived also from Sparks' breadth of vision. In contrast to some of the travelers and most of the New England men of letters, he never separated, after the fashion of Longfellow or Howells, the Castilian and the Spanish-American cultures. Sparks knew his Cervantes, but he was also tireless in collecting data from the South American countries. Out of these came his long and intelligent articles on history, government, and inter-American relations, and into his columns flowed the contributions of writers plagued by a similar curiosity—those of Caleb Cushing, Edward Everett, or Willard Phillips.[15]

Of all our major literary figures, Bryant alone (traveling in Cuba and Mexico and writing of South America in the *Evening Post*) would have approved the integration as parts of the same Spanish pattern of such different elements as Lope de Vega, Humboldt, Irving, or the grammar of Mariano Cubí y Soler. In his isolation Longfellow was wrong, and in his breadth of view Sparks was, as events have proved, right. It was to be one Spanish world. We can return to the literary content of the *North American Review* with more comprehension of its influence in this world if we recognize the high quality of Sparks' definitions of Spanish America. From Boston on September 24, 1825, he pleaded for more understanding:

The increasing stability [he writes Tudor] of the South American Republics makes it highly important, that as much knowledge as possible respecting them should be diffused among the people in this country. The difference of language, and the infrequence of communication, have thus far kept the people of the United States in almost total ignorance of what has been doing at the South. Our newspapers, the only vehicle of communication, have sent out as many errors as truths. Hardly an editor in this country knows the Spanish language, and there is not to this day taken in Boston a singular regular file of a newspaper from the whole South American continent, or Mexico. Our news is principally obtained from private letters of ignorant or disappointed adventurers.[16]

A year later Sparks was thinking not of South America but of Spain itself. In reviewing Cubí y Soler's *El traductor español* he expressed his ardent hope of the example and spirit of the best Spanish writers operating on our literature.[17] In this country [he says] little is known of the elegant letters of Spain; it is a field unexplored, but it is wide and fertile, rich in the fruits of genius and of cultivated intellect. The language of Cervantes and Calderon, of Lope de Vega and Feijoo . . .[18]

In contrast to the separation of the two, which we shall perceive so often, Sparks offered this fusion of Spain and Spanish America. So, after this tribute to the classics, let him finish his letter to Tudor in Lima:

Under these circumstances I have thought it might be serviceable to the interests of both countries if the most important intelligence could be embodied from time to time in the *North American Review,* and for this purpose I have taken measures to obtain, from the best sources in the different republics, papers and printed documents from which a pretty accurate knowledge of passing events may be derived. I shall esteem it as a favor if you will procure for me in Peru a copy of all the documents which have been printed during the revolutionary movements, both in the time of San Martin and more recently. I wish also to procure an entire file of a Lima newspaper.[19]

The newspapers of Lima and the plays of Lope de Vega! Apart from the variety of its contents, the *Review* strengthened this sense of the underlying unity of the Spanish civilization.[20]

THE magazine, whether it was the authoritative *North American Review* or some ephemeral, obscure monthly, outshone the travel book in the multiplicity of its offerings about Spain. Although an entity, the travel book could subdivide and write of scenery, inns, customs, art, or literature, but the magazine could exploit these in thousands of separate articles and, in addition, could print miniature histories and essays on politics and commerce. James Fenimore Cooper is said to have remarked that the male American of his day had only two interests: business and politics. For this American the magazine was important. Few travel books were likely to reach the hardheaded audience which read Jared Sparks' remarkable reports in the *North American Review* on the commerce of South America. In the pages of the magazine, too, appeared long excerpts from Spanish and Spanish-American prose and poetry. Here were prolonged discussions of Spanish themes in reviews and critical essays; adaptations of Spanish poems; novelettes on Spanish or Mexican subjects; or recondite bits of Peruvian history. The periodicals seemed to include everything; nothing Spanish was unimportant.

This variety of subject rendered the magazines, despite their distressingly uneven quality, unique transmitters of Spanish influence. Nor was there ever in these other periodicals, thanks perhaps to the *North American Review,* a narrow separation of the Peninsula from our own hemisphere although at first, naturally, articles on Spanish America were less numerous. In the same issue one might read either of Calderón or of the pampas of the Argentine. Therefore in the present chapter no division of the two interests will be made, for to the editors this hardly existed. We may trace the influence in the magazines very simply through six or seven topics: the description or analysis of Spain or Spanish-American countries; historical articles; political essays; critical pieces and reviews; creative writing on Spanish themes; and studies of the fine arts (including, for convenience, the theater). Following these types, with in each case some attention to chronology, we may, I think, estimate the force of this medium until about the close of the century, and in subsequent pages until 1950.

As ALREADY hinted, the most elementary but recurrent reporting on Spain in the magazines throughout the nineteenth century was the *description,* whether this was a simple cluster of four anecdotes on Spanish character in 1802 [21] or Mrs. Elizabeth Robins Pennell's "Lights and Shadows of the Alhambra" in 1896.[22] The early descriptions are childishly factual, relying chiefly on the novelty of the material: "Madrid"; "Description of Madrid"; or "Description of Malaga." [23] Not unlike these, the records of Spanish America and the borderlands are arid summaries of physical resources or bare notes on commerce, agriculture, or geological products. For bulletins equally naïve in our own time perhaps we must wait for the first explorers' literal accounts of rocket-visited Mars! Thus

"Characteristic Traits of the Spaniards" in the *Lady's Magazine and Repository* in March, 1793,[24] is nothing more than an extract from Jean François Burgoing's travels. Nor does the earliest narrative by an American make the pulse beat faster: the "Journal of a Tour from Cadiz to Seville. By a Bostonian." This reckless "Bostonian," who may have been George Washington Erving, then American chargé d'affaires, is abject before the marvels of Seville.[25]

Still more daring, eleven years later, was the "lady of sixteen" who pressed on beyond Seville to Madrid.[26] Firm, accurate descriptions, resembling those from the pens of Caroline Cushing or S. T. Wallis, hardly begin until the publication in the same year (1825) by Ticknor of his substantial "Amusements in Spain." [27] A little later Bryant's articles on Cuba prepared us for prolonged discussions of Spanish-American relations in this troublesome island, and "Centennial Sketches" may have been the first study of California and the missions.[28] By writing in 1842 with some discernment of Aranjuez,[29] Alexander H. Everett, minister to Spain from 1825 to 1829, seems to have initiated a new type of desultory, friendly description. This fashion of relating in casual, semipersonal reminiscence experiences in Spain and Spanish America was to continue. It culminated in the light pieces so popular in the eighties and nineties—"Madrid from Noon till Midnight"; "A Day in the Escorial"; "San Sebastian, the Spanish Newport"—or in *feuilletons* (on Spain, Mexico, or South America) more numerous than perceptive.

Everett's article was superior, as befitted a diplomat and man of letters. On the other hand, most of the descriptions between 1840 and 1865, though more limber than the writing of the "lady of sixteen," were tiresomely sentimental, like those of George Cheever [30] whose velvet prose has already been quoted as one depressing extreme. Or they were matter-of-fact and somber like Robert T. Maccoun's travelogues of 1852.[31] The earlier journey from Malaga to Granada by carriage in 1842 offered opportunities for realistic description undreamed of by the rhetorical Cheever, and Maccoun's anti-Catholic prejudices darkened his outlook even in his exposition of the paintings in the Madrid galleries. This is slack writing, even less engaging than that of the semiprofessional travelers such as John Mackie and Alexander Slidell Mackenzie, who now reappear in, respectively, "Cosas de España" and "Gipseys of Granada." [32] A long letter from the Alhambra; a comment on the Spanish Cortes; an excerpt from the English traveler John Ford; a translation from Prosper Mérimée [33]—as late as 1855 these were still enough, with the support of the travel books, to fascinate the readers of the magazines.

In contrast to these infantile effusions, the later discourse on Spain in *Harper's* and the *Atlantic Monthly* is more mature. One might assemble a moderately exciting anthology of descriptions written during the last three decades of the century. In the seventies and eighties dilettante compositions were still plentiful. We hurry by a pretty fancy called "Snow-Bound in a Basque Posada"; an essay candidly christened "A Cook's Tourist in Spain"; or a paper entitled "On Foot in Navarre," whose playful, anonymous author insists on our remembering him as "Fred." [34] These descriptions, which by 1880 may be numbered in the hundreds, differ from those of the early years not so much in the craft of writing, which was improved, as in their widened scope. Instead of a public building, we now read of the Carlists; instead of robber-infested roads, of the Catholic temper of Spain; instead of the cliffs of Ronda, of the Spanish political parties. This larger horizon resulted partly from the increase in American travel and from the proliferation of our periodicals. There was another reason. To study the various Spanish revolutions, notably that of 1868, many capable journalists boldly sought out the country to render specific reports to democratic America. Descriptions now transgressed the bounds set by the rococo Cheever and the pedestrian Maccoun and by 1890 included all contemporary Spanish life.

These active, subliterary men, such as Bayard Taylor, Charles Dudley Warner, Hobart C. Chatfield-Taylor, or Poultney Bigelow, were in quest of magazine script which, like the amoeba, might multiply itself and eventually become a popular book: *By-Ways of Europe* or *Saunterings* or *The Land of the Castanet.*[35] Into the corners of Spain they pushed and from wherever they could lay their restless eyes they forwarded to their magazines, now blessed with a hungry clientele, their impressions of gardens, vagrants, summer resorts, hill towns, Holy Week, or pelota. This material, as informative to their contemporaries as a book on backward, mysterious Tibet would be to us, they crowded into their spineless articles. Surveying this long bibliography, it is difficult not to believe that they exceed in number and excel in quality similar descriptions of other Continental countries. This cheerful chat of Spain, however, was merely a segment of the whole, a symptom of American curiosity about the panorama of Europe. France, Germany, and Italy,[36] if less remotely magical, evoked still more literature of this transient species—but that relating to Spain was abundant. On all phases of its life there were indeed by the close of the century articles enough.

These later articles displayed range, in "Spanish Vistas," a series of clever papers by George Parsons Lathrop, or in "A Day in Literary Madrid," lively, bookish gossip by W. H. Bishop.[37] Together these essays offered a thinly tinted canvas of Spain from the Pyrenees to Cadiz. What they omitted, however, was essential. This was the inner, the elusive Spain, not unfolding itself willingly to the journalist. The most conspicuous lack in all this reporting throughout the entire century was its isolation from the Spanish people. From first to last these writers of descriptions in the magazines see the Spaniard in the posadas (later in the hotels), in the stagecoaches (later on the railroads), as guides in the museums and cathedrals, or in the crowds in the Puerta del Sol or Vivarambla. Where they seldom see him is in his home, in the intimacy of friendship. To all of them, save to a very few, the Spaniard's mind, like the faces of the Moorish women, remained veiled and mysterious. So general was this ignorance that whatever is said in the earlier period by exceptional observers like S. T. Wallis is important. Victor Clay Barringer knew the upper-class Spaniards,[38] as did James Russell Lowell; and W. H. Bishop, acquainted with the language and the literature, could speak with some authority on the personal lives of Pérez Galdós, Palacio Valdés, and Juan Valera.[39] Others could be named but none distinguished enough to qualify strongly the general pattern of this shallow, facile reporting.

The most interesting variations among the conventional descriptions are not those dealing more thoughtfully than does the hurried Bayard Taylor with the daily routine of the Spaniard but those rare critical essays which strive for ingress into his mind. One essay of this kind is Irving Babbitt's extraordinary "Lights and Shades of Spanish Character," written two years before the end of the century.[40] This is an invasive analysis of that "something Spanish in the Spaniard which causes him to behave in a Spanish manner." [41] As might be expected from a philosopher, it is an examination of the criteria for living which motivate the Spanish mind. It is a psychological penetration. In particular, our humanist probes the Moorish element which, fused with the European, produces many anomalies and extremes. He studies the capacity for solitude and isolation; the imagination transcending fact; the pride and idealism; the inability to cooperate; the impatience of organization and discipline; the feralism and the indifference to bodily comfort, which must be in part an inheritance from the medieval contempt for the body. Other traits receive attention, but most of all Babbitt, like the very different Ticknor before him, is impressed by the magnificent basic qualities in the Spanish peasant. In him Babbitt reposes, as did Ticknor, his hope for the future of the nation. This is an acute and fearless essay, prophetic of twentieth-century analyses of the "soul of Spain." [42]

IRVING BABBITT's brilliant meditation on the modern Spaniard's mind was based upon a mastery of the past unknown to such casuals in history as Bayard Taylor or Charles Dudley Warner. Midway between description and history (and philosophy), his essay is neatly transitional to our consideration of another important office of the magazine: the interpretation of Spain through the historical essay. No one could accuse Warner's or Taylor's cheerful transcripts of Spanish life of any oppressive sense of tradition. For Irving, Longfellow, Ticknor, and Prescott, as well as for many less talented Americans, it was this intrusion of the past upon the present which made Spain so enchanting, so provocative. In our growing sensibility to Spanish culture the historian's function in the magazines was to define for the layman, that is, for the intelligent but unprofessional reader, this interrelation of past and present. Not only Irving and Prescott but later Henry Charles Lea, Henry Coppée, and Edwin L. Godkin, going behind the immediate present of the description, told the story of Spain's past and even hazarded a guess or two about her future. Less acceptable, no doubt, to the popular taste than such pieces as "Madrid from Noon till Midnight" or "A Peep at Cadiz," [43] these sinewy essays on government, colonial empire, or religion enriched thoughtful minds in their endeavor to comprehend Spain.

About 1850 there appeared in the magazines the first truly historical studies of Spain and, less frequently, of Spanish America. Naturally, not all of these essays were as elaborate as Mills' survey of Conde [44] or Hazewell's "The Rehabilitation of Spain." [45] Available also were snacks of history, designed as an hour's reading for those who quailed before the long course dinners of Prescott or Lea. Some of these topics seem trifling, some amusing. The Armada, for example, retains its immortal lure; this ancient morsel is served up again and again with new sauces. On April 17, 1830, in the *New York Mirror and Ladies Literary Gazette,* a mysterious specialist, "W," reviewed the strategy of the famous fleet, and seventy years later no less a sailor than Admiral Mahan speculated on the technical causes of the disaster.[46]

The surrender at Granada; obscure reasons for the massacre at Alcoy; Las Casas and the slave trade; the testament of Hernando de Soto; gossip concerning the statesman and writer, Martínez de la Rosa—these essays revealed curious facts in Spanish history.[47] Some of them were shining little nuggets of heroic action and dramatic incident. Even now we may find diverting the paragraphs on the *mogiganga* during the visit of Ferdinand VII to Zaragossa, on the murder of Escobedo, secretary and counselor of Don Juan of Austria, and on the deathless valor of Torrijos. In passing we recall this Spanish patriot's associations with Robert Boyd, John Sterling, and Carlyle.[48] One phase of the interpretation in the magazines of Spain's history was anecdotal.

Most of these oddments, besides the various essays on Spain in America,[49] postdated the middle of the century. It is surprising that the *North American Review,* so curious in respect to Spanish literature, should have printed during its early years so little of an

NORTH AMERICAN REVIEW.

No. LXV.

NEW SERIES, NO. XL.

OCTOBER, 1829.

Art. I.—*A Chronicle of the Conquest of Granada. By Fray Antonio Agapida.* 1829. 2 vols. 12mo. Philadelphia. Carey, Lea, & Carey.

ALMOST as many qualifications may be demanded for a perfect historian, indeed the Abbé Mably has enumerated as many, as Cicero stipulates for a perfect orator. He must be strictly impartial; a lover of truth under all circumstances, and ready to declare it at all hazards; he must be deeply conversant with whatever may bring into relief the character of the people he is depicting,—not merely with their laws, constitution, general resources, and all the other more visible parts of the machinery of government, but with the nicer moral and social relations, the informing spirit, which gives life to the whole, but escapes the eye of a vulgar observer. If he has to do with other ages and nations, he must transport himself into them, expatriating himself, as it were, from his own, in order to get the very form and pressure of the times he is delineating. He must be conscientious in his attention to geography, chronology, &c., an inaccuracy in which has been fatal to more than one good philosophical history; and mixed up with all these drier details, he must display the various powers of a novelist or dramatist, throwing his characters into suitable lights and shades, disposing his scenes so as to awaken and maintain an unflagging interest, and diffusing over the whole that finished style, without which his work will only become a magazine of materials for the more

A page of Prescott's review of Irving's
A Chronicle of the Conquest of Granada,
from the *North American Review,* volume 29, page 293,
October, 1829.

authoritative historical character about Spain. The earliest historical investigations, appearing often in the least distinguished journals,[50] were mere extracts from foreign periodicals. The few original
studies were too lightened by romance; [51] and the conventional
surveys were too weighed down by old prejudices—for instance,
William Davis Robinson's "Spain and her Colonies (1821)" [52] or
Robert Southey's "Siege of Zaragoza in Spain, June, 1808 (1823)."
This last article was lifted bodily from the poet's *History of the
Peninsular War*.[53] One might conjecture that these puerile beginnings found less favor than the descriptions. In any case, the success
of Prescott's volumes in the thirties and forties and his painstaking
estimates of Irving and others in the *North American Review*,
were preliminary to a long series of solid essays on historical subjects.[54]

All of Irving's three important Spanish books reflected his
studies in the Moorish civilization, and in their wake followed
article after article on similar themes. This interest reached a
climax in the scholarly work of Henry Coppée in the *Penn
Monthly* in 1873 [55] as well as in this author's less learned explorations into the records of the Moslem empire.[56] Although these
essays, besides those on Columbus, owed much to Irving [57] and
Prescott, this fact was less true of the historians who were absorbed
in interpreting modern Spain in terms of its past. As Cuba became
more and more a problem in our national affairs, this kind of political definition was attempted repeatedly in the magazine essay.
The growing dissatisfaction with outworn concepts of Spain as the
land of romance or the arsenal of cruelty has already been mentioned in the chapter on the travel books. The most vigorous historical essays were those which tried to dispel the "black legend"; [58]
those which strove to delineate the effect of the past on the present;
those which were eager to pierce through the Antaeus-like myths
enveloping this great, retarded nation. Our more enlightened
curiosity found expression in analytical essays not only on Spain's
governmental development [59] but on her religious psychology.
Catholic magazines, sometimes through Spanish writers, discussed
the status of the Church, of Protestantism, or of the Jews, and other
periodicals enlarged upon these subjects. It was the *Baptist Review*

which in 1881 overwhelmed its readers by a treatise called "A Study of the Inquisition." [60]

THE drift of all this analysis of Spanish government was typically American. It inclined toward the belief that a modern people had been reborn and that we could now help to establish a democratic nation. These last two words formed the title of one representative essay.[61] The revolutions of 1868 and 1873 had strengthened the conviction in America that the old thrones were collapsing. We were sure that monarchical Spain was obsolescent, a relic of the Inquisition, and that profound economic changes were at hand.[62] Charles Creighton Hazewell's challenging article in the *Atlantic Monthly* for March, 1862, conceded that "Spain walks in a circle, and she repeats the follies of her past with a pertinacity that would seem to indicate, that, while she has forgotten everything, she has learned nothing." [63] The historian admitted this weakness but pointed out the continual purging of government in the country, and its resilience even under "domestic decay." Everything suggested the emergence of a new nation. Even Spain's intervention in Mexico and her sympathy with the South in the American Civil War could not dampen this hope of ours. It was, indeed, on our need for comprehending a revived Spain (especially since her hands were still in Cuba, Mexico, and South America) that the historian in the magazines often based his plea for an understanding of her past.[64]

This charity for Spain's past and faith and hope for her future marked the temper of many historical essays during the two decades following our Civil War. Spain had atoned for her profligacy by the Revolution of 1868, and there had occurred if not quite a betrothal to democracy at least a flirtation. Our essays on possible meanings of this revolution were fervently optimistic. In an "Address of American Citizens to the Spanish Government and People" in the *Magazine of History* for March, 1869, the signers, among them celebrities like Peter Cooper, Horace Greeley, Charles A. Dana, and Elizabeth Cady Stanton, declared their "joy and gratification" at the news of this "liberation and emancipation from a tyrannical and corrupt government." Another step toward the fulfillment of Whitman's dream of a universe under the eagle of American democracy! The "Address" was sent to Spain, but the American friends of incipient Spanish democracy were disappointed. Nothing more was heard of it.[65] About this incident there was, on both sides, something extremely characteristic.

Next we may follow, not without a sense of the ironical change, the hostile articles on the policy of Spain in Cuba with their reflections of America's growing anger and, finally, their tirades on the war of 1898.[66] Writers who had never really credited the happy theory of Spain's enlightenment now spoke again; the caption of one of Lea's articles was, in contrast to those of a few years earlier, "The Decadence of Spain." [67] Though others, such as "The Débacle of Spain" by Peter MacQueen, were unabashed propaganda,[68] we are certain, if we study these later essays, that the past of Spain had now a grimmer meaning than American optimism had conceded it just after the Revolution of 1868. Old myths and old hatreds sprang up. Lea attributed the unfortunate war of 1898 to Spanish pride, conservatism, clericalism, and, in accordance with the central interest of his life, the pernicious Inquisition.[69] This, he believed, had isolated the country, checked the development of its people, and brought its colonial enterprises to ruin. These veering winds of opinion blew through the historical essays. Though less entertaining than the descriptions, they are, even more than the full-length histories, a dramatic record of mercurial attitudes in America toward the interrelated past and present of Spain.

IN THESE ways the periodicals offered their ever-changing approaches to Spain. Closer to the human spirit than descriptions of cities which one might never see, more intimate than the essays of historians, more imaginative than the studies of politics and war, fragments of Spanish literature, at once alien and haunting, were conveyed to Americans in the pages of their magazines. The infiltration of this rich and beautiful literature was slow, more so than the recognition of Spain through the descriptions as an actual country of village, plain, and mountain, even more so than that of the historical Spain now being revealed by Prescott or Coppée. In regard to Spanish authors, except for Cervantes, the editors could count upon an impressive ignorance. The literary beginnings in the magazines were sketchy, tentative. Nevertheless, the formal study of Spanish literature today is under obligation to these intermittent, often amateurish, but sometimes stimulating evaluations in nineteenth-century magazines of the ballad, of the drama, of Cervantes, of Pérez Galdós. There were firsthand versions of this literature, that is, translations of tale, poem, or proverb. There was criticism, particularly in the form of reviews, and as early as 1830 compact summaries of poetry, fiction, and the drama.[70] Finally, American writing introduced Spanish themes and backgrounds. All these materials prepared American readers for Ticknor's *History of Spanish Literature* in 1849 and for modern scholarship on Cervantes or Lope de Vega.

That such translations as the "Story of Amadis de Gaul" in the *Literary Magazine and American Register* in October, 1805,[71] rocked the English tradition in our literature we may doubt. Yet of the excerpts from Cervantes, Lope de Vega, and Calderón, which by the year 1850 were abundant,[72] there must have been some readers. Ballads, legends, fables, and even proverbs [73] supplemented the more familiar materials from England and France. In the first two of these four provinces Bryant was active before 1830.[74] His orotund "Niagara" was in debt to Heredia's sonorous poem.[75] Some of the numerous prose legends "from the Spanish" were vapid enough, but in the sixties the fiction of Spanish novelists excited a genuine interest. Possibly *La Familia de Alvareda* by Fernán Caballero, Washington Irving's Andalusian friend, was the first contemporary Spanish novel to appear in translation in an American periodical.[76] At last, in this decade, the dikes were down. American tastes had broadened. The novelty of an adaptation from Quevedo or Iriarte had passed. Instead the translations centered, especially in the final years of the century, in the new school of fiction introduced so ardently by William Dean Howells: Valdés, Valera, or Galdós. Later, as the books of these novelists became more accessible in America, quotation was accompanied by criticism.

Hence by 1880, instead of specimens of this foreign literature with an elementary use of plot and quotation as in Matthew Arnold's introduction of Tolstoi's novels into England,[77] criticism of Spain's classic figures, past and present, was plentiful, both for the popular and the sophisticated levels of opinion. Gradually the function of the magazine as a repository of texts (though this has recently been revived by a periodical or two) became obsolete. To read Cervantes or Galdós one laid hands on their books. As the translations and the prosy summaries in the magazines dwindled in number, the critical essays multiplied. The beginnings of this criticism were humble, but the road continued on steadily from the brief, anonymous sketch, "The Life of Miguel Cervantes de Saavedra," in the *New England Quarterly Magazine* for October–December, 1802,[78] to Howells' essay on his idol in the *Century* for June, 1898.[79] Within these ninety-six years matured the periodical criticism of Cervantes, of Lope de Vega, of Quevedo, and of many other authors now staples in our university curricula or in any planned reading of European literatures.

We should stop for a moment over the history of this criticism. Although three years after the biography of Cervantes in the *New England Quarterly Magazine* there appeared in the *Literary Magazine* an "Account of Lopez de Vega" [80] and although in 1821 the *New-York Literary Journal* reprinted from London a respectable little paper called "Spanish Literature, Political and Periodical," [81] we must make obeisance again to the *North American Review*. Once more it was to lead the way, this time in literary criticism. In October, 1827, Alexander H. Everett played with the perennial problem of *Gil Blas*,[82] and the next volume of the magazine included a review of *Cartas marruecas* [83] as edited by that pioneer teacher Francis Sales, whose name now begins to appear in the journals. Almost immediately, as if prodded by Everett, other magazines evaluated early Spanish drama, early fiction, and also early poetry, a subject in which these periodicals of a century ago showed a particular interest.[84] Among all these first forays into criticism Longfellow's "Spanish Devotional and Moral Poetry" [85] remains the boldest with its illustrative passages from the original texts and its English metrical translations. This article and the poet's "Spanish Language and

Literature" [86] helped to found the tradition of American scholarship in Spanish literature.

So the ties between the scholar and the magazine grew ever firmer. Sustained by Ticknor's scholarly history, by the scores of reviews [87] which spread the fame of this book throughout America, and by the study of Romance languages, the relationship has continued to thrive, in such an article as Joakim Reinhard's "Spanish Fiction from Caballero to Pereda" in the *Sewanee Review* for April, 1900,[88] or in the learned studies which we now encounter daily.[89] This writing was presumably the solid substratum of our criticism; it was underpinning for more impressionistic estimates of Spanish literature. Surely this scholarship was a proof of the deepening of our civilization, this new, serious study of the major European languages. We may take pleasure, too, in the reviews of books on Spanish America like Madame Calderón de la Barca's [90] and in the easygoing criticism which played over the masterpieces, especially *Don Quixote*. Many an American critic of Spanish literature now thrilled to a sense of discovery and possession. Was there not, he felt, something almost commonplace in a knowledge of the French and German literatures in comparison with a study of this little-known, mysterious Spanish? Perhaps for this reason, perhaps because his name had long been known to Americans, perhaps as a protest against this stiff learning in the *North American Review,* much of the writing on Cervantes now became charmingly light-hearted.

Crude as they were, the early sketches of Cervantes stole a kind of light from the great humorist. Most of them, like that in the *Knickerbocker* in 1851, were devoid of real criticism. In this article the author's aim was to share with others so hilarious, so unmatchable an experience as an evening with Don Quixote and Sancho Panza.[91] Unconsciously he prepared us for Brander Matthews' effusion in 1893, "Cervantes, Zola, Kipling & Co." [92] To write merrily of this sublime merrymaker is not always easy, but some of the essays re-emphasize the reasons for the hold of Cervantes upon us, reasons allied to our love for Mark Twain, whom he directly influenced.[93] A happy mixture of civilized scholarship and appreciation permeates Henry Dwight Sedgwick's "Don Quixote" in the

Atlantic for February, 1896.[94] This essay pleads for a sound English translation of the masterpiece. Is not English a language well constituted to give us the true Cervantes? Is not this the best of all books for the English-speaking boy? Is not *Don Quixote* the first great novel, and should it not therefore enjoy an appropriate English version? Moreover, since laughter is now at last recognized as a divine attribute, Cervantes must have his rightful place in the estimation of man through adequate translation. Implicit in the wisdom of this essay is the growth of our understanding (partly through the periodicals) of what the *American Monthly Magazine* had referred to quite simply in 1836 as "Cervantes and His Writings." [95]

This mood of happy discovery seems to me to be ingrained in much of our free-ranging criticism of Spanish literature in the latter years of the nineteenth century. Something of this feeling exists even in the anonymous article, "The Modern Spanish Theatre," in the *New-Yorker* for January 25, 1840; [96] this essay was an early precursor of many studies of the drama in the eighties and nineties. It certainly may be sensed, this pleasure, this spirit of adventure in the study of contemporary Spanish fiction, as critic after critic writes of Valera, Valdés, Galdós, or Emilia Pardo Bazán.[97] In themselves Rollo Ogden's friendly, personal essays and William Henry Bishop's chitchat on these novelists command little respect.[98] Yet they are lively repercussions from the world of letters which Howells insisted, as he read the novel in Italian, in French, and, with particular delight, in Spanish, must strive to be international. Unquestionably the bond between Spain's realistic novel and our own was strengthened by these roving articles in the magazines.[99]

IT WOULD have startled such lovers of the classic Spanish authors as Longfellow and Howells had they realized the steady growth of an interest in Spanish-American literature in the magazines. To be sure, the curiosity was at first restrained and even a little patronizing. In a very brief summary we might begin with a biographical sketch written in 1823 of Sor Juana Inés de la Cruz, the Mexican poetess.[100] It was, however, our scholarly conscience, the *North American Review,* which finally in 1849 sanctioned American study of this writer's *autos* and which added long expositions of the love songs of Alpuche (of Yucatan), of Mendive's *Pasionarias,* and of the work of the Cubans, Heredia and Milanes.[101]

After we become aware of Bryant's fondness for Heredia and Moreno and of his reviews in the *Evening Post,* we look back with more understanding at this thirty-one-page analysis in the *Review* of eight volumes of Spanish-American poetry. The article was an obvious sequel to the manifestoes of Jared Sparks of some fifteen years earlier. Toward this expansion of our Spanish interests a few leaders, among them Ticknor and Prescott, were sympathetic, but neither of these scholars wrote much for the magazines concerning literature.[102] Despite these directives from the *Post* and the *Review,* serious study of Spanish-American literature made slow headway. Even at the end of the century George Washington Cable's gossipy papers on the Spanish regime in Louisiana [103] were quite as acceptable as criticisms of the poets of South America. Extended and learned study of Spanish-American literature was to wait until the twentieth century.

MEANWHILE, some contributors to the magazines converted their interest in Spain into creations of their own. Into the periodicals they poured hundreds of sketches, tales, and poems, all with Spanish or Spanish-American themes, characters, and settings. Far more interesting than these attenuated literary products themselves is the fact that they were written, that Spanish subjects were popular in the periodicals. It is useless to study or even to list these cobwebs. We may read the anonymous "Donna Aminta de Bux-heda: A Spanish Story" in the *Port Folio* for September, 1821; [104] "Lazarilla, or the Gipsey Girl. Imitated from the Spanish" in the *New York Mirror* of June 30, 1832; [105] or, somewhat later, "Dona Paula; or, The Convent and the World. A Tale of Peru." [106] All these were spindrift.

Nevertheless, the editors found them printable. They were evidently designed for that soft-minded reader envisaged by William

Gilmore Simms when he published in the *Southern Literary Messenger* for August, 1838, a trial extract of his forthcoming *Pelayo: A Romance of the Goth*.[107] The craving for Spanish narratives increased rather than declined. The tales of bloody headsmen, robbers, and bullfighters [108] amplified into serious novels such as the Mexican "Chata and Chinta" in 1886 in the *Overland Monthly* [109] or developed into finished tales similar to "The Alcalde's Visit" in the *Atlantic Monthly* [110] for November, 1898. The use in the magazines of these Spanish traditions of our Southwest was to reach its fulfillment in the tales of Bret Harte.

Toward poetry, too, these scribblers turned with their fancies concerning Spain and even toward dramatic forms. Indiscriminately they sang of Seville, Granada, Ávila, the Alhambra, the Cid, Charles V, Saint Teresa, Quevedo, the cachucha,[111] or of Columbus, tirelessly of the peerless, half-legendary explorer.[112] Or, remembering the Spanish Southwest, they versified "El Vaquero" or "El Caballo de Mi Querido-Santa Cruz." [113] All these fugitive, mildly imaginative pieces were inspired by trifles, by some incident of travel, by the reading of a proverb, by the strumming of a Mexican guitar.[114] This is phantom verse, but like the tales it reemphasizes the important part played by the periodicals in this interpretation on the popular level. "Over the Sea Lies Spain" [115] was the characteristic title of a poem written in 1893. Nor are these lyrics always without distinction. Among them are the verses of Bryant [116] and successively in 1842, 1877, and 1882 Longfellow's "The Spanish Student," his "Castles in Spain," and his valedictory poem, "The Bells of San Blas." [117] Poe reviewed "The Spanish Student" as a *drama*. This poetizing of Spanish subjects included long extracts from the tragedy "Alhamar" by an unidentified playwright and a few plays with Spanish scenes and characters.[118]

MEANWHILE, as Spanish scenes, Spanish history, Spanish political life, and Spanish literature were discovered by the magazines, their editors seem guilty of a peculiar neglect. What of the fine arts, which received homage in so many of the travel books? Opportunities to read in the early periodicals of Spanish music, architecture, painting, and sculpture were comparatively rare.[119] The "Editor's Table" in the *Knickerbocker* for May, 1844, speculates on a Murillo brought to New York from an old convent in Lima, and in 1867 the paintings of this artist (to whom Washington Irving had expressed his devotion in Seville) were discussed in the *Ladies' Repository*. Other references to the arts are hardly more significant, and until the last twenty years of the century the silence in the magazines concerning Velázquez and other major artists remains almost unbroken. In the nineties studies of this painter, among others, began to appear, possibly as a belated accompaniment to the evaluation of Spanish literature.[120] Edward Prescott Bowen's long study, "Modern Spanish Art," in *Harper's* in March, 1888, resembles a landmark, and seven years later in the same magazine Royal Cortissoz contributed "The Museum of the Prado." [121] Other perceptive essays were written, but as late as 1893 a critic denounced Spanish painting as crude, brutal, and theatrical.[122] For a full appreciation in the periodicals of Spanish art we must again wait until the next century.

WHAT, finally, these nineteenth-century periodicals contributed to our consciousness of the Spanish mind cannot be easily synthesized. Certainly their range and persuasion on the popular plane were immense. Browsers who seldom owned a travel book or mastered a tough history glanced through the descriptions, the fragments of the past, the criticisms, the romances of Spain and Spanish America. Like the cinema goer or the radio listener today—in some ways the magazine reader was the forerunner of these—they drank in impressions of this far-off region. To such readers Spain meant the Malaga described in the *Port Folio* in 1814 or the city and palace introduced to them by Irving in 1832 or by Chatfield-Taylor in his "Granada and the Alhambra" in 1896. To some readers of 1840 this nonsense of "Caballero Ladrone" represented the life of Spain as persuasively as today the cowboy and the gangster of the films symbolize America to certain Europeans. Until the end of the century the magazines fostered the indomitable illusions of Spain as the land of the fiesta and siesta. Its history was the Armada, the Inquisition, and the dishonor of Cuba and its literature the tales of scimitar and highway pistol.

Nevertheless, as we have seen, some of these magazines spoke to critical readers. Certain southern publications and some Catholic periodicals acquainted us with a more spacious, more veritable Spain. These described a country with a puzzling but noble past, a nation, if one could trust its liberals, with a new future. With guidance from such students of Spain and Spanish America as Sparks, Ticknor, Irving, and Prescott, a few magazines like the *North American Review* encouraged scholarship. With similar principles and blessed by the good sense of S. T. Wallis, the *Southern Literary Messenger* posed the problems, social, intellectual, and literary, which were to absorb our scholars, historians, and men of letters. This audience applauded not Cheever but Babbitt, not Peter MacQueen but Lea, not the doggerel on Columbus but criticism and creative writing in debt to Cervantes, Lope de Vega, or Quevedo. This audience grew in numbers and strength throughout the century until it read the novels of Galdós and the criticism of Lowell. In preparation for the learning of the next century the magazine became the ally of the teacher, scholar, and critic.

AT LAST we reach the twentieth century. In estimating the Spanish influences in the periodicals in our own time we face a more difficult task. In the year 1900, of eighteen hundred monthly magazines published in the United States only one had a circulation of a million copies.[123] How different is this situation today! The labyrinths of antiquity seem plain paths compared with our present maze of magazines. We support some seven thousand periodicals of which twelve to fifteen claim more than two million readers and seventy to eighty more than one million.[124] This stupendous expansion of the periodical press is indeed another form, as one of its chroniclers says, of American "big business." [125] The causes of the change lie in the lowering of prices through the revenues of advertising, in the astute comprehension of the reading tastes of Americans by editors, publishers, and contributors, and—we long to believe—in the higher intellectual attainments of our people.

This complicated story of Brobdingnagian growth, whose various stages cannot be precisely dated, must be reduced here to an outline. Even this is likely to deceive us, to betray us into the conviction that because the magazines had now made European cultural influences more widespread they had caused them to penetrate more deeply. This is not necessarily so. In studying these recent magazines we should consider the last fifty years, as in other chapters, in the full perspective of our century and a half. Without mentioning every allusion to Spaniard or Uruguayan in the countless periodicals (whether professional journals or pulps), our purpose is to detect modern trends in American magazines toward Spanish and Spanish-American culture. These trends are conspicuously different from those of the nineteenth century.

We must study these tendencies in history, in literature, in the fine arts, or in other subjects, but we must first acquaint ourselves with twentieth-century changes in the magazines other than that of numerical increase. For by 1920 the periodicals resembled very little those of the preceding century. The reader of this chapter will recall the scholarship of the *North American Review* and the dignified discourse on literature and art in the other great quarterlies and monthlies. In general, these magazines had been high-minded tutors of the American Philistine. They hoped to purge him of his congenital provincialism. To accomplish this end they were inclined to turn away from commonplace America to the culture of England and of the Continent. It is unjust to their vigor but not to their ideals to say, in the words of a contemptuous modern critic, that they were preoccupied with "what was really cultural and academic shop-talk and upon the other blameless intellectual topics that they considered proper to nice people." [126]

One fact was certain: twentieth-century readers were not to be restricted to "nice people." During the rise of the Curtis publications or during the crusade of the muckrakers, individuals whose pabulum had been the almanac, the farm journal, or the daily paper discovered with delight the reconditioned periodical. Stirred

126

by the events of the day, these readers, especially during the first World War, craved the condensed, vivid news which enterprising journalists (Briton Haddon and Henry Luce of *Time* or De Witt Wallace of the *Reader's Digest*) were to give them. Democracy "En-Masse," as Whitman had christened it, absorbed through the huge circulation of the periodicals brief but intelligent summaries of the complex questions of the era. Simultaneously other magazines became what George Harvey of the *Independent* called as early as 1910 "national newspapers." [127] Against such a trend, intensified by the shattering events between 1918 and 1950, no "cultural and academic shop-talk" could possibly survive. Of the so-named "quality" magazines of the 1890's only the *Atlantic Monthly* and *Harper's* still live on, and these William Dean Howells, we might guess, if he looks down from paradise, would hardly recognize. In their pages, too, reverberate world crises.

If this dedication of our general magazines to our troubled times did not actually mean the complete exclusion from their pages of such subjects as history or the arts, it hinted plainly that these had better seek shelter in more specialized quarters. So exponents of particular fields of knowledge appeared. Nearly every form of art (poetry or the drama) had its own snug little medium, and almost every Continental country had its designated channels in the United States for literature or learning. To mention all these periodicals is impossible, either those established solely for Spanish and Spanish-American interests or those, broader in character, to whom the Spanish-speaking regions and peoples have proved intermittently attractive. For example, the *National Geographic Magazine*, the "teacher of geography to the nation," [128] included between 1899 and 1940 some twenty-five essays on Spain. In addition, the "little magazines," represented by *Poetry*, the *Mentor*, *Art and Archaeology*, and many others, linked their own particular hobbies with these European interests of the day.

Meanwhile, a few periodicals became the appointed guardians of Spanish learning. Never again were the general magazines to publish the equivalents of Ticknor's "Early Spanish Drama" or Longfellow's "Spanish Language and Literature." Erudition now found cover in such professional journals as the *Modern Language*

Review or *Modern Language Notes* [129] and also in the *Hispanic Review,* in a sense the successor of the *Revue Hispanique,* or in *Hispania,* the oracle of the newly formed American Association of Teachers of Spanish (1917). Less technical than the *Hispanic Review,* its purpose was to foster "a complete and sympathetic understanding of the history and culture of Spain and Spanish America." [130] *Hispania* was, in short, a catholic and practical magazine. It intended to help all teachers of Spanish rather than to become "an excessively learned and theoretical review." [131] It was a happy venture. How this magazine would have charmed some of the earlier students of Spanish literature, for instance, James Russell Lowell! For thirty-six years it has informed us concerning the teaching of Spanish and Portuguese, biography, Spanish and Spanish-American literature, travel in Spanish lands, and Spanish history. How many have turned to it for aid, to its surveys, reviews, and current bibliographies!

Meanwhile, the *Hispanic Review,* more erudite and fifteen years younger than *Hispania,* embraced the "literary history and linguistics of all Romance languages spoken throughout the Hispanic Peninsula and Latin America." [132] This intensified interest in Latin America was accentuated by the founding in February, 1918, of the *Hispanic American Historical Review,* a journal created for the historians of Latin America. Looking back from the thirtieth anniversary of this distinguished magazine, one scholar thought its roster of contributors read like a "Who's Who of Latin Americanists." [133] Another pointed out that of its pages twenty-four per cent had dealt with Mexico, eleven and a half with Brazil, another eleven and a half with the Antilles, ten per cent with regions now within the United States, and only eight per cent with Spain. [134]

In this preliminary word to our topical survey of Spanish influences in twentieth-century magazines, we are brought to this fresh emphasis: instead of the Iberian Peninsula, our own hemisphere. Classical Spanish literature or the Civil War in Spain still interests us, but what Jefferson foresaw and what William Dean Howells thought preposterous seems to have occurred. Our eyes are now fixed on Spanish America. Neither the influences of two world wars nor our propaganda can account in any substantial measure for the curiosity of North Americans to know more, especially through travel and the magazines, of these other nations at our very door. These picturesque and dynamic regions are exciting in their past and present, and their future is bound up with our own. This belief, now proclaimed by traveler, historian, scholar, and artist, is nowhere made clearer than in our study of these twentieth-century periodicals.

Again a few statistics are helpful. A tabulation of ten nonspecialist magazines shows that in one brief period from December, 1941, through February, 1942, these printed no fewer than thirty-nine articles on Latin America.[135] In the New Series of the *Yale Review* from 1911 to the present time appeared twenty-two on the same regions and only five on Spain itself, while in the *American Mercury* a ratio similar in emphasis was three to one. If we add to these illustrations the existence of numerous periodicals like *Inter-America*,[136] entirely concerned with Spain in the Western Hemisphere, the shift in balance is plain. Only with the perspective of these backgrounds can we now turn, in approximately the same order as in our earlier pages, to the place in the twentieth-century magazines of the description, of history, of Spanish and Spanish-American political affairs, of literature (fiction, poetry, and the drama), and of the fine arts.

Above the descriptions still gleam the familiar, tinseled captions ("Portugal of the Porcelain Sky" or "Little Window into Seville" or the unavoidable "Castles in Spain").[137] Yet the twentieth-century description is often sobered by scholarship and is now concerned more than ever before with Spanish America. Carrie Evangeline Farnham's record of travel in Spain in the *Romanic Review* is a carefully documented article,[138] and various studies, such as "Franco's Spain" or "Report on Franco's Spain," are solid, realistic examinations of the country today.[139] Chapters of some novels, notably those of John Dos Passos, appeared first as separate essays in the periodicals. His *Rosinante to the Road Again* incorporated twenty separate articles.[140] In addition to the twenty-five accounts of Spain already mentioned, the *National Geographic* has issued thirty on Latin America as a whole besides sixteen on Argentina, ten on Bolivia, sixteen on Chile, seven on Colombia, and seventy-one on Mexico. All of these are as close to truth as professional writing and expert photography can make them.[141] So far has the description or essay come since in 1802 the *New England Quarterly Magazine* favored its readers with its naïve little vignette called "Spaniards."

HISTORY, too, in these twentieth-century magazines, deserted to the scholar. Far more than the description, it became the property of the specialist, and essays in the general magazines comparable to those by Prescott, Lea, or Coppée are almost nonexistent. Articles on Spanish history sometimes fled the orthodox areas of the *American Historical Review* to the sanctuary of the *Hispanic American Historical Review*. In this subject of history both these magazines were apostate from the Peninsula. During its first twenty years the former periodical published sixty-one articles on Great Britain and Ireland and thirty on France but only sixteen on Italy and Spain.[142] In its pages Henry Charles Lea [140] and Roger Bigelow Merriman [144] wrote with insight of Spain itself, but in this journal, too, Spanish-American relations and Spanish America now commanded easily the interest which a century earlier the *North American Review* had striven so earnestly to inspire. As for the other magazine, its more than fifteen thousand pages during its first twenty-five years, its 308 monographs by 186 contributors [145] all re-emphasize the Latin-American direction of research.[146]

Nevertheless, Spain itself was discussed in the magazines, especially during the third decade of the century. It almost seems as if curiosity, which had slackened in regard to the past of Spain, now increased concerning her present. The humanitarian hopes and democratic enthusiasms for her struggling people, which had mounted high at every successive revolution, reached fever pitch in the conflict of 1936–39 with all its idealisms, brutalities, and international repercussions. Or earlier, the publication in 1929 in the *Yale Review* of Salvador de Madariaga's essay, "New Life in Spain," offering glimpses of the so-called "Generation of 1898," reminds us again of the undying interest of Americans in a reborn Spain.[147]

During the Civil War the magazines tried, not without passion, to make clear the issues between Republican and Franquista. The impact of this war upon the travel books has already been described, and in a later chapter we shall study its effects upon our fiction and poetry. Month after month the bitter conflict crowded into the magazines. Its fascination for us all is evident in eight hundred articles which these published during the three dreadful years.[148] Yet it would be foolish to think that all this writing derived from an interest in Spain as a nation. The unhappy country had become a laboratory not only for the experimenters in war but for the theorists on the class struggle. These meanings the magazines were bound to report. The innumerable articles focused attention, even while the scholars retreated to the specialized magazines, upon the governmental problems and the contemporary history of the Peninsula.

EVEN before the Civil War, which called attention to poets like García Lorca,[149] the excitement concerning contemporary Spain had not ignored its fiction, poetry, and drama. Howells' advocacy, discussed in a later chapter, of the Spanish novelists reached its climax just before his death in 1920 in his enthusiasm for Blasco Ibáñez.[150] Probably the fame of this writer in America was inevitable. In 1911 his novels began here their long cycle of translation and publication,[151] and three years earlier he had been introduced in an American magazine as "An Apostle of New Spain." He was, declared the author of this essay, the leading exponent "of a new group of novelists less competent as artists, to be sure, but inspired with a more virile craving for progress, a more violent spirit of protest against the torpor of Spain." [152] Exactly ten years later Charlotte Brewster Jordan's translation of *The Four Horsemen of the Apocalypse* made a Spanish novel for the first time a household word in the United States. In 1925 an article in the *Nation* on Blasco carried the ridiculous but suggestive title of "The Man Who Is Rocking a Nation." [153] Looking back on our fifty years, we find in the magazines of various kinds other novelists of Spain and Spanish America [154] but none with so universal a popularity as Blasco Ibáñez.[155]

In contrast to the increased currency of Spanish-American poetry, to be discussed in a moment, Blasco represents a peak in the influence of fiction in the magazines.[156] Numerous Spanish-American stories have appeared in *Inter-America,* which pleaded for a "community of ideas between all the peoples of America," [157] and in all our magazines may now be read tales with Spanish and Spanish-American backgrounds. Nevertheless, whether in the *Overland Monthly* [158] in 1911 or in the *New Mexico Quarterly* [159] in 1932 or in *Story,*[160] a periodical established in 1931 by two American expatriates and for a time printed in Spain, these tales lack power. Even if they exhibit our greater proficiency in the manipulation of this form, they show hardly more vitality than the superficial uses of similar materials in the preceding century.[161] Exceptions occur, as in a story of Spain during the Civil War written by the Brooklyn-born son of Spanish parents [162] or in the tales which appeared in the *Smart Set* under the editorship of Henry L. Mencken and George Nathan.[163] In the magazines, however, no voice of novelist or storyteller was heard so insistently as that of the great Blasco Ibáñez.

IN COMPARISON with the many studies of Blasco, the interest in contemporary poetry, as revealed in the magazines, seems less focused in single individuals. The verse of García Lorca and of others who lost their lives in the Civil War was published in our pages, and some of our own poets wrote on related themes. Our scholars continued to compose articles for the learned journals on the poets of the past, but in general our interest has swung more decisively in the poetry than in the fiction toward our neighbors. Is it possible that the home of poetry in Spanish is to be in the Western Hemisphere? Must the advances of the poetry of Spain itself be credited, as some critics assert, to Spanish-American poets, to Rubén Darío or José Santos Chocano? [164] The Peninsular poets look, they declare, toward Spanish America. Whether or not this is true, whether or not water now runs uphill, a survey of poems from the Spanish appearing in representative magazines during the last twenty years shows most of the originals to have been Spanish-American.[165] The impress of this verse upon any single major American poet is, as will be indicated in a later chapter, difficult to demonstrate, but its vitality in the "little" magazines is impressive.

Within the last twenty-five years *Poetry* has issued two Spanish-American numbers. The first of these (June, 1925) contained thirty-two poems selected and translated by Muna Lee and enriched by criticism from Luis Muñoz Marín (her former husband), Ernesto Montenegro, Harriet Monroe, and Constance Lindsay Skinner. All the poets honored by this volume were still writing except Rubén Darío, José Asunción Silva, and Julio Herrera y Reissig, and these were still living in spirit—so strong had their influence been upon the somewhat younger artists. The continuance of the same trend in the magazines is plain in the second issue eighteen years later (May, 1943) with its gallery of other poets. In a sense, the readers of this verse were also specialists, that is, young American craftsmen and experimenters. This Spanish-American influence has been limited but real, and in this magazine it has been ardently encouraged. The latter issue was preceded by a long essay by Jorge Carrera Andrade called "The New American and His Point of View Toward Poetry," an illuminating analysis of recent poetical movements in Latin America.

MEANWHILE, from the beginning of the twentieth century our magazines' curiosity regarding that noble province of Spanish literature, the drama, is important, not only in their reporting of contemporary plays but also in their perspectived writing on the theater of the past. As an illustration, Lope de Vega has received not only the continued attention of the scholars but on his three hundredth anniversary the memorial of a special number of the *Theatre Arts Monthly*. This popular magazine offered studies of his life and times, a new translation of a comedy, and valuable bibliographical apparatus.[166] Over this classic dramatist now hovered momentarily an air of popularity. Nor must we forget Julius Bronta's historical articles in *Drama* on "The Spanish Stage" and on Benavente, whom this writer discussed under the caption "Spain's Greatest Dramatist." [167] At about the same time, during the second decade, John Garrett Underhill paid tribute in "The One-Act Play in Spanish" to the perfection of this form in the Peninsula.[168] The criticism of plays in the magazines has retained throughout the half-century both its philosophical and its practical points of view, whether it dealt in 1929 with "The Spanish Theatre," in 1935 with "The Theatre in the Spanish Republic," or in 1933 with "Argentine Drama." [169] Again we are tempted to a contrast, this time of these stimulating pieces with, about 1830, the meager synopses of ancient Spanish plays.

The magazine of our time, besides such special treatment of the description, the historical or political essay, and the various forms of literature, interprets also, with some sophistication, architecture, music, and, in particular, painting. We remember how at the end of the nineteenth century the *Century* and *Scribner's* led the way in the dignified criticism of the last-named art. These magazines now continued with keener judgments and better illustrations to familiarize their cultivated clienteles with studies of Goya and Velázquez and of Sorolla and Zuloaga.[170] Timothy Cole's *Old Spanish Masters,* published in New York in 1907, first appeared as a series of plates in the *Century.*[171] The achievement of the new pictorial magazines was that they popularized, so to speak, the masters; they also told the layman about Picasso and the sensational Mexican painters.[172] Both the Spanish and the Spanish-American fine arts have become known not merely to the readers of the special magazines but to the browsers in train or waiting room who thumb casually the elaborate weeklies. On both planes these periodicals helped to bring to Americans the preoccupations, aesthetic and otherwise, of the Spanish-speaking peoples. This is really the point of this somewhat statistical but necessary chapter. For it was this dual approach to all subjects, this hold upon both the dilettante reader and the scholar, this communication with a few and with a public of millions, which throughout our 150 years, has made the periodical a more versatile conveyer of Spanish influence than the travel book.

THE magazines in their receptivity to Spanish influences were broad in scope, reaching several levels of our reading public. Sometimes, as in the case of the *North American Review*, they were distinguished in both authors and clientele. Nevertheless, this medium lacked, like the travel books, the dignified authority of the American histories of Spain.[1] For Americans Spanish history has always held a particular fascination, whether in the pages of Las Casas or of Prescott, whether or not it was relevant to either our national or our individual experiences. From the days (and earlier) when the works of Robertson or Jeremy Belknap were serialized in the periodicals [2] through those which witnessed the sweeping popularity of Irving, Prescott, and Motley down to our own times with their impressive monuments of scholarship [3] in both Spanish and Spanish-American history, the mere story of the Peninsula and of its titanic empire has stirred our imaginations in ways rivaling that of the story of our parent Britain. It was Jefferson, we remember, who pointed out that the histories of "a great part of America" were written in the Spanish language.

The fascination of Spanish history was linked with that romantic concept of Spain which has been mentioned so often in this book. The country's relative remoteness, emphasized in the chapter on the travelers; the barbaric opulence of its medieval past; the persistence of this past into the nineteenth century—all these factors excited us. However blessed with the utilities of life, our daily lives could hardly be termed rich in legend and story. We think in this connection of the discouragement of the artists, Hawthorne and Henry James, in America. Spanish history, so inextricably blended with legend, as Washington Irving shrewdly perceived,[4] offered not only the epic of the colonization but also the fabulous glories of Mexico and the Incas. During the nineteenth century, partly as a result of the drama of successive revolutions in the Peninsula, there was reborn in America that old notion of an eternal, chivalric Spain with its far-flung empire. Exiles in France, England, and even in America re-created for us the image of that ancient Spain of the seventeenth century.[5] King Boabdil of Granada, Philip II, or Torrijos, republican patriot memorialized today in the Plaza de Riego in Malaga; [6] the Armada, the Inquisition, the Carlists—in the nineteenth century all these became varied strands in the same gorgeous tapestry. The hunger for such romance could be mitigated by the travelers or the magazines but satisfied, perhaps, only by the historians.

This romantic vision of Spain included Columbus. Despite his erudite footnotes Irving had represented the discoverer, so someone said, as the protagonist in a nautical melodrama. Yet the re-creation of Columbus was not entirely romantic. The attraction of Spanish history for Americans was bound up in an honest desire to learn everything possible concerning the great navigator. This curiosity was personal and possessive. Although Genoese by birth and Spanish in his other associations, Columbus remained somehow our own. When the elaborate meetings of the three hundredth anniversary of the discovery were held in 1792 in New York, Boston, and Baltimore,[7] he had already been celebrated in Joel Barlow's mammoth epic *The Vision of Columbus*,[8] and in Boston two years later he became the subject of a historical drama.[9] Basic in the study of Columbus was the release (and Irving's use) of the manuscripts of Navarrete in the second and third decades of the century. The spate of novels, poems, portraits, brochures, and memorials flowed on through the next centenary [10] and has recently reached a kind of culmination in a twentieth-century scholar's symbolic re-enactment of the voyages.[11] For many Americans Spanish history has centered in the attempt to recapture the life experience of the arch-explorer.[12]

THUS Spanish history enthralled us by its romance, and it enriched the annals of our country by its new facts concerning the discovery. In addition, it illumined the spectacular events in three continents. It described the scramble for independence in Mexico, Cuba, and the South American nations or at the close of the century our inauspicious war with the mother country. In the late eighteenth century we encounter in the newspapers columns of "Spanish Affairs." Journalists, politicians, and businessmen kept a watchful eye on the stratagems of Spain, especially in America. Nevertheless, these matter-of-fact motivations for studying the history of Spain were hardly stronger than the characteristically American belief (briefly described in the previous chapter) that this misguided nation, repenting her misdemeanors, would soon join the fellowship of democratic countries. This delusion was already chronic on January 24, 1809, when in Boston, "at a public festival given in honour of the Spanish patriots," Americans lustily sang Robert Treat Paine's ode, "Spain, Commerce, and Freedom." [13] The fancy persisted throughout the century. The dream of an ennobled Spain struggling from its age-old bondage toward democratic liberty deceived us at the time of the Revolution of 1868 and again in 1936 as we christened ourselves the friends of "Spanish democracy." Besides its romance, its Columbian story, and its useful definition of our neighborhood problems, Spanish history has long been linked with our none too modest conviction that we ourselves could refashion it according to our own blueprint for a better world. I speak now not of the historians, to be discussed in the following pages, but of the politician and the everyday citizen. The true nature of Spanish nationalism, with its conflicting aims of the traditional and individualistic (sometimes the anarchistic), we have never really understood.

For these various reasons the allurement of Spanish history, beginning in the days of Cotton Mather and Samuel Sewall and provoking both knowledge and curiosity, formed a constantly growing public for our historians of Spain and Spanish affairs. Stimuli of precisely the same quality did not exist for the writing by Americans of histories of the other Continental nations. At first the spacious panorama, against which move the heroic figures created by Prescott and the others, startles us, as if these classic historians of Spain were without foreground. Nothing could be farther from the truth. The attractions of Spanish history, just described, had antedated these literary prospectors by many years and had encouraged, long before Irving examined in 1825 the manuscripts of Navarrete, a sensitivity to the story of Spain.[14] Indeed, the rushes for this triumphal procession of Irving and Prescott had been strewn in the seventeenth and eighteenth centuries. A measurable awareness of Spanish history existed prior to *The Life and Voyages of Christopher Columbus* (1828) or *The History of Ferdinand and Isabella* (1837).

The chapters concerning the two earlier centuries have shown how libraries contained both originals and translations of the best-known histories of Spain. Importations and reprintings of these standard chroniclers, like Bernal Díaz del Castillo whom Irving used with a plausible air of discovery, actually never ceased. All these had been widely read before they were popularized by him and by Prescott. As very different instances of this vogue, it might be observed that Las Casas was discussed in one periodical in 1823 and Llorente's *Histoire critique de l'inquisition d'Espagne* in another in 1825.[15] As early as 1770 Robert Bell published in Philadelphia an edition of Robertson, the most persuasive of all the eighteenth-century English historians of Spain, on this occasion his *History of the Reign of Charles the Fifth*.[16]

By 1840 three more editions of this history had appeared, and during this decade its introduction became a textbook for Jared Sparks' course in modern history at Harvard.[17] Robertson was by no means alone. In 1818 the first American editions of Robert Watson's accounts of Philip II and Philip III were issued in New York.[18] At about the same time appeared the histories of the Peninsular War, narratives which stirred both England and America; the articles in the periodicals in increasing variety; the semihistorical accounts of the primitive peoples of South America; and fiction and drama on Spanish historical themes. It is clear that long before Washington Irving toiled in Obadiah Rich's Madrid library or Prescott made his fateful decision to renounce Germany and Italy for Spain the way was prepared.

MEANWHILE, the young Republic itself, without predilections for Spain or for any other European country, was slowly developing its own school of historians. Prior to the Revolution history had been chiefly the business of the recorder or annalist.[19] Though

THE

TRUE HISTORY

OF THE

CONQUEST OF MEXICO.

BY

Capt. BERNAL DIAZ del CASTILLO,

ONE OF THE CONQUERORS.

WRITTEN IN THE YEAR 1568.

————*Labore, et expensis, et damno,*
Tempore, veritatis cognitio adquiritur.

Translated from the original Spanish,
BY MAURICE KEATINGE, Esq.

IN TWO VOLUMES.

VOL. I.

PRINTED IN LONDON:
REPRINTED AT SALEM, BY JOSHUA CUSHING,
FOR CUSHING & APPLETON.
1803.

Title page of *The True History of the Conquest of Mexico,*
by Bernal Díaz del Castillo, Salem, 1803.

the great upheaval had caused some intellectual confusion, it had inspired competent biographies of the country's leaders, among them Marshall's life of Washington. Besides, there were state histories such as Jeremy Belknap's and popular histories such as Mason Weems' or the brilliant burlesque account of Dutch New York by Washington Irving.[20] In the early attempts at histories of the nation as a whole, like Ebenezer Hazard's or Benjamin Trumbull's, analysis was unborn.[21] Patriotism and wooden narration were adequate. Until the advent of George Bancroft one may reasonably deny the creation by an American of any distinguished history, either of our own country or of a European nation.[22] What is the critical point in this post-Revolutionary development of historiography? The War of 1812? The year 1826, approximately the time of Jared Sparks' self-dedication to history? It is difficult to say. At any rate, in the 1830's this adolescent intellectual life of the country turned, not without hesitation, toward European history.

The appearance in New England in the thirties and forties of a group of capable historians was a natural result of the growing wealth and culture of this region.[23] For this was the "Golden Day": Emerson and Thoreau; Longfellow and Whittier and Hawthorne; and in history Bancroft, Motley, Prescott, and Parkman. "History" was the first caption in Emerson's most remarkable book, *Essays, First Series* (1841).[24] Here in New England the independent fortunes, like those of Prescott and Ticknor, made research in Europe possible. Here, too, were the most fertile libraries in America,[25] and here was a book-buying public.[26] In all these libraries this curious public found shelves of history; simultaneously in the bookstores this "middle group" of historians now provided others. The reading of history was fashionable; there was, one historian laments, little else to read. History adorned the cultivated reader's library; it was so obviously "polite and entertaining literature." In Boston, in 1837, Prescott's *Ferdinand and Isabella* was a standard Christmas present. As we look back now from our own machine age in scholarship with its professionals and steel filing cabinets, this phase of the "Renaissance of New England" resembles a gentleman-scholar's paradise. These rich and talented men collected manuscripts and hired agents abroad to explore the archives.

They assembled priceless libraries, and they wrote history which, at least so they believed, was literature.[27]

Indeed, these famous historians were really a literary coterie. Most of them lived in Massachusetts,[28] were associated with Harvard University, used the libraries of Boston, and were intimate friends, as in the case of Ticknor and Prescott. All were learned, gifted writers, working together in a medium partly scientific, partly belletristic. They wrote biographical articles, they annotated manuscripts, and they imported books. In particular, they were able to initiate colossal projects demanding prolonged research, extensive travel, and uninterrupted periods of writing. Notably absent were the formal organizations, the foundations, the professional connections between university and investigator. Nor did these skillful amateurs, like some modern scholar-historians, compose merely for each other.[29] They wrote for this book-buying, history-reading, genteel public which in turn accorded their productions an admiration unparalleled today for works equivalent in solidity of scholarship. For a brief moment, above the crude layers of business and politics in American life, above what one critic calls our "mercantile culture," flourished this union of learning and popular taste. It was the "Golden Day" for history, too.

That these writers should turn from the short and somewhat simple annals of America to the spacious subjects of Europe seems on reconsideration inevitable.[30] Prescott, a born historian, philandered with all subjects save those of his own country. He contemplated histories of the ancient world and of the literature of Italy before finally wedding his true love, Spain. Romantic in temperament, literary in taste, these "Golden Day" historians loved gorgeous fruits not available here in the green days of our Republic. It may even be argued that they were primarily men of letters, that each was by some accident deflected from literature to history. Prescott was the creator of some sentimental essays and Motley the author of a novel. That pioneer in this American exploration of Europe's past, Washington Irving, outside the Massachusetts set but allied to it by common interests, had won his fame as a master of the essay. This essay of manners, romantic in tone and akin to history, he had developed in English themes, German folk history, and slightly later in Spanish legend. Among these "literary" historians were exceptions. Some, like Francis Parkman, did indeed look westward. The others faced across the Atlantic. If for such temperaments the re-creation of European history was predestined, certainly among the nations celebrated would be immemorial Spain.[31]

For Spain presented, especially in its relation to the New World, a story incomparable in passion and color. Moreover, this tale was now elaborated. About the year 1825 and afterward throughout the century, long-forgotten episodes in the story and fresh versions of the thousand years' pageant came to light. In other words the widely scattered and jealously housed manuscripts in the Peninsula became gradually available to scholars, and by the year 1844 the guards surrounding these treasures had greatly relaxed.[32] For the American scholar in the Peninsula it was a beginning. No one who reads Irving's journals can forget his mounting excitement as he examined in the Madrid libraries manuscripts for his biography of Columbus. S. T. Wallis, devoted student of Spain, re-echoes in the *Southern Literary Messenger* for March, 1841, the stir among American historians created by the publication of Navarrete's superb documents.[33] Little by little, access to the Archives of the Indies, to the Archives of Simancas, even to the treasures of convent and private palace was permitted. More important than the wealth or the particular abilities of these historians, than the German researches in Spain with which they were familiar,[34] was this timely collapse of prohibitions in the libraries. Restrictions, as modern scholars know, were by no means ended. Nevertheless, the first shafts had been dug in the veins of Potosí.

As is sometimes the case, this precious metal was first seized not by the scholar but by the man of letters. It was characteristic of Irving that, having accepted Alexander Hill Everett's invitation to translate the manuscripts of Navarrete, he ended by writing a smoothly flowing, semifictionized history of Columbus.[35] In the same fashion he constructed from the old Moorish chroniclers his mild epic of the conquest of Granada, as related by an imaginary

monk named Fray Antonio Agapida. This book was a curious
blend of history and legend. "He is not the man," declared Lockhart of Irving, "to paint tumultuous war." [36] Irving used, however,
original sources and never strayed too far from established truth.
From his boyhood he had cherished a love of learning. An abundance of antiquarian lore adorned his history of New York, and
the subsoil of *The Sketch Book* and *Bracebridge Hall* was his respectable knowledge of Elizabethan England.[37] Irving loved the
stillness of a library, and presumably he never enjoyed happier
hours than those spent in the assembly of the materials for his four
or five Spanish books. In them, despite their thinness of content,
we must not underestimate his patience in a kind of amateurish
research. Nor was he indifferent to the basic problems of the historians, such as the winnowing of facts from masses of legend. He
loved to muse over an old story and would tell it with some accuracy, too—if, of course, truthtelling did not mar the tale!

It was to be expected that in his histories Irving would show, as
the reviews testified of both the *Columbus* and the *Granada*,[38]
power in narrative and sensitivity to imagined scenes and emotions
of the Spanish past. The stories of Columbus' voyage of discovery
and of Boabdil's farewell to Granada are well told, and we share
with Irving his fanciful re-creation of Columbus' joy at the first
sight of America and of Boabdil's sorrow at his last of Granada.
Though repetitious, the stories never halt. On and on they flow
with an enchanting ease, postponing from chapter to chapter the
challenges of scholarship or the knotty questions of doctrine, belief, or institutional development. Indeed, the philosophical elements of history are always blandly absent. Perhaps it is difficult
today to respect these books as authentic history. Like *The Alhambra,* these chronicles of Christian knight and Moorish castle, of
Atlantic storm and Indian chieftain, resemble glamorous, rather
intricate fairy tales of ancient Spain. Irving's achievement was, in
the end, a brilliant but dilettantish interpretation of priceless materials. He was the "discoverer," as one historiographer calls him,
"of the fascination of Spain." [39]

Such a dismissal, however, of our first modern historian of Spain
is too debonair. What historiographer fails to mention his name

with respect? In all the more exacting tasks of the scholar he was presumably unsuccessful, but the *Columbus* remains on sound recent authority "an excellent piece of historical work." [40] Perhaps its signal contemporary service, even if we dissent from the extravagant reviews, was to put flesh on the skeleton; or, better, Irving's *Columbus* gave a body to the tenuous ghost of legend regarding the discoverer. Investigators were to analyze and demolish much that he had written, but it was Irving who first submitted in English a fully rounded narrative out of which could be sifted the truth. We cannot be rid of Irving the historian of Spain by laughing at his references to princesses and rivers of gold. His position is secure. *The Conquest of Granada* was less fortunate than the *Columbus.* Irving's oscillation, to which he himself confesses in his preface, between a history and a romance damns the book as neither. Nevertheless, here, as in the *Columbus* and the *Voyages of the Companions of Columbus,* he exploited another grand historic theme. If he himself could not write history, he was, at any rate, the godfather of historians of Spain.

IN WILLIAM HICKLING PRESCOTT, Irving the historian had aroused admiration and on one occasion an intense anxiety which ended in Irving's generous renunciation of the theme of the Conquest of Mexico.[41] For everyone—including, perhaps, the deeply disappointed Irving—this was a lucky incident. The wide scope of the two continents was more appropriately Prescott's, with his relentless research, his extended vision of Spanish America, and his austere consecration to the art of the historian. Indeed, however important Irving's services as a historian of Spain, in comparison Prescott's were gigantic. In this group of magnificent amateurs he was first, and the rest were nowhere.[42] Prescott lacks philosophic profundity. He has little significant to say on politics, government, institutions, or on ideas in general. Nevertheless, his story is splendidly vast; he displays the entire Spanish world in the fifteenth and sixteenth centuries. His judgments are fair; who would suspect his personal detestation of Philip II? His stately style, less subtle and personal than Irving's, is well integrated with the dignity of his subjects. For all these reasons, among them the memory of the beautiful heroism of his own life, his great books live today. On the whole they might be regarded as the most powerful single source of Spanish influence on our culture during the forties and fifties.

The full record of Prescott's dedication to the study of the Spanish past will be told elsewhere in this book. We should, however, observe at this point in our story that the wealth and talents which led him abroad at an early age (without visiting Spain) and to a knowledge of the Spanish language at twenty-eight did not bring him to his colossal themes until years later. The momentous decision resulted from varied causes. Moved by Ticknor's exhortations, by his own growing distaste for classical, Italian, or French subjects, and possibly by the hazard for his unfortunate eyes in reading German script, he began in 1826 his history of Ferdinand and Isabella. Then followed research, with the aid of friends like Ticknor and Gayangos and of agents in the archives of Spain, and throughout the ensuing decade his ceaseless hours of composition. By Christmas, 1837, his three volumes were off the press to enjoy their immediate and overwhelming success. Almost at once their author's mind was absorbed in plans to re-create Spanish history upon an even grander scale.

In the tracery of influences we are considering, *A History of the Reign of Ferdinand and Isabella* is central. For the interest in Spanish subjects was instantly strengthened among all kinds of readers by this impressive record of a powerful and majestic Spain. Among the panegyrists of the book there were a few dissenters, notably Theodore Parker, who handled it severely for its omissions.[43] Nevertheless, even if the reviewers were sometimes friends of Prescott, the evidence of achievement was conclusive—never more so than in the cold testimony of publishers' receipts. The sales of the book were an earnest of Prescott's popularity for a generation. His contract for *Ferdinand and Isabella* called for 1,250 copies to be sold within five years and for an advance payment of one thousand dollars. Within five months the first edition was exhausted, and others followed in swift succession. The fate of Prescott's other books was equally blessed. On the day of its publication

The Conquest of Peru fetched 7,500 dollars for a corresponding number of copies and also eight hundred pounds for the English edition.[44] No traveler's reminiscences, no series of magazine articles could approach in sheer magnetism these solid histories of two centuries of Spanish empire.

Ferdinand and Isabella, anticipating by twelve years George Ticknor's *History of Spanish Literature,* was, in conjunction with Irving's studies, the first book of its kind to awaken European respect for American scholarship concerning Spain. As a historical work Richard Ford declared it inferior to no other published during the first half of the century,[45] and Count Adolphe de Circourt, a distinguished historian in the field, permitted himself to speak of it, none too briefly, in a twenty-four-page review in the *Bibliothèque universelle* of Geneva.[46] Spanish criticisms of the book have been interesting,[47] and so marked was its success in the Peninsula that Prescott's subsequent research on kindred matters was materially aided. If we add to this conspicuous recognition the circulation of the countless reviews, of the excerpts, of the biographies of the author, we arrive at some notion of Prescott's eminence in 1838, even prior to his other writings, as a historian of Spain.

A formidable element in Prescott's influence was his breadth of subject. No traveler, no translator, no romancer, no essayist has ever in writing of Spain rivaled him in scope. After the spacious *Ferdinand and Isabella* he created another panorama. For six years he was engaged upon *The Conquest of Mexico* (1843), "the most poetic subject," he asserted, "ever offered to the pen of the historian." [48] In unity of interest, in dramatic movement, this excelled the earlier triumph. It was also more varied, more thrilling in action, and more erudite. One lack, however, has dogged this famous book until this very day. Despite Prescott's prodigious labors, the sections on the pre-Cortesian civilizations have turned out to be, quite naturally, vulnerable to modern specialists. The problem of the accurate re-creation of these prehistoric cultures proved equally troublesome in *The Conquest of Peru* (1847). *The Reign of Philip the Second* (1855–58), episodic and colorful, Prescott left unfinished. The mere mention of the titles of these histories brings to mind their transcendent sweep though not their marvelous par-

ticularity of detail. Among all the historians of Spain none surpasses Prescott in epic proportions or in vivid, tiny incident. We
behold the armies of Spaniards and the hordes of Moors, Mexicans,
and Peruvians, or we pause in conversation with a single peasant.

THE anecdote of Irving's sacrifice for Prescott of his project on
Mexico is beautifully paralleled by the story of Prescott's insistence
that John Lothrop Motley take for his own the subject of Philip
II.[49] Motley was also a "literary" historian, learned and under the
spell of Carlyle. He was as zealous in research and more fervid in
style than the well-poised Prescott.[50] More ardent, too, concerning
the issues of politics, which inclined to bore the latter, he took sides
and wrote of them with eagerness, sometimes with violence.[51] Especially in his *Rise of the Dutch Republic* (1856) Motley's partisan-
ship for all things republican, his excessive passion for the Dutch
liberals, betrayed him into extremes. He announced, for example,
that the careers of William of Orange and George Washington
were essentially akin in their selfless devotion to freedom.[52] Indeed,
he very nearly formed the conviction, it would seem, that Philip
II, and perhaps everything represented by Spanish rule, was evil
itself. His *Rise of the Dutch Republic* became an eloquent polemic
for liberty and republicanism and at the same time a vigorous
diatribe against Catholicism and Spanish absolutism.[53]

Motley's Philip II plays the role of Satan in the moral drama of
the liberation of Holland. The historian's awareness of Spain itself
appears secondary in comparison with the insatiable curiosity of
Irving and Prescott about all phases of Spanish life. Though widely
traveled he never entered the country, and though during his long
residence in Brussels he read endlessly in Spanish manuscripts relating to Dutch history (documents drawn by the Belgian government from the Archivo general de Simancas),[54] he never sought out
the archives of the Peninsula. Nor is there evidence that he shared in
regard to Spain either the romantic feeling of Irving, the interest
in her colonial empire of Prescott, or the perceptions concerning
her institutions of Henry Charles Lea, the analyst of the Inquisition. In Motley's studies of the growth of republicanism Spain was

necessarily involved but became for him primarily the wicked oppressor, through Philip II, of true liberty. One could wish for Motley a participation in the judicial quality of Prescott's mind. Under the influence of George Bancroft's conceptions of liberty, of his own ancestral traditions, of his country's past struggles for freedom, Motley eventually bordered on fanaticism in his hatred of the Catholic church in Spain.[55] In spite of the high quality of his scholarship and the vivacity of his writing, he became, at least in the perspective of these nineteenth-century patterns, reactionary. In contrast to the more liberal evaluations by Irving and Prescott, he recalled those old, familiar prejudices against Spain of the seventeenth and eighteenth centuries.[56] These are evident even in his superb chapter on the destruction of the Armada.[57]

So IN 1828 in his *Columbus* Irving made his debut as the first freelance scholar-historian of the Peninsula, and forty years afterward, in the year of the last volume of Motley's *History of the United Netherlands,* this period of the brilliant amateurs may be said to have ended. For during the fifties, even while Prescott's *Philip the Second* was in process of publication, the scientific methods of German scholarship were beginning to seep into the United States. When in 1856 at Harvard Jared Sparks, who had retired in 1849, was followed by H. W. Torrey the event seemed a symbol of the arrival of new and sterner historical techniques. These subversive changes do not, of course, date themselves readily. Something will be said a few pages later of the timing and of the results of this revolution.

At the moment we are interested in the stubborn persistence of the romantic tradition among historians of Spain, on and on throughout the century. Long after Prescott had laid down his pen, his volumes encouraged the imitators and lesser historians. We recall as a parallel the echoes of Irving in fiction or of Longfellow in poetry. The reverberations, inevitable in any intellectual movement, sometimes seem particularly characteristic of American romantic literature. Similar repercussions now occurred in this kindred art. History followed history, true to the temper of the founders of the school but lacking conspicuously both their scholarship and their felicities of style.

It may, indeed, be argued that the deeper currents in American historical scholarship now avoided Spanish subjects until the twentieth century. Until the advent of Henry Charles Lea, by his contemporaneity and by his scientific scholarship a brilliant hybrid of the classical and modern schools, American historians of Spain were content to tell and retell the old stories of the master-amateurs, sometimes making the histories merely plated versions of the events related by Irving, Prescott, and Motley. Of five relevant titles in the *American Catalogue* in 1876 of histories by American authors, four were editions of Irving's *The Conquest of Granada*.[58] Yet these figures are misleading. Although seventeen years after his death Irving's histories were still admired and although reprints of English narratives of the Peninsula were current, a number of new American historians had appeared. These imitators wrote readable versions of the familiar tales, varying in scholarship and talents from the pretentious rhetoric of John S. C. Abbott to the ambitious but second-rate studies of the Moorish civilization by Henry Coppée. Unintentionally the pioneers in "literary" history had initiated a cult of romantic history dealing with Spain, history with the principles of genteel scholarship and the practices of popular journalism.

One is impressed by Abbott's bold achievement just ten years after Prescott's death (1859); he wrote the first American one-volume history of Spain. For reasons clear to all except, apparently, Abbott himself, none of the great amateurs had hitherto essayed this feat. A Congregational clergyman of New Haven, Connecticut, Abbott indicated the quality of his book by including it in a series concerned with various countries and naming it *The Romance of Spanish History* (1869). In a rather foolish preface he explained that "romance" was not "fiction" and that no one could possibly compress all the events of Spanish history between two covers. He had, therefore, tried "to glean, from the many centuries which have passed away, those well-authenticated incidents which, in his judgement, would prove most interesting and instructive to American readers." [59] Since Abbott is rhetorical at the end of every chapter and sentimental on nearly every page, he has little in reserve for such incidents as "El último suspiro del moro." [60] His narrative is valuable chiefly as an index to a type of shallow interest in Spain, already encountered in the travel book and magazine article. Popularization of Spanish history could hardly go further.

Another clergyman's skirmishes in Spanish history were bolder although the booty was scarcely more enriching. Edward Everett Hale, the nephew of Edward and Alexander H. Everett, describes his youthful hope, never realized, of becoming the amanuensis of Prescott.[61] While editor of the Boston *Advertiser* he had studied the language and had delved into Spanish-American history, and in 1882 he visited the Peninsula.[62] His *Story of Spain* (1886), a work done in collaboration with his sister Susan Hale (known also for her water colors of the country), tries to crowd into a single volume, as had Abbott, "the proud record of Spain in literature, in adventure, in discovery, in statesmanship, and in war." [63] Even Hale's enthusiasm could not accomplish the impossible; his *Story of Spain* is a book for the novice. He touched too lightly on the complicated intrigues of Spanish history as well as on the achievements of a great people. Reviews of this superficial book, in contrast to the eulogies of Abbott's rhetoric, were neutral in tone.[64] Nevertheless, it has had its day; it remained on the publishers' lists until 1929.

Popular or semipopular narratives of Spanish history were inspired in part by the commercial rewards of the subject, as in the case of Abbott, but partly also by the demand for the whole fascinating story from readers similar to those who devoured the travel books and magazine articles. For such readers the Hales wrote, and to some extent the Everetts, who were plainly a Hispanophile family.[65] An interest in the Peninsula was more deep-rooted in Charles Étienne Arthur Gayarré, whose lifelong passion for Spain was intensified by three additional factors: Spanish ancestry, Spanish backgrounds in Louisiana (his native state), and a long stay in Spain, apparently for the sake of enlarging his knowledge of the country. In contrast, Prescott's and Motley's unwillingness to live in Spain despite the difficulties of travel in their era is still regrettable.[66] For Gayarré Spain was a homeland, as definitely as Britain for Irving. We are sorry that he never attempted an interpretation of his feelings for Spain as had Irving for England in the opening pages of *The Sketch Book*.[67] Gayarré's grandfather had come to Louisiana in 1766 with Antonio de Ulloa. The historian knew three languages: English, French, and Spanish. It was entirely natural that he should become both the annalist of his own Louisiana and the biographer of Philip II.

Gayarré was sensitive to the French and Spanish traditions of Louisiana by reason of his antecedents and of his education at the College of New Orleans. He was also alive to the state's contemporary problems through his prolonged participation in politics and through his own impoverishment by the Civil War. He was well equipped to analyze the European origins of Louisiana and to trace its growth. The author of novels and plays, he infused into both his *Histoire de Louisiane* (1846) and his *Romance of the History of Louisiana* (1848) [68] a "passionate provincialism." [69] To this Louisiana of the past, says Grace King with appropriate sentiment, Gayarré "consecrated his first ambitions . . . through manhood, he devoted his pen to her; old, suffering, bereft by misfortune of his ancestral heritage, and the fruit of his prime's vigour and industry, he yet stood ever her courageous knight . . . He held her archives not only in his memory but in his heart." [70]

After reading Gayarré's later *History of Louisiana* (1854–67), we might easily believe that the faults of his *Philip II*, a far less successful book, were in some degree caused by the distractions of its creator during the Civil War. This is a peculiar narrative, sometimes not even mentioned by bibliographers in lists of works on the same subject, like those of Prescott, Motley, or Watson. Portions are highly rhetorical, justifying even William Dean Howells' devastating comment that one cannot tell whether the book was written in "the extravagant and curious English it now wears, or whether he produced it in Spanish, and [it] has been too literally translated." [71] *Philip II* was a depressing instance of the general tendency which we are now studying. Avoiding the principle of "a minute chronicle," it sought "a philosophical retrospect of what was most memorable in Spain during that period." [72] Gayarré himself christened it a "historical essay." [73] In debt to the famous "amateurs," it displayed a morbid preoccupation with the character of Philip. Howells thought the violence of Gayarré's hatred, despite his own Spanish blood and Catholic faith, toward the famous monarch the mainspring of the book's interest for the modern reader.[74] Everything follows naturally from the early description of the horror of Philip's life and death, and few readers will forget the author's macabre story of the latter.[75] *Philip II* hints at the disintegration of Gayarré's historical talents.

By the last quarter of the century "popular" histories of Spain or of Spanish regions were in constant demand, and among these Gayarré's were not the least admired. His popularity rivaled that of Henry Coppée, well known for his two-volume *History of the Conquest of Spain by the Arab-Moors* (1881). Inevitably this epochal invasion, whose sequel Irving had described in *The Conquest of Granada,* was included in this wholesale popularization of Spanish history. Coppée, soldier, educator, and miscellaneous writer, was shrewd enough to rely on Pascual Gayangos' translation of al-Makkari. He invested his exciting story in a mantle of scholarship.[76] None of his material, however, antedated the middle of the seventeenth century, and there is something specious about the learning in his deft narrative. In observing the increasing tolerance in the nineteenth century toward the saga of the Mohammedan peoples, the *Nation* stressed Coppée's willingness to countenance traditional stories even in the absence of strong evidence and praised his skill in making dubious anecdotes appear "possibly true and certainly interesting!" [77]

In his introduction Coppée admits that his visit to Mexico from 1846 to 1848 (the two years following Irving's final stay in Spain) had directed him, full of admiration for the historian of Granada, to Gayangos and to other standard sources. Their influence may be traced on nearly every page: "The valiant deeds," he says, "of the *Conquistadores* led me back to the mother country of such heroes, and to the earlier days of its romantic and brilliant annals, especially under the domination of the Arab-Moors. The interest thus excited was greatly increased by a visit to Spain in 1870, with a special purpose." [78] The "special purpose" of this journey was "glimpses of scenery, and of classic localities" [79] which he might introduce with authority into his ambitious book. Nevertheless, like Abbott, Hale, or Gayarré, Coppée really spoke to the undiscriminating reader. His prolific annotation, his allusions to Conde and other traditional scholars, or even his pioneer use of these Arabic sources cannot conceal the fact that the *History of the Conquest of Spain* differs little from the superficial records of Abbott and Hale. Of all these fluent narratives, these aftercurrents of Irving, Prescott, and Motley, presumably those of Gayarré deserve the most respect. [80]

How many more historical tales of the Peninsula would the nineteenth-century reader absorb? Irving, Prescott, and Motley had evidently unlocked the Spanish chest. There seemed to be no end. Modern catalogues of books in print attest the continuance of this type of Spanish history, and we encounter Abbott, Hale, or their kind even now. The war of 1898 released another series of histories, most of them preposterously partisan, like James C. Fernald's *The Spaniard in History* (1898). This book promises, in the midst of other nonsense, not to sheath the American sword "till Spanish power has ceased to touch with its blight the Western World"! [81] After 1900 these banal narratives still commanded an audience, but we may bid them farewell after a reference to Henry Dwight Sedgwick's layman's history, with its accounts of literature and the arts. [82] It has been said that the vogue of these popular nineteenth-century historians delayed the application of the best critical scholarship until the second or third decade of the twentieth. Perhaps so. They inherited that ideal of pictorial Spanish history originated by Prescott and Irving. New theories and new professional scholarship were needed for a real rejuvenation of this genre. In the work of the historians, Bourne, Bolton, or Merriman, to be discussed presently, the great Spanish themes of Prescott were to be broadened and deepened by fresh approaches, and for such a rebirth it was high time.

These new historical techniques, beginning not long after the Civil War, were to develop steadily side by side with the deterioration of the school of Prescott. Despite the presence abroad of many of our students, the real commitment to German scholarship did not come until later.[83] In the eighties, in at least three great universities German-trained historians started their momentous work of initiating young Americans into the new faith. From Johns Hopkins University poured out to the various seats of learning the pupils of Herbert Baxter Adams, who, indoctrinated in the methods of Germany, introduced in 1880 institutional history as a distinct branch of study.[84] For our purposes it is unnecessary to trace the movement much further. In 1884 the organization of the American Historical Association provided in the learned journals repositories for these scientific investigators.[85] The era brought with it the not unmixed blessings of the article on sources, of the monograph, of the intense cultivation of small segments of knowledge, of the young university teacher zealous for a reputation—in a word, of the professional historian as we know him today.[86] A modern writer points out that the distrust of "literary" historians made these "scientific" writers revert, in effect, to the attitude of the colonial historians. Again style became less important than fact and objectivity.[87]

Presently we shall see how this new scholarship was to alter the character of histories of Spain and Spanish America in the professional work of such scholars as Bourne and Bolton. Just now let us realize that these methods sent out their waves of influence beyond the universities, stimulating investigators as different as Henry Charles Lea and Hubert Howe Bancroft. We must consider briefly these historians, some of them almost professionals in the university sense and others, really scientific in attitude, who served as a kind of bridge between the amateurs of the earlier school and the single-minded devotees of German scholarship. Of such compromises the most dramatic example was Henry Charles Lea, and with him we shall now be concerned.

AT FIRST glance the remarkable career of Lea as a historian of Spain seems encased in contradictions and inconsistencies. His enduring works on the Inquisition were published in the late nineteenth and early twentieth centuries,[88] but his preliminary research on Spain, focusing in a documentation of the Inquisition,[89] was accomplished in 1839, hardly more than a decade after Irving's *Columbus* and only two years later than Prescott's *Ferdinand and Isabella*. Lea appears to have been unaffected directly by the university tradition; he was educated by tutors and by the compulsions of his own omnivorous mind. He was, however, the most meticulous of scholars, the most learned of students, and the most tireless of linguists. A master of ancient tongues, he was also at ease in French, in Italian, and, of course, in Spanish. He learned German at the age of sixty and Dutch at eighty. During his many years as a busy publisher—he was a grandson of Mathew Carey—his devotion to history was avocational, but the scientific quality of his investigations places him among the professional historians. His objectives were special, and he could even say: "Spanish history has never had any attractions for me." The ensuing sentences explain his meaning, making the entire statement a key to his purposes: "I cannot help," he added, "taking it up, for the Spanish Inquisition is the controlling factor in the career of modern persecution. I have become intensely interested in the curious problem of the profound modification wrought in the Spanish character by the Inquisition." [90]

Like the earlier historians in his happy possession of a fortune, Lea's free-ranging education permitted him to discover and indulge his deepest interests. His tutorial instruction, blessed with guidance from his mother in French and Greek, revealed successively his gifts for languages, for science, for literature, and for history, particularly for that of the Middle Ages. The scientific interval in his studies was basic. From science rather than from Germanic scholarship he acquired his allegiance to original manuscripts [91] and also his habits of patient search for these in the libraries and archives of Europe.[92] Between the appearance of his *History of the Inquisition of the Middle Ages* (1887) and his peerless *History of the Inquisition in Spain* (1906–7) he published four important works in six volumes,[93] besides magazine articles, which on the whole he was inclined to regard as annoying interruptions.

Henry Charles Lea, from the painting by Robert W. Vonnoh, 1895.

Slowly, one by one, he brought out his massive studies of the Spanish past.

The intimacy of Lea's knowledge of Spanish history is well demonstrated by the unique story about his essay (mentioned in the previous chapter), "The Decadence of Spain," which was printed in the *Atlantic Monthly* for July, 1898.[94] He wrote this brief but acute study at the request of Walter Hines Page while he was at the Delaware Water Gap without access to any books whatever. When someone expressed astonishment at this achievement, Lea explained that twenty years earlier he had become convinced that war between Spain and the United States was unavoidable and that the causes could be laid bare by a study of the Catholic church in the Spanish colonies. For this reason he had sought out the records of the friars, mastered these, and then put them aside. In the emergency, far from libraries, his retentive memory enabled him to write this brilliant essay without references or verifications.[95]

It is, then, superfluous to remark that in his interpretation of Spain Lea moved in a world of his own. He cared nothing for the romantic, legendary Spain even if toward the end of his life he became more interested for their own sake in contemporary Spanish affairs.[96] Although his army of scribes sacked the archives and although he had agents in Mexico, Peru, Guatemala, and Argentina, he never traveled in Spain or Spanish America. Furthermore, he derived little from the illustrious "amateurs" (in one sense his contemporaries) [97] who were the fountainheads of the popular histories. Compared with his learned discourse, the pages of Prescott, however honest in scholarship, seem lacquered and mannered. As a matter of fact, Lea's boredom with the "romance of Spain" was not the only difference between himself and these royal, poetic historians. He was also a pioneer, as far as American historians of Spain were concerned, in certain philosophic conceptions of history. Presumably Lea's interests were part of a general awakening among thinking men in regard to the importance of institutional history.

Philosophic in approach, Lea was never deliberately literary. In his choice of subjects he never seized upon a compellingly dramatic period or upon a group of personalities.[98] Instead he selected a particular institution, one veiled in secrecy, one deeply corrosive in its stamp upon humanity.[99] Although it presented insuperable difficulties in the representation of its inner truth, Lea was enamored of this story of the Inquisition. It cut beneath into the spiritual life of mankind. Medieval law, medieval religion, the medieval mind itself—these were the intellectual arcana which he explored. Spain itself became almost a by-product in his sustained philosophic examination of these mysterious institutional problems. The Inquisition was an episode in the life of humanity, incredibly revealing and profoundly illustrative. The Roman church was a momentous fact, leaving a scar on our modern society. Indeed, Lea believed this church to be the "great fact which dominates the history of modern civilization." [100] After reading his closely knit logic we turn less happily to Prescott, who seems in comparison almost a Robert Louis Stevenson among the historians of Spain.

Lea's was a spacious career. For sixty-eight years, inclusive of his forty active years in business, he lived the life of a productive scholar.[101] At his death he left, besides more than forty articles or papers in learned and in scientific journals, ten historical works, amounting in all to seventeen volumes.[102] Since he ardently believed that history which laid bare the recesses of institutional life aided the comprehension and perhaps the solution of modern problems, he became the first of our historians to perceive in the past of Spain analogies to the dilemmas of his own country.[103] In this way Lea differs vitally from other nineteenth-century historians. In reading Irving, Motley, or Prescott we are translated almost to another planet. In reading Lea we perceive in the Spaniard not so much differences from ourselves as resemblances left unexplored by the more superficial historians. His study of the institutions of humanity brings us in the end to the application of general and profound psychological principles.

Finally, it must be added that Lea's frank analyses of the inquisitorial processes, confessions, or *autos-da-fé* do not make pleasant reading. He had little sympathy for the Roman Catholic church, and partly for this reason he won fewer plaudits in Spain than either Irving or Prescott. Nevertheless, his learning, his tem-

156

perate spirit, and his lack of polemic zeal (such as Motley's or Gayarré's) have called forth the admiration of some Spaniards. Without conceding that Lea's studies of the Inquisition are definitive, a modern Spanish critic thinks them more complete than those of all his predecessors.[104] Probably it is true that his *History of the Inquisition of the Middle Ages* is, as Lord Acton declares, "the most important contribution of the new world to the religious history of the old." [105]

IN MOST of these nineteenth-century historians a curious bias, as it now seems to us, existed. Their eyes were fixed primarily on Spain itself. What of the vast empire now partly lost? What of Spain in the Americas? As we know, one may trace from the beginning of the eighteenth century a growing historical interest in Central and South America. Besides Robertson and besides Abiel Holmes, chroniclers already mentioned, the English edition of Francisco Javier Clavijero's *History of Mexico* was reprinted in the United States in 1806 and 1817 and was followed in 1832 by Thomas Francis Gordon's *The History of Ancient Mexico*. Eleven years later Prescott's engrossing story of the Conquest established a new emphasis on the colonies. By mid-century had appeared various histories of Guatemala, Peru, Paraguay, Chile, and of South America as a whole:

Spanish America [said the *North American Review* in 1849] at the present hour, looms up to us on the far horizon of the political world in a mist of lurid light, which veils her from the general gaze about as effectually as the darkness of her old estate. Her condition, her destinies, —these are problems too much unheeded, and yet unsolved . . . Very few persons have bestowed any serious observation and thought on the character and resources of these mysterious tropical nations, with whom it is the "manifest destiny" of our country to be more and more closely connected.[106]

This estimate of American ignorance of Spanish America was not exaggerated. The popular historians spoke with little authority, and although Prescott had unrolled the pageant of the conquerors and was sympathetic toward the South American peoples, his *point d'appui* was, after all, Madrid. The greater and even the lesser historians of Spain had ventured chapters on the discovery of the New World and on Spanish settlements within the United States, but these sections were maimed by the perennial prejudices.[107] For one corollary of the romantic attitude of Prescott's imitators was a blind spot for the actual in the life of Spanish America. After 1800 exceptions to this point of view were more numerous. Presumably the studies of Hubert Howe Bancroft (to be discussed in a moment) with their center in the Southwest turned the tide of interest. The full implications of Spanish rule in our hemisphere were not sharply defined prior to Edward Gaylord Bourne's *Spain in America,* which did not appear until the year 1904.[108]

The basic prejudice, virtually unqualified in these historians' asides on Spanish America, was the wickedness of Spain as a colonizer. Las Casas and Antonio de Ulloa [109] continued to be the unimpeachable sources for such judgments, whether in George Bancroft's *Colonial History of the United States* (1834–40) or John Fiske's *The Discovery of America* (1892). So impregnable was this preconception that for many historians it became a rigid assumption. Las Casas' *Breuissima Relacion* (like the *Noticias secretas de America* of Jorge Juan y Santacilia and Antonio de Ulloa) was, says a modern critic, for all sound Protestant historians a "veritable godsend" and "wherever the Spanish name was hated . . . found a ready sale and a readier credence." [110] Spain's depravity might be difficult to prove, but the assertion remained sweetly acceptable to those who had inherited the fear, jealousy, and hatred aroused in the sixteenth and seventeenth centuries. This mood of distrust is suggested forcefully by Edward Everett Hale's colloquial summary of the indomitable legend:

The Spain [he laments] which broke faith with John Hawkins in 1567, which poisoned Delaware and his companions at Madeira in 1611, which had hanged the Huguenots on the coast of Florida; the Spain of the Inquisition; the Spain of Pizarro and of Cortes, was the same Spain to the friends of Philip Nolan and his companions when the century began. When in 1870 a Spanish governor shot seventy passengers from the *Virginius* in Santiago without even the form of a trial, those men

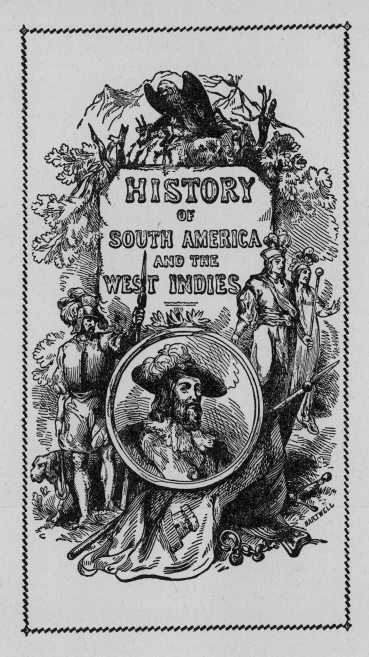

Illustrated title page of *History of South America and the West Indies*, by S. G. Goodrich, Louisville, Ky., 1848.

in the Southwest said, "This is the same old Spain!" When in 1897 Weyler committed worse atrocities, these people said, "It is the same old Spain." [111]

Thus the "black legend" [112] perpetuated itself even in reliable histories, waiting to be dispelled or modified by the scholars of the twentieth century. "The same old Spain!" Even if the historians of the nineteenth century happened to be curious about the Spanish colonies, they were apt to concentrate upon their own special interests. Lea extended to these regions his study of the Inquisition,[113] but he was hardly the man to exonerate Spain of cruelty. Moreover, linked with this bias was the assumption that the Spanish settlements in the United States were merely local phenomena; their essential unity with Mexico and South America was not yet taken seriously.[114] Since the local historians and antiquarians shared this delusion, some irreplaceable source materials were lost. In considering this story of American historians looking eastward toward Spain rather than toward Spanish America, we are irresistibly drawn to a parallel, however inexact in some particulars. We think of the men of letters in the United States neglecting the indigenous materials of their country and turning to England. We recall, for instance, James Russell Lowell's misunderstanding of Thoreau and Whitman. It is a commonplace that many of our early nineteenth-century writers (Irving or Longfellow) were indifferent to our native riches. In like fashion many historians minimized the significance of the Spanish-American civilization.

There is, indeed, a kind of pathos in the insecurity in their own day of some of these scholars, such as Buckingham Smith, one of the first Americans to make Spanish-American materials available to historians. At one time Smith was aided in his work by a sympathetic millionaire; at another he became a hack writer for Sparks, Bancroft, and Parkman.[115] Smith had a passion for the foundations of history. His devotion to the discovery and publication of untranslated versions of Spanish exploration in Florida developed naturally from his boyhood in this region and from a visit to Mexico about 1824 at the impressionable age of fourteen. At forty, following an education which included Trinity College and the Harvard Law School, he became secretary of the United States

Legation in Mexico, where he remained from September, 1850, until February, 1852. In 1855 he served for three years in the legation in Madrid, and here he knew that friend of scholars, Pascual de Gayangos. After the Civil War he was again in the Peninsula, engaged in the work he loved best, in the research which had produced books like *The Narrative of Alvar Nuñez Cabeza de Vaca* (1851) or *Letter of Hernando de Soto, and Memoir of Hernando de Escalante Fontaneda* (1854).[116] The twenty-five volumes of his Spanish documents, the maps, and the five volumes of his Florida papers [117] confirm the impression that Smith was less a historian than an invaluable exhumer of materials for history. He ranged far; he started the hare for other hunters.[118]

OF THESE no one hunted the grounds of the Southwest, with his myrmidons, more zealously than the fantastic Hubert Howe Bancroft. He was "the first to undertake to chronicle its history comprehensively and exhaustively." [119] A New Englander without any initial positive interest in Spain, he was to be remembered, in spite of his peculiar techniques, as an authoritative historian of both the Southwest and of Spanish America. Reaching California in 1852, he was evidently not unaffected by the spirit of the western pioneers in more robust fields of endeavor. He became successively an aggressive stationer and bookseller and a collector who rummaged the libraries and bookstalls of America and Europe. Finally, we see him as the executive head of a complex, departmentalized business, whose aim was nothing less than writing a multivolumed history of western, southwestern, and Spanish America.[120] Bancroft's is the familiar American story of the poor boy who became famous, except that in this bizarre version the successful hero sits among his collections of Americana directing the cooperative writing of history through some six hundred research assistants.[121] Bancroft organized historical writing as an industry. By introducing himself to eminent men of letters, by planning favorable reviews, and by a dozen originalities in method, Bancroft alienated orthodox scholars even as he created for them the histories which they could not ignore and the assemblies of books and manuscripts which were to be their indispensable guides. Simultaneously he inspired both laughter and respect.

Perhaps his copious contribution to our culture and even his magnificent library, the sustenance of so many modern scholars, will never entirely silence the disdain of Bancroft as a "compiler," as a writer of "reference" histories, to use the terms so often applied to his methods and to his thirty-nine volumes.[122] Perhaps he will never live down his business techniques.[123] Nevertheless, he referred devoutly to the creation of history as "among the highest of human occupations," [124] and his aims are now better comprehended. In contrast to the open attacks upon him or the veiled contempt from the professionals, we remark the present tolerance toward his eccentricities and the belated recognition of his achievement—"the most stupendous compilation," says Charles Edward Chapman of his books in the aggregate, "in the history of American historiography." [125] Even if we turn away, appalled, from the long shelf of his writings with their rhetoric and their encyclopedic documentation in fine print, there remains the collection itself. Beginning with books about California, Bancroft assembled thousands of western and Spanish-American items, for he considered the Southwest to be without boundaries. He extended his studies to adjacent sections of the country until, as his recent biographer says, he surveyed "a modest one-twelfth of the land surface of the earth." [126]

Throughout all these activities, not unlike in their violence the gold rushes of the period, Bancroft became involved in Spanish and Spanish-American history—a fact closer to our purposes than his experimental methods as an investigator. Eventually his collections sheltered many Mexican manuscripts reflecting the affairs of the mother country's colonial empire, and in the end his zeal as a collector led him to Spain. His biographer offers an amusing picture of him in Burgos before two small shops containing trinkets and books. While certain "miserable specimens of muffled humanity" looked on, Bancroft examined ruefully the "few pamphlets which spoke of Mexico." [127] Had he only visited the Casa Lonja in the Archivo de Indias in Seville he might have found manuscripts dealing with the colonization, thus deepening the content of his own writing and aiding indirectly other historians of Spanish America.[128] Meanwhile, like others, he fell in love with Prescott's breathless story. He had come to think Cortés' subjugation of the Aztecs the most brilliant episode in the history of the Americas.[129] It is natural, then, that in all his writings, even those on Utah or Alaska, we are constantly aware of the golden chronicles of the Spanish past.

In a chapter called "Spanish Americanist" Bancroft's recent biographer defines his secure place among the historians of Spain in America.[130] Of the twenty-eight volumes allotted to specific regions, from the *History of Central America* in three volumes or the *History of Mexico* in six to that of Alaska in one, about one half of Bancroft's content deals with the Spanish influence on this continent. In addition to the first two histories just mentioned, Spain is more or less present in his protracted accounts of the north Mexican states, in those of Texas, of Arizona and New Mexico, of California, and, with less emphasis, in his books relating to the Northwest coast.[131] Nor must we forget his life of Porfirio Díaz and his popular history of Mexico in one volume.[132] To create all these Bancroft's patience was infinite and his workmanship varied. He exhumed and studied obscure newspapers, or he took down the reminiscences of pioneers and old-timers. No labor was too great, no gossip too trivial.

In mere inclusiveness Bancroft's survey of these various areas has never been equaled. To go farther is to suffer misgivings. His style is often tumid and his philosophy of history thin and unconvincing. Are these books, after all, more than a gigantic encyclopedia? They are. Much more. The narratives are frequently sustained with power; the proportions are just, as evidenced by later versions of the same material; and the manuscript items are valuable. The best proof of the vitality of this historical writing lies in the fact that in only a few cases have attempts been made to do the work again, and in such instances the new histories must always begin with Bancroft.[133] We cannot approach the study of Mexico or the borderlands without him.

What if Bancroft, blessed with little Spanish, was not really responsible for the essential portions of these histories? [134] What if his entire "industry" was, in the opinion of one critic, a "factory"? [135] It hardly mattered. His volumes were to remain, to quote Frank W. Blackmar, "a mine of historical wealth," [136] and whatever his faults, through him the study of Spain in America was altered forever. From now on the serious American historians of the Spanish civilization were to turn not merely to Ferdinand and Isabella, Columbus, and the Moors but also to our own Southwest, to Mexico, to all Spanish America—and with infinitely more assurance. For the readers of literature, too, there were repercussions from the "factory." Bancroft's researches were to render more comprehensible translations of the Spanish folklore of New Mexico as well as novels or tales of Spanish California. His studies kindled our interest in all the arts connected with Spain. Most of all, we think of the library. Numbering one thousand volumes in 1862, sixteen thousand in 1869, thirty-five thousand in 1881, fifty thousand in 1890, this became in 1907 the possession of the University of California [137] and an accessible, fertile seed plot for scholars in the subject of Spain in America.

WE CANNOT discuss here all the modern historians who have exhibited again and again the spectacle of Spain in America, who have shown her strong presence in our cultural past. With or without the aid of Bancroft's library these scholars intensified our curiosity concerning the pueblo, the padre, the Spanish song, the Spanish word. Though in the popular mind romantic feeling for the tale of the Spanish Conquest has never entirely passed, there has developed since 1880 a remorseless scrutiny of facts. Adolph Francis Alphonse Bandelier devoted much of his life to opposing what he called, in a memorable paper delivered in 1885, "The Romantic School in American Archaeology." [138] A critic of Bancroft,[139] a student from his earliest days of the ethnology of Spanish America, an indefatigable scourer of original sources for archaeological knowledge, and, finally, a damaging skeptic concerning the old chroniclers, in whom he had once placed some credence, he tried to know the actual past of those remote days.[140] Not only scientific but literary, he sought to puncture the ancient myths in a novel. His

Delight-Makers relates with more archaeological truth than distinction in plot and character the story of the Indian tribes, particularly of the Pueblo Indians, with whom the early colonizing Spaniards had mingled.

There were other realists. In the year of Bandelier's *Contributions to the History of the Southwestern Portion of the United States* (1890), Blackmar, trained at Johns Hopkins, issued his *Spanish Colonization in the Southwest* and a year later his *Spanish Institutions of the Southwest.*[141] His work sprang from his conviction, then so daring and so far from general acceptance, that these Spanish-American subjects demanded thorough investigation! [142] Blackmar became a historian of California, but Woodbury Lowery, a lawyer who retired at the age of forty-three to devote his life to historical research, planned a "synthetic treatment" of Spain's career in North America. He would show "the reasons for her preliminary success, her later apathy, and her final decadence." [143] Lowery's story is that of a scholar assembling materials in Spain, with the help of his brother-in-law, the Duke of Arcos. He published two important books in this field before his early death in 1906. Let the studies of these typical scholars suggest—Lowery wrote particularly of Florida [144]—the marked change in attitude toward New Spain since the days of the amateur historians.

DESPITE their merits, the contributions of Bandelier, Blackmar, or Lowery seem cramped, even special, compared with the services of two or three later scholars. One of these, Edward Gaylord Bourne of Yale University, in his succinct book already mentioned, *Spain in America,* arrived at vigorously fresh conclusions in respect to the Spanish civilization in the New World. This acute volume restates and occasionally solves old problems, some of which centered in the explorations of Columbus, Amerigo Vespucci, or Magellan.[145] But the strength of Bourne's judgments (freed from bondage to Las Casas) resides in his later chapters on the Spaniards as colonizers.[146] He makes clear their restrictions in trade and their lack of initiative in self-government but also one dramatic fact of particular interest to us. In the colonies had developed a Spanish culture [147] richer far than that dreamed of by our nineteenth-century historians.[148] Other and greater books would surely have followed, but unhappily Bourne died at the age of forty-eight.

Almost simultaneously appeared Herbert Eugene Bolton, sponsor of scholars and the expounder of a principle which was to re-emphasize the study of Spain in America. His impressive career, identified with so many regions of the country, began with his first position as a teacher at the University of Texas.[149] In this critical hour he was vouchsafed a kind of vision. He suddenly perceived what a scholar might accomplish with the manuscript treasures of the Southwest and of Spanish America. Bolton's study of Spanish, his thirteen years in the Mexican archives,[150] and his articles and books [151] were episodes in a life experience which made him the mentor of fifty doctors of philosophy and of two hundred masters of arts.[152] This summary is neglectful of hundreds of other pupils, of the bibliographies of his more eminent students,[153] and of his historical purposes. We may take the title of one of his numerous books, *The Spanish Borderlands*, as a magic phrase suggesting what Spanish history in the finest professional sense meant to Bolton and his followers. "The Southwest," he declared, "is as Spanish in color and historical background as New England is Puritan, as New York is Dutch, as New Orleans is French." [154] For this historian the settlements in the United States were the borderlands of a vast Spain unified by the Peninsula and the far-flung colonies.

Bolton's basic idea, destined to reshape the writing of Spanish history in America, may be indicated by another title, namely *Greater America,* a book published in his honor in 1945 with a bibliography of the writings of his students. In this volume some 375 scholars subscribed to the principle of "Western Hemisphere history." [155] Looking back now upon this "Epic of Greater America," [156] we share the excitement experienced in 1932 when Bolton proclaimed his beliefs at the Toronto meeting of the American Historical Association.[157] Although this iconoclastic yet constructive plan for history reappears throughout his writings, it is most persuasive in his *Wider Horizons of American History,* four essays published in 1939. These emphasize and explain the theory's larger implications for the future history of the New World.[158]

Bolton's researches taught him that no historical problem of America could properly remain within national limits. It was false to think, as had historians for centuries, of the colonizations of New England and Mexico as unrelated. To master intelligently the history of any single American country, we must comprehend that of the others. We must understand inter-American relations, and we must employ an "all-American background for the study of the separate history of any of the various American nations." [159] Bolton infused this idea into his teaching. At the University of California his course in the Americas was "a general survey of the history of North America, South America, and Central America, from the discovery to the present time." [160] In his classroom [161] and in his books he analyzed comparatively the growth of the colonies of the various nations, the international competition for continents, the associated wars for independence in English America and Spanish America. In addition, he dwelt upon the important fact of the simultaneous development of republican forms of government in both continents. Indeed, the quantity of Bolton's work is somewhat overpowering. In scope nearly cosmic, in potential ramifications endless, the theory terrifies by what it demands of the historian. Actually, like some other theories of history, it can never be fulfilled. Nevertheless, even if the historian returns to narrower ways, it has implanted in him an ideal of an undivided America. This ideal has been accentuated by others. We think of the traveler-historian, Waldo Frank, who re-created imaginatively the spiritual temper of Spanish America [162] in its relation to the entire hemisphere.

ROUGHLY concurrent with the work of Bourne and Bolton there developed an interest in university courses of study concerning Spanish America.[163] By 1917 at least ten different institutions had committed themselves to this type of instruction.[164] It was merely the beginning; this was a "pioneer period" followed by a time of "expansion." [165] By 1930 the number of universities encouraging these programs had increased to 209 and in 1948–49 to 875 (with the courses numbering in all 3,346).[166] Equipped, unlike their predecessors, with texts, biographical dictionaries, photostats, or microfilms, this army of teachers attacked and conquered new areas of history. Their books lacked Prescott's epical sweep, Lea's concentrated analysis of an institution, or Bourne's originality, but they were varied, solid, and accurate. In the end their composite influence may prove enduring.[167] These professional historians of the Spanish-American regions were to inform our men of letters not only of the proximity of rich materials but of particular writers, for example, Luis Carlos López of Colombia or Jacinto Fombona Pachano of Venezuela.[168]

FINALLY, what of histories of Spain itself by twentieth-century scholars? In this chapter we have moved naturally from such a story as Irving's *Conquest of Granada,* with its indifference to the Western Hemisphere, to histories like Prescott's *Ferdinand and Isabella* or *The Conquest of Mexico,* with their dreams of empire. We have glanced at the popular histories of the Peninsula with their conventional sketches of settlements in America. We have shared the discovery of the Southwest by Hubert Howe Bancroft and, after Bourne's acute analysis of particular problems, come to Bolton's presentation of the "epic of America" against the backdrop of a hemispheric unity. In brief, we have now reached in our survey of the American historians of Spain those who wrote of all the Americas with Spain as a point of reference. For these Castile and León were still important but hardly more so than were England and France in George Bancroft's history of the growth of the United States. Did our rediscovery of Spanish elements in California, in New Mexico, in Arizona and of our relationships with Mexico, Central America, or Chile mean a cessation of history of the Peninsula for its own sake? Or if we continued to write histories of ancient Spain, were these to be dedicated to a special purpose, as in the institutional studies of Lea?

Lea is hardly a case in point. He confessed to little interest in

Spain proper. Were, then, the twentieth-century recorders of the Spanish civilization occupied primarily with Spanish America? Not all. Simultaneously there flourished a few others, inheritors of the older traditions of our historiography. We cannot limit the later interest in the Peninsula to the sentimental storybooks or to the works of propaganda inspired by the war of 1898. Distinguished among relatively recent histories of the mother country is Charles Chapman's *A History of Spain* (1918), a condensation of Rafael Altamira y Crevea's *Historia de España y de la civilización española*.[169] Altamira himself remarked of this work, which Chapman supplemented by two chapters on the period after 1808, that it was "a quite faithful portrait of Spain, instead of a caricature drawn in ignorance of the facts or in bad faith." [170] Evidently Americans had emerged from the transient madness of the war. Scholars were again attracted to the history of Spain [171] and now wrote with fresh insight of her cultural life.[172]

In fact, the most impressive twentieth-century book mentioned in the present chapter directs our attention not to Spanish America but chiefly to the Peninsula. This was Roger Bigelow Merriman's four-volume *Rise of the Spanish Empire* (1918–34). Merriman, for forty-three years a member of the department of history at Harvard, created his first two volumes not only from the standard printed sources but from the manuscripts and marginalia of Prescott, to whom he dedicated his book. For the second two volumes he had access to more manuscripts, and in all four he was continually mindful of the scientific scholarship [173] of his youth rather than of the psychological and sociological theories which had inclined to supplant it.[174] His book traced the growth of the Spanish empire to its apogee in Europe and overseas and held to the theory that the empire was the logical continuation of the Spain of the Middle Ages. It was a historian's history,[175] bold in form, meticulous in detail. We can only regret that Merriman abandoned his larger plan which included the decline of the empire.[176]

This lasting monument to Spain brings our story of the historians to a not inappropriate end. We need not recapitulate. Merely to turn Merriman's pages is to perceive what has happened in the American historiography of Spain since Washington Irving, writing his urbane pages on the wars of Granada and the explorations of Columbus, toiled in 1826 and 1827 in the libraries of Madrid. *The Rise of the Spanish Empire,* says an authority,

is a great work, worthy of a lifetime of effort on the part of a great scholar. Leaving Spanish America out of the discussion, it entitles him to rank with Prescott and Lea, also Americans, as one of the three outstanding writers in English on Spanish history, Prescott, Lea, and Merriman. It is an honor for each of them to have his name coupled with the others, and to American scholarship to have produced the three. Aside from Spain itself, what other country can show an equally distinguished group of historians of the Iberian peninsula? The answer is: *not any!* [177]

IN OUR studies of the travelers, the writers for the magazines, or the historians, all purveyors in their manifold ways of Spanish culture to the literature of the United States, we have encountered from time to time the occasional individual in love with the Spanish language and literature. The enthusiasm of that intrepid fellow, Alexander Slidell Mackenzie, in the 1820's is warming even if a little ridiculous:

In its present state [he declared], the Spanish language is perhaps the most excellent of all. Like the Italian, full of vowels, it lends itself with ease to the uses of poetry, and furnishes the most graceful garb to a happy idea . . . As a spoken tongue, the Spanish is unequalled; for while its graceful inflections and sonorous cadences please the ear, even of one who does not understand them, the mind is delighted and self-love flattered and gratified by a thousand happy proverbs and complimentary expressions, which have grown into use among a witty and courteous people. In the pulpit the Spanish is dignified and solemn, requiring but a little skill and feeling to kindle it into eloquence; at the head of an army it is prolonged, powerful, and commanding; in ordinary discourse it is expressive, sprightly, and amusing; from an enraged voice, its gutturals are deeply expressive of hatred and detestation; as the language of a lover, as the vehicle of passion, the Spanish has an earnest eloquence, an irresistible force of feeling; in the mouth of a woman it is sweet, captivating, and fraught with persuasion.[1]

Not everyone's passion for Spanish was exactly like Mackenzie's —fortunately. Nevertheless, to those who are sensitive to the power of the Castilian there is something pleasurable in discovering persons reading it in lonely devotion. During the early years of the nineteenth century, knowledge of the language for its own sake was meager. In 1826 the half-blind Prescott sought in vain for a capable reader of Spanish. Reviewing Cubí's Spanish grammar in 1825, the *United States Literary Gazette* was defensive in tone. It argued the obvious; it announced the usefulness of the language

to merchants trading in South America.[2] Today Salvador de Madariaga urges us to forget such matters, to neglect "the pitiless statistics which prove its dominions to be second in area and third in
population among those of the other languages of Europe, and
think of it purely as an instrument for the expression of man.
Where among living tongues is there one more beautiful?"[3] In
these first years doubtless some few would have echoed Madariaga's
implied answer: "Nowhere." This early drift toward qualifying the
ignorance and indifference of the majority of American readers
may be an additional proof of the subterranean forces at work in
disseminating Spanish culture.[4] Henry Adams thought that if he
were beginning life in 1894 (instead of 1854) he would have asked
no more from education than a mastery of four tools: mathematics,
French, German, and Spanish.[5]

The persistence of this quiet interest in speech, writing, and
reading is by no means irrelevant to our study of Spanish influences
upon American literature. The marrow of a culture is its language.
From the progressive curiosity[6] in America regarding the language
itself, as well as concerning its classic manifestations in literature,
and from the increase in Spanish-speaking persons in the United
States have evolved the changes so visible today. That is, from these
beginnings have grown the courses in this language and literature
in the universities and schools, the thousands of textbooks, the
more ingenious methods of instruction, the closer relations in
travel with the Spanish countries, and the research. More recently has developed the mastery of conversational Spanish for
business and, under the pressures of two world wars, for economic
and political purposes.[7] The study of the language for science followed rapidly,[8] as did the growth of the Spanish language press,[9]
the art of reading Spanish for enjoyment, and the translation by
scholars, journalists, and hack writers of novel, short story, critical
essay, poem, or play.

No longer is knowledge of the language limited to the shipmaster
unloading his lumber on the docks of Cadiz or in (as Cortés called
it) "La Villa Rica de la Vera Cruz." No longer is the acquisition of
Spanish considered an oddity peculiar to travelers[10] like S. T.
Wallis, bitter at his countrymen's misunderstanding of Spain, or

to lonely scholars like James Marsh in Germanophile New England.[11] As an additional factor, the legacy of the language in the Southwest has now become a professional cult. In 1891 F. W. Blackmar, in submitting a list of words such as adobe, cañon, tules, bonanza, fandango, corral, sombrero, or hacienda, pleaded for "an exhaustive and accurate study of the Spanish elements which have in this country entered our language." [12] Since the day of Cotton Mather or even since that of Thomas Jefferson the attitude toward this spinal element in Spanish influence has changed immeasurably. If we are to comprehend our men of letters' use of Spanish culture, we must examine scholarship in the United States in relation to both the language [13] and the literature.

The motives existing in the seventeenth and eighteenth centuries for the acquisition of the Spanish language were, as we have seen, primarily practical. We recall Cotton Mather's ludicrous scheme, born of his ethnological ignorance, of Protestantizing the Spanish-American countries. We remember also Thomas Jefferson's prophetic wisdom about our need of Spanish for political and international purposes. In both these centuries, records are comparatively scarce in America in respect to the study of Cervantes or of Lope de Vega. Later, in the nineteenth century, those best acquainted with the language and literature, such as Irving, Longfellow, Lowell, and Ticknor, were virtually to ignore Spanish America. It is, therefore, not without irony that the preliminary zeal for speaking and reading Spanish was connected with these regions. The causes were economic. By the middle of the eighteenth century many Americans in the large commercial centers on the eastern seaboard were demanding instruction in Spanish. In defiance of the Spanish patrols, Anglo-American vessels had swarmed into the southern ports, especially in the Caribbean. To trade, one must speak; and to speak, one must know the language. As early as 1735 the advertisements of the first teachers of Spanish appeared in the colonial newspapers.[14]

However matter-of-fact these aims, it is dangerous to assert that the study of Spanish in the eighteenth century never led to the reading of Spanish literature in the originals. As early as 1828 Ticknor commented both on the speaking of Spanish in the southern sections of the United States and on the publication of Spanish books in the North.[15] Some students of Spanish, having completed their apprenticeships in bills and accounts, may well have sampled history, the drama, or poetry. Evidence has survived, moreover, of the inclusion of Spanish in a few eighteenth-century schools and colleges,[16] whose objectives were certainly more broadly cultural than those of Garrat Noel. He, it will be recalled, published in 1751 the first American textbook for the study of the language.[17]

Paul Fooks, for example, was from 1766 to 1797 professor of the French and Spanish "tongues" in the Academy and Charitable School of the Province of Pennsylvania,[18] and shortly after 1779 Jefferson was successful in establishing a professorship of modern languages at William and Mary College.[19] Farther south in these same years the *State Gazette of South Carolina* of May 28, 1794, advertised for an assistant at Nixon's Academy qualified to teach English, French, and Spanish.[20] During the first decades of the nineteenth century Spanish was probably more generally taught in the schools than we have realized.[21] The curriculum of the famous Round Hill School, founded at Northampton, Massachusetts, in 1823 by Joseph Green Cogswell and George Bancroft,[22] included this language. In 1827 the English visitor, Mrs. Basil Hall, inspected Round Hill with interest. "From thence," she says, "we went to the High School, which is framed pretty much in the mould of the High School of Edinburgh. In one room there was a Spanish Class, as that is considered useful for boys who are to be brought up as Merchants owing to the Commerce with South America." [23]

THESE, in summary, are the beginnings. They are important in that they are the first step toward a "Golden Age" in the study of the Spanish language paralleling that of the literature under the sponsorship of Irving, Prescott, Longfellow, and Lowell. Meanwhile, the struggle of the language for its rightful place in America was not without its engaging incidents. One thinks of the mysterious and farseeing Abiel Smith of Harvard, who will be discussed shortly, or of an episode with which we may end these preliminaries. Father Peter Babad, a French émigré priest, after five years in Spain commenced his work at St. Mary's College, originally a boys' academy of the Sulpicians near their seminary in Baltimore. What textbooks Father Babad used or what methods he employed as a teacher we are not likely ever to know. At any rate, for twenty years he taught two Spanish courses, at first to the sons of French émigrés and to Spanish-American boys from the West Indies who had been cheated of a European education by the Napoleonic Wars. When in 1820 Father Babad left St. Mary's to return to France, he was succeeded by Mariano Cubí y Soler, a Catalan, who after serving here for seven years became a member of the faculty of the College of Louisiana.[24] It is difficult to believe that this remarkable priest's objectives in education were limited to ledgers and bills of lading.

Ten years before Father Babad reached St. Mary's College, Abiel Smith, a graduate of Harvard College in the class of 1764 and an unassuming businessman, had retired to spend the balance of his life in the enjoyment of the "fruits of his industry." [25] We know little more about Smith save that he was

a man of strong sense and steady purpose, guiding his life by his own convictions of duty, with little esteem for popular opinion or post-humous fame; scrupulously just and honest, practising habits of frugality less from regard to wealth than out of respect to the example.[26]

Sometime during the twenty-five years before his death in 1815 Smith arrived at some "conviction of duty" about these problems which interest us. In the light of his integrity we can hardly attribute his advocacy of Spanish in the Harvard curriculum to participation, along with some of his less scrupulous fellow New Englanders, in the illicit trade with the West Indies! Nor can we suspect that he was fomenting revolutionary movements in the Spanish colonies! There is no evidence for these explanations or for the wild guess that during his retirement he had conceived a passion for the Spanish novel or drama. Had he, perhaps, resolved that Harvard undergraduates of the future should not escape Cervantes and Lope de Vega? There is no answer.

The reasons underlying Smith's bequest continue to be obscure. We know merely that his will bequeathed to Harvard University the sum of twenty thousand dollars in the three per cent. funded stock of the United States, as a fund, the interest or income to be appropriated to the maintenance and support of a Teacher or Professor of the French, or French and Spanish languages, at said University, either singly or in company with any other fund, which may be given or appropriated to the same purpose.[27]

We admire this providential wisdom of Abiel Smith. His testament provided further that if at the time of his death the condition of his estate permitted the university might appropriate for this fund the additional sum of ten thousand dollars. Amused, we compute that today this tiny legacy would pay but a fraction of the salaries of one of our university departments in Romance languages. Yet in a very real sense this businessman's provision made possible or at least hastened the existence of all such departments. The creation of the famous Smith Professorship heralded the introduction of Spanish into Harvard's curriculum and therefore into those of other universities. It meant, though this may have been another happy accident, that the first three occupants of the chair were to be men eminent in both the scholarship and literature related to Spain: George Ticknor, Henry Wadsworth Longfellow, and James Russell Lowell. "What," says a modern Hispanist, "could Abiel Smith . . . have done better with his money?" [28]

It went far. From 1816 on, for three quarters of a century, our story of the expanding knowledge of the Spanish language and literature in the United States became a history of the Smith Professorship and its incumbents. In this year the Overseers of Harvard earmarked the money, designating that it should be used to "pay the expense of private instruction and recitation in the French and Spanish languages, and in part to the support of a Professor who should give lectures on the Literature, as well as the Languages of these nations." [29] "Literature, as well as the Languages"! At this moment the day of Romance languages dawned. Within a few years French, Italian, and Spanish were to be subjects as orthodox as mathematics.

On June 30, 1817, the duties of the new professorship were carefully defined, and instructorships were created in French and Spanish. The teachers in these new fields were to give lessons in both languages (three days a week in one term and two days a week in the other terms) to heretical students desiring additional work in these subjects and to iconoclastic members of the junior class who made bold to substitute French or Spanish for Hebrew.[30] On August 10, 1819, George Ticknor was formally inducted into the Professorship of French and Spanish Languages and of the Belles Lettres. It was a critical moment. To understand the ensuing felicitous union of man and opportunity we must turn thoughtfully to the career of this extraordinary scholar.

ALTHOUGH the famous educational sense of Ticknor was to leave its mark at Harvard on both teaching and scholarship, the application of this "sense" to modern language study seems in retrospect the result of a series of lucky chances. This father of the teaching of modern languages had studied French and a modicum of Spanish (under Francis Sales) in 1803 before his journey to Göttingen. He had been led to this university by a reading of Madame de Stael's *De l'Allemagne* and by a friend's description of its superb library. There, having abandoned the study of the law, he planned to devote himself to a life of scholarship. No evidence exists that in this appenticeship to learning Ticknor cherished any overwhelming leaning toward Spanish: "My chief objects," he wrote his father in June, 1816, "are still Greek and German, my subsidiary objects Italian and French, my amusement literary history, chiefly ancient, and books that will fit me for my future travels." [31] Nevertheless, at this very time he received from President Kirkland his invitation to become Smith Professor.

Ticknor's delay of a year before his acceptance of the appointment does not suggest eagerness, nor does the only surviving letter, to his father, which discusses the question. On this point he is still uncertain; he speculates on November 9, 1816, about

the Spanish part. Here is at once a new subject of study proposed to me, to which I have paid no attention since I have been here, and which I have not taken into the plan of my studies and travels in Europe. If I am to be a professor in this literature, I must go to Spain . . . This winter I must remain here, of course; the next summer I must be in

France, and the next winter in Italy. I willingly give up Greece, but I still find no room for Spain.[32]

He was, however, tempted, for the letter contains also a scheme for study at the University of Salamanca. What finally determined his decision? Did he talk over the problem with his beloved Bouter-wek, in whose house in Göttingen he was then living? [33] In the end the motivations for his election of Spanish must have been complex. Probably the educational opportunity, his innate love of learning, and the German scholars' interest in Spain were all persuasive factors.[34] At last, from Rome on November 6, 1817, he wrote to President Kirkland his letter of consent. Thus this great leader came into power, and so began a new era in the instruction of modern languages in the United States.

The originality and force of Ticknor as an educator are emphasized by his imaginative interpretation of certain bare clauses in the Smith Foundation, particularly that respecting "the two courses of lectures its statutes demand, one French and the other on Spanish Literature, until they should be completed." [35] For Ticknor's principle of alternating lectures and linguistic study was in advance of his time. On February 10, 1820, his letter to Jefferson, who was almost as much interested in such problems as his young friend, records, with its delightfully ambiguous conclusion, the relation of this exciting pedagogical adventure to his own intellectual experience:

I am [he writes] now established as Professor of Belles Lettres at Cambridge, with permission to reside in Boston, where I constantly live—that my duties consist entirely in lecturing—that in a month I shall begin a course of forty lectures on French Literature and in the autumn one of about thirty on Spanish Literature—that afterwards I shall prepare a course of sixty or eighty lectures on the Belles Lettres generally —and when all these are ready, conclude the circle of instruction by a course on Italian and a course on English Literature . . . And in each course I shall always deliver three or four a week, so as to keep up an interest in the subject—and when I have finished the whole, I shall look about for something else to do, as I have no idea that a Professor should ever be doing anything but preparing to teach.[36]

The last rigorous sentiment, which cynical members of the profession might now interpret as irony, really intimates how genuine a philosophy of education entered into this first instruction in modern languages. Ticknor's later letters show the development of his ideology of teaching. Four years after his appointment he summarized his achievements. In two years he had finished fifty or sixty lectures on French literature, in all equal to three octavo volumes, and to these he had added a syllabus for use in the Harvard Library. He had also been at work on the Spanish lectures with a published syllabus.[37] Since everything a professor does should be part of his preparation for teaching, Ticknor had also been collecting books. He was a born bibliographer and he was soon able to declare concerning his library: "For the Spanish portion I believe my collection of books is unrivalled—certainly there is nothing so complete in Spanish belles lettres to be found in the great libraries of England, France, Germany, or even Spain itself." [38]

He had been thinking, too, about what happens in the classroom. Attendance should be voluntary, and he determined also that his own teaching should cleave to the following faith: "To communicate genuine knowledge rather than exhibit the subject in rhetorical declamation." [39] He was evidently familiar with perennial types among teachers. Were particular colleagues in his honest, powerful mind? "But," he added rather sadly, "the Professors still keep on in the beaten track, and will not probably soon be induced to change." [40] He himself was always dogmatic. Yet how wise he was in his learning, in his philosophy of education, and in his hard sense as he now assisted at the birth of modern language teaching and scholarship!

Ticknor's belief in cooperation from the student and his trust in knowledge itself ramified into special convictions about methods of instruction and also concerning American university education in general as he experimented with it at Harvard. Before examining these opinions of Ticknor's in their relation to the dissemination of Spanish influence, we need to see the scholar himself clearly, if momentarily, in the classroom as he interpreted the literatures of

France and Spain. Fortunately for us, Josiah Quincy, who was present, observed in his journal:

In the evening I attended Ticknor's lecture, which was most beautiful and delightful, and on a subject as dry as possible. He explained to us on the map how languages progressed, and what was their origin. There is something very pleasing in his style and delivery, and he introduced figures very appropriately. But independently of this, there is a melody in his voice truly delightful. When describing the softness and beauty of the Provençal, it seemed as if he spoke in that delicious language. When he said of St. Louis, "whether he desired canonization or not, he certainly was one of the truest patriots, one of the bravest knights, and one of the noblest gentlemen who ever lived," it seemed as though this eulogy was complete. These words seemed to express all that was virtuous, lovely, and honorable, so that no addition could be made to his character.[41]

In our effort to define the indefinable, that is, to appraise Spain in our literature, we must think of many interpreters. We must weigh fairly the thousand intangibles which have made its presence real in story, history, picture, poem, or play. We must take into account not only the gossipy traveler returned from Andalusia, the facile or the serious contributor to the magazines, the historian, and the novelist, but also the scholar. We must think of George Ticknor lecturing to, let us boldly assume, intelligent young men in his Harvard classroom. Seriously, this assumption is justified. Lowell and Motley studied in the department which Ticknor now founded. There were many others, among them Henry David Thoreau, although in the end the poet-naturalist turned to literatures other than Spain's. Here, then, Ticknor stood, the serene founder of an enduring tradition. Here, said his nephew, George Ticknor Curtis,

he always, in my time, fixed and kept the attention of his class; indeed, there was never any movement or sound in the lecture-room that evinced an absence of attention . . . He followed the very exact and methodical order of his syllabus, introducing discussions which were always animated and sometimes eloquent . . . On all occasions his diction was both copious and precise. The sum of my testimony is, that his lecturing was as successful *teaching* as I have ever listened to.[42]

Besides his techniques of teaching which dealt with Spanish, besides his educational reforms at Harvard, which concern us far less, Ticknor was excited also by the intellectual growth of his students as they grappled with modern languages. In the year 1825–26 in a department which included, in addition to himself, Francis Sales, Charles Folsom, Pietro Bachi, and Charles Follen, the total undergraduate enrollment was 234. Of this number fifty-eight (about one quarter) had elected Spanish. If this group was smaller than that of the undergraduates preferring French it was at the same time more formidable than those in the German and Italian courses. The textbooks, whose development will be discussed later, now included Augustin Louis Josse's *A Grammar of the Spanish Language,* Tomás de Iriarte's *Fábulas literarias,* the *Colmena española, ó, piézas escogídas, de vários autóres españóles,* and Antonio de Solís' *Historia de la conquista de Mexico.*[43] During Ticknor's sixteen years as Smith Professor both texts and enrollments rose and fell, but when he finally retired in 1835, for a complex of reasons, Spanish had been expertly taught to many gifted students,[44] who were in turn to influence others. Meanwhile, out of the interrelated experience of student and lecturer emerged Ticknor's own philosophy of the teaching of modern languages, among these Spanish.

This philosophy is embodied in his *Lecture on the Best Methods of Teaching the Living Languages,* delivered in 1832, published in Boston in 1833, and reprinted in 1937 by an admirer of its vitality and contemporary relevance.[45] Today this little book may lack novelty, but the experienced teacher speaks in every sentence. We begin to understand the irresistible, directive power of this pioneer, Ticknor. These languages, he insists, are *living.* If possible, the apprentices in a language should "reside where it is constantly spoken." For such students it should be "the minister to their hourly wants, and the medium of their constant intercourse." These opportunities, he admits, do not exist for us all, and we must often fall back upon other methods which are "somewhat more artificial and indirect." Ticknor reaffirms his belief that "there is no *one* mode of teaching languages." From the wisdoms of various methods the teacher must learn to select, and he must "accommodate and arrange what he has thus selected . . . to the individual capacities, dispositions, and wants of each." [46] Two years after the first publication of this lecture Ticknor's services as Smith Professor ended. Presently we shall examine his attainments in scholarship, but we must now glance at his successors at Harvard.

BY THE year of Ticknor's retirement from Harvard the teaching of Spanish had made comparable progress elsewhere: at the University of Virginia, at Bowdoin, at Yale, and at the University of Pennsylvania. Yet we may do well for the time being to follow the history of the Smith Professorship through until the last decade of the century and then return to the general conditions in other American universities. Even if we violate the chronology of Longfellow's academic experience, whose beginnings we may summarize later in connection with modern language teaching at Bowdoin, we should see him late in November, 1836, now Ticknor's successor as he had previously been his protégé. According to an exchange of letters between President Quincy and Longfellow, he had orders, "to superintend, to instruct, and to lecture": [47]

His regular duty [wrote Edward Everett Hale, one of his students] was the oversight of four or more instructors who were teaching French, German, Italian, Spanish, and Portuguese to two or three hundred under-graduates. We never knew when he might look in on a recitation and virtually conduct it. We were delighted to have him come. We all knew he was a poet, and were proud to have him in the college, but at the same time we respected him as a man of affairs.[48]

The influence of Longfellow as an interpreter of Spain was multiform; he was a traveler, a contributor to the magazines, a translator, and (some still believe) a poet. Although his reputation as a Spanish scholar had probably inspired his appointment as Smith Professor, his role in the classroom differed from Ticknor's. His actual connection with the teaching of Spanish was, indeed, that of "man of affairs." More exactly, his immediate duty was "to superintend." Apparently, as Hale implies, he substituted informally in these Spanish classes, and he probably taught some of them continuously.[49] Only one of his public lectures dealt with Spanish literature. This lecture, on the Spanish drama, he delivered in the autumn of 1838 and again in the spring of 1840.

The breadth of Longfellow's teaching and a classroom in modern languages about a century and a quarter ago are made vivid for us in a delightful letter which he wrote Ticknor (then in Munich) from Cambridge on September 28, 1837:

Meanwhile I sit here at home, and do the things you wot of;—namely go up the stone-steps of University Hall, darkening the door of No 5 on summer mornings, and wearing, on Commencement days, the black mantle you let fall upon me, when you were translated into English,—not by fire, but by water:—for all which I thank you.—And now let me bear witness to the gentlemanly deportment of the Corporation in all things relating to me, thus far. They do not require me to hear recitations—but to Lecture—four courses a year; namely; oral, explanatory lectures on the most distinguished authors in Modern Literature—all the year through, once a week, at least: and in the Summer term, a course on Literary History—on what I choose. This year, I take as follows: Autumn term:—Göthe's Faust:—Spring term, Dante;—Summer term, the Spanish Drama;—and for the more elaborate written Lectures German and Northern Literatures. I say written, but they are not. Last Summer I spoke from notes: and I believe did pretty well.—The fourfold team of instructors jogs on its wonted pace;—but during yr absence the harness got very much out of order. The young men treat Surault, as the frogs did King Log: they leap upon him—run over him; and he, fat lord says nought but "My friend, my friend!—go on—go on!" meaning, with the lesson.—with ancient Sales it is hardly otherwise; except that the language of expostulation is changed to "My soul! —By George!" As to Bokum (the Portuguese word is *boquim*—signifying the mouth-piece of a wind instrument.) I fear matters go still worse with him. He stalks up and down the room, braying, and switching his books with a small black cane,—the students laughing all the while, and trying to persuade him to sing the Ranz des Vaches in *Deutsch* . . . The President frequently honors my Lectures with his presence; and as soon as I begin, he gives his spectacles three whirls (you remember the gesture) and then falls into a deep sleep, highly flattering to the lecturer, and highly conducive to decorum among the students.[50]

A scholar has recently asserted that the strongest trend in Long-fellow's teaching was toward German and Italian literature. He was eager to see the masterpieces of these countries appreciated, as were already, so he thought, those of France and in a few cases those of Spain.[51] Possibly we may attribute to this amiable neutrality in Longfellow's European studies, if we contrast it with the more con-centrated enthusiasm of Ticknor, one of the intermittent declines in the enrollment in Spanish studies during this period.[52] In 1849–50 (about a century ago) there were only thirteen seniors and sixteen juniors in the Spanish courses at Harvard. Nevertheless, Longfellow protested the rule limiting the study of modern lan-guages,[53] and his love for the Spanish language and literature is beyond question. Among our Hispanophile men of letters he and Irving were leaders, both in point of time and in devotion.

The basic teaching during the regimes of Ticknor and Long-fellow was actually performed by another, not by a "man of affairs" like the latter, not by a philosopher of the classroom like the brilliant Ticknor, but, as the academic world often finds its best work done, by just "an instructor." For the dust and heat of elementary teaching were reserved for Francis Sales. From the cir-cumstances surrounding the Smith Professorship this kindly drill-master became the most famous "instructor" in the history of modern languages in America. Born in Perpignan, Sales had lived in Spain and had come to Boston about 1790. Here he had given lessons in both French and Spanish long before the bequest of Abiel Smith. Among his students had been Ticknor himself.[54] Along with his eminent pupil, in 1817 Sales came, we might say, into office at Harvard. He was to offer "lessons in both languages, in one term on three days, and in the other two terms on not less than two days in each week, to such Students as wish to attend him at private hours out of either of the classes, and by those Juniors who choose to study French and Spanish instead of Hebrew." [55] His indenture was protracted. For thirty-five years virtually all the routine instruction in Spanish at Harvard lay in the hands of Francis Sales.

Thirty-five years! The work of Sales became the solid subsoil of the Abiel Smith Professorship and of the beginnings of Romance language study in the universities of the United States. Sales did more than lecture; he *taught*. And since he taught he was throughout those thirty-five years gnawed by the hunger of the good teacher for good texts. Probably Sales did not require the income from his meticulous editions of Spanish masterpieces more urgently than he needed these versions themselves when he faced his young gentlemen in the classroom.[56] Many of these texts were his own. His earliest venture was his adaptation of Josse's *Grammar* in 1822,[57] and the most successful his *Colmena española; ó, piézas escogídas, de vários autóres españóles, moráles, instructivas y divertídas*,[58] published in 1825. This volume, with excerpts from Feijóo, Padre Isla, Cervantes, *Lazarillo de Tormes*, Montengón, and Solís, revealed not only his intimacy with the Spanish classics but also his friendly comprehension of the young men whom he saw across his rostrum.

What, on the other hand, these same students saw behind the desk they never forgot, and there is reason to believe that some even remembered what they heard. They recognized in this teacher of Spanish one of those wise eccentrics who reach their full stature only in the classroom. It was fortunate for the teaching of Spanish in America that for so long a time its champion was humble Francis Sales. What Ticknor once remarked apropos of Sales' essay on the drama seems relevant in more particular terms. Ticknor had hopes concerning the early Spanish drama of attracting "some attention to its peculiar spirit and characteristics" and of recommending it "to the lovers of Spanish literature in our own country." [59] This was exactly it; this was how Sales felt about all the Spanish classics. He wished to make them better known in America. So Sales merely by being Sales compelled attention to Spanish literature.

For confirmation we might turn to the perceptive sketch of him by Lowell, another admirer, in his "Fireside Travels." [60] Thomas Wentworth Higginson's portrait is even more engaging:

We had [he reminisces] that delightful old Francis Sales, whom Lowell has commemorated, as our teacher of Spanish. In him we had a man who might have stepped bodily out of the Gil Blas and Don Quixote he taught. We never knew whether he was French or Spanish. He was then about sixty-five, and his robust head and shoulders, his pigtail

Francis Sales, from a daguerrotype by an unknown artist.

and powdered hair, with his quaint accent, made him seem the survival of some picturesque and remote age. He was, moreover, especially
indulgent, gave the highest marks for recitations, and was in all respects a favorite. A classmate who sat next to me, George Hay, took
delight in inflicting upon the innocent old man the most incredible
or old-fashioned English oaths as equivalent to the quaint Spanish
expletives; and when he gravely introduced "Odds' fish" or "Gog-
zounds," Mr. Sales would look bewildered for a moment, and then roll
out his stentorian "Ha! ha! ha! By Jorge!" in a way to add still further
to the list of unexpected phrases, and make the dusty room in Massachusetts Hall jubilant for that day.[61]

BY 1855 when Longfellow, in his turn, resigned the Smith Professorship, the teaching of modern languages had won, as we shall
see presently, a permanent place in other universities. The singular
distinction, however, of this triple foundation in modern language
study in America can be best realized by inspecting now the third
incumbent, James Russell Lowell. In him, and in all three teachers,
though the European languages were more nicely balanced in the
second appointee (Longfellow), the predilection for Spain was emphatic. Formed of scholars and men of letters of eminence in the
Republic, this triumvirate lent a weight and sanction to Spanish
studies comprehensible to us only if for a moment we try to fancy
that it never existed. This association of the study of Spanish with
creative American literature (there were Irving, Prescott, and Motley, too) was now close. Like the older men, Lowell was at once
literary and Hispanophile. In February he wrote his friend W. J.
Stillman that he had been appointed, that he was to give two courses
of lectures each year, and that during the rest of the time he was
to be his own master.[62] More than either of his predecessors he was
already entangled spiritually with a few great writers, especially
with Cervantes and Calderón.

Like both his forerunners, Lowell was permitted a year abroad
in which to prepare himself for his new position; he began his
duties as Smith Professor in September, 1856. He was not, like
Ticknor, a born lecturer or, on the other hand, like Longfellow,
easily fagged by the teacher's burdens. He was a free-ranging

scholar and literary man, pleasantly at ease in the classroom, way-
ward and witty in comment, humorous, and interested primarily
in discovering from a poem or prose piece what life had meant to
the writer. More than Longfellow he took part in the actual instruction in both Italian and Spanish, and apparently until the
enlargement of the department of modern languages in 1869–70
he was available for the elementary courses.[63] Most refreshing of
all his offerings were his advanced studies in Dante and Cervantes.
Barrett Wendell has described delightfully the little intimate dramas of these classes: the translation of a few lines and the welcome
interruptions of Lowell's eloquence on the poetic qualities of these
passages.[64] He poured out a "viva voce translation of 'Don Quixote' " and " 'got after the commentators'!" [65]

William Roscoe Thayer, who elected both the course in Dante
and that in Cervantes, was impressed by Lowell's inexhaustible,
minute knowledge of these authors and by his alternation of close
study of the texts with his informal talks on related or, quite as
often, unrelated subjects. He would strive to explain to Thayer an
obscure sentence; it was Lowell's last year, and Thayer was the only
member of the Cervantes class. Then he would "ramble on, passing
from Cervantes to Calderon . . . and so on to his own experiences
in Madrid and London." [66] Clearly, for the New Englander Lowell,
Don Quixote was not only a masterpiece of mirth but also an en-
chiridion for human behavior. He kept reminding Thayer how
Cervantes contrived to keep his hero a "perfect gentleman" who
conducted himself as a man of delicate courtesy and honor would
even when those about him were utterly commonplace.[67]

Lowell held the Smith Professorship for a period of thirty-six
years until his death in 1891. His glance backward, a year earlier,
is both entertaining and informative, especially in the last phrases
quoted:

For nearly two hundred years [he says of America] no modern language
was continuously and systematically taught here. In the latter half of
the last century a stray Frenchman was caught now and then and kept
as long as he could endure the baiting of his pupils. After failing as a
teacher of his mother-tongue, he usually turned dancing-master, a call-
ing which public opinion seems to have put on the same intellectual

level with the other. Whatever haphazard teaching of French there
may have been was, no doubt, for the benefit of those youth of the better
classes who might go abroad after taking their degrees. By hook or by
crook some enthusiasts managed to learn German but there was no
official teacher before Dr. Follen about sixty years ago. When at last a
chair of French and Spanish was established here, it was rather with an
eye to commerce than to culture.[68]

In a moment we must retrace our steps. Chronologically we are
ahead of our story, for by this year the teaching of Spanish was no
novelty in America. Yet only through this continuous survey of the
seventy-five years at Harvard, following the establishment of the
professorship in 1816, can we perceive the strength of this particular
caryatid in the building. Was it not, indeed, the central pillar of
the whole structure? It opened to all three holders of this chair
new doors of intellectual experience. For Ticknor the professorship was a stimulant and one of the originating forces of his great
History of Spanish Literature. For Longfellow, despite his Teutonic learnings, it solidified his romantic and scholarly interests in
Spanish. For Lowell, it helped prepare for his later career in Spain
and for his scholarship in Spanish subjects. Again we should observe the connection through all these literary leaders of Spanish
studies with American literature. Their writings on Spain and
their enthusiasm for Spanish masterpieces bore the stamp of authority and must have affected in various if intangible ways the
temper of our growing literature. It has been well said that:

When Ticknor began his work modern literature was virtually unknown to America; when Lowell died, modern literature was as familiar
to this whole continent as ever were the classics. Meanwhile almost all
the literature which our continent has yet produced, and certainly all
the memorable literature of New England had come into existence.[69]

One other related fact must not be overlooked. Since the Spanish
interests of Ticknor, Longfellow, and Lowell were scholarly and
literary, the Peninsula, with its archetypal writers, continued to be
their fount of inspiration. Indeed, the devotion of Longfellow and
Lowell to Spain now seems in retrospect not unlike an extension
of our literature's prolonged subservience to England. By the thrill-

ing history of the transference of this Peninsular culture to Mexico or South America they remained unmoved. No translations from the poets of these regions, comparable to Bryant's of the Cuban Heredia or of the Mexican José Rosas Moreno, sullied this reverence for the "Golden Age" of Spanish literature.[70] For all these three Spanish America hardly existed as a cultural entity. Although we now realize that Ticknor knew something of Spain in America, apparently neither he, Longfellow, nor Lowell ever contemplated a visit beyond our southern borders. Nor did the available texts for students concern themselves, as today, with Mexico and other Spanish-speaking nations.[71] Even the most elementary of the lesson books used as illustrations the eternal riches of Peninsular literature—enough, yet not enough. What of the new, vigorous literatures of Mexico and South America? They were ignored. The vision of the essential union of Spain and Spain in America was hidden until a later generation of writers and scholars.[72]

IN PASSING, several allusions have been made to the simultaneous study of Spanish in other universities. Second only to Harvard in point of time and in achievement was the department of modern languages at the University of Virginia, where the ideas of both Thomas Jefferson and George Ticknor took root and flourished. This promising young scholar, as he then appeared to be at their first meeting in 1815, Jefferson had never forgotten, and as a proof of his regard he had offered him in 1817 the professorship "of Idealogy, Ethics, Belles-Lettres and Fine Arts." [73] Despite the magnificence of this title and his friendship with Jefferson, Ticknor had declined the post. His father was old and ill, and he himself was already committed to Harvard. This "road not taken" provokes speculation. What if he had done his pioneering in Spanish at the University of Virginia? Perhaps his amends to Jefferson for refusing the post was his recommendation of Georg Blaettermann of Leipzig, the first to fill the chair (1825–40), whose incumbents included the remarkable Maximilian Schele de Vere (1844–95), Joachim Reinhard (1895–96), and James A. Harrison (1896–98).[74] Jefferson's fundamental plan, toward whose fulfillment Ticknor evidently lent his advice, centered in a School of Modern Languages (the second of eight schools), in which were to be taught Anglo-Saxon, French, Italian, German, and Spanish.[75]

This exchange of ideas between Ticknor of Harvard and Jefferson of Virginia influenced the teaching of modern languages in both institutions and may have hastened the success of this Jeffersonian system of "schools." [76] We observe the resemblances in method: the elementary classes; the lectures on the literature by the professor; and the use by the academic year 1880–81 of the *Colmena española,* Lope de Vega's *Estrella de Sevilla,* and Ticknor's *History of Spanish Literature.*[77] Apparently from its inception Jefferson's program for the study of modern languages at the University of Virginia was popular. As early as 1825 there were seventy-three students in the School of Modern Languages in comparison with fifty-seven in the more orthodox School of Ancient Languages and seventy-three in the School of Mathematics. During the year 1870–71 more than one student in three enrolled in the School of Modern Languages, and among these, doubtless, were some specialists in Spanish.[78] Virginia had its Ticknor in Schele de Vere, who directed its study of modern languages for fifty-one years. Born in Sweden and a student at Bonn and Berlin, he had emigrated to America in 1843, stimulated by the reputation abroad of Ticknor and of Longfellow, who had helped him on his arrival toward his career at Virginia. Although dealing with pupils probably inferior in linguistic background to those at Harvard, Schele de Vere left a lasting impression on hundreds of these early American students of Spanish.[79]

In estimating the growth of Spanish at the University of Virginia we necessarily returned to Ticknor, and in surveying its development at Bowdoin we must relive the early career of Longfellow. In this institution the trustees voted in September, 1825, to establish "a professorship . . . for the instruction of the Junior and Senior classes in the modern languages of Europe, particularly in French and Spanish." [80] A temporary instructor was appointed, but it remains a Bowdoin tradition that a certain young man, by his excellent rendering of an ode of Horace, had attracted the attention of the trustees to his literary ability.[81] So began the professional career of Longfellow, whose years at Harvard have already been described. Though we now consider it in retrospect, we may recognize in this novitiate the same qualities of mind, the same indecision or, if we prefer the euphemism, the same comprehensiveness, in regard to the four great modern languages, which was to be so characteristic of his teaching at Harvard. Though a true scholar and a not ineffective teacher, Longfellow could never, like the positive Ticknor, plan, select, and emphasize.

The vote of the trustees, just quoted, stressed Spanish, but young Longfellow was already fascinated by the literary opportunities of German literature. He had written to his father, hinting broadly that he might profitably give up Spanish for German. It would be helpful to know whether Stephen Longfellow, lawyer and businessman, was strongly influenced by the value of Spanish for trade. We cannot say with certainty, but his reply hints at this fact. The letter also illumines the character of the professorship, of his son—and his own:

Your ulterior objects [he wrote] cannot be accomplished unless you obtain an *accurate* knowledge of the *French & Spanish* languages. The *situation you have in view cannot be obtained unless you qualify yourself to teach both these languages correctly.* Such are the relations now existing between this country & South America that a knowledge of the Spanish is quite as important as the French, and as those relations are rapidly increasing, the acquisition of the Spanish language is a *sine qua non* with you . . . Permit me however to say that I consider the knowledge of the *Spanish* of more importance to you than *German & Italian* both. These latter languages are very desirable but are by no means so important to *you* as the *French & Spanish.* Indeed if you neglect *either of them* your whole object will be defeated, and *you may be sure of not obtaining the station which you have in view.* And I should never have consented to your visiting Europe, had it not been to secure that station.[82]

Does this exhortation imply Longfellow's distaste at this time for Spanish studies? Probably not. In some ways his mastery of these was to excel that of Ticknor or of Lowell. Behind the father's letter, however, is an intimation of the literary character of his son's mind. His objectives differed, perhaps unconsciously, from those of his ambitious father. Just now he was not eager for the linguistic disciplines of French and Spanish.

This literary bias in Longfellow's teaching of Spanish was more conspicuous in these early days than later at Harvard, where he was committed to a more formal scholarship and where, as we have seen, his mandate was to "superintend." Moreover, after his intensive study of Spanish in Europe and after his induction in 1830 into his new duties [83] at Bowdoin, he became a persistent investigator of the writers of the Peninsula. Possibly his purpose was stiffened by his father's letter or by his realization of some hard facts in his professional situation: an academic dispute delayed for a time his appointment to the proper rank on the Bowdoin faculty.

Perhaps, too, in minor details of his personal regime he now imitated his revered Washington Irving. Though permitted to yield more freely than Longfellow to any sort of reading which aided his writing, Irving had shown during some periods of his life a zest for learning and a surprising capacity for self-discipline. When Longfellow knew him in Madrid in 1827 it was Irving's habit to rise at five and to work tirelessly all day on his *Life and Voyages of Christopher Columbus*. So Longfellow, too, now learned to toil. On June 27, 1830, he described his own program of study, teaching, and writing:

The intervals of college duty, I fill up with my own studies. Last term I was publishing books for the use of my pupils, in whom I take a very deep interest. This term, I am writing a course of lectures on Modern Literature—or rather on French, Spanish, and Italian Literature—which I am to deliver in Portland next winter.[84]

One of the most interesting sources of these books for his students was a little volume (now a bibliographical rarity) called *Tareas de un solitario,* which included Spanish versions, adapted from the English by George Washington Montgomery, of two of Irving's stories, "Rip Van Winkle" and "The Mysterious Picture." [85]

Meanwhile, during these years Longfellow strengthened the foundations of his scholarship and enriched his general reading

191

in Spanish literature. An ancient motivation in the seminomadic profession of teaching now goaded him on; he hoped to escape "laboring on in this little solitude." [86] He was tormented by longings for a more sophisticated academic world in which he need not order by mail European books to satisfy his hungry mind. He sought Ticknor's help in applying for a Spanish chair at New York University, and he lamented to his friend that he had "grown very tired of Brunswick." [87] On the other hand, Bowdoin liked Longfellow. No doubt existed there concerning the quality of his teaching in these modern languages. When at last in 1834 he received the invitation from President Josiah Quincy to succeed Ticknor at Harvard, it was an accepted fact that Spanish at Bowdoin meant Longfellow and that there he was to be canonized as the patron saint of such studies. Despite capable teaching by those who came after him, the interest in modern languages at the college, after his exit, declined.[88]

LOOKING backward in summary over the seventy-five years embraced by the fertilizing Smith Professorship, we discover no university so ardent in the introduction of Spanish into its curriculum as Harvard, Virginia, and Bowdoin. In this concentration the double functioning of Ticknor and Longfellow, each influential at two of these three universities, was a powerful factor. Even if less ambitious and less picturesque in academic and literary personalities, the story elsewhere has interest and for the sake of completeness should be outlined. Spanish was first made available at Yale in the year 1826–27 in a course in the third term open to members of the junior class at the "option of the student" and at his own expense.[89] Whatever enthusiasm the novice retained after this cordial invitation was to be satisfied by M. Charles Roux or, about two years later, by José Antonio Pizarro. The former was apparently the first foreign instructor in the college and was known as "a gentleman well qualified to teach the French and Spanish language." [90] Even this mild beginning lacked a vigorous sequel in the following decades. At Yale during the thirties and forties Spanish seems to have been deliberately neglected.[91]

Again it was the man who conquered. The appointment in 1879 of William Ireland Knapp, the first American professor after Ticknor and Longfellow to prepare in Spain for his career, ushered in a creditable era of Spanish study at Yale. In the classroom Knapp's up-to-date textbook, *Grammar of the Modern Spanish Language,* was effective, while outside in the world of scholarship his editions of Juan Boscán and Diego Hurtado de Mendoza moved the Spanish government to official recognition.[92] The contents of the courses during Knapp's last years—he retired in 1892—are illuminating. The elementary course used his own grammar, Fernando de Castro's *Historia profana general, y la particular de España,* novels by Juan Valera, Pérez Galdós, and the prose fantasies of José Selgas y Carrasco. The advanced students read *Lazarillo de Tormes, Don Quixote de la Mancha,* and also Cervantes' novels, *La Gitanilla* and *Rinconete y Cortadillo.* This acceleration of interest at Yale is almost dramatic if we recall the earlier apathy and if we remember that between 1830 and 1843 no Spanish instructor was listed in the college catalogues. For some thirty years after 1846 little or no mention had been made of Spanish.[93]

This study of Spanish at Yale, timid and uneven until the appearance of Knapp, is paralleled by its destiny at the University of Pennsylvania. In spite of a false dawn—the college is said to have offered a course in Spanish during the eighteenth century—and in spite of the distinction of twentieth-century studies in Spanish at the university, these did not attain real power prior to the dynamic leadership of Hugo Rennert in the last decade of the nineteenth. In 1830 French, German, and Spanish could be pursued if— another hazard—"required by parents." [94] Nevertheless, from this time until the year 1870–71 when the subject became an elective for juniors and seniors references in the catalogues to Spanish are rare. Pennsylvania's position in relation to the subject was, like Yale's, that of toleration, different indeed from the aggressive, forward-looking experiments at Harvard, Virginia, and Bowdoin.[95] Nor can the University of California be regarded in these earlier years as a pioneer institution. Here, almost immediately after the founding in 1868, Spanish studies took on some life, but the hour was late. By the year 1885–86 the university boasted two courses in Spanish, but both of these were taught by an instructor in French.[96] Nevertheless, these preliminaries at Pennsylvania and California during the seventy-five years under consideration show that studies in Spanish in these places also were maturing rapidly. In the succeeding century these beginnings were to reach spectacular culminations dwarfing in many ways the achievements at all other universities.

THE foregoing estimate of Spanish in the universities has been occupied with the period between 1816 and 1891, the year of Lowell's death. Within this era of three quarters of a century the exploratory studies of Harvard, Virginia, and Bowdoin were, it will be conceded, impressive, whereas those of Yale, Pennsylvania, and California were definite harbingers of their twentieth-century attainments in the field. All these programs of study have been used merely as illustrations; elsewhere there was proportionate activity. One authority names six other institutions into which Spanish was introduced before 1832 and twenty-nine more which added this subject to their curricula between 1846 and 1896.[97] In 1872 G. F. Comfort, professor of modern languages at Syracuse University, published in *Scribner's Magazine* his radical essay, "Should the Study of Modern Languages Precede That of Ancient Languages?" [98] Four years later Professor Edward S. Joynes of the University of South Carolina advocated at a meeting of the National Education Association that modern languages be elevated from their tutorial rank to a dignity commensurate with their real value.[99] If we now return briefly to the great institutions which actively nourished the beginnings of these studies we shall find them at the turn of the century quickened and oriented toward teaching and scholarship in Spanish in ways familiar to us today.

For instance, during the year 1895–96 there flourished at Harvard three courses in Spanish, two of which admitted graduate students.[100] In the *Harvard Graduates Magazine* of March, 1899, Professor C. H. Grandgent commented upon the large enrollment in the university of 150 students in Spanish 1.[101] Needless to say, this popularity grew during the tenure of J. D. M. Ford, the fourth of the Smith Professors at Harvard.[102] Although activity slackened somewhat at Virginia and Bowdoin after the retirement, respectively, of Schele de Vere and Longfellow, the Spanish studies in these places were more than competently directed and taught. Meanwhile, at Pennsylvania in the twentieth century Hugo Rennert, the "dean of American Hispanists," conferred on the work of that university an enduring fame.[103]

At the University of California, not entirely, as in some of the older institutions, out of fealty to the "Golden Age" of Spanish literature, the interest deepened into almost a crusade. In 1928 fourteen hundred boys and girls were studying Spanish, and of this small army one hundred undergraduate and thirty-eight graduate students were majoring in the subject.[104] In the same year was founded "Casa Hispana," one of the earliest of the now innumerable organizations created to encourage conversation in the language.[105] Regardless of fluctuations, despite sensitivity to depressions, to wars, or to other madnesses of the modern world, Spanish increased yearly in importance.[106] In 1910, 171 out of 340 colleges and universities in the country gave instruction in the subject.[107] By 1919 it had become routine in the programs of all of the better institutions of learning, and by 1940 at least ninety-two colleges in the South were offering Spanish.[108] We lack space to record its contagious spread to the secondary schools.[109] For to argue now the value of Spanish as an aid for commerce or as an adornment for culture is to preach without opposition. One wishes that Ticknor could have known of this fulfillment of his dream.[110]

LIKE two streams rising parallel in the barren cultural soil of eighteenth-century America, the teaching of Spanish and the scholarship in Spanish subjects developed steadily throughout the nineteenth century until both attained the professional character with which we are familiar today. At first, scholarship encountered more pitfalls than teaching. The legend concerning Emerson's difficulty in locating a German grammar hints at the dearth of textbooks in all the modern languages during the era of Ticknor. This lack was to be overcome, but there developed another problem: a kind of schism between scholarship and teaching. Ticknor's remark, that a professor should always be "preparing to teach," had little relevance to hours spent in study for a particular lecture. He would be puzzled by the present dichotomy in teaching and scholarship. He was thinking of these two as one.

Ticknor's self-counsel had a broad base. He meant that to teach effectively the teacher must be an investigator and, if possible, he must be a collector and even a forger of the weapons of scholarship. The teacher must acquire and systematize his own knowledge. No bibliographies, no handy guides, and few convenient editions were then available to lead him through the forest of the unknown. Ticknor and Prescott and, in a lesser degree, Longfellow and Lowell assembled their own libraries and built their own texts. Ticknor's comments on the *Syllabus* of his Spanish lectures reflect his conviction concerning the essential unity of teaching and scholarship. These "lectures" were really pieces of research or "works on Literary History": "I read," he says, "portions to my classes without regard to any fixed division into lectures, and as such, they are the first attempt made in this country." [111]

Books for the classroom and books for the scholar's workshop! Most of the great teachers of Spanish in the nineteenth century won their spurs also in the world of scholarship. Although several lesser items may be credited to Ticknor, such as his introduction to an edition of Cervantes, the culmination of his career was one book. This grand fusion of his teaching, investigating, and book collecting occurred in his epoch-making *History of Spanish Literature,* published simultaneously by the Harpers in New York and Murray in London in the year 1849. Ticknor's gradual absorption in this subject and its particular place in his intellectual life are discussed in detail in another chapter, but in the present résumé of the scholarship of the century we may pause over a few general characteristics of this noble work.

Almost at once the *History* became a unique masterpiece through the vastness and minuteness of its erudition (so admired by the English Hispanist, Robert Southey),[112] through its study of Spanish literature as a reflection of the national character, and through its invitation to American readers to enjoy what Barrett Wendell called "a fresh range of learning." [113] Ticknor had "handled" as well as read these books; [114] in every way the *History* was authentic bibliographically. Perhaps the oft-quoted compliment was justified: that there were not six persons in the United States capable of reviewing it. After its appearance all previous writing on the subject in English seemed elementary, and the *North American Review* compared Ticknor's resultant status as a historian with that of Sismondi. [115] Not even in the country whose literature it defined so completely existed a volume remotely like it. It instantly served, Edward Everett Hale declared, as "the working book of reference in the Royal Library at Madrid." [116]

The intimate association of Ticknor's scholarship with his passions for teaching and library making is demonstrated by the early use of his book as a classroom text in many universities. He had derived the descriptive content of the *History* from the volumes on his own shelves and from his experience in his own teaching. Yet somehow he had also ensnared the clientele which delighted in Prescott's histories. [117] Less popular, less comprehensible than these to the gentlemanly readers of Boston and New York, the book nevertheless found its way into their libraries. Everyone liked the simplicity of Ticknor's writing and the direct, expositional, tripartite structure. He told the story from the earliest Spanish document to the sixteenth century of Charles V, from the beginning to the end of the "Golden Age," and from the day of the Bourbons until the day of the book's publication. [118] Everywhere in the work were order, clarity, good sense.

These virtues imply the faults in this *History of Spanish Literature*, faults predictable from what we already know of the solid, meticulous Ticknor. Its knowledge is formalized, exterior. Even the reader who knows little of Spanish literature will sense in his chronological definition of writer after writer a wearing defect. This missing flower is an imaginative insight into the Spanish character and into Spanish literature: [119] "The style of the work," said E. P. Whipple, "is excellent of its kind, clear in statement, manly in tone, but somewhat hard and cold in its sustained elegance." [120] In brief, the *History of Spanish Literature* is a tower of scholarship in the German pattern but hardly a work of the creative imagination. Nevertheless, this verdict appears captious. The externality is merely the obverse of the large merits already noted. The magnificence of the book resides in its bibliographical achievement and in its revelation to American readers of a literature hitherto symbolized for most of them by two familiar words: "Don Quixote." [121]

IN COMPARISON with the massive scholarship of Ticknor, that of Longfellow, romancer and poet, appears at first glance incidental and meager. This illusion—for illusion it is—has been sustained by the relatively slight content of his scholarly productions. He left us the readable articles in the *North American Review* on Spanish devotional poetry and on the Spanish language, the pleasant textbook, *Novelas españolas,* with its fragile preface for his students, and the translations of the *Coplas* and of the ballads. We should be glad that Longfellow's true interests lay outside the confines of a rigorous scholarship. Often, as in *The Spanish Student,* the rough, tangled roots of his learning blossomed in story or poem. "If," he exclaimed of *La estrella de Sevilla,* "I can only interest the youngsters in this, and make them see the beauties more than the defects!" [122] In both his teaching and his scholarship lingers that flavor of the popular which made him the bourgeois laureate of his generation. Behind his investigations lies almost always an ulterior literary purpose. He is forever searching for the charming tale, the quaint background, the picturesque incident. Although a donor of books to the Bowdoin and Harvard libraries, he was never afflicted by a bibliographical fervor like Ticknor's. Should not all learning, he seems to imply, be consecrated to the creation of literature?

Yet Longfellow was sincerely and deeply learned. Though in his poems he sometimes played with facts, his erudition was firm, exact. The truth of this statement appears in his voluminous notes made in Germany during his prolonged study of Spanish literature [123] or in his conscientious translations. For both his theory and practice in translation have excited the admiration of modern Spanish critics. Today his two essays in the *North American Review* seem pedestrian in method and sentimental in tone. Their paramount purpose was to provide American readers with a window on the world of Spanish literature. Nevertheless, if old-fashioned in spirit, these essays remain capable expositions of classic material. As a student Longfellow loved Spanish words, Spanish phrases, Spanish proverbs.[124] In another field, his translation of Dante shows his complete mastery of the Italian language. Finally, the most authoritative warning not to minimize his learning may be found in the tribute of the scholar who chose him as his successor:

He writes [said Ticknor] & speaks Spanish with a degree of fluency & exactness, which I have known in no other American born of Parents speaking the English as their vernacular. His knowledge of Spanish literature is extensive & is to be relied upon; and several publications he has made in the subject, have been accompanied with poetical translations of much spirit & fidelity.[125]

The fact is that the poet Longfellow possessed an insight denied the more extrovert Ticknor into Spanish ways of thought, into Spanish techniques in writing, or even into some Spanish institutions such as, surprisingly enough, the Spanish Catholic church.[126] These intuitions rendered his little temples of scholarship more attractive, if less Olympian, than Ticknor's mighty acropolis of learning. One is tempted to say that Ticknor loved Spanish books and Longfellow Spanish literature. Although he could speak with authority on the beginnings of the language or on the primitive writing of Spain, Longfellow's natural tastes centered in the "Golden Age": "Worked away," he wrote in his Journal in 1840, "at the early Spanish drama. Hard work. I long to get down to Lope, Cervantes, and Calderon." [127] His *Novelas españolas,* his translation of the *Coplas* with its addenda of graceful versions of sonnets, and even *The Spanish Student,* an imaginative reconstruction from many sources, made agreeable reading for college students. We may believe also that his urbane, scholarly articles on the early periods of the literature delighted some who would have been lost in the thornier pages of Ticknor.

Both Ticknor and Longfellow were German trained, and it would be interesting to learn more of Bouterwek's direct influence upon the former. Both, like Lowell whose excellent scholarship never memorialized itself in grammar, reader, or literary history, were relatively experimental, free-ranging, trail blazing. This is true even if now their texts seem archaic [128] in their lack of the pedagogical apparatus found in today's study of Spanish in secondary school, college, and university seminar. Innocent of the terrifying consequences, the three Smith Professors prepared the way for the modern complexities of journals, learned societies, and documented texts. For the classroom *The Spanish Student* and even the *History of Spanish Literature* proved inadequate, and so eventually did Sales' adaptation of Josse's *Grammar* or the widely studied *Colmena española.* Yet the scholarship of these three pioneers remained a light upon difficult seas. Their learning drew students toward the study of Spanish. More students meant more investigation, more teachers, and more specialized training. So evolved the pattern as we know it now of graduate schools, technical problems, and dissertations with all that is good and bad in the scholarship of our own time.

ALTHOUGH a course in Spanish may have been a starting point for the enthusiasm of a novelist or poet, it is impossible to assess precisely the weight of this type of influence upon the literature of the United States. It is equally impracticable to record here the many professional scholars [129] who, though distinguished specialists, lay few claims, as had Ticknor, Longfellow, or Lowell, to a larger, freer audience. Organization, technical methods, and professional advancement through publication represent a situation with which these early discoverers enjoyed hardly a bowing acquaintance. Nevertheless, these conditions had come to stay. Indeed, they were to dominate an academic world which was to become ever more intricate and more compartmentalized.

Possibly the subsequent trends in scholarship may be best comprehended by remembering some climactic moments during this time of exploration. Let us recall that in 1892 Hugo Rennert prepared his doctoral thesis on Spanish pastoral romances under Gottfried Baist, Germany's leading Hispanist.[130] In 1894 Charles Carroll Marden, one of the most famous of modern scholars, chose

SELECCION

DE

OBRAS MAESTRAS DRAMÁTICAS.

POR

CALDERON DE LA BARCA, LOPE DE VEGA, Y MORETO.

CON NOTAS, ÍNDICE Y REGLAS ESENCIALES; AL USO DE LOS COLE-
GIOS Y UNIVERSIDADES DE ESTOS ESTADOS UNIDOS.

———◆———

*Preparado, Revisado y Corregido, conforme á las decisiones mas re-
cientes de la Academia Española sobre la Ortografía,*

POR F. SALES,

*Instructor de Frances y Español en la Universidad de Harvard,
en Cambridge.*

————————

BOSTON:
DE LA IMPRENTA DE MUNROE Y FRANCIS.
Se vende en las principales Librerías de esta Capital.
....
1828.

Title page of Longfellow's copy of Francis Sales' edition
of *Seleccion de obras maestras dramáticas*, Boston, 1828.

for his topic "The Phonology of the Spanish Dialect of Mexico City," [131] and in 1897 J. D. M. Ford wrote the first dissertation on a Spanish subject at Harvard, namely "The Old Spanish Sibilants." [132] The emphasis was to be upon learned investigation. This scholarship in Spanish was to be molded by those "scientific" tendencies already discussed in our estimate of the historians of Spain.[133]

Gradually the early grammars introduced by Francis Sales, by Mariano Velázquez de la Cadena,[134] by Schele de Vere, and by Francisco Javier Vingut [135] were superseded. "Each year," wrote a critic in the year 1950, "sees new additions to the already staggering total number of Spanish grammars for use in the first year." [136] Gradually the pioneering works in Romance languages of Thomas Frederick Crane [137] gave way to the sophisticated scholarship of Rennert, Grandgent, and Ford.[138] The last-named, equipped with a minute knowledge not only in French, Italian, and Spanish but also in Catalan, Provençal, Rumanian, and Portuguese, issued in 1906 the first edition of his collection of *Old Spanish Readings* and in 1918, at the Lowell Institute, delivered his series of lectures, *Main Currents of Spanish Literature*. Ford was also the inspirer of two books with a promise for the future: Isaac Goldberg's *Studies in Spanish American Literature* [139] and Alfred Coester's *Literary History of Spanish America*. Less eminent as a man of letters than his predecessors, the fourth Smith Professor was superior to them all in his vision of the study of Spanish in regions other than the Peninsula. For in the twentieth century Spanish America [140] and also our own Southwest and California were to engross the professional scholars. In New Mexico and in adjacent areas these new experts were to turn to history, legend, song, and play.[141] At the moment we should notice merely the increasing interest in the languages and dialects of Spanish America.

Through this scholarship extraordinary changes had occurred; Spanish studies had been broadened, diversified, and professionalized. Perhaps the danger now existed that they might, like other American products, become standardized. If these studies were less literary than Longfellow's and Lowell's they were better planned and better geared to the needs of various types of modern students.

In 1926 Marden's *First Spanish Grammar,* as unlike the primers of Sales or Knapp as the eras which produced them, offered "a clearer and more scientific statement of the principles of Spanish grammar." [142] Later, between 1920 and 1950, there developed for the study of history "the essential bibliographies, ground-breaking monographs and the texts." [143] This professional scholarship turned vigorously to the literature of Spain [144] and, with more emphasis, to that of Spanish America. In 1945 a bibliographer and critic declared that the books published in the United States on the literature of Spanish America exceeded the total number published in England, Germany, France, and Spain and equaled these in quality.[145]

In this reorientation of Spanish scholarship in America, we can merely mention as examples (for the achievements of others are equally impressive) the brilliant contributions of Sylvanus Griswold Morley, an authority on the Spanish ballad; John Driscoll Fitz-Gerald, student of Gonzalo de Berceo; Lawrence Wilkins, tireless worker in the methods of teaching Spanish in secondary schools; or James Pyle Wickersham Crawford, Rennert's distinguished pupil and one of the founders of the *Hispanic Review.*[146] With such modern scholars we end this outline, our brief survey of backgrounds which could not have been wholly unknown to American men of letters. It is more than a coincidence that Ezra Pound, once a professional student of Lope de Vega, later translated Spanish verse.

THE indispensable weapons of the teachers and of the scholars were books and still more books, and in the history and use of these, too, twentieth-century progress has been startling. Little imagination is needed to conceive of the riches in print and manuscript now assembled in public and private libraries in contrast to the scanty hoardings of the seventeenth and eighteenth centuries. For easily comprehensible reasons the collections of ancient Spanish books grew steadily in numbers and rarity, and at the same time in our twentieth-century bookstores one might find readily enough the novels of Blasco Ibáñez or the verse of García Lorca. The change is amazing. We recall Ticknor's anxious insistence a century earlier on the need of Spanish books. We remember, too, the precedent he set—his own peerless library.

The detailed story of the growth of Spanish collections has been told elsewhere.[147] In our particular study we need only recognize the utterly different point of view. With the immeasurable increase in the availability of Spanish books had come the deepened understanding on the part of librarians, collectors, teachers, and scholars of the value of all books and manuscripts pertaining to Spain or to Spain in America. As merely one remarkable antithesis, we might turn from the shelves of the Boston Athenæum in 1807, where among the few Spanish volumes donated were *Retratos de españoles ilustres* (1791) and *El ingenioso hidalgo Don Quixote de la Mancha* (1780),[148] to those of the American Antiquarian Society in 1919 with its early Spanish-American imprints, including seven hundred examples of typography from 1555 to 1800 in Mexico City, Puebla, or Lima.[149] Such contrasts, which might be duplicated in nearly every important library, demonstrate the swift multiplication in America of both books in Spanish and books connected with Spanish subjects.[150]

THE immediately preceding pages have shown, in contrast to the more informal, heterogeneous studies in Spanish during the first three quarters of the nineteenth century, the marked organizational trend in twentieth-century teaching, scholarship, and book collecting. Appropriately enough, the interest in Spanish books found its embodiment in 1904 in the Hispanic Society of America, which now secured its unique place in Spanish-American intellectual life. From this time on other societies and federations took form.[151] Our interrelations with the intellectuals of Spain and Spanish America were strengthened through the American Philosophical Society.[152] The Hispanic Institute in the United States strove to coordinate the work of all institutions for the study of Spanish culture in America,[153] and the American Association of the Teachers of Spanish studied with professional zeal new methods of instruction.[154] More than these and all other groups, the Hispanic Society of America influenced our scholars and writers and proclaimed our sensitivity to all the arts of Spain. For a period of fifty years its library, museum, and galleries have continued to reflect those particular qualities of the Spanish imagination which have so often captivated our men of letters from Washington Irving to John Dos Passos.

For the Hispanic Society is

not merely a museum, nor a library, nor a Société des Savants; it is all that and much more. It is the crystallization of the whole soul of Spain. It is presented to the Americans as a unique pageant, entirely apart from teaching fellows, schools and universities; apart from merchants and travelers, but open to teaching fellows and travelers and merchants to help them apprehend what they generally do not perceive—the very spirit of the country.[155]

The Society originated in a collection of Spanish books begun by Archer M. Huntington in 1885. In its present form its object is no less than to communicate the entire history of Hispanic culture by books, manuscripts, objects of art, and crafts.[156] We may study in its library, or we may read its reprints or magazines, or we may rely in our work on its bibliographies.[157] We must wander within its halls to realize the glories of its assembly of the arts, its wealth of books, its documents, and its paintings. With our particular purpose in mind—that is, the relations of all these to our literature— we can hardly help speculating on the thoughts of some of our men of letters had it existed in their day. We may easily imagine Irving, Ticknor, Prescott, or Lowell within its library or before the murals of Sorolla. In a sense they were the ghostly founders of its splendors.

TEACHING, scholarship, collections—all these fostered a special craft, one of the most effective means of communicating Spanish and Spanish-American culture to the United States. This was the art of translation. Among all the teachers and scholars mentioned in this chapter few neglected this kind of interpretation. Every year, in constantly increasing numbers, the translators responded to our interest in Spain, whether in the sustained work of the pro-

Museum Court (southwest view) of the Hispanic Society of America.

fessional poet Longfellow with his theory of the translator's techniques or in the beautiful renditions of Spanish poetry for its own sake by Sylvanus Griswold Morley or in a painstaking text from some young college teacher. Translation was, indeed, a kind of universal plaything—of the travelers such as Hay, of the historians such as Lea, of the poets such as Bryant, of the romancers such as Irving, or of the many scholars who tried their hands at versions of *Don Quixote*.[158]

Translators, therefore, cannot be isolated as translators; they appear and reappear in all the groups discussed in our Spanish backgrounds of American literature. Nevertheless, through teaching and scholarship translations received a definite impetus. The editors of texts and the investigators not only translated but introduced free-lance writers to this pastime. As, year after year, thousands of students equipped with adequate Spanish (or with another modern language) were graduated from the universities, the techniques of translation ceased to be the property of the specialists. Quickened with new life, the talent passed to the desks of writers indifferent to the drab pursuits of the scholar. During the twentieth century, in all the living languages, translation became a fashion, a popular as well as a scholarly art. Over the general aspects of these interpreters of Spanish culture we should for a moment delay.

In some of these translations the aims were artistic as in a fresh version of a play, a short story, or a poem. In others the purposes were historical or scientific as in articles on archaeology or on ornithology. These translations were often designed for an audience quite as cultivated as that presided over by the academic translator with his redactions of, say, the early Spanish drama. Other translations, however, were frankly journalistic and commercial, the result of chance or a casual tip from an editor or publisher. So in the twentieth century bloomed these scores of amateurs, whose hundreds of translations now form a dense bibliographical thicket. Some, indeed, were the authors of only a single item. Presumably these separate twigs have little meaning, but the vast extent of the shrubbery cannot be ignored. The translators were conveying to American readers infinite variations in the complex pattern of Spanish culture.[159]

As in the cases of the teachers, the scholars, and the books, the vogue of the translator in the twentieth century was a result of a new attitude toward this Spanish and Spanish-American culture. Prior to the last decade of the preceding century when the instruction in Spanish began to leave an accumulative impress upon our culture, the translators of Spanish had been isolated, almost as special as Richard Alsop in his early nineteenth-century version of Juan Molina. Soon afterward the traveler Caleb Cushing or the anthologist Samuel Kettell or that strange bilingual adventurer George Washington Montgomery (so interesting to both Irving and Longfellow) had experimented with this little-known foreign language. Thereafter consuls,[160] antiquarians, historians, librarians, instructors, and a few Spaniards themselves, among them George Santayana,[161] translated diversified Spanish materials in lonely fashion, with little hope of a reading public. William Elliot's translations from the *Visions* of Quevedo were regarded in 1832 as a delightful oddity.[162] Not until the end of the nineteenth century did it become a commonplace activity to translate Spanish poetry, history, and drama. Of the 1,108 items listed in Sturgis E. Leavitt's valuable bibliography only thirty were published before 1900.[163]

One vigorous stimulus for the translation of contemporary Spanish literature was William Dean Howells' eloquent appeal, described in a later chapter, in behalf of such realists as Pérez Galdós, Juan Valera, or Palacio Valdés.[164] Readers ignorant of everything Spanish enjoyed the English text of *Doña Perfecta* with its introduction by Howells. Katherine Lee Bates gave us the legends of Bécquer, and many a translator now forgotten showered on us famous short stories.[165] Instead of an unusual exercise, such as Bryant found it, in the twentieth century the translation of these multifarious Spanish materials became a passion. Everywhere we encounter scientific works, philosophy, ethnology, fiction, or contemporary poetry, as in the distinguished renderings by Eleanor Turnbull.[166] Everywhere we find tales on Mexican themes, as in Katherine Anne Porter's version of Fernández de Lizardi's picaresque novel, *El Periquillo Sarniento*. Or we may read in English, to cite only a few instances of works published during the last two decades (1930–50): Manuel Chaves Nogales' *Heroes & Beasts of*

Spain (the Civil War stimulated translation); *Plays of the Southern Americas; The Araucaniad* of Alonso de Ercilla y Zúñiga; *Anthology of Contemporary Latin-American Poetry; III Tragedies* by Federico García Lorca; *Martín Fierro, the Argentine Gaucho Epic* by José Hernández; or translations of Cervantes, of Alarcón, of Ramón José Sender, or of *Marcela, a Mexican Love Story*—the list is endless. Don Quixote compared the art of translation to "gazing at a Flemish tapestry with the wrong side out," but in the twentieth century he himself has been brilliantly retranslated in styles which avoid both the antiquated and the flippant.[167]

The vogue of Spanish drama in New York City will be described in another chapter; among the many translators of Spanish plays John Garrett Underhill excelled. Meanwhile, the scope of all the translators was broadened not only by the discovery of Spain within the United States but by the location of Spanish books and documents dealing with the ancient past of California and the Southwest.[168] We cannot distinguish here between the innumerable species of these translators. We can only fasten once more upon the fact that the translation of Spanish writing was now no longer exceptional. Instead it was an authentic part of our national literary life.[169] When these translations rose above the journalistic, as in those by Ezra Pound or by John Dos Passos [170] or in versions of established poetry like Walsh's *Hispanic Anthology*,[171] we cannot doubt that they exerted an influence upon our fiction and our verse.

From all this activity of the teacher, the scholar, the collector, and the translator has there been a distillation? In other words, has there occurred the most important result, that of a distinguished criticism? The question may well be asked as we conclude this chapter whether American authors have pronounced on Spanish or Spanish-American literature judgments as perceptive as those which they have occasionally rendered on English and on some Continental writers. Although our recognition of Spanish literature is tardy, we are tempted to look for criticism comparable to that of John Livingston Lowes on Coleridge or of Irving Babbitt in his *Masters of French Criticism*. A knowledgeable grasp upon Spanish literature has been, as we have seen, of slow growth. There are now many workmanlike estimates. We are curious to know if there is more.

To answer the question fairly we must for a brief moment again look backward; to search for critics we must begin in the early years of the nineteenth century. If we do so and if we extend this scrutiny until 1910, the verdict is sadly negative. By rigorous standards there is little first-rate criticism. This is not surprising, for no province of American literature during this century was, except the drama, more barren. Our acute critics may be limited to the fingers of one hand, perhaps in the middle years to Poe and Lowell and in the latter decades to Howells and James. Amid this general sterility in criticism, Spanish literature could hardly fare well. Ticknor was historical and expository; Longfellow was appreciative and descriptive; and the great historians were only obliquely critical of the literary aspects of Spanish culture. In his reviews of Spanish books Poe wrote at second hand with no real knowledge of the subject.[172] Only two mid-nineteenth-century literary critics compel our attention. These were Lowell on Cervantes (and, in his letters, on Calderón) and Howells on the novelists Valera, Valdés, Galdós, and Blasco Ibáñez.

In Lowell's essays the allusions to Cervantes and to Calderón are abundant,[173] and his article (or lecture) on Cervantes is still tolerable reading.[174] Like his studies of Chaucer and Milton, Lowell's wisdom on Cervantes shocks us into no fresh view either of the author or of the immortal book. It recapitulates what we already know and emphasizes moral issues. It lacks altogether that free play of thought which distinguishes, let us say, Matthew Arnold's critical essays on French and Russian literature.[175] Howells' estimates of the Spanish realists are sensitive, and they illumine the ties of these novelists with the world movement of modern realism. Nevertheless, the paragraphs on Valdés and Valera in his *Criticism and Fiction* are frequently illustrations of a theory rather than forthright analyses of Spanish fiction.[176] It would appear that Ticknor's encyclopedic history laid the groundwork for a thorough knowledge of Spanish literature. It called tacitly for critical minds and for penetrative critical essays either upon the writers of the "Golden Age" or upon later Spanish drama, fiction, and poetry—or even, by implication, for evaluations of Spanish-American literature. Yet in the nineteenth century no such critic appeared to lead us on into fields beyond those of the historian and scholar.

What, finally, of the twentieth century? Astute, luminous passages occur in introductions to editions of Cervantes, Lope de Vega, and other Spanish masters. Rennert (on Lope de Vega), Buchanan (on Cervantes), Schevill, Carolina Bourland, and other persons of learning, to whom the admiring Romera-Navarro devotes so many pages, may be called critics as well as scholars, and Ford's *Main Currents of Spanish Literature* is comparable to some of our critical writings on the literature of England. Moreover, the twentieth-century anthologies, essays, and biographies are both numerous and provocative.[177] All these writings are fine flowers of the interests discussed in this chapter on the teacher, the scholar, the collector of Spanish books, and the translator. Nevertheless, most of the studies are, it must be said, investigatory, informative, preparing for criticism rather than brilliantly critical themselves. In like fashion, the exhaustive work of Frederick Bliss Luquiens in the Spanish-American field is chiefly bibliographical, and the contributions of Isaac Goldberg and Alfred Coester are historical in principle.[178] Analysis of this Spanish-American literature in prefaces is necessarily slight, in, for example, H. R. Hays' *12 Spanish American Poets;* and the many estimates of the oral literature of the Southwest, of the religious drama, the ballads, the children's songs, and the folk tales are hardly criticism of the first order. After this summary the first question still remains, I think, unanswered—whether among all these we may find the great literary critic. Or, perhaps, it *is* answered. He is not yet here.

IN THE accelerating development of American belles-lettres, after the 1830's Spanish culture became a vital force. We have already observed how close some of the travel books were to the essay and to the romance. The magazines included tales, and some histories, in their gilded accounts of the ancient peoples and folklore of Spanish America, were not unlike novels. Spanish themes, beckoning to our poets, found varied expression, from trivial verses on Columbus to the scholarly Longfellow's adaptations of Jorge Manrique with their echoes of Spanish prosody. Spanish idioms brought back by travelers in the Southwest or by soldiers in Mexico became current in our newspapers. These phrases were to reappear in the fiction of Bret Harte and Willa Cather and even in the poetry of James Russell Lowell.[1] In the drama the imprint was registered more slowly. Nevertheless, Spanish plays, from Lope de Vega to Benavente, entered vigorously into our literary consciousness. More vividly than the other mediums discussed in preceding chapters, our literature revealed the richness of this Spanish coloring in ideas, moods, and forms.[2]

Our writers refashioned these in stories, poems, and plays. They created interrelated patterns of Spanish inlay, brilliant but so encyclopedic that in this general chapter they must be simplified. In story we range from Washington Irving to John Steinbeck, in poem from William Cullen Bryant to Archibald MacLeish, in drama from William Dunlap to Ernest Hemingway. Innumerable minor authors were sensitive to the Spanish influence, and few major figures escaped it completely. Besides those fully discussed in the biographical chapters of this book, it laid its spell at various times on James Fenimore Cooper, William Gilmore Simms, Edgar Allan Poe, Walt Whitman, Mark Twain, Herman Melville, and Willa Cather.

Not only are these literary expressions of Spanish influence varied and different in their aims, but the precise quality of the

imprint is never twice the same. Simms dwells on Spanish backgrounds in the Carolinas whereas Mark Twain borrows directly
from Cervantes. Meanwhile, Melville selects as the setting of a tale
"the harbour of St. Maria—a small, desert, uninhabited island
toward the southern extremity of the long coast of Chili." [3] In our
time Hemingway has written of violent death in war or in bull
ring. Or the poet Hart Crane, who in Mexico seems to have had a
kind of foretaste of his tragic death, recalled his schoolboy reading
when he

> . . . walked with Pizarro in a copybook,
> And Cortez rode up, reining tautly in—
> Firmly as coffee grips the taste,—and away! [4]

To classify these writers as in debt to the Peninsula, Spanish America, and the Southwest,[5] as in the case of the travel books, would
be misleading. Instead the story will be told, whatever the particular quality of the influence, in three parts, each chronologically
from 1800 to the present time: first the novelists, then the poets,
and finally the dramatists.

BEFORE telling this story, however, we must pause over subliterary
patterns which elude such precise classification, namely the fiction,
poetry, or drama arising out of the folklore in our Spanish regions.
In our study of the seventeenth and eighteenth centuries and in
the chapter on the scholars occurred allusions to the Spanish culture of Florida and the Southwest.[6] It is now clear that, besides
architecture and other crafts, a legacy to American literature has
been accumulated in these areas in tale, ballad, or play.[7] In thinking later in the present chapter of Bret Harte or of Willa Cather
or of Maxwell Anderson's *Night over Taos* we must always remember this subsoil. It flowered in only a few instances into literature
(as we conceive of it in this book) but was always present as a background for our writing. It is still potentially our richest body of
native material for novelist, poet, and playwright. "No informed
person," says an authority on the region, "would hold that the
Southwest can claim any considerable body of *pure literature* as its

own. At the same time, the region has a distinct cultural inheritance, full of life and drama." [8] We should survey this "cultural
inheritance" briefly from its origins until the present day [9] before
returning to the particular achievements of leading novelists, poets,
and dramatists.

This seed time began in the sixteenth century, in the *relaciones*
of the explorers, in the writings of Cabeza de Vaca or of Hernando
de Soto, or in Espejo's account of his journey to New Mexico,
printed in Madrid in 1586.[10] These books both recorded and stimulated history and legend and helped to create a body of enduring
folklore. It has often been observed that, when in 1598 Oñate
crossed the Rio Grande and released the inundation of colonists
from Mexico, in Spain Lope de Vega and Cervantes had not
reached the fullness of their powers and Calderón was still unknown.[11] Notwithstanding, in native story, song, and play it is
possible to imagine some faint tints from the glory of the "Golden
Age" of Spanish literature.[12] At any rate, there survived in southern
Colorado, New Mexico, Arizona, and California these patterns
which took shape in the sixteenth and seventeenth centuries. Here
live on the *canciones, romances,* songs (religious and secular), proverbs, and especially dramas not unlike the mystery and morality
plays of England.[13] In this folklore priceless materials resided for
later generations of novelists, poets, and dramatists.

During the eighteenth century both facts and myths were enriched by the reports, records, and memoirs of the mission period.
Ultimately all this tangled weave found a lively expression in the
nineteenth and twentieth centuries, chiefly in fiction and in works
which were at once historical, descriptive, and interpretative. One
might wonder why the early relaciones or the *documentos* or the
autos produced during the era of the missions no authentic piece of
great Spanish literature in the Southwest. But nonreligious writing
was sometimes burned in the courts of the missions. Soon after the
law of secularization in 1833 the tide of American invaders flowed
through the Southwest, contemptuous of everything which might
have inspired an indigenous poet, novelist, or dramatist. The story
of this debasing wave, almost drowning the Spanish culture, is told
in Helen Hunt Jackson's *Ramona.* Further echoes of the extinction

occur later in Willa Cather's *Death Comes for the Archbishop* and in Anderson's *Night over Taos*. Perhaps the failure of the drama to separate itself, as in England, from the Church was a factor.[14] Whatever the causes, no Spanish-American work of genius appeared.

Nevertheless, throughout the nineteenth century there flourished in an oral literature and also in a growing body of fiction the legends and the history of the conquistadores, of the colonists, and of the missions. All these narratives suffer from the inflation of which recent critics have complained. Forlorn bands in search of a little wealth became armies engaged in a heroic quest for mountains of gold. Adobe chapels grew into cathedrals. Skirmishes with the Indians expanded into epical battles. Legends multiplied, of "buried treasure," "lost" mines, people in golden cities, lovers on the brinks of cliffs united in suicide pacts, and flowers, streams, and dismal chasms.[15] The stories drawn from Villagra's *Historia de la Nueva Mexico,* published in 1610, were hardly more exaggerated than those of the Texan novelists who about 1850 celebrated the more recent glories of the Alamo.[16]

For a full century, until the present moment, the inviting themes of this Spanish past inspired hundreds of novels. All these were definitely short of immortality, but some of their authors were capable of handling story and background (seldom character) with competence. Charles W. Webber's *The Gold Mines of the Gila* (1849) or Augusta J. Evans' *Inez: A Tale of the Alamo* (1855) were standardized melodrama with a southwestern flavor.[17] Gertrude Atherton's *The Splendid Idle Forties* (1902) dramatized meetings of the Mexican and Spanish inhabitants with the American intruders. Mary Austin's *Isidro* (1905) was a tale of the missions, and Harvey Fergusson's *The Blood of the Conquerors* (1921) related the history of Ramon Delcasar, a modern man with roots in the past. Such representatives of modern American fiction revealed an ever-increasing sophistication in depicting the Spanish tradition of the Southwest.

Actually, the best prose writers of the region have not been, either in aims or essential interests, primarily novelists. This is true of the gifted Mary Austin who was folklorist, social critic, scholar, humanitarian, "mystic," and more—much more.[18] For

many of these storytellers the subject has centered on the background itself. This interest in the Spanish and Indian past and
present has expressed itself in some delightful books with fusions
of description, travel, and with imaginative re-creation of the older
days. We think of Ruth Alexander Laughlin's *Caballeros* (1931)
or of Harvey Fergusson's *Rio Grande* (1933), which was, its author
says, "an attempt to portray a region, both as it is today and as it
has been." [19] Somewhat earlier, as a roving journalist, "O. Henry"
had studied the Spanish language and had known the Mexicans at
first hand. He reported their dress, manners, and dialects with accuracy but with a fillip of humorous exaggeration.[20] Through these
writers in the early twentieth century a custom of candid reporting
of scenes and traditions had grown up in a way to rebuke charlatans
with their patter of Spanish names and places for the sake of specious coloring. With this writing in mind, the good and the bad,
we may comprehend more clearly in their respective epochs the
achievements of Bret Harte and Willa Cather.

Meanwhile, the soldiers, explorers, and missionaries had bequeathed to the Southwest not only stories but songs. Many of
these, like the narratives and plays (of which they were occasionally
a part), have survived. We may read them in their ancient forms
or in versions enriched by new associations. Like the stories, the
homespun lyrics of Texas or New Mexico enjoy adaptations in the
recent poetry of the Southwest. Their variety is astonishing. They
may be connected with a famous event or with a humble incident in
the life of plain and mountain: a wedding, a funeral, or a fiesta.[21]
They record in changing meters the changing moods of an emotional people. "I have," says a student of this poetry, "travelled in
Southern Colorado and Northern New Mexico in an effort to collect *décimas, cuandos, corridos, romances, inditas, versos, alabados,
canciones, adivinanzas, pastorelas.*" [22]

The list suggests a diversity within the simple art of this early
poetry, and the problems of its versification are still challenging.
These songs, so close to the life of the Southwest, belong in a broad
sense to American literature, but the impulse to write lyrics on
this life of the past seems to have diminished in the light of our
modern day. In the nineteenth century few poets of the Southwest

dealt with Spanish themes, and then without unusual power. The poetry written in English in these regions has absorbed new and exciting elements into American verse, in theme, in the nomenclature of places and persons, and in vocabulary.[23] Nevertheless, it remains minor poetry, from R. M. Potter's "Hymn of the Alamo" or Mirabeau B. Lamar's "The Daughter of Mendoza" [24] (both written about a century ago) to John Gould Fletcher's "Mexican Quarter." An attenuation of ideas seems characteristic of the verse of Witter Bynner, of Arthur Davison Ficke, or of the brilliant young priest, Fray Angelico Chavez.[25] Their poetry demands respect but does not convince us that the tradition of Spanish song has yet been reborn in modern American writing.

The richest vein in the quarry of Spanish folklore in the Southwest is the religious drama in Texas, Colorado, Arizona, California, and in New Mexico.[26] It is difficult to find a better relation of its beginning than Mary Austin's:

The landing of the Pilgrims on the coast of Massachusetts was dramatic in situation; the entrada of the Spanish Colonists by way of the Chihuahua Trail was so by intention . . . Arriving at the crossing of the Rio Grande amid hardships before which the Pilgrim crossing pales, the expedition sat down on the bank of the Rio Grande and witnessed a comedy of their adventures written by Captain Farfán and played by his company. Thus on the 29th of April, 1595, modern drama began in our Southwest, which was taken possession of next day with a pageant of banners and ritual in the name of all the Blessed Personages, the King of Spain, and St. Francis. The founding of their first capital, now Chamita, New Mexico, was celebrated by a horseback pageant of Christians conquering the Moors before an audience augmented by two pueblos of Indians.[27]

Under these circumstances was acted for the first time in the Southwest the now venerable play, *Los moros y los cristianos*.[28]

In the wake of explorers followed the missionaries. Their campaign of evangelization depended in part on plays now linked by scholars not only with the primitive religious drama of Gómez Manrique, Juan del Encina, and Gil Vicente but also with the plays of Lope de Vega and Calderón.[29] The warriors themselves brought acting versions into New Mexico, where they took deep root. Others came with the missionaries, who changed them to suit their special purposes. These "mysteries," such as *Adán y Eva* (performed in Mexico in 1538 and later many times in New Mexico), were acted and re-acted throughout the centuries.[30] Though they survived for years only "in the folk mouth," [31] they have now been set down on paper from the lips of participants. We may now read *Los pastores* or *Los reyes magos*,[32] plays first conceived in Spain, or we may study the secular play, *Los Comanches,* composed in New Mexico during the latter half of the eighteenth century.[33] The religious drama, a colossal subject in itself and the focus of much scholarly activity, has little direct bearing on the playwriting discussed in the last pages of the present chapter, but, like the tales and the songs, it must be borne in mind as related to our literary interest in Spanish subjects and forms.

So WE end this general, introductory view of the novel, the poem, and the play in the nineteenth century and of the backgrounds of literary Spanish folklore within the United States. Let us now return to the main stream, to our beginnings in orthodox fiction. Washington Irving, interpreter of Spain as traveler, contributor to magazines, and historian, reappears as a short-story writer in *The Alhambra* (1832). Storytelling, however, despite "Rip Van Winkle" or "The Legend of Sleepy Hollow," was never Irving's forte. He had learned this unhappy truth eight years earlier by the failure of his *Tales of a Traveller.* At the same time the incidental narratives in his essays on the famous palace were popular and stimulated the continuance of writing on Spanish legend.[34] As in architecture, "Alhambraism" became a fashion.[35]

If Irving's stories (half essay, half tale) lacked precision, they nevertheless exhaled a special quality to which later narrators were sensitive:

As I stood there that night [wrote one of these of the Alhambra] my thoughts reverted to the time when, with childish eagerness, I pored over the fascinating pages of Irving wherein are recounted the traditions of this grand old palace of the Moorish kings. Then arose the remembrance of the weird tales of the Gate of Justice; of the tower whence the

Princesses descended into the arms of their expectant lovers; of magic scrolls read by the light of tapers compounded with a hundred charms in the secret cave of the astrologer; of subterranean chambers, where lines of grim warriors mounted, armed, and motionless as statues, awaited in mysterious silence the breaking of some potent spell; of the talismanic hand of jet; and of Gallego with his jars of gold.[36]

These brief plots, imbedded in the long descriptive and historical sections of *The Alhambra,* were mere fragments of a "Spanish Sketch Book," but they were powerful agents. After 1832 short story and novel emulated these tales of Irving.

William Cullen Bryant, whose role as a translator and poet will be discussed presently, must have been conscious of Irving as he wrote his "Moriscan Romances" and his tales concerning a Spain he had not yet visited.[37] There were others. It is certain that Cooper, in spite of his enmity toward Irving, borrowed from his *Conquest of Granada* (and, like everyone else, from Prescott) for his tedious story of Columbus, *Mercedes of Castile* (1840).[38] At about the same time Hawthorne, though by no means a disciple, could speak in one of his tales of "the profound, pathetic humor of Cervantes" and in *Our Old Home* of "Sancho Panza's dip out of Camacho's caldron." [39] As a reviewer Poe had his fling at Irving's and Long-fellow's writings on Spain, and he analyzed various translations from the Spanish.[40] A student of the language at the University of Virginia, he acquired an interest in the literature, particularly in Cervantes, whom he quotes with surprising frequency. He refers, among other classical writers, to Lope de Vega, Quevedo, and Calderón.[41] Was his "William Wilson" under the spell of "El embozado," the reputedly lost play of this dramatist? [42] Spanish authors were certainly in Poe's mind as he wrote some of his tales, notably "Morella" and "The Pit and the Pendulum." [43] It is, indeed, easy to imagine a peculiar affinity with Spain in our melodramatic story writer with his Spanish titles, Spanish characters, and Spanish oaths. The contribution of Spain to Poe's writings was chiefly *décor.* Delighted by his craftsmanship, Rubén Darío called him "that celestial Edgar." [44]

These founders of our belles-lettres sponsored the use of Spanish themes in fiction. Partly through their example, side by side with

217

the travel book, the magazine article, and the history flourished the novel, the romance, and the short story associated in some way with Spain or Spanish America. The fashion was accentuated by the persistence among American readers of the passion for Cervantes. He was present in Tabitha Tenney's widely read *Female Quixotism* [45] and in the cheap romances (the counterparts of the "popular" histories) which were to continue into the next century—and perhaps forever. [46] The natural drift of our early fiction toward Spanish themes is reflected in pretentious, florid novels now of interest only to the antiquarian and to the specialist in literary history. In this era of beginnings the authors of these were read and applauded and in our study are not without importance. Although interested in subjects connected with the Southwest and Mexico, by background and affiliation these writers belonged to the school of eastern novelists.

IN THIS connection, Timothy Flint is remembered both as a novelist and a traveler in the Southwest. [47] His *Francis Berrian, or The Mexican Patriot* (1826) was probably the first novel written in English with a setting in New Mexico and Mexico. A graduate of Harvard, an editor, and for ten years a missionary in the Mississippi Valley, Flint crossed the frontier in 1825 and lived for a time in the typical Spanish village of Adayes. Knowing nothing at first hand of Mexico, he related his story, half realistic, half romantic, of wanderings there, in New Mexico, and in the Southwest. He was ambitious; he was in quest of a new Eden. In his pages are Spanish names and characters (and quotations from Quevedo) against the background of Sante Fe, San Antonio, Durango, Vera Cruz, or Mexico City. In this elementary novel narrative power is not entirely lacking, but the mixture of truth and fancy renders it a curious hybrid. Its significance is historical. [48] In some ways *Francis Berrian,* which could boast of a second printing in a second edition, [49] anticipates the local-color novels of half a century later.

Many of these minor novelists, earnest but ephemeral, expressed their interest in Spanish and Spanish-American subjects in several mediums. Robert C. Sands, a Knickerbocker storyteller, completed for translation into Spanish a history of Cortés which enjoyed a wide circulation among the South American populations.[50] He composed also a blank-verse poem on the famed sister of Monte-zuma, Papantzin, whose amazing story was, avers Clavijero, "universally known." [51] Almost at the same moment he regaled his public with his novel *Boyuca* (1832), a lurid version of the some-what frayed legend of the Fountain of Youth.[52] An accomplished linguist, Sands knew French, Italian, and other tongues: "After," remarks his biographer, "he acquired the Spanish language very critically, and after studying its more celebrated writers [he] read very largely all the Spanish historians and documents he could procure touching American history . . . [and] years later acquired the Portuguese." [53] For these lesser romancers the voyage in our English-speaking, English-reading America was, just now, up-stream. This fact they fully realized, but they struggled manfully to communicate their enthusiasm in story, poem, and play. The novelists Robert Montgomery Bird and William Gilmore Simms composed poems on Spanish America, and Bird's plays, which will receive comment in a moment, were elaborate illustrations of his Spanish-American studies.

Like that of Sands, Bird's excitement concerning the Spanish-American countries endured. In 1833 he abandoned reluctantly plans for a journey to Mexico and South America.[54] Ingenious in devices directing attention to the themes he loved, he prefaced his first novel *Calavar* (1834) with an introduction recording a dia-logue between a friar, armed with a manuscript, and a "pobre Yankee." [55] Even if Bird borrowed this trick from Irving's *Conquest of Granada*,[56] it was effective. In the same section he begged his readers to realize that "Nature, and the memory of strange deeds of renown, have flung over the valley of Mexico a charm more ro-mantic than is attached to many of the vales of the olden world . . . This is the proper field of romantic musings." [57]

It was indeed, as later fiction and poetry demonstrated. Bird's novels on Spanish themes were amateurish, and *Calavar*, antedat-ing *The Conquest of Mexico* by three years, was pretentious. Al-though his Mexican fiction was mildly successful, he admitted, prior to Prescott's mighty wave of influence, that the odds were against him. His friend James Lawson had warned him of this: "I fear the novel-reading world do not feel the same interest in the semi-civilized portion of our hemisphere, which you entertain." [58] In a moment of discouragement Bird agreed, not without petulance, that his subjects were "too far-offish and Hebraic for our Johnny Raws of the States, who know and care as little about Mexico as they do about the moon." [59]

This was not altogether true, even in 1834. In the same letter Bird remarked enviously on Simms' success with Spanish materials. Actually, *Calavar* was not entirely a failure with its mysterious knight bearing this lofty name, with its young Don Amador, with Cortés himself, and with its thrilling scenes of battle and massacre.[60] Behind *Calavar* lay Bird's solid knowledge of the Spanish language, his tireless reading, and his passionate delight in everything connected with the Conquest:

> Escucha, pues, un rato, y diré cosas
> Estrañas y espantosas, poco á poco.

So runs the motto from Garcilaso de la Vega. The novel is too proliferated, too ostentatiously learned, and too melodramatic. Yet parts of it, particularly the scenes of warfare, are alive. Prescott paid it a tribute in his great history,[61] and it was translated into German.[62] Finally, there remains the powerful word of the hypercritical Poe that *Calavar* was "certainly the very best American novel, excepting perhaps one or two of Mr. Cooper's, which [he had] ever read." [63] Nor was Bird himself really frightened away from his beloved Spanish subjects. In the very next year he published *The Infidel; or The Fall of Mexico* (1835). The final episode of the earlier novel had been the battle of Otumba; this other relates, as the subtitle intimates, the events following the return of Cortés. Among the characters is the famous priest himself, Bernal Diáz del Castillo, not to mention the extraordinary dog "Befo." [64]

Far superior as a novelist to Sands or Bird (with whom he probably discussed Spanish themes), William Gilmore Simms surpassed them both in his portrayal of the Spanish civilization in America. In general, Simms resembled James Fenimore Cooper, whom perhaps he hoped to excel in the use of foreign subjects, in his bold appropriation of history for the gist of an enthralling story. As a boy his reading in history was substantial, and he began very early the study of foreign languages. Years later, at the age of fifty-three, he urged his young friend Mary Lawson to make every effort to acquire German, Italian, and Spanish.[65] Everything suggests a passion for Spanish: the phrases in his letters, the allusions in his fiction to Andalusian, Cuban, or Mexican, his translations of the poetry, and especially the numerous reviews, either from his own hand or from those of his lieutenants on the *Southern Quarterly Review*. All these facts, recently brought to light,[66] qualify sharply impressions of Simms as merely a novelist of the South and his native South Carolina. His intelligent comments on Ticknor's *History of Spanish Literature* (he thought it "singularly dry & costive—cold and tame") as well as his friendships suggest that he was the center in meetings and correspondence of a little group of southern Hispanists (naturally less closely organized than the New Englanders), whose membership included Bird, Gayarré, Waddy Thompson, Brantz Mayer, and Joel Roberts Poinsett.[67]

How many Spanish books enriched Simms' library we cannot be certain, for most of its 10,700 volumes were burned in 1865 by stragglers from Sherman's army, but among the survivals are works of Gayarré, Prescott, and John L. Stephens. By temperament Simms was drawn to Spanish stories. Carried away at the age of seventeen by the tale of Roderick the Goth, he wrote a juvenile play on this legendary hero. In 1840 at the age of thirty-four he began an ambitious drama concerning Don Carlos, of which there survives today in manuscript about an act and a half.[68] At about the same time he rediscovered among his papers his story of Roderick. Stirred by seeing in Mississippi a rude cross—did this not mark the grave of some soldier of De Soto? [69]—he composed, neglecting his study of the law, his long novel *Pelayo* (1838) and portions of its sequel *Count Julian* (1845). Both deal with the Saracenic invasion of Spain and the career of Roderick. Perhaps the young druggist's apprentice should have left his play in his "lock-up," as he called it.[70] Nevertheless, Simms' wanderings from his chosen paths of Revolutionary and post-Revolutionary days show the seductive power of these Spanish subjects.

Besides his poetry and numerous sketches,[71] lesser novels on Spanish-American themes testify to Simms' intermittent participation in this Spanish revival of the thirties and forties. A year after *Pelayo* he had issued a weaker romance, a story "of the New World," so ran his dedication to James K. Paulding, "—of the perils and privations of early discovery—of its bold adventures, wondrous triumphs, and inadequate rewards." [72] For this novel, *The Damsel of Darien,* he had been reading Irving's *The Voyages of the Companions of Columbus.* "The scene," he wrote Paulding, "is partly laid upon the isthmus of Darien, and the material is drawn from the events attending the discovery by Vasco Nunez." [73] *The Damsel of Darien,* perhaps designed as a rival for Bird's fiction, was a failure. Poe called it flatly Simms' worst novel.[74] In 1853 he tried once more, this time under the pseudonym of "Frank Cooper," [75] in his elaborate narrative *Vasconselos.*

The famed De Soto was the hero of this novel, and something of the talent which has earned Simms a belated reputation in the twentieth century entered into its composition. Like James Fenimore Cooper, he possessed a flair for a romantic story. This feeling for the past is strongly evident in the dedication of a later edition of *Vasconselos,* dated October 20, 1856:

As a drama [he says], embodying a most curious and interesting progress, during a singularly-attractive period in our ante-colonial history, the invasion (not the conquest—very far from it!) of the empire of the Floridian (Apalachian) savage, by Hernan de Soto, affords a vast and fertile region for him who works in the provinces of art in fiction. It is, in brief, one of the most magnificent of episodes in the history of progress and discovery in the western world." [76]

In his descriptions of De Soto's tournaments and battles Simms is competent—perhaps not more. Nevertheless, unlike his fairy tales about Spain itself (*Pelayo* and *Count Julian*), *Vasconselos* reveals his mastery of a text on which eventually he was to preach with authority. For after he had seen the Spanish settlements in South Carolina [77] he no longer wrote of Spain as the fanciful land which he had never beheld. Instead he described its relation to the struggling Republic, of which in his long series of novels he was to become a distinguished interpreter. *Vasconselos,* despite some sentimental nonsense, is based upon Simms' matured interest in Spanish America. His youthful enthusiasm for the past of Spain was revitalized by her actual presence in the world he knew. So Simms' story of "Hispaniola" became a fascinating prelude to a true history of the United States. Long before Bourne or Bolton, he believed that American history (and the novel) must record the role played by Spain. And—most important—he thought the theme inexhaustible "for him who works in the province of art in fiction."

IF WE now glance back at this group of early American novelists and storytellers who turned to Spanish themes simultaneously with the travelers, the writers for the magazines, and the historians, we perceive at once underlying motivations. Apart from Irving and possibly Sands, none of these is enamored of classic Spanish literature. Only Cervantes attains recognition in their pages, and the experience of such learned poets as Longfellow or Lowell is never theirs. The first impulse of these pioneer nineteenth-century novelists was to exploit the Spanish stories. From this point of view Russian legend,[78] had it been available, would have served as well. In these six or seven novelists, therefore, is again evident that literary adolescence, that flaccid romanticism not uncharacteristic of the American novel prior to the masterpieces of Hawthorne and Melville. Second, we recognize in every volume written after 1837 the magnetic influence of the historian of Mexico, himself an experimenter in fiction. In dedication, preface, footnote, and in content, all echo and emulate the peerless Prescott. Finally, we sense the excitement in these writers as they discover for themselves the boundless materials for fiction in Spanish America. If we consider them all, their enthusiasm for Spain in America is uneven. We encounter both the indifference of Irving and Cooper and the ardent curiosity of Sands and Bird.

This naïveté—for such it seems to us—in the interpretation of Spain in fiction could not last. After mid-century the travelers and the historians increased our knowledge of Spanish America, and the teachers, scholars, and translators revealed to us a literature in Spain beyond that familiar masterpiece, *Don Quixote*. Like the art of the novel in America, like, indeed, America itself, the story-tellers' management of Spanish themes became gradually more sophisticated [79] until these romantic motivations, persisting into the twentieth century, inspired far subtler explorations. Although the shallow tale of Spain or of Peru would never really cease to appear and although stylized Spanish characters would continue to weaken even such superior writing as Bret Harte's, occasionally the romantic associations with Spain were to be manipulated with delicate meanings and philosophic enlargement. This was true of Herman Melville's *Moby-Dick* and of his remarkable tale with a South American background, "Benito Cereno." [80]

In Lenox, on August 1, 1851, while reading the newspapers, Hawthorne saw approaching "a cavalier on horseback." The "cavalier," he says, "saluted me in Spanish; to which I replied by touching my hat and went on with the newspaper. But the cavalier renewing his salutation, I regarded him more attentively, and saw that it was Herman Melville!" [81] No one would submit this incident or the fact that Melville marked passages in Calderón's Spanish texts as proof of his mastery of the language.[82] Nevertheless, on his voyages he must have known Spanish-speaking sailors; the odds are in favor of both his conversational and reading knowledge. The shore leaves in Lima and other South American ports hint at the former,[83] and his devotion to "Don Quixote, the sagest sage that ever lived," makes probable the latter.[84] Melville's purchase of the Jarvis edition in 1855 [85] appears to date not the beginning but the maturing of his interest in Spanish literature. He had bought *Guzmán de Alfarache* in 1849, and in the following year he had borrowed *Lazarillo de Tormes*.[86]

Aside from the question of his exact knowledge of the language and literature, it is plain that Melville was a victim, like so many of his contemporaries, of the provocative mystery of the Spanish world. "Spain," so he quoted Edmund Burke in *Moby-Dick,* "a great whale stranded on the shores of Europe," [87] and in some very early writing he alluded to the "dark-glancing daughters" of Spain.[88] Or he mused: "the very word Spaniard has a curious, con-a mistress is like a tree without leaves, a building without cement, a shadow without a body that causes it."—"There is no more to be said!" interrupted the duchess; "but for all that, if we are to believe the history of Signor Don Quixote, lately published, with the general applause of all nations [480], we are to collect from thence, if I remember right, that your worship never saw the lady Dulcinea; that there is no such lady in the world; that she is only an imaginary lady, begotten and born of your own brain, and dressed out with all the graces and perfections you pleased."—"There is a great deal to be said upon this subject!" answered Don Quixote; "God knows whether there be a Dulcinea or not in the world, and whether she be imaginary or not imaginary; and this is one of those things the proof whereof should not be too nicely inquired into. I neither begot nor brought forth my mistress, but I contemplate her as a lady endowed with all those qualifications which may make her famous over the whole world, as beautiful without a blemish, grave without pride, amorous with modesty, obliging as being courteous, and courteous as being well-bred; finally, of high descent, because beauty shines and displays itself with greater degrees of perfection when matched with noble blood than in subjects that are mean of extraction."— "True!" said the duke; "but Signor Don Quixote must give me leave to say what the history of his exploits forces me to speak. We must thence infer that, supposing it be allowed that there is a Dulcinea in or out of Toboso, and that she is beautiful in the highest degree, as your worship describes her to us, it must, I say, be inferred that, in respect of high descent, she is not upon a level with the Orianas, the Alastrajareas, Madasimas [481], and a hundred others of the same sort, of whom the histories are full, as your worship well knows."—"To this I can answer," replied Don Quixote, "that Dulcinea is the daughter of her own works, that virtue ennobles blood, and that a virtuous person, though mean, is more to be valued than a vicious person of quality. Besides, Dulcinea has endowments which may raise her to be a queen with crown and sceptre; for the merit of a beautiful virtuous woman extends to the working of greater miracles, and though not formally, yet virtually she has in herself greater advantages in store."—"I say, Signor Don Quixote," retorted the duchess, "that you tread with great caution, and, as the saying is, with the plummet in hand. For my own part, henceforward I will believe, and make all my family believe, and even my lord duke, if need be, that there is a Dulcinea in Toboso, that she is this day living and beautiful, that she is especially well born, and well deserving that such a knight as Signor Don Quixote should be her servant, which is the highest commendation I can bestow on her. But I cannot forbear entertaining one scruple, and bearing a little grudge to Sancho Panza. The scruple is, that the aforesaid history relates that the said Sancho Panza found the said lady Dulcinea, when he carried her a letter from your

---

[480] In several passages of the second part of his book, Cervantes strives to connect it with the first; and with this view he supposes between them, not a lapse of ten years, but only an interval of a few days.

[481] Oriana, the mistress of Amadis of Gaul; Alastrajarea, the daughter of Amadis of Greece and queen Zalara; and Madasima, daughter of Famongomadan, the Giant of the Boiling Lake, are ladies of chivalric creation.

spirator, Guy-Fawkish twang." [89] But more important than the conventional mood of romance, we sense his perception of meanings for particular use in his fiction. In *Moby-Dick* Elijah warns Ishmael not to speak of Captain Ahab's "deadly scrimmage with the Spaniard afore the altar in Santa." [90] This was one of Ahab's secrets and also one of Melville's, but the allusion is understandable, as we shall see in a moment in our study of "Benito Cereno."

To Cervantes, whose *Don Quixote* he mentions so often, Melville may have been in debt for the quasi-picaresque form of *Moby-Dick* or for its talk of knight-errantry.[91] Markings in Melville's own copy of *Don Quixote,* though acquired four years after the publication of *Moby-Dick,* reveal his interest in the knight's "monomania," [92] in the latter's need of a kind of heroine or ideal,[93] and in Cervantes' comments on the "intrinsic worth" of chivalry:

That you may see, Sancho . . . how fair a prospect its meanest retainers have of speedily gaining the respect and esteem of the world, I will that you sit here by my side, in company with these good folks, and that you be one and the same thing with me, who am your master and natural lord; that you eat from off my plate, and drink of the same cup in which I drink; for the same may be said of knight-errant[r]y, which is said of love, that it makes all things equal.[94]

Other alleged obligations are nebulous. The coexistence of romance and realism in Melville's writings can hardly be construed as a dependence upon the Knight and Squire as models. In his vivid presentation of heavenly time and Greenwich time (*Pierre*) or in his contrasts of the "monomania" of Ahab with the "reason" of Starbuck, Melville receives, as far as we can tell, only confirmatory sustenance from Cervantes.[95]

It might be argued that the Spanish influence upon the poetic, philosophic Melville was exerted less through Cervantes than through a special concept of the Spaniard formed in his mind both by his reading and by his association with Spanish-American countries. This concept is conspicuous in certain sketches in "The Encantadas" and especially in "Benito Cereno." There is, for instance, a curious emotional insistency in his allusions to everything connected with the white city of Lima. He refers to the harbor of Lima, to the walls of Lima, to the women of Lima. The melancholy Spanish captain, Benito Cereno, treads the deck of the *San Dominick,* once graced by "the Lima Viceroy's daughters," and in *Moby-Dick* we are told of "tearless Lima, the strangest saddest city thou can'st see." [96] Through books and through his experience on the sea, Spain and the "Spaniard" had come to be identified by Melville with something singular. As in so many situations and qualities in life, Melville read into Spain his own private meanings. The heart of his concept was both religious and social. The Spaniard stood both for an illustrious, if decadent, civilization and also for a form of Christianity for which he felt alternately attraction and repulsion. In *Mardi* he had already revealed his ambivalence toward ancient European civilizations and toward this ancient Catholic faith. Benito Cereno, unable to face life, takes refuge in a monastery. In contemplating his hero Melville is, I think, both contemptuous and a little envious. For the weak the Church still offers sanctuary.

As he meditated on the history of the Spanish civilization—there was a copy of Prescott's *Ferdinand and Isabella* in the library of the frigate, the *United States* [97]—and on Spanish Catholicism, these concepts entered as concrete characters or objects into his beautiful, fluid symbolism, real but unconfinable within precise limits. Captain Benito Cereno, "so Spanishly poetic," [98] represents this proud but crippled civilization of Spain. Benito wears an empty scabbard. Observe further that to shave his master the conquering, primitive man, Babo, uses the royal, bright-colored flag of Castile and Aragon as a towel. [99] There are three "civilizations" represented on the *San Dominick*. On the ship we meet the Negro, the Spaniard, and, in almost comic contrast to Benito, the practical, philosophically immature Captain Amasa Delano, symbol of our own brash Republic. [100] Melville's sense of the glory and disintegration of the Spanish empire becomes a factor in his symbolism and in his thinking concerning the contemporary world.

Melville's symbolism and his thought are affected even more by the history of Catholicism in Spain. In this masterpiece, "Benito Cereno," whose backdrop is Lima and the Chilean coast, the broken sea captain is associated in his mind with the decline of the Roman Catholic church. The name of the ship suggests the terrors of the Inquisition. At a distance it resembles a blanched, moldering convent. Later we become conscious of the ironical resemblance of the blacks to monks, of the missal, of the crucifix, and of the friars' girdles in the ship's cuddy. Finally, the death of Benito Cereno in the Mount Agonia convent is profoundly symbolic. Through such images and incidents Melville is telling us in his connotative language what he believes about man's oldest fabric, the Catholic church. He admires a splendor (so he implies) that is no more, a sublime faith that is now impossible. The severed head of Babo, implacable even after death, glares out from the market place toward the monastery where lived and died his victim, Benito Cereno. Captain Ahab, the free and rebellious mind—this is the meaning of the earlier incident—engaged in deadly struggle with a Spanish believer even "afore the altar in Santa!" For these magical moments in the writings of Herman Melville the Spanish influence is a precious, indispensable constituent.

MEANWHILE, in the years after the Civil War Prescott's influence, growing steadily, reached a peak in the last two or three decades of the century. His histories spawned novels, among them General Lew Wallace's brilliant but diffuse re-creation of the Aztec civilization, *The Fair God* (1873). During the same twenty or thirty years with, respectively, technical skill and moral enthusiasm Bret Harte and Helen Hunt Jackson contributed their stories of California. In the eighties (and earlier) Cervantes found a spiritual descendant in the frontiersman Mark Twain, and William Dean Howells introduced to his countrymen Juan Valera, Palacio Valdés, Pérez Galdós, and other great Peninsular realists. These names will reappear in our later record of the novel, until about 1900. In this fiction the Spanish strain cannot be ignored: Mark Twain is not fully understood without Cervantes, nor Howells apart from Galdós.

Two intense personal experiences breathed life into Wallace as he wrote *The Fair God*. During his service with the army in Mexico he had become deeply curious about the Aztec antiquities.[101] The other and equally causative experience was his intimacy in his father's library with Prescott's *The Conquest of Mexico*. We can comprehend better the influence of this historian upon the readers of his generation by reliving for a moment young Wallace's delight as he studied this book. He "devoured it, preface, text, notes, and appendix," and he virtually destroyed the first volume by his scribblings in English and Spanish.[102] With Prescott constantly in mind, Wallace mastered the language, extended his reading to Bernal Díaz and other authorities, and spent happy hours on Spanish volumes in the Library of Congress.[103] Throughout the composition of his long romance based on the coming of the conquistadores to the lovely plateau of Mexico, Prescott remained his inspiration:

As a history [Wallace exclaimed], how delightful it was! as a tale, how rich in attractive elements!—adventure, exploration, combat, heroisms, oppositions of fate and fortune, characters for sympathy, characters for detestation, civilization and religion in mortal issue . . . I would write, and the Conquest of Mexico should be my theme.[104]

The success of *The Fair God* was not immediate, but readers turned back to it expectantly after the phenomenal fame of *Ben Hur* (1880).[105] Reminiscent of Scott and of Bulwer-Lytton, the endless combats, love episodes, prophecies, and mythologies pall long before the last of the 586 pages in the seven long books. Nevertheless, *The Fair God* remains an enchanting version in fiction of the coming of Cortés and the fall of the House of Montezuma. After the usual transparent device, a translation from the Spanish of a mysterious "Don Fernando de Alva, a Tezcucan," [106] the story begins with the appearance of Hualpa and the rise of Guatamozin. It ends with the horrors of "La Noche Triste." The narrative itself, in spite of its swollen dialogue and its archaic language, does well enough for an evening by the fire. The charm of the book resides in Wallace's perception of the poetic elements in the story: the gorgeous court by the fragrant lake; the subterranean caverns of the hieratic priests; the glamor of a civilization which, to repeat Wallace's hyperbole, "might have instructed Europe." [107]

LEW WALLACE was, after all, a child of Prescott; his exposure during his military service to Aztec and Cortesian history was tangential. Knowledge of another aspect of the Spanish past was more precise in Francis Bret Harte, who dignified in fiction the traditions of California. Harte's imitation of the methods of Irving in re-creating the Spanish legends of this region, as Irving had arrested the Dutch memories of the Hudson, haunts the reader. He became "the Washington Irving of the Pacific Coast." [108] This discipleship to Irving (or in other ways to Charles Dickens) did not impair Harte's firsthand observation of the far western frontier. Out of its conglomerate of gamblers, miners, Indians, Chinamen, Spaniards, Mexicans, and "greasers" he fashioned his bizarre, sharply drawn personalities. He valued particularly one stripe in the colors of this disappearing frontier civilization—namely the Spanish.

Bret Harte studied for himself the residual phases of this migration from Mexico. Though he came to them late, he mastered their texture. When he reached the West in 1853 he probably already knew something of the Spanish language, and it is certain that by this year he was a reader of Cervantes. One of his most delightful tales, "A Knight-Errant of the Foothills," is alive with echoes of *Don Quixote*.[109] Harte's knowledge of Cervantes was natural; from boyhood he had been incurably bookish. In his fiction he conventionalized Spanish characters, but artful writing did not conceal his understanding of these men and women as individuals. Even after 1821, the year of Mexican independence, Spanish families continued to live in California while the infiltrating Mexicans enriched further the cultural design.[110] All in all, for the keen ears and keener eyes of this talented literary prospector, there was still much to hear and see. The record of what he saw and heard, as well as of his reading, may be found in his tales and sketches of Spanish California.

In these move his priests, working patiently for the triumph of the true Church. Here his dark-eyed young women fall in love, wearing their mantillas and flowers in their black tresses. Here his courtly government officials preside with their formal, military customs.[111] One part of Harte's achievement as a precursor of the regionalists was this portraiture. He shows the padre, making gentle but persistent war on the Devil; the *señorita* in her satin slippers; or an "Enriquez Saltello" with his strange Spanish-Californian dialect.[112] Harte polished these characters with an art known only to the creator of Colonel Starbottle or Oakhurst.[113] They are "literary" Spaniards, designed to give the American reader exactly what he expected: Spanish "honor"; Spanish generosity and pride; the fandango; the *vaquero;* the hacienda; the mission church; the presidio; the pueblo; the serenade; the fiesta. Even if Harte's effects are calculated, his tales have a kind of authenticity. He loved his Spanish subjects and wrote of them until the end of his life. After him came other literary explorations of America's foreign past, of French and Spanish Louisiana by George Washington Cable and Kate Chopin [114] and, in our time, of Californian backgrounds by John Steinbeck. Sands, Bird, and Simms seem experimental in comparison with Harte. He was the first distinguished interpreter in fiction of Spanish traditions in America.

IF SPANISH tradition was basic in Bret Harte's writing, if under his skillful hand it became pictorial, decorative, nevertheless he probed no depths. He analyzed none of the problems raised by the conflict of three such diverse peoples as the Spaniard, the Indian, and the dispossessing American. It was the destiny of another author to record this unhappy warfare—in a single novel. *Ramona* by Helen Hunt Jackson aroused the emotions of thousands of readers indifferent to Harte's subtler techniques of writing. Such accidents occur; we think of Harriet Beecher Stowe. Appropriately enough, the preface of the translation of *Ramona* for Cubans christens it "la Cabaña del Tío Tom de los indios," [115] and the popularity of this sentimental study of old California parallels the success of Mrs. Stowe's famous novel. Almost at once *Ramona* became a bourgeois classic. It passed into the speech, the literary criticism, and the travel lore of the West. It was translated into foreign languages. It has appeared on the stage and on the screen, and by 1903 more than a half-million copies of the book had been sold.[116] In its pages lived again the sleepy yet savage California of the era of the missions. No scholarly investigation, skeptical of its accuracy, could efface the impression left upon the popular mind by its ranchos and Franciscan priests.

Angered by the sufferings of the Indians, Mrs. Jackson had defined their wrongs specifically in her earlier volume, *A Century of Dishonor* (1881).[117] Later she listened at the Coronel Rancho in the Los Angeles Valley to Don Antonio and to Doña Mariana, with her "soft, Spanish-voiced broken English," as they poured out to her their memories of the past.[118] She now found prototypes for several of her characters (Señora Moreno, Alessandro, and Felipe), and perhaps at this time she first thought of her Spanish-Indian heroine, the beloved Ramona.[119] Moral in purpose, journalistic in method, but sensitive to the somnolent life of the homestead or to the beautiful "Invocation to the Virgin," [120] she composed this painting of the transition, of the old civilization of Spain yielding reluctantly to "the hated Americans." [121] Despite its rhetoric and melodrama, the story had warmth; it reminded a writer in the *Atlantic Monthly* of "a Murillo in literature." [122] Nevertheless, as a re-creation of Spanish California *Ramona* seems far from reality. No evidence exists either in her life or in her writings, save a sketch or two,[123] that Mrs. Jackson had any interest whatever for its own sake in the Spanish civilization in America. She had not bothered to learn Spanish, and she was never conscious, like Bret Harte, of what this Spanish past might mean to the American novel. A fortuitous triumph, and hardly more than a sentimentalized social document, *Ramona* became the layman's poetic version of ancient California.

The problem which so disquieted Mrs. Jackson belongs to the past. The heated arguments about the originals of the characters have cooled.[124] The bitter denunciations in California of the book as "a tissue of falsehoods" [125] are forgotten. What remains? As literature *Ramona* is an inferior romance. A few powerful episodes, such as the quarrel between Ramona and the Señora Moreno, the heroine's flight with Alessandro, or the scenes with Father Gaspara, may possibly escape oblivion. More memorable are the glimpses of the idealistic Franciscans, incarnate in Father Salvierderra, or of the backgrounds of sheep shearing, canyon, and Indian village.

In these explicit ways the book opened our eyes still wider to the richness of Spanish tradition in the West. *Ramona* may well offend a modern taste; it is diffuse, lush. Yet so passionately absorbed was the creator in her creation that the book is full of sincere feeling, and in scope, in contrast to the hard cameos of Bret Harte, it is like an elaborate mural of old California. In reading it we share not only the world of the transition but also the dreams of Father Junípero Serra for his heavenly kingdom on earth.

MEANWHILE, an infinitely greater writer, Mark Twain, indifferent in his fiction to frontier padres or señoritas, types so attractive to both Bret Harte and Mrs. Jackson, was creating his picaresque masterpieces. These were in debt far more than we have realized to at least one of the enduring Spanish classics. How deeply he was moved by his short stay in southern Spain in 1867 is uncertain, but a clue to his delight in the country is offered in his assertion that it was still, so he had discovered for himself, the land of Don Quixote and Sancho Panza.[126] This direction in his reading in his thirty-third year (*The Innocents Abroad,* 1869) is confirmed by his later allusions to Cervantes in *Life on the Mississippi* (1883), in *Huckleberry Finn* (1885), and in many another book, letter, and conversation.[127]

Mark Twain's robust habits in reading, about which we now know so much more than in his own lifetime,[128] included this loyalty to Cervantes. His saturation from his earliest boyhood in *Don Quixote* has induced one scholar to define it as, next to the Bible, the most causative influence in Mark Twain's literary life.[129] Our humorist, our satirist, our amateur philosopher, our humanitarian, our dreamer never ceased to browse in the writer who now seems in some ways to have been his kinsman in the sixteenth century. This lasting debt to Cervantes, surprising, perhaps, in a frontiersman, together with the enthusiasm for Spanish literature of the midwesterner Howells, forms an interesting complement, in our second group of writers of fiction, to the work of Bret Harte and Mrs. Jackson.

Our difficulties in assessing precise literary impacts on Mark

Twain's writings arise primarily from the *un*literary character of his mind.[130] He was, to adapt Emerson, Man *writing*. From boyhood to old age he remained absorbed in the life about him: the West, travel in Europe, the post-Civil War America. Even after the East and Europe had iced the cake, had introduced him to new worlds in music, painting, sculpture, architecture, and literature, he continued to find his bread in the broad, plenteous human writers, in Plutarch, in Shakespeare, or in Browning. These strong, human geniuses became part of him, and among them was his adored Cervantes. These immortals reappear in his writings less in repercussions of particular passages than in points of view, in attitudes of mind, in conceptions of life. Some episodes in *Huckleberry Finn,* our most successful picaresque novel (perhaps influenced also by *Lazarillo de Tormes* and *Guzmán de Alfarache*),[131] are reminiscent of particular chapters in *Don Quixote.* The debt, however, is more vigorously evident in resemblances in ways of thought in the idealistic Tom Sawyer and in the Knight of La Mancha. In the same fashion *A Connecticut Yankee at King Arthur's Court* (1889) [132] veils thinly Mark Twain's awareness of the eternal conflict between realist and romantic. Indeed, this might well affect him; within his own breast this identical battle was daily joined.

In *Huckleberry Finn,* as in the related books (*Tom Sawyer,* 1876, and *Tom Sawyer Abroad,* 1894), the antithesis is sharp between the imaginative Tom, the romance-loving knight of the Mississippi plain, and the hardheaded Huck, a buckram, American Sancho Panza. Outside the magic raft the darkness menaces; on the shores of the river lurks evil. Tom Sawyer confronts these perils with his books and his dreams; earthy Huck Finn faces them with dogged common sense. No doubt this American saga could have been written—so ageless is the warfare portrayed—without its author's intimacy with *Don Quixote.* Nevertheless, the tragic and humorous realities are so vividly suggestive of Cervantes that, remembering again Mark Twain in the act of reading, self-consuming and self-identifying, we can hardly challenge the essential obligation. In addition, besides the resemblance in spirit of the two books, other parallels haunt the memory. Scholars have pointed out the kinship between the long arguments of Tom and Huck and those of Don Quixote and Sancho, and the resemblance of the "A-rabs" who turned out to be picnickers to the ingenious Knight's army which proved to be sheep.[133] Or, turning again to the *Connecticut Yankee,* we note the exploitation of the "armor." George Santayana compared the unselfish missions of Tom Sawyer to those of Don Quixote.[134] Indeed, says a recent investigator of the problem, Mark Twain was "a sort of adolescent Cervantes." [135]

IN OUR evaluation of Spanish influences on the American novel in the late nineteenth century, we must stress the leadership of William Dean Howells. His dedication to Spain is fully described elsewhere in this book. In his endless conversations on literature with Mark Twain, did the two friends discuss Cervantes? It seems certain. For both, the source of their Spanish interests was never the southwestern frontier or Spanish America, of which Howells seems to have had a kind of horror, but the established literature of Spain. If Spain meant to Mark Twain, as we have seen, the large, free genius of Cervantes, a mirror of life reflecting its illusions, tragedy, and laughter, to Howells it signified the spaciousness of Cervantes and, later, direct inspiration from *Don Quixote* for loosely knit stories of everyday life. Discovering him at the age of ten, planning a biography of him at fifteen, and renewing his vows to him in Madrid at the age of seventy-four, Howells knew Cervantes intimately—and perhaps more comprehensively than his crony Mark Twain. From Cervantes it was easy to pass to *Lazarillo de Tormes* and to American writers who had already paid their tributes to *Don Quixote.* So Howells reinforced his youthful interest in Spain through the pages of Irving and Longfellow.

In Howells' busy life his passion for Spanish literature was intermittent; the Italians, the Germans, and the Russians shared at various times the admiration of this theorist of the novel. Nevertheless, his early experience of Cervantes was formative. He studied him historically and examined his relation to the *novella.* He sought out in reference to Cervantes the reasons for this beautiful new light in Spanish fiction, in Valdés, Valera, Emilia Pardo Bazán,

Pereda, Alarcón, and, after a time, in Blasco Ibáñez.[136] Most of these, like Cervantes, like Howells himself, scorned "efectismo." [137] So for thirty years he championed them,[138] letting them confirm him in his carefully wrought philosophy of the novel without, presumably, inspiring directly particular creations of his own.

For example, the scenes on the northern coast of Asturia in Valdés' *Marta y María* might be the originals of settings for similar communities in New England.[139] Such a link, however, is undemonstrable. With some knowledge of Spanish fiction, one may search the novels of Howells and discover fewer resemblances than differences. In the writings of the Spaniards are the religious or ethical skepticism, the moods of passion or of "mysticism," [140] the occasional extravagance of language, and the paganism, like that of Valera, so distasteful to Howells.[141] What we find is an approximation in points of view, each arrived at, it would seem, independently. In the important essay on Valdés in the *Atlantic Monthly* for April, 1900, the following words seem to describe not merely the Spaniard but also Howells: "He shows us," says Sylvester Baxter, "the things of every day and of common life as they are, but we are made to see them with his sense of proportion; and while we recognize them as the things we have always known, he endows them with unsuspected interest, and reveals their inherent character in a wealth of illustrative detail." [142]

Although close parallels are elusive, the influence of the Spanish novel upon Howells was penetrative. Realism was in the air, in Russia, Norway, Italy, France, and Spain. Spanish realism reassured him in his theory, and this theory, in turn, affected the writing of fiction in America as perhaps no other American's philosophy of fiction has ever affected it. Hence among the novelists discussed in the present chapter the nature of this Spanish influence is unusual. For the first time in America Spanish critical theory was not regarded as "foreign" by reason of race, religion, and a national point of view. Was not Emilia Pardo Bazán, if one thought about her a little, comparable to our own realists? In the criticism of the novel Howells seems to have been the true internationalist rather than Henry James, who shared Howells' interest in the French and Russians but paid slight attention to the great Spaniards.[143] With

Valdés Howells enjoyed a warm friendship, discussing with him in a long correspondence the common problems of Spanish and American fiction.[144] When in 1911 he finally visited Spain, to regard reverently the home of Cervantes and to talk with Valdés,[145] he might well have claimed that of all American novelists up to that hour he had been the most fully aware of the importance of Spain for the development of our fiction.

DURING the thirty years which have passed since his death in 1920, no novelist has appeared more conversant than Howells with the classics of Spanish literature. It may be added that since 1900 no writers of fiction have interpreted Spain in America in ways so varied as those devised by Lew Wallace, Bret Harte, and Helen Hunt Jackson. The torrent of narratives has flowed on; not volume but distinction has been missing. One might pause at the end of the century over the staccato war stories of Stephen Crane [146] with their fabricated Spanish and Cuban backgrounds, over F. Marion Crawford's gaudy romance, *In the Palace of the King* [147] (1900), or over Gertrude Atherton's *The Splendid Idle Forties* (1902),[148] shallow, diverting stories of the transition: "It is," says Pio Pico, "the gayest, the happiest, the most careless life in the world. But how long will it last? Curse the Americans! They are coming." [149]

Or we might choose at random from stories based on the worn-out themes of the fall of Granada, the discovery of America, Columbus, Pizarro, and the conquest of Peru or from ephemeral novels whose background was Spain or Spanish America.[150] The pioneering days of Sands, Bird, and Simms belonged to the past; their subjects were now common property. So sensitive a story of Mexico as Katherine Anne Porter's "María Concepción" [151] suggests a change, but emphasis on Spain or Spanish America has been lacking in the writings of our most eminent novelists. Preoccupation with our villages, cities, and the problems of our own civilization crowded out European subjects in Theodore Dreiser, Sinclair Lewis, or Sherwood Anderson. There have been dramatic exceptions, such as Ernest Hemingway and John Dos Passos (to be discussed in a moment), but in other leaders in fiction the influence seems a by-product, as in Stephen Vincent Benét's touching story of Sebastian Zafortezas and the Minorcans in Florida.[152]

On July 20, 1714, on the road between Lima and Cuzco the bridge of San Luis Rey collapsed, carrying five persons to death.[153] Peru is a background for this novel by Thornton Wilder, and the southern Californian country is a setting for John Steinbeck's stories of the *paisanos,* those picturesque peasants of "Spanish, Indian, Mexican and assorted Caucasian bloods." [154] The Peruvian civilization and Spanish California are, however, only incidental to Wilder's sensitive studies in character and to Steinbeck's perceptive writing concerning the dispossessed. In this introductory glance at twentieth-century fiction we think again of the powerful undercurrent of folklore and of its modern interpreters.[155] And we think even more often of Hemingway and Dos Passos and of Willa Cather, who published in 1927 her matchless chronicle of old New Mexico, *Death Comes for the Archbishop.*

Two brilliant novelists of our own time, John Roderigo Dos Passos (of Portuguese descent) [156] and Ernest Hemingway, have been stirred by the struggles of the liberal in the Peninsula. In different ways their novels register its class warfare; [157] in different ways for each of them Spain has been both an escape and a means of self-comprehension. The former's *Rosinante to the Road Again* [158] shows no exhaustive knowledge of Spain or Spanish culture any more than the latter's *The Sun Also Rises* with its bullfighters and fiestas reveals a subtle understanding of the lives of the common people. Nevertheless, Dos Passos' novels reflect a characteristic attitude of the thoughtful mind in America. They reveal its dual passion, for the past ages of Spain (Cervantes, El Greco, or Goya) and at the same time for the new Spain, Spain of the aroused peasant, Spain straining at the bonds of the oppressor.

The second interest (not the first) absorbed Hemingway and has given us his character studies in primitivism, human loneliness, and death. The postwar disillusionment of both these novelists intensified their sympathy for these unhappy workers, by-passed during European reforms of the nineteenth century. In Dos Passos this mood is even deeper. In his *Adventures of a Young Man* Glenn Spotswood's death in the Spanish Civil War symbolizes the martyrdom of the true liberal caught in the feuds of the extremists.[159] At various times both these writers lived in this backward Spain and talked with farmers, workmen, and anarchists. The sensitivity of Dos Passos to the problems of these people can hardly be unconnected with his stays among them. We recall, too, his Portuguese ancestry.[160] During the strife of 1936–39 Hemingway served as a war correspondent for the Republican army,[161] and for him, as for his hero, Robert Jordan, the attempted revolution was evidently an "education." Nevertheless, this dream of a free, democratic Spain was not new. We remember how in 1805 the patriots of Boston listened with cheers to Robert Treat Paine's ode on "Republican Spain."

THE bitter plight of the half-fed worker who must give what he wrests from the soil to some callous landlord is vigorously reported in *Rosinante to the Road Again,* especially in such a chapter as "Cordova No Longer of the Caliphs." [162] This thread is only one in the bright-colored skein of this clever book. With Telemachus (Dos Passos' name for himself) and Lyaeus, a kind of up-to-date Don Quixote and Sancho, we travel the country roads past wine shops and inns, over turbulent streams and through blue mountains, meeting on burro or on foot, as in a picaresque tale, the villagers of Spain. Nature and man are described with the tension and the hard, bright imagery inherent in this novelist's art. Pausing, we muse on the various contrasts in this nation of paradoxes. Dos Passos compares this modern Spain, just waking from its lethargy, with ancient Iberia and opposes the idyllic world of these peaceful towns to strident, far-off America. Once more we are invited to reflect on the slowness of change in virtually changeless Spain: "It was all so mellow, so strangely aloof from the modern world of feverish change, this life of the peasants of Almorox. Everywhere roots striking into the infinite past. For before the Revolution, before the Moors, before the dark, furtive traders, the Phœnicians, they were much the same, these Iberian village communities." [163]

Rosinante is at once a travel book, a poetic fantasy, a work of social criticism, and a proof of Dos Passos' delight in contemporary

238

Spanish literature. Simultaneously, through its exposition of Pío Baroja's ideas it is a confession of his faith in the worker. We may even think of it as Dos Passos' *Walden*. To these scenes he flees from the mechanistic civilization which, we know from his other writings, has long weighed so heavily upon his hopes for mankind. In *Rosinante to the Road Again*, as in his novels on America, we sense his imperious demand for justice. We meditate on his tribute (the old theme of Irving and Ticknor) to the nobility of the Spanish peasant, or we pause over the chapter called "Benavente's Madrid," a colorful focus of the contrasts already mentioned.

I think that we are most interested in what Dos Passos says of his fellow writers, of, for instance, Pío Baroja with his "intense sense of reality." [164] Or he denounces Blasco Ibáñez, who through his clattering typewriter has become in his later work just "one more popular novelist." [165] Blasco has been vulgarized for an America already oversupplied with authors of this kind. In a savage attack on the Spanish novel of the nineteenth century Dos Passos remarks: "Everything was good humour, taste, and gentility . . . Facetiousness and *genre* were the keynotes. The genial fatuity of the novels of Valdes and Juan Valera is almost incredible. A tremendous epic sense of events hardly saved Galdós from the same doldrums." [166] As a modern man Dos Passos prefers Pío Baroja, and he is in love with the poets, Antonio Machado of Castile and Juan Maragall of Catalonia. The verse of the former, with its beautiful feeling for the old Spanish towns, and that of the latter, with its love of the family, he translates with a spirit worthy of this fictionized yet truthful book on Spain.[167]

HEMINGWAY's dedication to Spanish liberalisms is less reasoned, more fiercely partisan, and not devoid of naïveté. His interest in Spain must be identified with his obsession with violence, with the physical life of men and women, and with a kind of pseudo primitivism, emphasized by his participation in war and by the teachings of Gertrude Stein.[168] Nowhere in Europe was there a better laboratory for his study of the passions of lust, hatred, and cruelty than in certain depths of human experience in Spain. The national sport of Spain had long been denounced in America, but Hemingway discovered that torment, which has always allured him, attained a theatrical reality in the bullfight.[169] The *plaza de toros* became a stage both for enjoyment and for careful analysis.[170] Here in the bull ring was violent death to delight the heart. Here the lover of hunting, football, and boxing could contemplate as a man and as a writer this extraordinary form of courage and terror, this truly "complicated art." [171] Here in his ironic conversations with "the old lady" he could discourse on all manner of terror and cruelty. Here he could exult in the peculiar, savage joy of the hunter, in the anguish of the hunted, in the bitter, ecstatic death of animal and man.

In Hemingway's exultation resides a strange irony or contrast if we recall the tradition of the cruelty of the Spaniard, if we re-member the "black legend," so often mentioned in the present book. This sportsman-writer, this superb stylist, is now infatuated with the brutality which his countrymen have so long deplored. For such tastes, unaccompanied by excessive curiosity regarding Span-ish history, Spanish culture, or Spanish ways of living, the Civil War in 1936 was a godsend. Uninhibited, pitiless death stalked through the land, and out of its horror came (a little later) Picasso's *Guernica* and Hemingway's most harrowing novel. From his study of primitive passions, from his sharing in the war, Hemingway evolved his story of killing and suffering, *For Whom the Bell Tolls* (1940).[172] Animal strength, triumphant lust, twitching death, ruth-less fate—all these forces dominate this story of the Spanish patriots. The *guardias civiles* turn their victims' faces to the wall. Then Pablo, placing his pistol at the base of the brain of each one, exe-cutes them all. In the plaza occurs the orgy of murder nearly un-bearable to the reader.[173]

The liberalism, always vague, of the young American school-teacher "Roberto," who gives his life for the Republican cause seems blurred in the physical excess of living and dying. Perhaps this earthy, sensuous conception of the Spaniard balances the senti-mentalizations which we have so often encountered, or perhaps it is a portrait of Ernest Hemingway rather than of Spain. Through all the novel's strain, with its denial of the life of the spirit save in

the primal virtues of courage and tenderness, runs a pervasive softness. Is not this essentially a romantic view of violence and death?
Life is "nada," and for the "dirty trick" of death Spain supplies illustrations, unforgettable not merely in themselves but in Hemingway's masterly manipulation of the Spanish language. He pours
this as from a living mold into English, in a kind of breathing, vital,
rough translation. The dialogue of *For Whom the Bell Tolls* is a
major instrument in making us sense intimately the relentless
forces which destroy Robert Jordan. Here is the rendering of primitive emotion through the strong language of the primitive people
who speak it and feel it. Here Spanish speech is transformed as
never before into its English equivalent. No use of Spanish discussed elsewhere in the present book can parallel it.[174]

AWARENESS of this language and of Spain was more psychologi-
cally penetrative (even if not always intelligible to the irritated
layman) in Hemingway's mentor, Gertrude Stein, novelist, poet,
critic, and playwright. The fancy that her books were really connected with "automatic writing" is outmoded.[175] More reasonably,
we may begin with her sensitivity to the pioneering thought of William James while she was his most brilliant student at Radcliffe
College.[176] From this time on she developed both the theory and
the practice of "the ideal function of language." [177] She created her
own version, at once original and powerful, of "the stream of consciousness," [178] her own "continuous-present" techniques in which
her characters have their existence in relation to "time." [179] All
that she has to say on "time," reality, seeing and not seeing, or, for
that matter, on grammar, nouns, verbs, connectives, prepositions,
"emotional sentences," repetitions, and all the structural elements
in language (which also deeply interested James) is provocative.
Yet her fearless, exploratory, and often delightfully humorous use
of them in her writings, is even more challenging.

Gertrude Stein adhered to and developed her principles in suc-
ceeding works, whether in *Three Lives* (in debt to Flaubert), in
Tender Buttons, or in *Four Saints in Three Acts.* She called
Tender Buttons "a conscious struggle with the problem of correlat-

ing sight, sound and sense." [180] At about the time of the composition of these bare little riddles (so they seem to the profane), such as
"Red Roses," "A Red Stamp," or "Nothing Elegant," she wrote:
"I began to wonder . . . just what one saw when one looked at
anything really looked at anything." [181]

Miss Stein's rejection of the stereotyped past and future for her
continuous present, her reporting of one instant even as it melted
into the next, her levels of symbolism, her record of this inner
experience of the mind first baffles, then stimulates, and finally
rewards the persistent student. The problem is oversimplified but
illumined for the unconsecrated reader by Sherwood Anderson's
homespun summary:

Miss Stein is a worker in words with the same loving touch in her strong
fingers that was characteristic of the women of the kitchens of the brick
houses in the town of my boyhood. She is an American woman of the
old sort, one who cares for the handmade goodies and who scorns the
factory-made foods, and in her own great kitchen she is making something with her materials, something sweet to the tongue and fragrant
to the nostrils . . .

She is laying word against word, relating sound to sound, feeling for
the taste, the smell, the rhythm of the individual word.[182]

Gertrude Stein's stays in Spain,[183] her friendships with Spaniards,
her strong interest, especially from about 1913 to about 1922, in
Spanish landscapes,[184] in Spanish arts, and in Spanish words can
lead us into nebulous assertions about this emphasis in her writing.
But Spain was confirmative of her unique point of view. It was
also during this period enriching and germinal. All the conventional evidences of Spanish influence which have so often engaged
us in other authors—particular works of literature, history, legend
—are virtually nonexistent. We are thrown back on speculation
concerning Miss Stein's sharing, so to speak, the Spanish mind.
That there was such a relationship is demonstrable not only in her
living into the country, in her intellectual affinity with Pablo
Picasso,[185] Juan Gris, and other Spaniards, but also in what she
says of the Spanish scenery and of the Spanish outlook on life.

On scenery we may cite a brief but revealing passage in her study
of Picasso:

Gertrude Stein, from the painting by Pablo Picasso.

The sadness of Spain and the monotony of the Spanish coloring, after the time spent in Paris, struck him forcibly upon his return there. Because one must never forget that Spain is not like other southern countries, it is not colorful, all the colors in Spain are white black silver or gold, there is no red or green, not at all. Spain in this sense is not at all southern, it is oriental, women there wear black more often than colors, the earth is dry and gold in color, the sky is blue almost black, the star-light nights are black too or a very dark blue and the air is very light, so that every one and everything is black.[186]

About the Spanish mind she makes a statement whose paradoxes may arouse some doubts in the reader. She says "that americans can understand spaniards. That they are the only two western nations that can realise abstraction. That in americans it expresses itself by disembodiedness, in literature and machinery, in Spain by ritual so abstract that it does not connect itself with any thing but ritual." [187]

Picasso is the focal point of influence: James, Whitehead, Bergson, Picasso. We see them together, Gertrude Stein and Pablo Picasso, at 27 rue de Fleurus, bending over pictures of the American Civil War. Suddenly Picasso recalled the Spanish-American conflict, and he "became very Spanish and very bitter and Spain and America in their persons could say very bitter things about each other's country." [188] This constant intimacy with twentieth-century Spanish painting, this endless talk with Picasso and Juan Gris of color, of composition, of the true inwardness of painting, could hardly help confirming Miss Stein in her own convictions concerning the continuous present. "The things," she says, "that Picasso could see were the things which had their own reality, reality not of things seen but of things that exist." [189] For Picasso declared that "there is no past or future in art. If a work cannot live always in the present it must not be considered . . . as art." [190] In this way the Spanish painter became part of *The Making of Americans* and of other writings by his friend.

There are some palpable refractions, too, in Miss Stein's work, of Spanish painting, of Spanish dances, of bullfights. One might cite the echoes of the dance in "Susie Asado" or in "Preciosilla." Or we may turn to the *Four Saints*, written in Paris but recapturing Spanish memories.[191] We must not, however, look too much for surfaces. In the end what matters is the psychological root which Gertrude Stein sank down into the Spanish mind. "In Spain," says the *Autobiography,* "Gertrude Stein began to write the things that led to Tender Buttons." [192] This is the real quest, this search for the psychological or philosophical union of Gertrude Stein with Spain. It is a search likely to defeat all of us if we attempt to define too sharply its precise meaning. Possibly only her teacher, William James, could have explained the value of Spain in the complete fulfillment of her complex aims.

WE MAY conclude our story of the influence of Spain upon the American novel with a far different illustration. Besides the Spain of Gertrude Stein other Spanish areas have invited the creation of fiction, among them the beneficent domain of the Catholic church in our own Southwest. Aspects of this story had already enthralled writers as diverse as Bret Harte and Helen Hunt Jackson. Now, continuing as a priceless essence in our American cultural heritage, it reached a new height of understanding in Willa Cather. In the year after Hemingway's vignettes of northern Spain and in the year in which he issued a group of typical stories on typical themes, *Men without Women,* Miss Cather, after stays in New Mexico and after prolonged meditation, gave us this particular fragment of what she called "the incommunicable past," *Death Comes for the Archbishop.*[193] It is one of her most poignant novels, and it has been acclaimed as her masterpiece. Surely none surpasses it in its sensitivity to this fabled age of priest and mission. *Death Comes for the Archbishop* is likely to remain in our fiction the most enduring interpretation of the Church in the nineteenth-century Southwest. For in contrast to the propagandist *Ramona,* its primary trait is its fidelity to certain spiritual values in the past of Spain in America.

Indeed, like her imaginative intimacies in the other novels with Ántonia Shimerda, Thea Kronborg, or Marian Forrester, Willa Cather's projection of herself into the pioneering Bishop Jean Latour and Father Joseph Vaillant accomplished two purposes. We see through their eyes the surviving Spanish and Indian civiliza-

244

tions, and we live not only with these priests but into their personal experiences. Miss Cather had long been in love with New Mexico. In childhood she had been fascinated by the magical tale of Coronado, and she had used this with exquisite art in *My Ántonia* (1918), to introduce the figure of the gigantic plough against the molten red of the setting sun. In *The Professor's House* (1925) her hero, Godfrey St. Peter, had toiled for fifteen years upon a work entitled *Spanish Adventurers in North America*.[194] The inner core of this novel had been Tom Outland's chronicle of his boyhood in the Southwest. The region moved her deeply, as if it had a personality: "During the twelve years," she says, "that followed my first year in New Mexico and Arizona I went back as often as I could, and the story of the Church and the Spanish missionaries was always what interested me; but I hadn't the most remote idea of trying to write about it." [195]

She was in search of pastures new. Her own Nebraska frontier had attained a fulfillment in her earliest books,[196] and now the Southwest, touched on in these other novels, seemed at first a backdrop strangely different from the bleak plains of the Middle West. Yet into her imagination entered even more deeply than had the prairies the beauty of the dome-shaped mesa, of the red sands, of the towering clouds, of the mysterious canyons. She studied documents,[197] but she relied chiefly on her belief in the novel *démeublée*.[198] That is, she created backgrounds in outline, essentially true but poetic. She described "without accent" [199] how the French priests, the patrician Bishop Latour and the warmhearted, practical Father Vaillant, went out in 1851 to found the diocese of New Mexico. The blue sky, the sun-baked soil, the adobe houses of Santa Fe, and the Spanish words which she used so artfully are real, but equally so are the legacies of Spaniard and Indian: turquoise, silver, wood carving.[200] Her own description of her method is suggestive: "While many of the episodes in this narrative actually occurred, and others are matters of popular tradition, I have used them as a rug-maker uses color rather than as a chronicler marshals events." [201]

So at Angelus we hear the clear tones of the bell of Moorish silver. With the priests we see the light of evening:

The sun had set now, the yellow rocks were turning grey, down in the pueblo the light of the cook fires made red patches of the glassless windows, and the smell of piñon smoke came softly through the still air. The whole western sky was the colour of golden ashes, with here and there a flush of red on the lip of a little cloud. High above the horizon the evening-star flickered like a lamp just lit, and close beside it was another star of constant light, much smaller.[202]

Landscape and details of the arts, all coalesced in the soft luster of her writing, are less important than Miss Cather's integration of her style with the minds of these heroic European priests. Their spiritual grace became part of her prose until, as was her desire, her language was lost in her "people," as she called them. All our many experiments in fiction with Spanish-American themes reach a culmination in this masterpiece, so deserving of recognition in Spain itself.

IF, AFTER this survey of the fiction, we now return to the beginning of the nineteenth century to examine the interpretation of Spain in our poetry, we shall encounter during the 150 years a similar contrast between triviality and distinction. In the novel we find Robert Montgomery Bird and Willa Cather; in poetry there are Mrs. Anna Mowatt Ritchie, creator of the six dreary cantos of *Pelayo: or, the Cavern of Covadonga*,[203] and Archibald MacLeish, modern poet of Cortés and the Conquest. As a matter of fact, much of the weak early poetry was written by the authors of the weak fiction. Bird, Simms, and Sands, whose prose concerning Spanish legends and Spanish history we have already considered, bequeathed us, respectively, *Oralloossa* (1832),[204] a blank-verse tragedy dealing with the Peruvians, *The Vision of Cortes* (1829),[205] and "The Dream of Papantzin" (1828).[206] This last poem, according to a memoir in Sands' collected works, represents "the fruits of his researches into Mexican history, and is remarkable for the religious solemnity of the thoughts, the magnificence of the imagery, and the flow of versification." [207] Equivalent eulogies are at hand for Mrs. Ellet's adaptations of Iriarte [208] or for Edward Maturin's ballads,[209] but in vain. The modern reader cannot admire this poetry. Nor can he be too sorrowful that Charles Brockden Brown never completed his projects of three historical poems: on the discovery of America, on Cortés, and on Pizarro.[210] The compelling fact is this simultaneous expression on Spanish subjects in both poetry and fiction.

Spain was interpreted in different ways through the two eminent poets of the day, Bryant and Longfellow. Bryant, whose story will be related in detail in Part III, is conspicuous in any general view of the Spanish-American intellectual scene. He became a traveler in Cuba, Mexico, and Spain. He had connections with these regions as a contributor to magazines, as a romancer, as a translator, and as a poet. He was, moreover, a thoughtful liberal concerning the rights of the oppressed in Spain and a supporter of the struggles for freedom taking form throughout Spanish America. It is this social and political imagination, evident for many years during his editorship of the New York *Evening Post,* which renders Bryant so unusual as an interpreter of Spain in poetry. For he was barely fifteen years old when he published, as an appendix to the second edition of his precocious satire, *The Embargo,* "The Spanish Revolution" (1809), a verse apostrophe to the patriots who had defied Napoleon.[211] In 1822 he wrote "Spain"; in 1826 "The Damsel of Peru" and "The Lament of Romero"; in 1867 "A Brighter Day"; and nine years later "Christmas in 1875." He devoted all these lyrics, besides others, to the liberties of Spanish peoples. Bryant's enthusiasm for these causes persisted; he continued to use his poetic talents to champion Spanish freedom.

In addition, his learning and literary taste enabled him to translate or adapt poem after poem on personal and on religious themes. We should turn more often to his graceful verses from Luis de León, Bartolomé Leonardo de Argensola, or Francisco de Rioja (or Caro). Most interesting of all, we observe his study of Cuban poetry. His special debt to José María Heredia will be discussed in the later chapter, but the immediate fact is his exploration of Spanish-American verse. For he was the first major American poet to recognize the achievements of his Mexican brothers: he adapted the *Fables* of José Rosas Moreno. At last in our literary history a poet of Mexico received in the United States the most substantial of recognitions, namely, adequate translation into the English

247

language. Although he lacked Longfellow's erudition and although he was attracted to Cuban and Mexican literature, Bryant sat at the feet of the Spanish masters. To aid the Spaniards in New York in celebrating the three hundredth birthday of the greatest of these he contributed his memorial stanzas, "Cervantes." [212]

No HUMANITARIAN zeal for the downtrodden Spaniard ruffles the tranquillity of Longfellow's ballads (not without their debts to Bowring and Lockhart),[213] the scholarship of his translation of the *Coplas*, or the sentiment of his *Spanish Student*.[214] It has been said that the poet's eight months in Spain stirred him more deeply than all his sojourns in France, Germany, and Scandinavia. Possibly so. Of his European experience these days in the Peninsula were certainly the most richly laden with poetic suggestion. They helped particularly his communication of the romantic past of Europe to the less intellectual of his countrymen. Everyone knows of Longfellow's submission to this beautiful lie. Everyone has heard of his imaginative flight, from American themes to the magic Europe he portrays in *Outre-Mer*, in "Nüremberg," and in other lyrics. In the poet's iridescent bubbles gleam Spanish tints. Side by side with the kindly burgomaster, the flaxen-haired maiden, the French troubadour move the Don, the toreador, the Andalusian gypsy.

Apart from the vogue of his poetry, of which Longfellow was shrewdly aware, he loved to let his imagination, so volatile in such externals but so incapable of attaining subtler meanings, play over the details of a world which never really existed. In his stanzas roam Spanish characters; in the cadences of his verse sound the bells of San Blas [215] (not unlike Bret Harte's bells of Monterey). The romantic concept of Spain becomes everywhere in Longfellow's poetry a premise masquerading as truth. Though not without opportunities to do so, he would never return to the Peninsula lest somehow he tarnish his first dream-impression, formed when he had browsed in the libraries or danced in the streets.[216] In caption and content his poem, "Castles in Spain," exemplifies a particular mood; it springs from his youthful experience. With little thought for South America, not at all anxious about the poor Peruvian, he embraced this inviolate illusion and transmitted to Americans what he himself felt, sincerely enough, about romantic Spain.[217]

As Longfellow's poetry sentimentalized the Indian and the village blacksmith, so it also sentimentalized everything Spanish. Besides the poems containing Spanish scenes and characters, besides translations in verse in the *New-England Magazine*,[218] he tried to popularize the medieval ballads of Spain.[219] In a gigantic anthology, *The Poets and Poetry of Europe*, he contributed translations or adaptations of Spanish poetry.[220] Finally, he created *The Spanish Student*, a mediocre drama but an engaging story of a youth in love with a gypsy. Despite the erudition involved in its several sources, this poetic play lacked body. Though thousands of readers would have agreed with Ticknor that it was "beautiful," [221] it merely showed us for the thousandth time the land of castanet and fiesta. It told once more the old stories and sang the old songs. Nevertheless, in any estimate of Longfellow *The Spanish Student* is important; it remained for literally millions of readers one of the most acceptable poems of this singer for the people. In prose Irving and his *Alhambra*, in poetry Longfellow and his lyrics of Spain!

All this is truth, but half-truth only. We have long since learned that behind the facile Longfellow of the domestic lyrics and the verse tales of New England dwelt the composer of the sonnets and the translator of Dante. Behind the misty dream of Spain, which he half believed, half exploited, flourished Longfellow's learning in Romance literatures and, indeed, in most European literatures. The author of these pretty songs of Spain was one of our first great scholars in Romance languages and one of the most learned men of his time. He had once contemplated writing a literary history of the Middle Ages.[222] Longfellow had extracted some of the ballads from Hernando del Castillo's *Cancionero general de muchos y diuersos autores* (1511). Few of his American contemporaries knew of the originals, and fewer still could have translated them.

Longfellow's scholarship is also visible in the translations embodied in his articles for the *North American Review*, such as "Spanish Devotional and Moral Poetry." [223] In particular, his first published work of verse, and thus virtually his first book, was his

capable rendering of the *Coplas* of Jorge Manrique, the fifteenth-
century warrior and poet. Among the various translations of the
Coplas his version is still esteemed. It was, as Washington Allston
declared, "so like an original!" [224] Longfellow's earliest poetry was
an adaptation not of the French or of the German but of the Spanish, and it was poetry born of his Spanish scholarship. Herein lies
the other facet of his interpretation of Spain through poetry. More
than any other American poet he spoke both to the everyday reader
and to the scholar.

BRYANT died in 1878, Longfellow four years later; in neither of
these poets did the zest for Spanish subjects ever really abate. Unlike the influence in the fiction, which seems to stop sharply between Simms and Bret Harte, that affecting the poetry was more
sustained until the close of the century, chiefly through these
pattern-shaping authors, Bryant and Longfellow, and also through
Lowell, who died in 1891. Although Spain or Spanish America left
imprints upon the writings of Lew Wallace, Mark Twain, or
Howells, the prose could never boast, like the verse, of three men
of letters for whom Spanish subjects were hardly less than an obsession: Bryant, Longfellow, and Lowell. For these three Spanish
literature was a primary interest. During the same period, from
Longfellow's translation of the *Coplas* in 1833 until 1900, the preoccupation with Spanish materials of minor versifiers, as well as
the incidental enthusiasms of a few major poets, demands a casual
word or two. After the briefest possible summary of these we may
return to a more significant poetic allegiance to Spain in the verse
of Lowell.

It is impossible to tabulate here the obscure nineteenth-century
poets interested in Spain. All these seem to form a cult reflecting
dimly the more substantial enthusiasms which we have been studying in traveler, historian, and scholar. They employ a kind of Spanish vocabulary: Spanish names; Spanish titles; Spanish characters;
Spanish words. These influences may be found in Rose Terry
Cooke's insipid stanzas, "Segovia," or Washington Allston's "The
Spanish Maid" or Joaquin Miller's pretentious "Songs of the

Mexican Seas." [225] The few—too few—poems by John Hay cut through the conventions in "Amor Mysticus," a translation from Sor Marcela De Carpio,[226] but the many—far too many—poems by Thomas Bailey Aldrich, like his sixteen-stanza "Pepita" or his "Palabras Cariñosas," are stereotyped.[227] This minor verse reveals nothing except the Spanish fashion of the day. On the other hand, occasional poems from writers of more power follow the fashion in order to express their own special meanings. Pertinent illustrations are Emerson's "Alphonso of Castile," [228] Poe's "Coliseum" (from Quevedo) and "El Dorado," [229] or Bret Harte's "The Miracle of Padre Junipero." These adaptations of Spanish materials to American ideas become, however isolated or trivial, a necessary part of our story.

The most amusing of these poetic vagabonds in Spanish territory was the unpredictable Walt Whitman. He could read Spanish; [230] he could discourse on Cervantes; [231] and he owned a copy of Ticknor's *History of Spanish Literature*. Fond of the euphony of words, he may have liked the language for the odd reason given by Slidell Mackenzie, that it was "full of vowels." Whitman was fond also of the Italian word, "romanza." [232] The frequency of Spanish phrases in his verse indicates what he heard as he walked the streets of his polyglot New York or during his visit to New Orleans. So Spanish words enlivened his chants for America: "Libertad" or "Americano!" For his interest in the language was related, like Bryant's, to his dream of a vaster America and also to his somewhat ridiculous doctrines of a democratic imperialism and of a vague internationalism. He was the author of a letter called "The Spanish Element in Our Nationality," [233] and he generously included all Spanish-speaking peoples in his vision of the eventual spiritual union of mankind.[234]

MEANWHILE, in more civilized ways, James Russell Lowell carried on with Bryant and Longfellow the established precedent of a Spanish flavor in our American poetry. His allusions to Spain, unlike those in the verse of Aldrich, rise from the solid knowledge of Spanish culture which we now know to have been his. He had been excited by the story of Columbus and by Prescott's histories, and he, too, had once planned the composition of an epic poem on Mexico.[235] Certain phrases in "To the Dandelion" come naturally from the imagination which later was to deal so sympathetically with every phase of Spanish life:

> Gold such as thine ne'er drew the Spanish prow
> Through the primeval hush of Indian seas.[236]

Again, in his estimate of Irving in *A Fable for Critics* (1848) the humor of the essayist reminds him of Cervantes:

> You bring back the happiest spirit from Spain,
> And the gravest sweet humor, that ever were there
> Since Cervantes met death in his gentle despair.

But he ends the famous verse criticism of his contemporaries with an apology for placing even Irving beside "matchless Cervantes." [237]

Lowell belongs with Bryant and Longfellow, but the quantity of his verse inspired by Spain cannot match theirs. Apart from a few other allusions, the poems, such as "Columbus," [238] "The Nightingale in the Study," or "Death of Queen Mercedes," appear slight in substance in comparison with Bryant's translations and with Longfellow's memorable contributions in the *Coplas* and *The Spanish Student*. Unlike Longfellow, Lowell never tried consciously to popularize Spanish subjects, unless *The Biglow Papers* may be regarded as chips from *Don Quixote*. The Spaniards evidently associated this work with Cervantes and humorously named the popular ambassador to Madrid "José Bighlow." [239] There is not much to build on, but one poem, "The Nightingale in the Study," a lasting testimonial of Lowell's love of Calderón, is worth all the more popular interpretations from Bryant and Longfellow. Within this charming lyric lie depths of perception into the seventeenth-century dramatist and also the most ardent devotion ever accorded Calderón by an American writer. What Calderón had meant to Lowell's spiritual life animates the poem. Perhaps in evaluating him as a poetic interpreter of Spain we read into his verse too easily his known associations with Spain: his critical essays; his entertaining letters and diplomatic dispatches; and the universal affection of the Spaniards. Actually his secure place in our category rests upon the few poems. These are enough.

WITH Lowell, this chronicle of the interpretation of Spain itself in our poetry properly ends. In reaching now the twentieth century, we think at once of George Santayana, poet, philosopher, and critic. Nevertheless, by the very fact of his birth in Madrid (in 1863) he hardly belongs to our congeries of influences, or perhaps even to Spain, where he spent only the first seven years of his life. World and other-world citizen, he has seldom spoken to us in his poetry of his native land. At the same time he has strengthened on the highest intellectual level our respect for Spain by a philosophic inquiry which is touched unmistakably by the irony and realism of his own people. His lofty agnosticism has never been inconsistent with Unamuno's Spanish man of flesh and bone, discussed elsewhere in this book,[240] "El hombre de carne y hueso."

Or if we turn from Santayana to such contemporary poets as Antonio Machado or Juan Maragall, to both of whom Dos Passos, in *Rosinante to the Road Again,* professes his devotion, or to García Lorca or to any other poets of the Peninsula, we find none, I think, who has affected deeply a twentieth-century major poet of the United States.[241] The scattered subjects and the trickle of allusion continue,[242] but we must regard as unusual Ezra Pound's knowledge of Lope de Vega [243] and also the Spanish echoes in his verse. The contribution of the Catholic poet, Thomas Walsh, who knew Spain well, is impressive in translation, anthology, and lyric poem and in its passion for the ideas of medieval Spain.[244] Nevertheless, the culture of Spain has exerted little pressure upon this twentieth-century poetry save in the "little magazines" or in some versifier electrified by the Spanish Civil War.[245]

For Spain is nearer, less mysterious than in the days of Ticknor and Lowell. In addition, most of our poets are concerned with our own back yard. John Dos Passos hints at still another cause for the decline in direct Spanish influence:

You cannot [he says] read any Spanish poet of to-day without thinking now and then of Rubén Darío, that prodigious Nicaraguan who collected into his verse all the tendencies of poetry in France and America and the Orient and poured them in a turgid cataract, full of mud and gold-dust, into the thought of the new generation in Spain.[246]

As a novelist Dos Passos himself wrote of Mexico and Guatemala. Today it is Hemingway who, in his interest in the Peninsula, is exceptional. And, like our novelists, our modern poets look less toward Spain than toward Spanish America.

The depth of this Spanish-American impact on our poetry is debatable. Once again the many allusions occur, and the many translations. On parallel pages we may read in the two languages (as in the Loeb classics) poems by Ramón López Velarde of Mexico, Eugenio Florit of Cuba, César Vallejo of Peru, or Jacinto Fombona Pachano of Venezuela,[247] and in the "little magazines" appear translations from Jorge Carrera Andrade or from young Mexican poets.[248] This activity suggests that our poets now shared in the rediscovery of Spanish America, of its color, its somnolence, its intensity.[249] While throngs in New York, San Francisco, or Detroit flocked to see the murals of Orozco or Rivera, some poets perceived the riches of Spanish-American subjects. We hear of Hart Crane living in Mexico City, and in 1929 Archibald MacLeish followed the route of Cortés from the coast and told once again the whole splendid story. In 1932 he published his *Conquistador,* derived from his own journey and from the narrative of Bernal Díaz.[250] Yet if these debts seem substantial, we must remember that to most of the major poets of our own time Spain and Spanish America still remained as unregarded as Afghanistan.[251]

Conquistador is a dazzling poem, full of color and light and breathing fresh life and tensions into the epical tale of Cortés. It is a stirring exotic, without much obligation to the civilization it depicts but with firm, harsh descriptions of the landscape:

> And we marched in the great plain under the sky-star:
> Close footing in steep sun: narrowly
> Laid we our feet along the wheeling light:

And the plain went up: rock-colored: barren:
Roses and wild plums over the waters:
Far south of us much snow: as in Arragon.[252]

To this none too extensive Spanish influence on our contemporary poetry, equivalent to hardly a single novel by Hemingway, we may add the Spanish tinge in verse written about our Southwest. We perceive in our more voluble, nationalistic poets, in fabulists like Vachel Lindsay or Stephen Benét, an awareness of this region, so rich in legend and history.

FICTION, poetry, and, finally, the stage; we approach the end of a long story. Irving loved the Spanish theater; Longfellow studied Lope de Vega; and Lowell visited Spain to see, so he professed, a *play* by Calderón. The borderline between these forms of the novel, the poem, and the drama is often tenuous,[253] and we may conclude our study of these literary mediums for Spanish influence by a brief examination of the debt of American playwriting to Spain and Spanish America. It will be recalled that several poems mentioned in the present chapter were written as dramas and were composed for acting—for example, Robert Montgomery Bird's *Oralloossa* and Longfellow's *The Spanish Student*. At least one famous novelist in the nineteenth century (Howells) and one in the twentieth (Hemingway) wrote successful plays on Spanish subjects. What great American playwrights turned to Spanish materials with an enthusiasm equal to Irving's in the essay or to Bryant's in poetry?

The answer is none, or almost none. One reason for this sweeping negative is that until the edge of the century, until the days of Clyde Fitch and Augustus Thomas, talented American playwrights, no matter what their subjects, were really nonexistent. In America power in the drama, like that in criticism, has developed late. Our professional dramatists of the nineteenth century have proved to be, according to the ruthless verdicts of posterity, minor personages. William Dunlap, John Howard Payne, or George Henry Boker, however competent, never attained as playwrights niches comparable to those held by Irving or Cooper in fiction or by Bryant or Lowell in poetry. In the current reconsideration of our nineteenth-century writers, we need expect in our drama no rediscovery or revival even faintly approaching those now centering in Melville and Henry James.

In the twentieth century this poverty has been happily supplanted by wealth; we now have an American drama. Nevertheless, like the poets, our most gifted dramatists have seldom turned to Spain. During our 150 years, of the scores of writers for the stage who have made trial of Spanish subjects, only two, Eugene O'Neill and Maxwell Anderson, are associated with the highest achievements of the American theater. *The Fountain* (1926) by the former, an adaption of the ancient story of Ponce de León, is not one of its author's masterpieces. *Night over Taos* (1932), in which Anderson dramatizes the coming of the "Americanos" in the late 1840's, attained only moderate success. Anderson shows the hopeless struggle of the strong ruler, Pablo Montoya, against the invaders, against the new era, and against his own nature:

> The Spanish blood runs thin. Spain has gone down,
> And Taos, a little island of things that were,
> Sinks among things that are.[254]

So obscure, compared with the leaders in our literature, have been the translators and adapters of Spanish plays—these adroit manipulators of Spanish data on our stage—that, though individually their plays are sometimes better than the trivial stories or the conventional poems, the Spanish influence on our drama has been strikingly different. From 1800 to 1950 it has continued to be diffuse, uneven. Scattered in a play here and a play there, it has lacked concentration in the achievements of a few talented writers. Although one might form a fair impression of Spanish influences on our novel by a study of, say, Irving, Howells, and Bret Harte, no such approach would do in the drama. For the influence reveals itself rather through the perpetuation, often in the work of forgotten hacks, of varied kinds of dramatic writing, such as an adaptation of Cervantes, a translation of Calderón, a melodrama, or an *opéra bouffe*.[255]

Therefore, we should now, in ending this chapter, think far less of authors than of types of influence. These are chiefly three: the Spanish influence manifested, first, through American productions of Spanish plays; next, through dramatic adaptations of Spanish legend and literature (including Spanish drama); and, finally, through miscellaneous borrowings. I refer to the use of a Spanish plot, a Spanish character, or Spanish music. This miscellaneous collection of plays, this rag bag of Spanish influences, from Robert Montgomery Bird's dreary, artificial *Pizarro in Peru, or the Death of Rollo,* acted on March 26, 1800, to the hilarious Spanish-American skit, *Mexicana,* performed in 1939, is important on the popular level. All three types of influence require mention in our story.

NO RECORD exists prior to 1797 of the production on the American stage of a play written by a Spanish dramatist.[256] This test, however, is narrow if we take into account the development of the theater in Mexico a century earlier [257] or even—it is a surprising fact—the acting of mystery plays in Spanish Colorado (and elsewhere in the Southwest) long before this date.[258] As will be evident in a moment, adaptations of Spanish themes on the stage were popular throughout the nineteenth century, but there occurred only occasional performances of Spanish plays themselves, of such standard dramatists as Lope de Vega or Calderón.[259] Naturally these playwrights, no matter how immortal, could not, any more than Molière or Schiller, rival Shakespeare, himself not always secure upon the American boards. We may, then, date active interest in the Spanish and Spanish-American drama as late, as roughly coincident with the furore stimulated by William Dean Howells about the great realists in Spanish fiction, Pérez Galdós, Juan Valera, or Palacio Valdés. For these reasons, the appearance in New York in the twentieth century of genuine Spanish plays was an event fresh and exciting in our literary history. Spanish musicians, singers, and dancers had at times delighted nineteenth-century theatergoers, but in seeing Spanish drama Americans now enjoyed an exhibition as unique as the bullfight—the Spanish play direct from Madrid with a Spanish cast.

What plays were performed? Well, at the turn of the twentieth century, José Echegaray, whose *El Gran Galeoto* was to charm theatergoers in adaptations,[260] was a favorite as was Ángel Guimerá. His *Terra baja,* in a translation entitled *Marta of the Lowlands,* ran for twenty-three nights at the Manhattan Theatre, beginning on October 13, 1903. In the second and third decades attention shifted to various plays of Jacinto Benavente and to those of Gregorio Martínez Sierra.[261] The latter's *Cradle Song* (1927) and *The Kingdom of God* (1929) were acted, respectively, for fifty-seven and ninety-three performances. The conspicuous (and mildly shocking) fact is that during the first three decades of the century only one great classic of the "Golden Age" (Calderón's *El alcalde de Zalamea*) seems to have been presented, in comparison with some twenty plays by writers like Martínez Sierra, the Quinteros, Benavente, or Echegaray.[262]

Although it is pointless to list many others, the startling change in conditions from those of the preceding century, as well as the energy of the stage as an instrument of this influence, is suggested by the appearance in April, 1932, at the New Yorker Theatre of a company from the Teatro Español of Madrid, headed by Fernando Díaz de Mendoza and María Guerrero. For forty performances these players delighted audiences with their renditions from the Quintero brothers, Benavente, Echegaray, Lope de Vega, and from other European dramatists, among them Henri Bernstein and Oscar Wilde.[263] Perhaps there was something precious in this twentieth-century fuss in America about Spanish plays. Nevertheless, even if there were necessary adjustments in the translations, our audiences were at last brought into intimacy with the traditional Spanish theater. Nor must we forget the success in 1927 of Camila Quiroga of Argentina [264] in a succession of Spanish dramas, and of various operas from Spanish America, most raffish of which was *Mexicana* with its thirty-five performances.[265]

THIS is the story, in brief, of the living transfer of Spanish drama to America. The history of adaptations, as we look back again at the 150 years, is interesting and not without some originalities. If

Jacinto Benavente y Martínez,
from the painting by Joaquín Sorolla y Bastida.

during the eighteenth and nineteenth centuries neither the facilities nor the demands for Spanish plays themselves were extensive, these lacks limited very little the adaptations of Spanish themes on the stage by American playwrights. Among the most popular of these were those based on *Don Quixote,* from Mrs. Susanna Rowson's fumbling use of the narrative in her *Slaves in Algiers* (1794) [266] to the glittering twentieth-century versions, like Melchior Lengyel's *Sancho Panza* (1923) or Paul Kester's dramatization, successfully assigned in 1908 to E. H. Sothern and Julia Marlowe.[267]

Probably the most successful adaptation during the entire nineteenth century was Fanny Kemble Butler's version of Lope de Vega's *La estrella de Sevilla* (1832). With death instead of separation for the lovers in the last act, with Shakespearean diction, with a genuinely English spirit, this adaptation was in several respects remote from the original, as the interested Longfellow probably discovered.[268] The character of Shakespeare himself was central in Augustin Daly's equally free adaptation of Tamayo y Baus' *Un drama nuevo.*[269] In *Yorick's Love,* however, which was Howells' translation for Lawrence Barrett of the same Spanish play, Shakespeare was supplanted by Thomas Heywood. In this clever version Howells' share was presumably more than his modesty would admit. It is probable that his talent was responsible for a lively spirit which made this play a popular nineteenth-century adaptation.

OUT of this solid trunk, so to speak, of actual plays, through these branches or adaptations, this tree of the Spanish drama blossomed (from 1800 to 1950) into thousands of leaves, into the ephemeral plays of quasi-Spanish origin—most of them just stories with a Spanish tang.[270] James Nelson Barker, one of the least boring of our early dramatists, commenced his career in 1804 with his unfinished *Spanish Rover* and laid the scene of his successful play, *How to Try a Lover* (1817), in Catalonia.[271] In the meantime, Robert Montgomery Bird tinkered with stage versions of the conventional yarns, and John Howard Payne wrote a few plays in which the Spanish setting was hardly more than atmospheric.[272]

Longfellow's *The Spanish Student,* popular as a poem, was never acted. Its fate illustrates the use of Spanish subjects for closet drama, in whose British vogue (Tennyson, Browning, and others) American literature had its inglorious share. There can, for instance, be no doubt about the moral elevation in the blank-verse tragedies of George Henry Boker. Nevertheless, although *Calaynos,* a tale of the taint of Moorish blood in Spanish veins, enjoyed forty performances in the year 1850 and although *Leonor de Guzman* (1853) presented lucidly the events relating to the succession to the Spanish throne after the death of Alfonso XI, both these plays were painfully "literary." [273] On the stage worse productions won greater success, notably Epes Sargent's ridiculous drama of blood and iron, *Velasco.*[274] We must look to the next century to enjoy the clever, actable sketches dealing with Don Juan [275] or Ernest Hemingway's timely war play, *The Fifth Column,*[276] written while high-explosive shells dropped at regular intervals on his Madrid hotel.

Among all these heterogeneous dramas appeared some with Spanish-American subjects. Robert Montgomery Bird's melodrama, *The Broker of Bogota,* was a favorite of Edwin Forrest's,[277] and William Dunlap corralled for the stage legends of both Castile and the Incas.[278] After 1850 all the familiar themes, worn so threadbare in the fiction and the poetry, had their day in the theater: Columbus, Cortés, Pizarro, De Soto, or Iturbide.[279] In the twentieth century the fashion of entertainment altered. As a result of more intimate associations with Spanish America, we applauded comedies with their national settings, light plays with laughter, music, and satire. For, as the travelers, scholars, historians, novelists, and artists have now persuaded us, the Spanish-American world, in Argentina or in Arizona, is no longer extraneous but part of our own. The hilarious *Nina Rosa* with its lyrics and its Peruvian background, which in 1930 registered in New York 137 performances, is but one instance of this inter-American alliance of the arts.[280] Perhaps in the future Spanish America will be so represented on the stage rather than in the heavily ambitious *Night over Taos* in which Maxwell Anderson merely retold the story of imperial Spain in New Mexico.[281] This play, so serious yet so different in subject from the formal, romantic drama of a century earlier, reflects our new comprehension of the history of Spain in our Southwest. In the drama, as well as in fiction and poetry, we are now less likely to write nonsense about it.

This intimacy of our modern drama with Spain in America is symbolic. As we look back over the 150 years, it is certain that our novelists and dramatists and, in a lesser degree, our poets are now really conscious of Spanish America. At the same time the various literatures of these countries, unlike their painting and architecture, touch our living writers only in incidental fashion. Rubén Darío or Ramón López Velarde can claim few imitators in the United States. In the present chapter we have observed also the continuing seal of Cervantes upon all these forms (novel, poem, and play) but only the intermittent importance to us, as in the tie between Calderón and Lowell, of other classic Spanish authors. Although the impress of the literature of Spain upon our scholars is, as we have seen, infinitely more vital now than earlier, upon our creative writers this imprint is less directly formative than a century ago. In general, although the use of all kinds of Spanish and Spanish-American materials in romances, verse, and plays has sometimes been meretricious and even ridiculous, we recognize the surprisingly large number of novelists, poets, and playwrights who since 1800 have used these same materials with distinction. More intellectual than the travelers, more stable than the writers for the magazines, more flexible and more imaginative than the historians, all these authors reflect the penetration into our belles-lettres of both Spain and Spain in America.

CHAPTER SIX / THE PAINTERS, SCULPTORS, MUSICIANS, AND ARCHITECTS

HENRY THEODORE TUCKERMAN, one of our mid-nineteenth-century critics of painting, speaks of the "constantly blended associations" among authors and artists.[1] Like Tuckerman, many of our writers from Prescott to Howells sensed the supplementary and eloquent expression of Spanish influences through painting and architecture and incidentally through sculpture and music. Even the poet-philosopher Emerson, whose associations with the fine arts were tenuous, took notes in the Louvre on the Spanish painters. He was convinced that Velázquez and Spagnoletto were strong, swarthy men, "good soldiers or brigands at a pinch." Did they not paint with a kind of ferocity?[2] Indeed, to estimate the full import of our writers' achievements we must have some knowledge of these mediums. Irving speaks of the Murillos and of the arches of the Alhambra. Bryant writes of the melodies of Andalusia. Longfellow is eager to hear Spanish music. Mark Twain praises the Alcázar. Bret Harte's tales of New Spain would be less without the mission belfries, without the low, soft line of hacienda and patio. A rare evaluation of Spanish sculpture comes, strangely enough, from William Dean Howells.

Some of our histories of Spain included the story of her arts. Coppée's *History of the Conquest of Spain by the Arab-Moors*[3] devotes one chapter and part of another to the architecture which was to flourish in our own Southwest. As we have seen, the historian, the traveler, the romancer, the poet, or the editor helped to popularize the fine arts of Spain.[4] Gradually, to many of our artists the strong English influences became less exciting than those of the Continent. Gradually among the European patterns in our arts those of Spain emerged. From the Peninsula and from New Mexico or California appeared a Spanish quality which indirectly affected writing: a song from the Alhambra; blacks and greys from a Velázquez; a gateway at Carmel Mission. All these crosscurrents of influence must be in our minds if we are to understand the uses by our men of letters of Spanish themes.

So as the writers talked of the painter or of the builder, in eager conversation, in history, in essay, or in story, Americans learned much of the arts of Spain [5] and of their rich flowering in the Western Hemisphere. A deeper understanding, however, of these crafts came not from painter to author but from painter to painter, from builder to builder, and so on. The influence of Spanish ideas and techniques upon American painting has been slight compared with those of the French. In our architecture the English influence has been dominant. Nevertheless, in both painting and architecture in America Spain has always been present. In any history of American painting we must reckon with, to mention only two or three representative examples, Velázquez, Goya, and Picasso. The famous Carolus-Duran, a French artist of Spanish descent, kept admonishing his students in Paris, among them John Singer Sargent: "Velasquez, Velasquez, Velasquez, étudiez sans relache Velasquez." [6]

In Paris, in Madrid, and possibly even in Germany during the reign of the Düsseldorf school in the fifties, our beginners stood reverently before the Spanish masters. The pictures which Thomas Eakins called the "big work," "the good Spanish work, so good, so strong, so reasonable, so free from affectation," [7] shaped the ideals of some of our greatest painters. An even stronger case can be made for architecture. "Alhambraism," which we encountered in literature, had its vogue in building, too. Finally, as everyone knows, the story of our architecture must always concern itself with presidio, mission, baroque chapel, and with the modern adaptations of Spanish and Mexican public and private structures.

This sophistication and this comprehension of the arts of Italy, France, and Spain could never have been prophesied from the beginnings of the colonial "limners" any more than Ticknor's interpretation of Spanish literature could have been predicted from Cotton Mather's limited knowledge of the Spanish language. In some ways the story of our painting resembles the story of our literature. We observe in both a preliminary sterility, a prolonged subservience to English tradition, a struggle for an intellectual independence, and a realization in a few painters and writers of a kind of "Golden Age." [8] One difference, however, in the history of this painting lies in the nature of the emancipation. The liberation encouraged American subjects, but freedom from England meant at the same time a vigorous embrace of Continental art. Naturally there could never be, as in our frontier literature, a bold break, even theoretically, with all tradition. Another difference in the two stories is also important. Though at times weakened, the English influence lasted longer upon our painting than on our literature. Through our "primitives," those extraordinary colonial portraits,[9] through Copley and through West, through Gilbert Stuart, John Trumbull, and other disciples of West, we began in the art of painting a long indenture to England. Despite occasional glimpses of the Spanish culture during war and exploration,[10] the colonists were inclined to remain true to the English traditions.

As IN literature, English criteria were never unimportant. Nevertheless, as our ties with our mother country declined by reason of the new, American-born generations, the nationalism, and the increased opportunities for travel on the Continent, a gradual change occurred in our attitude toward English painting. In the early nineteenth century Romney and Lawrence enjoyed in the Republic no such fame as had earlier the school of Reynolds and Gainsborough. We were more conscious, too, of what our own amazing continent of mountains, plains, and rivers offered to the artist. We now hear of the "Hudson River School." Instead of the allegories of West appeared Thomas Cole's poetic landscapes. More than the realistic Durand and Kensett, Cole cherished the elevated hope, so familiar to Americans through their first aspiring poets and novelists, of making the native glories of our scenery as worthy of veneration as the hallowed hills of Europe. Bryant, either blind or indifferent to Cole's faults, evident enough in comparison with Constable or Corot, praised the painter when he died in 1848 for "pictures which carried the eye over scenes of wild grandeur peculiar to our country, over our aerial mountain-tops with their mighty growth of forest never touched by the axe, along the banks of streams never deformed by culture, and into the depth of skies bright with the hues of our own climate; skies such as few but Cole could ever paint." [11]

This is grandiose enough. In the vernacular of his time Bryant was expressing the ever-strengthening belief among writers and painters in American subjects, a faith reaffirmed by our truly great landscapist, George Inness. We must not forget this passion for American themes if we are to see the European, especially the Spanish, influences in proportion. The ideal remains cogent in the genre or storytelling pictures (we think of Longfellow's verse tales), in Winslow Homer's seascapes, or even in the revolutionary painters of the twentieth century.[12] For our purposes the chronological history of American painting is less essential than the recognition of one crucial fact: the existence of a conflict, sometimes resolved by American subjects using European techniques, between the mandates of professional European art and our uneasy ambitions for authentic masterpieces of our own. As we reflect on the Spanish influences in painting we must carry in our mind's eye, by way of balance, pictures created between the Revolution and the present day, such as John Trumbull's *The Battle of Bunker's Hill,* Thomas Cole's *Conway Peak,* William Sidney Mount's *Bargaining for a Horse,* Winslow Homer's *Canoe in Rapids,* Frank Duveneck's *The Blacksmith,* John Sloan's *In the Wake of the Ferry,* Edward Hopper's *Corner Saloon,* or Thomas Hart Benton's *Homestead.*[13] We must expect to see paintings of prize fighters, New York streets, or southwestern Indians. All these differ from each other, and all take account of European art. Nevertheless, all possess a loyalty toward American subjects which seems to make the influence of the Spaniard, Velázquez, belong to a different world.

In a sense it did. Sometimes the Spanish influence appears special, even exotic. It seems divorced from the main development of American painting though occasionally, as in Velázquez' effect on W. T. Dannat and others, it elicited or intensified the search for actual life. It may even be argued that Spanish influences on American painting are twice removed. They are separated from the emphasis on American materials, and they are often communicated through the art of another nation, namely France. Naturally some American artists acquired their intimacy with the Spanish masters through the famous teachers in Paris. From colonial days France, if sometimes through England, has been a shaping force in American painting: "But apart," says a French historian of art, "from these anglicized Americans we must not forget that there were from this time on a number of Americans more or less gallicized who made long stays in Paris and whose works call forth unmistakably the memory of David and of Ingres." [14]

It was true. Later, as we shall see, a few Americans studied in the Prado, but many more sat in Paris under teachers who had themselves been inspired by great Spaniards. It was also true that this mass flight of the American artists to Paris had some unhappy consequences. One result was the inability of these expatriates to sell or exhibit in America what their French training had produced. One thinks of Henry James; his experience with his Europeanized fiction was not altogether dissimilar. Sargent (a friend of James) and some other artists were reluctant to return to an America where their fellow countrymen would expend their wealth on the work of Parisian artists but not on that of Americans blessed with the same advantages. Another consequence is more to the point: the exposure of the best artists of America through the best teachers of France to the old masters of Spain. Although in a sense second-hand, this contact with Spanish art created a high expression of Spanish influence upon American painting. An example might be Velázquez through Carolus-Duran to Sargent. Later the French middleman was eliminated, but when we consider the total effect we cannot wholly regret his intrusion.

For all these teachers, such as Gérôme, Bouguereau, Boulanger, Bonnat, Manet, or Carolus-Duran, had themselves, at one time or another, succumbed to the Spaniards. Manet advocated a new method acquired directly from Velázquez, and of this his pupil, Carolus-Duran, was the interpreter. Manet and his followers were certain that Velázquez' power was connected with his determination to paint only what he could see and not what he knew was there in the subject.[15] In other words, he painted a pictorial summary or a synthesis recording his impression. By this theory, as communicated to them by their French teachers, the American students were strongly affected. They employed new uses of colors (for instance, subdued blacks and grays) and simple lines and large colored masses, varied by breaking them into several different tones.[16] In these and other ways the American painters learned how the "actual craftsmanship of the brush" [17] might be restored. These gospels, originating in the age of Velázquez, were likely to engage so free a spirit as Dannat, and artists like Whistler, Sargent, and William Merritt Chase became, so remarked a critic in 1903, "postulants at his shrine." [18]

LEAVING, then, techniques, which concern us little, and the history of American painting, which interests us only as a frame of reference, we may now turn to a general survey of American artists, from the colonial Robert Feke to the contemporary Waldo Peirce, who have been sensitive in one way or another to Spanish influences. We must begin in colonial days, in the seventeenth and eighteenth centuries. Much has been written to dispel the myth that the Puritans were insensitive to art forms. We have now assembled abundant evidence of their skills in silver, gold, pewter, woodwork, and in architecture. Before the Revolution of all the arts (save sculpture) painting seems to have been least in favor. Its menial position is vigorously suggested by an advertisement in the *South Carolina Gazette* for May, 1735, in which a certain Mr. B. Roberts informs possible customers that "Portrait painting and Engraving, Heraldry and House painting are undertaken and performed expeditiously in a good manner, and at the lowest rates." [19] Evidently the eighteenth-century painters were versatile: a coach, a house, or a human face. In the latter half of the century, however, there developed more skillful "face-painting," thanks to such craftsmen as Robert Feke, John Smibert, or John Watson. Colonial portrait painting culminated in the more than respectable work of Copley and West.

The sources of these primitive yet often sensitive beginnings in painting were English, and they were likely to remain English for many years to come, even after Copley and West had revealed to the colonists large areas for the imagination in history and allegory. In this very period painting, sculpture, music, and, in particular, architecture took on in distant Mexico new and beautiful forms, half Christian, half pagan. Nevertheless, under the difficult relationships of trade between the English and the Spanish colonies works of art would naturally be the very last commodity. Not even in England itself in the eighteenth century was the knowledge of Spanish art extensive.[20] Indeed, to a strongly Protestant people it was barely acceptable. Religious passion, sensuous or mystical feeling, the pallid faces of saints, or florid murals could never suit the English temper.[21] Nor were Spanish masterpieces numerous in Britain. Not until Napoleon's hordes overran Spain was the Peninsula's artistic isolation broken. Only then, in these early years of the nineteenth century, did the paintings by the Spanish masters begin to leave the walls of palace and monastery to make their long, halting journeys into the other nations of Europe. Even if such pictures had been plentiful in England, how many of them would have been retransported to America? Such a situation explains the dearth in the writings of the colonies of even casual references to Spanish art. In Massachusetts or in Virginia one might find a copy of Cervantes far more easily than a canvas by Velázquez or Murillo.

Nevertheless, it is exciting to continue the search, as if for a volume of Quevedo or for a copy of Cotton Mather's Spanish pamphlet. In this austere Anglo-Saxon world every allusion takes on romance. Robert Feke, our earliest native-born portraitist and the author of the group painting of Isaac Royal and his family, ran away to sea. Taken as a prisoner from his ship, so the story runs, he was carried off to Spain, where in his cell he learned the art of painting.[22] The tale is more than doubtful, and we look in vain in Feke's portraits for confirmation. Although excellent enough to be mistaken sometimes for Copley's, these paintings reveal no trace of his singular adventure or of his foreign training.[23] Somewhat later we encounter another legend. In the collection of Governor James Hamilton of Pennsylvania hung a portrait of Saint Ignatius, once salvaged from a Spanish prize ship.[24] This picture Benjamin West was permitted to copy, unsuspecting at the time that it might be a Murillo. Murillo and West! The American made a creditable duplicate, but there is no evidence that the painter of soft-eyed

268

madonnas shook, even slightly, the orthodoxy of the painter of Biblical and pagan story.[25]

Soon the very remoteness of Spain and the mysterious differences in Spanish life were to fascinate painters as well as writers. After the American artist, weary of being a mere "face-painter," turned to the historical and the contemporary, the terrible Spaniard of the "black legend," that mythical, picturesque bigot, became as desirable a subject for a canvas as for a printed page. The first influence was born not of the study of Spanish painters but of the adaptation, as in poetry and fiction, of Spanish subjects. In the eighteenth century the Spaniard was still famous for his empire and for his invincibility in war. It was natural that John Singleton Copley should include in his gallery of historical events *The Siege of Gibraltar*,[26] as natural as that John Wilson should in the seventeenth century celebrate in verse the glory and destruction of the Armada. Still more natural was it that a younger artist, the "painter of the American Revolution," John Trumbull, a born delineator of military action, should become infatuated with an episode in battle between Englishman and Spaniard. He called his popular painting *Sortie from Gibraltar*.[27]

For Trumbull the origin of this painting was not in art but in life. That he knew anything whatever of Spanish artists is doubtful. Like so many writers discussed in this book, his imagination was stimulated by the Spaniard in his more glittering guises. We see him in the twilight of that May afternoon in 1787, walking down Oxford Street in London with Antonio Poggi. The Italian artist is telling the story to the rapt American, who could not sleep that night until he had drawn a small sketch of what happened: "I was pleased," he declared later, "with the subject, as offering, in the gallant conduct and death of the Spanish commander, a scene of deep interest to the feelings, and in contrast to the darkness of night, with the illumination of an extensive conflagration, great splendor of effect and color." [28] The picture was immediately acclaimed for this "splendor" of color. Although this and the composition were inferior in comparison with Trumbull's other works, the painting was remarkable in its drama and in its able execution of the portrait heads, for one of which Lawrence served as the model. *Sortie from Gibraltar* was so popular that Trumbull duplicated it in no fewer than five different sizes.[29] One of these obtained wide currency through William Sharpe's engraving. We might almost say that *Sortie from Gibraltar* marked, at least on the popular level, the first stage of Spanish influence on American painting.

As OUR national consciousness took form, no dramatic deed of the Spaniard could compare with one, that is, his discovery of America. This subject, re-enacted in our history, fiction, poetry, sculpture, and music, our painting was unlikely to ignore. The same scenes dear to the romantic narratives of Irving or Cooper, from Columbus' first dream of a New World to his disgrace and death, now found their way into many representations on canvas.[30] One of the most famous was John Vanderlyn's *Landing of Columbus* (1834), created in Paris for a panel in the Capitol at Washington and so strangely uncharacteristic of the American that it was rumored to have been the work of a French artist in our expatriate's employ.[31] Robert W. Weir, who was for a time Whistler's teacher in drawing at West Point, varied the setting by showing the explorer before the Council at Salamanca.[32] Again, these painters had never been in Spain and knew nothing appreciable of Spanish art. Nevertheless, since Trumbull had been disturbed by discovering an error in the Spanish uniforms in his *Sortie from Gibraltar*, we may conjecture that artists had begun to be curious about details of Spain's dress, inhabitants, and, presumably, her painting.

During the first decades of the century more and more artists shared this curiosity. Before 1840 a number of painters had turned to Spanish scenes or characters, among them that disciple of the Venetian masters, Washington Allston. Since then (rightly or wrongly) this painter, sitting among his unfinished canvases, has often served as a tragic illustration of Henry James' thesis that the artist cannot survive in America.[33] In the exhibitions of the Athenæum Gallery of 1833 and 1839 respectively, George W. Newcombe displayed his charming miniature, *A Spanish Musician Tuning a Mandoline* and George Harvey his *Spanish Lady*.[34]

A Quartette, from the painting by William T. Dannat.

These works of art lacked reality. They resembled Bryant's prose sketches of patio and señorita before he had visited Spain rather than Irving's more faithful vignettes drawn from his study of peasants in the Alhambra. Yet, however conventional these representations of Spanish persons, they imply a further penetration by American artists by way of subject into the relatively unknown world of art in the Peninsula.[35] Was this not to be, these painters were asking themselves, as rich a field for them as for the novelists and poets?

The mandolinist did not help much, nor the Castilian lady; these paintings were conspicuously empty. Allston, however, who had lived long in Italy, managed in his famous picture, *A Spanish Girl*, to convey a meaning.[36] At the edge of the lake, with the Sierra Morena rising above it into the heavens, sits the fair Inez, awaiting the return from the wars of Isidore, her lover.[37] The painting was not without a certain Spanish content, like the same artist's *Donna Mencia in the Robbers' Cavern*, which illustrated a scene from *Gil Blas*. We cannot help remembering Allston in Italy in 1805 with Washington Irving, trying to persuade the young writer to turn painter. In this artist's work was a conscious moralizing and a grandiose sentiment, but critical respect for him has risen steadily. Despite the inadequacy of the Spanish pictures of Newcombe, Harvey, or Allston, these announce plainly that later painters would strive to reflect actual Spanish life. The vital, honest scenes of Spanish living, such as the four musicians in Dannat's *Quartette*, were to reveal progress far beyond the *Sortie from Gibraltar*.

THIS progress included, but even more slowly, Spanish America. By the middle of the century Madame Calderón de la Barca and other travelers had relayed to our artists impressions of the Mexican civilization. Most of these records seemed to depict a squalid society against a sublime natural background. The infinite wealth of subject which was to fascinate our later painters did not yet allure, but these glories of cloud, sky, and snow-capped volcano attracted our thriving landscape artists, already enchanted by the sweep of western plain and mountain. To this interest, rather than to anything definitely Spanish-American, we must attribute the two bold visits to South America in 1853 and 1857 of Cole's pupil, Frederick Edwin Church. Linked with the general nineteenth-century passion for landscape, his paintings remind us forcibly of the prose panoramas in Prescott's *Conquest of Mexico*. During his first stay Church made the sketches for his colossal canvas, *The Great Mountain-Chain of New Granada,* and during the second he conceived such paintings as *The Heart of the Andes, Cotopaxi, The Rainy Season in the Tropics,* and *Chimborazo.*[38] Accustomed now to the light of impressionism and to the bright colors of expressionism, we find Church's paintings somber and often, in the tropical scenes, inadequate. Nevertheless, it is easy to believe that these ambitious panoramas exerted influence in inter-American relations in art. Presently our painters were to borrow subjects from all the Americas.[39]

In a history of Spanish influences in our painting Church's South American landscapes are peripheral. The mid-century witnessed no eager turning to Spanish America for fresh subjects but rather an exodus of artists to Europe for study, to Düsseldorf, to Munich, or to Paris and less frequently, usually after a Spanish inoculation in Paris, to Madrid. This drift away from London to the Continent for invigorating instruction represented a phase of the expanding drive of the romantic movement in its reaction against neoclassical ideals. In Munich in the seventies American painters shared in the new-found interest in the feelings of the heart, earlier extolled by Bryant in his theories of poetry.[40] Here Frank Duveneck studied German techniques, and here he dedicated himself to the old masters, to Hals and to Rembrandt, and also to Velázquez—though he never entered Spain. Duveneck lacked brilliance of color, but much of his work was human and enlivening, like his *Whistling Boy,* which in 1875 so edified the art circles of Boston.[41] The specific obligations of the Düsseldorf group to the Spaniards were probably slight, but Duveneck's debt to Velázquez is suggestive.

From now on, through the French teachers, through increased travel in the Peninsula, through the romantic temper inviting a return to the old masters, and (this must be remembered) through an increased production of books on art,[42] Spain began in earnest to influence America's greatest painters.[43] We shall return later to the varied shades of meaning in these influences, but we should now appraise quickly the associations with Spain of these major artists. William T. Dannat, although he was trained in Munich and in Paris, studied devotedly the craft of Velázquez.[44] Even more ardent was William Merritt Chase, who made three journeys to Spain between 1881 and 1884 and who in 1896 took his class there for six months of study. Artist after artist now fell under the spell of what Eakins called the "big work."

Chase's fearless pursuit of whatever charmed his artistic soul found a kind of climax in his love of Spanish painting. In boyhood he had been a worker in his father's Indiana shoeshop, next a sailor, and eventually an eager painter of still-life objects. In 1877 he left Munich to study in Venice, but in the following year he returned to America to commence a long professional career. We must not linger too long over his volatile nature, over his picturesque history. We hear of his dinner parties, his exquisite dress, his wit, his studio overflowing with animals and birds—and his magnificent debts. He loved to pick out for his friends Velázquez types in the crowds, and he never tired of talking of the techniques of the Spaniards. The essential fact is that he became a leader, a teacher, and that after 1881 into all that he said and thought entered his enthusiasm for Spanish art.[45] A new era had begun; it was now fashionable to imitate Spanish painting.

In their approaches to the "big work" some artists hastened to Madrid; some did not. Eakins himself, who had previously worked under Bonnat[46] and Gérôme, arriving there in December, 1869, "discovered the sunlight of the south, southern life and character, and Spanish art."[47] Despite the mute testimony of the familiar butterfly autograph in the pension guestbook of the Señora Carmona Dolores,[48] it appears certain that Whistler never knew Spain. Perhaps he was fearful of domination by the "big work,"[49] but this seems unlikely. Whistler was sensitive to many kinds of painters, among them the Pre-Raphaelites, the impressionists, the Japanese, and the Spaniards, but he was not easily thrown off balance. Furthermore, he could have taken the infection in the Louvre, where he was often seen studying the paintings by Velázquez, especially that of the little *Infanta,* at which he would look "long and earnestly." [50] Whistler shared the general passion; his admiration of "the good Spanish work" was deep and genuine. [51]

The lure for these questing Americans was the simplicity and truth of the old Spanish masters: "What," said a critic, "is the somber, splendid charm of this wonderful Andalusian? Partly, I think, that he dared to tell the truth as no other man has told it before or since." [52] Robert Henri, twenty-one years younger than Eakins and nine years younger than Sargent, spent hours in the Louvre, as had Whistler, before the grandeur of these paintings. Weary of academic rules, he experienced the same sense of rebirth. [53] Mary Cassatt, too, who eventually became the foremost woman among the American impressionists, bowed down before Velázquez. While traveling in Spain during her student days, she had formed a friendship with Sorolla, whose exhibition in 1909 was to make such an indelible impression in America. [54] It was, however, in Sargent himself that the reality of these influences seemed to center. His knowledge of Spain and, presumably, of Spanish art, was deeper than Whistler's. Born in Italy of American parents, he did not visit America until he was twenty years old. Then and later he did not stay long, and what he thought of his country can be deduced only from his long absences and from his patrician portraits of eminent American contemporaries. [55] Europe was his habitat, and we must quote the well-known description of him as "an American born in Italy, educated in France, who looks like a German, speaks like an Englishman, and paints like a Spaniard." [56]

This last was true enough. Like the others, Sargent studied under Carolus-Duran [57] when the teacher was still aglow with inspiration from the Velázquezes in the Prado, but, unlike some of the others, the pupil sealed his bond with the Spanish masters by frequent and productive stays in Spain. The earliest visit occurred when he was twelve years old; he then formed his first impressions of Madrid, Valencia, Cordova, Seville, Cadiz, and Gibraltar. [58] He was there again in the autumn of 1879. We must forgive its exaggeration for the sake of the wit and insight in Henry James' description of this gifted young American at the age of twenty-three. The two were congenial spirits:

Here [says this other Europeanized American], even more than he had already been, the great Velasquez became the god of his idolatry. No scenes are more delightful to the imagination than those in which we figure youth and genius confronted with great examples, and if such matters did not belong to the domain of private life, we might entertain ourselves with reconstructing the episode of the first visit to the museum of Madrid, the shrine of the painter of Philip IV., of a young Franco-American worshipper of the highest artistic sensibility, expecting a supreme revelation and prepared to fall on his knees. It is evident that Mr. Sargent fell on his knees and that in this attitude he passed a considerable part of his sojourn in Spain.[59]

The passage is Jamesian and delightfully provocative. But is it true? As will be suggested in a closer analysis of the influences of Spain on our painters, James' somewhat ridiculous image may be askew; that Sargent "fell on his knees" before Velázquez remains controversial.[60] Modern critics regard the influence of Velázquez upon him as exaggerated. Nevertheless, if Sargent did not worship he learned; the aims and craftsmanship of these demigods remained forever in his soul: "Begin," he told Miss Heyneman, "with Franz Hals, copy and study Franz Hals, after that go to Madrid and copy Velasquez, leave Velasquez till you have got all you can out of Franz Hals." [61] Or we recall his lasting passion for El Greco. As late as 1914 he declared: "Ingres, Raphael, and El Greco, these are now my admirations, these are what I like." [62]

Goya, too, during these days in the Prado, stirred Sargent. It has been said that even in his last paintings there are traces of Goya [63] and that he may truly be called one of "Goya's artistic descendants." [64] Nevertheless, in this survey of Sargent's preferences and debts, we keep returning to Velázquez, always to Velázquez, the incomparable Velázquez. Such a universal orienting of so many of our better painters cannot be unimportant. Sorolla once remarked that the real founder of American art was Velázquez. On February 13, 1909, the New York *World*, commenting on eighty-six water colors by Sargent shown at Knoedler's, declared that Sorolla's assertion was now validated. The Spanish influence upon Sargent was enduring. Before he began the design for the mural of the *Dogma of the Redemption* for the Boston Public Library, he made a special journey to Spain. Only here, he thought, could he absorb, in preparation for his difficult task, the spirit of medieval Christianity.[65]

EAKINS died in 1916, Sargent in 1925, Mary Cassatt in 1926. The intimacy of these artists with Spanish traditions and techniques included also the beginnings of modern Spanish painting, which in our time was to reach the startling apex of Picasso. In her volume on this painter Gertrude Stein declared characteristically: "Painting in the nineteenth century was only done in France and by Frenchmen, apart from that, painting did not exist, in the twentieth century it was done in France but by Spaniards." [66] We have already noticed Mary Cassatt's friendship with Sorolla, and in these transitional years it is difficult to winnow old influences from new. Early in the twentieth century American artists were familiar with the old masters but also with such painters as Fortuny, Madrazo (the brother-in-law of Fortuny), Pradilla, Álvarez, Casado, Valles, or Galofre.[67] Study in Spain was now more usual. As in travel, the periodicals, history, or fiction, the Peninsula was no longer out of bounds. Monographs on the classic figures appeared, and articles on contemporary painters were numerous. Handbooks, biographies, exchange students and professors, and traveling fellowships broke down whatever barriers remained between the inquisitive American and the art of Spain.[68] Histories devoted solely to Spanish art told the story with completeness and even magnificence.[69] Meanwhile, we must not forget the Spanish and Spanish-American artists,[70] notably Mexicans, who sifted into the United States, not merely to learn about our civilization but to remain and to teach our young painters. In brief, in our general survey we have reached the modern age.

During this period American art has experienced a radical, even a violent transformation in new uses of the American scene. In this art we must expect to find the industrial age and the machine, and must master the daring forms of abstractionism, expressionism, or surrealism.[71] In the midst of these new materials and fresh techniques the influence of Spanish painting is still distinct but possibly less concentrated on particular painters. Some American artists have been as strongly affected by Picasso (or by Juan Gris and others) as were Whistler and Sargent by Velázquez. Nevertheless, in contrast to the select group in Paris in the mid-nineteenth century, the influence of some of these contemporary painters, like Picasso, covers a far wider area. It orients many, many craftsmen. Few modern American artists are unaware of Picasso.

In the beginnings of this modern period we might pause over Leopold Seyffert,[72] who had been trained under Chase at the Pennsylvania Academy of the Fine Arts and who depicted Spanish peasant types in a fashion which would have rejoiced the pioneer Washington Irving with his notebook of Andalusian drawings.[73] Like Seyffert's paintings, the early work of Waldo Peirce, to cite another twentieth-century example, shows the handiwork of Ignacio Zuloaga: "Of course," Peirce said, "the landscapes and everything there look a lot like Zuloaga—one can't help painting Zuloagas." [74] The vigorous Peirce represented precisely this mood: the savage landscape of the country and the earthy life of the people. His *Bull Loose in Pomplona,* which was in debt to Goya, belonged as realistically to the modern life of Spain as the stories of his friend Ernest Hemingway, whom he accompanied there in 1927.

If we continue the story of Spanish influences to the present hour, we shall still be sensible of the force in America of Spanish and also of Spanish-American painting. This is true even if we cannot name American artists of genius who owe as much to it as did Sargent to Velázquez. The Museum of Modern Art exhibited recently many distinguished paintings of eight Spanish-born artists [75] and twenty-one Mexicans.[76] Of these twenty-nine artists it is tempting to see leadership in five or six, say, Dali, Picasso, Orozco, Rivera, or Siqueiros because theirs became household names. Dali, who called his paintings "hand-done color snapshots," [77] has a qualified professional following although the crowds before his work at the World's Fair in 1939 attested also the general curiosity.[78] Possibly Picasso's "Rose Period" is well illustrated by the figure pieces in Alexander Brook's *The Tragic Muse*,[79] and other traits of this "pace-setting" [80] radical appear in the violence of form and color in the performances of John Graham.[81] For clear and interesting examples of the influence of Picasso's rose and blue periods we may turn to Bernard Karfiol's *Two Figures* or Max Weber's *Composition with Three Figures*.[82] Let us, however, for our purposes, be content to observe the vogue of these Spanish artists in American galleries and leave speculation concerning subtle influences to the technicians.[83]

Among them all, Pablo Picasso is supreme. In 1945 more than 160 of his works were to be seen in twenty-six American museums, and at least seventy-seven exhibitions of his art have been held in this country since the year 1911.[84] In these collections we may study at our leisure Picasso's "formidable and defiant genius." [85] In his paintings we feel, however untrained we are in the craft, the dynamism and originality of this great Spaniard. We respond with delight to the wonder of his color and line, the daring, the heterodoxy of his pronouncements, indirect and direct, on life and particularly on modern life.[86] The magic of his genius carries us on with him through the "Blue Period," which took form about the turn of the century when he was a youth of twenty,[87] through the short "Rose Period," that is, his first classical style, into the "Negro Period" with its African sculpture and primitivism.[88] But Picasso was just beginning. In 1908 when he was twenty-seven, he envisaged, as a leader of the cubist movement,[89] "the independence of the world of forms from optical reality"; [90] through abstract art man might move freely in a new world.[91] Since 1925 his paintings have reflected both abstract and surrealistic tendencies.[92] His range is wide, from his *Demoiselles d'Avignon* [93] to *Guernica,* in which he is plainly rent in twain by the horror of the modern world.[94] This painting is a protest, to use his own words, against "brutality and darkness." [95]

His subtlety of draftsmanship, his use of both the esoteric and the human, and his highly specialized expression of the terror of being alive today makes it difficult to estimate Picasso's influence on either painting or literature.[96] The intensity of his depiction of evil (as well as the difficulty of his forms) suggests William Faulkner

278

and other agonized interpreters of modern life in fiction or poetry. His ruthless revelation of genocide in *Guernica* reminds us of Hemingway's descriptions of cruelty in the Civil War. Is it not probable that this painting has deeply moved our writers? Whether or not the "Blue Period" with its "poetry of misery" [97] molded other painters we cannot say. The "Rose Period," reminiscent of the deep classical past of which Picasso as a son of ancient Spain was a natural legatee,[98] was closer to the general trend of our painting.[99] The primitivism in the "Negro Period" seems to have cognates in Vachel Lindsay and also in twentieth-century music and drama. All our painters interested in abstractionism and surrealism derived help from this master. Some say that in renouncing the phenomenal he has achieved not the universal but merely the abstract.[100] Picasso is, of course, *sui generis*. No American artist of the first magnitude has been made in his image. Nevertheless, he has affected the temper of our painting as a whole and, presumably, particular areas in our literature.

IN THIS chronicle of our painters we have proceeded rapidly from Robert Feke, who (according to the legend) mixed his colors in a seventeenth-century Spanish prison, to surrealists who studied Dali and Picasso. So far there has been only incidental mention of the growth of kindred aesthetic influences in our own hemisphere. We must return for a few moments to the nineteenth century. We must retrace our steps, back to the time of the traveler-landscapist Church with his *Cotopaxi* and *Chimborazo*. The ensuing blank in respect to Spanish-American art has literary parallels. It will be recalled that Irving, Longfellow, Ticknor, Lowell, and Howells thought little worth their attention below the Rio Grande. Somewhat later than Church, Leopold Seyffert inclined toward Guatemalan subjects,[101] but the true revelation of Spanish-American art was to come in the twentieth century from three great Mexican muralists. These gave aid and stimulus to young American painters and eventually settled for long periods in the United States.[102] Living here, they left memorials of their genius.

This Mexican influence, which belonged almost wholly to the

twentieth century, was twofold. It conveyed to our painters Mexican techniques, and it led to the use of Mexican artists and Mexican patterns of art in the decoration of American buildings. The almost simultaneous appearance in various parts of the country on our public walls of magnificent paintings, gorgeous in the colors, designs, and ideas of an alien culture, was spectacular. The reasons are interesting. They include the availability of vast areas of wall space, the novelty, in our standardized American scene, of this color and strangeness, and, above all, the social cause. For the downtrodden, the rejected, the uprooted, the homeless, the unemployed or rather for the intellectuals who spoke for them, these canvases of Orozco, Rivera, and Siqueiros had intense emotional meaning. Here, not without portraits of their prophets, were their eloquent panoramas of the worker and of industry. Through their articulation of the political unrest which was common not only to both countries but to the entire world, these muralists wielded a powerful weapon. Nor were they alone. Other less theatrical artists, like Rufino Tamayo [103] and Miguel Covarrubias,[104] loving New York not less than Mexico City, strengthened the influence from the neighboring nation, as if to make up for the long years lost in mutual neglect. The first extensive show of Mexican art in New York City occurred in 1930.[105] From this year on we may trace through these painters an influence without parallels in sculpture or literature. The poet Ramón López Velarde is known in the United States, but Orozco, Rivera, and Siqueiros are renowned—and justly so.

"Two strong painters," José Clemente Orozco and Diego Rivera, have shaken, says a critic, a "Mexican pepper castor" on American art.[106] Orozco, who lived in this country for two different periods totaling nine years, enlivened several universities with his frescoes.[107] His painting, which reveals traces of both El Greco and Goya,[108] is alternately admired and detested. Rivera, not averse to publicity, is even more daring in subject and more provocative of hosannas and curses. It is impossible to discuss here in detail his frescoes, with their fusion of nationalism and politics. We are startled by their stylized Mexican characters, their inclusion of the figures of Lenin, Helen Wills, and (like a modern Fra Lippo

Hispano-America. The Rebel and His International Enemies.
The eleventh panel of the Orozco murals at Dartmouth College.

Lippi) himself. They attain a near-sublimity in the allegorical pattern of California surrounded by the symbols of her agricultural and mineral resources.[109] Nor can we pause over the controversies which follow Rivera wherever he goes, as in the "battle of Rockefeller Center." [110]

This "battle" centered in Rivera's depiction of Lenin in an elaborate grouping of the workers of the world.[111] The painting was destroyed, but Rivera re-created it for the Palacio de Bellas Artes in Mexico City. Here each year thousands of Americans look at it and comment, variously, according to their political color, aesthetic maturity, or temperament, on its banishment from the United States. The mural suggests the magic of Rivera for some of our younger painters. Not less magnetic and not more conservative in politics or in the use of the brush, David Alfaro Siqueiros also commands a large following, partly because he has lived long in the United States. His subjects in murals are revolutionary, and his techniques are his own. Among these is the use of synthetic resins and automobile paints, applied with a spray gun. An outdoor mural, which probably hastened his departure from Los Angeles, shows the Latin-American peoples bound to a cross, which is surmounted by the American eagle.[112]

The work of these Mexican painters is functional; the arresting designs on massive buildings point to the problems of our time. Destiny calls the common man! Moreover, apart from their proletarian temper, these paintings pulsate with the expanding nationalism of Mexico, which is now as bumptious as her northern neighbor a century ago. It is not strange that young, ambitious painters responded to this robust, expressive art.[113] Paul O'Higgins, a Californian who toiled with Rivera on the Chapingo and Ministry of Education murals, tried his hand at independent frescoes on Mexican buildings.[114] The influence, however, is more than libertarian. If we pause for a few days on the Pan-American Highway at, say, the sleeping town of Jacala, we share the mood of ancient, timeless Mexico. Besides the Mexico of Hollywood neon signs and the Reforma, we may find this quiet temper from the past: "[It] gave my work," wrote Howard Cook concerning Mexico, "a tremendous stimulus allowing me freedom to develop new techniques, including my first fresco, as well as to attempt to realize a *portrayal of the serenity and beauty of the lives of the common Mexican people.*" [115]

This discipleship of some American painters to Mexico predicates a relationship between the two cultures.[116] Is it prophetic of the future? Will it eventually extend to literature? Sometimes the work of imitation is done in a comprehending civilization, that is, in the Southwest. At other times it appears in ludicrously inappropriate settings, in the northern city of Detroit or in the New England village of Hanover, New Hampshire. Peter Hurd was "much stirred by the works of the Mexican muralists" [117] during several stays in their country. Later he was commissioned to design a triptych for the buildings of the New Mexico Military Institute. It was an exciting incident, this renewal in the Southwest of inspiration at the ancient fountainhead, this study of "three dominant racial stocks of New Mexico—the aboriginal, Spanish, and Anglo-Saxon —the pageant of their conflicts and changing relationships through the centuries." [118] This Mexican influence, recorded in these murals, breathed new life into old cultural concepts.

It is illogical to expect through the revival of the Spanish tradition in architecture and in the handicrafts (from Florida to California) that a vigorous development would now occur in painting —and in literature. Our eclecticism in architecture has not been paralleled by an eclecticism in the graphic arts; there is, for example, no painted equivalent (*laus Deo*) for university Gothic. Nevertheless, the animated intrusion of Mexican architecture into the Southwest and into our industrial centers has hardly been more awakening than the mere splendor of Rivera. This is so even if the influences of the Mexican painters (among them Rivera) was strongest in the 1930's and has since declined. We see with mingled feelings the young American painter, David Fredenthal, watching Rivera in admiration as the famous Mexican paints the frescoes in the Detroit Institute of Arts. Attempting to make a sketch of his hero at work, Fredenthal was threatened by the guard with eviction. But Rivera intervened. "He is," he said, "all right. He is a friend." [119] Fredenthal was more than a friend. He represented the illumination of young American artists as they realized what the art of the Mexican fresco might be. The incident is symbolic of a remarkable phase of Spanish influence on our art and on our cultural life.

The painter has many adjutants. Whether Mexican or Spanish, whether in the nineteenth or twentieth centuries, in his wake thrive the engraver or the illustrator, the private collector, the director of the museum, the organizer of the exhibition. These functionaries deserve a word or two. Not every American lover of painting could stand before Eakins' *Street Scene in Seville* or Sargent's *El Jaleo*. Even today, when the social and industrial changes of life have made such experiences more possible, we cannot all see the murals of Orozco. Indeed, for many years the curious American could not examine even adequate reproductions of American masterpieces. During the last quarter of the nineteenth century, however, to which we must again revert, the subsidiary art of illustration increased in importance in both books and periodicals. Through continuous invention, as in the new method of reproducing plates, this attained excellence and bred brilliant illustrators.[120] Moreover, Americans with a talent for illustration would turn naturally to Spain; we think of Mariano Fortuny and Martín Rico.[121] It was a Spaniard, Daniel Urrabieta Vierge, who was called the "father of modern illustration." [122] Vierge, declared Joseph Pennell, was responsible for most of the advances in the technique of American draftsmanship.[123]

Vierge's devotees were numerous. Among them was Robert Frederick Blum who, by the way, accompanied William Merritt Chase on his first journey to Spain. One day in a museum of his native Cincinnati young Blum stumbled on some drawings of Fortuny [124] and Rico and was overcome by the "spell of their gemlike brilliance of coloring and the exquisiteness of their technique." [125] This flirtation with Spanish art became a serious love affair when Stephen Ferris showed Blum his beautiful reproductions of Rico, Fabres, and Casanova and spread before him his etchings by Fortuny. Ferris, a teacher at the Pennsylvania Academy of the Fine Arts,[126] talked with him incessantly of the Spanish artists. Out of these experiences evolved Blum's characteristic Spanish techniques, so evident in his sketches of colonial life in Virginia published in *Scribner's Monthly* in 1879. Here is an odd juxtaposition of materials, but the costuming is plainly in debt to the famed master, Fortuny.[127] He drew, says a critic, "stunning Fortuny-like things . . ." [128]

Does not the Spanish influence seem more unified, more concentrated, if narrower, in these illustrators than in the painters? For it was through Stephen Ferris that Joseph Pennell also owed his introduction to Fortuny; the Spaniard gave him both "inspiration" and craftsmanship. Anointed by this high priest of etching, Fortuny, he could trust himself to illustrate books on Spain. Perhaps he was right about this. There is a pertinence in what Pennell did for *The Alhambra* and for *Castilian Days;* [129] editions of these now seem incomplete if without his drawings. We recall that in 1903 he made a special trip to the Peninsula to illustrate Hay's book, but his best work took form during his first journey in 1896 when he lost himself in the brilliant light over landscape and building. Or perhaps he dreamed his dream of Spain during his preparation under Ferris for these very moments:

In my drawings [he recalled] it can be seen how much, even then, I had studied and tried to imitate the techniques of Rico and Fortuny. Vierge's work, curiously, I did not know till long after . . . But I thank Heaven I had such good and sound technical masters of the art of pen drawing for reproduction. The pen drawings by these men and Casanova, Fabres and Vierge . . . have never been surpassed and are not approached now.[130]

In this summary we cannot trace this subtle and beautiful art further, through the other illustrators of the nineteenth century, through the successors of Blum or Pennell. We cannot linger over the abundance of twentieth-century illustration or the friendly, emulous invasion of the Mexicans and of the South Americans, such as F. Luis Mora [131] of Montevideo. Rivera, too, showed that he could draw as deftly for a printed page as for a mural.[132] Our purpose has been merely to suggest how the illustrators widened still further the Spanish influence on our art.

DURING the nineteenth century paintings, engravings, etchings, and illustrations found their way more and more into the hands of the private collector. Supported by his henchman, the dealer,[133] the collector was destined both to elicit and to satisfy the increasing demand for pictures of all kinds. Prior to the Revolution American collections, both public and private, were few, and within these the Spanish items were at first almost nonexistent. Possibly the earliest known collection was that of John Watson who, returning from Europe in about the year 1725, brought with him portraits of kings and heroes to hang in his home at Perth Amboy, New Jersey.[134] At nearly the same time the painter Smibert formed a collection of engravings, done after masterpieces by Raphael, Michelangelo, and Rubens.[135] Other groupings of pictures receive passing allusion in colonial records.[136] Among them we find in our particular search only the Saint Ignatius, which had aroused the zeal of West, and, in the possession of New York State, a portrait of Columbus by a Spanish artist.[137] Naturally, the expansion of collections followed the rise of interest in painting. The availability of Spanish pictures in America became noticeable after the French invasion of the Peninsula and the consequent dispersal of some of its art treasures. In those years few indeed could have predicted accurately how many such paintings were eventually to find a permanent home in America.

We must imagine a shrewd American merchant in London or in Cadiz in approximately the year 1830, realizing his opportunity and bringing back, besides the staples of his business, an occasional Spanish portrait for some wealthy agent or for an enterprising dealer.[138] Out of similar incidents began some of the early collections. One of the first truly great American collections, assembled by James Bowdoin, minister to Spain from 1804 to 1808, included an anonymous work called *Fish Shambles* besides a drawing which has recently been ascribed to Velázquez.[139] Even more prophetic of the future was the presence during these lean years in Richard Worsam Meade's collection [140] of Murillo's *Roman Daughter,* a painting with a checkered, an almost comic history. Godoy had received it as a gift from Charles IV of Spain, and when his house was looted by a mob in 1808 it fell into the hands of the engraver Enguidarrus. To protect the picture, Enguidarrus rolled it inside an inferior painting assigned to a village church.[141] Eventually reaching Cadiz, it became part of Meade's collection, which could already boast of several other Spanish items. The story is typical of the period and of galleries whose Murillos, Riberas, and Velázquezes so often mysteriously disappeared.

The great collections lacked dimensions until well after midcentury when the changes already discussed were well under way. We recall the progressive interest in painting, the study of genre at Düsseldorf and Munich,[142] the hegira of our artists to Paris, and the emergence of our most talented painters. Not least important was the accumulation of fortunes, whose owners coveted, fortunately, the art treasures of Europe.[143] The collectors themselves enjoyed advancing stages of sophistication. One critic has suggested that they passed from the Düsseldorf School to the Paris Salon to the Barbizon School (through William Morris Hunt) to Monet and thence to the old masters.[144] Another way of appraising the change in these collections (and in American taste) is to leaf through Edward Strahan's (i.e. Earl Shinn's) *Art Treasures in America* (1886). This book describes the paintings then owned by more than 170 wealthy Americans.[145] Here are the famous names: Fortuny, the Madrazos, León y Escosura, Villegas, and Zamacois. Then, gradually, we encounter the old masters: a Velázquez, a Murillo, a Moro, or a Goya. In 1888 in Seville Mrs. Jack Gardner bought her *Madonna* by Francisco de Zurbarán [146] and in 1896 her portrait of Philip IV by Velázquez. Both remain invaluable parts of an invaluable collection.[147] Meanwhile, in respect to our neighbors of the South, one of the most surprising and influential collections of the century in Spanish-American painting was R. H. Lamborn's, formed in Mexico City between 1881 and 1883.[148]

For a private collection, like Mrs. Gardner's, to become semipublic or public was not unusual. Partly from these origins the museums and galleries multiplied in number and scope. Public art galleries had been established almost simultaneously with the private collections, but their real growth occurred after the Philadelphia Exposition of 1876.[149] In this year the Pennsylvania Academy of the Fine Arts [150] and the Boston Museum of Fine Arts [151] were founded, and the Metropolitan Museum,[152] which had come into existence six years earlier, began to expand. It would be easy to show the creation of similar institutions in city after city and to demonstrate in each the accelerating interest in Spanish painting. In 1915 one critic, restricting her fact finding to the works of El Greco, Murillo, Ribera, and Velázquez and, among the moderns, to Sorolla, listed Spanish paintings in the collections of Boston, Brooklyn, Chicago, New York, Philadelphia, Pittsburgh, Rochester, Sacramento, and Saint Louis.[153] What this might mean to any student of Spanish painting need not be explained. Here at home he could study professionally El Greco, Velázquez, or Goya. In 1930 Royal Cortissoz asserted that he could find and absorb the essential Velázquez in this country.[154] This situation marked an amazing advance from the days when Chase made his first journey to Madrid or Whistler stood long and intently before the *Infanta* in the Louvre. And now, too, flourished everywhere the museums of modern art with their collections of Dali and Picasso.[155]

After 1900 the acquisition of Spanish pictures carried with it a kind of distinction.[156] The trend reached a culmination in the magnificent assembly of materials begun by Archer M. Huntington when he himself was a collector of Spanish Moorish pottery. In 1904 he founded, as indicated earlier, the Hispanic Society of America. Here he gradually transferred his treasures, to this "free public library, museum, and educational institution, containing objects of artistic, historic, and literary interest." [157] Into this central repository were poured paintings, drawings, sculpture, wood carvings, silver, ironwork, pottery, glassware, textiles, laces, embroideries, incunabula, first editions of Spanish books, maps, prints, and manuscripts. A catalogue published in 1930 describes in the field of painting alone the work of some two dozen Spanish artists of the fourteenth and fifteenth centuries.[158] Here, without the agency of steamer or airplane, we can be in Spain.

Dealers, collections, museums and galleries—and, of course, exhibitions. During the first half of the nineteenth century, these verged on the pitiful,[159] but like the museums they took on new life after the Exposition of 1876.[160] In the twentieth century the

287

exhibitions became an informative guide not only to the aggregate riches of Spanish art in the United States but also to the popular interest in the subject. In 1909 when Joaquín Sorolla y Bastida [161] made his first visit to America and directed an exhibition of his paintings in New York, the public was responsive:

Three hundred and fifty paintings [wrote a critic] big and little, all by one man, all in one building, and not an uninteresting one in the lot! Standing in the presence of this amazing display, it is impossible for anyone with a grain of art in his nature to remain unmoved . . . Have a care how you drink of the wine of life which this wonderful Spaniard offers you.[162]

The Hispanic Society followed this exhibition with another in the same year, this time of Zuloaga.[163]

To these many thousands of art lovers, Sorolla, "this wonderful Spaniard," and Zuloaga offered, on the whole, a less mellow "wine of life" than the exhibitions of the Metropolitan which were consecrated to the old masters. Here the exhibition of 1928 consisted of sixty-seven masterpieces including thirteen El Grecos, seven Murillos, six Riberas, seven Velázquezes, four Zurbaráns, and twenty-two Goyas—all assembled from many corners of the country.[164] In this connection, statistics mean something. During the fifty-nine days of the exhibition nearly one hundred thousand visitors looked at the pictures, and more than ten thousand copies of the catalogue were sold.[165] The spectators were rapturous, like a first-night audience at a much heralded play.[166] They were eager to behold with their own eyes "the good Spanish work, so good, so strong, so reasonable, so free from affectation." The enthusiasm of Thomas Eakins, many years earlier, was now shared by thousands of those Americans who, to quote the newspaper's condescending phrase, had within their natures "a grain of art."

WE HAVE been considering the scope of Spain's influence upon American painting and its interlocked artistic interests. Now, as we look back, we conclude that though this breadth has increased immeasurably in the vogue of Picasso and others there was a particular

depth in the Spanish influence upon a few painters of the nineteenth century. This focus of influence seems to parallel the concentrated devotion of our Hispanophile men of letters: Irving, Prescott, Ticknor, or Longfellow. The debts of such moderns as Robert
Henri, Waldo Peirce, or Leopold Seyffert are not comparable individually to those of Chase, who in difficult times visited Spain three
times, or of Whistler, who was directed by Manet and Courbet to
Velázquez. We remember especially Sargent, who in the studio of
Carolus-Duran meditated constantly on the work of the Venetians
and the Spaniards. He studied their "bold yet learned manipula-
tions." [167] Before we leave painting and turn to sculpture, we must
inquire a little more exactly into the effects of Spanish art upon
these painters.

Among them Chase seems to have been responsive to all great
painters. He was, indeed, always so passionately absorbed in his
deity of the moment that it is difficult to name his permanent god.
Van Dyke puts it well: "Before Velasquez at Madrid," he says, "everything was just as it should be. He was the greatest of them all—
the master craftsman of the craft; in the Louvre he protested that
no one had ever equalled or approached such still-life painting as
that of Chardin; at Haarlem he was just as unstinted in praise of
Frans Hals." [168] This volatility in Chase worked toward a study not
merely of various German or Italian masters but also of the sharply
differing Spaniards. The somewhat casual quality of his early appreciation is reflected in *A Spanish Lady*,[169] the product of his first
summer's stay in Spain. During his fourth sojourn, however, he
became the slave of Velázquez and made one of his famous copies,
Las Meninas.[170] Evidently the masters now affected him deeply. He
became an authority on El Greco [171] and fanatical about the craftsmanship of Velázquez and Ribera.

Convinced that for him Velázquez held some precious secret,
Chase was tireless in his discipleship. One day as he worked in the
Prado, two distinguished Spaniards paused to watch him. One remarked significantly: "Velasquez lives again!" [172] Perhaps this was
true in a special sense. For in Chase Velázquez passed through an
alembic which produced somehow "a new thing and his own." [173]
The Spanish qualities were there, but hardly definable:

In the painting [says his biographer] of face, hair, or figure, in the treatment of the actual Spanish subject, in the masterly handling of blacks and whites, one glimpses the Velasquez lesson; but the trail that contact with the art of Spain left upon the painter's imagination is something less specific than the influence of any one painter, however great. It is an essence like the rhythm of a Spanish dance. One can trace it to the pose of a figure not Spanish, as in the portrait called *Dorothy,* or just in some indefinable manner or detail of treatment.[174]

Upon the genre painter, Thomas Eakins, inadequately recognized during his lifetime, the influence of Velázquez was definite though Eakins was characteristically less articulate about the experience than Chase.[175] After he had gazed long at the Spanish masters, he said simply: "Now I have seen what I always thought ought to have been done and what did not seem to me impossible." [176] These painters strengthened his love of realism; he became a careful student of their methods. Although he did not consciously imitate the masterpieces in the Spanish galleries, he experimented with them in mind, particularly in the medium of oil.[177] He adopted, for instance, the old way of "building up his pictures by successive paintings and glazes, the solid forms being painted most heavily, the recessions more transparently." [178] In Eakins' paintings, even in those completed after his return to America, lingers a subtle Spanish influence, like that of Velázquez in *Margaret in Skating Costume* [179] or of El Greco in the portrait of Signora Gomez d'Arza.[180]

For the layman, speculative about these resemblances, Whistler and Sargent are fascinating subjects; to move directly from a painting by Velázquez to one by Whistler is a painless sequence. Although various strains from the past and present meet in this modern artist, Velázquez is evident in Whistler's stately figures: "Yes," he once remarked coolly, "there is Velasquez, Hokusai, and—myself." [181] He does not imply influence, but surely it exists, in the "grand line" or in the blacks and greys.[182] Is it not, for instance, discernible in the celebrated, if somewhat shopworn, painting of the artist's mother? Nevertheless, in this nineteenth-century painter his own strong individuality is always present.[183] Even in the following tribute to the Spaniard we may infer his independent use of what he found in him:

Look at Velasquez [he says], are you conscious, in his paintings, of the hands as a detail? Do you see them step out of their proper place; do they force themselves upon your attention? And yet they are as well drawn and as admirably placed as Van Dyck's, only they are part of a whole and preserve a subordinate position always.[184]

Velázquez was in his mind and in his art, but in any prolonged analysis of this relationship the influence was strongly counter-balanced. Whistler was like Velázquez in this, too: he remained himself. His ends were his own. His debt to Velázquez was not deeply central.[185]

Finally, to complete our story of the painting and the related arts, we recognize in the work of Sargent, although he, too, re-mained "himself," other insights into Velázquez. Modern criticism modifies strongly the acclaim of Sargent as the "heir to Velásquez" and also his attainments as a painter.[186] He has been judged no artist and without distinction even as an illustrator. Nevertheless, in his ears he did hear the counsel of Carolus-Duran, already quoted: "Étudiez sans relache Velasquez." In 1879, during his second visit to Spain, occurred what might be called a spiritual union with this genius of the past, who was not wholly unlike, oddly enough, this nineteenth-century American. Presumably Sargent did not "fall on his knees." James' subsequent comment is nearer the truth. The novelist, whose understanding of painting was con-siderable and who had at least thought of a stay in Spain, declared that for some time Sargent meditated in regard to every subject "just how Velasquez would have treated the theme." [187] Both the austerity and the naturalism of Velázquez were relevant to the development of Sargent's art. The kinship of mind was already there. The two, so different in race, era, and personal traits, be-longed to the same artistic family. As one biographer says wisely, "the essence of what Velasquez and Goya had to teach him was already in some degree present in his purpose and conscious-ness." [188] Or, as this critic adds, the influence of Velázquez was "rather a confirmatory force . . . than a revolutionary revelation."[189]

As in the galleries we surrender ourselves to these resplendent performances of Sargent in the painter's art, we forget our psychological problem concerning the nature of Velázquez' influence.[190] Instead we delight in the wonder and beauty of the living Spain on his canvases: the *Fumée d'Ambre-Gris* (so admired by James); *Spanish Beggar Girl; Spanish Courtyard; The Alhambra; The Court of the Lions; The Spanish Dance;* or *El Jaleo.*[191] How difficult it is to define a kind of essence in these, that of Spain seen through American eyes! Yet this temper is both real and familiar; it recalls Irving's *Tales of the Alhambra* or Hay's *Castilian Days.* In these paintings and in this literature recurs that strain of which we are in search, that unique, yet elusive, quality which our men of talent have borrowed from the culture of Spain and have blended into our various arts.

One particularly fine illustration of this quality is *El Jaleo,* which was the cynosure of the Paris Salon of 1882 and which now daily perpetuates its fame in the "Spanish Cloister" of Fenway Court. In this painting Sargent is aware not merely of the dancer but of the traditions of her race. Was he not, indeed, to draw illustrations for a book on Italian and Spanish folklore?[192] *El Jaleo* has been described as "a piece of naturalistic painting," in which

every ingredient of visible passion, grace and Spanish glamour which belongs to the famous dance, as I have seen it again and again in Seville and Madrid, is reflected as in a mirror; but there is no tincture of the photograph there . . . Put its veracity aside and you still have what is, after all, the thing most worth having in the circumstances,—a beautiful work of art, beautiful in its rich darks, its luminous yet restrained yellows, its grouping of some eight or ten figures in a design which seems simplicity itself—until you take the trouble to analyze the balance of its movement and the subtle co-ordination of its values.[193]

El Jaleo and *Carmencita* represent an unconditional, direct register of a particular type of Spanish influence. Henry James could not wholly approve *El Jaleo.* He was ruffled by this "lithe, inspired female figure, given up to the emotion of the dance . . . circling round incommoded by her petticoats."[194] In his estimate

El Jaleo, from the painting by John Singer Sargent.

James is namby-pamby as he recoils from the vigor of the moment. Nevertheless, even as he protests that the picture "has a want of serenity," [195] he cannot deny its energy and its boldness of conception and execution. Some critics think *Carmencita* Sargent's masterpiece. The restless, living model could not stand still or pose quietly before him, but the painter caught her and in so doing was in debt to his Velázquez: "In no other picture by Sargent," says a biographer, "is the suggestion of suspended movement so direct and convincing . . . In the treatment of the dress . . . there is a very definite reminder of Velasquez. The shimmer of silver, the notation of pattern, the suggestion of texture, the crispness of touch, all are reminiscent of the portrait of Philip in the National Gallery." [196]

PAINTING and architecture! In these the Spanish and Spanish-American patterns are extensive, definite, and infinitely varied. The Spanish influence in painting seemed to shift in the twentieth century to Mexico, and in architecture it emanated almost wholly from that region. In both these arts in America Spain, directly or through Mexico, is constantly present. This is not so of two other arts, to be surveyed briefly before we turn to architecture. In comparison sculpture and music give only faint echoes either from the Peninsula or from Spanish America. For this fact perhaps both Spain and the United States must take the blame. Though a list of Spanish sculptors, past and present,[197] might be submitted, it would by no means rival a roster of the painters, and in America the musicians of Spain must bow to those of Germany or Italy. Yet the major fault is ours. In America sculpture came late, and in music—well, we cannot name many great composers before the 1890's. Nevertheless, intercommunication through the two arts exists.

There has been much lively conjecture about the relative insensitivity of the Anglo-Saxon race to plastic expression. In this obtuseness the American of the nineteenth century apparently excelled even the Englishman. One finds, for example, a kind of naïveté in Hawthorne's descriptions in *The Marble Faun* of the expatriate sculptors in Italy [198] and of their work. In 1820 John Trumbull, the painter, must have been thinking of this lack of ours when he remarked to the marble cutter, Frazee, that "nothing in sculpture would be wanted in this country for yet a hundred years." [199] In 1756 William Rush was born, our able pioneer sculptor, and in 1805 Horatio Greenough, "our first professional sculptor." In 1833 Ball Hughes finished his bust of Hamilton. (His head of Washington Irving is an interesting superficial link between the two arts, sculpture and literature.) In 1853 Clark Mills offered to the world with fanfare his ugly equestrian statue of Andrew Jackson.[200] To us, a century later, these events do not indicate a dazzling beginning for American sculpture.

Nor is the later story of American sculpture exhilarating; in effect it brings to pass Trumbull's dismal prophecy. As this art pursued its rather ineffectual course, our few sculptors worked in a medium nearly incomprehensible to Philistine America. It is curious, however, that in some ways their aims resembled those of the painters, architects, and men of letters. In their works appear the sentiment or the idealism, the struggle for the communication of *fact* (like that of Emerson or Emily Dickinson in poetry), and the subservience to European modes. With a few exceptions (the realistic John Quincy Adams Ward or the cobbler and brilliant anatomist, William Rimmer),[201] this last tendency persisted long after the indigenous had won its place in painting and literature. Our sculpture remained unashamedly "European," and in a limited sense. This adjective always meant in sculpture, in contrast to painting and architecture, criteria which were French and Italian and virtually never Spanish. Their Parisian period did not, as in the case of the painters, lead the sculptors beyond the Pyrenees to the Prado. Where Greenough had studied, Florence and Rome, there flocked the others. American sculptors sought usually, except for the occasional apostasies of Ward or Rush, to achieve an Italianate, neoclassic style.

This allegiance to France and Italy does not mean that Americans had never heard of Spanish and Spanish-American sculpture. As early as December, 1821, the *Port Folio* referred to the sculptural achievements of the artist, Sola,[202] and about a century later the Uruguayan-born sculptor and illustrator, Jo Mora, carved the monument in Golden Gate Park in San Francisco to commemorate the tercentenary of the death of Cervantes.[203] That sponsor of artistic (as well as commercial) fertility, the Centennial of 1876, exhibited twenty-seven pieces of Spanish sculpture, including carvings.[204] The Metropolitan Museum, to cite other examples, contains what is probably a twelfth-century relief from the Church of St. Leonard at Zamora,[205] and in 1928 it acquired the fourteenth-century tomb of Armengol VII, Count of Urgel.[206] In our time the Museum of Modern Art displays the cubistic sculpture of Picasso or the wood and metal of Miró.[207]

So the story is not a complete blank. No doubt our nineteenth-century sculptors were aware of Mariano Benlliure y Gil, Jerónimo Suñol, Aniceto Marinas, or Montañés. The links, however, are fragile. Occasionally, from some unexpected source, comes evidence of American discovery of the unique qualities in Spanish sculpture, as in this tribute from Howells in 1913, written after a visit to Valladolid:

Pictures you can see anywhere, but not statuary of such singular interest, such transcend[e]nt powerfulness as those carvings of Berruguete and other masters . . . But far beyond this is the motionless force, the tremendous repose of the figures of the Roman soldiers in the part of sleeping at the Tomb . . . Beyond all other Spanish sculptures they seemed to be expressive of the national temperament; I thought no other race could have produced them, and that in their return to the Greek ideal of color in statuary they were ingenuously frank and unsurpassably bold.[208]

Whereas classical Spanish sculpture made only slight headway in the American civilization, the allied craft of wood carving conquered Mexico and later the Southwest. Related also to architecture, it will be briefly surveyed in connection with monastery and chapel, in connection, too, with the trades of gold- and silversmithing, tin, and weaving. As we leave the art of sculpture itself, we should remember that side by side with the workers in marble and stone flourished the Flemish and German wood carvers brought to Spain by Charles V. These artists, mingling with the Moorish and Moro-Spanish handicraftsmen, absorbed the delicacy of the Arabian and the realism (emulated by the American painters and builders) of the Spaniard. Perhaps it was this union of the luxuriant and the practical [209] which the wood carvers of New Mexico strove to attain. Studying these carvings in the churches of the Southwest (*santos, bultos,* or *retablos*),[210] we are carried back in imagination to Spain. There in church or chapel are the originals, and during Holy Week in Seville the worshipers bear aloft on their floats the beautiful images of the Virgin and the saints. We cannot be too sure that Spanish sculpture left but a little mark upon our civilization until these peripheral influences are fully assessed.

HARDLY less than sculpture, American music, lacking the springs of ancient folklore and dominated by European standards, has been insecure. In the midst of imitation it has groped persistently toward an authentic native expression, sometimes experimenting with Negro spirituals, with Indian music, or with resounding national themes.[211] Here is the story of a receptive audience rather than of a dynamic American art or of a series of triumphantly original American composers. In the creative achievement of our musicians, the Spanish influence is not impressive. There is, furthermore, a hint of our indifference in the fact that in America preparation for a composer's career seldom impels teachers or pupils to Spain for study or travel. The strongest trends have been German, Italian, and French, presumably in this order.

Something in Spanish music seems to forbid transplantation. Perhaps original and noble compositions will eventually come out of the Southwest, where Spanish songs are being constantly exhumed,[212] and also out of our younger composers' curiosity regarding Spanish-American rhythms. At present only through its assimilative power, which is remarkable, is American music really in debt to Spain; our music has absorbed and combined some Spanish elements. For, in contrast to the other arts, Spanish influence on American music seems to lack largeness and permanence. It stimulates not creation but merely the enjoyment of Spanish music. We

296

listen to it as we listen to that of Russia or Poland. It is unusual, and we never tire of it. But it has not, I think, shaped the work of any great American composer.

"Our musical Columbus," Manuel del Popolo García (with his daughter), performing *Il Barbiere di Siviglia* 125 years ago at the New York Park Theatre, began our long history of listening to Spaniards in operas, in concerts, in dance halls.[213] For this incredible García, composer, singer, and founder of a family of singers, appeared in the first opera rendered in New York in a foreign language. Later Lucrezia Bori and Madame Terzi acted before overflowing audiences at, respectively, the Metropolitan and the Madison Square Amphitheatre. The famous Aurelio Cerulos performed at the piano, and only some twenty years ago the matchless Raquel Meller charmed New Yorkers night after night. These were representative moments in the story of Spanish music in America.[214] We have listened to the religious music and the folk songs of Spanish composers, and we have watched the dancing and the zarzuela, a short musical drama with its roots deep in Spanish life.[215] We have heard our own compositions on Spanish themes, and we have been hospitable to Spanish musicians, when living here or on tour.[216]

We delight in the adventures of Isaac Albéniz who worked in New York as a dock porter and who played the piano in water-front dives, sometimes with his back to the piano and his arms crossed behind him. By these musical acrobatics he earned enough money to travel to San Francisco and to return to Europe.[217] In retrospect the anecdotes of these Spanish musicians in America have a special quality. In the seventies and eighties we hear of the violinist Pablo Sarasate (immortalized after a fashion in Whistler's painting) and in the next century of the brilliant young cellist Pablo Casals. Among others, Americans have listened to the singer Emilio de Gorgoza, the pianist Enrique Granados y Campiña (who suffered a tragic death at sea), Gustavo Durán, the commander of a Republican army corps in the Civil War, and the popular Spanish-speaking musicians of today, including Enrique Fernández Arbós, José Iturbi, or Andrés Segovia.[218] Long ago in Spain Washington Irving became "fanatico por la musica," [219] and like him we have been captivated by the Spanish pattern in this art. It has done this to us —but little more. Compared with painting and architecture, it has not penetrated deeply into our culture.

These operas, concertos, or zarzuelas made definite use of the native folklore which so charmed Ticknor, Irving, and Longfellow. They adapted the legends, set to music, and the ballads. Without confusing them with the vulgarizations always available to us on our short-wave radios from Cuba or Mexico, we must admit the insistent influence of these native melodies and dances upon our assimilative musical minds. Anyone who has heard at nightfall the Andalusian sing his songs, wild, melancholy, strained, but entirely natural in their self-expression, knows that, in spite of exploitation, the old airs of Spain are still beautiful.[220] Thoughtful Americans have always felt so; some songs have entered into the minds of our composers. It is impossible not to respond to the *seguidillas,* the melodies used for dancing, with their three-line refrain; the *malagueñas* and *rondeñas* of Moorish origins; the *carceleras* or prisoners' chants; or the melancholy *peteneras.*[221]

The old songs with their haunting words ("Oh, lonely days!"; "Oh, Christ upon the cross!"),[222] the heartfelt expressions of the lowly, these once heard we never forget. They are from the soul of the people; they are incorruptibly Spanish or Moorish. They describe restless passion or unconquerable despair. They sing of unhappy love or of the distant Moorish past. They communicate their meanings to us with strange tensions of the voice and with facial expressions inappropriate for any other type of lyric.[223] Although their strangeness borders on the grotesque and although they have been artificialized by song writers and orchestra leaders until their repetition and their melancholy are intolerable, these songs are part of our Spanish heritage. They have been brought back by the travelers from Andalusia, and they have drifted across the Rio Grande. They are still sung in the Southwest.[224] They are as authentic as the old churches of Mexico. It is well that they have found their way, even in diluted form, into the writing of our men of letters, of Longfellow (in his *Spanish Student*), of Bret Harte, of John Hay, of John Dos Passos.

Today on the popular level the influences in music express themselves more and more through Spanish America. As early as 1847 Havana sent excellent operatic companies to New York,[225] and in the fifties and sixties Louis Moreau Gottschalk, sometimes dignified with the title of "the first American musical ambassador," gave concerts in Spain (at the invitation of the queen), in Cuba, and in South America. In many of his compositions Gottschalk used Spanish-American folk themes.[226] Probably the first official attempt to link the two regions musically occurred in 1924 in the radio broadcasts and recitals of Spanish-American musicians at the Pan-American Union.[227] The old stories of Mexico reappear. *Azora, Daughter of Montezuma* is no longer a novel or a solemn blank-verse play but an opera performed in Chicago.[228] Instead of the señorita, whose spirited dancing shocked Henry James even in a picture, instead of *Carmencita*,[229] we watch wilder antics. We see the *zamacueca* or the *cueca*, introduced by the Chileans into California in 1849. We learn the tango from Argentina (via Paris), the maxixe and the samba from Brazil, the *jarabe* from Mexico, the rumba and conga from Cuba.[230] We may now turn to architecture but with the realization that music, too, has helped to solidify Spanish influence in the United States.

IN CONTRAST to painting, sculpture, and music, Spanish architecture has inspired, as Ruskin would say, by bodily presence and by daily use. Despite reproductions in engraving or print, the masterpieces of painting and sculpture must remain esoteric, sometimes even unknown, except to the devotee, and music lacks the enduring persuasions of the visual arts. Whether Romanesque or Georgian, whether Fanueil Hall or the Alamo, the influence of architecture seems larger, more directly formative of public taste. Spanish Renaissance architecture, which in 1573 took a majestic form in the great cathedral of Mexico City,[231] may be held responsible for buildings as diverse as the priceless little church of San Xavier del Bac near Tucson or for the modern railway station at Ajo [232] or for the Roman Catholic Chapel at Colorado Springs.[233] Sargent's *El Jaleo* is inaccessible compared with Father Serra's missions, which, long after their apogee, have continued to affect archi-

tectural aims. Particular buildings have been subjects for description in our literature. Just as the Salem architecture appears in the
stories of Hawthorne [234] in ways impossible for painting or sculpture, so the patio, the hacienda, the rancho,[235] the church become
backgrounds and sometimes personalities in the writing of Bret
Harte, Helen Hunt Jackson, or Willa Cather.

The most interesting fact about Spanish architectural influence
in America is connected with its origins. It came for the most part,
unlike painting, not directly from Spain but from sixteenth-century
Mexico and later from adjacent regions. It brought with it into our
Southwest all the variations inevitable in a transplanted art.[236]
Whereas our artists hardly knew Spanish painting until the middle
of the nineteenth century when they invaded the studios of Paris
and Madrid, there were missions or churches during the seventeenth and eighteenth in the regions which were to be Florida,
Texas, New Mexico, Arizona, and California.[237] Although the
Spanish and the English civilizations remained for centuries widely
separated, in these areas Spanish architecture was established early,
with its incalculable effects upon thought and feeling. The ancient
buildings of the invaders, such as the Fort of San Marco at Saint
Augustine, Florida, or the Cabildo at New Orleans or the missions
in California,[238] carried within them, still unborn, the designs of a
twentieth-century American architecture.

This broad dichotomy in architectural aims in America was
predestined. Even if communication had early permitted an exchange of ideas, the climatic conditions of New England (and even
of the South, as far as Florida) would have made Spanish types of
building impracticable, even exotic.[239] To the twentieth-century
New Englander in California, like one astray in a foreign land, the
stucco, tiled houses now seem a natural product of the environ-
ment. He accepts instinctively what the pioneer Yankee learned
from experience when he tried a century ago to rear his "frigid,
wood-begotten New England types" [240] of dwelling on the inhospitable mountains and in the suffocating deserts of the West. Both
types of architecture have developed vigorously, reacting and
counterreacting to many influences but never effectively to each
other, for no real compromise of principles has been thinkable.

Indeed, the two styles now seem symbols of the chasm between the two cultures. Not until the end of the nineteenth century, as a kind of experimental corollary of the mighty Spanish revival in California, did Spanish architecture attain a serious place in the East.[241] It belongs to Texas, New Mexico, Arizona, and California. Though in debt to old Spain, and so to Rome and to Africa, it is a legitimate child of the Southwest.[242]

Meanwhile, in the East, in New England, and in Virginia during the seventeenth century, the English colonists, with no real knowledge of the ornate cathedral then raising itself to the sky on the site of the pre-Cortesian Aztec temple, built their huts, their palisades, their ocher-colored houses of hewn timber. The eighteenth-century story is also familiar: in New England the farmhouse and in Virginia the porticos and columns of Mount Vernon. These buildings are now a precious heritage, competing easily with the relics of later taste, with the legacies of the "Greek," the "Gothic," or the "Egyptian" revivals. Out of the chaos of forms and bad taste which persisted until about the year 1880 occurred a rebirth,[243] somewhat difficult to define. The new era was indulgent toward the Romanesque, the Italian Gothic, and other styles, but through all its vagaries it restored certain classical principles. It turned our thoughts again to the loveliness of Georgian homes and public buildings. We must remember all this, and then we must see clearly the long, broken, yellow ribbon of Spanish Renaissance architecture stretching from Florida to the Pacific Coast. We must consider this peculiar geographical distribution. We must understand this alien ideal of bare brown wall and baroque ornament and also the antiquity of the Spanish architecture. Some New Mexican houses are said to be older than any buildings on the eastern coast.[244] These two contrasting patterns should be, for the remainder of this chapter, always in our minds.

APART from any Spanish-American influence, these jumbled criteria help us to understand the astonishing presence about a century ago, in the conservative city of Philadelphia, of buildings adorned with delicate Moorish decorations. An Arabesque gateway in a world of Federalist façades and Victorian gingerbread ornament! Among the heretical specimens, evidently under a direct Spanish influence, were the Moorish arches on the pulpit enclosure of the Pine Street Presbyterian Church and the Cordovan façade of the North Presbyterian Church at Sixth and Green streets. Here was the "fantastic arabesque gateway in blue marble," which admitted to the colonial burying ground in Germantown. Here were Horticultural Hall and the Old Broad Street Theatre.[245] The Spanish influence in the East and Southeast (not to be entirely dissociated from Mexico and the Southwest) became most conspicuous during the triumph of eclecticism in the last third of the century in buildings like the Ponce de Leon Hotel in Saint Augustine.[246] The Moorish temper was emphatic in the tower of the Old Madison Square Garden in New York.[247] No one who had ever visited Seville or had read Washington Irving's description of the Giralda could miss the resemblance.[248] Everyone knew *The Alhambra,* and to "Alhambraism" we must ascribe these Moorish madnesses of Philadelphia and New York and even of Cincinnati. In this city in 1829 Mrs. Trollope's elaborate "Bazaar" sprang up, with Moorish pilasters and Spanish "scenery"—a devastating if unintentional travesty of "Alhambraism." [249]

Moreover, a few architects were now visiting Spain, perhaps without the ardor of the painters in the Prado but with intelligent curiosity.[250] Although there developed in architecture no causative experience similar to that of the painters in their discipleship to Velázquez, some Spanish traits appeared in buildings inspired from abroad. Possibly Richardson's solution of his dilemma in constructing the crossing tower of Trinity Church in Boston was symptomatic of a current attitude toward Spanish architecture. It was special but useful.[251] Trinity Church was derived in part from the Romanesque churches which he had seen in Provençal France and northern Spain. Like most of Richardson's work, it was not a conscious imitation of any one building, and it contained new American designing. The original plan for the crossing tower had baffled the builders until Richardson, chancing on a photograph of Salamanca Cathedral, hit upon an expedient. Stanford White, who made the drawing, retained the design for the earlier square lantern but added an additional story of arched openings and above it the Salamanca dormers and octagonal tiled roof. Thus the rich intricacy of Trinity Church tower proclaimed its ancient prototype in Spain. Finally, in estimating the element of direct Spanish influence, we must never forget the increasingly detailed studies by art historians of the architecture (and related crafts of Spain), some of which attained, as in the work of Georgiana King, a high intellectual distinction.[252]

THE architectural influences from the Peninsula seem meager compared with the dynamic radiations from Mexico City. These began in the sixteenth century. The impact of the Spanish Renaissance upon the arts of peoples already skillful in building and decoration set its mark upon palaces and churches throughout Mexico. Farther north, in the satrapies of the mighty empire, it left for thousands of miles an afterglow of ornament and color. If, after examination of the edifices of the Southwest, we stand in Mexico City before the cathedral, which was some 240 years in construction [253] and which itself records the changing forms of colonial Spanish architecture, we shall know that we have come to a primary source. Everywhere in Mexico we may study buildings which are the predecessors of our own architecture. Examples are the Church of San Sebastián y Santa Prisca in Taxco, the "almost perfect gem of the Ultra-Baroque at its height." [254] Or we may look at Puebla's many churches (preferably at sunset) with their gleaming tiles. Out of Mexico came the cathedral at Saint Augustine, the church at Chimayo, New Mexico, or the old houses in Santa Fe. Although the luxuriant culture of the period proliferated into other forms (carvings, portraits, chests, or delicate traceries in silver, gold, and tin), the full force of the influence was transferred from building to building. No Spanish pattern in the United States is more tangible, more lasting, or more inspiring than the far-flung line of presidios, houses, and missions from Florida to California.

If we could have seen these buildings at the close of the eighteenth century or in the 1850's when Bret Harte dreamed away the hours in their patios, we should have been amazed at the beauty of these islands of old Spain in the American deserts. Or if, at about this time, we had left New England and passed south along the eastern coast, amid a conglomeration of architectural forms, and then fared west from Florida, we should have felt, also, the serene antiquity of this world. We might have paused before the cathedral of Saint Augustine (looking up at the open belfry) or at the Franco-Spanish Cabildo in New Orleans or at the Alamo in San Antonio or, farther west, in New Mexico and Arizona, at the mission church of Santo Domingo or the Church of San Xavier del Bac. On this imaginary journey we are here before the days of restoration or the fashionable revival of the 1890's. In Santa Fe we see the Governor's Palace, the Church of San Miguel, and the oldest Spanish house in the United States.[255] Next we pick up the straggling missions of Father Junípero Serra's epical conquests, and we yield, like Harte, to the magic of old Spanish California. The mere existence of these beautiful buildings is moving. The later revival is admirable yet secondary. No doubt we are now being sentimental. We must not forget the matter-of-fact elements in this conquest: the meager armies; the scattered outposts; the mud villages.[256] Nevertheless, no architectural pageant in the United States is more thrilling to the imagination than this spectacle of the separate yet united memorials of a vanished civilization.

Many of these buildings show, as we recall to mind the cathedral in Mexico City, the three great styles of the Spanish Renaissance, namely, the plateresque, the Griego-Romano, and the ultrabaroque.[257] The last-named (sometimes called inexactly the Churrigueresque) left, with multiple gradations of ornateness,[258] ineradicable traces on these buildings of ours. The Spanish style was, at bottom, an orderly style. It offered vast, bare walls but made these changeful by labyrinthine carving in stone, wood, and metals.[259] Unlike the stiff New Englanders, the Spaniards were curious and hospitable in regard to the indigenous cultures and in regard to the native peoples themselves. They used both adroitly in rebuilding the Aztec cities.[260] On the other hand, the Indian workmen,[261] finding the Spanish art not entirely dissimilar to their own decorative techniques, employed it willingly enough, not without eloquent

additions. Like adjustments, similar combinations were to occur
wherever these organizing, town-building, church-establishing
leaders laid down their lines of travel, whether beside the Rio
Grande, among the Zuñi Indians, or along the shapely crescent of
Santa Barbara Bay. It is this adaptation of the two styles to each
other, different in every locality, which has varied and enriched
Spanish-American architecture.

Bret Harte describes vividly the altars of old California churches
which exhibit the mingling of Spanish and Indian crafts. It might
be said that this combined art is less firm, less definite, but quickened with a certain freshness of spirit. So to analyze is not our task
but only to suggest the fact that this union occurred. In the Southwest building materials were scarce, and methods were crude. Sometimes the soldiers and the padres, themselves becoming for the time
being architects, builders, and woodworkers, toiled with the Indians, bequeathing to them their recollections of spacious and
beautiful structures or of ingenious carving in Mexico or Spain.[262]
Whatever the standards, Spanish Renaissance carving suffered
changes and modifications. It may be myth that into the symbolism
crept occasionally another tradition. Everyone who has been in
Mexico has heard tales of the invincibility of pagan rites under an
overlay of Christian doctrine. Indians tell some visitors that secretly
the heathen mysteries are at times interchanged with the Christian.
For us such legends, however extravagant, are part of the tale. The
mocking, satirical phrases, said to have been found in the Gothic
cathedrals, seem to have analogies in this story of symbols on the
doors, lintels, altars, or vigas of these ancient Mexican buildings.

To speak of these interiors reminds us again of the handicrafts,
already briefly alluded to apropos of Spanish sculpture. In the
churches and chapels could be found the most ambitious specimens
of these arts, which from the days of the Conquest continued to
engage the colonials both in Mexico and in their vassal states beyond the Rio Grande. Taking advantage of Spanish designs and
Indian workmanship, these people embellished their places of
worship with panels, pulpits, columns, lintels, or colored altar backs

and wrought with skill gold, silver, and iron ornaments.[263] Inevitably, these techniques were easily divorced from the ecclesiastical and diverted into secular fields. From the Spaniards the natives enriched their folk arts.[264] The carving of church furniture led to the ornamentation of domestic tables and seats or to the adorning of pieces suggestive of some far-off Moorish originals, for houses and public buildings.[265] Vegetable paints were employed,[266] and wood carving, not crude but reminiscent of very simple tools, was used, not merely on the altars but on old cupboards and chests, on chairs, and on doorways.[267] These were the crafts which were to last long after the fall of the empire, until, indeed, the present instant.[268]

Which pleases us most, the work in wood, in gold, in silver, or in cloth? [269] In a moment, as we study the modern return to Spanish architecture, we must remember that its revival embraces all these arts. In the different modifications of the architecture from Florida to California, these experienced their appropriate variations. Like the old buildings, old jewelry in native silver and gold has survived.[270] Ancient silver pitchers, plates, basins, trays, bowls, mugs, spoons, and forks (all made in Spain) may be seen in New Mexico,[271] besides the "Rio Grande Silver," which the seventeenth- and eighteenth-century smiths forged from Mexican ores.[272] This delicate gold and silver filigree tempts the imagination back into the Middle Ages. Some of these patterns were first conceived and first given reality centuries ago. The poor man's silver, tin,[273] and the weaving offer further evidence of the alliance of different types of art and also of the importance of these ancillary skills to the total effect of Spain upon our culture.

THE particular proportions in these unions of Spanish and Indian craftsmanship are provocative. Sometimes the Spanish builder was compelled to fall back almost completely on the materials and methods of native artisans. The alleged "oldest house" in the European tradition is of crude Indian construction and differs from the primitive dwellings of the country only in extended spaces for windows and doors.[274] On the other hand, possibly in Arizona more

San José y San Miguel de Aguayo (main façade),
from a photograph by Harvey Patteson.

San Xavier del Bac (exterior; side),
from a photograph by Wayne Andrews.

than in New Mexico, richness and intricacy of ornament in the churches are impressive even if the workmanship is less subtle than in the mother country. In the tangle of Indian influences we cannot help looking for these convincing proofs of Old Spain in New Spain, of Spanish ideas and of Spanish execution pure and undefiled. The reredos at Chimayo,[275] the window and the portal of the mission of San José y San Miguel de Aguayo, or the carved door of the mission church of Santo Domingo, New Mexico [276] excite the lover of Spanish art and stir his memories. Is he not once more in a little church of Castile or Andalusia? So deeply loyal to its pristine origins is the Church of San Xavier del Bac [277] that the imagination is quite ready to accept it as a part of Spain itself.

We must remind ourselves that the honors we now bestow upon these relics of Spain were not always theirs. As the aggressive Republic pushed its boundaries ever farther west, the fortress-church and the mission fell on evil days. One mood of the American settler in the Southwest is reflected in the novel, *Ramona:* his contempt for the declining civilization of Spain.[278] The lack of sympathy in these new conquerors for the old Spanish way of living, which was mirrored both in *Ramona* and in the stories of Bret Harte, included an insensitive disdain for the ancient architecture. The "Americanos" recognized neither the grace of the buildings nor their friendly life of family and servant nor their happy suitability to the climate. So the invaders built their "frigid" New England houses and let the priceless landmarks sink into disrepair, whether governor's mansion or "casa de campo," whether the beautiful San Juan Capistrano or the graceful Santa Barbara Mission. The troubled history of the Governor's Palace at Santa Fe makes suggestive reading. The perpetual sieges, fortifications, dismantlings, and reconstructions [279] illustrate the unhappy relations of the three races during the first half of the nineteenth century. The quarrels of the Mexican Spaniard, the Indian, and the American frontiersman left no time for reverence for these irreplaceable architectural monuments.

The neglect was to change to veneration as California and the Southwest experienced the transforming architectural revival of the late nineteenth century. This revival was to reconsecrate the very buildings which had been scorned by the American pioneers. The beauty of Spanish architecture had long been known to artists in the East. It had, we remember, been described in literature, in *The Alhambra* and *Castilian Days,* books well known at the end of the century. Even then a few perceptive writers had advocated a modified Spanish architecture. The beginnings of the change were functional. After the "Monterey style," an odd farrago of Yankee and Spanish building, appeared in the thirties,[280] there followed a re-emphasis upon the practical merits of the Spanish dwelling. Then, in the early years of the twentieth century, as the Southwest became culturally self-conscious, a sudden flash of illumination made clear the meaning of these treasures.[281] Why not make them the center of a Renaissance?

So the revival began. It was suddenly realized that no colonial house in Massachusetts or in Virginia opened such vistas of an architectural past as the Church of San Xavier del Bac or Carmel Mission. More and more architects were converted. Why not construct out of these relics the architecture of the future? Why not adapt the old to the new? [282] For space, shade, sunshine, coolness, warmth, light, mood, and the essence of an aesthetic tradition centuries old, the architect turned to these ancient buildings as models. He created new structures, sometimes from the originals, sometimes from study in Mexico or Spain. There now appeared in the twentieth century in the Southwest and California the new, simple churches, reminiscent of the mission and also, eventually, buildings with "all the glitter and theatric charm of full-fledged Spanish baroque." [283]

IT IS amusing to discover that almost the first child of this self-analysis was the California bungalow.[284] The new architecture was to satisfy a functional need, but it was to accomplish much more. That infallible gauge to American progress, the exposition, was to prophesy the nature of the Spanish revival in architecture. In 1876 the Centennial Exposition had revealed the pulse and temperature of the fine arts in America. In 1893 the Chicago Fair reflected the return in the country as a whole to classical forms.[285] Now the drift toward Spanish architecture was intimated in the Buffalo Pan-American Exposition in 1901; its "Electric Tower" resembled the Giralda.[286] The reassessment of Spanish influences, architectural and otherwise, had begun, just as the fair at Saint Louis four years later appraised French backgrounds in our civilization.[287] Hence one could almost predict the temper of the two great fairs in 1914 and 1915 at San Francisco and San Diego. These summarized vividly the new ideas regarding the Spanish tradition in architecture. They soon fanned the architectural interest in the subject into fires which swept, perhaps too early, through California and the Southwest.

The Panama-Pacific Exposition at San Francisco re-emphasized the classicism now so indispensable to Americans in their public buildings [288] but tempered it with color and modernistic patterns.[289] At this exposition the Spanish plateresque was suggested by "The Cloister," [290] but the architectural future of the Southwest was more accurately revealed in the companion festival, the "Panama-California" Exposition at San Diego. This exposition made no compromises with architectural fads.[291] It set out to crystallize the aims of California in building, and to accomplish this it presented an idealized conception of a Spanish colonial city of the seventeenth and eighteenth centuries [292]—nothing less. Alternating simplicity with luxuriance of ornament, according to the type of building, the exposition showed all forms of the Spanish Renaissance: mission, baroque, Churrigueresque. "We have," said the consul-general of Spain to the president of the exposition, "buildings in Spain just as beautiful, we have gardens just as fine, but nowhere in my country have I seen such a perfect blending of the two. You have *out-Spained Spain!*" [293]

PERHAPS the spirit of this exposition, which apparently objectified a particular concept in the American mind, at least in the southwestern American mind, is summed up in one man and one building. The man, Bertram Goodhue, had long been an "avid absorber" [294] of all things Spanish, a passionate lover of ornament. He had been an apostle of the Gothic, but he had visited the Orient and had studied the architecture of Spain. A journey to Mexico revealed to him the full possibilities of Spanish architecture. Two stays there convinced him that its architecture was more dramatic in its contrast of surface and detail and superior in its domes.[295] If for this architect the exposition was his supreme opportunity, he realized this, presumably, in his California building, particularly in its disposition of masses and ornamental detail. Goodhue's genius seemed at its best in its capture of the inner quality of these ancient forms.[296] His basic principle was the Spanish colonial of Mexico, with marked attention to the ultrabaroque.[297] In the California building he attained a near perfection, not only in the scrolls, in the ornaments, in the richness of the doorway, but in the tower, reminiscent of the belfries of past ages. Perhaps he had, as one critic said, created "a masterpiece . . . finer than anything in Spain." [298] In any case, it epitomized a new and brilliant eclecticism.[299]

This statement invites qualification, but after 1914 one fact was undeniable: the enthusiastic revival of the Spanish style for both public and private buildings. New respect for the old meant also conservation of the old. Restoration became fashionable. The falling wall was buttressed, the tottering tower fortified, and the patio cleared and replanted. The cloisters of Santa Barbara were rehabilitated, and the Alamo became a historical museum. The functional ultimate of this movement, as applied to domestic architecture, may be visualized in the countless dwellings, some of them beautiful, in such cities as Albuquerque or Pasadena. Inevitably, interest begot excess, and presently one might have seen

evidences of this unthinking attempt to out Spanish the Spanish. Candy-stick twisted columns, broken pediments, and iron grilles burgeon over and around doors and windows, and vie with over-rustic tile roofs and windows and panels and niches to give these buildings their strange and repellent appearance of a particularly new and artificial unreality.[300]

Eventually, in railway station, hotel, shop, and wayside stand, vulgarity in this style was to attain a new comprehensiveness. Probably no movement of the sort ever escapes such cheapening. "More architectural crimes," wrote Irving Gill, a California architect, "have been committed in the name of the missions than in any

other unless it be the Grecian Temple." [301] Today in the Chapultepec Heights of Mexico City and even in Peru, this fashion in domestic building is blessed with the name of "the California style."
Nevertheless, these grotesques were unimportant in comparison
with the attainments of the new architecture. In it lived again, with
a fresh beauty, the dreams of Indian, Mexican, and medieval Spaniard.[302]

From Florida to California! The golden trail of buildings, like
their now-honored predecessors, spread from coast to coast. In
various sections of the country, the new Spanish-American architecture flourished, undergoing local modifications and eliciting indigenous traits. Throughout the revival Florida used a varied kind
of Spanish colonial, appropriate to its somewhat complex Spanish
history. For we think of Ponce de León, of the Anglo-Spanish wars,
of the Minorcans (who were so interesting to the poet Bryant), and
of the not too distant neighbor, Cuba. One critic finds in the Floridian architecture traces of Moorish Spain, North Africa, and Mexican colonial.[303] These buildings are more theatrical than reproductions of the severe, early Spanish-Indian houses of New Mexico. A
provocative example of this modern adaptation of the Spanish style
is the Alcazar Hotel of Saint Augustine, constructed in 1896.[304]
Such a building, not too subtle in conception if compared with
certain brilliantly conceived residences,[305] suggests the elaborations
in the Spanish fashion in Florida. These have passed through all
phases from baroque to comparative academic correctness, from
structures on a huge scale to simple, informal, tiny dwellings.[306]

Northeast of the fountainhead of this influence, in southern
Louisiana, the Spanish accent is distinct but, for various reasons, less
emphatic than in Florida, New Mexico, Arizona, and California.
Spanish governmental control in Louisiana began in 1762 and
lasted forty years. Its influence seemed to confirm the Latin temper
of the architecture and to solidify French characteristics rather than
to establish, as in New Mexico, a quality basically Spanish.[307] Case-
ment windows, balconies, steep slate roofs, large dormer windows,
as well as the symmetry of the compositions, speak of France.[308] If
we wander through the streets of old New Orleans, we shall find
the Spanish influence, as in reading the romances of George Wash-

ington Cable and Grace King, real enough yet somehow elusive. We shall discover it in an interior, in a half-French courtyard, in a half-Spanish patio, in the mass of some exterior, such as the Old Absinthe House, whose windows, again, are French. Perhaps the Cabildo,[309] if we shut our eyes to its depressing Mansard roof, speaks most definitely of Spanish ancestry. It was natural that in Louisiana the modern revival should combine both French and Spanish forms.[310]

Spanish was spoken in Louisiana, and at different times Spanish customs overlaid the French. We must look for the deeper stamp of Spanish influence in religious rather than in political domination. Into Texas came almost exclusively the Franciscans. Their missions were fewer than in California but more elaborate in decoration. Although their hold upon these regions was less tenacious than upon those farther west, their priests left here memorials far more distinctive than had the politicians in Louisiana.[311] The Franciscan mission of San José Aguayo [312] has bequeathed to us a portal and a window which are arresting products of the Spanish Renaissance, and besides—well, there is always the Alamo. Let us for a moment forget its intrusive battles and study its architecture. The front, says a modern critic, is

perhaps the most striking example in the United States of the remarkable persistence of Spanish-Renaissance forms. In it no trace of eighteenth-century classicism betrays its real date; instead, its composition is typical of the Spanish *baroque* feeling, and its shell-headed niches, its flatness of ornament, and the flat wide frame of its central upper window are reminiscent of an even earlier style—the Spanish plateresque of the sixteenth century.[313]

In Texas the modern revival has a special flavor in a city hall and a railway station in San Antonio.[314] These buildings reflect, not without a certain incongruity in this brash state of Texas the Franciscan tradition and the architecture of the old missions.

If the presence of the Spanish tradition in our architecture now seems, in our recent, more sophisticated estimates of our past, a blessing, then of all these regions, with the possible exception of California, New Mexico was the most fortunate. For here, as already suggested, the Indian hospitality to Renaissance forms resembled that first afforded the Spaniards by the Aztecs at the time of the Conquest of Mexico. In New Mexico, too, the Spaniards persuaded the native craftsmen, even as they retained their own methods of construction,[315] to incorporate ideas, including Christian patterns, from Old Spain. In this way was maintained a continuity from Spain to New Mexico and, after the blending, some uniformity. In the nineteenth century modern workmen perpetuated the old styles, unconfused, as in Texas, by a Greek revival or, as in Louisiana, by a competing French tradition. In New Mexico more than in Spain itself, some have asserted, the folk art of early days survived, unchanged by a "fusion with outside artists." [316] The old is still revered, and near it rises the new in forms worthy of its lineage.[317]

Nowhere in the United States can one encounter a more dignified, a more admirable cult dedicated to the Spanish past than in New Mexico with its cyclonic center in Albuquerque and Santa Fe. This community was not, like California, endowed with a Bret Harte or a Helen Hunt Jackson to memorialize in fiction Spanish nineteenth-century history. Its literary flowering came later. Besides sheltering Willa Cather during the creation of one of her most remarkable books,[318] New Mexico inspires today a band of capable novelists and poets. Closely knit together as authors and artists, the New Mexico group is intelligently aggressive in its reclamation of the past and in its insistence on the relation of the past to the living present. In 1907 Santa Fe set a dramatic example to the Southwest by restoring the Governor's Palace, one of the two official buildings remaining from the eighteenth century, and by converting it into the distinguished Museum of New Mexico.[319] Thus the past was honored. Yet only two years after the stimulus of the San Diego Exposition, two artists designed the art gallery with its skillful union of Pueblo and Spanish styles. This is an architectural composite of six Spanish missions built in New Mexico by the Franciscan friars and Indian laborers.[320] Here, within a few steps of each other, stand the antique palace and the new gallery. The latter is obviously the child of the former but in its differences is a building of today.

These buildings reflect the wisdom of Santa Fe and of New Mexico. Much of this modern architecture seems a completely natural inheritance from the Spanish past. Whether, in Santa Fe, we study the post office or the La Fonda Hotel or the private homes on Cañon Road, we find ourselves in the presence of a convention as firmly rooted as the trees in the sleepy old plaza (not unlike another in Puerto de Santa María, Spain). This architectural consanguinity is an astonishing achievement. If Father Latour himself of *Death Comes for the Archbishop* were to confront us in this plaza, we should hardly be surprised. The types of domestic architecture in New Mexico are chiefly three, all related: Pueblo, Mexican, and American-Spanish.[321]

From the old manor houses, one-storied groups of rooms rambling pleasantly over the countryside, was derived the Mexican style.[322] Bret Harte's tales describe similar haciendas in California. This type of building was functional, with uses for climate and for defense,[323] but after the peonage ended, the manors were subdivided into private homes.[324] Carrying on these principles, the modern dwellings, like those on Cañon Road in Santa Fe, exhibited the same plain exteriors and the same distrust of ornamentation. The Americans, without blurring the original plan, have added forms and colors which may be justly called "American Spanish." [325] These buildings have the true Spanish flavor: the brick cornices, the lime plaster, the painted shutters, the Spanish doors, windows, and "portales." Within, in the dark lines against rough sand plaster tinted white or cream, in iron grills, carvings, and tiles, the Spanish tradition lives on. These are twentieth-century American houses.[326]

California and Arizona, too, show clearly the special adaptations in different areas to the noble tradition. In Arizona we may visit the churches of San José de Tumacacori and San Xavier del Bac or, at the other extreme in point of time, the modern railway station at Ajo.[327] Or in California we may admire the restored missions: elaborate San Juan Capistrano, stately Santa Barbara, domed Carmel, and Carlos de Borromeo's tomb of Father Serra.[328] Wealthy California, almost a nation in itself, bestowed the bungalow [329] on her Philistine and the palace on her elite. Her climate with its bright sunshine and deep shadows,[330] her pride in her romantic past, her riches, and her (so we are told daily) fabulous future—all these have encouraged magnificent adaptations of Spanish patterns in private homes.[331] On a spacious scale, with lavish ornament, with beautiful contrasts of simple wall and exquisite portal, these buildings reveal their architects' understanding of the Spanish past. These indeed, as the consul general remarked, "out-Spained" the Spanish and proved the abundant possibilities of modern Spanish architecture.

Above all, the freedom of the Californian use of the Spanish tradition appears in public buildings. Museums, hotels,[332] and churches—for example, the imaginative experiment with the baroque style in the Riverside Congregational Church [333]—show, with a scope unrealized in any other state, these modernized Spanish principles. The high school at National City is Spanish in its stucco walls and cloisters,[334] and Goodhue's plans for the California Institute of Technology at Pasadena included "planted patio and shaded portale, . . . rich decoration concentrated in the Spanish way, . . . iron grills and brilliant tiles, . . . sheltering walls and Persian pools." [335] Of all such adaptations in educational buildings, that of Stanford University is the best known, especially in the alien East where, in contrast, in the universities the Georgian has been mingled with all the architectural vagaries of the nineteenth century.

In encouraging, if indirectly, American literature in its use of Spanish elements, it is evident that architecture has been a more compelling force than sculpture, music, or even painting. This is said with a full realization of the constant kinship in writing (as in Hawthorne or James) between the author and the painter. Irving was presumably influenced by the sentiment of the Murillos, which he knew so well, and the revolutionary murals of Orozco have probably made some of our proletarian writers more conscious of the Spanish tradition. The influence of Velázquez may be recognized in our painting, but his connection with fiction or poetry is intangible. On the other hand, the mere physical existence of presidio or mission throughout the centuries has touched the imaginations of some of our writers. How true this is we shall perceive in the chapter on Bret Harte, but a word or two may be added here. San Gabriel Mission, visited by hundreds of writers, has been sung in verse by both Harte and Charles Warren Stoddard.[336] Historic buildings appear in tales whose setting is Florida, Texas, or California. In this fiction we stand before the Cabildo or the Alamo—often before the Alamo. Of all these the storytellers speak repeatedly, from Sands to Simms, from Bret Harte to the present. Yet even such uses are less important than the strong psychological effect upon writers of the actual presence in our country of the varied forms of Spanish architecture.

For as we survey the Spanish imprint, from its beginnings in the eighteenth century, on our arts (painting, sculpture, music, and architecture) we become aware that on intellectual levels it was a vital force in enlarging a public only mildly curious about writers on Spanish subjects and in educating vividly and decisively those already converted. To mention only two instances, Sargent's *Carmencita* and Pennell's etchings and lithographs gave visual definition to scenes, moments, and characters of Spanish life in our prose and poetry. Simultaneously architecture created authentic backgrounds for our fiction and verse inspired by Spain or Spanish America. We cannot, I think, grasp the full significance of the eight writers now to be studied as interpreters of Spain without an awareness of the growth through the centuries of American delight in Spanish art.

Notes

CHAPTER 1: SPANISH CULTURE IN THE SEVENTEENTH-CENTURY
COLONIES (1607–1700)

1. "More than one half of the present territory of the United States has at
one time or another been under Spanish dominion." E. G. Bourne, *Spain in
America, 1450–1580* (New York, Harper & Brothers, 1904), p. xix.

2. See A. J. Riley, "Catholicism and the New England Mind," *Pub. Col.
Soc. Mass., 34* (1943), 397–8.

3. See E. B. Greene, *Provincial America, 1690–1740* (New York, Harper &
Brothers, 1905), p. 150.

4. T. J. Holmes, *Cotton Mather, A Bibliography of His Works* (Cambridge,
Harvard University Press, 1940), *3*, 1022. For other links of Cotton Mather
with Spain, see *ibid., 1*, 385–7; 2, 483, 692, 904; *3*, 936–7, 1084.

5. See Harry Bernstein, *Origins of Inter-American Interest, 1700–1812*
(Philadelphia, University of Pennsylvania Press, 1945), chap. i, "The Contest
for the New World."

6. See *ibid.*, p. 2.

7. Greene, p. 150.

8. S. E. Morison, *The Maritime History of Massachusetts, 1783–1860* (Boston,
Houghton Mifflin & Co., 1921), p. 9.

9. Bernstein, *Origins*, p. 15.

10. *Diary of Samuel Sewall, 1674–1729*, Mass. Hist. Soc. Col., 5th Ser. (Boston,
1878–82), *1*, 152.

11. Hakluyt, who used Spanish, was probably well known. A copy is listed
in W. C. Ford, *The Boston Book Market, 1679–1700* (Boston, Club of Odd
Volumes, 1917), p. 109. See also W. D. Houlette, "Plantation and Parish Libraries in the Old South," Iowa University, *Abstracts in History*, 2 (1934), 93.
For works of travel which may have been known to the colonists in the seventeenth century, see E. G. Cox, *A Reference Guide to the Literature of Travel*
(Seattle, University of Washington, 1935–49), *1*, chaps. i–v.

12. "These great expeditions of DeSoto and Coronado . . . mark the highest reach of Spanish energy in our own country; nor have they ever been surpassed as exhibitions of skillful leadership and enduring labor by any similar
enterprises by the French or English in North America." Bourne, p. 174. For
a discussion of the prejudiced view of the English colonization of the Americas,
read *ibid.*, chap. xiii, "The Achievement of Three Generations (1492–1580),"
and also the opening paragraph of chap. xiv, "The Beginnings of Spanish
Colonial Policy (1493–1518)."

13. John Wilson, *A Song of Deliverance for the Lasting Remembrances of
God's Wonderful Works* (Boston, 1680). See *Handkerchiefs from Paul*, ed. K. B.
Murdock (Cambridge, Harvard University Press, 1927), pp. 34–5. See Cotton
Mather's comment on the Armada in his *History of Seasonable Interpositions
of Divine Providence, on the Fifth of November* ([Boston, 1719]), p. 29, men-
tioned by Holmes, 2, 483. See also *ibid.*, p. 692.

14. See Julián Juderías, *La leyenda negra* (Barcelona, Editorial Araluce [1943]), pp. 242–5.

15. R.-N., p. 278. This attitude persisted long after the colonial period. See, for example, *NAR* (Oct., 1828), in which are announced for publication *Records of the Spanish Inquisition*, translated from the original MSS; and in *ibid*. (April, 1828), *A Narrative of Don Juan Van Halen's Imprisonment in the Dungeons of the Inquisition and His Escape in 1817 and 1818*. See Helman, p. 342 n. 13.

16. See Bourne, pp. xviii, xix.

17. See S. E. Morison, *The Puritan Pronaos* (New York, New York University Press, 1936), pp. 14, 205.

18. See *ibid.*, p. 15.

19. See H. I. Priestley, *The Coming of the White Man, 1492–1848* (New York, Macmillan Co., 1929), pp. 141–6. These dates are subject to correction. The first known book, the *Doctrina christiana*, was not printed until 1539. For a discussion of the beginnings of printing in Mexico, see D. C. McMurtrie, *Civilization Follows the Press* (Chicago, 1934), pp. 3–4; and *Colonial Printing in Mexico . . .* (Washington, Govt. Print. Off., 1939), pp. 3–4.

20. For an interesting study of such resources, see Harry Bernstein, "A Provincial Library in Colonial Mexico, 1802," *HAHR*, *26* (May, 1946), 162–83. Professor Bernstein analyzes the "Lista de los libros pertenecientes a D. Joseph Pérez Becerra." "There are," he says, "only seventy titles which, even by the broadest interpretation, could be put in a religious category. The number of scientific works (physics, chemistry), on the other hand comes to sixty-eight, while there are seventy-seven works that could easily come under the heading of literature and the classical humanities . . . Great names of Spanish literature and history are conspicuously present." *Ibid.*, pp. 164–5. Other articles confirm the humane element in these libraries. See, e.g., I. A. Leonard, "A Frontier Library, 1799," *HAHR*, *23* (Feb., 1943), 21–51; José Torre Revello, "Bibliotecas y librerías coloniales, 1585–1694," Mexico, Archivo general de la nación, *Boletín, 10* (1939), 661–1006; etc. For similar records, see Bernstein, *Origins*, p. 163 n. 4 and O. H. Green and I. A. Leonard, "On the Mexican Booktrade in 1600," *HR, 9* (Jan., 1941), 1–40.

21. For an analysis of the literary backgrounds of the Conquest and of the influence of Cervantes during this period, see I. A. Leonard, *Books of the Brave* (Cambridge, Harvard University Press, 1949).

22. The libraries of these colonists contained Spanish books. Adam Winthrop, father of John Winthrop, owned the works of Fray Luis de Granada (*Winthrop Papers* ([Boston] Massachusetts Historical Society [1929–47]), *1*, 82) although there is no evidence that these were brought to America. See Harold Jantz' forthcoming article on the library of John Winthrop the Younger in the *Proceedings of the Massachusetts Historical Society*.

23. For summaries of the historical associations with Spain, region by region, in what is now the United States, see H. W. B., pp. 23–32.

24. See H. E. Bolton, *Coronado, Knight of Pueblos and Plains* (New York, Whittlesey House [1949]).

25. See Mary Austin, "Folk Plays of the Southwest," *Theatre Arts, 17* (Aug., 1933), 599–606. See below, p. 215.

26. Chilton was possibly the first Englishman to visit the Southwest. See Richard Hakluyt, *The Principal Navigations, Voiages, Traffiqves and Discoueries of the English Nation* (London, 1598–1600), *3*, 456–7.

27. See J. F.-K., pp. 8–10. See below, pp. 9–10.

28. See *The Literary Diary of Ezra Stiles,* ed. F. B. Dexter (New York, C. Scribner's Sons, 1901).

29. *Ibid., 3,* 131, July 28, 1784.

30. See below, pp. 171–2.

31. Anna Eliot Ticknor, "Manuscript Notes furnished to Mr. Winsor, Supt. of the Boston Public Library, 1868–77 . . ." (B. P. L.). Thomas Morton's *New English Canaan* (Amsterdam, 1637) mentions *Don Quixote.* See p. 128.

32. On April 29, 1700, Sewall alludes to "An Account of the first Voyages into America by don Barthol de las Casas." Sewall, *Diary, 2,* 13.

33. J. F.-K., p. 10. See Thomas Fowler, *The History of Corpus Christi College* (Oxford, 1893), pp. 370–1.

34. See J. F.-K., p. 12.

35. See Arturo Farinelli, "España y su literatura en el extranjero," *Ensayos y discursos de crítica literaria hispano-europea* (Roma, Fratelli Treves [1925]), *1,* 45–108. See also the review of this book by J. D. M. Ford, *Journal of Comparative Literature, 1* (July–Sept., 1903), 284–6.

36. J. F.-K., p. 16.

37. See *ibid.,* p. 26; and *The Poetical Works of Edward Taylor,* ed. T. H. Johnson (New York, Rockland Editions [1939]).

38. See J. F.-K., pp. 20–1.

39. See Martin Hume, *Spanish Influence on English Literature* (London, E. Nash, 1905), p. 179.

40. See Morison, *Puritan Pronaos,* entire; *The Puritans,* ed. Perry Miller and T. H. Johnson (New York [1938]), etc.

41. Morison, *Puritan Pronaos,* p. 146.

42. Even in Emerson's early writings may be found the vocabulary of the frontier and a sense of its constant presence as an influence on American thought. A similar feeling haunts the reader of Tolstoi: the backdrop is the vastness of the Russias. In somewhat the same way one may divine in Lowell, Thoreau, and in others not actively interested in Spain in America a consciousness of its forceful existence.

43. "Nor shall there be a Popish *Alva* to brag, that in the space of one Six years he had Executed Eighteen Thousand People, by the Ordinary Minister of Justice, besides a Million other Butcheries." Mather alludes to Fernando Álvarez de Toledo (1508–82). See Holmes, *3,* 1084.

44. *Diary of Cotton Mather,* Mass. Hist. Soc. Coll. 7th Ser. (Boston, 1911–12), *1,* 420, March 4, 1702.

45. Sewall, *Diary, 2,* 53, Feb. 21, 1702.

46. For a discussion of the "intangible" character of Spain in relation to English literature, see Rudolph Schevill, "On the Influence of Spanish Literature upon English in the Early 17th Century," *Romanische Forschungen, 20* (1907), 604–34.

47. Apparently by the year 1615 there were Spanish mission stations in Florida, Georgia, and South Carolina. See H. E. Bolton, *The Spanish Border-*

lands (New Haven, Yale University Press, 1921), p. 160. For attempts at set-tlement in 1526 and 1566, see M. C. S. Oliphant, *The New Simms History of South Carolina* (Columbia, S. C., State Co., 1940), pp. 21–32. Although the power of Spain in South Carolina centered in the earlier century, "the first words that the English heard from the Indians in 1670 were a welcome in broken Spanish." D. D. Wallace, *The History of South Carolina* (New York, American Historical Society, Inc., 1934), *1*, 55. Another instance is the case of "Francis Maguel, a Spanish subject who had passed eight months at James-town sometime previous to 1610." See P. A. Bruce, *Economic History of Virginia in the Seventeenth Century* (New York, Macmillan Co., 1907), *1*, 32.

48. See below, pp. 28–9.

49. See below, pp. 174–5; 2, 243–5.

50. See Morison, *Puritan Pronaos*, p. 85.

51. See L. B. Wright, "The 'Gentleman's Library' in Early Virginia," *HLQ, 1* (Oct., 1937), 14, 36, 44, 60. See also "Libraries in Colonial Virginia," *WMQ, 2* (Jan., April, 1894), 169–75; 247–51. The *Catalogue of the Library of Rev. Thomas Prince* (Boston, 1846) lists at least two items connected with Spanish: Ambrogio Calepino, *Dictionarivm vndecim lingvarvm* (Basileæ, 1598) (p. 49); and John Minsheu, . . . *Ductor in linguas, The Gvide into Tongves* (Londini, 1617) (p. 50). Dates of accession are uncertain. See also P. A. Bruce, *Institutional History of Virginia in the Seventeenth Century* (New York, G. P. Putnam's Sons, 1910), *1*, 425–6; G. K. Smart, "Private Libraries in Colonial Virginia," *AL, 10* (March, 1938), 38.

52. See E. G. Jaeck, *Madame de Staël and the Spread of German Literature* (New York, Oxford University Press, 1915), pp. 21–5.

53. M. D. Learned, *The Life of Francis Daniel Pastorius* (Philadelphia, W. J. Campbell, 1908), p. 241. Among the manuscripts of Pastorius is a poem called "Maravillas de Peru."

54. *Ibid.*, pp. 256, 257. In alluding to "100 Emblems" Pastorius probably means Diego Saavedra Fajardo's *Idea de un príncipe politico christiano,* a work which appeared, beginning in 1640, in various editions in Spanish and Latin.

55. Bruce's "conclusion that there were at least one thousand libraries in the colony and at least twenty thousand volumes (not titles) before 1700 is a conservative estimate." Smart, p. 27 n. 13.

56. See Morison, *Puritan Pronaos*, p. 145. See also C. A. Herrick, "The Early New Englanders: What Did They Read," *Library*, 3d Ser., *9* (Jan., 1918), 1–17. At the early date of 1640 the library of John Winthrop the Younger contained more than a thousand volumes. This number presumably increased before his death in 1676. Morison, *Puritan Pronaos*, p. 130.

57. See Hume, pp. 186–92.

58. The famous *Breuissima relacion de la destruycion de las Indias* ([Seuilla, 1552]), widely read and translated, became a standard source for historians. Bourne's warning is pertinent: "It is forgotten that his book was the product of a fierce agitation, or that it was written before the Spanish had been fifty years in the New World, where their empire lasted three hundred years. Two centuries of philanthropic legislation has [*sic*] been thrown into the background by the flaming words which first gave it impulse. Las Casas was the Lloyd Garrison of Indian rights . . ." P. 257.

59. See Smart, p. 39. Although John Winthrop's library contained twenty-three German items and only one Spanish, German books were, in general, rare. See *ibid.*, and for the account of Winthrop's library see Morison, *Puritan Pronaos*, pp. 130–2. See also Harold Jantz' forthcoming article, mentioned in n. 22, p. 320.

60. "Books in Colonial Virginia," *Va. Mag. Hist. and Biog., 10* (April, 1903), 402.

61. See below, p. 17. Some Spanish works of a political character were in the colonial libraries. The library of John Carter II, for example, contained Bartolomé Felipe, *Tractado del conseio y de los conseieros de los principes,* 2a imp. (Torino, 1589). See Wright, p. 52. The *Republicas del mundo* by Hieronymo Roman was in the Harvard College Library at an early date. Morison, *Puritan Pronaos*, p. 144.

62. See J. H. Tuttle, "The Libraries of the Mathers," *Proc. Am. Antiq. Soc. N. S., 20* (April, 1910), 294.

63. See T. G. Wright, *Literary Culture in Early New England, 1620–1730* (New Haven, Yale University Press, 1920), pp. 59, 60. The item in Bradford's library might be *St. Avgvstine, Of the Citie of God: with the Learned Comments of Io. Lodovicvs Vives Englished First by J. H.* (London, 1620). Morton used *De orbe novo* . . .

64. See "Libraries in Colonial Virginia," p. 170. This library contained also "a Discourse touching the Spanish monarch," p. 174.

65. See *Catalogue of the Library of Rev. Thomas Prince*, p. 109. In the library of the Rev. Benjamin Bunker was a Portuguese work, "an English translation (London, 1653) of the *Peregrinação* of Mendez Pinto in the Far East." Morison, *Puritan Pronaos,* p. 135.

66. H. H. Brackenridge, *Modern Chivalry* (Philadelphia, 1792–97); and Washington Irving, *A History of New York* (New York, 1809). See below, pp. 45–6.

67. See below, in the Index, "Cervantes."

68. See Morison, *Puritan Pronaos,* p. 146: "The mere fact that there is no mention of Shakespeare, Dryden, or Donne in lists found hitherto is no proof that these books were unknown in New England."

69. "Libraries in Colonial Virginia," p. 174.

70. S. E. Morison, "The Library of George Alcock, Medical Student, 1676," *Pub. Col. Soc. Mass., 28* (1935), 351, 352, 356 n. 7.

71. *Magnalia Christi Americana* (Hartford, 1855, 1853), *2*, 497. See also T. G. Wright, p. 148.

72. The first illustration of its use given by the *New English Dictionary* is dated 1688.

73. See E. B. Knowles, *Four Articles on Don Quixote in England* (New York, 1941).

74. See Morison, "The Library of George Alcock," pp. 354–6.

75. See Morison, *Puritan Pronaos*, p. 146.

76. *1*, 208.

77. See L. B. Wright, "The Purposeful Reading of our Colonial Ancestors," *ELH, 4* (June, 1937), 110.

78. See Ford, App. VII, "List No. III. Sold to Mr. John Iue March the 3d,

1683–84," p. 125. "2 Queuedos Visions Compl. both parts 8° sh. The Visions of Dom (Francisco) [Gomez] de Quevedo Villegas, Knight of the Order of S. *James,* made English by R. L. . . ." Quevedo aroused considerable interest among American readers of the nineteenth century. See below, p. 217.

79. Quevedo's vision of the empire of Death, with its sophisticated blend of the lofty and the absurd, is different indeed from the orthodox, flaming hell in Wigglesworth's *Day of Doom.*

80. See Morison, *Puritan Pronaos,* p. 144. See also S. E. Morison, *Harvard College in the Seventeenth Century* (Cambridge, Harvard University Press, 1936), *1,* 285–97. John Harvard's library, with more than three hundred titles, gives no sign of Spanish books except "the commentary on Aristotle's *de Generatione et Corruptione by* Domingo Bañez." See S. E. Morison, *The Founding of Harvard College* (Cambridge, Harvard University Press, 1935), pp. 264–5.

81. In speaking of certain grotesque passages in the poetry of Anne Bradstreet, Moses C. Tyler refers to a "literary disease . . . originating in Italy in the fifteenth century . . . desolating for a time the literature of Spain, of France, and of England." See his *A History of American Literature* (New York [1878]), *1,* 282.

82. Some of these mystics, such as Fray Luis de Granada, remarkable for his pulpit rhetoric, were not particularly Catholic in doctrine or tone and, if known, might have attracted Puritan readers. See Hume, p. 226.

83. E.g., see *The Poetical Works of Edward Taylor,* pp. 65, 106, 109, 148, etc.

84. See Morison, *Puritan Pronaos,* p. 14; I. A. Leonard, "A Great Savant of Colonial Peru: Don Pedro de Peralta," *PQ, 12* (Jan., 1933), 54–72.

85. *Letter-Book of Samuel Sewall,* Mass. Hist. Soc. Col., 6th Ser., (Boston, 1886–88), *1,* 239, 297. Sewall owned a folio copy of Cipriano de Valera.

86. Quoted in Bernstein, *Origins,* p. 69.

87. See *ibid.,* p. 67.

88. See *ibid.,* pp. 66–71. Professor Bernstein discusses the use of Spanish by Mather and Sewall to establish communications with Mexico in chap. v of this book, "Inter-American Political Ties." See also his two other articles, "Las primeras relaciones intelectuales entre New England y el mundo hispánico: 1700–1815," *RHM, 5* (enero, 1939), 1–17, and "Some Inter-American Aspects of the Enlightenment," in *Latin America and the Enlightenment,* ed. A. P. Whitaker *et al.* (New York, D. Appleton-Century, Co. [1942]), pp. 53–5.

89. Sewall, *Letter-Book, 1,* 297.

90. Quoted in Bernstein, *Origins,* p. 69.

91. Mather, *Diary, 1,* 206.

92. *Ibid., 1,* 284–5. See also *1,* 296, March 4, 1699; *1,* 302, May 21, 1699; *1,* 420, March 4, 1702; 2, 455, May 22, 1717.

93. *Ibid., 1,* 302, May 21, 1699.

94. Sewall, *Diary,* 2, 53, Feb. 21, 1702.

95. *Ibid., 1,* 485, copy of a letter to the governor, Sept. 19, 1698.

96. *Ibid.,* 2, 110, July 1, 1704.

97. Mather's original title. As published in Boston in 1699 the little book

was called *La fe del christiano: . . .* Por C. Mathero, siervo del Señor Jesu Christo. On p. 10 is "La religion pura . . ." (H.)

CHAPTER 2: WIDENING CONSCIOUSNESS OF SPANISH CULTURE IN EIGHTEENTH-CENTURY AMERICA (1700–1800)

1. *History of the United States of America* (New York, 1889–91), *1,* 340.

2. See G. L. Rives, "Spain and the United States in 1795," *AHR, 4* (Oct., 1898), 62–79; and A. P. Whitaker, *The Spanish American Frontier: 1783–1795* (Boston, 1927).

3. Friction between England and Spain and disagreement between England and the colonies in regard to a joint Spanish policy may be followed in Peter Zenger's *New-York Weekly Journal.* In 1706 a combined French and Spanish fleet attacked Charleston, S. C. The colonists, for example, disapproved of the treaty between Great Britain and Spain signed in January, 1739. See E. C. Cook, *Literary Influences in Colonial News-papers, 1704–1750* (New York [Columbia University Press], 1912), pp. 140–1.

4. For a brief, colorful account of the settlements, see Bolton, *The Spanish Borderlands.*

5. Spanish place names of cities or towns in the United States number about two thousand. "California leads with more than four hundred Spanish names of cities and towns alone, New Mexico has more than two hundred and fifty, and Texas has about the same number." For other facts concerning place names of towns, rivers, mountains, etc., see H. W. B., pp. 16–18; 221–36. See also N. Van de G. Sánchez, *Spanish and Indian Place Names of California* (San Francisco, 1914).

6. See H. W. B., Introduction.

7. See below, pp. 211–12, and n. 7.

8. See Priestley, *The Coming of the White Man,* "Spanish Colonial Life and Letters," pp. 157–61.

9. See *ibid.,* p. 178.

10. See *ibid.,* pp. 177–8.

11. *The United States and Spain in 1790,* ed. W. C. Ford (Brooklyn, 1890), p. 12.

12. *Autobiography and Letters of Benjamin Franklin,* ed. John Bigelow (London, 1891), p. 69. Franklin arranged for the inclusion of Spanish in the course of study of the Philadelphia Academy, established in 1749. See Helman, p. 349 and n. 43. For interesting discussions of the use of Spanish materials in American literature during the eighteenth century, see F. S. Stimson, "Spanish Themes in Early American Literature in Novels, Drama, and Verse, 1770–1830" (unpub. diss., University of Michigan, 1952). The main topics in this book, which may be used to supplement the present chapter and others in Pt. II, are "Columbus and the Discovery," "The Black Legend," "The Noble Savage," "Emancipation of Spanish America," "Peninsular History and Legend," "Spanish Language and Literature," "Quixotism," "The *Comedia,*" "A Spanish Backdrop," "The Call of the Caribbean." For Frank-

lin's interest in Spanish, see *ibid.*, pp. ii, 104. See also *passim* for informative studies of Freneau, Susanna Haswell Rowson, Barlow, Brackenridge, Robertson (the historian), and other writers who appeared before 1830.

13. *The Works of John Adams,* ed. C. F. Adams (Boston, 1850–56), *3,* 234. "I . . . purchased Sobrino's Dictionary, in three volumes in quarto, and the Grammatica Castellana, which is an excellent Spanish grammar in their own tongue, and also a Latin grammar in Spanish, after which, Monsieur de Gras made me a present of a very handsome grammar of the Spanish tongue in French, by Sobrino." *Ibid.* See also *Familiar Letters of John Adams and His Wife Abigail Adams, during the Revolution* (New York, 1876), p. 372.

14. J. Adams, *Works, 3,* 234.

15. About 1740 feeling ran particularly high against Spanish America, and the possibility of war to conquer this region was not wholly fantastic. See Cook, p. 141.

16. F. L. Humphreys, *Life and Times of David Humphreys* (New York, G. P. Putnam's Sons, 1917), *2,* 82–90.

17. E.g., "A Poem on the Industry of the United States," in *The Connecticut Wits,* ed. V. L. Parrington (New York, Harcourt, Brace & Co. [1926]), p. 393.

18. Jefferson to Carr, Paris, Aug. 10, 1787. *The Writings of Thomas Jefferson,* ed. A. A. Lipscomb (Washington, D. C., Thomas Jefferson Memorial Association, 1903–4), *6,* 257.

19. See Emilio Goggio, "The Dawn of Italian Culture in America," *RR, 10* (July–Sept., 1919), 250–62.

20. Jefferson to Carr, Paris, Aug. 19, 1785. *Writings of Thomas Jefferson, 5,* 87.

21. See L. H. Boutell, *Thomas Jefferson* (Chicago, 1891), p. 11. Apparently *Don Quixote* was the only novel Jefferson selected for his collection of books for the University of Virginia. See *1828 Catalogue of the Library of the University of Virginia* (Charlottesville, 1945), p. 92. The library, whose catalogue Jefferson began to compile in 1824, contained a number of books relating to Spain and Spanish, among them Ercilla's *Araucana,* published in Madrid, in 1776.

22. Jefferson to Carr, Paris, May 28, 1788. *Writings of Thomas Jefferson, 7,* 44.

23. Jefferson to Carr, Paris, Aug. 10, 1787. *Ibid., 6,* 257.

24. *Ibid.*

25. See H. S. Randall, *The Life of Thomas Jefferson* (New York, 1858), *1,* 24. *The Literary Bible of Thomas Jefferson,* ed. Gilbert Chinard (Baltimore, 1928), a record of his youthful reading, does not mention Spanish.

26. In his diary, on Oct. 25, 1775, John Adams wrote: "Duane says that Jefferson is the greatest rubber off of dust that he has met with; that he has learned French, Italian, Spanish, and wants to learn German." J. Adams, *Works, 2,* 430.

27. Randall, *1,* 25.

28. *Ibid.,* p. 24.

29. Humphreys, *2,* 100. Jefferson had a standing order for books in European capitals, including Madrid. See F. W. Hirst, *Life and Letters of Thomas Jefferson* (New York, Macmillan Co., 1926), p. 503.

30. See Helman, p. 349, and below, pp. 188–9.

31. Dec. 6, 1813, *Writings of Thomas Jefferson, 14,* 21.

32. E.g., see H. E. Bolton, *Wider Horizons of American History* (New York [1939]).

33. See the comment on the "History of America" in T. P. Peardon, *The Transition in English Historical Writing, 1760–1830* (New York, Columbia University Press, 1933), p. 25. See also J. B. Black, *The Art of History* (London, Methuen & Co. Ltd. [1926]), pp. 120 ff.

34. See *ibid.,* p. 25 n. 36.

35. See L. N. Richardson, *A History of Early American Magazines* (New York, T. Nelson and Sons, 1931), p. 350 n. 54.

36. See T. A. Zunder, *The Early Days of Joel Barlow* (New Haven, Yale University Press, 1934), pp. 87, 220. The fourth and seventh volumes of Robertson's work dealt with the civilization of early peoples in South America.

37. See Bernstein, *Origins,* pp. 25, 30.

38. "Hardly a port of Europe there was, from Archangel to Trieste where the Yankee trader was not as familiar as the seasons . . . George Loring, of Hingham, married a beautiful Spanish girl in the seventeen-nineties; her sons formed the firm of Loring Brothers of Malaga, which fifty years later was operating Massachusetts-built clipper ships under the Spanish flag." Morison, *Maritime History,* pp. 180–1.

39. Note, for example, the silence about Spain in Michael Kraus, "Scientific Relations between Europe and America in the Eightenth Century," *Sci. Mo., 55* (Sept., 1942), 259–72.

40. Numerous isolated instances of the study of Spanish during the century are available. E.g., C. R. Fish, *The Rise of the Common Man, 1830–1850* (New York, Macmillan Co., 1927), p. 294.

41. In his *History of New York* Irving shows his awareness of the Dutch and (apparently) of the Swedish languages but not of the German.

42. See H. M. Jones, *America and French Culture, 1750–1848* (Chapel Hill, University of North Carolina Press, 1927), chap. vi. See also Michael Kraus, "Literary Relations between Europe and America in the Eighteenth Century," *WMQ,* 3d Ser., *1* (July, 1944), 226–7. See also A. H. Jaffe, *Bibliography of French Literature in American Magazines in the Eighteenth Century* (East Lansing, Mich., 1951).

43. *The Diary of William Bentley, D. D.* (Salem, Mass., Essex Institute, 1905–14), *1,* 307, Sept. 21, 1791.

44. *Ibid., 2,* 299–300, April 10, 1799. See also *ibid., 3,* 23, May 14, 1803. Bentley probably refers to Nathaniel Bowditch, who made between 1795 and 1803 five long voyages to Lisbon, Cadiz, Madeira, Manila, etc.

45. "Trait of Spanish Character," *NAR, 5* (May, 1817), 30. Quoted by Helman, p. 342.

46. See R. F. Seybolt, "Notes on the Curriculum in Colonial America," *J. Ed. Res., 12* (Nov., 1925), 275; and *The Evening School in Colonial America* (Urbana, University of Illinois, 1925), p. 31: "There seems to have been a steady demand for evening instruction in French, Italian, Portuguese, and Spanish." See also the same author's "The Teaching of French in Colonial New York," *RR, 10* (Oct.–Dec., 1919), 364–76.

47. J. R. Spell, "Spanish Teaching in the United States," *Hisp.*, *10* (May, 1927), 147–8.

48. Silas Deane to Ezra Stiles, Philadelphia, July 29, 1778, *Literary Diary of Ezra Stiles*, *2*, 296–7.

49. See Seybolt, "Notes," p. 275.

50. *Ibid.*

51. *Ibid.*, pp. 275–6.

52. *Ibid.*, p. 276.

53. For a brief account of schools, tutors, libraries, and other cultural links with Spain, see Bernstein, "Las primeras relaciones intelectuales," *RHM*, *5* (enero, 1939), 1–17.

54. This precedence applies also to French literature and other forms of French culture. See H. M. Jones, "The Importation of French Books in Philadelphia, 1750–1800," *MP*, *32* (Nov., 1934), 157–77; "The Importation of French Literature in New York City, 1750–1800," *SP*, *28* (Oct., 1931), 767–83.

55. From Garrat Noel's preface.

56. "Two other language masters . . . Francis Humbert de la Roche and Anthony Fiva. De la Roche, 'having taught the French Language in this City for a few Years,' announced, in 1772, that he would 'also teach to read Latin and Spanish.' [*New York Gazette and Weekly Mercury*, March 2, 1772]. In the following year, Fiva 'gave notice' that he 'continues to teach grammatically, at his house in Dutch Church Street, opposite Captain Berton's the French, Spanish, and Italian languages in their greatest purity.' " Seybolt, "Notes," p. 276.

57. *Ibid.* The advertisements are in Rivington's *New York Gazetteer, or Connecticut, New Jersey, Hudson's River, and Quebec Weekly Advertiser*, July 22, Aug. 12, Dec. 9, 16, 1773. *Ibid.*, n. 8.

58. *Ibid.*

59. *Ibid.*, n. 9. Seybolt lists numerous advertisements.

60. *Ibid.*

61. See John Locke, *Philosophical Works*, ed. J. A. St. John (London, 1889), *2*, 497–504.

62. An examination of a number of eighteenth-century library catalogues shows that copies of these works were available in such public collections as the Harvard College Library, the Redwood Library, and the Library Companies of Burlington, N. J., and Philadelphia, as well as in the private collections of the Rev. Thomas Prince of Boston and of John Logan of Philadelphia. For a description of these libraries and the titles of their catalogues see Bernstein, *Origins*, chap. iv, "The Formation of Cultural Interest."

63. See *ibid.*, pp. 53, 54.

64. See H. S. Tapley, *Salem Imprints, 1768–1825* (Salem, Mass., Essex Institute, 1927), pp. 377, 387.

65. The availability of Spanish dictionaries is noticeable. Jefferson, for instance, sent one to his nephew. Various references occur as early as 1732 to "Pinder's Spanish Grammar." See Cook, pp. 251–2. See also *Catalogue of the Books Belonging to the Loganian Library* (Philadelphia, 1795–1829), *1*, Pt. 1, 14,

22; *1*, Pt. 2, 13. Five different dictionaries are listed in the Harvard College catalogue for 1790.

66. See Bernstein, *Origins*, p. 53 n. 6, p. 54 n. 11. See *The Charter, Laws, and Catalogue of Books, of the Library Company of Burlington* (Philadelphia, 1758), p. 9.

67. Copies of *Don Quixote* in Spanish, French, or English were to be had in the following libraries, public or private: Redwood, Burlington, Loganian, Harvard, Yale, Williamsburg. By 1790 the Harvard library recorded three copies of *Don Quixote*. In the South, too, were private owners—for example, John Hodgson of North Carolina. See S. B. Weeks, "Libraries and Literature in North Carolina in the Eighteenth Century," *Am. Hist. Assoc. Ann. Rep., 1895*, p. 206.

68. Michael Kraus, *Intercolonial Aspects of American Culture on the Eve of the Revolution* (New York, Columbia University Press, 1928), p. 191.

69. See Bernstein, *Origins*, p. 57 and n. 19.

70. See *ibid.*, p. 58.

71. See *ibid.*

72. E.g., see "Books in Williamsburg," *WMQ, 15* (Oct., 1906), 108; *A Catalogue of the Library of Yale-College in New-Haven* (N[ew] London, 1743), p. 44. The Salem Library contained a copy of Jarvis' two-volume *Don Quixote*, and Samuel Orne's books, sold in 1774, included two copies of this work, one in the original. See Tapley, pp. 236, 295, 296. Motteux's translation appeared in 1700.

73. See Jones, "The Importation of French Books," p. 172.

74. Cervantes was discussed in the *Tatler*, No. 252, and in the *Spectator*, Nos. 249, 288, 466. See M. F. Heiser, "Cervantes in the United States," *H.R. 15* (Oct., 1947), 410 and nn. 4, 5, 6.

75. See *The Diary of Francisco de Miranda*, ed. W. S. Robertson (New York, 1928), p. 21: ". . . pues jamas he encontrado sugeto tan apasionado admirador del merito y buen gusto de nuestro inimitable Miguel de *Cervantes* . . ."; p. 113: "Doct^r *moyes* que me aguardava para el proposito, en que hablamos de Siencias y Artes, y Particularm^{te} de la Poesia Española de que es sumamente apasionado."

76. *Hamilton's Itinerarium, Being a Narrative of a Journey from Annapolis, Maryland*, ed. A. B. Hart (St. Louis, 1907), p. 23.

77. *Ibid.*, pp. 115–16.

78. See Richardson, p. 293.

79. The years between 1750 and 1770 in Germany have been described as a period of "slowly growing interest" in Spanish literature and the years between 1771 and 1800 as a period of "established interest." See H. O. Lyte, *Spanish Literature and Spain in Some of the Leading German Magazines of the Second Half of the Eighteenth Century* (Madison [Wis.], 1932), Contents.

80. See Bernstein, *Origins*, pp. 60–1. In the growth of cultural relations with Spanish America in the late eighteenth and in the nineteenth century, the book trade, the intercommunication of learned societies, and the devoted efforts of a few public-spirited men (scholars, publishers, scientists) were important factors. See *ibid., passim* (with its accounts of Samuel Latham Mitchill

and Isaiah Thomas), and for a history of the later relationships and of other leaders (e.g. John Russell Bartlett or the geologist Charles Hartt) see Harry Bernstein, "The Latin American Book Trade before 1900," *Pub. Week., 148* (Dec. 1, 1945), 2416–19. See also his forthcoming book, *Making an Inter-American Mind.*

81. *New American Magazine,* Feb., 1758—May, 1759. See Richardson, p. 99.

82. From February to October, 1789, the *Gentlemen and Ladies' Town and Country Magazine* serialized "The History of the Conspiracy of the *Spaniards* Against the Republick of Venice." See *ibid.,* p. 354.

83. On March 5, 1785, *Carey's Pennsylvania Evening Herald* published "Columbia to Her Genuine Sons, on the Prospect of a Spanish War." On October 13, 1787, the *Georgia State Gazette* included the lines:

> We'll force our trade, and fear no evil,
> And drive the Spaniards to the devil . . . !

For these and other instances, see L. M. Miner, *Our Rude Forefathers. American Political Verse, 1783–1788* (Cedar Rapids, Torch Press, 1937), *passim.*

84. *Columbian Magazine,* July, Nov., 1788. Numerous libraries sold during the eighteenth century contain other items relating to the conquest of Spanish America. E.g., see Cook, p. 119; J. T. Wheeler, "Reading and other Recreations of Marylanders, 1700–1776," *Md. Hist. Mag., 38* (June, 1943), 168; Tapley, p. 295. For additional Spanish items in the magazines, see Bernstein, *Origins,* p. 60.

85. See Bernstein, "Some Inter-American Aspects of the Enlightenment," p. 57; and *Origins,* pp. 63–5.

86. Ezra Stiles, *3,* 131, July 28, 1784.

87. See Bernstein, *Origins,* p. 56.

88. See Carita Doggett, *Dr. Andrew Turnbull and the New Smyrna Colony of Florida* ([Florida, Drew Press, 1919]). Apparently some Minorcans came earlier: "Some share they also had in planting the *American* colonies." John Armstrong, *The History of the Island of Minorca* (London, 1752), p. 211.

89. On April 1, 1788, Governor Miró of Louisiana informed the Council of the Indies that "the introduction of the Spanish language in the province was difficult work." See Jones, *America and French Culture,* p. 114. For the influence of Spanish culture in this region and in parts of the Southwest, see below, pp. 311–12.

90. See Jonathan Carver, *Three Years Travels through the Interior Parts of North America* (Boston, 1797).

91. E.g., see the article cited above, n. 81.

92. The American prejudice concerning the corrupting tendencies of European travel was still strong. Some English travel books (relating to Spain) were in the libraries. E.g., *The Charter, Laws and Catalogue of Books, of the Library Company of Burlington,* pp. 21, 45.

93. An exceptionally fine description of John Jay's journey from Cadiz to Madrid is contained in a letter to his father written on May 23, 1780. *The Correspondence and Public Papers of John Jay, 1763–1781,* ed. H. P. Johnston (New York [1890–93]), *1,* 333–5.

94. There is reason to believe that he visited Jamaica. See J. P. Mitchell, *St. Jean de Crèvecoeur* (New York, Columbia University Press, 1916), p. 25.

95. Merle Curti, *The Growth of American Thought* (New York, Harper & Brothers [1943]), p. 13.

96. M. G. St. J. de Crèvecœur, *Sketches of Eighteenth Century America,* ed. H. L. Bourdin, R. H. Gabriel, and S. T. Williams (New Haven, Yale University Press, 1925), p. 65.

97. M. G. St. J. Crèvecœur, "Sketch of a Contrast between the Spanish & the English Colonies," ed. H. L. Bourdin and S. T. Williams, *Univ. Calif. Chron., 28* (April, 1926), 157.

98. "The first three books of his original plan corresponded rather closely in structure with the sections of Robertson's *History of America* on which they were based. But, as the poet began to look more closely into the 'uncommon ornaments' of poetry offered by the new Indian civilization of South America, he became captivated by new material to such an extent that he revised his outline and increased the hemispheric part of his work by an entire book in order to interpolate an episode 'in epic form' dealing with the Incan hero Manco Capac." Leon Howard, *The Connecticut Wits* (Chicago, University of Chicago Press [1943]), p. 148.

99. See *ibid.,* p. 146.

100. London, 1688, an English translation by Sir Paul Rycault. For an account of this interesting volume, see *ibid.,* p. 148.

101. E.g., see *The Columbiad.*

102. See W. H. Prescott, "Life of Charles Brockden Brown," *The Library of American Biography,* ed. Jared Sparks (New York, 1839), *1,* 123.

103. Dunlap's *Don Carlos,* an adaptation from Schiller, was acted at the Park Theatre, New York, on May 6, 1799. See F. W. C. Lieder, *The Don Carlos Theme* (Cambridge, Harvard University Press, 1930), p. 29.

104. *The Virgin of the Sun* was acted on March 12, 1800, *Pizarro in Peru; or The Death of Rolla* on March 26, 1800, and an opera, *The Knight of the Guadalquivir,* on Dec. 5, 1800.

105. Acted on Dec. 22, 1794. See A. H. Quinn, *A History of the American Drama, from the Beginnings to the Civil War* (New York, Harper & Brothers, 1923), pp. 121–3. Versions of Cervantes, which were to be popular throughout the nineteenth and twentieth centuries, began to appear in the first half of the eighteenth. Among such productions were Henry Fielding's *Don Quixote in England* (acted in Philadelphia, May 21, 1766) and Isaac Bickerstaffe's comic opera, *The Padlock,* from "El celoso estremeño" (acted frequently after 1769). For descriptions of various versions, see Heiser, pp. 417–18. See also J. R. Spell, "Hispanic Contributions to the Early Theater in Philadelphia," *HR, 9* (Jan., 1941), 192–8. Royall Tyler was the author of a farce (never produced or published), "The Island of Barataria," inspired by *Don Quixote.* For comment on later versions of Cervantes, see below, p. 259.

106. Duyck., *1,* 173.

107. For a useful survey of the growth of scholarship and history concerning Columbus, see Bourne, pp. 322–8.

108. See *Catalogue of the Books Belonging to the Loganian Library,* p. 18.

109. See Richardson, p. 126.

110. See W. C. Cairns, *British Criticisms of American Writings, 1783–1815* (Madison [Wis.], 1918), pp. 68–72.

111. See Bourne, pp. 82–3.

112. *Daily Advertiser* (New York), Feb. 11, 1791. For other articles, see *ibid.*, Nov. 12, 1790; *United States Magazine, 1* (Feb., 1779), 81–8; *Freeman's Journal*, Aug. 21, 1781; *National Gazette*, March 12, 1792; *Jersey Chronicle*, Nov. 21, 1795.

113. Published in the *United States Magazine, 1* (June, 1779), 282–3. See Richardson, p. 208. See *The Poems of Philip Freneau*, ed. F. L. Pattee (Princeton, University Library, 1902–7), *1*, 46–8.

114. *Ibid.*, *1*, 89–122.

115. Freneau, apparently long interested in the romantic conception of Columbus, wrote of the burial of the admiral in the West Indies. See Philip Marsh, "Freneau and the Bones of Columbus," *MLN, 60* (Feb., 1945), 121–4. For other poems of Freneau relating to Columbus and for Freneau's identification with the "black legend," see Stimson, pp. 3–4, 17–18. In his satire Freneau was in debt to Cervantes. For evidence of Freneau's reading of *Don Quixote*, see Heiser, pp. 418–19.

116. See B. H. Bissell, *The American Indian in English Literature of the Eighteenth Century* (New Haven, Yale University Press, 1925), pp. 16–19.

117. Quoted in Kraus, "Literary Relations," p. 213. See also H. N. Fairchild, *The Noble Savage* (New York, Columbia University Press, 1928), p. 10.

118. For discussions of this concept, see Fairchild, Bissell, Kraus, "Literary Relations," pp. 213–14.

119. For the connection of Las Casas with this tradition, see Fairchild, pp. 10–12.

120. See Bissell, p. 16.

121. Garcilaso de la Vega includes an idealization of the Peruvian government and poetic accounts of the Indians. See *ibid.*, pp. 17–19. In this way the influence of Garcilaso de la Vega may have been greater than that of Las Casas.

122. See Fairchild, p. 11.

123. "Montaigne illustrates the third and final stage in his development. By fusing the more or less objective and irreflective narrations of the explorers and various long-current traditions, the philosopher arrives at important generalizations about the virtue of savage man and the deteriorating effects of civilization." *Ibid.*, p. 21.

124. See *ibid.*, p. 12.

125. For the representation in this play of the "Golden Age of the Incas," see *ibid.*, p. 33.

126. In one of these speeches occurs the first use of the term "noble savage." See *ibid.*, p. 29.

127. The scene is not Peru but Moorish Spain, and the cruelty of the Spaniards is emphasized.

128. See Fairchild, p. 10.

129. J. I. Molina, *The Geographical, Natural and Civil History of Chili*, tr. Richard Alsop (Middletown, Conn., 1808). Alsop, like Charles Brockden Brown, was interested also in Italian literature.

130. See Howard, p. 150. Barlow's early biographer suggests that he may

have used Marmontel's *The Incas; or the Destruction of the Empire of Peru.*
See the biographical sketch of Barlow by Elihu H. Smith in the *Monthly
Magazine,* 6 (Oct., 1798), 251, quoted by Howard, p. 149.

131. Freneau, *1,* 117.

132. See *Correspondence of John Adams and Thomas Jefferson,* ed. Paul
Wilstach (Indianapolis, Bobbs-Merrill Co. [1925]), p. 149.

133. *The Letters of Joseph Dennie, 1768–1812,* ed. L. G. Pedder (Orono,
Me., University Press, 1936), p. 20.

134. Sometimes called the first American novelist. Born in New York in
1720, Mrs. Lennox went to England in 1735. Here she spent the remainder
of her life.

135. See *ibid.,* pp. 40, 70, 81, 88, 93, 96, 148.

136. See Heiser, pp. 418–19 and notes.

137. See Heiser, p. 417 n. 30.

138. *W. Bentley, 1,* 17, 32, 36, April 16, 1785; March 19, May 2, 1786. On
September 28, 1791, Bentley formed a plan for the study of French, Spanish,
German, and Italian. *Ibid.,* p. 310. His *Diary* reflects his speculations regarding Spain. He owned "Spanish books on Purgatory" (Quevedo?) and, as noted,
meeting three Spanish officers on September 21, 1797, received from one of
them an addition to his Spanish library.

139. *CHAL, 1,* 236.

140. See the example given by Heiser, p. 420, and nn. 43, 44. *Don Quixote
at College or, A History of the Gallant Adventures Lately Achieved by 'the
Combined Students of Harvard University* (Boston, 1807). Probably at about
this time copies of *Don Quixote* became more numerous in the libraries. A
copy, for example, was acquired about 1805 by the Farmers' Library of
Wheatland, one of several private subscription libraries organized in western
New York after 1796. See P. B. Daghlian, "The Farmer's Library," *Rochester
Univ. Lib. Bul.,* 2 (Nov., 1946), 6.

141. *Port Folio,* 2 (Feb. 13, 1802), 44–5.

142. For Irving's debt to Cervantes in this work and in the earlier *Salma-
gundi,* see Heiser, pp. 421–3; and S. T. W., *1,* 114. See also *Diedrich Knickerbocker's A History of New York,* ed. S. T. Williams and Tremaine McDowell
(New York, Harcourt, Brace & Co. [1927]), Introduction, pp. xxxviii–xli.

143. See S. T. W., *1,* 114.

144. Trumbull was familiar with Cervantes. See Alexander Cowie, *John
Trumbull, Connecticut Wit* (Chapel Hill, University of North Carolina Press,
1936), p. 147.

145. H. H. Brackenridge, *Modern Chivalry,* ed. C. M. Newlin (New York,
American Book Co. [1937]), p. 406. The book was originally published in parts
in the years 1792, 1793, 1797, 1804, 1805, 1815.

146. Brackenridge's first intention was to tell his story in Hudibrastic couplets. See *ibid.,* p. xxiii.

147. *Ibid.,* p. 43.

148. For a detailed comparison of *Don Quixote* and *Modern Chivalry,* see
Heiser, pp. 413–17.

NOTES FOR PART 2

CHAPTER 1: THE TRAVELERS

1. Letter of Mary E. Fenno to G. L. Verplanck, New York, Dec. 29 [1810] (N. Y. H. S.).

2. *A Journal of Travels in England, Holland and Scotland, and of Two Passages over the Atlantic, in the Years 1805 and 1806*, 3d ed. (New Haven, 1820), "Preface to the First Edition—1810," *1*, 3–4.

3. Travel books about Spain and Spanish America by other than American authors had currency in the United States. Humboldt's influence was incalculable. Our discussion is limited to travel books written by Americans. See "Commentators on Europe," Spiller, *3*, 356–7.

4. In both fiction and poetry of the mid-nineteenth century narrative was popular.

5. A few books, whose right to the name of "travel book" might be called controversial, are referred to briefly here. Some, such as Irving's *The Alhambra*, are discussed in other chapters.

6. As another type, see C. A. Bartol, *Pictures of Europe, Framed in Ideas* (Boston, 1855).

7. See Bayard Taylor, *Rhymes of Travel, Ballads and Poems* (New-York, 1849).

8. E.g., Bernard Romans, *A Concise Natural History of East and West Florida* (New-York, 1775); Thomas Anburey, *Travels through the Interior Parts of America* (London, 1789); William Bartram, *Travels through North & South Carolina, Georgia, East & West Florida* (Philadelphia, 1791).

9. For a discussion of these conditions of travel, see R. E. Spiller, *The American in England during the First Half Century of Independence* (New York, H. Holt & Co. [1926]), chap. i.

10. Irving was frequently reproached for his long stays abroad.

11. Some of Irving's manuscript notes were written in pencil during travel by stagecoach.

12. (New York), p. 8.

13. "I can hardly realize as yet that we are in Spain . . . I feel at home amid these familiar names, recalling as they do many a story and legend of romance, of knight and cavalier and Moorish warrior . . . I am thoroughly imbued with Spanish legend and romance." H. T. Allen, *Travels in Europe and the East: during the Years 1858–59 and 1863–64* (New Haven, 1879), pp. 462–3.

14. See, besides *The Innocents Abroad*, D. R. Locke, *Nasby in Exile* (Toledo, 1882).

15. *Cosas de España; or, Going to Madrid via Barcelona* (New York, 1855). Mackie, who refers playfully to himself as "a loiterer" and says that he treats only of "pleasing Spanish matters," writes such trash as his chapters, "My Rooms at the Fonda," "My Balcony," "My Table," or "The Rambla and the Muralla de Tierra." He was warmly praised by the Duyckincks, who said these "clever sketches" represented successful writing in a field in which

334

several American travelers, such as Irving, Mackenzie, Wallis, and others, "have gathered distinguished laurels." Duyck., *2*, 483. Many of these travel essays appeared in *Putnam's Monthly Magazine* in 1854, a year before their assembly as a book.

16. By the middle of the century Europeans had perceived the financial potential of the American tourist. The great exhibition in 1851 at the Crystal Palace in London and later exhibitions in Paris announced that they would not exclude American travelers!

17. In his fiction James depicts repeatedly the American in Europe holding fast to the cultural and social criteria of his native land.

18. A brief summary called "Americans in Italy" may be found in Camillo von Klenze, *The Interpretation of Italy during the Last Two Centuries* (Chicago, University of Chicago Press, 1907), pp. 145–7. Until the thirties and the forties the pattern was similar to that of American travelers in Spain. We hear, for example, of *Letters from Europe, during a Tour through Switzerland and Italy* (Philadelphia, 1805). Among the distinguished literary travelers in Italy were Cooper, Charles Eliot Norton, Hawthorne, Howells, and James. See also H. N. Maugham, *The Book of Italian Travel (1580–1900)* (London, 1903), Pt. II, and, in particular, the bibliography in Giuseppe Prezzolini, *Come gli Americani scoprirono l'Italia (1750–1850)* (Milan, 1933).

19. *Correspondence of James Fenimore-Cooper*, ed. J. F. Cooper (New Haven, Yale University Press, 1922), *1*, 96.

20. *Gleanings in Europe [France]* (Philadelphia, 1837); *Gleanings in Europe. England* (Philadelphia, 1837); *Gleanings in Europe. Italy* (Philadelphia, 1838).

21. In 1852 W. W. Story declared in a letter to James Russell Lowell: "We must take some untravelled paths which the English have not spoiled . . ." See Henry James, *William Wetmore Story and His Friends* (Boston, Houghton Mifflin & Co., 1903), *1*, 253.

22. For Johnson's comment, see *Boswell's London Journal*, ed. F. A. Pottle (New York, McGraw-Hill Book Co. [1950]), p. 285. For conditions of travel see C. E. Farnham, "American Travellers in Spain, (1777–1867)," *RR, 13* (Jan., July, Oct., 1922), 44–64, 252–62, 305–30. Allusion is made to these chapters as part of a projected larger work. Miss Farnham wrote me (Feb. 4, 1946) that Vol. *1* (1777–1867) was completed and Vol. *2* (1867 to the present time) was in preparation. See also *Todd Memorial Volumes*, ed. J. D. Fitz-Gerald and Pauline Taylor (New York, 1930), *1*, 129–39. See also Raymond Foulché-Delbosc, *Bibliographie des voyages en Espagne et en Portugal* (Paris, 1896), and Arturo Farinelli, *Viajes por España y Portugal desde la édad media hasta el siglo XX* (Roma, 1942–44).

23. Alexander Slidell Mackenzie describes the various routes. See *A Year in Spain*, 3d ed., enl. (New-York, 1836), Vol. *1*, chap. i.

24. See *ibid.*, vol. *1*, chap. iii. Irving wrote of Mackenzie: "He has been robbed. I expected the event. The dilligence in which he started had been attacked on its way to Madrid . . ." Irving to Mrs. T. W. Storrow, May 5, 1827 (H.).

25. Irving's Spanish notebooks and letters allude frequently to these unhappy memorials, so full of meaning to the lonely traveler.

26. See, for example, George Ticknor's description of the "General Hospital" in Madrid as "very dirty and ill kept." G. T., *1*, 194.

27. In 1813 Mordecai M. Noah's relief after crossing the border from Spain into France was voluble: "Every thing was changed; we had but just left a country, through which we had journeyed for many days, under privations the most painful, and in tedious monotony: we now, were seated around a table plentifully supplied." In particular, Noah rejoiced that he no longer saw "the Priests swarming in every direction, as in Spain." *Travels in England, France, Spain, and the Barbary States* (New-York, 1819), pp. 195, 242. "As you walk the streets of a Spanish city," wrote E. C. Wines, "priests and friars, next to beggars, appear to be the most numerous class of inhabitants." *Two Years and a Half in the Navy: or, Journal of a Cruise in the Mediterranean and Levant* (Philadelphia, 1832), *1*, 163.

28. *Saunterings* (Boston, 1872), pp. viii–ix.

29. For example, Italy's art affected Landor, Browning, and Longfellow, its revolutionary spirit Shelley, Byron, and Margaret Fuller.

30. J. J. Jarves, *Art-Hints, Architecture, Sculpture, and Painting* (New York, 1855), p. 276.

31. John William De Forest, author of travel books and novelist, and George William Curtis, essayist and orator, serve as illustrations of the young, cultivated American traveler who neglected Spain. Curtis, who remained in Europe from 1846 to 1850, visited France, Italy, Germany, Egypt, and Palestine, but not Spain.

32. One example is William Henry Bishop, whose books on Spain and Mexico were popular in the latter half of the century. In the twentieth century the acquaintance of travelers with many Spanish-speaking countries was a commonplace.

33. Among the travelers describing Mateo Ximénez or Irving in Spain or both were H. T. Allen, W. H. Bishop, Walter Channing, Madame Le Vert, Frances Schroeder, C. A. Stoddard, Bayard Taylor, and Julia Sands Bryant (the poet's daughter).

34. These four volumes, published between 1862 and 1864, were read by thousands of Americans.

35. John Calhoun's inadequate phrase for Madame Octavia Walton Le Vert, whose *Souvenirs of Travel* appeared in Mobile in 1857. Madame Le Vert described also England, France, Germany, Italy, and Cuba. Near Valdepeñas, during a moonlight journey to Argamasilla del Alba, she recorded an old monk's "glowing expressions of admiration of Washington Irving," whom he had known in Granada.

36. Bryant visited Cuba in 1849 and 1872, Spain in 1857 and 1866, Mexico in 1872. Long before these journeys, in 1828, he wrote: "I remember that one afternoon I was returning from a solitary excursion along the skirts of the Sierra Morena . . . ," etc. "Recollections of the South of Spain," *The Talisman for MDCCCXXIX*, p. 45.

37. "After having seen every State and Capital in his own country, his desire was to visit every Capital in Europe." Vassar's first letter is dated Havana, Feb. 10, 1839. He traveled to California, South America (Caracas, Buenos Aires, Lima, and Quito), and was apparently in Spain from Feb. 28, 1853, to

May 23 of the same year. This gigantic book, first published in 1861, was popular. A fourth edition appeared in 1891.

38. Théophile Gautier, *Tra los montes* (Paris, 1843), reprinted under title *Voyage en Espagne;* Richard Ford, *A Hand-Book for Travellers in Spain, and Readers at Home* (London, 1845); S. E. Widdrington, *Sketches in Spain during the Years 1829, 30, 31, & 32* (London, 1834).

39. This is only part of the book's protracted title. Spain is discussed in Pt. 2, pp. 60–194. Noah's previous knowledge of Spain was limited, being, in fact, hardly more than his memory of the younger Colman's play, *The Mountaineers.* He "commenced singing the stanzas aloud:

> Ye high-born Spanish Noblemen
> Ye Dons and Cavaliers . . ."

See p. 136. Noah names "Morton" as the author of the play and misquotes the song.

40. *Ibid.,* p. 189.

41. "The great effort of Spain at present, is to check the independence of South America; this is impossible." *Ibid.,* p. 193.

42. *Ibid.,* p. v.

43. *Ibid.,* p. 134.

44. Dedicated to the secretary of the United States Navy.

45. "I have never read the English version, but am confident that no translation can do more than feebly shadow forth the exquisite and incomparable beauties of the original." Wines, *1,* 210.

46. *Ibid.,* Preface, p. v.

47. When Irving left Granada in August, 1829, he carried with him the incomplete manuscript of *The Alhambra* (1832).

48. *Letters, Descriptive of Public Monuments, Scenery, and Manners in France and Spain* (Newburyport, 1832).

49. See *NAR, 37* (July, 1833), 84–117.

50. Gayangos to Prescott, Nov. 17, 1841, Wolcott, p. 271.

51. *Reminiscences of Spain* (Boston, 1833), *1,* 21. "Once again the scene shifted. I imagined myself, as I was, reclining in an alcove of the Court of Lions. It seemed half a reverie, half a dream . . ." *Ibid.,* p. 41.

52. *Ibid.,* "Advertisement," p. v.

53. Cushing's learning in Spanish history and literature is evident. He prefaced the chapter called "Francisco de Toledo" by a section from Garcilaso de la Vega's *Historia general del Peru,* and that called "Fortune, a Vision of Time" by stanzas from the *Coplas* of Jorge Manrique and the *Lusiadas* of Luiz de Camões. This quality in Cushing's book elicited no particular appreciation in the reviews. See, e.g., *Am. Mo. M., 1* (June, 1833), 225–7, or *Am. Mo. R., 3* (June, 1833), 466–73.

54. See her statement in "Carta á mi lector de las Batuecas" in *Clemencia* (Madrid, Hijos de M. Guijarro, 1902), p. xxxii.

55. See Irving to S. A. Allibone, Sunnyside, Nov. 2, 1857. S. A. Allibone, *A Critical Dictionary of English Literature and British and American Authors* (Philadelphia, 1859–71), *1,* 943.

56. References to the book as a guide to the palace are innumerable. As

late as 1896 H. C. Chatfield-Taylor, in recording a visit there, was sensible of the "presence of the American writer who, more than any other man, has preserved the memory of the Moor." *The Land of the Castanet* (Chicago, 1896), p. 161.

57. See L. T., p. 367–8. Passages in the letters describing Spain may be read in I. L. W., chap. ii.

58. E.g., "The Village of El Pardillo." See *Outre-Mer* (New-York, 1835), 2, 27–44.

59. One section is called "Ancient Spanish Ballads." Longfellow discusses or alludes to Jovellanos, Berceo, Lope de Vega, Calderón, Quevedo, and, of course, Cervantes.

60. Duyck., 2, 179. A brother of John Slidell, with the name Mackenzie added at the request of a maternal uncle, Mackenzie made two stays in Spain while on active duty with the American navy in the Mediterranean. Serving also in South American waters, he became an intimate of General Rosas and wrote a pamphlet describing his experiences as an eyewitness of political events on the Rio de la Plata. He was the author of several biographies of naval heroes and of a popular work on nautical subjects. Mackenzie's political interests are evident in his two books on Spain. See A. K. Shields, "Slidell Mackenzie and the Return of Rivas to Madrid," *HR*, 7 (April, 1939), 145–50. References to Mackenzie's *A Year in Spain* in the present work are to the revised, enlarged edition of 1836. The book was dedicated to "Alexander H. Everett, Esq., Late Minister Plenipotentiary of the United States to Spain."

61. For Mackenzie's associations with Irving, see S. T. W., *1*, 468–9, 476–7. For his friendship with Longfellow, see below, 2, 157, 158.

62. *New-York Evening Post,* April 30, 1831. For Hoffman's interest in the Spanish language and literature, see H. E. Barnes, *Charles Fenno Hoffman* (New York, Columbia University Press, 1930), pp. 30, 72, 100, 145.

63. See, for example, the review of *Spain Revisited* in *Western Mo.*, 5 (July, 1836), 436–40.

64. *1* (Aug. 6, 1836), 317.

65. *So. Lit. Mess.*, 2 (Aug., 1836), 503. This review and the one on *Spain Revisited* (less certainly) in 2 (May, 1836), 389–92, are assigned to Poe by D. K. Jackson, *The Contributors and Contributions to the Southern Literary Messenger (1834–1864)* (Charlottesville, Va., Historical Publishing Co., 1936), p. 15.

66. *Am. Mo. M.*, N. S., 2 (Aug., 1836), 204.

67. "Royal Order excluding the Author from Spain." "Esta indigesta produccion esta llena de falsedades y de groceras [sic] calumnias contra el Rey N. S. y su augusta familia . . ." *Spain Revisited* (New-York, 1836), *1*, 375–6.

68. *A Year in Spain, 3*, 263. Nevertheless, Mackenzie knew *Don Quixote* (see ibid., p. 264), and Longfellow respected his knowledge of literature.

69. *Ibid., 1*, vii.

70. "My motives for going to a country which travellers ordinarily avoid, were a wish to perfect myself in a language which is becoming so important in the hemisphere which it divides with our own, and a strong desire to visit scenes so full of interest and attraction." *Ibid., 1*, 15–16.

71. In 1826, in Madrid, Irving was fascinated by Mackenzie's experiences. See S. T. W., *1*, 476–7.

72. *A Year in Spain*, 2, 86.

73. Poe was quick to point out these foibles. See *So. Lit. Mess.*, 2 (May, 1836), 389–92.

74. G. R. B. Horner, *Medical and Topographical Observations upon the Mediterranean; and upon Portugal, Spain, and Other Countries* (Philadelphia, 1839), p. 46.

75. Walter Channing, *A Physician's Vacation* (Boston, 1856), pp. 459–506.

76. See this flamboyant dedication in *The Lands of the Saracen* (New York, 1855).

77. *At Home and Abroad: A Sketch-Book of Life, Scenery, and Men* (New York, 1860), p. 487.

78. Quoted in Spiller, 2, 831.

79. Severn Teackle Wallis (1816–94) was a Baltimore lawyer, who for nearly fifty years was the leading member of the Maryland bar. His collected works, published in 1896, filled four volumes. He made his first visit to Spain in 1847 and his second in 1849, when he was appointed by the government to report on the titles to public lands in Florida.

80. *Glimpses of Spain* (New York, 1849), p. 334.

81. *Ibid.*, p. 14.

82. Wallis refers to "Fray Luis de Leon, the greatest of the Spanish lyric poets." *Ibid.*, p. 46.

83. *Ibid.*, pp. 362–5.

84. *Ibid.*, p. 365. For more on the "bloody-minded grand-inquisitor," that is, on the "black legend" of Spain, see below, pp. 158–9.

85. *Ibid.*, Preface, p. vi.

86. *Ibid.*

87. *Ibid.*, p. 337.

88. 7, 441–51. In this important article Wallis mentions the following interesting reasons for unfavorable American opinions of Spain: first, the illustrations in the elementary geographies recalling the Inquisition or the horrors of the bullfight; second, the general inaccuracy of textbooks and their failure to mention the achievements of present-day Spain; third, the inability to admit that basically both English and Spanish colonists were actuated by the same motives.

89. Wallis, Preface, p. v.

90. 3d Ser., *1* (July, 1853), 366.

91. Wallis, p. 365.

92. Apparently at this time ignorance of Catalonia was nearly complete. *Am. Whig R.*, N. S., *5* (March, 1850), 292–300, praised Wallis for his sections on this region.

93. Wallis, p. 373.

94. See *By-Ways of Europe*, p. 162.

95. "A Glimpse of the Alhambra," *Appleton's, 6* (Dec. 16, 1871), 683.

96. See W. H. Bishop, "San Sebastian, the Spanish Newport," *Scrib. M., 22* (Sept., 1897), 267–81.

97. *Keel and Saddle* (Boston, 1872), p. 51.

98. See St. George Mivart, "Notes on Spain," *Am. Cath. Q., 5* (April, 1880), 288.

99. E.g., see "Borrow's Bible in Spain," *Ecl. Mus., 1* (Feb., March, 1843), 252–

67, 338–43; "The Bible in Spain," *Cath. Expositor, 4* (June, 1843), 197–211; W. I. Knapp, "George Borrow in Spain," *Nation, 42* (Feb. 11, 1886), 121–3; *The Bible in Spain* was first published in 1842. "By the end of the year, 1843, six editions of the book had been issued in London, thousands of copies sold in America . . ." G. H. Stephen, *Borrow House Museum* (Norwich [Eng.] Norwich Public Libraries Committee, 1927), p. 7. It was pirated in America by three publishing houses and issued in New York in 1843, 1848, 1851, 1887, etc.

100. See also W. H. Bishop, *A House-Hunter in Europe* (New York, 1893), p. 156.

101. The other four volumes were W. H. Downes, *Spanish Ways and By-Ways* (Boston, 1883); M. R. Vincent, *In the Shadow of the Pyrenees from Basque-Land to Carcassonne* (New York, 1883); Henry Day, *From the Pyrenees to the Pillars of Hercules* (New York, 1883); G. P. Lathrop, *Spanish Vistas* (New York, 1883).

102. Allen, p. 459. For other narratives of this type in the latter half of the nineteenth century, see M. H. Elliott, *Three Generations* (Boston, Little, Brown, 1923), pp. 253–5, 317–20. In this book journeys to Spain in 1894 and 1905 are described. See also C. A. Stoddard, *Spanish Cities* (New York, 1892).

103. Henry James, *Portraits of Places* (Boston, 1884), p. 1. Both Howells and Lowell urged James to visit Spain, but without success. See below, p. 399, n. 143; 2, 194.

104. Howells published *Venetian Life* in 1866 and *Italian Journeys* in 1867. His *Familiar Spanish Travels* did not appear until 1913.

105. Howells noted the sardonic tone of these essays. See "John Hay in Literature," *NAR, 181* (Sept., 1905), 343–5. In praising the book Howells referred to its "forcible and brilliant style"; "a certain polished hardness of manner"; etc.

106. See C. E. Norton, *Notes of Travel and Study in Italy* (Boston, 1860), pp. vi, 7, 37, 38, 47, etc.

107. *Atlan., 28* (Nov., 1871), 637.

108. From the early description in George Ticknor's "Amusements in Spain," *NAR, 21* (July, 1825), 52–78, to the climactic *Death in the Afternoon* by Ernest Hemingway, American writing on tauromachy is endless, in travel books, articles, and novels. Most ancient and most indomitable of Spanish pastimes, it seems likely to live forever.

109. "No other book in English [wrote Howells in 1871] about Spain can compare with it, and we know of none on the subject which offers, with such easy and charming grace, so much that we may be all the wiser for knowing." *Atlan., 28* (Nov., 1871), 638.

110. The fourth American edition of this unique work appeared in 1872.

111. *G. T.'s Travels.*

112. Had this record been published immediately after the journey (1818), it would have balanced and qualified the superficial travel books of the period. Ticknor's delight in travel in Spain was genuine: "It seems to have been with real enjoyment that he changed the ease of his early journeyings for the hardships of traveling in this comfortless land; and although the inns were miserable, the fare uncertain and meagre at the best, and there were many other afflictions to vex the tourist, he evidently enjoyed this expedition to the full."

T. S. Perry, "The Life of George Ticknor," *Lippinc.*, *17* (May, 1876), 631. This book, including the Spanish sections, was widely reviewed.

113. G. T., *1*, 197.

114. E. E. Hale, *Seven Spanish Cities, and the Way to Them* (Boston, 1883), p. 48. For a time Hale was "South American Editor" of the Boston *Advertiser*. See below, p. 149.

115. *Ibid.*, pp. 33, 56. In spite of this declaration for realism, Hale was a disciple of Irving, and his estimates of the older writer were sympathetic. See *ibid.*, pp. 83, 89–90, 114–17.

116. *Ibid.*, p. 34. This somewhat peculiar tribute was reprinted by the reviewer of "Books about Spain" in the *Lit. W.*, *14* (Nov. 17, 1883), 384. For Howells' comparison of Palacio Valdés to a typical Vermonter, see below, *2*, 253.

117. Lowell arrived in Spain as minister in Aug., 1877, and remained until Jan., 1880.

118. It would seem from dispatches and letters that Lowell had contemplated the writing of a travel book. On March 4, 1879, he wrote Grace Norton: "Since I have been here I have been reading a good many travels in Spain, beginning with a Bohemian knight of the fifteenth century and ending with Théophile Gautier" (H.).

119. *Critic, 33* (Oct., 1898), 263.

120. *Impressions of Spain,* compiled by J. B. Gilder (Boston, Houghton Mifflin & Co., 1899), p. 11.

121. For a study of American travelers in Spain during the late nineteenth and early twentieth century, see R.-N., pp. 397–433. The author summarizes travelers' opinions concerning the Spanish landscape, women, children, country people, the traits of courtesy, pride, and industry, democracy and political corruption, the future, etc.

122. E.g., see P. S. Marden, *Travels in Spain* (Boston, Houghton Mifflin & Co., 1909), p. 4.

123. *Spanish Highways and Byways* (New York, Macmillan Co. [1900]), p. 11.

124. In the *United States Catalog* for 1912 eighty-four titles were listed under the subjects: "Spain—Description and Travel" and "Spain—Social Life and Customs." During the next five years twenty-three additional titles appeared. Between 1918 and 1922, eleven were noted, whereas in the following five years there were twenty-eight new works. The period of greatest activity was that between 1928 and 1932 with forty-five titles. Thirty-seven more appeared in the next five-year period. Between 1938 and 1942 this figure shrank to thirteen, and from 1943 to 1947 only three new books were published, of which none was written by an American. Interest in Spain had not diminished, but it had shifted from travel to the Civil War. On topics related to this the *Cumulative Book Index* listed for 1933–37 forty-four titles, and during 1938–42 eighty-four. Many of these works were the narratives of American reporters, soldiers in the Lincoln Battalion, government representatives, or other observers of the war. In happier days some of these authors would probably have written travel books.

125. (Y.)

126. "I think it should be clearly understood . . . [writes Marden] that my

aim has not been to pose as an interpreter of Spain or of the Spanish character . . . The book is simply the record of my own Spanish experiences—
experiences which proved so enjoyable that the temptation to describe them
has been too strong to resist . . . This is but the simple narrative of what I
myself saw and of how I saw it." p. v. G. W. Edwards, in the opening pages of
a similar book, says that this "is just what it seems to be . . . a most truthful
chronicle of the experiences of the author in the land of 'Poco Tempo,'—of
'Mañana.' " *Spain* (Philadelphia, Penn Publishing Company, [1926]), p. 12.
Edwards' book is illustrated with "Drawings in Color" and "Drawings in
Monotone." Some books, lacking such accessories, resembled those of the nineteenth century. E.g., H. A. Franck "covered a thousand miles of the Iberian
peninsula on foot, twice that distance by third-class rail," and computed the
cost of the journey as $172. *Four Months Afoot in Spain* (New York, Century
Co., 1914), "A Foreword," 3d prelim. leaf.

127. For example, P. S. Marden's book contains beautiful photographs
showing the detail of the Alhambra. Edward Penfield's *Spanish Sketches* (New
York, 1911) includes colored illustrations showing the influence of Spanish
techniques. Ernest Clifford Peixotto, another magazine illustrator, adorned his
Through Spain and Portugal (New York, 1922) with his drawings of archi-
techural antiquities. "Merely to turn these pages," said a reviewer, "is to step
into enchantment," *Int. Bk. R., 1*, No. 1 (Dec., 1922), 35. Vernon Howe Bailey's
Little Known Towns of Spain (New York [1927]) was a collection of sixty-
seven plates from water colors and drawings, and his *New Trails in Old Spain*
(New York [1928]) was also illustrated. The work of the artist-travelers is
discussed on pp. 79–81.

128. F. T. Rogers, *Spain: A Tragic Journey* (New York, Macaulay Co.
[1937]), Preface, p. vii.

129. *Ibid.* Rogers was a newspaper publisher in Manila who had spent many
vacations in Spain and who had toured the country for five months before the
outbreak of hostilities. Other typical newspaper accounts were H. R. Knickerbocker's *The Siege of Alcazar,* which described the fighting in Spain from the
"Loyalist" point of view between August 22 and October 1, 1936. See also
H. E. Knoblaugh, *Correspondent in Spain* (London, 1937), which reported
both from the trenches of the "Loyalists" and from the "hide-aways" of the
"Rightists." In mentioning (without bias) in this and later chapters books
and articles connected with the Spanish Civil War it has been difficult to
choose from the various names of the opposing factions: Loyalist, Leftist,
anti-Franco, Republican, Falangist, Rightist, pro-Franco, Franquista, etc.
Meanings alter, and the word "Loyalist," for example, carries a different
significance today from that of 1936–39. For clarity it has seemed best to use
hereafter the contrasting words of "Republican" and "Franquista."

130. Rogers, plate facing p. 1.

131. *The Life and Death of a Spanish Town* proved to be one of the
memorable books connected with the Spanish Civil War. "Without the poetry
in Paul's prose," says a reviewer, "we could not suffer this greatly moving
experience. It was his gift to translate directly to the sensibilities of the English-
speaking peoples the innate dignity, the nobility in the individuals making up
the Spanish people, however humble; and thereby to demonstrate how mon-

strous is the crime of war against them." *C. Sc. Mon.*, Aug. 16, 1937, p. 18. See also *Books,* Aug. 1, 1937, pp. 1–2.

132. For varying receptions of these two books, see *N. Y. Herald Tribune Wkly. Bk. R.,* Dec. 2, 1945, p. 3; *New Repub., 113* (Nov. 26, 1945), 718; and *ibid., 114* (May 20, 1946), 739. Hayes called his book "a personal account of [his] diplomatic mission in Spain from May, 1942, to January, 1945," and "an historian's candid and factual record of what he saw and knew at first hand."

133. R. M. McBride, *Spanish Towns and People* (New York, R. M. McBride & Co. [1925]), p. vii.

134. Bates, p. 2.

135. *Rambles in Spain* was "built up from letters written by the author during two visits to Spain," in 1899 and from 1900 until 1902, preface. For an estimate of this book see *R. of R., 42* (Nov., 1910), 638.

136. *N. Y. Times Book Rev.,* Oct. 24, 1937, p. 16. In London *TLS, 36* (Dec. 25, 1937), 982, was less approving.

137. See E. V. Greenfield, *Spain Progresses: The Impressions and Experiences of a Student and Traveler in Spain* (Boston, R. G. Badger [1932]), pp. 212–13. This book contains an estimate by a professor of modern languages of what he owed to Spain.

138. Bates, p. 39.

139. See *Bookm., 14* (Sept., 1901), 89–90.

140. See *TLS, 19* (Dec. 30, 1920), 890.

141. See Miss King's edition of G. E. Street's *Some Account of Gothic Architecture in Spain* (London, 1914). As a distinguished historian of Spanish art, Miss King is discussed below, pp. 428–9, n. 252.

142. This book was six years in preparation.

143. *Heart of Spain,* ed. Agnes Mongan (Cambridge, Harvard University Press, 1941), pp. 94–5.

144. See Federico Sánchez in *Hisp., 10* (March, 1927), 126.

145. In this group belong, presumably, G. W. Edwards, *Spain* (Philadelphia [1926]); Nancy Cox-McCormack, *Pleasant Days in Spain* (New York [1927]); the two books, already cited, by Vernon Howe Bailey; and E. C. Peixotto's volumes.

146. Bates, p. 1.

147. See below, Conclusion, 2, 287–91.

148. In a preface to *America Hispana* (New York, C. Scribner's Sons, 1931), p. ix, Frank says: "Like its predecessors in that division of my writings which I call History, this book must be taken as a work of art. The subject is a people, rather than—as in that division which I call Story—a person or group of persons. But the aim is not primarily to give facts or information: it is to create for the reader an image of the living organism about which the facts are recorded, to give him an experience of the truth which this collective living being represents." This concept of Frank's should be remembered in reading *Virgin Spain, The Re-Discovery of America,* and *America Hispana.*

149. See *Virgin Spain,* p. 2.

150. *New York World,* April 11, 1926, p. 6m. See also *The Book Review Digest,* 1926, pp. 248–9; C. E. Laughlin, *So You're Going to Spain* (Boston,

Houghton Mifflin & Co., 1931), p. 467. See also *SRL*, *2* (April 17, 1926), 720: "Despite certain repetitions, despite language that at times is overdrawn and over emphatic, and at times abstruse and almost incoherent,—or, perhaps, rather because of this vivid color in his words, his book is instinct with life, vivid, clean-cut, and at times as baffling as a modernistic picture."

151. See above, p. 343, n. 148.

152. See T. B. Jones, *South America Rediscovered* (Minneapolis, University of Minnesota Press [1949]), p. 8. Through such subjects as "The Outward Voyage," "Buenos Ayres," or "The Conquest of the River Plate," the author reconstructs "southern South America as foreigners saw it in the years from 1810 to 1870" and discusses the sources for this reconstruction.

153. See *ibid.*, pp. 3–4. This book was Alexander Von Humboldt, *Personal Narrative of Travels to the Equinoctial Regions of the New Continent*, tr. H. M. Williams (Philadelphia, 1815).

154. *Glimpses of Spain*, p. 365.

155. W. C. Bryant, *Letters of a Traveller*, 2d ed. (New York, 1850), pp. 114, 105.

156. *National Era*, *4* (July 4, 1850), 106.

157. P. 487.

158. *Eldorado, or, Adventures in the Path of Empire* (New York, 1850), *1*, 3. On returning from California in 1849 Taylor crossed from Mazatlán to Vera Cruz. Paying thirty dollars for a mule and five for a saddle and bridle, he set out for Guadalajara, pausing at various posadas and inns. Outside this town he was robbed. Continuing by diligence, he arrived in Mexico City in six days. His entire journey across Mexico consumed some twenty days.

159. Another reason was the distaste of Americans for the poverty, disease, and warfare of these struggling peoples of Spanish America. Travel would have brought knowledge of the color and of the antiquities of these civilizations and in this way have replaced indifference with interest. Eventually this change in attitude took place.

160. "Madame Calderon's Life in Mexico," *NAR*, *56* (Jan., 1843), 138.

161. See U. S. Bureau of Statistics (Dept. of Commerce and Labor), *Transportation Routes and Systems of the World* (Washington, 1907), pp. 23–4.

162. See Jones, pp. 10, 246. Gradually rail and ship communications improved. As late as 1859 it took one group of travelers fifty-five days to reach Montevideo from New York (by sail and steam), but in the year 1865 Mrs. Agassiz reached Rio de Janeiro quickly and comfortably. *Ibid.*

163. *A Narrative of Voyages and Commercial Enterprises* (Cambridge, 1842), *1*, v–vi.

164. Cleveland's recollections of Madrid appeared in the *Literary Gazette* of Boston. See *ibid.*, *2*, 230.

165. This book dealt incidentally but vividly with Spanish scenes and customs. See chaps. xvii, xviii, xxi, xxvi, xxvii.

166. E. R. Sill, *Around the Horn*, ed. S. T. Williams and B. D. Simison (New Haven, 1944). Not until 1790 did an American merchantman complete what was probably the first successful voyage of this kind to the Oregon coast by way of Cape Horn. See E. R. Johnson, *History of Domestic and Foreign Commerce of the United States* (Washington, D. C., Carnegie Institution, 1915), *2*, 26.

See also George Coffin, *A Pioneer Voyage to California and Round the World 1849 to 1852* ([Chicago? 1908]), and C. M. Welles, *Three Years' Wanderings of a Connecticut Yankee in South America, Africa, Australia, and California* (New York, 1859).

167. Alexander von Humboldt, *Political Essay on the Kingdom of New Spain, Containing Researches Relative to the Geography of Mexico,* tr. John Black (New-York, 1811). See also his *Personal Narrative of Travels to the Equinoctial Regions of the New Continent.* The historian, Robertson, was still popular. See below, p. 135.

168. Between 1815 and 1865 the American navy was distributed throughout the seven seas to protect our merchant marine. See C. S. Alden and Allan Westcott, *The United States Navy* (Philadelphia, J. B. Lippincott Co. [1943]), pp. 113–14. For this reason naval men became our greatest travelers. Some of them took part in Wilkes' Antarctic Expedition (1838–42), in William Lewis Herndon's exploration of the Amazon Valley (1850–52), and in Thomas J. Page's exploration of the Parana and Paraguay rivers (1853–55).

169. "Madame Calderon's Life in Mexico," p. 139.

170. During the 1820's a few travel books provided lively descriptions of Chile, Colombia, and Argentina. Small trading vessels carried a few passengers, who sometimes worked for their accommodations. See, in particular, Washington Chase, *A Voyage from the United States to South America,* 2d ed. (Newburyport, 1823); William Duane, *A Visit to Colombia, in the Years 1822 & 1823* (Philadelphia, 1826). Valparaiso was a "favorite port" of the Pacific squadron of the navy, chiefly on account of the hospitality of the English and American colony. See Walter Colton, *Deck and Port* (New York, 1850), p. 201; W. S. W. Ruschenberger, *Three Years in the Pacific Including Notices of Brazil, Chile, Bolivia, and Peru* (Philadelphia, 1834), pp. 106–7.

171. John Russell Bartlett's *Personal Narrative of Explorations and Incidents of Travel in Texas, New Mexico, California, Sonora, and Chihuahua* (New York, 1854) dwells on the Spanish books and documents in Texas. Walter Colton's *Three Years in California* (New York, 1850), relating his experiences as alcalde of Monterey, is sometimes more entertaining than fiction. We remember Colton's accounts of the Christmas celebration with the "shepherds." He writes of the egg breaking, the old Mexican laws, the "Spanish courtesies," the Spanish friends, and the missions. Everywhere he heard "the Castilian." "Saturday, Aug. 15 [1846] To-day the first newspaper ever published in California made its appearance . . . One-half of the paper is in English, the other in Spanish." Pp. 32–3. Peter H. Burnett was annoyed that there were laws in Spanish which he could not understand. *Recollections and Opinions of an Old Pioneer* (New York, 1880), p. 294. Bayard Taylor had done his shallow best for these regions. E.g., *Eldorado* . . . (New York, 1850).

172. Poinsett was sent by President Monroe on a secret mission to Mexico in 1822, but his *Notes on Mexico* was not his official report. He returned through San Juan del Rio, Queretaro, Guanajuata, the valley of San Felipe, San Luis Potosí, and Tampico. In 1835–36 the *American Monthly Magazine* published a series of anonymous articles, "Extracts from the Journal of a Mexican Tourist," which show that the facilities for travel had improved considerably since Poinsett's visit. The journey from Vera Cruz to Mexico City

was accomplished by diligence in seven days, with a stopover of one day at Puebla. An interesting correspondence between Poinsett and Prescott survives (M. H. S.).

173. In the same year Thomas J. Farnham published *Mexico: Its Geography —Its People—and Its Institutions* (New-York [1846]).

174. See *Recollections of the Last Ten Years* (Boston, 1826), pp. 151, 365–8, 370, 372.

175. *Incidents of Travel in Egypt, Arabia, Petræa, and the Holy Land* (New-York, 1837); *Incidents of Travel in Greece, Turkey, Russia, and Poland* (New-York, 1838).

176. For a map of the route in Yucatan, see V. W. Von Hagen, *Maya Explorer, John Lloyd Stephens and the Lost Cities of Central America and Yucatán* (Norman, University of Oklahoma Press, 1947), facing p. 174.

177. See *ibid.*, pp. 186, 191, 198–9.

178. Quoted by von Hagen in *ibid.*, p. 200.

179. See *ibid.*, p. 197. For recent interest, see Pál Kelemen, "The Stephens Centenary," *El Palacio, 48* (May, 1941), 97–110; and H. E. Mole, "John L. Stephens, Traveler," *N. J. Hist. Soc. Proc., 61* (April, 1943), 98–115.

180. Cleveland, pp. v–vi.

181. With Richard Alsop. See Juan Ignacio Molina, *The Geographical, Natural and Civil History of Chili* (Middletown, Conn., 1808). One of the first Americans to know Spanish America at first hand, Shaler continued in his later career his enthusiasm for these regions. See R. F. Nichols, "William Shaler, New England Apostle of Rational Liberty," *NEQ, 9* (March, 1936), 71–96. See also William Shaler, *Journal of a Voyage between China and the North-Western Coast of America* ([Philadelphia, 1808]).

182. *Two Years before the Mast* (New York, 1840), pp. 98–9.

183. G. R. Stewart, *Bret Harte, Argonaut and Exile* (Boston, Houghton Mifflin & Co., 1931), p. 211.

184. *Two Years before the Mast*, p. 97.

185. Another non-American travel book which exerted some influence was Basil Hall's *Extracts from a Journal, Written on the Coast of Chili, Peru, and Mexico, in the Years 1820, 1821, 1822* (Edinburgh, 1824).

186. Mr. and Mrs. Howard T. Fisher of Winnetka, Illinois, are engaged on a new, illustrated edition of *Life in Mexico*, with a biography of Madame Calderón de la Barca. Mrs. Fisher writes (letter to me, November 5, 1953) that about a century ago the book enjoyed a wide circulation in England.

187. The travel books published between 1865 and 1900 showed relatively little interest in the arts. One exception is W. H. Bishop's *Old Mexico and Her Lost Provinces* (New York, 1883), which discusses briefly the art and literature of this country.

188. It might be more correct to say that American trade with the Spanish-American nations did not expand at the same rate as that with Europe. Isaac N. Ford, an American journalist in Brazil just after the overthrow of Don Pedro, noticed the absence of American flags in the La Plata and the age of the two warships stationed there. He thought these facts indicative of the "degeneracy" of the United States in Spanish-American affairs. See *Tropical America* (New York, 1893), p. 77. See also W. E. Curtis, *Between the Andes and the Ocean*

(Chicago, H. S. Stone & Co., 1900), *passim*. See also a volume written by a naval officer, W. H. Beehler, *The Cruise of the Brooklyn* (Philadelphia, 1885).

189. For routes, costs, and conditions of travel in these years, see A. Z. Gray, *Mexico As It Is* (New York, 1878), pp. 28–9, 36–7, 148. Gray described the three possible routes from New York and spoke of the trip from Vera Cruz to Mexico City as "one of the wonders and delights of the world."

190. See "A Diligence Journey in Mexico," *Cent.*, *23* (Nov., 1881), 1–14.

191. E.g., see Michael Wineburgh, *Where to Spend the Winter Months* (New York, 1880); and T. A. Janvier, *The Mexican Guide* (New York, 1886).

192. E.g., see H. W. Baxley, *What I Saw on the West Coast of South and North America* (New York, 1865).

193. Pp. 325–33, 615–21. The first edition of this work appeared in New York in 1870. The third edition included an account of a second expedition in 1873, up the Amazon from Pará to Yurimaguas, over the Andes to the Pacific Coast and Lima, with a side trip to Lake Titicaca by way of Arequipa.

194. In 1877 Squier was already known for his writings on archaeological research in Central America. He went to Peru in 1863 as a special commissioner of the United States to settle conflicting claims between the two countries. See *Peru; Incidents of Travel and Exploration in the Land of the Incas* (New York, 1877).

195. In 1884 Curtis was appointed secretary of the United States commission to the Central and South American nations to report on a method for securing more effective international and commercial relations with the United States. In 1900 he published another book, *Between the Andes and the Ocean,* describing in some 430 pages his journey in 1899 along the west coast of South America as far as the Straits of Magellan.

196. Vincent published *Around and about South America* (New York, 1890) and *In and Out of Central America* (New York, 1890). See also Isaac N. Ford's *Tropical America,* already mentioned, and Davis' *Three Gringos in Venezuela and Central America* (New York, 1896).

197. See Samuel Hazard, *Cuba with Pen and Pencil* (Hartford, 1871); J. L. M. C. Woodruff, *My Winter in Cuba* (New York, 1871); R. J. Levis, *Diary of a Spring Holiday in Cuba* (Philadelphia, 1872); Gray, *Mexico As It Is;* F. H. Smith, *A White Umbrella in Mexico* (Boston, 1889); etc.

198. In these years Venezuela, in particular, attracted tourists. See Davis, p. 245.

199. H. J. Sanborn, *A Winter in Central America and Mexico* (Boston, 1886), pp. 190–1. Miss Sanborn adds: "And now, while we think of that country with affectionate interest, we can but say our pleasure in seeing Guatemala is to *have* seen it; and, should we ever go there again, we should take the Pacific Mail from New York and content ourselves with a visit to the capital and vicinity, the most interesting part of the republic."

200. *Ibid.*, pp. 315–16.

201. Hudson Strode, *South by Thunderbird* (New York, Random House [1937]), p. 189.

202. *Ibid.*, p. xxi.

203. See J. T. Trippe, "The Importance of Inter-American Air Transport," U. S. Travel Bureau, *Official Bulletin, 13* (Sept. 10, 1939), *1.*

204. W. D. Frank, *South American Journey* (New York, Duell, Sloan and Pearce [1943]), p. 227. Copyright, 1943, by Waldo Frank.

205. Walt Whitman wrote a letter, dated Camden, N. J., July 20, 1883, to "Messrs. Griffin, Martinez, Prince, and other gentlemen at Santa Fe," in reply to their request for a poem in commemoration of the 333d anniversary of the founding of that city. He declared with characteristic vagueness: "To that composite American identity of the future, Spanish character will supply some of the most needed parts. No stock shows a grander historic retrospect— grandeur in religiousness and loyalty, or for patriotism, courage, decorum, gravity, and honor." "November Boughs," W. W., *6*, 117.

206. For a discussion of racial differences in the various countries, see Frank, *South American Journey*, pp. 360–1.

207. See A. R. Hager, *Wings over the Americas* (New York, 1940), and L. R. Freeman, *Discovering South America* (New York, 1937).

208. Even Waldo Frank's solid travel book, *South American Journey*, begins: "At fifteen thousand feet, in a stratoliner . . ."

209. New York, 1935.

210. *South by Thunderbird* was so popular that it was reprinted in 1941 and 1945. This book originated in certain "alluring cross references to South America" which Strode encountered as he was doing research for a history of Cuba. His object was to "present a clearer comprehension of our Southern neighbors." See pp. xx–xxi.

211. See *The Cumulative Book Index*.

212. See Hudson Strode, *Now in Mexico* (New York [1947]), and H. A. Franck, *Trailing Cortez through Mexico* (New York, 1935). See also H. A. Phillips, *New Designs for Old Mexico* (New York [1939]), with its descriptions of Mexico City.

213. *Village in the Sun* (New York, G. P. Putnam's Sons [1945]), 5th prelim. leaf.

214. For reviews of these books, see *New Yorker, 18*, No. 28 (Aug. 29, 1942), 57; *SRL, 38*, No. 41 (Oct. 13, 1945), 46. See also John Collier Jr. and Aníbal Buitrón, *The Awakening Valley* ([Chicago, 1949]). This book is an account of the Indians in the town of Otavalo near Quito.

215. For lists of these books, see Mary Tucker, *Books of the Southwest* (New York City [1937?]), and J. L. Rader, *South of Forty* (Norman [Okla.], 1947).

216. See the selected bibliography in Carey McWilliams, *North from Mexico* (Philadelphia, J. B. Lippincott Co., 1949), pp. 307–8, with its descriptions of works by W. P. Webb, J. F. Dobie, R. N. Richardson, C. C. Rister, G. I. Sánchez, R. E. Twitchell, Haniel Long, Ross Calvin, Harvey Fergusson, or Ruth Laughlin. These important books are closer to scholarship, history, the interpretive essay, or the romance than to the travel book.

217. See *Our Southwest* (New York, 1940); *Albuquerque* (Albuquerque [1947]).

218. *N. Y. Herald Tribune Wkly. Bk. R.*, Nov. 24, 1946, p. 7.

219. *Journey to Manaos* (New York [1938]) combined "present adventure, historical perspective, economic and philosophic comment." *Books*, April 24, 1938, p. 3. We think also of the Roosevelt-Rondon Scientific Expedition of 1913–14, and the Yale Peruvian Expeditions of 1911–15, out of which came such books as Hiram Bingham's or Theodore Roosevelt's *Through the Brazilian*

Wilderness (New York, 1914). William Beebe's *Edge of the Jungle* (New York, 1921) and *Galapagos: World's End* (New York, 1924) were similar in their purposes.

220. *Across South America* (Boston, Houghton Mifflin & Co., 1911), pp. vii–viii.

221. The author's description suggests the character of this travel book: "This book follows closely the pattern of *Inside Europe* and *Inside Asia* . . . It attempts to give a picture of the political situation in each Latin American country, an appraisal of its personalities, and a survey of its more pressing problems. It is a job of reporting." Later this amazing, almost comic record follows: "To write this book I traveled 18,938 miles by air and I don't know how many other miles by train, boat, and car . . . I was lucky enough to see seventeen out of the twenty available Latin American Presidents or Acting Presidents, and I saw eighteen of the twenty Foreign Ministers. In each country I talked to countless journalists, scholars, men of affairs, business leaders and politicians—in and out of office." Introduction, pp. ix–x.

222. Among these is *Day of Immense Sun* (Indianapolis, Bobbs-Merrill Co. [1936]), "the story of certain imaginary characters living in Peru at the time of the Spanish Conquest," "Author's Note," p. 7. See also *A Journey in Time, Peruvian Pageant* (Indianapolis [1937]).

223. Blair Niles, *Journeys in Time* (New York, Coward-McCann, Inc. [1946]), p. 3.

224. *Ibid.*, p. 2.

225. *Ibid.*, p. 12.

226. For Mrs. Niles' reading and for her plan for this book, see *ibid.*, pp. 1–12.

227. See *N. Y. Herald Tribune Wkly. Bk. R.*, Dec. 29, 1946, p. 5.

228. Publisher's note quoted in the *Book Review Digest*, 1931, p. 367.

229. "He had spent much time in Spain, his *Virgin Spain* being considered by Spaniards to excel even Havelock Ellis' *Soul of Spain*, which had previously held first place among all works on the subject by foreign authors." Niles, pp. 138–9.

230. "Here Frank the novelist, Frank the poet, and Frank the philosophic interpreter are fused together; and the final result is a book that will live." *N. Y. Times Book Rev.*, May 23, 1943, p. 5.

231. *South American Journey*, pp. 379–80.

232. For the direct influence of the travel book upon fiction, see Stimson, "Spanish Themes in Early American Literature," pp. 177–8.

CHAPTER 2: THE WRITERS FOR THE PERIODICALS

1. See Bernstein, *Origins*, pp. 60–1.

2. *Western Mo. R.*, 3 (July, 1829), 25. Quoted by F. L. Mott, *A History of American Magazines, 1741–1850* (New York, D. Appleton Co., 1930), p. 191. See *ibid.*, pp. 178–80, 397–401 (English literature), 190–1 (French literature), 191–2 (German literature).

3. For the magazine as "a reliable chronicle of the intellectual tendencies,

the prevailing tastes, the current thought, of the time which produced them," see S. H. Goodnight, *German Literature in American Magazines* (Madison, 1907), p. 7.

4. *NAR, 30* (Jan., 1830), 237–59.

5. See *Cent., 57* (Nov., 1898), 140–8; *Critic, 33* (Sept., 1898), 171–83. Of the legends in M. T. H. Middlemore's *Round a Posada Fire* (London, 1881), all but one had previously appeared in magazines.

6. The extent of Irving's use in the magazines of his Spanish studies is seldom realized. In them after his return to America in 1832 he published some dozen stories and sketches on Spanish themes. See Williams and Edge.

7. *Knick., 19* (Feb., 1842), 127.

8. The Catholic magazines tried systematically to interest American Catholics in Spain through articles on religion and the saints and through translations from such novelists as Fernán Caballero. Even for Protestants religion in Spain, past and present, held a strange enticement. E.g., see "Observations on the State of Religion in Spain," *Christian Spectator, 6* (April, 1824), 193–7. This essay is a bigoted study of the evils of Catholicism in Spain.

9. "The *North American Review,* prints long quotations from the address in the Cortes of Dr. Antonio Ruiz de Padrón, who had been in the United States and met eminent American literati at Benjamin Franklin's home; it quotes at length, too, from the vitriolic article, 'Bread and Bulls' which it attributes to Jovellanos." Helman, p. 343. These passages were in the issue of May, 1816. Possibly the Hispanophile attitude of the *North American Review* was influenced by the earlier *Port Folio*. See, in this magazine the vigorous passage which begins: "Nothing can be more deplorably stupid than the *vulgar* idea which has been cherished respecting the character and habits of the modern Spaniards." *Port Folio*, N.S., 2 (Sept., 1809), 282–3.

10. *NAR, 28* (Jan., 1829), 103–34; *29* (Oct., 1829), 293–314; *35* (Oct., 1832), 265–82.

11. Sparks had held the editorship briefly in 1817–18. See F. L. Mott, *A History of American Magazines, 1850–1865* (Cambridge, Harvard University Press, 1938), p. 231.

12. *NAR, 34* (April, 1832), 277–315.

13. *Ibid., 30* (Jan., 1830), 26–61.

14. Tudor was probably well grounded in the Spanish language. See Helman, p. 349.

15. See *ibid.*, p. 345.

16. Quoted in Helman, pp. 344–5.

17. This magazine helped to accomplish his "operating on our own literature."

18. *NAR, 22* (April, 1826), 451. Quoted by Helman, p. 346.

19. See *ibid.*, p. 345.

20. For other representative articles and reviews of books connected with Spain in this magazine, see Helman, pp. 346–7.

21. "Spaniards," *New England Quarterly Magazine, 3* (Oct.–Dec., 1802), 89–91.

22. *Cent., 52* (June, 1896), 198–215. This article was elaborately illustrated by Joseph Pennell.

23. E.g., *Polyanthos, 4* (May, 1814), 98–100; *U. S. Lit. Gaz., 2* (Sept. 1, 15, 1825), 424–7, 452–9; *Port Folio,* 5th Ser., *2* (Oct., 1816), 284–90.

24. This article was followed by an extract from Philip Thicknesse's *A Year's Journey through France and Part of Spain* in *American Moral & Sentimental Magazine, 1* (Dec. 4, 1797), 353–7.

25. Erving, frequently confused by the Spaniards (and by others) with Washington Irving, set out from Cadiz, then the seat of the government during the French occupation of northern and central Spain. He describes his journey, with stops at Jerez and Lebrija in *Monthly Anthology, 7* (Nov., Dec., 1809), 305–10, 361–6; *8* (Jan., Feb., 1810), 6–11, 75–80. The "Sketch of a Journey in Spain" in *Literary Magazine, 6* (Aug., 1806), 153–158, may have been written by an Englishman.

26. The "lady," unidentified except that she was an American, recorded her impressions of Cadiz, Cordova, and Aranjuez. See "Journal of a Tour from Cadiz to Madrid," *Port Folio,* 5th Ser., *20* (Nov., 1825), 365–74. See also "Description of Madrid," *U. S. Lit. Gaz., 2* (Sept. 1, 15, 1825), 424–7, 452–9; and "Description of Malaga," *Port Folio,* 5th Ser., *2* (Oct., 1816), 284–90.

27. *NAR, 21* (July, 1825), 52–78.

28. *Appleton's, 15* (Jan. 22, 1876), 105–7.

29. *Boston Miscellany, 2* (July, 1842), 1–8. Everett describes the town and palaces and reminisces concerning his sojourns in Aranjuez in 1827 and 1829.

30. See G. B. Cheever, "Grenada and the Alhambra," *Knick., 19* (Feb., March, April, 1842), 120–7, 197–203, 329–42. Cheever spells "Granada" in his own fashion. Apparently this was the first article on travel in Spain prepared expressly for publication in a periodical. Cheever's florid writing has a strong Protestant bias.

31. R. T. Maccoun, "Journeyings in Spain in 1852," *Knick., 41,* 95–103, 316–22, *42,* 1–5, 160–9, 331–7, 497–505 (Feb., April, July, Aug., Oct., Nov., 1853).

32. J. M. Mackie, "Cosas de España," *Putnam, 3,* 482–93, 583–93, *4,* 14–21, 518–24 (May, June, July, Nov., 1854). Mackenzie's article, from an unpublished book, appeared in *Knick., 1* (Jan., 1833), 45–9.

33. W. H. Bidwell, "Reminiscences of the Alhambra," *Ecl. M., 46* (March, April, 1859), 434–6, 581–4; M. J. Quin, "The Spanish Cortes and the Holy Alliance," *Mus., 3* (Nov., 1823), 472–6; John Ford, "A Journey in the Pyrenees, in 1813," *Anglo-American, 2* (April 13, 1844), 585–6; Prosper Mérimée, "A Bull-Fight at Madrid," *New Eng. M., 9* (Oct., 1835), 252–61.

34. See *Western Mo., 3* (May, 1870), 383–8; *Atlan., 54* (July, Aug., 1884), 33–51, 191–206; *Lippinc., 9* (May, 1872), 544–52.

35. Bayard Taylor spoke of the Balearic Islands as seldom "represented in the journals and sketchbooks of tourists," *Atlan., 20* (Dec., 1867), 680. Warner wrote of Tangiers. See "Around the Spanish Coast," *ibid., 52* (Aug., 1883), 257–66.

36. See Goodnight; also E. Z. Davis, *Translations of German Poetry in American Magazines, 1741–1810* (Philadelphia, Americana Germanica Press, 1905). For similar books on France and Italy, see Mott, *History of American Magazines.*

37. See *Harper, 64,* 641–62, 801–20, *65,* 205–22, 371–92, 546–66 (April, May,

July, Aug., Sept., 1882); *Scrib. M.*, *7* (Feb., 1890), 187–201. Bishop was the author of various other articles on bullfighting, summer resorts, etc.

38. See "Twelve Months in Spain," *Land We Love*, 2, 100–2, 282–7, 314–23, 425–31, *3*, 47–53, 130–5, 285–90, 376–9 (Dec., 1866—Sept., 1867). Barringer enjoyed unusual opportunities; he was secretary to his brother, Daniel M. Barringer, minister to Spain from 1849 to 1853.

39. See "A Day in Literary Madrid."

40. *Atlan., 82* (Aug., 1898), 190–7.

41. *Ibid.*, p. 190.

42. See below, Conclusion, 2, 287–91.

43. *Putnam*, N. S., *5* (April, 1870), 427–36, and *New-Eng. M.*, *9* (Nov., 1835), 313–20.

44. H. Mills, "The Saracenic Civilization in Spain," *Nat. Q.*, *2* (March, 1861), 297–320. José Antonio Conde's *Historia de la dominacion de los Arabes en España*, published in Madrid in 1820–21, was translated into French in 1825 and into English in 1855.

45. C. C. Hazewell, "The Rehabilitation of Spain," *Atlan.*, *9* (March, 1862), 351–65.

46. "The Spanish Armada," *Cent.*, *56* (June, 1898), 204–20. (Introduction by Admiral Mahan; second part by W. F. Tilton.) See also Tilton, "The Defeat of the Spanish Armada," *Atlan.*, *76* (Dec., 1895), 773–87.

47. "The Surrender of Granada," *Yale Lit.*, *11* (Dec., 1847), 60–3; E. W. Very, "A Terrible Revenge. An Episode of the Spanish War," *Galaxy*, *22* (Oct., 1876), 544–52; "Las Casas and the Slave Trade," *Mus.*, *2* (Feb., 1823), 147–55; "Will of Hernando de Soto, Adelantado of Florida," *Hist. M.*, *5* (May, 1861), 134–7; "Spain and Her Politicians," *Am. Whig R.*, *13* (June, 1851), 494–500.

48. See "La Mogiganga," *New-Eng. M.*, *5* (Dec., 1833), 453–8; "The Murder of Escovedo," *Harper*, *38* (Jan., 1869), 238–47; "Torrijos and His Companions" *Knick.*, *19* (Jan., 1842), 52–5. There was much sympathy for Torrijos in the United States.

49. E.g., Charles Gayarré was now writing of Spanish rule in Louisiana. See *De Bow*, *13* (Oct., 1852), 383–90.

50. The first of a series of articles in *Port Folio*, 5th Ser., *16* (Nov., 1823), 374–83, under the heading "History of Modern Europe," was devoted to Spain during the year 1819. In a similar series in the *New-Eng. M.*, *7* (Nov. 1834), 385–95, "Spain" was the subject.

51. An example of the hybrid essay, part history, part romance, is "Almene. A Spanish Legend," *Yale Lit.*, *5* (Nov., Dec., 1839), 31–40, 93–107. This piece, recounting the story of Almene, sister of King Boabdil, includes various poems: "Moorish War Song"; "Almene's Song"; and "The Serenade."

52. *Port Folio*, 5th Ser., *11* (June, 1821), 378–80. This article, an excerpt from Robinson's *Memoirs of the Mexican Revolution*, denounced the tyranny of the Spanish government and prophesied the emancipation of its entire colonial empire.

53. *Mus.*, *2* (April, 1823), 357–71.

54. The founding of the *Magazine of American History* was important as preliminary to the scientific study of history. By the nineties this magazine was

printing documents and source material. E.g., Otto, Comte de Mosloy, "Memoir on the Discovery of America," *28* (Nov., 1892), 358–67.

55. "The Conquest of Spain by the Arab-Moors," *Penn Mo., 4* (March–Dec., 1873), 133–56, 207–26, 320–38, 398–420, 457–81, 535–57, 622–44, 777–95, 843–67. This work was published in 1881 as *The History of the Conquest of Spain by the Arab-Moors.* The most ambitious of Coppée's writings, it dealt with the period prior to that described by Irving and Prescott. Coppée used Spanish sources and fresh translations of Arab chronicles.

56. See "The Moors in Spain," *So. R.,* N. S., *14* (Jan., 1874), 26–53; S. P. Scott, "The Moslem Empire in Spain," *Overland, 15* (Aug., 1875), 172–80; Edward Thompson, "The Moorish Empire in Spain," *Potter Am. Mo., 8* (June, 1877), 8–17.

57. To the *Knickerbocker* Irving contributed articles which were republished in the *New-Yorker* and the *Rover* and which were later collected and reprinted in book form.

58. See H. G. Doyle, "The 'Black Legend' of Spain," *Hisp., 16* (Oct., 1933), 341–6.

59. "Spain and her Politicians," *Am. Whig R., 13* (June, 1851), 494–500, offers reasons for the ignorance of Spain both in Europe and America.

60. J. C. Fernald, "A Study of the Inquisition." *Bapt. R., 3* (July–Sept., 1881), 341–65. For typical articles in the Catholic magazines, see those by José Ignacio Rodríguez, "Protestantism in Spain," *Am. Cath. Q., 12* (Oct., 1887), 612–36; and Pérez Villamil y García, "The Jews in Early Spanish History," *Cath. World, 54* (Oct., Dec., 1891), 86–96, 360–71; "The Jews in Spain during the Middle Ages," *ibid., 55* (Aug., 1892), 649–61; "Expulsion of the Jews from Spain in the Fifteenth Century," *ibid., 55* (Sept., 1892), 851–9.

61. Emilio Castelar, "Spain a Democratic Nation," *Forum, 11* (May, 1891), 276–90; F. S. Fiske, "Spain a Republic," *O. & N., 7* (April, 1873), 474–8. This writer was convinced that the Spaniards were ready for republican institutions.

62. See E. L. Godkin, "Economic Results of the Spanish Revolution," *Nation, 8* (March 25, 1869), 225–6.

63. *9,* 360–1.

64. See J. C. Welling, "The Monroe Doctrine," *NAR, 82* (April, 1856), 478–512; "Our Relations with Spain," *De Bow,* N. S., *7* (Dec., 1869), 998–1024; "Cuba and Spain," *Putnam,* N. S., *5* (Jan., 1870), 9–22; "How We Escaped War with Spain," *Scrib., 1* (Jan., 1871), 297–303.

65. Perhaps there was no reply because the American minister, John P. Hale, was disapproving, or perhaps because the action of these estimable men and women was slightly premature. Probably Henry C. Kingsley appraised the situation accurately. See "Spain, and the Late Revolution," *New Englander, 28* (April, 1869), 308–18. See Lyman Abbott, "The Spanish Revolution," *Harper, 40* (Jan., 1870), 262–73, an article describing fully the historical background of the changes. See also E. L. Godkin, "The Spanish Revolution," *Nation, 7* (Dec. 17, 1868), 496–9.

66. "Our Relations with Spain," *De Bow,* N. S., *7* (Dec., 1869), 998–1024; "Cuba and Spain," *Putnam,* N. S., *5* (Jan., 1870), 9–22; "History As It Is Made," *Chaut., 27* (June, 1898), 313–20; E. A. Walcott, "The War between Spain and

the United States," *Overland*, 2d Ser., *31* (June, 1898), 528–45; Peter MacQueen, "The Débacle of Spain," *Nat. M., 9* (Dec., 1898), 204–10.

67. *Atlan., 84* (July, 1898), 36–46.

68. *Nat. M., 9* (Dec., 1898), 204–10. See also J. H. Bridge, "The Collapse of Spain and the Rise of the Anglo-Saxon," *Overland*, 2d Ser., *32* (July, 1898), 87–9. In contrast, one should read the temperate and kindly article by Edmond Kelly, "An American in Madrid during the War," *Cent., 57* (Jan., 1899), 450–7.

69. See below, pp. 155–6.

70. See George Ticknor, "Early Spanish Drama," *Am. Q., 4* (Dec., 1828), 308–49. This was an able article tracing the history of this form to the year 1700, with particular attention to Cervantes, Lope de Vega, and Calderón. See also "Early Spanish Ballads," *So. R., 5* (Feb., 1830), 62–99; "Spanish Literature," *American Monthly, 64* (Nov., 1864), 460–5. See also "Spanish Popular Poetry," *NAR, 54* (April, 1842), 419–46. For later studies, see "Calderon, the Spanish Poet," *Graham's, 49* (Sept., 1856), 248–51; and "The Poetical Literature of Spain," *Nat. Q., 3* (Sept., 1861), 205–34.

71. One of the earliest pieces of this kind was a translation in *American Register, 2* (1817), 183–200, from Simonde de Sismondi called "Fragment on Spanish Literature."

72. See the translations of Lope de Vega in *New-York R., 2* (Feb., 1826), 228–30. *Boston Lyceum, 1* (April, 1827), 197–9, contained an abstract of Calderón's *El médico de su honra*.

73. "Little Flowers of Spain," *Cath. World, 9* (Aug., 1869), 706–10, was a translation of one of Fernán Caballero's "cosas humildes de España." This was an article on the derivation of popular expressions and proverbs.

74. See "Recollections of the South of Spain," *The Talisman for MDCCCXIX*, pp. 43–9; "A Moriscan Romance," *ibid.*, pp. 49–51; "Story of the Island of Cuba," *ibid.*, pp. 163–220; "Early Spanish Poetry," *The Talisman for MDCCCXXX*, pp. 227–9. For attribution of these poems to Bryant, see R. M. Peterson, "Bryant as a Hispanophile," *Hisp., 16* (Nov.–Dec., 1933), 401–12.

75. *United States Review, 1* (Jan., 1827), 283–6. See below, 2, 145–6.

76. "Perico, the Sad; or The Family of Alvareda," *Cath. World, 3* (July, Aug., Sept., 1866), 497–517, 660–79, 787–804. For translations and criticism of Fernán Caballero, see "Doña Fortuna and Don Dinero," *ibid., 13* (Apr., 1871), 130–3; "Lucas Garcia," *ibid., 13,* 785–97, *14,* 49–62, 189–99 (Sept., Oct., Nov., 1871). Since few if any translations of this novelist appeared in other magazines, it may be conjectured that one reason for these versions was the desire to introduce this Catholic novelist to Catholic readers. Catholic periodicals published many accounts of eminent Spanish figures in particular relation to their religious interests. See, for example, the sketch of Father Felix Varela by José Ignacio Rodríguez, *Am. Cath. Q., 8* (July, 1883), 463–76.

77. *Essays in Criticism, Second Series* (London, 1906), pp. 252–99.

78. For other early writings by or about Cervantes, see *Monthly Anthology, 6* (Feb., 1809), 86; *Portico, 1* (March, 1816), 244–51; *New-Eng. M., 2* (May, 1832) 381–90; *Am. Mo. M.*, N. S., *1* (April, 1836), 342–54; and (W. H. Prescott), *NAR, 45* (July, 1837), 1–34.

79. "Pictures for Don Quixote," *Cent.*, *56* (June, 1898), 177–85, discusses the characteristics of the proposed edition of *Don Quixote* with illustrations by Daniel Vierge.

80. *Literary Magazine, 4* (Dec., 1805), 458–9.

81. *New-York Literary Journal, 4* (Jan., 1821), 232–3. This article, which appeared originally in the London *New Monthly Magazine,* analyzed the effect of the current revolution in Spain upon literature.

82. "Who Wrote Gil Blas?," *NAR, 25* (Oct., 1827), 278–307. Everett examined J. A. Llorente's *Observations critiques sur le roman de Gil Blas* and J. F. de Isla's *Aventuras de Gil Blas de Santillana.*

83. "Cadalso's Moorish letters," *NAR, 26* (Jan., 1828), 248–58. This review by E. Wigglesworth included a brief account of the author, "el Coronel Don José Cadalso," analyzed both the original work and this edition, submitted five extracts, and contained a tribute to the Spanish language. See also Wigglesworth's outline of Navarrete's life of Cervantes. *Ibid., 38* (April, 1834), 277–307.

84. See *So. R., 5* (Feb., 1830), 62–99, for a long, confused article entitled "Early Spanish Ballads," with a review and an outline of an English publication, the *History of Charles the Great and Orlando . . . Together with the Most Celebrated Ancient Spanish Ballads . . . with English Metrical Verses by Thomas Rodd* (London, 1812).

85. *NAR, 34* (April, 1832), 277–315.

86. *Ibid., 36* (April, 1833), 316–44. This article deals with the several languages or dialects of Spain, with translations. "The Specimens of Castilian" for the twelfth, thirteenth, and fourteenth centuries was taken from Tomás Antonio Sánchez' *Coleccion de poesias castellanas anteriores al siglo XV* (Madrid, 1779–90).

87. Among the many reviewers of this work, the following have been identified: J. D. B. DeBow; C. C. Felton; G. S. Hillard; W. H. Prescott. See, in particular, the long review by T. C. Reynolds, *So. Q.*, N. S., *2* (Sept., Nov., 1850), 85–123, 273–313.

88. *8,* 156–69. The writer discusses also Alarcón and Trueba. See B. W. Wells, "Realism in Early Spanish Fiction," *ibid., 5* (July, 1897), 257–76.

89. The professional journals began to come into being in the eighties. E.g., see H. R. Lang, "On Spanish Grammar," *AJP, 6* (1885), 79–85. In this early period articles of a semischolarly character were published. See A. M. Huntington, "A Spanish Romeo and Juliet," *Bookm., 5* (Aug., 1897), 493–6. This article describes the origin of the "Lovers of Teruel" and lists the various forms in which the romance had appeared from the sixteenth century until 1894.

90. See W. H. Prescott, "Madame Calderon's Life in Mexico," *NAR, 56* (Jan., 1843), 137–70. See also *Ecl. R.*, N. S., *13* (June, 1843), 642–54. See also the reviews of Theodore Irving's *The Conquest of Florida, So. Lit. Mess., 1* (July, 1835), 648; *Am. Q., 18* (Sept., 1835), 238–9.

91. R. J. Cordova, "The Don Quixote of Cervantes," *Knick., 38* (Sept., 1851), 189–203.

92. *Cosmopol., 14* (March, 1893), 609–14.

93. See below, pp. 232–4.

94. *Atlan., 77* (Feb., 1896), 256–64.

95. *Am. Mo. M.*, N. S., *1* (April, 1836), 342–54.

96. This article describes the plays of various nineteenth-century dramatists. In *Graham's, 39* (Dec., 1851), 360–4, appeared an article on Carolina Coronado, the friend of Bryant. The earliest review of an English translation of a work by a contemporary Spanish author was that of J. L. Starr's translation of Fernán Caballero's *La Gaviota* in *Nat. Q., 10* (March, 1865), 386–7. The *Nation*, in particular, devoted space to modern Spanish novelists.

97. See "Modern Spanish Fiction," *SR, 1* (Nov., 1892), 41–51.

98. See Rollo Ogden, "Emilia Pardo Bazán," *Bookm., 5* (June, 1897), 300–3; and his article "In the Spanish Cortes," *Critic, 17* (Sept. 13, 1890), 134–5. This author includes extracts from Galdós' *La Incógnita* showing the similarity between Spanish and American public men. These judgments were probably based on his own experience as a representative of Puerto Rico in the Spanish Cortes. See also Ogden's "Leading Writers of Modern Spain" in *Cosmopol., 9* (June, 1890), 222–8; Emilia Pardo Bazán, "The Women of Spain," *Ecl. M.*, N. S., *50* (July, 1889), 91–107; W. H. Bishop, "A Day in Literary Madrid," *Scrib. M., 7* (Feb., 1890), 187–201; "Female Writers of Spain," *Nation, 51* (July 31, 1890), 87–8, in which is discussed an article by Emilia Pardo Bazán in the *Fortnightly*. This article in the *Nation* mentions particularly Doña Faustina Sáez de Melgar, Doña María del Pilar Sinués de Marco, Doña Concepción Arenal, Doña Gertrudis Gómez de Avellaneda, Fernán Caballero, and Emilia Pardo Bazán.

99. The acquaintance of American readers with Galdós is suggested by the publication in *Bookm., 5* (May, 1897), 220–2, of A. M. Huntington's article, "Perez Galdós in the Spanish Academy."

100. See *New York Mirror, 1* (Aug. 30, 1823), 36–7.

101. See W. H. Hurlbert, "The Poetry of Spanish America," *NAR, 67* (Jan., 1849), 129–60. Hurlbert discusses the three-volume edition of the Mexican poetess, published in Madrid in 1689. Other poets mentioned in the review (with excerpts) are Don Mariano Irujillo of Yucatan, Gabriel de la Concepción Valdés of Cuba, José Joaquín de Olmedo of Lima, and Estéban Echeverría of Buenos Aires.

102. See Stuart Cuthbertson, "George Ticknor's Interest in Spanish-American Literature," *Hisp. 16* (May, 1933), 117–26. Selections from Prescott's *The Conquest of Mexico* were published in the magazines.

103. Articles on the fine arts in Spanish America were still rare. See, however, C. H. Shinn, "Spanish Pioneer Houses of California," *Mag. Am. Hist., 23* (May, 1890), 353–60.

104. *12*, 102–24. A foolish story of the Napoleonic era but important as an example of the early use of Spanish themes.

105. *9*, 409–10.

106. *Am. Whig R., 13* (May, June, 1851), 419–42, 509–33.

107. *4*, 535–8. Published as a book by Harper's in the same year.

108. See H. F. Harrington, "Caballero Ladrone," *Godey, 21* (July, 1840), 38–41; or "The Spanish Headsman," *ibid., 5* (Nov., 1832), 234–8. Many of these sketches bordered on history. E.g., see Professor Ingraham's "The Vestal of Saragossa. A Tale of the Moorish Invasion," *Catholic Expositor, 4* (April, 1843),

21–5; or J. R. Browne, "The Disguised Heretic. A Sketch of the Inquisition," *So. Lit. Mess.*, 7 (Jan., 1841), 60–4.

109. By Louise Palmer Haven. See *Overland*, 2d Ser., 7, 561–9, 8, 1–11, 179–90, 279–91, 393–409, 509–19, 634–52, 9, 51–64, 162–71, 294–310, 413–25, 522–39, 577–87, 10, 2–23, 187–204, 291–310, 420–33, 518–32 (June, 1886—Nov., 1887).

110. A short story whose scene is laid in the West Indies.

111. Some pieces were translations (from Lope de Vega, Quevedo, and others), and some were merely verses inspired by Spanish themes.

112. E.g., "The Legend of Christopher Columbus," *Port Folio*, 5th Ser., *11* (June, 1821), 470–510; and Will Carleton, "Three Scenes in the Life of Columbus," *Nat. M.*, *17* (Jan., 1893), 212–28.

113. *Overland*, *10* (March, 1873), 279; *ibid.*, *15* (Dec., 1875), 546–7.

114. E.g., see the poem by T. A. Janvier inspired by the Spanish proverb,
> Quien á buen árbol se arrima,
> Buena sombra la cobija.

Cosmopol., *17* (June, 1894), 202.

115. By Charles Washington Coleman. See *Cent.*, *46* (May, 1893), 160.

116. See "The Lament of Romero," *The Talisman for MDCCCXXIX*, pp. 158–61; "Eva," *The Talisman for MDCCCXXX*, pp. 230–7.

117. See "The Spanish Student," *Graham's*, *21* (Sept., Oct., Nov., 1842), 109–13, 176–80, 229–34; "Castles in Spain," *Atlan.*, *39* (May, 1877), 601–3; "The Bells of San Blas," *ibid.*, *50* (July, 1882), 42–3.

118. See *Am. Mo. M.*, N. S., *3* (Feb., 1837), 129–39. See the account of La Tirana, a Spanish actress, in the *Literary Magazine*, 6 (Aug., 1806), 152–3. See *So. Lit. Mess.*, *5* (Feb., 1839), 150–1, for a review of Epes Sargent's *Velasco; a Tragedy*, produced in New York and Philadelphia in the preceding December. For Poe's review of N. P. Willis' *Tortesa, the Usurer* and Longfellow's *Spanish Student*, see "The American Drama," *Am. Whig R.*, 2 (Aug., 1845), 117–31.

119. See, however, Nina Sturgis, "Traditional Music of the Spanish Pyrenees," *Scrib.*, *14* (June, 1877), 237–41.

120. E.g., C. C. Cooper, "A Spanish Painter," *Lippinc.*, *51* (Jan., 1893), 75–82. This article offered a critical estimate of Velázquez with illustrations from his paintings. See also A. F. Jaccaci, "The Father of Modern Illustration. Daniel Vierge Urrabieta," *Cent.*, *46* (June, 1893), 186–203; Elizabeth (Robins) Pennell, "Velasquez in Madrid," *Nation*, *59* (Nov. 1, 8, 1894), 323–4, 339; Cornelia Van Rensselaer Dearth, "An Artistic Treasure from Spain," *Cent.*, *56* (July, 1898), 436–8; Octave Thanet, "A Spanish Court Painter and His Times," *Dial*, *10* (Oct., 1899), 133–5.

121. *Harper*, *90* (May, 1895), 921–39.

122. For this opinion in full, see below, p. 414, and n. 68.

123. J. P. Wood, *Magazines in the United States* (New York, Ronald Press Co. [1949]), pp. 103–4.

124. See *N. W. Ayer & Son's Directory [of] Magazines and Periodicals* (1949), p. 11; and Wood, p. 263.

125. *Ibid.*

126. F. L. Allen, "The American Magazine Grows Up," *Atlan., 180,* No. 5 (Nov., 1947), p. 79.

127. "The Magazines in Journalism," *Harp. W., 54,* No. 2778 (March 19, 1910), p. 8.

128. Wood, p. 279.

129. See, for example, S. G. Morley, "Fondo en . . . A Rare Spanish Idiom," *MLN, 32* (Dec., 1917), 501–3; W. J. Entwistle, "The Spanish Mandevilles," *MLR, 17* (July, 1922), 251–7; S. G. Morley, "Notes on the Bibliography of Lope de Vega's Comedias," *MP, 20* (Nov., 1922), 201–17; W. S. Jack, "Development of the 'Entremes' before Lope de Rueda," *PMLA, 37* (March, 1922), 187–207.

130. A. M. Espinosa, *Hisp.,* Organization Number (Nov., 1917), p. 19.

131. L. A. Wilkins, "The First Annual Meeting," *Hisp., 1* (Feb., 1918), 17.

132. Ronald Hilton, *Handbook of Hispanic Source Materials and Research Organizations in the United States* (Toronto, 1942), p. 366. This magazine printed many articles in Spanish and was published by the University of Pennsylvania Press. Its first editor was J. P. Wickersham Crawford.

133. See C. W. Hackett, "Discussion of Lesley Byrd Simpson, 'Thirty Years of *The Hispanic American Historical Review,*'" *HAHR, 29* (May, 1949), 213–18. Among the authors represented in the first volume of this periodical were Herbert Eugene Bolton, Charles E. Chapman, Chester K. Jones, Philip Ainsworth Means, Herbert I. Priestley, James A. Robertson, William S. Robertson, William L. Schurz, William R. Shepherd, and Mary W. Williams.

134. See L. B. Simpson, "Thirty Years of *The Hispanic American Historical Review,*" *ibid., 29* (May, 1949), 192.

135. K. C. Wade, "Recent Articles Relating to Inter-American Affairs in Periodicals Published in English in 1941," *Inter-Am. Bibl. R., 1* (Winter, 1941–42), 262–9, quoted by E. R. Hutton in H. G. Doyle, *A Handbook on the Teaching of Spanish and Portuguese* (Boston [1945]), pp. 10–11. The magazines selected for this tabulation were the *Christian Science Monitor Magazine, Collier's, Fortune, Good Housekeeping, Harper's, Life, Nation, Reader's Digest, Saturday Evening Post,* and *Time.*

136. E.g., *Bulletin of the Pan American Union,* 1893–1948; *Inter-American Quarterly,* 1939–41; *Inter-American,* 1942–46; *Americas,* 1945 to date.

137. Mrs. Frances Parkinson Keyes' *Silver Seas and Golden Cities* (1931) was first published in *Good Housekeeping* between Aug., 1929, and Nov., 1930. See her "Portugal of the Porcelain Sky," *ibid., 89,* No. 2 (Aug., 1929), 46–57, 166–70. "A Little Window into Seville," No. 3 (Sept., 1929), 34–5, 280–93; "Castles in Spain," No. 4 (Oct., 1929), 28–9, 270–80, etc. In this category of the description appeared some of the work of Edward Penfield and Ernest Clifford Peixotto. Howells' records of travel in Spain appeared in the magazines, and John Driscoll Fitz-Gerald's *Rambles in Spain* was first issued (*Chaut., 55* [Aug., 1909], 311–477), as part of its home-study program. Sometimes a magazine financed a journey, as in the case of Mrs. Keyes, to secure desirable material. Other periodicals solicited from writers already known for their books or articles on Spain. See John Dos Passos, "Spain Gets Her New Deal," *Am. Merc., 31* (March, 1934), 343–56.

138. C. E. Farnham, "American Travellers in Spain (1777–1867)," *RR, 13*

(Jan., July, Oct., 1922), 44–64, 252–62, 305–30. Other scholarly journals published travel essays. E.g., G. P. Hammond, "Some Impressions of Spain," *Quarterly Journal of the University of North Dakota, 14* (Nov., 1923), 70–81; J. O. Swain, "On Foot in the Pereda Country," *Hisp., 19* (Feb., 1936), 61–8.

139. See Marya Mannes, "Spain Today," *Am. Merc., 60* (Feb., 1945), 213–19; M. L. Pflaum, "Franco's Spain," *ibid., 66* (Jan., 1948), 29–36; E. A. Paulin, "Report on Franco's Spain," *Cath. World, 165* (June, 1947), 218–19; Richard Pattee, "A Little Common Sense about Spain," *ibid., 166* (Nov., 1947), 107–15.

140. See Jack Potter, *A Bibliography of John Dos Passos* (Chicago, Normandie House, 1950), pp. 21, 38–9, 48–9.

141. *Cumulative Index to the National Geographic Magazine, 1889 to 1940 Inclusive* (Washington, D. C. [1941]).

142. *AHR, 21* (Oct., 1915), 194. Examples of this interest in Spanish-American relations are G. L. Rives, "Spain and the United States in 1795," *ibid., 4* (Oct., 1898), 62–79; I. J. Cox, "General Wilkinson and His Later Intrigues with the Spaniards," *ibid., 19* (July, 1914), 794–812; E. G. Bourne, "The United States and Mexico, 1847–1848," *ibid., 5* (April, 1900), 491–502; J. H. Smith, "The Mexican Recognition of Texas," *ibid., 16* (Oct., 1910), 36–55.

143. "The First Castilian Inquisitor," *ibid., 1* (Oct., 1895), 46–50; "Ferrand Martinez and the Massacres of 1391," *ibid., 1* (Jan., 1896), 209–25; "Lucero the Inquisitor," *ibid., 2* (July, 1897), 611–26; "A Letter of Ferdinand of Aragon to Diego Columbus, 1510," *ibid., 3* (Oct., 1897), 83; "Hidalgo and Morelos," *ibid., 4* (July, 1899), 636–51; "Molinos and the Italian Mystics," *ibid., 11* (Jan., 1906), 243–62.

144. "The Cortes of the Spanish Kingdoms in the Later Middle Ages," *ibid., 16* (April, 1911), 476–95; "Charles V.'s Last Paper of Advice to His Son," *ibid., 28* (April, 1923), 489–91.

145. See Hackett, p. 213. Among the eminent contributors five men have accounted for more than twelve per cent of the total number of articles (W. S. Robertson, eleven articles; J. F. Rippy, ten; P. A. Martin, seven; A. P. Whitaker, six; W. W. Pierson, five). See *ibid.,* p. 214.

146. Other special periodicals have published many articles on parts of the United States formerly under Spanish rule. E.g., see J. G. Johnson, "The Yamassee Revolt of 1597 and the Destruction of the Georgia Missions," *Ga. Hist. Quar., 7* (March, 1923), 44–53; H. E. Bolton, "Spanish Resistance to the Carolina Traders in Western Georgia (1680–1704)," *ibid., 9* (June, 1925), 115–30; W. H. Siebert, "Spanish and French Privateering in Southern Waters, July, 1762, to March, 1763," *ibid., 16* (Sept., 1932), 163–78. See also Adele Ogden, "The Californias in Spain's Pacific Otter Trade, 1775–1795," *Pac. Hist. R., 1* (Dec., 1932), 444–69; C. E. Quainton, "Colonel Lockhart and the Peace of the Pyrenees," *ibid., 4* (Sept., 1935), 267–80.

147. See *YR*, N. S., *19* (Autumn, 1929), 67–84. See also Robert Sencourt, "The Burning Question of Spain," *Atlan., 136* (July, 1925), 108–16.

148. The *Readers' Guide to Periodical Literature* lists between 1936 and 1939 849 articles on the war. Of these 138 appeared in *Time* and a substantial number in *Newsweek*. Sympathy for the Republicans is indicated by ninety-one articles in the *Nation* and seventy-six in the *New Republic*. During the same period 101 articles concerning the Spanish government were

published, of which ten were in *Time,* ten in the *Nation,* and seven in the *New Republic.*

149. See below, p. 253.

150. Howells began these discussions of Blasco Ibáñez in the "Editor's Easy Chair," *Harper, 131* (Nov., 1915), 957–60.

151. *The Blood of the Arena* (Chicago, 1911).

152. R. H. Keniston, "An Apostle of New Spain," *Nation, 87* (Dec. 24, 1908), 622–3. See also "Blasco Ibañez a Spanish Zola," *Cur. Lit., 52* (May, 1912), 588–91.

153. *120* (April 15, 1925), 414–15.

154. E.g., W. W. Comfort, "Modern Spanish Fiction," *Atlan., 99* (March, 1907), 398–404; Ramón Jaén, "Spanish Fiction in the United States," *Nation, 106* (March 7, 1918), 261.

155. See e.g., the *Delineator,* the *North American Review,* the *New Republic,* the *Catholic World,* etc.

156. A number of Spanish stories have appeared in the *Living Age* and in the *Golden Book.* See, in the former magazine, *328* (Feb. 13, 1926), 370–5; *329* (May 1, 1926), 281–6; *333* (Nov. 1, 1927), 830–3. Among the stories in the latter magazine may be noted P. A. de Alarcón, "Captain Veneno's Proposal of Marriage," *1* (Jan., 1925), 13–14; Serafín Estébanez Calderón, "An Andalusian Duel," *1* (April, 1925), 513–14; Emilia Pardo Bazán, "The Last Will of Don Javier," *4* (Nov., 1926), 659–61.

157. *Inter-America, 1* (Oct., 1917), verso of front cover. This periodical, established in 1917 through the influence of the Carnegie Endowment for International Peace, alternated monthly in publishing translations into Spanish of articles in the periodicals of the United States and translations into English of articles written in Spanish and Portuguese. For examples of Latin-American stories in this magazine see the issues of Dec., 1917; June, 1919; Aug., 1919; or Oct., 1924.

158. See the issues of Feb., May, June, July, Aug., and Dec., 1911.

159. See the issues of Aug., 1932; Aug., 1934; Summer, 1947.

160. See the issues of Oct., 1933; Dec., 1934; July, 1936; March–April, 1940; Jan.–Feb., 1943; Jan.–Feb., 1946; Sept.–Oct., 1946. See also the *Partisan R.,* July–Aug. and Nov., 1936. Both these magazines include stories and poems by the Philippine author, José García Villa.

161. This fact is also true of the stories in the "quality" magazines. See *Harper, 160* (April, 1930), 587–94; or *Scrib. M., 102,* No. 3 (Sept., 1937), 26–31.

162. Prudencio Pereda, "The Spaniard," *Story, 10,* No. 58 (May, 1937), 9–18.

163. See, for example, L. R. Massey, "The Voice of Urraca," *Smart Set, 73,* No. 1 (Jan., 1924), 55–8.

164. See Thomas Walsh, "The Progress of Poetry: Spanish—I–II," *Nation, 113* (Sept. 14, 21, 1921), 292–3, 317–18.

165. Since 1929 109 such poems have appeared. See *Readers' Guide to Periodical Literature* under the heading "Poetry—Translations from the Spanish."

166. This issue contained also rare and new illustrations and a chart indicating events in the world during the dramatist's lifetime.

167. See *Drama, 4* (May, 1914), 245–63. Bronta discusses what he calls the

"Renaissance Epoch," which began in Spain about the middle of the nineteenth century. See also *ibid.*, 5 (Nov., 1915), 555–66. In the same issue appeared Underhill's translation of Benavente's *The Bonds of Interest, ibid.*, pp. 567–643.

168. See *ibid.*, 7 (Feb., 1917), 15–24. This article was followed by translations of five one-act plays, to illustrate different types of subject and method: Serafín and Joaquín Álvarez Quintero, "By Their Words Ye Shall Know Them"; Gregorio Martínez Sierra, "Love Magic"; José Echegaray, "The Street Singer"; Jacinto Benavente, "No Smoking"; and Santiago Rusiñol, "The Prodigal Doll."

169. For these and other articles on various phases of the Spanish and Spanish-American theater, see *Theatre Arts*, April, 1920; June, 1929; March, 1932; August, 1938; and May, 1939. See also Elizabeth Wallace, "The Spanish Drama of To-Day," *Atlan., 102* (Sept., 1908), 357–66.

170. See "Two Great Spanish Painters, Sorolla and Zuloaga," *Cent., 78* (May, 1909), 26–36; Christian Brinton, "Ignacio Zuloaga," *Scrib. M., 57* (May, 1915), 647–50. See also H. C. Candee, "Certain Goyas in America," *ibid., 62* (Oct., 1917), 428–38; William Walton, "Some Notes about Velasquez," *ibid., 69* (March, 1921), 380–4.

171. *62–69* (Nov., 1901—Jan., 1905).

172. See "Modern Mexican Art," *Life, 20*, No. 22 (June 3, 1946), 58–60, and C. C. Wertenbaker's article on Picasso, *ibid., 23*, No. 15 (Oct. 13, 1947), 92–8, 100, 102, 104. See also the pictures of Goya's *Retouched Goddess* in *ibid., 26*, No. 13 (March 28, 1949), 86.

CHAPTER 3: THE HISTORIANS

1. Some of the historians discussed in the present chapter wrote also for the magazines, among them J. S. C. Abbott, Coppée, Fiske, Gayarré, and Lea. For a time many influential editorial positions in the magazines were held by historians. It must also be remembered that the books of all the well-known historians, particularly those of Irving, Prescott, and Motley, were widely reviewed.

2. For an excellent account of Robertson's influence, see H. E. Barnes, *A History of Historical Writing* (Norman, University of Oklahoma Press, 1937), pp. 156–8. Besides the Spanish chroniclers of America, such as Bernal Díaz del Castillo, Antonio de Herrera y Tordesillas, Antonio de Solís y Rivadeneyra, or Garcilaso de la Vega, there were available in the nineteenth century, including Robertson, various English historians of the Conquest. E.g., see S. A. Dunham, *Spain and Portugal* (London, 1832–33). Here is further evidence that an audience was prepared before Americans turned to writing histories of Spain.

3. Many of the historians were scholars in the true sense of the word, and some of the scholars were historians. The boundaries between this and the following chapter are not sharp but are divisions of convenience. The two chapters should be considered together.

4. E.g., *The Conquest of Granada*, etc.

5. See Martin Hume, *Spanish Influence on English Literature*, p. 308.

6. For an account of the Torrijos affair, see Thomas Carlyle, *The Life of John Sterling* (London, 1851), chap. x, pp. 86–95.

7. See C. T. Thompson, "Columbus Day One Hundred Years Ago," *Chaut., 16* (Nov., 1892), 188–93.

8. *The Vision of Columbus* (Hartford, 1787).

9. Thomas Morton, *Columbus: or, the Discovery of America* (Boston, 1794). This was an American edition of a play first published in England in 1792. For novels, poems, and other literature inspired by Columbus, see O. A. Bierstadt, "Columbus in Romance," *Mag. Am. Hist., 28* (Oct., 1892), 272–9.

10. See M. J. Lamb, "A Group of Columbus Portraits," *Mag. Am. Hist., 26* (Oct., 1891), 241–60. See also W. E. Curtis, "The Columbus Monuments," *Chaut., 16* (Nov., 1892), 138–46; W. E. Curtis, "The Columbus Portraits," *Cosmopol., 12* (Jan., Feb., 1892), 259–67, 409–20.

11. S. E. Morison, *Admiral of the Ocean Sea* (Boston, 1942).

12. See A. P. Dunlop, "The Real Character of Christopher Columbus," *Arena, 6* (Oct., 1892), 603–20. For this article, almost unique in disparaging Columbus, Dunlop used unimportant references from well-known works to build up his case. In 1891 an eight-page quarto edition of the letter of Columbus was sold for $4,300, a sum then about the value of a Shakespeare folio, of one volume of the Mazarin, or of the Gutenberg Bible. See J. G. Wilson, "Spanish Memorials of Columbus," *Nat. M., 17* (Dec., 1892), 144.

13. A critic, analyzing this ode in the *Port Folio*, N. S., *2* (Dec., 1809), 497–502, referred to it as "sublime, prophetic, and unintelligible." According to the *Monthly Anthology, 6* (March, 1809), 185–6, the poem was preceded by "a brief sketch of Spain," also by Paine.

14. See Charvat, pp. xxx–xxxvi. Presumably the antiquarianism of Bishop Hurd and of the Wartons stimulated in scholars an interest in Spanish medieval life.

15. "Las Casas and the Slave Trade," *Mus., 2* (Feb., 1823), 147–55, and the *Port Folio, 20* (Nov., 1825), 388–400. For an account of the Spanish historians of America in the originals or in translations, see Barnes, pp. 140–3.

16. Later editions appeared in 1812, 1822, and 1840.

17. See H. B. Adams, *The Study of History in American Colleges and Universities* (Washington, 1887), p. 19.

18. *The History of the Reign of Philip the Second* (New York, 1818); *The History of the Reign of Philip the Third* (New York, 1818).

19. A. B. Hart, "The American School of Historians," *Internat. M., 2* (Sept., 1900), 298–302.

20. Despite its humorous exaggeration, Irving's *jeu d'esprit* commanded some respect as a history. See J. S. Bassett, *The Middle Group of American Historians* (New York, Macmillan Co., 1917), p. 22.

21. "The first American historian to write an important general history was Rev. Abiel Holmes, who published the first edition of his 'American Annals,' in two volumes in 1805." *Ibid.*, p. 45.

22. Albert Bushnell Hart believed that until 1830 there was "no account of the development of America which is now read as a classic, and still less any first-hand American history of a foreign country." See p. 305. For a definition of three main phases in American historiography, see C. H. Haskins,

"European History and American Scholarship," *AHR, 28* (Jan., 1923), 217.

23. See the comments on libraries, a book-buying public, etc., in Hart, p. 308. See also W. C. Lawton, "An Earlier Apostle of American Culture," *Dial, 32* (May 1, 1902), 307.

24. "Broader and deeper," concluded this transcendental essay, "we must write our annals—from an ethical reformation . . ." R. W. E., 2, 40.

25. J. G. Palfrey believed that the valuable collections of history in the public libraries of Boston and Harvard drew Prescott, Motley, and himself into research in this subject. See E. E. Hale, *Memories of a Hundred Years* (New York, Macmillan Co., 1902), 2, 45–6.

26. See Bassett, pp. 303–4.

27. These were the famous "literary" historians. In their day this designation was common. It must not, of course, be confused with the same words used in this book with a different meaning: i.e., historians of literature.

28. See J. F. Jameson, *The History of Historical Writing in America* (Boston, 1891), pp. 91–2.

29. See Michael Kraus, *A History of American History* (New York, Farrar & Rinehart [1937]), p. 183.

30. Nevertheless, Jameson said of the period following 1861: "The devotees of European history are not numerous in the United States." See p. 134.

31. The only American writers on European history whom G. P. Gooch considered worthy of extended estimates in his *History and Historians in the Nineteenth Century* (London, Longmans, Green & Co. [1935]) were Irving, Prescott, and Motley. All of these were deeply interested in Spanish history. In discussing with Jared Sparks the possibility of publishing *Ferdinand and Isabella,* Prescott expressed doubts, saying that "the subject was not one likely to interest American readers: it related to Spain and times long past." "Prescott Memorial," *Hist. M., 3,* Supplement (1859), p. v.

32. For a study of the liberalization of the Spanish libraries, see W. R. Shepherd, "The Spanish Archives and Their Importance for the History of the United States," *Am. Hist. Assoc. Ann. Rep., 1903, 1,* 145–83.

33. See below, 2, 302, n. 165. See also "New Documents concerning Columbus," *NAR 24* (April, 1827), 265–94; and J. C. Brevoort, "Spanish American Documents, Printed or Inedited," *Mag. Am. Hist., 3* (March, 1879), 175–8.

34. See below, p. 177 and n. 34.

35. "His clear and well-proportioned narrative, coupled with enough accuracy to satisfy the age in which he wrote, made him a force for good historical interest in the first half of the nineteenth century." Bassett, p. 23.

36. See Samuel Smiles, *A Publisher and His Friends* (London, 1891), 2, 258.

37. See S. T. W., *1,* 182.

38. See "Irving's Life of Columbus," *Am. Q., 3* (March, 1828), 173–90; "Irving's Life of Columbus," *So. R., 2* (Aug., 1828), 1–31; A. H. Everett, "Irving's Life of Columbus," *NAR, 28* (Jan., 1829), 103–34; "Irving's Conquest of Granada," *Am. Q., 5* (March, 1829), 190–221; W. H. Prescott, "A Chronicle of the Conquest of Granada," *NAR, 29* (Oct., 1829), 293–314.

39. Gooch, p. 412.

40. Jameson, p. 99. See also Gooch, pp. 410–12.

41. See below, 2, 30.

42. Tributes to Prescott as a historian are innumerable. See, in particular, C. K. Adams, *A Manual of Historical Literature*, 3d ed. (New York [1888]), pp. 437–8; R. B. Merriman, *The Rise of the Spanish Empire* (New York, Macmillan Co., 1918–34), *1*, xii; Gooch, pp. 415–16.

43. "The author seems to know nothing of the Philosophy of History, and little even, of Political Economy. He narrates events in their order of time, with considerable skill, but the causes of the events, their place in the general history of the race, or their influence in special on the welfare of the nation, he does not appreciate . . ." *Mass. Q.*, *2* (March, 1849), 247. For further discussion of Parker's hostility, see below *2*, 103. For an estimate from the Spanish point of view, see R.-N., pp. 27–42.

44. See Bassett, pp. 312–13.

45. "Prescott's History of Ferdinand and Isabella," *Quar.*, *64* (June, 1839), 58.

46. "William H. Prescott," *Bibliothèque universelle*, *4* (avril, 1859), 597–620.

47. See J. De L. Ferguson, *American Literature in Spain* (New York, Columbia University Press, 1916), pp. 148–57.

48. In a section called "Arrangement of the History of the Conquest of Mexico," following a diary entry of July 14, 1839 (M. H. S.).

49. See O. W. Holmes, *John Lothrop Motley* (Boston, 1879), pp. 62–6; Bassett, pp. 223–4; Gooch, p. 416.

50. "The United States found its most distinguished representative of the school of Carlyle and Froude in John Lothrop Motley." Barnes, p. 191.

51. *Ibid.*, pp. 191–2. See also *John Lothrop Motley: Representative Selections*, ed. C. P. Higby and B. T. Schantz (New York, American Book Co. [1939]), pp. lxxx–lxxxii.

52. J. L. Motley, *The Rise of the Dutch Republic* (New York, 1856), *3*, 625.

53. Barnes, p. 191.

54. See Motley to F. H. Underwood, March 4, 1859, in Holmes, p. 88. In *The Correspondence of John Lothrop Motley*, ed. G. W. Curtis (New York, 1889), there occurs hardly a mention of Spain.

55. Barnes, pp. 191–2.

56. He added "one more to the long chain of English writers, who out of ancestral prejudice, have dealt hard measure to all Spaniards." Jameson, p. 121.

57. *History of the United Netherlands* (New York, 1861–68), Vol. *2*, chap. xix.

58. The other was John S. C. Abbott's *The Romance of Spanish History* (New York, 1869). The total number of histories of Spain listed was seventeen. See the *American Catalogue, Subject Entries* (1876), p. 390. In the *United States Catalog of Books in Print* (Jan. 1, 1912), thirty-four titles were listed, among which was this item of Abbott's, Hale's *Story of Spain*, and the works of Prescott. The inter-American book trade during this period was extensive, and included many works in the Spanish language published in the United States. "A thousand different titles on Spanish America were printed here in English and Spanish from 1800 to 1900." Harry Bernstein, "The Latin American Book Trade before 1900," p. 2416. For the popular histories, romances, and children's stories see *ibid.*, p. 2418.

59. Abbott, Preface, p. vii. See H. O. Ladd, *A Memorial of John S. C. Abbott* (Boston, 1878).

60. See Abbott, pp. 186–9.

61. Hale enrolled as a special student in Spanish under Francis Sales.

62. See *Lit. W., 14* (Nov. 17, 1883), 384.

63. E. E. Hale and Susan Hale, *The Story of Spain* (New York, 1886), p. iv.

64. Hale introduced anecdotes, legends, and translations from Spanish poetry. See *Lit. W., 17* (Oct. 2, 1886), 330–1.

65. The services of the Everetts as interpreters of Spain were extensive rather than deep. See Index.

66. For Prescott ill health was the primary reason.

67. Gayarré named his home "Roncal" after the region in Spain where his ancestors had lived for centuries and where they had taken their stand against the Moors. G. E. King, *Memories of a Southern Woman of Letters* (New York, Macmillan Co., 1932), p. 43.

68. Gayarré's first historical work was written in French, "Essai historique sur la Louisiane" (1830). He had studied the history of Louisiana during a stay in Paris. See also his series of lectures, *Romance of the History of Louisiana,* 1848, 1851, etc. See Bassett, pp. 49–56.

69. *CHAL, 4,* 597.

70. G. E. King, *New Orleans, the Place and the People* (New York, 1895), pp. 403–4.

71. W. D. Howells, "Philip II of Spain. By Charles Gayarré," *Atlan., 19* (May, 1867), 638. See also Bassett, p. 55.

72. Charles Gayarré, *Philip II of Spain* (New York, 1866), p. iii.

73. *Ibid.*

74. See Howells, "Philip II of Spain," p. 639.

75. E.g., see *Philip II of Spain,* pp. 6–7.

76. al-Makkari, *The History of the Mohammedan Dynasties in Spain,* tr. Pascual de Gayangos (London, 1840).

77. W. M. Ferries, "Coppée's Conquest of Spain," *Nation, 32* (April 21, 1881), 282–3.

78. Henry Coppée, *History of the Conquest of Spain by the Arab-Moors* (Boston, 1881), *1,* vii.

79. *Ibid.*

80. Interest in Moorish themes was sustained by numerous articles in the magazines. Samuel Parsons Scott, who lived long in Spain, spent some twenty years on his ambitious *History of the Moorish Empire in Europe* (Philadelphia, 1904). During the last twenty-five years of his life he devoted himself to translations into English of records of "the Spanish and the Civil Law." These translations have been judged inaccurate, and the histories have been described as too monotonous and too uncritical. For a review by F. W. Williams see *AHR, 10* (Jan., 1905), 372–4.

81. J. C. Fernald, *The Spaniard in History* (New York, 1898), p. 4. This book depends heavily on Irving, Prescott, Motley, and Lea. See also as typical J. B. Crabtree, *The Passing of Spain and the Ascendency of America* (Springfield, Mass., 1898); and Mary Platt Parmelee's *A Short History of Spain* (New York, 1898). Mrs. Elizabeth W. Latimer's *Spain in the Nineteenth Century*

(Chicago, 1897) is slightly superior to these works. See also J. A. Harrison, *Spain in Profile* (Boston, 1879) and *Spain* (Boston, 1881); and E. H. Strobel, *The Spanish Revolution, 1868–1875* (Boston, 1898).

82. In this respect the book may represent a new tendency in historians of Spain. Probably the author's remark in the preface is only half serious, that his book "is intended for the ignorant and the indolent, for passengers in steamer chairs, bound on their first voyage to Vigo or Barcelona . . ." but its superficial character evoked some hostile estimates. See, e.g., *Revista de estudios hispánicos, 1* (julio–sbre., 1928), 286.

83. The introduction of German methods into American historical scholarship was evident when Torrey succeeded Sparks at Harvard and when Lieber and White were appointed at, respectively, Columbia and Michigan. In 1876 Adams founded at Johns Hopkins a training school for historians. See Barnes, p. 259. For an attempt to define and date the change, see Bassett, pp. viii–ix. See also Jameson, pp. 122–45. Torrey was not German-trained but was hospitable toward this new scholarship.

84. See E. N. Saveth, "Race and Nationalism in American Historiography," *Pol. Sci. Q., 54* (Sept., 1939), 427.

85. See Bassett, p. ix. "We may say that the new spirit existed fundamentally in the minds of scholars about the middle of the century and that it was not revealed to public view until the cloud of sectional feeling lifted. In this view the year 1884 may well be taken as the dividing point between two points of historical endeavor in our country." *Ibid.*

86. Nevertheless, until the end of the century various aspects of European history were still treated in the old-fashioned manner. W. A. Dunning, "A Generation of American Historiography," *Am. Hist. Assoc. Ann. Rep., 1917,* p. 351. See also Hart, pp. 311–15.

87. See R. H. Shryock, "American Historiography: a Critical Analysis and a Program," *Proc. Am. Phil. Soc., 87* (1943), 39.

88. *A History of the Inquisition of the Middle Ages* (New York [1887]); *Chapters from the Religious History of Spain Connected with the Inquisition* (Philadelphia, 1890); *The Moriscos of Spain; Their Conversion and Expulsion* (Philadelphia, 1901); *A History of the Inquisition of Spain* (New York, 1906–07); *The Inquisition in the Spanish Dependencies* (New York, 1908).

89. See E. S. Bradley, *Henry Charles Lea* (Philadelphia, University of Pennsylvania Press, 1931), p. 71.

90. Lea to W. E. H. Lecky, April 9, 1888, quoted in *ibid.,* p. 328.

91. Much of Lea's research was done in America in a collection of original sources and transcripts which he began to assemble in 1843 and which are now parts of the collections of the University of Pennsylvania. See E. P. Cheyney, "The Henry C. Lea Library," *University of Pennsylvania Library Chronicle, 1* (March, 1933), 4–5.

92. Lea's labors in folio collections of law and theology, in ancient tracts and pamphlets, were ceaseless. He often declined to read modern writers lest they make him false to his own vision of the past. See C. H. Haskins, "Tribute to Henry Charles Lea," *Proc. Mass. Hist. Soc., 43* (1910), 185.

93. The reviews were extravagant: e.g., he is "the only American historian

who, by reason of the extraordinary volume of his work, the inherent intricacy and obscurity of his chosen subject, and the fundamental character of his research, deserves to be ranked with the greatest historians of the century. Beside his astonishing achievements the popular treatises of Prescott and Motley sink, from the scholar's standpoint, into relative insignificance." *Nation, 72* (May 9, 1901), 376.

94. *82*, 36–46.

95. See Bradley, pp. 307–8.

96. *Ibid.*, p. 293; *Minor Historical Writings and Other Essays by Henry Charles Lea,* ed. A. C. Howland (Philadelphia, University of Pennsylvania Press, 1942), p. 203.

97. Lea was eleven years younger than Motley and twenty-nine years younger than Prescott.

98. See E. P. Cheyney, "On the Life and Works of Henry Charles Lea," *Proc. Am. Phil. Soc., 50* (1911), xiii.

99. *Ibid.*, p. xiv.

100. Haskins, p. 184.

101. Lea retired from business in 1880 at the age of fifty-five.

102. Lea, *Minor Historical Writings,* p. vii.

103. *Ibid.*, p. 203.

104. R.-N., p. 310.

105. "A History of the Inquisition of the Middle Ages. By Henry Charles Lea," *The History of Freedom and Other Essays* (London, Macmillan & Co., Ltd., 1919), p. 551.

106. W. H. Hulbert, "The Poetry of Spanish America," *NAR, 68* (Jan., 1849), 130–1.

107. Note, in particular, besides editions of Robertson, Prescott, H. H. Bancroft, etc., Abiel Holmes, *American Annals; or, A Chronological History of America* (Cambridge [Mass.], 1805); F. J. Clavijero, *The History of Mexico,* tr. Charles Cullen (Richmond, Va., 1806); J. M. Niles, *A View of South America and Mexico* (New York, 1825); T. F. Gordon, *The History of Ancient Mexico* (Philadelphia, 1832); S. G. Goodrich, *History of South America and the West Indies* (Louisville, 1848); E. G. Squier, *Nicaragua* (New York, 1852); Brantz Mayer, *Mexico* (Hartford, 1852–53); etc.

108. L. B. Simpson, "The Encomienda in New Spain," *Calif. Univ. Pub. Hist., 19* (1929), 14–15. Bourne was almost the first American historian who did not emphasize Spanish greed and Spanish cruelty. See *AHR, 11* (Jan., 1906), 394–7.

109. In 1735 the Spanish government sent two naval officers, Jorge Juan y Santacilia and Antonio de Ulloa, with the French scientific expedition to South America to measure the arc of the meridian. In addition to the account of their travels, *Relacion historica del viage à la America Meridionàl* (Madrid, 1748), they prepared for the secret instruction of the king and his ministers an elaborate report on the government of the Spanish colonies, on their military and naval strength, and on conditions among the Indians. This report, which was a scathing indictment of the corruption among the Spanish colonial officials, was first brought to light in England in 1826 when

David Barry published it under the title *Noticias secretas de America.* An abridged edition in English by "an American" was published at Boston in 1851 and reprinted there in 1878.

110. Simpson, p. 2.

111. *Memories of a Hundred Years, 1,* 85. For a history of this tradition, see H. G. Doyle, "The 'Black Legend' of Spain," *Hisp., 16* (Oct., 1933), 341–6. Some modification of the "black legend" is apparent in the last decade of the century. See, in particular, the review of Lummis' *The Spanish Pioneers,* in *Nation, 58* (June 14, 1894), 453–4, and Chatfield-Taylor's "The Capital of Spain," *Cosmopol., 21* (June, 1896), 124. See also H. M. Skinner, "The Spanish-Speaking World Today," *Nat. M., 23* (March, 1906), 617–22.

112. See J. M. Gallardo, "Los hispanistas y la historia de América," *Hisp., 20* (Feb., 1937), 73.

113. *The Inquisition in the Spanish Dependencies* (New York, 1908).

114. Gallardo, p. 73.

115. *DAB, 17,* 243–4. Buckingham Smith, who anticipated Bolton in his advocacy of a common history for the Americas, Spanish as well as English, was a strong influence in directing historians toward Spanish America. Incidentally, he helped bring Amador de los Ríos into the membership of the New-York Historical Society. In this shift from Spain to Spanish America the historical societies were now an important factor. For an interesting account of these and for much supplementary information concerning topics discussed in the present chapter, see Harry Bernstein's forthcoming book, *Making an Inter-American Mind.*

116. In this volume errors, for which Smith was probably not to blame, aroused criticism.

117. (N. Y. H. S.)

118. See also *Memoir of Dº d'Escalante Fontaneda respecting Florida,* tr. Buckingham Smith, ed. D. O. True (Coral Gables, Fla., 1945).

119. J. W. Caughey, "Hubert Howe Bancroft," *AHR, 50* (April, 1945), 461.

120. Bancroft relates the story of his career as a collector and historian in his *Literary Industries,* The Works of Hubert Howe Bancroft, Vol. *39* (San Francisco, 1890). See also H. L. Oak, *"Literary Industries" in a New Light* (San Francisco, 1893). William H. Knight's request for certain volumes in compiling his *Hand Book Almanac* for 1860 suggested to Bancroft the idea of collecting books concerned with California, Oregon, Washington, and Utah.

121. For the complete story, see J. W. Caughey, *Hubert Howe Bancroft; Historian of the West* (Berkeley, University of California, 1946).

122. Bancroft's interest in writing history grew out of his experiences as a collector. As he said, "with the growth of the collection came the purpose." See Bancroft, p. 176.

123. E.g., "It is regrettable that the task of utilizing the priceless collection of sources should have been intrusted to a literary bureau and supervised by an inexperienced amateur." Gooch, pp. 408–9. See also Jameson, pp. 152–5.

124. See Caughey, p. 90.

125. *Colonial Hispanic America* (New York, Macmillan Co. [1933]), p. 368.

126. Caughey, p. 71.

127. *Ibid.,* p. 73.

128. *Ibid.*, pp. 73–4.

129. *Ibid.*, pp. 170–1.

130. See *ibid.*, p. 159.

131. See *ibid.*

132. See *ibid.* Caughey regards as a serious fault the fact that "Bancroft did not take full advantage of the rich store of original documents in the official archives of Mexico and Spain," p. 169.

133. See C. E. Chapman, *The Founding of Spanish California* (New York, Macmillan Co., 1916), p. 437. "Es su crítica la que, rompiendo con la tradicional leyenda de nuestra torpe y bárbara conquista y colonización de América, restablece, en parte, la verdad histórica e inicia la nueva orientación tan favorable a la causa española." R.-N., p. 325.

134. For Bancroft's share in the writing, see Oak. It is possible that Bancroft himself composed no one complete volume and that in the thirty-three volumes his own effort would total hardly more than the equivalent of five of these. It has been said that he wrote only seventy-five pages of *Central America*. For accounts of the other contributors, such as Oak, Savage, Nemos, and Harcourt, see *ibid.* Savage was the Spanish expert. Born of New England parents in Havana, he read *Don Quixote* in Spanish before he had learned the alphabet. At the age of nine he spoke Spanish fluently. After more than twenty-one years in the consular service in Spanish America, he arrived in San Francisco in 1873 and was engaged by Bancroft. He was the author of *Central America* and *Mexico* besides several other volumes. See Oak, and W. A. Morris, "The Origin and Authorship of the Bancroft Pacific States Publications," *Oreg. Hist. Quar., 4* (Dec., 1903), 362–3. Savage studied the Spanish manuscripts and supervised the copying of these in public and private archives.

135. "The stamp of the factory system of production that marks Bancroft's work should not make the student insensitive to his real achievement." Kraus, p. 575.

136. F. W. Blackmar, *Spanish Institutions of the Southwest* (Baltimore, 1891), p. vi. For another estimate of Bancroft's significance, see Gooch, pp. 408–9.

137. See Bancroft, pp. 173–97, 206–10. See also C. E. Chapman, "The Literature of California History," *Southw. Hist. Quar.*, 22 (April, 1919), 350–1.

138. See *Mag. Am. Hist., 13* (April, 1885), 409.

139. Bancroft was ridiculed by Lewis H. Morgan for depicting the ancient Mexicans as a feudal monarchy, as a kind of "Oriental empire." Bandelier, therefore, after his conversion to Morgan's opinions, shot a "number of poisoned shafts in Bancroft's direction." On one occasion he wrote: "The great wholesale Book-manufactory at San Francisco threatens the world with another volume" (1876). Again he said: "The descriptions are simply disgusting, and I cannot conceive that I was once blind enough to believe such stuff" (1879). A. F. A. Bandelier, *Pioneers in American Anthropology* (Albuquerque, University of New Mexico Press, 1940), *1*, 89. See also F. W. Hodge, "Biographical Sketch and Bibliography of Adolphe Francis Alphonse Bandelier," *New Mex. Hist. Rev.*, 7 (Oct., 1932), 353–70.

140. Bandelier, born in Switzerland, had traveled among the native peoples of New Mexico, Arizona, and Bolivia. More an archaeologist than a historian,

he had at first apparently accepted the accounts of the old Spanish chronicles. See his *Pioneers, 1,* 13. His ideas, however, were altered by his friendship with Morgan. See *ibid., 1,* 15–18. In 1881 he published his *Historical Introduction to Studies among the Sedentary Indians of New Mexico,* Archaeological Institute of America, Papers, American Ser., *1* [Pt. 1] (Boston, 1881). See also *The Final Report of Investigations among the Indians of the Southwestern United States,* Archaeological Institute of America, Papers, American Ser., *3–4* (Cambridge, 1890–92); and *Contributions to the History of the Southwestern Portion of the United States,* Archaeological Institute of America, Papers, American Ser., *5* (Cambridge, 1890). For an account of Bandelier's novel, see A. H. Noll, "The Pueblo Indians," *Dial, 12* (Aug., 1891), 104–7. This novel, *The Delight-Makers,* first written in German, was a story of pueblo life and was published in both English and German in 1890. See the review in *Critic, 17* (Dec. 20, 1890), 318. For hints concerning the rather strange personality of Bandelier, see Paul Radin's introduction to his *Unpublished Letters* (New York, C. P. Everett, 1942), pp. ix–xv.

141. *Spanish Colonization in the Southwest* (Baltimore, 1890). *Spanish Institutions of the Southwest* (Baltimore, 1891).

142. See *The Literature of American History,* ed. J. N. Larned (Boston, Houghton Mifflin & Co., 1902), p. 110; and C. E. Chapman, "The Literature of California History," *Southw. Hist. Quar.,* 22 (April, 1919), 339–40.

143. *The Spanish Settlements within the Present Limits of the United States, 1513–1561* (New York, 1901), p. vi. See *Engl. Hist. R., 17* (July, 1902), 616–17.

144. See *The Spanish Settlements within the Present Limits of the United States. Florida, 1562–1574* (New York, G. P. Putnam's Sons, 1905).

145. See E. G. Bourne, *Spain in America,* chaps. iii–xii.

146. *Ibid.,* chaps. xiii–xx.

147. See *ibid.,* "Editor's Introduction," p. xvii.

148. For an account of Bourne's achievements (and limitations), see *AHR, 11* (Jan., 1906), 394–7. See also *R. hisp., 15* (1906), 906–8.

149. See F. C. Lockwood, "Adventurous Scholarship: Dr. Herbert E. Bolton," *Cath. World, 138* (Nov., 1933), 187. In 1895 Bolton received his bachelor's degree from the University of Wisconsin, where he studied with Turner, Haskins, and Ely. His graduate work was done at the University of Pennsylvania under McMaster, Cheyney, and Munro.

150. One product of this experience was his *Guide to Materials for the History of the United States in the Principal Archives of Mexico* (Washington, D. C., 1913).

151. For bibliographies of Bolton's writings, see *New Spain and the Anglo-American West* ([Los Angeles, 1932]), 2, 245–52; and *Greater America* (Berkeley, University of California Press, 1945), pp. 537–48.

152. See Lockwood, p. 190. In 1933 it was estimated that his class in the History of the Americas at the University of California had enrolled 1,258 students. See Chapman, *Colonial Hispanic America,* p. 354. For a summary of Bolton's career, see *New Spain and the Anglo-American West, 1,* ix–xii.

153. A long series of articles on Spanish backgrounds in the Carolinas,

Georgia, and Florida, published in *Ga. Hist. Quar.*, shows the interest in local history aroused by Bolton's teachings.

154. Bolton, *The Spanish Borderlands,* p. x.

155. See *Greater America,* pp. 549–672. A few of the names suggest the wide distribution and the distinction of Bolton's influence: Caughey, Chapman, Dunne, Espinosa, Hammond, Lanning, Leonard, Rippy.

156. See *AHR, 38* (April, 1933), 448–74. For an interesting endorsement and extension of these ideas, see Gallardo, "Los hispanistas y la historia de América."

157. The theory has been compared in its importance to Turner's concerning the frontier. See Chapman, *Colonial Hispanic America,* pp. 357–8. For its genesis, see W. R. Shepherd, "Report of the Conference on the Contribution of the Romance Nations to the History of America," *Am. Hist. Assoc. Ann. Rep., 1909,* pp. 221–2.

158. See, in particular, pp. xiii–xv. See also W. C. Binkley, "Have the Americas a Common History?," *Can. Hist. R., 23* (June, 1942), 125–32. Apart from Bolton's influence, the twentieth-century study of the Spanish borderlands was destined to thrive. The question was agitated at meetings of the various historical associations and appears in the numerous histories of the Spanish origins of California, Texas, and Florida. Many years earlier Edward Everett had advocated the study of the history of the Americas.

159. H. E. Bolton, *Wider Horizons of American History* (New York, D. Appleton–Century Co. [1939]), p. xv. His first attempt at synthesis was produced in collaboration with one of his students, Thomas Maitland Marshall, in his *Colonization of North America, 1492–1783* (New York, 1920). His most recent book is a biography, *Coronado, Knight of Pueblos and Plains* (Albuquerque, N. M. [1949]).

160. California University, *Register, 1919–20,* Pt. III, p. 120.

161. No textbook was used, but in 1928 a syllabus entitled *History of the Americas. A Syllabus with Maps* was published. Bolton urged a broader treatment of American history and, in particular, two types of college courses: an introductory, synthetic course on the entire Western Hemisphere, to be followed by courses in the history of the United States or of any other individual nation. See also Chapman, *Colonial Hispanic America,* pp. 354–5.

162. For a discussion of Waldo Frank's books, see above, pp. 81–2, 100.

163. The preliminary work in Spanish-American historiography has already been outlined. This development occurred after 1900 partly by reason of the Spanish-American War, the building of the Panama Canal, and the increased interest in the United States after World War I in international affairs. The real cause, as in the cases of the travelers, writers for the periodicals, scholars, novelists, and artists, was inherent in a general transference of interest from Spain itself to Spain in America. The first lectures in Spanish-American history were delivered at Columbia University by Daniel De Leon between 1883 and 1886. See L. U. Hanke, "The First Lecturer on Hispanic American Diplomatic History in the United States," *HAHR, 16* (Aug., 1936), 399–402. Other pioneer courses were given by Elizabeth Wallace at the University of Chicago in 1892, by Bernard Moses at the University of California in 1895,

by others at the University of Texas and Columbia University in 1904 and at the University of Pennsylvania in 1907. See Pan American Union, Division of Education, Department of Cultural Affairs, *Courses on Latin America in Institutions of Higher Education in the United States, 1948–1949* (Washington, D. C., 1949), pp. xi–xii.

164. Namely California, Texas, Columbia, Pennsylvania, Yale, Stanford, Chicago, Harvard, Illinois, Michigan. See catalogues of these universities.

165. Pan American Union, pp. ix, xx–xxiii.

166. For these statistics and others, see *ibid.*, pp. v–vi, xx–xxiii, xliii–xliv.

167. Among these only a few historians of the "pioneer period" can be mentioned. Bernard Moses, whose first publication in this field occurred in 1898, was the author of six books, of which the last, *Spain Overseas* (1929), appeared in his eighty-fourth year. C. E. Chapman regarded Moses as better acquainted with the printed works on colonial Spanish America than any Anglo-American scholar of his time. See *Colonial Hispanic America*, p. 352. Although William Robert Shepherd was the author of three important works on Spanish America (*Guide to the Materials for the History of the United States in the Spanish Archives*, 1907; *Latin America*, 1914; *The Hispanic Nations of the New World*, 1919), he was most useful in his teaching of generation after generation of Columbia students. See J. T. Shotwell, "William Robert Shepherd," *Pol. Sci. Q.*, *49* (Dec., 1934), ix–x. For Leo S. Rowe's work as an inspirer of the younger historians at the University of Pennsylvania, as director of the Pan American Union, and as a writer, see R. S. Hill's account of him in *HAHR*, 27 (May, 1947), 187–8, and the special number of the *Bul. Pan. Am. Union*, *81* (April, 1947), 181–286. James Alexander Robertson's massive work, *The Philippine Islands*, and his achievements as librarian, editor, and writer are described in *Hispanic American Essays* (Chapel Hill, University of North Carolina Press, 1942), pp. 3–14, and in Pan American Union, pp. xx–xxiii. Necessary (and distinguished) textbooks appeared, such as W. W. Sweet's *History of Latin America* (1919), Robertson's *History of the Latin American Nations* (1923), or Mary W. Williams' *People and Politics of Latin America* (1930). During what Jorge Basadre calls the "second expansion," from 1933 to 1945, there were many advances in professional instruction, textbooks, and bibliography. These authors of handbooks, textbooks, bibliographies, geographies, and diplomatic histories cannot be mentioned by name or by their specific titles, which are numerous and of startling variety (if one looks, in contrast, at the past). For accounts of them, see Pan American Union; L. U. Hanke, "The Development of Latin-American Studies in the United States, 1939–1945," *Americas*, *4* (July, 1947), 32–64; C. E. Chapman, *Republican Hispanic America* (New York, 1937); A. C. Wilgus, *Histories and Historians of Hispanic America* (New York, 1942), etc.

168. See *12 Spanish American Poets*, ed. H. R. Hays (New Haven, 1943).

169. Chapman's purpose was to relate the important events in Spanish history from the point of view of America and at the same time to record the growth of the civilization or institutions of Spain.

170. Rafael Altamira, in his introduction to this work, p. xv. In 1949 Muna Lee published a translation of the second edition of Altamira's *Manual de*

historia de España entitled *A History of Spain from the Beginnings to the Present Day.*

171. See E. D. Salmon, *Imperial Spain* (New York [1931]); J. A. Brandt, *Toward the New Spain* (Chicago, 1932); Pierre Crabites, *Unhappy Spain* (Baton Rouge, 1937). Studies of the Moorish civilization continued. See above, p. 365, n. 80. S. P. Scott gave as one reason for attempting this history his conviction that the writings of Irving and Prescott "swarm with errors." See p. vi.

172. See, in particular, N. B. Adams, *The Heritage of Spain* (New York, 1943). See *Hisp., 29* (Feb., 1946), 154–5; and *N. Y. Times Book Rev.,* March 5, 1944, p. 7.

173. See C. E. Chapman, *HAHR, 1* (Nov., 1918), 435–41. Some critics found the narrative of events less successful than the analysis of institutions. See *AHR, 24* (Oct., 1918), 83–5. See also among the many reviews *ibid., 40* (Jan., 1935), 325–7. Another review calls it "an account of Spain in the Old World with generous attention to her expansion in the New rather than a balanced narrative of her activities in both hemispheres." *Nation, 123* (Aug. 4, 1926), 109.

174. See Garrett Mattingly, "The Historian of the Spanish Empire," *AHR, 54* (Oct., 1948), 32–48. This study contrasts the influences in Merriman's youth (of Henry Adams, MacVane, Channing, Hart, and Coolidge) with the combination in British scholars of exactitude and the "gentleman amateur." The reviewer finds Merriman's Oxford years important and describes how he fell in love with Spanish history while he was teaching a course in the subject at Harvard.

175. *Ibid.*

176. *Ibid.*

177. C. E. Chapman in *HAHR, 15* (Aug., 1935), 355.

CHAPTER 4: THE TEACHERS, SCHOLARS, TRANSLATORS, AND CRITICS

1. *A Year in Spain,* 3d ed. (New York, 1836), *3, 296*–7. See also the more sophisticated estimate of the language by Edward Wigglesworth in his review of Sales' edition of Cadalso's *Cartas marruecas, NAR, 26* (Jan., 1828), 248–58.

2. *U. S. Lit. Gaz., 2* (April, 1825), 35. See also the following: "Next to our own language, the Spanish will be likely at a future day to become the most important in this country. The new theatre of enterprise, which is opening to the whole world in the vast extent of the South American republics, and the intimate intercourse, which, from proximity of situation, and similar principles of government, must necessarily grow up between those republics and the United States, will make the language a desirable, if not an essential acquisition to our men of business, as well as to scholars and politicians." Jared Sparks in *NAR, 20* (April, 1825), 450. Cubí's grammar, first published in Baltimore in 1824, went through six editions by 1847. See Harry Bernstein, "The Latin American Book Trade Before 1900," p. 2418.

3. *The Genius of Spain and Other Essays* (Oxford, Clarendon Press, 1923), p. 10.

4. The number of books connected with Spain in early nineteenth-century bookstores is suggestive. See *Catalogue of Books, for Sale, by Isaac Beers & Co.* (New-Haven, 1801); and the auction list of Howe & Spaulding (New Haven, 1824), with grammars, histories, etc.

5. *The Education of Henry Adams* (New York, Modern Library [1931]), p. 348.

6. In 1833 Longfellow spoke of Spanish as "that language so justly popular among us." Quoted by Helman, p. 342.

7. The war, demanding immediate performance in conversation rather than the old disciplines in Spanish and Portuguese, probably retarded orthodox scholarship for a short time. See L. U. Hanke, "The Development of Latin-American Studies in the United States," *Americas, 4* (July, 1947), 58–60.

8. See Marshall Nunn, "The Growing Importance of Spanish in Science," *Hisp., 29* (Feb., 1946), 38–44.

9. The Spanish language press is now active in the circulation of news and ideas in the Southwest, in New York (among the Cuban and Puerto Rican colonies), in Tampa, and elsewhere in the United States. The first of foreign presses in number of publications, in all about 140, it indicates the growth of Spanish in this country. New York, for example, publishes seventeen regular periodicals and twenty-four trade journals. Tampa, with twenty thousand Spanish-speaking inhabitants, supports five periodicals in the language. See R. F. Brand, "A General View of the Regular Spanish Language Press in the United States," *MLJ, 33* (May, 1949), 363–70. See also Bernstein, "The Latin American Book Trade," p. 2417.

10. The following comment on Jan. 16, 1838, reflects the new interest: "The Spanish is a very easy and nobly sounding language. It is so full of the spirit of Chivalry that I cannot but admire it." See Herbert Thoms, "Some Letters of Edmund Randolph Peaslee," *Yale Jour. Biol. and Med., 17* (July, 1945), 689.

11. In his diary on Feb. 21, 1821, Marsh wrote: "In Spanish too, I have done something, and shall conquer it within the year." *The Remains of the Rev. James Marsh, D.D. . . . with a Memoir of His Life* [by Joseph Torrey], 2d ed. (New York, 1845), p. 38.

12. F. W. Blackmar, "Spanish American Words," *MLN, 6* (Feb., 1891), 91–8. See also his *Spanish Institutions of the Southwest* (Baltimore, 1891), pp. 273–7.

13. Despite Madariaga's comment, just quoted, on "pitiless statistics," these are often informative, and in this chapter I shall turn to them from time to time. For instance, 21,996,240 persons in the United States speak as their mother tongue some language besides English. The fourth largest group, numbering 1,861,400, speak Spanish. The three larger groups are German, Italian, and Polish. See *Hisp., 30* (Feb., 1947), 135.

14. For accounts of the beginnings of the study of the Spanish language, see C. H. Handschin, *The Teaching of Modern Languages in the United States,* U. S. Bureau of Education, Bulletin, 1913, No. 3 (Washington, 1913); E. W. Bagster-Collins, *The History of Modern Language Teaching in the United States* (New York, Macmillan Co., 1930); H. G. Doyle, *Spanish Studies in the United States* (Washington, D. C., Govt. Print. Off., 1926); J. R. Spell, "Spanish Teaching in the United States," *Hisp., 10* (May, 1927), 141–59. See also Bern-

stein, *Origins,* chap. iv, "The Formation of Cultural Interest"; and Robert F. Seybolt, *Source Studies in American Colonial Education, The Private School* (Urbana, 1925), pp. 11, 31.

15. See below, 2, 303–4, n. 1.

16. Spanish was one of the languages mentioned in the constitution of the Academy and Charitable School of the Province of Pennsylvania. See T. H. Montgomery, *A History of the University of Pennsylvania* (Philadelphia, G. W. Jacobs & Co., 1900), pp. 46–51.

17. *A Short Introduction to the Spanish Language* (New York, 1751).

18. Montgomery, p. 474. See also Spell, p. 148.

19. See R. J. Honeywell, *The Educational Work of Thomas Jefferson* (Cambridge, Harvard University Press, 1931), pp. 54–6. See also L. G. Tyler, "Early Courses and Professors at William and Mary College," *WMQ, 14* (Oct., 1905), 77.

20. J. F. Shearer, "French and Spanish Works Printed in Charleston, South Carolina," *PBSA, 34* (1940), 145.

21. For an interesting summary of such teaching, see Helman, p. 349. Mrs. Helman speculates on ways in which the New Englanders of this period learned Spanish, in particular regarding the niece of William Tudor, who in Peru received from this young girl charming letters in the language. Mrs. Helman quotes from one of these written in idiomatic Spanish. *Ibid.,* p. 349 n. 42.

22. See *ibid.,* p. 350.

23. Quoted *ibid.,* p. 350 n. 46.

24. See R. C. Smith, "A Pioneer Teacher: Father Peter Babad and His Portuguese Grammar," *Hisp., 28* (Aug., 1945), 330–63. During the year 1814–15 Claudius Berard was referred to as a professor of French, Spanish, Italian, and German at Dickinson College, but it is not certain that he taught Spanish. See *Spanish Studies,* p. 1.

25. See Josiah Quincy, *The History of Harvard University* (Cambridge, 1840), 2, 323.

26. *Ibid.*

27. "Extract from the Will of Abiel Smith, Esq.," Harvard University, *Report of a Committee of the Overseers of Harvard College, January, 6, 1825* (Cambridge, 1825), p. 34. It has been hinted that Smith's motives were commercial rather than cultural. In any case, he gave liberally of his wealth. In 1798 he was one of the contributors of $1,500 each for the frigate *Boston,* and in 1812 he founded a school for colored children. See *Professional and Industrial History of Suffolk County, Mass.* ([Boston], 1894), *3, 424;* and Nathaniel Dearborn, *Boston Notions* (Boston, 1848), p. 173: and the obituary in *Columbian Centinel,* Nov. 25, 1815.

28. T. F. Crane, "Three New England Professors," New England Society of Pennsylvania, *Annual Festival, 34* (1914), 81.

29. Harvard University, p. 35.

30. See *ibid.,* p. 36.

31. G. T., *1,* 95.

32. *Ibid., 1,* 117.

33. C. H. Hart, *Memoir of George Ticknor* (Philadelphia, 1871), p. 8. Bouterwek, a favorite professor at Göttingen, published his history of modern

literature, *Geschichte der Poesie und Beredsamkeit*, during the years from 1801 to 1819.

34. German scholars' interest in Spain took definite form in the Middle Ages, but the really enthusiastic study of Spanish literature developed during the nineteenth century. Jacob Grimm introduced Spanish ballads, and Herder translated them. Friedrich Diez laid foundations for the study of the language. Lessing was interested in the Spanish drama, Goethe in Calderón, and Tieck translated *Don Quixote*. Among others who shared the experience in various ways were A. W. Schlegel, Chamisso, and Heine. See Adalbert Hämel, "The Spanish Movement in Germany," *MLJ, 12* (Jan., 1928), 261–71. Of this revival our American Hispanophiles, especially those who had been in Germany, were much aware.

35. See O. W. Long, *Thomas Jefferson and George Ticknor* (Williamstown, Mass., McClelland Press, 1933), p. 30. In a letter to President Kirkland on Aug. 9, 1819, Ticknor outlined his plans: two distinct courses of literature, one in French literary history and criticism and one in Spanish.

36. *Ibid.*, p. 29.

37. George Ticknor, *Syllabus of a Course of Lectures on the History and Criticism of Spanish Literature* (Cambridge [Mass.], 1823).

38. Long, pp. 30–1.

39. *Ibid.*

40. *Ibid.*, p. 31.

41. Josiah Quincy, *Figures of the Past* (Boston, 1883), p. 22.

42. G. T., *1*, 326. See also S. E. Morison, *Three Centuries of Harvard* (Cambridge, Harvard University Press, 1937), pp. 236–7.

43. See Harvard University, President, *Annual Report, 1825–1826*, pp. 24–9, 33. All but the last-named of these texts were prepared by Francis Sales. This peculiar system for the accentuation of Spanish words in some of Sales' texts was his own invention and is best explained in his own words: "to facilitate the reading of Spanish by accenting every word, that could produce the least hesitation in the minds of learners, in regard to its pronunciation." See his *Colmena española*, p. iii.

44. In 1830–31 Folsom had been replaced by F. M. J. Surault, but other members of the department remained unchanged. At this date students were not compelled to study a foreign language but, if they elected one, were required to continue it until mastery was attained. During this year the regular students taking Spanish were in the sophomore and junior classes. Out of a total undergraduate enrollment of 237, in the first term there were sixty-seven students, in the second thirty-four, and in the third thirty-three. For further details, see Harvard University, President, *Annual Report, 1830–1831*, p. xviii, and *ibid.*, *1834–1835*, pp. ix–x.

45. By H. G. Doyle, as an appendix to his pamphlet, *George Ticknor* (Washington, D. C., 1937).

46. *Ibid.*, p. 16.

47. C. L. Johnson, *Professor Longfellow of Harvard* (Eugene, Ore., University Press, 1944), p. 23. In a letter to his father on Aug. 23, 1837, Longfellow described his duties as follows: "1. One Oral Lecture per week the year through. 2. Superintendance [*sic*] of studies & Instructors, by being present at least once

a month at the recitation of every student in each Language. 3. In the Summer Term Two lectures on Belles Lettres or Lit. Hist. per week in addition to the Oral Lectures, as above" (L. H.).

48. S. Longfellow, *1*, 274.

49. During 1838–39 Longfellow taught French to some 115 students and German to thirty. This teaching, he complained in a letter to the Corporation, gave him little time for the superintendence of the department and "no leisure for the prosecution of those studies which are absolutely requisite for the proper discharge of the duties originally prescribed to me." Johnson, p. 36.

50. (D. C.).

51. See Johnson, p. 87.

52. See Harvard University, President, *Annual Report, 1840–1841*, p. viii; *ibid., 1845–1846*, p. 27; *ibid., 1849–1850*, p. 28.

53. Letter, Cambridge, June 24, 1845. The rule declared that "no student will be allowed to take more than one Modern Language at a time, except for special reasons assigned, & by express vote of the Faculty." "Longfellow— Records of Harvard Classes—1837–54" (L. H.).

54. See Alfred Coester, "Francis Sales—a Forerunner," *Hisp., 19* (May, 1936), 283–302.

55. Harvard University, *Report of a Committee of the Overseers*, p. 36.

56. In his later years Sales had difficulties with discipline in the classroom, and at one time the Corporation desired to remove him from his position.

57. This book contained also a vocabulary and the "Dialogues" of Felipe Fernández, which Fernández had taken from H. S. J. Giral del Pino, *A New Spanish Grammar*, 2d ed. (London, 1777). See Coester, p. 289.

58. The book included eighty-eight *chistes* or short anecdotes, selected for their intrinsic value, and a vocabulary. Other publications from Sales' hand were: José Cadalso's *Cártas marruécas y poesías seléctas* (Boston, 1827); *Seleccion de obras maestras dramáticas por Calderon de la Barca, Lope de Vega, y Moreto* (Boston, 1828); Tomás de Iriarte's *Fábulas literarias* (Cambridge [Mass.], 1830); and an edition of *Don Quixote* (Boston, 1836). Ticknor reviewed the *Seleccion de obras maestras* in *Am. Q., 4* (Dec., 1828), 308–49. Sales also edited for his classes George Washington Montgomery's *El bastardo de Castilla*. See F. S. Stimson, "Spanish Themes in Early American Literature," p. 109.

59. Ticknor's comment. See *Am. Q., 4* (Dec., 1828), 310.

60. See *Putnam, 3* (May, 1854), 481–2.

61. "Cheerful Yesterdays," *Atlan., 78* (Dec., 1896), 763.

62. *Letters of James Russell Lowell*, ed. C. E. Norton (New York, 1894), *1*, 223.

63. See C. W. Eliot, "James Russell Lowell As a Professor," *Harvard Grad. Mag., 27* (June, 1919), 492–7.

64. "Mr. Lowell As a Teacher," *Scrib. M., 10* (Nov., 1891), 645–9.

65. See Ferris Greenslet, *James Russell Lowell* (Boston, Houghton Mifflin & Co., 1905), pp. 123–4. Lowell gave his famous course in Cervantes for the last time in 1885. See Morison, *Three Centuries*, p. 352.

66. W. R. Thayer, "James Russell Lowell As a Teacher," *Scrib. M., 68* (Oct., 1920), 477.

67. *Ibid.,* p. 478.

68. See "Address," *PMLA, 5,* No. 1 (1890), 5. In a footnote to the same address Lowell declared: "Mr. George Bancroft told me that he learned German of Professor Sydney Willard, who, himself selftaught, had no notion of its pronunciation." *Ibid.*

69. Barrett Wendell, *A Literary History of America* (New York, C. Scribner's Sons, 1931), p. 381.

70. See Spell, pp. 151–2.

71. In contrast, see the account of modern texts in José Padín, "Latin American Literature in North American Schools," *Harvard Ed. R., 13* (Oct., 1943), 323–34.

72. For sixteen years after the death of Lowell the Smith Professorship remained vacant. In 1905 President Eliot offered it to Bliss Perry, suggesting that he select the work he preferred "within this great field of literature— English, French, Italian, and Spanish." Since Perry was not a specialist in Romance literatures, this was an exceedingly broad interpretation of the original purposes of the Smith bequest. Perry did not accept this appointment. See Bliss Perry, *And Gladly Teach* (Boston, Houghton Mifflin & Co., 1935), pp. 235–7. In 1907 J. D. M. Ford was appointed "Smith Professor of the French and Spanish languages."

73. Long, p. 25.

74. See *ibid.,* p. 26. See also J. S. Patton, *Jefferson, Cabell, and the University of Virginia* (New York, Neale Publishing Co., 1906), pp. 334–5; Honeywell, p. 272; H. B. Adams, *Thomas Jefferson and the University of Virginia* (Washington, 1888), pp. 124, 126–9. In 1898–99 the School was divided into the School of Teutonic Languages and that of Romance Languages with Richard H. Wilson directing the latter.

75. Honeywell, p. 269.

76. Jefferson explained his opinions on this subject in a letter to Ticknor on July 16, 1823, in which he invited Ticknor to come to the university. See *The Writings of Thomas Jefferson, 15,* 454–7. In Dec., 1824, Ticknor visited Virginia and reported to Prescott: "It is more practical than I feared, but not so practical that I feel satisfied of its success." H. B. Adams, p. 124.

77. An examination of the University of Virginia catalogues, beginning in the year 1832–33, reveals that at this time French, Italian, German, Anglo-Saxon, and Spanish were taught. Although no special mention of Spanish is made, we learn that in some of these subjects there were two classes, of which the senior was taught by the professor and the junior by the tutor. The latter was then J. Hervé, a native of France, who had taught languages in Richmond. A system of both written and oral translations was used, and lectures on the literature were delivered by the professor. In 1836–37, 1846–47, 1850–51, and 1855–56 the same methods were still employed. In 1890–91 one group of students read aloud in order to practice pronunciation, to acquire idioms, and to appreciate the classic writers. More and more modern authors were assigned as outside reading and lectures on syntax were given. In 1895–96, after James A. Harrison had become professor of Romance languages, the work in Spanish was divided into two courses. The course for the B. A. used Edgren's *Spanish Grammar,* Knapp's *Modern Spanish Readings,* Todd's *Don*

Quixote, with selections from Lope de Vega and Calderón, Valera's *Pepita Jiménez,* Harrison's *Spain,* and Seoane's *Dictionary.* In the course for the M. A. Knapp's *Grammar* was used, with lectures based on Paul Foerster's *Spanische Sprachlehre* and Wiggers' *Grammatik der spanischen Sprache.* Included also were selections from the lyric and dramatic poets and from the great prose writers, Ticknor's *History,* Isla's edition of Le Sage's *Gil Blas,* the *Romancero del Cid,* and Seoane's *Dictionary.* I shall not trace the development of instruction in Spanish in each university, but the foregoing may be helpful in indicating the character of the study of Spanish in a university with a predilection for this language and literature. The courses given in the year 1900–1 are interesting but will not be outlined here. For further details, see Virginia University, *Catalogues, 1832–1833,* p. 18; *1859–1860,* p. 26; *1870–1871,* p. 32; *1880–1881,* p. 27; *1890–1891,* pp. 6–7; *1895–1896,* pp. 11–12; *1900–1901,* p. 65.

78. This figure declined to one in four during the year 1880–81, one in five in 1890–91, and one in seven in 1895–96. The catalogue for 1900–1 lists ten students in Spanish.

79. For accounts of Schele de Vere, one of the great practical teachers of Spanish, see P. A. Bruce, *History of the University of Virginia* (New York, Macmillan Co. [1920]–22), *3,* 82, 84; A. C. Gordon Jr. in *DAB, 16,* 423–4; P. B. Barringer, *University of Virginia* (New York, Lewis Publishing Co., 1904), *1,* 134–5. Proof of Longfellow's power to attract Spaniards or teachers of Spanish to America is contained in a series of interesting letters to him from José Cortés y Sesti (L. H.). See below, *2,* 338, n. 29.

80. L. C. Hatch, *The History of Bowdoin College* (Portland, Me., Loring, Short & Harmon, 1927), p. 61. In 1825 Mrs. Henry Dearborn, the widow of James Bowdoin Jr., a former minister to Spain and the son of the man for whom the college was named, gave one thousand dollars to establish a professorship of French.

81. Bowdoin College, *Memorial of the Hundredth Anniversary of the Incorporation of Bowdoin College* (Brunswick, Me., 1894), p. lx.

82. Stephen Longfellow to Longfellow, Dec. 3, 1826 (L. H.).

83. It was not until he had finished his second year of teaching that Longfellow was formally inducted as professor of modern languages. On Sept. 18, 1830, he delivered his inaugural address, "Origin and Growth of the Languages of Southern Europe and of Their Literature." This lecture was published in pamphlet form by the Bowdoin College Library in 1907.

84. Longfellow to George W. Greene (W. C.).

85. Longfellow borrowed the two stories for his *Novelas españolas.* To the best of my knowledge, only three copies of *Tareas de un solitario* survive. See S. T. Williams, "The First Version of the Writings of Washington Irving in Spanish," *MP, 28* (Nov., 1930), 185–201.

86. Longfellow to George Greene, June 2, 1832 (L. H.).

87. (D. C.) Two years prior to his appointment at Harvard Longfellow sought eagerly an appointment as secretary of the legation in Madrid. See his letter to G. W. Pierce [Brunswick, July, 1833] (L. H.).

88. Longfellow was succeeded by Daniel Rayne Goodwin, an "assiduous, fearless, and most efficient teacher." See Hatch, p. 62. For indications of the fate

of Spanish at Bowdoin after Longfellow's departure, see Bowdoin College, *Catalogues, 1833,* p. 22; *1834,* pp. 20–1; *1836–1837,* p. 20; *1861–1862,* p. 19.

89. Yale University, *Catalogue, 1826–1827,* pp. 24–5.

90. *Ibid.*

91. Between 1830 and 1843 no Spanish instructor was listed in the catalogues. From 1843 to 1849 François Turner taught both Spanish and French. In 1845–46 the title of the course was changed to "Modern Languages," and both seniors and juniors could elect a language in the second term. See *Catalogue, 1845–1846,* p. 29.

92. Juan Boscán Almogáver, *Las obras de Juan Boscan repartidas en tres libros* (Madrid, 1875); and Diego Hurtado de Mendoza, *Obras poéticas de D. Diego Hurtado de Mendoza. Primera edicion completa* (Madrid, 1877). For accounts of Knapp, see Doyle, *Spanish Studies,* p. 6; and Joseph Seronde in *DAB, 10,* 453–4.

93. See Yale University, *Catalogue, 1889–1900,* p. 41. In 1892–93, after Knapp had been succeeded by Henry Roseman Lang, two courses were again offered. See *ibid., 1892–1893,* pp. 48, 147. See also J. D. M. Ford, "Henry Roseman Lang," *HR, 3* (Jan., 1935), 70. The first Ph. D. in romance languages was granted to George Pomeroy Otis, B. A., 1861, in 1873. The title of his dissertation is unknown. In 1894 the third Ph. D. in the field was given to Cornelia Hephzibah Bulkeley Rogers, whose dissertation was called "Sinalefa, sinéresis, é hiato en los romances del Cid." See Yale University, Graduate School, *Doctors of Philosophy of Yale University* (New Haven, 1927), p. 179.

94. Pennsylvania University, *Catalogue, 1830,* p. 21.

95. The fortunes of Spanish at the University of Pennsylvania may be traced in the following catalogues: *1870–1871,* pp. 33, 34, 35; *1871–1872,* pp. 5, 32, 33, 34; *1875–1876,* p. 39; *1890–1891,* p. 95; *1895–1896,* pp. 145, 193; *1900–1901,* pp. 139, 211.

96. For information concerning the teaching of Spanish at this institution, see California University, *Register, 1870–1871,* pp. 5, 58–9; *1875–1876,* p. 6; *1876–1877,* p. 49; *1885–1886,* pp. 31–2; *1890–1891,* p. 48; *1895–1896,* pp. 98, 142; *1900–1901,* pp. 185–6, 270. By the year 1901 there were five courses in Spanish.

97. Spell, pp. 152–4.

98. *Scrib., 4* (Aug., 1872), 414–24.

99. Doyle, *Spanish Studies,* pp. 3–4.

100. See Harvard University, *Catalogue, 1895–1896,* pp. 90–1.

101. 7, 438–9. In the same article Professor Grandgent speaks of the need for a new Spanish course dealing with modern prose and poetry and "bridging the gap between the elementary work and the scientific study of Renaissance letters." See also *ibid., 1* (Jan., 1893), 281–2, and *8* (Dec., 1899), 236–7.

102. See Harvard University, *Catalogue, 1900–1901,* pp. 372–3, 425. An indication of the popularity of Spanish at this time is the fact that an elementary course was offered in the summer session. See also, for an account of Professor Ford's remarkable contribution to the teaching of Spanish, H. G. Doyle, "Jeremiah Denis Matthias Ford," *Hisp., 19* (May, 1936), 153–62.

103. See J. P. W. Crawford, "Hugo Albert Rennert," *Gen. Mag. and Hist. Chron., 30* (April, 1928), 373.

104. See *Revista de estudios hispánicos, 1* (enero-marzo, 1928), 84. For the development of the teaching of Spanish in this institution during the last years of the century, see the following representative catalogues: 1875–76; 1885–86; 1890–91; 1895–96. See also the *Harvard Grad. Mag., 1* (Jan., 1893), 281–2; 7 (March, 1899), 438–9; *8* (Dec., 1899), 236–7.

105. See A. M. O'Brien, "Casa Hispana," *Hisp., 15* (May, 1932), 261–6.

106. See Coester, pp. 300–2; and H. G. Doyle, "Progress in the Teaching of Spanish and Portuguese," *Harvard Ed. R., 13* (Oct., 1943), 335–41.

107. See Handschin, p. 84.

108. The departments of Spanish in these schools now included, besides the ordinary language courses, thirty-five survey courses in Spanish literature, fifteen in the "Golden Age," eight in Cervantes and *Don Quixote,* two in old Spanish, etc. See Terrell Tatum, "General Survey of the Study of Spanish," *Hisp., 23* (Dec., 1940), 384–90. The war emphasized conversational aims and between 1943 and 1948 caused changes in methods of teaching. See W. H. Rice, "Teaching Foreign Languages," *R. Ed. Res., 16* (April, 1946), 139–60. For the increase of popular interest in this period, see Doyle, *Handbook,* p. 4.

109. See Bagster-Collins, p. 32, and *Report of the Commissioner of Education,* 1917, 2, 12, 13, 14. See also Dorothy Meyer, "Enrollment Trends in Foreign Languages in the Public and Private Secondary Schools of the United States" (unpublished master's essay, University of New Mexico, 1930). See also C. A. Jessen and L. B. Herlihy, *Offerings and Registrations in High School-Subjects, 1933–34,* U. S. Office of Education, Bulletin, 1938, No. 6 (Washington, D. C., 1938). According to these statistics more than two fifths of the total registration in Spanish was in the southwestern states. See also *Hisp., 28* (Nov., 1945), 624, for figures on the Spanish enrollment in the schools of New York City.

110. The present fulfillment of the dream is interesting. In their catalogues for 1948–49 or later the colleges previously considered offered the following courses in Spanish (on various levels): Bowdoin, six; the University of California, thirty-two; Harvard, thirty-nine; Pennsylvania, nine; Virginia, nineteen; Yale, twenty-five. These listings do not, of course, mean that all these courses were given every year.

111. Long, p. 30.

112. See below, 2, 305, n. 15.

113. See his *A Literary History of America,* p. 392.

114. See W. I. Knapp, "The Ticknor Spanish Library," *New Englander, 39* (May, 1880), 389. This review of the *Catalogue of the Spanish Library and of Portuguese Books Bequeathed by George Ticknor to the Boston Public Library* (Boston, 1879) included an account of its contents.

115. See *NAR, 70* (Jan., 1850), 4. For a summary of the European predecessors of Ticknor in the field, see T. F. Crane, "Ticknor's Spanish Literature," *Nation, 14* (June 6, 1872), 377–8. Recently E. L. Furness in "A Tentative Chronology of Spanish Literary History (1780–1941)" listed only the histories of Ticknor, Ford, and Northup. See *MLJ, 33* (Jan., 1949), 23–6.

116. *James Russell Lowell and His Friends* (Boston, 1899), pp. 126–7.

117. The *Christian Examiner* spoke of this book as addressed to "all classes of intelligent and cultivated men." *48* (Jan., 1850), 122.

118. See *So. Q.*, N. S., *2* (Sept., Nov., 1850), 85–123, 273–313; *NAR, 70* (Jan., 1850), 1–56, by W. H. Prescott; and *Meth. Q., 32* (April, 1850), 292–324.

119. E. P. Whipple, "George Ticknor," *Internat. R., 3* (July, 1876), 458.

120. *Ibid.*, pp. 457–8. "He is seen at his best in such literary magnates as Cervantes, Lope de Vega, Calderon, etc. His defects are most apparent in his treatment of purely poetic subjects—Gongora, for instance." T. F. Crane, "Ticknor's Spanish Literature," p. 377.

121. "Spanish literature, prior to 1849, was known generally only by one masterpiece, 'Don Quixote,' a book universally talked about, little read, and not at all understood." *Ibid.*

122. Journal, Sept. 14, 1838. "First Lecture on Lope's Star of Seville" (L. H.).

123. (L. H.)

124. I. L. W., pp. 102–5.

125. This passage is from a letter to, presumably, Chancellor James M. Matthews of New York University. Dated Harvard University, June 18, 1834, it recommends Longfellow "for the chair of Spanish Literature, vacant in the University of New York by the resignation of Professor Calvara" (D. C.). Other letters from Longfellow in this collection attest his close personal and intellectual ties with Ticknor. See also the numerous letters from Ticknor (L. H.) on *Novelas Españolas, Outre-Mer*, etc.

126. See W. V. Gavigan, "Longfellow and Catholicism," *Cath. World, 138* (Oct., 1933), 42–50.

127. See S. L., *1*, 350.

128. Some of these old textbooks are interesting today. Francis Butler's *The Spanish Teacher and Colloquial Phrase Book*, published by D. Appleton and Co. in 1849, was brought out in a new edition in 1892, revised and arranged according to the rules of the Spanish Academy. See A. M. Brady's article on Butler's work in "One Hundred Years," *MLJ, 33* (Feb., 1949), 115–21. This article reprints "Advice to the Student, on the Method of Studying a Foreign Language."

129. The present chapter is not designed in any way as a complete record of Spanish scholarship but as a background for Hispanism in American literature. I have made no attempt to define the attainments of all twentieth-century scholars or to mention all living scholars of distinction, though an awareness of many of these will be apparent from citations in the notes.

130. See Crawford, p. 372. See also H. A. Rennert, "The Spanish Pastoral Romances," *PMLA*, 7, No. 3 (July–Sept., 1892), 1–119.

131. See, in addition to Doyle's *Spanish Studies*, p. 5, "Charles Carroll Marden, 1867–1932," *PMLA, 47* (Sept., 1932), 609–12; F. C. Tarr, "Charles Carroll Marden," *HR, 1* (Jan., 1933), 70–2; and "A Bibliography of the Publications of Charles Carroll Marden," *MLN, 47* (Dec., 1932), vii–xi.

132. In 1895 Ford won both the Sales Prize in Spanish and the Dante Prize in Italian. His subject for the latter was "Dante's Influence on Spanish Literature in the Fifteenth and Sixteenth Centuries." See Doyle, "Jeremiah Denis Matthias Ford," pp. 153–62; "A Great Teacher Retires," *Hisp., 26* (Oct., 1943), 320–1; and H. G. Doyle, "J. D. M. Ford Honored by Friends and Former Students," *ibid., 31* (Aug., 1948), 348–9.

133. In contrast to these beginnings in formal investigation, W. M. Miller

in his "American Doctoral Degrees Granted in the Field of Modern Languages in 1949" lists "nineteen dissertations on Spanish topics out of a total of seventy-eight accepted in some twenty-one universities." See *MLJ, 33* (Dec., 1949), 624–9. For other figures, see *HAHR, 27* (Aug., 1947), 570–1; L. L. Barrett, "Theses Dealing with Hispano-American Language and Literature—1946," *Hisp., 30* (May, 1947), 200–2. See also D. D. Walsh, "The Status of Spanish and Portuguese in American Colleges and Universities," *ibid.* (Aug., 1947), pp. 346–50.

134. See Mariano Velázquez de la Cadena, *Elementos de la lengua castellana* (Nueva-York, 1820), and 2 ed., corr. y aum. (Nueva-York, 1824). Velázquez de la Cadena was professor of Spanish language and literature at Columbia University for thirty years (1830–60). In a review of Miguel Romera-Navarro's *El hispanismo en Norte América,* J. L. Gerig says: "Beginning with the gifted Ticknor and the early lexicographer Velásquez . . . Spanish scholarship in America has shown a varied, if not steady, development. With the publication of the grammars of W. I. Knapp (1882) and A. Hjalmar Edgren (1891) the study of Spanish received a new impetus here. Later on came M. M. Ramsey's *Text-Book of Modern Spanish,*" *RR, 10* (April–June, 1919), 184.

135. Vingut, a Cuban, came to the United States in 1848 and taught modern languages at New York University, from 1848 to 1857. He edited papers, called *La Aurora* and *La Indiana,* in Spanish and English and published grammars and phrase books for learning Spanish, English, and French. With his wife, a Philadelphian, he edited an anthology, *Gems of Spanish Poetry,* containing both Peninsular and Spanish-American authors.

136. See *Hisp., 33* (Aug., 1950), 281. For the increase of textbooks, see D. K. and J. H. Arjona's *A Bibliography of Textbooks of Spanish Published in the United States (1795–1937)* (Ann Arbor, Mich., 1939).

137. Crane was indirectly under Ticknor's influence. In 1867, while he was studying in an Ithaca law office, he began to read Spanish with Edward Curtis Guild, Ticknor's nephew. At Cornell he was successively assistant professor of South European languages (1868–73), professor of Spanish and Italian (1873–81), and professor of Romance languages and literatures (1881–1927). See G. I. Dale, "Ticknor and Crane," *Hisp., 19* (Feb. 1929), 83–4; and W. T. Hewett, *Cornell University* (New York, 1905), 2, 32–3.

138. See Doyle, "Jeremiah Denis Matthias Ford." Ford was one of the first American scholars to be interested in Spanish-American literature.

139. Goldberg's contribution was substantial. Although he never visited Spanish or Portuguese countries, his knowledge of their literatures was thorough and creative. "Words to me," he said, speaking of his interest in language during boyhood, "words and structures of words—are, and always have been, among the miracles of the universe. As fleeting as the breath that shapes them and warms them with meaning, they yet remain as perdurable as the emotion that first sought for them a healing utterance." See his "Notes from a Multilingual Career," *BA, 7* (July, 1933), 272. See also Allen Crandall, *Isaac Goldberg, an Appreciation* (Sterling, Colo., 1934), pp. 39–50; and S. M. Waxman, "Isaac Goldberg," *RI, 1* (mayo, 1939), 107–9.

140. We should compare the limited knowledge of Spanish-American literature at the time of Goldberg's book with the enthusiasm for the subject thirty

years later. See Thomas Walsh, "The Spanish-American Masters," *Bookm., 51* (April, 1920), 235–7.

141. Some of the most important scholarship concerning legend, song, or language may be found in historical or in state and sectional journals. Typical studies are: Mary Austin, "Spanish Manuscripts in the Southwest," *SWR, 19* (July, 1934), 402–9; A. M. Espinosa, "Studies in New Mexican Spanish," *Bulletin, University of New Mexico Language Series*, Vol. *1*, No. 2 (Dec., 1909); A. L. Campa, "Sayings and Riddles in New Mexico," *ibid.*, Vol. *5*, No. 2 (Sept. 15, 1937); F. M. Kercheville, "A Preliminary Glossary of New Mexican Spanish," *ibid.*, Vol. *5*, No. 3 (July 15, 1934); G. R. Stewart, "Two Spanish Word Lists from California in 1857," *AS, 16* (Dec., 1941), 260–9.

142. See "Charles Carroll Marden," *PMLA, 47* (Sept., 1932), 611.

143. See Howard Cline, "Reflections on Traditionalism in the Historiography of Hispanic America," *HAHR, 29* (May, 1949), 203–4.

144. For the continuance of scholarship in Spanish literature itself, see O. H. Green, "A Critical Survey of Scholarship in the Field of Spanish Renaissance Literature, 1914–1944," *SP, 44* (April, 1947), 228–64.

145. See Sturgis E. Leavitt, "Latin American Literature in the United States: Retrospect and Prospect," *ibid., 42* (July, 1945), 716–22. This informative article praises the early study by M. M. Ramsey in Warner's *Library of the World's Best Literature* (1896–97) and notes the pioneering translations. It points out as the initiator of systematic study of the subject Alfred Coester's *Literary History of Spanish America* in 1916, with its second edition in 1928. The article records in detail the rapid appearance of dissertations, research in special fields, and bibliographies. See also Arturo Torres-Ríoseco's *The Epic of Latin American Literature* (New York, 1942) and E. H. Hespelt, I. A. Leonard, and others, *An Outline History of Spanish American Literature* (New York, 1941).

146. For accounts of these and other scholars, see Doyle, *Spanish Studies; R.-N.*, pp. 330–56; and H. G. Doyle, "J. P. Wickersham Crawford," *MLJ, 24* (March, 1940), 457–8. For accounts of Cecil Knight Jones (1872–1945), bibliographer and pioneer teacher of Spanish-American literature, see the obituary notice by J. B. Childs in *HAHR, 25* (Nov., 1945), 411–12, and H. G. Doyle, "A Modest Scholar Passes," *Hisp., 28* (Nov., 1945), 556–8; of William Samuel Hendrix (1887–1948), see *HR, 16* (July, 1948), 245–9; of Frederick Bliss Luquiens (1875–1940), see J. A. Buendía, "Methods of Teaching Spanish at Yale University," *Hisp., 27* (May, 1944), 178–208. Meanwhile, living scholars carry on the tradition, among them eminent Spaniards and Spanish Americans, such as Federico de Onís; Miguel Romera-Navarro, Arturo Torres-Ríoseco, and Pedro Henríquez-Ureña.

147. See Bernstein, *Origins*, chap. iv, "The Formation of Cultural Interest."

148. See Helman, p. 348. For Obadiah Rich's aid to American libraries, see *ibid.* See also the *Catalogue of Books in the Boston Atheneum* (Boston, 1827).

149. *Proc. Am. Antiq. Soc.*, N. S., *29* (April, 1919), 12–13.

150. In addition to the catalogues of the libraries, one may consult with profit those of the universities discussed in the present chapter. See also *Cata-*

logue of the Library of the Athenaean Society of Bowdoin College (Brunswick, 1834). In the Catalogue of Books, Belonging to the Library of the University of Pennsylvania (Philadelphia, 1829) only two Spanish books were listed: Francisco Sobrino, Dicionario nuevo de las lenguas española y francesa (Brussels, 1721); and Bernal Díaz del Castillo, The True History of the Conquest of Mexico (London, 1800). See also Gonzalo de Reparaz Ruiz, "Les Études hispaniques aux États-Unis jusqu'en 1939," B. Hi., 47, 103–122, 48, 14–43, 147–69 (1945–46).

151. For an account of the Hispanic Foundation of the Library of Congress (1939), see Hutton, "Popular Interest in the Study of Spanish and Portuguese," Doyle, Handbook, p. 6; and the Information Bulletin of the Library of Congress for July 19–25, 1949, pp. 4–5. See also L. O. Wright, "The Spanish National Honor Society, Sigma Delta Pi," Hisp., 9 (Nov., 1926), 297–8.

152. The Proceedings and Transactions of the society record many instances of these interrelations, from José Joaquín de Ferrer's "Memoir on the Occultation of Aldebaran by the Moon on the 21st of October 1793," Transactions, 6 (1809), 213–21, to Santiago Ramón y Cajal's "Recollections of My Life," Memoirs, 8 (1937), 1–638. See Bernstein, Origins, pp. 59–60.

153. Founded in October, 1920, as a result of meetings representing the Junta para Ampliación de Estudios del Ministerio de Instrucción Pública de España, the Institute of International Education, the American Association of Teachers of Spanish, and several Spanish and American universities. See its Memoria del curso 1920–1921 (Madrid–Nueva York, 1921). See also its Bulletin, No. 1 (Jan., 1931), p. 2; and RHM, 10 (enero y abril, 1944), 180–3.

154. Founded in 1917, the association had a membership of fourteen hundred by 1926. For an account of its activities, see Doyle, Spanish Studies, pp. 11–12. See also the description of the Inter-American training center in H. G. Doyle, "Practical Inter-Americanism," Bul. Pan. Am. Union, 78 (Aug., 1944), 429–36.

155. Joseph Pijoan, "Collections of the Hispanic Society," Int. Stud., 96, No. 4 (Aug., 1930), 70.

156. See The Hispanic Society of America (New York, 1952) and Ronald Hilton, Handbook of Hispanic Source Materials and Research Organizations in the United States (Toronto, University of Toronto Press, 1942), pp. 284–7.

157. See Bibliographie hispanique (1905–17); Revue hispanique (1905–33); Notes Hispanic (1941–45); Hispanic Notes and Monographs; Essays, Studies, and Brief Biographies (1919–date).

158. The most recent is Samuel Putnam's scholarly translation (New York, 1949), with a critical text based upon the first editions of 1605 and 1615 and with variant readings. Dudley Fitts says of this: "It is more than a translation: it is a kind of redemption" in its power to communicate "the freshness, the divine limpidity of the original." See Hisp., 33 (Feb., 1950), 87–8. See also Putnam's translation, Three Exemplary Novels (New York, 1950), and The Portable Cervantes (New York, 1951). For an account of Putnam as a translator see Time, 54, No. 14 (Oct. 3, 1949), 76–8. For Putnam's other translations, see Who's Who in the East, 2, 1375–6.

159. For lists of translations, see R. U. Pane, English Translations from the

Spanish (New Brunswick, 1944); S. E. Leavitt, *Hispano-American Literature in the United States* (Cambridge, Mass., 1932), and his supplements published in *Hispania* and elsewhere.

160. George William Erving (1769–1850), a diplomat, translated a part of Erro's treatise, *The Alphabet of the Primitive Language of Spain* (Boston, 1829).

161. George Santayana translated selections from *Don Quixote*. Among the various translators during the nineteenth century were Samuel Eliot (1821–98), who offered versions from the poet Zorrilla (Boston, 1846); Mrs. S. G. C. Middlemore, author of the controversial *Round a Posada Fire* (London [1881]); Rollo Ogden, translator of Spanish-American stories; or Mrs. Mary Jane Serrano, translator of Emilia Pardo Bazán.

162. William Elliot's translation was a direct result of his intense delight in the original. Apparently this is the latest English translation of this work although there have been versions in French and other languages.

163. See Leavitt. Among twentieth-century translations of particular interest are *The Lay of the Cid*, tr. R. S. Rose and Leonard Bacon (Berkeley, 1919), and Thomas Walsh, *Hispanic Anthology* (New York, G. P. Putnam's Sons, 1920).

164. See the review in *Harper*, 92, No. 2 (Jan., 1896), sup. p. 4, of Mary J. Serrano's translation of *Doña Perfecta* (with Howells' introduction) in "clear and forcible English."

165. See Antoinette Ogden, *Christmas Stories from French and Spanish Writers* (Chicago, 1892); C. B. McMichael, *Short Stories from the Spanish* (New York [1920]); and Max Lieber and B. C. Williams, *Great Stories of All Nations* (New York, 1927).

166. For accounts of some of these translators and their works see Dudley Fitts, *The Book Review Digest, 1948*, pp. 271–2; Ángel Flores, *Hisp.*, 26 (Feb., 1943), 114–17; Muna Lee, *ibid.*, 33 (May, 1950), 179–80; Harriet de Onís, *ibid.*, 26 (Feb., 1943), 114–17, and *The Book Review Digest, 1945*, p. 545; Eleanor Laurelle Turnbull, *Hisp.*, 28 (Aug., 1945), 474–5; etc.

167. See *Don Quixote*, 2, 923, and Preface.

168. E.g., Charles Fletcher Lummis (1859–1928), who lived five years in the Indian pueblo of Isleta in order to learn Indian languages and customs; or, Henry Raup Wagner (1867—).

169. See, for example, Gusta B. Nance's and Florence J. Dunstan's translation of Carlos González Peña's *History of Mexican Literature*, rev. ed. (Dallas, 1943).

170. Pound translated excerpts from Lope de Vega's *Los pastores de Belén*. Dos Passos translated various poems of Antonio Machado y Ruiz. See Pane, p. 138.

171. (New York, 1920). See also his *The Catholic Anthology*, rev. ed. (New York, 1932).

172. See below, p. 217, and n. 40.

173. These allusions, compiled from the first six volumes of J. R. L., number at least seventeen for Cervantes or *Don Quixote* and ten for Calderón.

174. Lowell's subtitle is "Notes Read at the Workingmen's College, Great Ormond Street, London." See J. R. L., 6, 115–36. In the light of modern criti-

cism this lecture or essay seems sound enough but hopelessly commonplace with its talk of the "savor of nationality" in *Don Quixote* and its none too original comments on humor, optimism, and cosmopolitanism. Lowell tells us, for example, that Cervantes is the "father of the modern novel."

175. For Lowell as a critic of Spanish literature, see Norman Foerster, *American Criticism* (Boston, Houghton Mifflin & Co., 1928), pp. 144–5; and J. J. Reilly, *James Russell Lowell As a Critic* (New York, G. P. Putnam's Sons, 1915), pp. 50–1, 141, 158–9, 206–7.

176. See *Criticism and Fiction* (New York, 1891), pp. 58–63, 70–2, 82–6.

177. E.g., H. C. Berkowitz, *Pérez Galdós* (Madison, 1948). See the review of this book in *HR, 18* (Jan., 1950), 78–86.

178. There are now numerous histories of Latin-American literature. E.g., Pedro Henríquez-Ureña, *Literary Currents in Hispanic America* (Cambridge, Mass., 1945); J. R. Spell, *Contemporary Spanish-American Fiction* (Chapel Hill, 1944); *Concerning Latin American Culture,* ed. C. C. Griffin (New York, 1940); Arturo Torres-Ríoseco, *The Epic of Latin American Literature* (New York, 1942); E. H. Hespelt, I. A. Leonard, and others, *An Outline History of Spanish American Literature* (New York, 1941). See also L. U. Hanke, "The Development of Latin-American Studies in the United States," *Americas, 4* (July, 1947), 58–60.

CHAPTER 5: THE NOVELISTS, POETS, AND DRAMATISTS

1. See H. W. B., pp. 62, 63, 64, 183, and especially "Vocabulary," in which our writers' use of Spanish words is discussed.

2. Until the third quarter of the century American interest in Spanish literature was inclined to center in the writers of the past. In an article introducing Carolina Coronado (see below, 2, 134–5, 136–7), *Graham's, 39* (Dec., 1851), 360, remarked: "Why are English readers so little acquainted with the works of their Spanish contemporaries? The names of Cervantes, of Lope de Vega, of Calderon, are as well known as those of Corneille, Racine, and Voltaire, or of Dante, Tasso, and Petrarch. The works of Lamartine, of Victor Hugo and Sue, are in the hands of every one, while it cannot be denied that there is a lamentable ignorance of modern Spanish literature."

3. "Benito Cereno," H. M., *10,* 66.

4. *The Collected Poems of Hart Crane,* ed. Waldo Frank (New York [1933]), p. 11. Copyright 1933 by Liveright, Inc. Published by Liveright Publishing Corp.

5. For bibliographies of literature of the Southwest and California, see Spiller, *3,* 197, etc. See also J. E. Stiff, "The Spanish Element in Southwestern Fiction" (unpub. diss., North Texas Teachers' College, 1928).

6. See Lyle Saunders, *A Guide to Materials Bearing on Cultural Relations in New Mexico* (Albuquerque, 1944). For a discussion of the inexact and varied uses of the term "Southwest," see J. W. Caughey, "The Spanish Southwest," *Regionalism in America,* ed. Merrill Jensen (Madison, University of Wisconsin Press, 1951), pp. 173–6. In the use of the term I have had in mind Professor Caughey's definition: "Out of this apparent jumble of geographic,

political, didactic and historical fact, a Southwest emerges, which . . . stretches from central Oklahoma and Texas to southern California. Much of Colorado, Utah, Nevada, and northern California belong, so that it embraces the lower left-hand quarter of the parallelogram that is the United States." *Ibid.*, p. 175.

7. See A. M. Espinosa, "Spanish Folk-Lore in New Mexico," *New Mex. Hist. Rev.*, *1* (April, 1926), 135–55; and J. M. Espinosa, "New Mexico As a Historical Laboratory of the Good Neighbor Policy," *Americas*, 2 (Oct., 1945), 211–19. See also *New Mexico Folklore Record*, *1946/47* (Albuquerque, 1948).

8. J. F. Dobie, *Guide to Life and Literature of the Southwest* (Austin, University of Texas Press, 1943), p. 9.

9. For a detailed study of this "important chapter in American literature" (p. 5), see Mabel Major, R. W. Smith, and T. M. Pearce, *Southwest Heritage, a Literary History with Bibliography* (Albuquerque, 1938).

10. See, for example, Haniel Long, *Interlinear to Cabeza de Vaca* (Santa Fe, 1936), for an imaginative reading "between the lines of Cabeza de Vaca's letter to his king." See also Theodore Irving, *The Conquest of Florida, by Hernando de Soto* (Philadelphia, 1835). In his dedication to his uncle, Washington Irving, the author says the book was written at the former's suggestion. In his preface he describes how, while he was studying Spanish in Madrid, he discovered "The Florida of the Inca, or the History of the Adelantado, Hernando de Soto . . . by the Inca Garcilaso de la Vega." Theodore Irving's use of the narrative and the history of various editions are discussed in the preface for a new text, *The Florida of the Inca,* tr. and ed. J. G. Varner and J. J. Varner (Austin, 1951).

11. E.g., see Mary Austin, "Folk Plays of the Southwest," *Theatre Arts,* *17* (Aug., 1933), 599. Oñate took formal possession near El Paso on April 30, 1598. His first extensive journey eastward from the Rio Grande into what is now Oklahoma and Kansas was in 1601. Books and articles dealing with this folklore and related more or less intimately to the Spanish traditions are innumerable.

12. Calderón's influence is evident in some of the *autos sacramentales.*

13. See A. L. Campa, "Spanish Religious Folktheatre in the Spanish Southwest," *University of New Mexico Bulletin, Language Series, 5,* Nos. 1–2 (Feb. 15, June 15, 1934).

14. See Major, pp. 39–40.

15. See *ibid.,* pp. 14–17. See also J. F. Dobie, *Legends of Texas* (Austin, Tex., 1924), and his *Coronado's Children, Tales of Lost Mines and Buried Treasures of the Southwest* (Dallas, Tex. [1930]). For an account of the Quivira Indians, who were believed to have vast hoards of gold, see C. F. Lummis, *The Land of Poco Tiempo* (London, 1893), pp. 285–310.

16. For the history of Texas as a source of fiction, see Stiff, pp. 23–5.

17. For other mid-century novels of Texas, see *ibid.,* p. 15. See also Major, pp. 75–9. *The Gold Mines of Gila* contains chapters dealing with Coronado, Cabeza de Vaca, and other explorers. This pattern of sentiment and melodrama continued in the twentieth century. See the novels of Andy Adams or Mrs. M. E. Ryan's *For the Soul of Rafael* (Chicago, 1907), a romance of the American invasion, or *The Dancer of Tuluum* (Chicago, 1924), with its scenes in twelfth-century Yucatan.

NOVELISTS, POETS, DRAMATISTS

18. The Spanish tradition was only one of Mary Austin's many interests. See D. T. Wynn, *A Critical Study of the Writings of Mary Hunter Austin* ([New York, 1941]).

19. (New York, A. A. Knopf, 1933), p. vii. See also Erna Fergusson, *New Mexico, a Pageant of Three Peoples* (New York, 1951).

20. The Spanish-American influence on O. Henry is thin but in its way authentic. See such stories as "The Cactus," "Hearts and Crosses," "Pimienta Pancake," etc. For an account of O. Henry's use of Spanish words, characters, and scenes, see F. M. Kercheville, "O. Henry and Don Alfonso, Spanish in the Work of an American Writer," *NMQ, 1* (Nov., 1931), 367–88. See also E. H. Long, *O. Henry, the Man and His Work* (Philadelphia, University of Pennsylvania Press, 1949), p. 30; and H. E. Rollins, "O. Henry's Texas Days," *Bookm., 40* (Oct., 1914), 156. Probably one should not overlook the little poem in *Rolling Stones* (Garden City, N. Y., Doubleday, Page & Co., 1912), p. 246:

> This is the Mexican
> Don José Calderon
> One of God's countrymen,
> Land of the buzzard.
> Cheap silver dollar, and
> Cacti and murderers.
>
> . . .

21. See A. L. Campa, "The Spanish Folksong in the Southwest," *University of New Mexico Bulletin, Modern Language Series, 4,* No. 1 (Nov. 15, 1933). See also F. S. Curtis Jr., "Spanish Folk-Poetry in the Southwest," *SWR, 10,* No. 2 (Jan., 1925), 68–73. See the collections of M. R. Van Stone in her *Spanish Folk Songs of New Mexico* (Chicago [1926]). See also C. F. Lummis, *Spanish Songs of Old California* (Los Angeles [1923]); and for descriptions, texts, and musical scores, the same author's *The Land of Poco Tiempo,* pp. 217–50. See also the folk songs in Nina Otero, *Old Spain in Our Southwest* (New York [1936]).

22. See A. L. Campa, "A Bibliography of Spanish Folk-Lore in New Mexico," *University of New Mexico Bulletin, Language Series, 2,* No. 3 (Sept., 1930), 3.

23. See R. V. Grant, "The Localized Vocabulary of California Verse," *California Folklore Quarterly, 1* (July, 1942), 253–90. The author of this article lists, for example, the words of Spanish origin in Joaquin Miller's poetry (p. 253) or, later, Charles Lummis' use of a Spanish phrase (p. 258):

> There in the long portal she stands,
> My dainty, doubting Spanish fairy—
> Counting the blush-rose in her hands
> With *"Si, me quiere, no me quiere!"*

24. See S. H. Dixon, *The Poets and Poetry of Texas* (Austin. Tex., 1885); and H. R. Greer, *Verse of the Southwest* (New York, 1923), pp. 1–2, 3–4. See also Philip Graham, *The Life and Poems of Mirabeau B. Lamar* (Chapel Hill, 1938), p. 303.

25. Father Angelico Chavez' verse, primarily poetry of the Catholic faith,

includes Spanish backgrounds and overtones. See, in particular, *The Single Rose* ([Santa Fe] 1948).

26. See Sister Joseph Marie, *The Role of the Church and the Folk in the Development of the Early Drama in New Mexico* (Philadelphia, 1948). For the many individual studies of tales, poems, and plays in the folklore of the Southwest, see the bibliography of this volume, pp. 159–72.

27. Mary Austin, "Native Drama in Our Southwest," *Nation, 124* (April 20, 1927), 437. For the original account of this incident, see Gaspar de Villagrá, *History of New Mexico,* tr. Gilberto Espinosa (Los Angeles, 1933), p. 129.

28. For a summary of this play, see Major, p. 36 n. 1. See the manuscripts in the collection assembled by Mary Austin in Santa Fe.

29. See Sister Joseph Marie, p. 44.

30. See C. E. Castañeda, "The First American Play," *Cath. World, 134* (Jan., 1932), 428–37. See also A. L. Campa, "Religious Spanish Folk-Drama in New Mexico," *NMQ, 2* (Feb., 1932), 3–13.

31. See Sister Joseph Marie, p. 1.

32. For accounts of these plays, see *ibid.,* pp. 40–5. *Los reyes magos,* probably first written in the thirteenth century, is still acted in New Mexico as one of a group of *autos* which includes also *Los pastores, La estrella,* and *El niño perdido.*

33. See "Los Comanches, a Spanish Heroic Play of the Year Seventeen Hundred and Eighty," ed. A. M. Espinosa, *Bulletin, University of New Mexico, Language Series, 1,* No. 1 (Dec., 1907). See also "Los Comanches, a New Mexican Folk Drama," ed. A. L. Campa, *ibid.,* 7, No. 1 (April 1, 1942).

34. Perhaps the best of such Spanish tales is "Prince Ahmed al Kamel or the Pilgrim of Love." See *New Eng. M., 3* (July, 1832), 81–2. See also A. H. Everett, "Irving's Alhambra," *NAR, 35* (Oct., 1832), 265–82. Although Irving is regarded as a pioneer in the use of Spanish themes, Charles Brockden Brown used them in his novel, *Wieland,* in 1798. See Stimson, "Spanish Themes in Early American Literature," pp. 173–4.

35. See M. A. Buchanan, "Alhambraism," *HR, 3* (Oct., 1935), 269–74. For "Alhambraism" in American architecture, see below, p. 302.

36. S. P. Scott, "Granada and the Alhambra," *Lippinc., 27* (May, 1881), 435.

37. Bryant first traveled in Spain in 1857.

38. It was characteristic of Cooper's breadth of vision that he foresaw the present close relations of North and South America. For this reason he urged Americans to master the Spanish language. He had, however, no real interest in Spanish history, and his *Mercedes of Castile,* dealing with the first voyage of Columbus, is a prolix and moralizing novel. See O. A. Bierstadt, "Columbus in Romance," *Mag. Am. Hist., 28* (Oct., 1892), 275. Fanny Calderón de la Barca wrote Prescott: "I cannot say I like the mingling of such grave subjects with the tale of a novel. It is a bold thing to introduce Christopher Columbus in such a way. Only Walter Scott could take such liberties with impunity." Wolcott, p. 222. For a definition of Cooper's debts to Irving and Prescott, see D. M. Goodfellow, "The Sources of Mercedes of Castile," *AL, 12* (Nov., 1940), 318–28.

39. See "The Hall of Fantasy," *Mosses from an Old Manse* (New York, 1846), *1,* 160; and *Our Old Home* (Boston, 1863), p. 371. Hawthorne speaks of reading

Cervantes aloud to his family (R. H. Lathrop, *Memories of Hawthorne* [Boston, 1897], p. 293), and during one period his sister Elizabeth was apparently at work on a translation of Cervantes' tales. See Julian Hawthorne, *Nathaniel Hawthorne and His Wife*, 3d ed. (Boston, 1885), *1*, 390, 440. See also *Hawthorne As Editor*, ed. Arlin Turner (University, La., 1941), p. 253. Possibly Cervantes' "El coloquio de los perros" influenced another story. See F. N. Cherry, "The Sources of Hawthorne's 'Young Goodman Brown,'" *AL*, 5 (Jan., 1934), 342–8. See also A. M. Brady, "One Hundred Years," *MLJ*, *33* (Feb., 1949), 116.

40. As editor of the *Southern Literary Messenger* Poe reviewed Mackenzie's two books and also *Madrid in 1835* (2 [May, Aug., Oct., 1836], 389–92, 593, 732). He wrote a review of Cooper's *Mercedes of Castile* for *Graham's, 18* (Jan., 1841), 47–8. He reviewed R. M. Bird's *The Infidel, The Conquest of Florida* by Theodore Irving, and Washington Irving's *Legends of the Conquest of Spain*. In addition, he commented on Don Tomás de las Torres, Mrs. Ellet's translations of Quevedo, Iriarte, and Longfellow's *The Spanish Student*.

41. He twice quotes an epigram of Cervantes. See Killis Campbell, "Poe's Reading," *Univ. Texas Stud. in Eng., 5* (Oct. 8, 1925), 190. For Poe's version of the epigram,

> Ven, muerte, tan escondida,
> Que no te sienta venir,

see his "Pinakidia," *So. Lit. Mess., 2* (Aug., 1836), 579. For Poe's play on the word "pinto," see *N & Q, 169* (Sept. 14, 1935), 189.

42. Perhaps through Byron's and Irving's interest in this idea of the "Döppelgänger." No real evidence, however, exists that Poe knew of this play. See S. T. W., *1*, 466–7.

43. Margaret Alterton has named as an influence on "The Pit and the Pendulum" Juan Antonio Llorente's *History of the Spanish Inquisition, MLN, 48* (June 1, 1933), 349–56; and T. O. Mabbott has suggested a source for Poe's heroine Morella, *N & Q, 172* (Jan. 9, 1937), 26–7. Possibly we should note, conversely, the enormous popularity of Poe (both prose and poetry) in Spain and in Spanish America. See J. E. Englekirk, "Plantando Dá," *Hisp., 32* (Nov., 1949), 444–5.

44. *Obras poéticas completas*, nueva ed. rev. (Madrid, M. Aguilar, 1941), p. 590.

45. *Female Quixotism: Exhibited in the Romantic Opinions and Extravagant Adventures of Dorcasina Sheldon* (Boston, 1808). Of the many evaluations of this widely read book, probably Duyckinck's is the most compact: "This is, as its title implies, one of the numerous literary progeny of Cervantes' immortal satire. It resembles in one respect more closely its original than most of its family, turning like Don Quixote on the evils of reading romances. In place, however, of the lean-vizored Don, we have a blooming delicate young lady . . . a sturdy, sensible, country-bred waiting maid, Betty, a female Sancho Panza." *1*, 521–2. For a discussion of this novel, see Heiser, pp. 411–13.

46. See Cony Sturgis, *The Spanish World in English Fiction* (Boston, 1927).

47. See R. L. Rusk, *The Literature of the Middle Western Frontier* (New York, Columbia University Press, 1925), *1*, 288. In *The Shoshonee Valley* Flint used materials he had secured from travelers in the Pacific regions, some of

whom were familiar with the Spanish regime in the Far West. One character in this story is "a Spanish lady carried captive from California." *Ibid.*, pp.
291–2.

48. See L. M. Walker, "Picturesque New Mexico Revealed in Novel As
Early As 1826," *New Mex. Hist. Rev., 13* (July, 1938), 325–8; and J. T. Flanagan,
"Mexico in American Fiction Prior to 1850," *Hisp., 23* (Dec., 1940), 309–10.

49. See L. H. Wright, *American Fiction, 1774–1850* (San Marino, Calif.,
1939), p. 68.

50. Sands' manuscript, translated into the Spanish by Manuel Domínguez,
did not appear in English until the collected edition of Sands' work was
printed two years after his death in 1832. Two letters in the prefixed "Memoir"
give us insight not only into Sands' methods of research but into the general
conditions of scholarship in respect to South American studies. Only the opening sentences of the first letter (Feb. 10, 1828) are quoted: "White, Gallaher,
and White, of this city [New York], are republishing, for the market of Mexico,
the letters of Cortes to Charles V. I have undertaken to write a biographical
notice of the Conquistador, with such reflections on his character and career as
may be summarily suggested by the accounts of conflicting historians and the
state of his age. I am very much troubled for want of books. I have read Robertson and Clavigero together, and am getting through De Solis. I want Guevara,
Bern. Diaz del Castilio, and Herrera, the two former especially, as the latter is
only a compiler. I found the second and third letters of Cortes in the N. Y.
Society Library, edited by an old fool of an archbishop of Mexico, in 1770."
The Writings of Robert C. Sands (New-York, 1834), *1*, 18. On Feb. 12, Sands
added: "Since I wrote you, I have seen the catalogue of books offered to Congress. Some of the manuscripts are forgeries, beyond all question . . . But
among the books and manuscripts, there is all that the heart of man could
desire (excepting B. Diaz del Castilio, which I do not find) in writing on the
conquest of Mexico." *Ibid., 1*, 19.

51. "The Dream of the Princess Papantzin," *ibid., 2*, 322. This poem was
originally published in *The Talisman for MDCCCXXIX*, pp. 291–306.

52. Sands' contribution in Bryant's *Tales of Glauber-Spa* (New-York, 1832).
See also Sands, *2*, 62–101. *Boyuca* is a melodramatic tale which ends as the
dying heroine murmurs, after extravagant adventures, "I see Bimini."

53. *Ibid., 1*, 16.

54. See C. E. Foust, *The Life and Dramatic Works of Robert Montgomery
Bird* (New York, Knickerbocker Press, 1919), pp. 55–6.

55. See *Calavar; or, The Knight of the Conquest*, new ed. (Philadelphia,
1835), pp. iii–xxviii. The date of the action of *Calavar* is about 1520, beginning with the battle between Narváez and Cortés which yielded the latter the
city of Zempoalla. A curious version or abridgment of this novel appeared in
London in 1839, *Abdalla the Moor and the Spanish Knight*.

56. Fray Antonio Agapida. See *A Chronicle of the Conquest of Granada*
(Philadelphia, 1829).

57. *Calavar*, p. iii.

58. Foust, p. 89.

59. *Ibid.*, pp. 89–90.

60. See R. M. Bird, *Nick of the Woods; or, The Jibbenainosay,* ed. C. B. Williams (New York [1939]), pp. xviii–xx.

61. See *History of the Conquest of Mexico* (New York, 1843), 2, 336 n.

62. In St. Louis in 1848. See Wright, p. 23.

63. See Poe's review of *Calavar* in *So. Lit. Mess., 1* (Feb., 1835), 315.

64. This novel contains elaborate descriptions of Cortés, the Indians, the Christians, the city of "Tezcuco," and also characters of Bird's own invention. The novelist pays a fulsome tribute to Bernal Díaz del Castillo.

65. See E. A. Duyckinck, *National Portrait Gallery of Eminent Americans* (New York [187?]), *1, 514.* See also Simms to Mary Lawson (daughter of John Lawson), Woodlands, Feb. 28, 1859 (S. C.). See also his letters to J. H. Hammond, Woodlands, March 2 [1859] and April 11, 1859 (S. C.).

66. Through the various collections of Simms' manuscripts which form the basis for the monumental five-volume edition of his letters, of which one volume has appeared. See *The Letters of William Gilmore Simms,* ed. M. C. S. Oliphant and others (Columbia, S. C., 1952). For Simms' interest in Spanish topics while he was editor of the *Southern Quarterly Review* (1849–54), for his reviews of Spanish subjects, and for other details concerning his Hispanism, see S. T. Williams, "Spanish Influences on the Fiction of William Gilmore Simms," *HR, 21* (July, 1953), 221–8.

67. For Simms' discussion of Ticknor, see his letter to Thomas Caute Reynolds concerning the latter's review, Charleston, June 6, 1850 (H.). Reynolds was chargé d'affaires at Madrid in 1847.

68. See *Count Julian; or, The Last Days of the Goth* (Baltimore, 1845), Preface, pp. v–vi; and Trent, p. 14. In the dedication of this novel Simms admits that he was wrong in looking for material for fiction outside his own immediate section of the country. The manuscript of Simms' play concerning Don Carlos is in the Charles Carroll Simms Collection (S. C.).

69. W. P. Trent, *William Gilmore Simms* (Boston, 1892), p. 15.

70. "I was reminded of my almost forgotten tragedy. I relieved it from its lock-up, reviewed it, and proceeded to convert the story into prose. The work grew beneath my hands. The material was copious. A certain duplexity in the action suggested its division into two parts, and the first of these parts took a definite form, before the public eye in the shape of a 'Story of the Goth,' in two volumes entitled 'Pelayo.' This work was written in the beginning of 1836. In the close of that year I wrote the greater part of the sequel . . . 'Count Julian, or the Last Days of the Goth.' " See *Count Julian,* pp. vi–vii. An extract from *Pelayo* appeared in *So. Lit. Mess., 4* (Aug., 1838), 535–8.

71. Simms' other works on Spanish themes include *Atalantis* (New-York, 1832), the story of a shipwrecked Spanish knight; "Ponce de Leon" in *The Book of My Lady. A Melange, By a Bachelor Knight* (Philadelphia, 1833), pp. 60–75; *Donna Florida* (Charleston, 1843), an imitation of Byron in which Ponce de León substitutes for Don Juan (see Trent, p. 143); and *The Maroon. A Legend of the Caribbees* (Philadelphia, 1855). See also *Views and Reviews in American Literature, History and Fiction,* 1st Ser. (New York, 1845), pp. 143–209.

72. *The Damsel of Darien* (Philadelphia, 1839), Dedication.

73. Charleston, S. C., June 16, 1839, in the possession of Mr. C. E. Walter, York, Pa.

74. See Poe's review of *The Damsel of Darien* in the *Casket, 15* (Nov., 1839), 283.

75. See W. G. Simms, *The Yemassee,* ed. Alexander Cowie (New York [1937]), p. xviii n. 32.

76. *Vasconselos* (New York, 1868), p. iv. J. H. Hammond asked Simms to write of Silver Bluff on Beach Island, S. C., where De Soto is believed to have crossed the Savannah River.

77. *The Cassique of Kiawah* (New York, 1859), a story with a Spanish heroine in which Simms describes the Spanish attack on Port Royal. *The Yemassee,* Simms' most famous novel, contains a slender vein of Spanish interest. For Simms' conviction that the novel should use Spanish history, see "The Epochs and Events in American History, As Suited to the Purposes of Art in Fiction," *Southern and Western Monthly Magazine, 1* (June, 1845), 391–2.

78. As a matter of fact, Russian influences on our literature have been more definite than is generally known. See Harvey Wish, "Getting Along with the Romanovs," *So. Atlan. Q., 48* (July, 1949), 351–8.

79. As merely one illustration of the change, we might consider the vogue of adaptations of Lope de Vega's *La estrella de Sevilla* and Longfellow's discussion in his classes concerning the differences between the original play and Fanny Kemble Butler's version.

80. For an analysis of the Spanish background in this story, see S. T. Williams, " 'Follow Your Leader'; Melville's 'Benito Cereno,' " *VQR, 23* (Winter, 1947), 61–76. *Don Quixote* is referred to on the following pages: *White Jacket,* H. M., *6,* 63, 284; *Piazza Tales, ibid., 10,* 9; *The Confidence-Man, ibid., 12,* 317; *Poems, ibid., 16,* 412. See *Journal up the Straits,* ed. Raymond Weaver (New York, The Colophon, 1935), p. 7. *See Clarel,* H. M., *14,* 251, in which for seven lines Melville discusses the helmet of "Malbrino."

81. Nathaniel Hawthorne, *The American Notebooks,* ed. Randall Stewart (New Haven, 1932), p. 220.

82. See M. M. Sealts Jr., *Melville's Reading, Offprinted from the Harvard Library Bulletin, 1948–1950* ([Cambridge, 1950]), No. 114. Passages are marked in both English and Spanish. See also Nos. 9, 124, 125. For Melville's markings in three plays of Calderón, see Jay Leyda, *The Melville Log* (New York, Harcourt, Brace & Co. [1951]), 2, 738. Books which may have been in the *Acushnet's* library when Melville was aboard included a "Spanish & English Dictionary," *ibid.,* p. 149 n. 32.

83. For Melville's acquaintance with South American and Mexican ports, see C. R. Anderson, *Melville in the South Seas* (New York, Columbia University Press, 1939), pp. 355–7. In the possession of Wilson L. Heflin of Annapolis, Maryland, is a chart which traces the voyage of the *Acushnet* and suggests Melville's opportunities for knowing these regions. "El contacto geográfico determinó incluso en *Melville* cierta erudición en cosas de estas regiones." Estuardo Núñez, "Herman Melville en la América Latina," *Cuadernos americanos, 68* (marzo–abril, 1953), 211. Mr. Heflin thinks Melville may have been familiar with Spanish through some of his seafaring relatives, such as Guert

Gansvoort, and he notes the presence of four Portuguese sailors on the *Acushnet* and of three on the *Lucy Ann.*

84. For allusions, direct and indirect (e.g., through Beaumont and Fletcher), to Cervantes, see Harry Levin, " 'Don Quixote' and 'Moby Dick,' " in *Cervantes across the Centuries,* ed. Ángel Flores and M. J. Benardete (New York, Dryden Press, 1947), pp. 217–26. See also *Realidad,* 2 (sbre.–obre., 1947), 254–67.

85. See Levin, pp. 220, 225 n. 9. On the flyleaf of Vol. *1* of Melville's copy of *Don Quixote* is written in pencil: "H. Melville, Sept. 18, '55."

86. Sealts, Nos. 9, 324. Melville may have derived some of his interest in Spain from Irving.

87. *Moby-Dick,* H. M., 7, xviii.

88. "Fragments from a Writing Desk, No. 1," *Democratic Press and Lansingburgh Advertiser,* May 4, 1839. Melville quotes Byron, *Childe Harold's Pilgrimage,* Canto I, stanza lix.

89. "Benito Cereno," H. M., *10, 113.*

90. *Moby-Dick,* H. M., 7, 116.

91. See *ibid.,* 7, 267. In 1856 Melville wrote: "At noon, off Algiers. In the vicinity beautiful residences among the hills. White house among gardens. Reminded one of passages in Don Quixotte [*sic*], 'Story of the Morisco.' " *Journal up the Straits,* p. 7.

92. See Melville's copy of *Don Quixote, 1,* lii. For an account of these markings, see Levin, pp. 220–1.

93. Part of a note written in by Melville reads: ". . . a knight-errant without a mistress is like a tree without leaves, a building without cement, a shadow without a body that causes it." Melville's copy of *Don Quixote, 2,* 215–16. In the margin Melville has added "Or as Confucius said 'a dog without a master,' or, to drop both Cervantes & Confucius parables—a God-like mind without a God."

94. *Ibid., 1,* 126.

95. "The relation of *Moby Dick* to *Don Quixote* is neither close nor similar; it is complementary and dialectical." Levin, p. 224. For other references, see Leyda, *1,* 173, 490, *2,* 508, 549.

96. See "Benito Cereno," H. M., *10,* 106, and *Moby-Dick, ibid.,* 7, 241. Melville's peculiar concept of the Spanish civilization as decadent is emphasized by his eloquent passage on the horror of white and waterless Lima: "Nor is it, altogether, the remembrance of her cathedral-toppling earthquakes; nor the stampedoes of her frantic seas; nor the tearlessness of arid skies that never rain; nor the sight of her wide field of leaning spires, wrenched cope-stones, and crosses all adroop (like canted yards of anchored fleets); and her suburban avenues of house-walls lying over upon each other, as a tossed pack of cards; it is not these things alone which make tearless Lima, the strangest, saddest city thou canst see. For Lima has taken the white veil; and there is a higher horror in this whiteness of her woe. Old as Pizarro, this whiteness keeps her ruins for ever new; admits not the cheerful greenness of complete decay; spreads over her broken ramparts the rigid pallor of an apoplexy that fixes its own distortions." See also Núñez, p. 216.

97. See Anderson, p. 358 and n., and p. 484.

98. Melville's phrase in describing the nailing of the doubloon to the mast in *Moby-Dick,* H. M., *8,* 189.

99. See "Benito Cereno," *ibid., 10,* 123.

100. Captain Amasa Delano was a whaleman. In *Moby-Dick* Melville suggests that South America was freed by the whalemen "from the yoke of Old Spain." See *ibid., 7,* 137. "Benito Cereno" is a notable example of the influence of the travel book on our fiction dealing with Spanish subjects. See H. H. Scudder, "Melville's *Benito Cereno* and Captain Delano's Voyages," *PMLA, 43* (June, 1928), 502–32. See also Núñez, pp. 217–21.

101. See *Lew Wallace, an Autobiography* (New York, 1906), *1,* 196.

102. *Ibid.,* pp. 88, 90.

103. *Ibid.,* p. 90.

104. *Ibid.,* pp. 88–9.

105. F. L. Pattee, *A History of American Literature since 1870* (New York, Century Co., 1915), p. 254. Pattee calls *The Fair God* "a blending of Prescott and Bulwer-Lytton."

106. See "Note by the Author," *The Fair God; or The Last of the 'Tzins* (Boston, 1873), p. iv.

107. From a quotation from J. W. Draper's *Intellectual Development of Europe,* which Wallace, violently anti-Spanish, published on the title page of *The Fair God.* The quotation continued: "It has been her [Spain's] evil destiny to ruin two civilizations, Oriental and Occidental, and to be ruined thereby herself . . . In America she destroyed races more civilized than herself."

108. Both writers dream of the legendary past. Both laugh a little in kindly fashion at padre or burgomaster. Both ponder on older civilizations from the perspectives of their own. See Pattee, p. 68. See also his *The Development of the American Short Story* (New York, 1923), p. 225; *CHAL,* 2, 377; and Harrison, p. 404. The "Legend of Monte del Diablo" is particularly reminiscent of Irving.

109. See John Erskine, "Bret Harte" in *Leading American Novelists* (New York, H. Holt & Co., 1910), p. 327. Carlos Vázquez-Arjona, "Spanish and Spanish-American Influences on Bret Harte," *R. Hispan., 76* (août, 1929), 573–621, is a pertinent study.

110. See H. C. Merwin, *The Life of Bret Harte* (London, 1912), p. 213.

111. See Vázquez-Arjona, pp. 575–98.

112. See *ibid.*

113. In these characters and in their experiences is something of that mechanical quality which the posthumous words of Mark Twain suggest about Harte: See *Mark Twain in Eruption,* ed. Bernard De Voto (New York, Harper & Brothers [1940]), p. 265: "pumping up the tear of sensibility."

114. The primary influence upon Cable was not Spanish but French. See W. S. Harwood, "New Orleans in Fiction," *Critic, 47* (Nov., 1905), 426–35. This is also true of Lafcadio Hearn in his connections with New Orleans. A few allusions to Spain occur in *Creole Sketches* (Boston, 1924). F. L. Pattee says of Harte's tales: "Meager and fragmentary as these Spanish sketches are, they nevertheless opened the way for a new school of American romance." *A History of American Literature,* p. 70.

115. See *Ramona, novela americana* (Habana, Impr. de Rambla, Bouza y cia., 1915). The editors describe the popularity of the book in Cuba and relate the circumstances concerning Martí's translation. One preface, dated Berlin, Sept. 7, 1914, is signed by Gonzalo de Quesada. In another preface, signed by Blanche Z. de Baralt, occurs the reference to the book as "la Cabaña del Tío Tom de los indios."

116. See Carey McWilliams, *Southern California Country* (New York, Duell, Sloan & Pearce [1946]), pp. 71–7. A dramatization by Virginia Calhoun and General Johnstone Jones was performed at the Los Angeles Opera House on February 27, 1905. Since 1921 three different motion-picture versions have been made. See *ibid.*, p. 75. See also the acting version of the novel by Ina Dillaye (Syracuse, N. Y., 1887).

117. Mrs. Jackson made four trips to California (1872, 1881–82, 1883, and 1884–85). See McWilliams, p. 72. On the second journey she was asked by Richard Watson Gilder, editor of the *Century*, to write about the Mission Indians. See Ruth Odell, *Helen Hunt Jackson* (New York, D. Appleton–Century Co., Inc., 1939), p. 171.

118. See *ibid.*, p. 175. See also C. C. Davis, "Ramona: the Ideal and the Real," *Out West, 19* (Dec., 1903), 575–96. Don Antonio had long been a friend of the Indians: "Many an afternoon [was] spent listening to Don Antonio's stories of the days of the Spanish and Mexican occupations, details of which went into her first *Century* article, under title of 'Echoes in the City of the Angels.' It was an alluring picture she drew of the one-hundred-year-old town —*El Pueblo de Señora la Reina de los Angeles* . . . with its certain indefinable, delicious aroma from the old, ignorant, picturesque times." Odell, p. 174.

119. See Davis, pp. 588–90.

120. See Odell, p. 175.

121. See *Ramona* (Boston, 1884), p. 18.

122. See H. E. Scudder's review, *Atlan.*, 55 (Jan., 1885), 127–30.

123. For *Century Magazine*. See McWilliams, p. 72.

124. Stories concerning the characters were various: that Señora Doña Ysabel del Valle was the original of Señora Moreno; that her son Reginald F. del Valle was Felipe. Ramona was said to be a composite of Blanca Yndart, a Spanish girl and a ward of Señora del Valle, and Guadalupe, a Mission Indian girl who had lived with the Señora since a child. Other hypothetical originals included one for Alessandro. See Davis, pp. 588–90, 593–4. The "jewels" of Ramona were rumored to be in the possession of a lady in Los Angeles. The "Rancho Camúlos" has become a literary landmark. See Odell, p. 177, and Rexford Newcomb, *The Old Mission Churches and Historic Houses of California* (Philadelphia, J. B. Lippincott Co., 1925), pp. 344–52. Possibly Mrs. Jackson paid only one visit to Rancho Camúlos. The currency of the book is shown by the amount of "Ramonana." See, for example, D. A. Hufford, *The Real Ramona of Helen Hunt Jackson's Famous Novel* (Los Angeles [1900]); G. W. James, *Through Ramona's Country* (Boston, 1909); M. V. Allen, *Ramona's Homeland* (Chula Vista, Cal. [1914]); C. C. Davis and W. F. Alderson, *The True Story of "Ramona"* (New York [1914]).

125. See McWilliams, p. 73.

126. This journey into Spain is described in a brief paragraph in *The In-*

nocents Abroad (Hartford, 1869). A letter dated Cadiz, Oct. 24, 1867, remarks: "The country is precisely what it was when Don Quixote and Sancho Panza were possible characters." He adds: "But I see now what the glory of Spain must have been when it was under Moorish domination." A. B. Paine, *Mark Twain* (New York, Harper & Bros., 1912), *1*, 340–1. Mark Twain spoke of himself as "carried away, infatuated, entranced with the wonders of the Alhambra and the supernatural beauty of the Alcazar," E. C. Wagenknecht, *Mark Twain* (New Haven, Yale University Press, 1935), p. 22. See also S. T. Williams, "Spanish Influences on American Fiction: Mark Twain to Willa Cather," *Hisp., 36* (May, 1953), 133–6.

127. These comments are not always favorable. For a summary of Mark Twain's allusions to Cervantes, see O. H. Moore, "Mark Twain and Don Quixote," *PMLA, 37* (June, 1922), 324–46. Possibly *Don Quixote* also influenced the conception of Colonel Sellers in *The Gilded Age*. See Friedrich Schönemann, *Mark Twain als literarische Persönlichkeit* (Jena, Frommann, 1925), p. 46. In a letter to his brother Orion, March 18, 1860, Mark Twain refers to Goldsmith's *Citizen of the World* and *Don Quixote* as his "beau ideals" of fine writing. See *Mark Twain's Letters*, ed. A. B. Paine (New York, Harper & Bros. [1927]), *1*, 45.

128. See Wagenknecht, pp. 32–49. See also S. T. Williams, *Tres escritores clásicos* ([México, 1948]), pp. 33–54.

129. See Wagenknecht, p. 44.

130. See W. D. Howells, *My Mark Twain* (New York, Harper & Bros., 1910), p. 17.

131. "One sees in Mark Twain's *Huckleberry Finn* a transparent intention to experiment with an American picaro, as near as circumstances could make him to Lazarillo, Guzman de Alfarache, and the rest of the goodly company of sharp-witted youngsters with pockets as light as their hearts, who sprang from the Spanish genius as a reaction from the wandering knights of chivalry." Martin Hume, *Spanish Influences on English Literature*, p. 183.

132. See Moore, pp. 338–40.

133. See *ibid.*, pp. 327–8, 346.

134. See his "Tom Sawyer and Don Quixote," *Mark Twain Quart., 9,* No. 2 (Winter, 1952), 1–3; see also Sister M. T. Roades, "Was Mark Twain Influenced by the Prolog to 'Don Quixote'?" *ibid.*, pp. 4–6, 24.

135. E. H. Templin, "On Re-Reading Mark Twain," *Hisp., 24* (Oct., 1941), 269–76.

136. See *CHAL, 3,* 81.

137. See W. D. Howells, *Criticism and Fiction* (New York, 1891), pp. 65–72.

138. In his preface to Galdós' *Doña Perfecta* Howells quoted with approval Clarín's opinion that the fiction of his own time derived from "the novel, large or little, as it was in the day of Cervantes, Hurtado de Mendoza, Quevedo, and the masters of picaresque fiction." (New York, 1896), p. v. See also *Criticism and Fiction*, pp. 59–63.

139. See Sylvester Baxter, "A Great Modern Spaniard," *Atlan., 85* (April, 1900), 557.

140. See *ibid.* See also E. S. Morby, "William Dean Howells and Spain,"

HR, 14 (July, 1946), 187–212. This article summarized effectively Howells' major debts to Spanish writers. See also R.-N., pp. 273–5, 361–2, 364.

141. See Morby, p. 204.

142. Baxter, p. 550.

143. When Howells urged James to go to Spain, the latter gave as his reason for declining his limited income. Writing to his brother William on May 24, 1903, he said: "I have practically never travelled at all—having never been economically able to; I've only gone, for short periods, a few times—so much fewer than I've wanted—to Italy; never anywhere else that I've seen every one about me here (who is, or was, anyone) perpetually making for. These visions I've had, one by one, all to give up—Spain, Greece, Sicily, any glimpses of the East . . ." *The Letters of Henry James,* ed. Percy Lubbock (New York, C. Scribner's Sons, 1920), *1,* 417. See also *ibid.,* p. 50. James once remarked that it was "the dream of one's life to visit the land of Cervantes." See his *Portraits of Places* (Boston, 1884), p. 177. Apparently he never went farther into Spain than Santander. There is no evidence of James' active interest either in Spanish literature of the past or in its contemporary writers of fiction. He admired in 1898 the courage of Spain: "so decent and picturesque and harmless a member of the European family." *The Letters of Henry James, 1,* 281. Lowell, too, begged James to visit Spain. For James' interest in Spanish painting, see below, pp. 274–5, 291–3.

144. See *Life in Letters of William Dean Howells,* ed. Mildred Howells (Garden City, N. Y., Doubleday, Doran & Co., Inc., 1928), *2,* 303, 313–14, and *passim.*

145. See *Spanish Travels,* pp. 72 ff.

146. See Stephen Crane, *Wounds in the Rain* (New York [1900]).

147. The quality or tone of Crawford's novel, which was popular in the home and on the stage, may be estimated by the following brief paragraph (p. 102): "After the guards came Philip the Second, a tall and melancholy figure; and with him, on his left side, walked the young Queen, a small, thin figure in white, with sad eyes and a pathetic face . . . The King was one of those men who seemed marked by destiny rather than by nature, fateful, sombre, almost repellent in manner, born to inspire a vague fear at first sight." Crawford wrote some forty novels with Italian backgrounds.

148. Among Gertrude Atherton's novels of California were *The Californians* (London, 1898); *The Doomswoman* (New York, 1901); and *Rezanov* (New York, 1906). She "was," says C. C. Dobie, "to do a romantic service to letters and her state by reconstructing the vanished Castilian era of the 'splendid idle forties.' Still later, she was to smash this very legend of the romantic infallibility of Spain that she had helped to create." *American Writers on American Literature,* ed. J. A. Macy (New York, H. Liveright, Inc. [1931]), p. 417.

149. "The Pearls of Loreto," *The Splendid Idle Forties* (New York, Macmillan Co., 1902), p. 4. For a compilation of the writing of Californians, see E. S. Mighels, *Literary California* (San Francisco, 1918). During the first decade Thomas A. Janvier wrote his friendly, witty tales centering in a "Latin-American Village hotel" in New York. E.g., *At the Casa Napoléon* (New York, 1914). Janvier was also the author of various romances with Spanish themes, such as *Stories of Old New Spain* (New York, 1891) with its touching story,

"Niñita"; *The Aztec Treasure-House* (New York, 1901); *Santa Fé's Partner* (New York, 1907); etc.

150. See Cony Sturgis, *The Spanish World in English Fiction*. An example of the light novel might be A. D. Ficke's *Mrs. Morton of Mexico* (New York [1939]).

151. See *Flowering Judas and Other Stories* (New York [1930]). This author, who has lived in Mexico, has used the country as a background for some charming tales. She is also a translator of Mexican literature.

152. See *Spanish Bayonet* (New York [1926]).

153. See Thornton Wilder, *The Bridge of San Luis Rey* (New York, A. & C. Boni, 1927), p. 15.

154. See *Tortilla Flat* (New York, Covici, Friede [1935]), p. 11. See also Steinbeck's *Of Mice and Men* (New York [1937]), *The Pearl* (New York, 1947), etc. See also for a study of Mexico *The Forgotten Village* (New York, 1941).

155. E.g., Mary Austin, Erna and Harvey Fergusson, etc.

156. "His paternal grandfather was an immigrant Portuguese shoemaker." See *SRL*, *32*, No. 2 (Jan. 8, 1949), 8. Dos Passos studied Spanish in school and lived in Spain in 1916 and also in 1919 after leaving the army. Letter to me, Westmoreland, Va., Oct. 30, 1951.

157. See J. T. Reid, "Spain As Seen by Contemporary Writers," *Hisp.*, *20* (May, 1937), 145–50. For a definition of the related but contrasting points of view toward the Spain of Dos Passos and Hemingway, see Maxwell Geismar, *Writers in Crisis* (Boston, Houghton Mifflin & Co., [1942]), pp. 89–90.

158. Large portions of this book, with the additions of chapters on the Civil War, are reprinted in his *Journeys Between Wars* (New York [1938]). For his account of Mexico, see "Land of Great Volcanoes," *In All Countries* (New York, Harcourt, Brace & Co. [1934]), pp. 73–116. *Rosinante* was the product of the two stays in Spain. Letter, Oct. 30, 1951. Many sections of these books appeared first in periodicals.

159. See Alfred Kazin, *On Native Grounds* (New York, Reynal & Hitchcock [1942]), p. 343. The Spanish scenes occur as a climax in the last few pages of the novel. See *Adventures of a Young Man* (New York, Harcourt, Brace & Co. [1939]), pp. 303–22.

160. "It was in Spain and Latin America that Dos Passos learned to prize men like the Mexican revolutionary Zapata, and the libertarian Anarchists of Spain," Kazin, p. 345.

161. Some of Hemingway's dispatches from the front are vivid. E.g., see "Hemingway Reports Spain," *New Repub.*, *90* (May 5, 1937), 376–9; *93* (Jan. 12, 1938), 273–6; *94* (April 27, 1938), 350–1; *95* (June 8, 1938), 124–6.

162. For further discussions of political problems in Spain, see the very different, ironic chapter, "The Republic of Honest Men," in Dos Passos' *In All Countries*, pp. 117–68. See also his article "Spain Gets Her New Deal," *Am. Merc.*, *31* (March, 1934), 343–56.

163. *Rosinante to the Road Again* (New York, G. H. Doran Co. [1922]), p. 52.

164. *Ibid.*, p. 100. Dos Passos was attracted by Pío Baroja's rejection of authority. See Milton Rugoff, "Dos Passos, Novelist of Our Time," *SR*, *49* (Oct.–Dec., 1941), 456–7. See *Bookm.*, *55* (July, 1922), 538. See his review, "Baroja Muzzled," *Dial*, *74* (Feb., 1923), 199–200.

165. *Rosinante to the Road Again,* p. 131. For Howells' praise of Blasco Ibáñez, see below, 2, 264.

166. Dos Passos, "Baroja Muzzled," p. 199.

167. *Rosinante to the Road Again,* pp. 140–75. See also "Andaluza," *Vanity Fair, 20* (April, 1923), 68. This is a translation of one of Antonio Machado's poems. The reader should notice Dos Passos' interest in Jorge Manrique. Ever since childhood he has read in *Don Quixote* and the *Novelas exemplares.* Letter, Oct. 30, 1951. For his paintings of Spain and other items, see Jack Potter, *A Bibliography of John Dos Passos* (Chicago, Normandie House, 1950), pp. 21 (a Spanish edition: *Rocinante vuelve al camino,* Madrid, 1930), 44–45, 62–4, 69–72, 90. This Spanish edition contains an amusing preface by Dos Passos.

168. That is, through her emphasis upon the primitive. Hemingway mentions Gertrude Stein in the opening pages of *Death in the Afternoon* (New York, C. Scribner's Sons, 1932). See his comment on the "morality" of the bullfight, pp. 4–5.

169. "The only place where you could see life and death, i.e., violent death now that the wars were over, was in the bull ring and I wanted very much to go to Spain where I could study it." *Death in the Afternoon,* p. 2. Hemingway's letters tell the same story of his feelings, not of revulsion but of curiosity and amusement, when the horses were killed.

170. Max Eastman refers to the book's "juvenile romantic gushing and sentimentalizing of simple facts." See his "Bull in the Afternoon," *New Repub., 75* (June 7, 1933), 94. See also Malcolm Cowley, "A Farewell to Spain," *ibid., 73* (Nov. 30, 1932), 76–7.

171. See Reid, pp. 148–9.

172. Hemingway's novel excels all other American fiction dealing with the Civil War. See, for example, Jenny Ballou, *Spanish Prelude* (Boston, 1937).

173. See *For Whom the Bell Tolls* (New York, 1940), chap. x, pp. 96–130.

174. For an illuminating study of Hemingway's use of Spanish, see Edward Fenimore, "English and Spanish in *For Whom the Bell Tolls,*" *ELH, 10* (March, 1943), 73–86.

175. See Rosalind S. Miller, *Gertrude Stein: Form and Intelligibility* (New York, Exposition Press [1949]), pp. 18–21, 50–3.

176. See *ibid.,* pp. 17–18.

177. Quoted *ibid.,* p. 52.

178. Originally the title of a chapter in William James, *Psychology* (New York, 1892).

179. See Miller, p. 90.

180. See *ibid.,* p. 51.

181. *Ibid.,* p. 54.

182. *Sherwood Anderson's Notebook* (New York, 1926), pp. 48–9. Copyright 1926 by Boni & Liveright. Published by Liveright Publishing Corp.

183. Gertrude Stein was "very fond of Granada. It was there she had her first experience of Spain when still at college just after the spanish-american war when she and her brother went through Spain." *The Autobiography of Alice B. Toklas* (New York, Harcourt, Brace & Co. [1933]), p. 145.

184. For her debts to Spanish landscape, see Donald Sutherland, *Gertrude Stein, a Biography of Her Work* (New Haven, Yale University Press, 1951), pp. 70–2.

185. "Their long friendship with all its sometimes troubled moments and its complications." *Autobiography of Alice B. Toklas,* pp. 18–19. See this basic volume for detailed accounts of Miss Stein's friendships with Picasso and Juan Gris. "Her two dearest friends, Picasso and Juan Gris, both spaniards," *ibid.,* p. 111. For Picasso's portrait of Miss Stein, see illustration facing p. 242, also Donald Gallup, "Picasso, Gris, and Gertrude Stein," San Francisco Museum of Art, *Picasso, Gris, Miro. The Spanish Masters of Twentieth Century Painting* ([San Francisco, Calif., 1948]), pp. 15–23.

186. Gertrude Stein, *Picasso* (London, B. T. Batsford [1938]), pp. 5–6.

187. *Autobiography of Alice B. Toklas,* p. 111. For other comments of this kind, see her *Picasso,* p. 12. Note the following: "Well, Don Quixote was a Spaniard, he did not imagine things, he saw things and it was not a dream, it was not lunacy, he really saw them. Well, Picasso is a Spaniard." *Ibid.,* pp. 17–18.

188. *Autobiography of Alice B. Toklas,* p. 19.

189. *Picasso,* p. 19.

190. Miller, p. 26.

191. See Sutherland, pp. 71 n. 6, 120–1 n. 27.

192. *Autobiography of Alice B. Toklas,* p. 141.

193. Willa Cather wrote the last chapters of this book in Mary Austin's "Casa Querida." See T. M. Pearce, *The Beloved House* (Caldwell, Id., Caxton Printers, 1940), pp. 176–8; and David Daiches, *Willa Cather, a Critical Introduction* (Ithaca, Cornell University Press [1951]), pp. 106–18.

194. Professor St. Peter looked like a Spaniard; he had lived in Spain; and he "was an authority on certain phases of Spanish history." See *The Professor's House* (New York, A. A. Knopf, 1925), pp. 12–13. This novel offers glimpses of Spain and New Mexico in Miss Cather's beautiful prose. See *ibid.,* pp. 106, 240, 250. Chap. x of Pt. II of *The Song of the Lark* (Boston, 1915), which includes "Spanish Johnny" and his songs, contains a charming description of Mexican dances.

195. See "A Letter from Willa Cather," *Commonweal,* 7 (Nov. 23, 1927), 713. The numerous, recent studies of Willa Cather discuss in detail her association with the Southwest, but see, in particular, E. K. Brown, *Willa Cather, a Critical Biography* (New York, 1953), for his comments on her use of her experiences in the Southwest (pp. xii–xiv) and of such topics as Coronado (pp. 41, 208–9), the "Mesa Encantada" (p. 149), and the ancient Spanish bell (p. 265).

196. E.g., *O Pioneers!* (Boston, 1913); *My Ántonia* (Boston, 1918).

197. The originals were Archbishop Lamy of Santa Fe and Father Joseph P. Machebeuf. For accounts of these churchmen, see Lester Raines, *Writers and Writings of New Mexico* (Las Vegas [N. M.], 1934), pp. 32–3. Although the events in the prologue are supposed to have occurred in 1848, the bishop did not reach Santa Fe until 1851, and he was not actually named Bishop of Santa Fe until July 29, 1853.

198. See *Not under Forty* (New York, A. A. Knopf, 1936), pp. 43–51.

199. Her own phrase. Quoted in Carl Van Doren, *The American Novel,* rev. and enl. ed. (New York, Macmillan Co., 1940), p. 290.

200. E.g., see *Death Comes for the Archbishop* (New York, A. A. Knopf, 1927), pp. 31, 39, 99, etc.

201. *Forum,* illustrated section, 77, No. 1 (Jan., 1927), xxx.

202. *Death Comes for the Archbishop,* p. 92.

203. (New York, 1836). This effusion, which has sometimes been attributed to William Gilmore Simms, bears on the title page quotations concerning Spain from Byron and Southey. "The following Romance," says the Preface, pp. v–vi, "is founded strictly upon historical facts. The name of 'Pelayo' to every Spanish ear, will long be a hallowed sound. Both Southey and Don Trueba (author of the Romance of Spain) have used their best endeavours to immortalize this renowned warrior . . . I have chosen for my tale the accounts which Don Trueba gives." This pedestrian poem of six cantos and 156 stanzas was well known in its day. Probably Mrs. Ritchie alludes to Joaquín Telesforo Trueba y Cossío, *The Romance of History. Spain* (New York, 1830).

204. Duyckinck says that *Oralloossa* was "well received." See 2, 200.

205. In his preface Simms expresses surprise that this rich field for poetry has been neglected. See Charvat, p. xxxii n. 83. Throughout his poetry one finds occasional pieces "from the Spanish." For a discussion of his poetry on Spanish themes, see Stimson, pp. 20–2. For his play, *Michael Bonham,* see *ibid.,* p. 75.

206. This pompous blank-verse poem describes Papantzin's death, her resurrection, her life after death, and her prophecy:

> it seemed she stood
> In an illimitable plain.

Waking, she finds herself in a coffin. Despite its absurdity, the poem communicates a mood of suspense and mystery. See Sands, 2, 320–35.

207. *Ibid., 1,* 22.

208. Mrs. Elizabeth Fries Lummis Ellet, the friend of Poe, was skilled in French, German, and Italian, and, apparently, in Spanish, for besides her adaptations from Iriarte, her sonnet, "Rome in Ruins," is in debt to Quevedo. *The Characters of Schiller* (Boston, 1842) shows her interest in the story of Don Carlos, many times a medium for Spanish influence. She was also the author of "The Prince and the Palm Tree," a tale based on the belief that Abderrahman transplanted the palm from the East into Spain. See her *Poems, Translated and Original* (Philadelphia, 1835), pp. 24–5, 61, 62–4. For Spanish elements in the poetry of the "Sweet Singer of Hartford," Lydia Huntley Sigourney, see Stimson, pp. 23–4.

209. *Lyrics of Spain and Erin* (Boston, 1850). The author was the son of Charles Robert Maturin, the Irish novelist. The first seventy-three pages of his volume contain Spanish ballads, including such poems as "Roderick after the Battle"; "The Banner of the Cid"; "The Foray of the Cid"; "The Cid's Farewell"; "Boabdil's Lament"; "Boabdil's Farewell." Maturin wrote a novel dedicated to Prescott: *Montezuma; the Last of the Aztecs* (New York, 1845).

210. See Duyck., *1,* 609. James Gates Percival (who knew Spanish) planned a tragedy to be called "Fall of Peruvians." See J. H. Ward, *The Life and Let-*

ters of James Gates Percival (Boston, 1866), p. 260. See, in particular, Percival's *Zamor,* his "Ode on the Emancipation of Spain," and his "Ode on the Emancipation of South America." For a discussion of Percival's poems on Spanish subjects, see Stimson, pp. 53, 69.

211. For accounts of this and the later poems on similar subjects, see R. M. Peterson, "Bryant As a Hispanophile," *Hisp., 16* (Nov.–Dec., 1933), 401–3.

212. *The Poetical Works of William Cullen Bryant,* ed. Parke Godwin (New York, 1883), *2,* 352.

213. See J. F.-K., p. 30.

214. The absence of social and contemporary issues in Longfellow's poetry is conspicuous.

215. For Spanish scenes, characters, and sources in Longfellow's poetry, see Paul Morin, *Les Sources de l'œuvre de Henry Wadsworth Longfellow* (Paris, E. Larose, 1913), pp. 389–431.

216. See Longfellow to his mother, Madrid, July 16, 1827 (L. H.).

217. See Longfellow to Alexander Slidell Mackenzie, Bowdoin College, Oct. 15, 1829 (L. H.).

218. E.g., "The Death of Agrican the Moor," *New-Eng. M.,* 2 (April, 1832), 332–3.

219. See the chapter "Ancient Spanish Ballads" in *Outre-Mer. A Pilgrimage beyond the Sea* (New-York, 1835), *2,* 1–26. In 1829 in Dresden Longfellow discovered with delight Hernando del Castillo's *Cancionero general.*

220. *The Poets and Poetry of Europe* (Philadelphia, 1845). See L. S. Livingston, *A Bibliography of the First Editions in Book Form of the Writings of Henry Wadsworth Longfellow* (New York, 1908), pp. 38–40, 78–9. A new edition appeared in 1870. For praise of his skill as a translator, see R.-N., pp. 54–68.

221. For the influence of this poem on Howells, see below, 2, 242–3.

222. See *Final Memorials of Henry Wadsworth Longfellow,* ed. Samuel Longfellow (Boston, 1887), p. 7.

223. *NAR, 34* (April, 1832), 275–315.

224. S. L., *1,* 340–1.

225. See E. C. Stedman and E. M. Hutchinson, *A Library of American Literature* (New York, 1892), *8,* 333–4. Or see J. G. C. Brainard, "The Guerilla"; Mrs. Maria Gowen Brooks, "Farewell to Cuba"; R. H. Dana, "The Buccaneer"; Sarah Ann Lewis, "Lament of La Vega"; Epes Sargent, "Cuba"; Elizabeth Stoddard, "Mercedes"; etc. Cincinnatus Heine ("Joaquin") Miller knew something of South America, but his use of Spanish themes was also conventional. See "Joaquin Murietta" and "The Sea of Fire," *The Poetical Works of Joaquin Miller,* ed. S. P. Sherman (New York, G. P. Putnam's Sons, 1923), pp. 120–5, 245–62. See also pp. 172–3, 438.

226. For the text of "Amor Mysticus," see *The Complete Poetical Works of John Hay* (Boston, Houghton Mifflin & Co., 1917), pp. 219–21. See also *ibid.,* pp. 38–9, and Sister Ignatius Ward, *The Poetry of John Hay* (Washington, D. C., Catholic Univ. of America, 1930), pp. 5, 7, for "The Surrender of Spain," a hexameter poem in which Hay exhorts Spain to renew her ancient glories.

227. See *The Poems of Thomas Bailey Aldrich;* household ed. (Boston, 1886), pp. 46–7, 146–8. See also pp. 227–66, *Mercedes,* a sentimental little tragedy in two acts and seven scenes, with its setting in Spain during the

Napoleonic campaigns. *Mercedes* was acted, with Aldrich himself in the title role, at Palmer's Theatre on May 1, 1893.

228. Emerson refers to Don Quixote's "impenetrable armour of witty courtesy," but he can hardly be claimed as a Hispanophile. In the Spanish classics his reading was probably limited to Cervantes and in history to William Beckford's *Italy, with Sketches of Spain and Portugal* (London, 1834), S. A. Dunham's history, *Spain and Portugal* (London, 1832–33), Southey's *History of the Peninsular War* (London, 1828–37), and J. G. Lockhart's *Ancient Spanish Ballads* (Edinburgh, 1823). In the *Dial, 4* (Oct., 1843), 270–1, he reviewed Longfellow's *The Spanish Student*. His brother William was familiar with Spanish as a translator for a newspaper and as a dweller in Puerto Rico, but Emerson himself showed no interest in the language, using in his letters only a few Spanish words. He did not care for the Spaniards whom he met at Saint Augustine. His indifference to Spanish was typical of his attitude toward all languages: he preferred translations to the originals, and he learned German only after fervent exhortations from Carlyle. "Do you study Spanish?" Waldo wrote Charles Emerson, who knew the language. Emerson read the *Chronicle of the Cid* by Robert Southey. For his allusions to Cervantes and to the Spanish language or literature, see K. W. Cameron, *Ralph Waldo Emerson's Reading* (Raleigh, N. C., Thistle Press, 1941), Index, and *The Letters of Ralph Waldo Emerson*, ed. R. L. Rusk (New York, Columbia University Press, 1939), *1*, xlix, 125; *2*, 289; *3*, 50. Thoreau "dreamed of being a postman in Peru." See Stimson, p. ii. He studied Spanish during his last two years at Harvard, using as a textbook Don José Cadalso's *Cartas marruecas*. His library contained Spanish grammars and copies of Florian's *Gonzalve de Cordoue* and of Iriarte. See F. A. Sanborn, *The Life of Henry David Thoreau* (Boston, Houghton Mifflin & Co., 1917), pp. 105, 511, 512. Thoreau used Sancho Panza as an illustration of the character of philosophers. See *The Writings of Henry David Thoreau*, Walden ed. (Boston, Houghton Mifflin & Co. [1906]), *16*, 344–5.

229. See Quevedo's sonnet, "Rome in Ruins." Poe's title, "El Dorado" (1849), suggests the currency of this phrase in this particular year.

230. The authority for Whitman's proficiency in Spanish is William H. Garrison. See "Walt Whitman," *Lippinc., 49* (May, 1892), 624; and R. M. Bucke, *Walt Whitman* (Philadelphia, 1883), p. 52.

231. See W. W., *5*, 276; *9*, 64–9. For a summary of these opinions of Cervantes, see M. O. Johnson, *Walt Whitman As a Critic of Literature* (Lincoln, Neb., 1939), p. 16.

232. See his "Song of the Answerer," W. W., *1*, 200–5. Miss Louise Pound believes that Whitman discovered the first of these words in the Waverley novels.

233. *Ibid., 6*, 116–19. Walt Whitman is popular in Spanish America. See Fernando Alegría, *Walt Whitman en Hispano-América* (México, 1954).

234. See his poem, "Spain, 1873–74," W. W., *2*, 264.

235. Rollo Ogden, *William Hickling Prescott* (Boston, Houghton Mifflin & Co., 1904), p. 137.

236. J. R. L., *7*, 225.

237. *Ibid., 9*, 78.

238. See Bierstadt, p. 274.

239. J. R. Lowell, *Impressions of Spain*, p. 12.

240. "To this day Santayana speaks without a trace of Spanish accent, has never written a book in Spanish . . . Neither the peasant nor the grandee finds a place in Santayana's work. One poem is addressed to Spain, but it is a rhetorical piece, chiding Spain for her dreams of world supremacy and for the evils which attended the colonization of America. 'Overheard in Seville' records a bit of local color; 'Avila' celebrates the uplands which were the scene of Santayana's early life; there are also an essay on Spanish drama, a discussion of Spanish opinion during the World War, an article on Cervantes, and an 'imitation' of Calderón. Seven pieces are a small number, though, for a man of letters to devote to his native land; in turn, his work is little known in Spain, only a few articles having been translated into Spanish." G. W. Howgate, *George Santayana* (Philadelphia, University of Pennsylvania Press, 1938), pp. 3-4. See also George Santayana, *Poems* (New York, 1923), pp. 39, 75-8, 101-4, 118-29.

241. E.g., Edwin Arlington Robinson's verse on Spanish themes seems to be limited to "Ponce de Leon." See his *Collected Poems* (New York, 1949), pp. 1187-99. García Lorca, who visited New York, aroused much interest among American readers. See *Poems, F. Garcia Lorca* (New York, 1939). See, in particular, the introduction (tr. Herschel Brickell) in *The Poet in New York, and Other Poems of Federico García Lorca* (New York [1940]).

242. See John Gould Fletcher's "Mexican Quarter" and "To Columbus," *Selected Poems* (New York [1938]), pp. 91-3, 150-5; Elinor Wylie's "Castilian," *Collected Poems* (New York, 1932), pp. 79-80; and Wallace Stevens' "The Novel," *The Auroras of Autumn* (New York, 1950), pp. 94-7.

243. After he left the profession of teaching, the chief Continental influence on Pound was Italian rather than Spanish. For other poems, see F. E. Pierce, "The Night before the Auto-da-Fé," *Poems of New England and Old Spain* (Boston, 1918), etc.

244. Walsh's poems include some related to Spanish monastic life. His interest in Spanish subjects was strengthened by seven journeys to Europe and South America, and he communicated his enthusiasm to a wide circle of artists and writers. His *Selected Poems* (New York, 1930), contains various verses on Spanish themes. See John Bunker, "The Poetry of Thomas Walsh," *Cath. World, 131* (Sept., 1930), 699-705; H. A. Allen, "Thomas Walsh, His Spanish Fantasies," *ibid., 113* (May, 1921), 192-202.

245. E.g., . . . *and Spain Sings; Fifty Loyalist Ballads Adapted by American Poets*, ed. M. J. Benardete and Rolfe Humphries (New York, 1937). The poet Edwin Rolfe served in Spain. See his *The Lincoln Brigade* (New York [1939]).

246. *Rosinante to the Road Again*, p. 145.

247. *12 Spanish American Poets, an Anthology*, ed. H. R. Hays (New Haven, 1943). Undoubtedly the influence of Spanish-American poetry began early. For example, Bernardo de Balbuena's *Grandeza mexicana* was published in the United States in 1828, and Roe Lockwood, at 411 Broadway, published again and again at about this time the verse of José María Heredia. See Harry Bernstein, "The Latin American Book Trade Before 1900," pp. 2416-17.

248. See *Quarterly Review of Literature, 1* (Autumn, 1943), 4-8. See also

Lloyd Mallan's translations from the Mexican poets in *New Directions, 9* (Norfolk, Conn. [1946]), 121–39.

249. See *The Collected Poems of Hart Crane*, p. xx. For Witter Bynner's interest in Mexico, see Harriet Monroe, "Pan-American Concord," *Poetry, 26* (June, 1925), 157.

250. "Where I have followed the historical chronicles of the Conquest of Mexico I have, in general followed the account given by Bernál Díaz del Castillo . . . in his *True History of the Conquest of New Spain* . . . I have however altered and transposed and invented incidents at my own pleasure . . . My account of the topography of the march from the sea-coast to the Valley of Mexico is based upon my own experience of the route and the country by foot and mule-back in the winter of 1929 and differs from that of the historians." Archibald MacLeish, *Conquistador* (Boston, Houghton Mifflin & Co., 1932), Note.

251. One may deduce the slight importance to American poets of contemporary Spanish and Spanish-American verse from the following article: F. M. Kercheville, "A Study of Tendencies in Modern and Contemporary Spanish Poetry from the Modernist Movement to the Present Time," *University of New Mexico Bulletin, Modern Language Series, 4,* No. 2 (Dec. 15, 1933). For an estimate of the influence of the prose and poetry of today, see Eliseo Vivas, "Recent Spanish Literature," *Nation, 124* (May 11, 1927), 530–1.

252. MacLeish, p. 62.

253. See Thomas Bailey Aldrich's *Mercedes*.

254. *Night over Taos* (New York, S. French, 1932), p. 199.

255. For example, in 1917 H. W. Lee published an opera entitled *El Cid Campeador* in three acts and eight scenes, based on *The Poem of the Cid, Gesta Roderici*, in Latin. See A. M. Coe, "Vitality of the Cid Theme," *HR, 16* (April, 1948), 134–6.

256. See G. O. Seilhamer, *History of the American Theatre* (Philadelphia, 1888–91). One of the earliest performances of a play of Calderón, probably his *El escondido y la tapada*, occurred in 1790. See J. R. Spell, "Hispanic Contributions to the Early Theater in Philadelphia," *HR, 9* (Jan., 1941), 192–8.

257. See Oscar Wegelin, *Early American Plays, 1714–1830* (New York, 1900), p. vii. See also Carlos González Peña, *History of Mexican Literature,* chaps. iv, vii.

258. See E. B. Place, "A Group of Mystery Plays Found in a Spanish-Speaking Region of Southern Colorado," *Univ. Colo. Stud., 18* (Aug., 1930), 1–8.

259. See C. C. Ayer, "Foreign Drama on the English and American Stage (Italian and Spanish)," *Univ. Colo. Stud., 10* (Nov., 1913), 149–59.

260. Among the most popular was *The World and His Wife*, a version which in 1908 ran for eighty-eight performances. *Mariana*, another play by Echegaray, was included in Mrs. Patrick Campbell's repertory in 1902.

261. Throughout these years Benavente's plays were especially popular.

262. For detailed accounts of the reception of the plays, see Florence Nicholson, "Spanish Drama on the American Stage, 1900–1938," *Hisp., 22* (May, 1939), 135–44.

263. See Burns Mantle, *The Best Plays of 1931–32* (New York, 1932), pp. 500–1.

264. See Burns Mantle, *The Best Plays of 1927–28* (New York, 1928), pp. 467–8.

265. See Burns Mantle, *The Best Plays of 1938–39* (New York, 1939), p. 471.

266. See A. H. Quinn, *A History of the American Drama from the Beginning to the Civil War* (New York, Harper and Bros., 1923), p. 122. About 1800 Royal Tyler wrote a popular farce in three acts, "The Island of Barrataria," based on six chapters in the second part of *Don Quixote.* See *ibid.,* p. 72. During the early decades of the nineteenth century pantomime versions were popular, and during the latter years operettas. See Heiser, pp. 417–18 and n. 35.

267. See *American Theatre, 39,* No. 2 (Feb., 1924), p. 16, and *Am. Merc., 1* (Jan., 1924), 119, for reviews of Lengyel's comedy. For Kester's version, see Burns Mantle, *The Best Plays of 1899–1909* (New York, 1944), p. 470.

268. See L. S. Driver, *Fanny Kemble* (Chapel Hill, 1933), pp. 49–50. This version of Lope de Vega's play, which delighted Longfellow, had an interesting history. See Lope Félix de Vega Carpio, *La estrella de Sevilla,* 2d ed. (Oxford, 1930), pp. xxiv–xxv.

269. See A. H. Quinn, *A History of the American Drama from the Civil War to the Present Day* (New York, F. S. Crofts & Co., 1936), pp. 32–4, 70–1.

270. Note that adaptations of *Don Quixote* continued to be acceptable in the twentieth century. Among the most popular of the plays concerning Spain was the version of Francis Marion Crawford's novel, *In the Palace of the King.* Opening at the Republic Theatre in New York on December 31, 1900, it ran for 138 performances. For further study of Spanish drama or plays with Spanish themes, see Stimson, chap. viii.

271. See Quinn, *A History of the American Drama from the Beginning to the Civil War,* pp. 137, 146–7.

272. Quinn's praise of Bird as a dramatist seems extravagant: "Before he was thirty years old he had lifted romantic tragedy to a level higher than it had reached in English since Congreve, and had written plays which even to-day can be placed on the stage with effect." *Ibid.,* p. 248. Besides *Oralloossa,* the blank-verse tragedy already mentioned, Bird was the author of *Isidora, or The Three Dukes,* a play whose action took place in Catalonia in about the year 1500. Payne's *The Spanish Husband* was unsuccessful, and his drama, "The Last Duel in Spain," remains in manuscript.

273. See E. S. Bradley, *George Henry Boker, Poet and Patriot* (Philadelphia, University of Pennsylvania Press, 1927), pp. 56–61. "As we grew older," says C. G. Leland, "Boker and I, from reading *Don Quixote* and Scott, used to sit for hours improvising legends of chivalry and marvellous romances." *Ibid.,* p. 9. Boker's collected *Plays and Poems,* published in 1856 in two volumes, contained four tragedies, two comedies, with other pieces, among them seventy-nine sonnets. These volumes passed through five editions, the last appearing in 1891. Evidently there was much interest among the reading public in Boker's romantic writings and in his Spanish plays. See J. W. Krutch, "George Henry Boker," *SR, 25* (Oct., 1917), 457–68. For a description of *Calaynos,* see Bayard Taylor, "George H. Boker," *Internat. M., 4* (Sept., 1851), 156–7. For

an analysis of *Leonor de Guzman,* see A. H. Quinn, "The Dramas of George Henry Boker," *PMLA, 32* (June, 1917), 233–66.

274. Produced at the Chestnut Street Theatre, Philadelphia, on November 29, December 26 and 28, 1838, and followed by, says Odell, "a surprisingly large number of repetitions." *Annals of the New York Stage* (New York, Columbia University Press, 1927–49), *4,* 280–1. See the review of this play in *So. Lit. Mess., 5* (Feb., 1839), 150–1.

275. *Don Juan,* an ironic comedy adapted from the French by Lawrence Langner, was acted at the Garrick Theater on September 5, 1921. The setting is in Spain in about the year 1620. *Last Night of Don Juan,* a play in prologue and two acts by Edmond Rostand, translated by Sidney Howard, was acted at the Greenwich Village Theatre, New York, on November 9, 1925.

276. See *The Fifth Column and the First Forty-Nine Stories* (New York, 1938). This play, dealing with counterespionage in Madrid during the Spanish Civil War, opened on March 6, 1940, in New York at the Alvin Theatre, where it ran for eighty-seven performances.

277. See also *Pizarro in Peru, or, The Death of Rollo.* For accounts of *Oralloossa,* another play on the Inca civilization, and *The Broker of Bogota,* see Quinn, *History of the American Drama from the Beginning to the Civil War,* pp. 238–43, and Foust, pp. 57–60.

278. E.g., the opera, *The Knight of the Guadalquivir,* produced on December 5, 1800; and *Virgin of the Sun,* from the German of A. von Kotzebue, first played at the Park Theatre, New York, March 12, 1800. The scene is Quito, Ecuador, and the story is about the Incas.

279. See R. F. Roden, *Later American Plays, 1831–1900* (New York, 1900).

280. See Burns Mantle, *The Best Plays of 1930–31* (New York, 1932), p. 415.

281. In 1847 Don Pablo Montoya, the last leader of the Spanish grandees in Taos, New Mexico, leads his people in defense of their ranches against the encroaching American government. See Burns Mantle, *The Best Plays of 1931–32* (New York, 1932), p. 492.

CHAPTER 6: THE PAINTERS, SCULPTORS, MUSICIANS, AND ARCHITECTS

1. *The Criterion* (New York, 1866), p. 87. See also his *Book of the Artists* (New York, 1867), Introduction, and *Artist-Life* (New York, 1847).

2. This was in the year 1848. See R. L. Rusk, *The Life of Ralph Waldo Emerson* (New York, C. Scribner's Sons, 1949), p. 348.

3. (Boston, 1881.) See 2, 401–31.

4. For recognition of the need for a study of Spanish influence in American painting, see Pedro Henríquez Ureña, review of Carl Van Vechten's *The Music of Spain* in *Hisp., 2* (Nov., 1919), 270.

5. Some of the articles were illustrated, and some illustrations were widely distributed in the United States, often without attributions, so that many knew the pictures but not the names of the artists. See Mary Lowe, "Murillo and La Caridad," *Ladies' Repository, 27* (May, 1867), 264–5. For a summary of the meager content of painting in the "Spanish-controlled" regions, see

Virgil Barker, *American Painting* (New York, Macmillan Co., 1950), pp. 3–4.

6. Evan Charteris, *John Sargent* (London, W. Heineman, Ltd. [1927]), p. 28.

7. Lloyd Goodrich, *Thomas Eakins* (New York, Whitney Museum of Modern Art, 1933), p. 28.

8. Further parallels might be drawn between the presence in both mediums of similar attitudes: sentiment, nationalism, idealism, and, in particular, the struggle of stronger and more original minds to achieve representation of fact, of authentic American qualities.

In reflecting on the Spanish element in our painting, the general history of the art should be kept in mind. In an outline of American painting a French critic suggests a "period of memory" until 1776; a "period of science or sentiment," 1776 until 1840; a "critical period," 1840 to 1876; and one of "extension and quality," 1876 to 1919. See René Brimo, *L'Évolution du goût aux États-Unis d'après l'histoire des collections* (Paris, J. Fortune [1938]). This author, who may be consulted for the location of paintings in this country, mentions persistent characteristics in the evolution of American taste: a preference for English art; an attachment to realism or exactitude of reproduction; the activity of dealers or agents in sustaining certain trends of taste. See *ibid.,* pp. 122–3.

9. Little convincing evidence exists for the well-known assertion that the colonial artist fitted his portraits to previously prepared "bodies."

10. See J. T. Flexner, *American Painting* (Boston, Houghton Mifflin & Co., 1947), pp. 24, 282.

11. *A Funeral Oration, Occasioned by the Death of Thomas Cole* (New York, 1848), p. 14.

12. See J. I. H. Baur, *Revolution and Tradition in Modern Art* (Cambridge, Harvard University Press, 1951), pp. 11–20.

13. See F. J. Mather Jr. and others, *The American Spirit in Art* (New Haven, Yale University Press, 1927), pp. 33, 40, 43, 153. See the section named "American Scene" in *Painting and Sculpture in the Museum of Modern Art,* ed. A. H. Barr Jr. (New York, Museum of Modern Art [1948]), pp. 154–62. See also Baur, chap. ii, illustrations.

14. Louis Réau, *L'Art français aux États-Unis* (Paris, H. Laurens, 1926), pp. 73–4. Vanderlyn spent five years in Paris. His debts, like Trumbull's, to David were chiefly technical but apparently represent the beginnings of French influence. See O. W. Larkin, *Art and Life in America* (New York, Rinehart & Co. [1949]), pp. 63, 112, 118–19.

15. See C. H. Caffin, *The Story of American Painting* (New York, F. A. Stokes [1907]), p. 238.

16. See *ibid.,* p. 241. See also C. C. Cooper, "A Spanish Painter," *Lippinc.,* *51* (Jan., 1893), 75–82. In 1906 only three paintings by Velázquez were known to be in the United States. For accounts of some of Velázquez' paintings and of his art, see Royal Cortissoz, *The Painter's Craft* (New York, C. Scribner's Sons, 1930), pp. 18–27.

17. See Caffin, p. 242.

18. N. H. Moore, "Spanish Art in the United States," *Chaut.,* *37* (June, 1903), 280.

19. See issue for May 7–10, 1735, p. 3.

20. As late as 1901 Mrs. E. R. Pennell commented in the *Nation* on the comparative ignorance in England of Spanish painting, saying that there were approximately twenty books on Italian art to one on Spanish. See her "A Survey of Spanish Art," *Nation, 72* (May 23, 1901), 411–13.

21. The following is exaggerated but suggestive: "All that is valuable in Spain—art, science, literature, monuments, institutions, manners, and even her language—is Catholic . . . The grand Raphaelic designs, as well as the famous Venetian coloring, were used by our painters to represent the ecstasies of saints, the labors and miracles of Jesus, and the ineffable beauties of the Virgin." Manuel Pérez Villamil y García, "Religion in Spain," *Cath. World, 49* (July, 1889), 495–6. See also C. H. Caffin, *The Story of Spanish Painting* (New York, Century Co., 1910), pp. 25–6.

22. See F. W. Bayley, *Five Colonial Artists of New England* (Boston, 1929), p. 294. It has been said that Feke had the benefit of nine years of study in Spain. See Homer Saint-Gaudens, *The American Artist and His Times* (New York, Dodd, Mead & Co., 1941), pp. 22–3. See H. W. Foote, *Robert Feke* (Cambridge, Harvard University Press, 1930), pp. 32–3.

23. Other incidents warn against assuming a complete lack of Spanish influence. For example, in 1825 a Catalonian miniaturist named Manuel Cil opened a studio in Charleston. See J. F. Shearer, "Agustín de Letamendi: a Spanish Expatriate in Charleston, S. C. (1825–1829)," *S. C. Hist. and Gen. Mag., 43* (Jan., 1942), 19.

24. See William Dunlap, *A History of the Rise and Progress of the Arts of Design in the United States,* ed. F. W. Bayley and C. E. Goodspeed (Boston, C. E. Goodspeed & Co., 1918), *3,* 270. For an alleged original Murillo captured from a Spanish vessel in the 1740's, see Barker, p. 192.

25. See John Galt, *The Life, Studies, and Works of Benjamin West* (London, 1820), *1,* 71. Other records of Spanish or Spanish-American artists living in colonial days are uncertain. In 1797 a landscape painter named Samuel Luzada lived in Division Street in New York, but nothing more is known of him. See G. L. McKay, "A Register of Artists, Booksellers, Printers and Publishers in New York City, 1781–1800," *BNYPL, 45* (June, 1941), 489. Although the Spanish-American influence on our painting was to appear much later, during the early Spanish days in California wandering artists traveled from one estate to another, painting the dons and their ladies or altarpieces. See Eugen Neuhaus, *The History & Ideals of American Art* (Stanford University, 1931), p. 240.

26. See Suzanne La Follette, *Art in America* (New York, Harper & Bros., 1929), p. 50. Gilbert Stuart's first commissions came from the groups of aristocratic Spanish Jews who had settled in Rhode Island. See Saint-Gaudens, p. 56.

27. See M. M. Swan, *The Athenæum Gallery, 1827–1872* ([Boston] Boston Athenæum, 1940), pp. 111–16.

28. John Trumbull, *Autobiography, Reminiscences and Letters* (New York, 1841), p. 148.

29. See J. F. Weir, *John Trumbull* (New York, C. Scribner's Sons, 1901), pp. 53–4.

30. The long and tangled European history of the pictures of Columbus was repeated in America, where many of the spurious canvases were dupli-

cated and widely used, even in such books as Irving's biography of the discoverer and Prescott's *Ferdinand and Isabella*. See W. E. Curtis, "The Columbus Portraits," *Cosmopol., 12* (Jan., Feb., 1892), 259–67, 409–20.

31. See Neuhaus, p. 47.

32. See *ibid.*, p. 62. In the forties, the paintings of the German-born Emanuel Leutze aroused interest: *Columbus before the Council of Salamanca; Columbus in Chains; Columbus before the Queen; Columbus Received at Barcelona;* etc. See *Bulletin of the American Art-Union*, Sept., 1851, pp. 95–6.

33. E.g., see Van Wyck Brooks, *The Pilgrimage of Henry James* (New York, E. P. Dutton & Co. [1925]), p. 29. For denial of the fact that Allston's talents were stifled in America, see E. P. Richardson, *Washington Allston* (Chicago, University of Chicago Press [1948]). For opposition to the belief that, in general, America was inhospitable to the artist, see M. L. Williams' review of this biography, *NEQ, 22* (June, 1949), 267–8.

34. See Swan, pp. 185, 187.

35. Throughout the century, apart from the strong influences exerted on such painters as Whistler and Sargent, we encounter Spanish subjects. In the *National Academy of Design Exhibition Record, 1826–1860* (New York, New York Historical Society, 1943) some paintings on Spanish subjects are listed. Examples are George Cooke's *Portrait of a Lady, in a Spanish Dress*, 1834 (*1*, 94); R. E. Launitz' *The Rose of the Alhambra*, 1843 (*1*, 286); or Joseph Biays Ord's *Spanish Bandit*, 1835 (*2*, 57). The most frequently recurring subjects are those connected with Columbus and Don Quixote. For typical paintings see *1*, 6, 10, 29, 50, 72, 74, 75, 81, 82, 164, 205, 247, 290; *2*, 6, 7, 23, 24, 73, 121, 133, 142, 155, 185, 189, 190, 192. Much may be learned of the growth of interest in Spanish painting during the fifties and sixties from certain periodicals. The *Crayon,* for example, discusses Velázquez in the issues of May 2, June 21, and July 11, 1855. For a criticism of Church's *The Heart of the Andes*, see *ibid., 6* (June, 1859), 193–4. See also *ibid., 3* (April, 1856), 123; *5* (March, 1858), 85; *6* (March, 1859), 132, (May, 1859), 153; *7* (March, 1860), 87; *8* (March, 1861), 69. See also *Bulletin of the American Art-Union*, April, 1850, p. 15, and Sept., 1851, pp. 95–6, 98; and in the *Cosmopolitan Art Journal, 1–4* (July, 1856—Dec., 1860), *passim.* When almost ninety, Thomas Sully made several copies of a small painting, *Spanish Boy,* possibly in continuation of his early interest in imitating Spanish subjects, among them Landseer's and Wilkie's work. See Edward Biddle and Mantle Fielding, *The Life and Works of Thomas Sully* (Philadelphia, 1921), pp. 385–7. In 1859 George Fuller studied Spanish painting in Europe but did not visit Spain. See C. H. Caffin, *American Masters of Painting* (New York, Doubleday, Page & Co., 1902), p. 106. Other artists who traveled in Spain include Samuel Coleman and George Henry Hall (1825–1913), A few Spanish-American artists living in the United States may have stimulated interest in Spanish painting: e.g., Thomas Codezo, who was born in Havana in 1839 and came to this country in 1869.

36. Caffin, *Story of American Painting,* plate facing p. 56.

37. See M. F. Sweetser, *Allston* (Boston, 1879), pp. 112–13.

38. See C. W. Sheldon, *American Painters,* enl. ed. (New York, 1881), pp. 12–13; and J. T. Soby and D. C. Miller, *Romantic Painting in America* (New York, Museum of Modern Art [1943]), p. 19.

39. Another painter who showed interest in Spanish themes was the illustrator of Washington Irving's tales, John Quidor, who in his early work portrayed scenes from *Don Quixote*. See J. I. H. Baur, *John Quidor, 1801–1881* (Brooklyn, Brooklyn Institute of Arts and Sciences [1942]), No. 1, "Dorothea." See Heiser, p. 429.

40. See S. T. Williams, *The Beginnings of American Poetry (1620–1855)* (Uppsala, Sweden, 1951), p. 76.

41. See R. L. Shoolman and C. E. Slotkin, *The Enjoyment of Art in America* (Philadelphia, J. B. Lippincott Co. [1942]), p. 682.

42. One of the first accounts of Spanish painting published in this country appeared in J. J. Jarves, *Art-Hints* (New York, 1855), pp. 269–83. In *Art Thoughts* (New York, 1869) Jarves again devoted a few pages to Spain. From this time on historians of Spanish art increased in number and importance. See A. G. Radcliffe, *Schools and Masters of Painting* (New York, 1876) pp. 336–68; and W. H. Goodyear, *A History of Art for Classes, Art-Students, and Tourists in Europe*, 3d ed. (New York, 1889), pp. 336–47. In 1877 M. F. Sweetser published the first American memoir of Murillo. See also C. B. Curtis, *Velazquez and Murillo* (New-York, 1883), and E. W. Washburn, *The Spanish Masters* (New York, 1884).

43. Perhaps the "master" best known to the average American art lover, through exhibitions and copies, was Murillo. Many travelers to Seville had described his paintings, and other pictures of his had been exhibited at the Athenæum. In "A Picture by Murillo," *Knick.*, 23 (May, 1844), 503, occurs an ecstatic account of an alleged original: "For the first time in our lives, we have enjoyed the delight of seeing . . . one of the grand pictures of MURILLO, which was obtained by a distinguished connoisseur at Lima, in 1828, from the cloister of an old convent, where it had hung for countless years in ignoble seclusion . . ."

44. See his *Contrabandier Aragonais* and *A Quartette*.

45. Chase put Spanish collars on his figures in the Valázquez manner and dressed his children as infantas. See Larkin, p. 301.

46. For the influence of Bonnat's studies upon Eakins and others, see Caffin, *Story of American Painting*, pp. 164, 230–1.

47. Goodrich, p. 28.

48. In Madrid. See K. M. Roof, *The Life and Art of William Merritt Chase* (New York, C. Scribner's Sons, 1917), p. 219.

49. See A. J. Eddy, *Recollections and Impressions of James A. McNeill Whistler* (Philadelphia, J. B. Lippincott Co., 1903), p. 71.

50. *Ibid.*

51. *Ibid.*

52. L. C. Moulton, "A Lazy Tour in Spain," *Cosmopol.*, 3 (July, 1887), 274. See also Octave Thanet, "A Spanish Court Painter and His Times," *Dial, 10* (Oct., 1899), 133–5.

53. See his *Spanish Gypsy Girl* (reminding us of Murillo's *Beggar Boys*); *Dancer with Castanet* (1904); *Little Spanish Dancer* (1910); or *Old Segoviana* (1924). See H. A. Read, *Robert Henri* (New York [1931]). For Henri's debt to Spanish painting, see Larkin, p. 329.

54. Mary Cassatt, who was a follower of Manet and of Degas, did not ac-

knowledge the influence of Velázquez upon her art. but it almost certainly existed. See Dorothy Grafly, "In Retrospect—Mary Cassatt," *Am. M. Art, 18* (June, 1927), 311; and Samuel Isham, *The History of American Painting,* new ed. (New York, Macmillan Co., 1916), pp. 411–12. Among others, Jane Peterson of Elgin, Illinois, studied under Sorolla in Spain. See L. M. Bryant, *American Pictures and Their Makers* (New York, J. Lane Co., 1917), pp. 277–8.

55. See, for example, his *The Four Doctors.*

56. See Neuhaus, pp. 221–2.

57. From Carolus-Duran Sargent learned the "sum total of an art that was a modern Frenchman's paraphrase of one of the biggest of the old masters, Velasquez." Caffin, *American Masters of Painting,* p. 57. Carolus-Duran's paternal grandfather was Spanish.

58. See Charteris, p. 10.

59. *Picture and Text* (New York, 1893), p. 100.

60. See W. H. Downes, *John S. Sargent, His Life and Work* (Boston, Little, Brown & Co., 1925), p. 11. See J. P. Leeper, "John Singer Sargent, a Revaluation," *Mag. Art, 44* (Jan., 1951), 11–15.

61. Charteris, p. 51.

62. *Ibid.,* p. 195.

63. Goya was, of course, closer than Velázquez to modern impressionism. See Caffin, *Story of Spanish Painting,* pp. 187–8. See also Christian Brinton, "Goya and Certain Goyas in America," *Art in Am., 3* (April, 1915), 85–103.

64. Bryson Burroughs, *Catalogue of an Exhibition of Spanish Paintings, from El Greco to Goya* ([New York, 1928]), p. xxiv.

65. F. J. Mather Jr., *Estimates in Art, Series II. Sixteen Essays on American Painters of the Nineteenth Century* (New York, H. Holt & Co., 1931), p. 245.

66. *Picasso* (London [1938]), p. 1.

67. See E. B. Prescott, "Modern Spanish Art," *Harper, 76* (March, 1888), 491–516.

68. See Brimo, pp. 121–2. See the comments on Spanish painting in Prescott, and in A. G. Radcliffe, *Schools and Masters of Painting,* 5th ed., rev. (New York, D. Appleton & Co., 1900), pp. 336–68. One interesting criticism of painting at the end of the century drew attention to the attempt "to show the life and manners of today that we welcome in Spanish fiction." "Editor's Study," *Harper, 84* (May, 1892), 967–8. The following comment from Cooper, p. 75, is typical of the transition period: "Modern Spanish art in general is disappointing: it is crude in color, brutal in technique and theatric in design, and stands in strong contrast to the genuine character of such of her masters as Coello, Greco, Moro, Murillo, Ribera, and others of the fifteenth and sixteenth centuries . . ."

69. Timothy Cole's reproductions of paintings (which had originally appeared in the *Century*) were collected in *Old Spanish Masters* (New York, 1907). Three years later Caffin issued his *The Story of Spanish Painting.* In the meantime the Hispanic Society had begun its long series of studies of all phases of Spanish art. Other books might be mentioned, but these pale before C. R. Post's *A History of Spanish Painting,* still in process of publication. Eleven volumes have now appeared of a "work sealed of that tradition of thoroughness and urbanity which Ticknor so admirably inaugurated." See F. J. Mather

Jr.'s review of this work, "The Rise of Spanish Painting," *Y. R.*, N. S., 20 (Autumn, 1930), 193.

70. E.g., Joaquín Torres-García; Xavier Martínez, a Mexican who moved to California; or F. Luis Mora, a Uruguayan from Montevideo who settled in Boston. In the last quarter of the century León y Escosura visited New York several times.

71. For the complete story during the last half century, see Baur, *Revolution and Tradition in Modern American Art*.

72. See Bryant, pp. 268–9. See also Pittsburgh, Carnegie Institute, Dept. of Fine Arts, *Survey of American Painting, October Twenty-Fourth—December Fifteenth, 1940* ([Pittsburgh, 1940]), No. 288.

73. See Notebook, 1829 (Y.).

74. Margit Varga, *Waldo Peirce* (New York, Hyperion Press [1949]), p. 64. Other comments of Peirce on Zuloaga are suggestive. In a recent interview he informed me that he now has little interest in this painter. Earlier Zuloaga seemed to satisfy in America a particular aesthetic craving. See A. P. McMahon, "Some Aspects of Ignacio Zuloaga," *Art Bul.*, 7 (June, 1925), 117–30.

75. See *Painting and Sculpture in the Museum of Modern Art*. These are: José de Creeft (1884— American, born in Spain); Salvador Dali (1904—); Pablo Gargallo (1881–1934); Julio González (1881–1942); Juan Gris (1887–1927); Manuel Martínez Hugué Manolo (1876—); Joan Miró (1893—); Pablo Picasso (1881—).

76. Among these attention might be called to Carlos Mérida for his use of abstract form. See R. M. Pearson, *Experiencing American Pictures* (New York, Harper & Bros. [1943]), pp. 210–12.

77. See A. H. Barr Jr., *What Is Modern Painting?* (New York, Museum of Modern Art [1943]), p. 32.

78. Dali was engaged to make surrealist drawings for the Hearst newspapers. It has been said that the most intelligent review of his exhibition in 1934 was in a tabloid newspaper. See J. T. Soby, *After Picasso* (New York, Dodd, Mead & Co., 1935), p. 7.

79. See Soby and Miller, p. 43.

80. S. M. Kootz, *New Frontiers in American Painting* (New York, Hastings House [1943]), p. 49.

81. *Ibid.*

82. See J. P. Slusser, "Bernard Karfiol," *Arts*, 6 (Aug., 1924), 79; and *Max Weber. Retrospective Exhibition, 1907–1930, Museum of Modern Art, New York* ([New York, 1930]). Weber seems to have been influenced by the "elongations" of El Greco. See Larkin, p. 357. For the influence of Picasso on Weber, Stuart Davis, Carl Knaths, and other painters, see Baur, *Revolution and Tradition in Modern American Art*, pp. 70, 72, 73, etc.

83. The Spanish-American artist, Federico Castellón, who was granted funds by the Republican government to study under Picasso in Spain, traveled to his door with letters but, overcome with doubts, went away without presenting them. In Spain he was influenced by the surrealists. See Pearson, pp. 214–17.

84. A. H. Barr Jr., *Picasso; Fifty Years of His Art* (New York, Museum of Modern Art [1946]), pp. 280–4; 278–9.

85. Barr, *What Is Modern Painting?*, p. 26.

86. When Hendrik Willem Van Loon visited the Picasso exhibition of 1939 he was "frightened" by what he saw, "the mink-coat-faces of the surging crowd so like the ghastly caricatures which grinned at me from the walls." For the pictures made sense: "magnificent works of art, born out of Picasso's hate for the world into which he was born." See Pearson, pp. 38, 40.

87. In his youth Picasso studied El Greco and later, in Paris, Cézanne.

88. See S. A. Lewisohn, *Painters and Personality* (New York, Harper & Bros. [1937]), pp. 107–10.

89. Although only one of several pioneers, Picasso is usually regarded as the leader of the movement. See K. S. Dreier, *Western Art and the New Era* (New York, Brentano's [1923]), pp. 80–2.

90. Alfred Neumeyer, "Picasso and the Road to American Art," *JAAC, 1,* No. 6 (1942), p. 32.

91. A world undisturbed by "humanist or Christian tradition." See *ibid.*

92. See *ibid.*, p. 37.

93. 1906. The first cubist picture. For Picasso's place in cubism, see Barr, *What Is Modern Painting?*, pp. 26–9.

94. The sale or possession of Picasso's paintings was banned by all totalitarian governments. *Guernica* is not propaganda, but it shows Picasso's emotional reaction to suffering and also his desire to tell the truth about it. *Ibid.*, pp. 36–7.

95. See Barr, *Picasso*, p. 12.

96. For Picasso's influence on Gertrude Stein, see above, pp. 242–3.

97. See Neumayer, p. 27. Although American artists have studied Picasso's forms and colors, some ideas of his seem alien to our thought. Our naturalists have shown the ugliness of misery and our social novelists its injustice, but it is difficult to believe its "poetry" congenial to the American mind.

98. See Walter Pach, "Picasso's Achievement," *Forum, 73* (June, 1925), 769–75. This critic compares Picasso with Don Quixote as a "divine madman" who triumphs "in our affections over the 'reasonable people' surrounding him." It is "natural that a Spaniard should be the man to incarnate the struggle of the pure ideal in a world obsessed with material values." *Ibid.*, p. 771.

99. "Contemporaneousness in him is fused with an awareness of the contribution of his predecessors." See Neumayer, p. 30.

100. See A. V. Churchill, "Picasso's Failure," *Forum, 73* (June, 1925), 776–83.

101. See Pittsburgh, Carnegie Institute, Dept. of Fine Arts, No. 288.

102. Before the time of these great muralists a few Mexican artists had entered California, among them the landscape painter Fortunato Ariola, who crossed the border in the sixties and became the first teacher of Toby Edward Rosenthal. See Neuhaus, pp. 154–5. Today there are many more, among them Carlos Mérida (1893—) or Jean Charlot (1898—), who since 1921 has been associated with Mexico.

103. The first exhibition of Rufino Tamayo (1900—) was held in Mexico City in 1926. For a history of his career, see MacKinley Helm, *Modern Mexican Painters* (New York, Harper & Bros. [1941]), pp. 136–42.

104. Although Miguel Covarrubias (1904—) was born in Mexico, he has lived so long outside the country that when he returned in 1940 someone

asked: "What does Covarrubias know about Mexican art today? He is never here, and besides he isn't Mexican." A caricaturist and witty book illustrator, he conveys the force of the Mexican movement on a popular level. See *ibid.*, pp. 195–7; and Howard Simon, *500 Years of Art & Illustration from Albrecht Dürer to Rockwell Kent* (Cleveland, World Publishing Co. [1942]), p. 320. For accounts of other Mexican painters, such as Julio Castellanos (1905—), José Chávez Morado (1909—), or Jesús Guerrero Galván (1910—), see L. E. Schmeckebier, *Modern Mexican Art* (Minneapolis, University of Minnesota Press [1939]), pp. 177–80.

105. See H. G. Dwight and A. M. Frankfurter, *Art Parade* (New York, Art Foundation Inc. [1943]), p. 104.

106. Saint-Gaudens, pp. 243–4.

107. He has done frescoes for Frary Hall, Claremont, Calif.; the New School for Social Research, New York; the Baker Library, Hanover, N. H. See Schmeckebier, p. 179.

108. See Justino Fernández, *José Clemente Orozco; forma e idea* (México, Porrua hnos. y cia., 1942), pp. 48, 50, 55, 116.

109. The alleged picture of Miss Wills is in the Stock Exchange fresco and the self-portrait in that of the California School of Fine Arts. See Schmeckebier, p. 144. For descriptions of the murals in Detroit and for Rivera's other work, see Helm, pp. 37–61.

110. Schmeckebier, pp. 147–51.

111. See Saint-Gaudens, pp. 243–4.

112. See Helm, p. 93. See also Schmeckebier, pp. 161–3. In New York Siqueiros became for a time a kind of unofficial artist for the Communist party. His painting of George Gershwin in the Museum of Modern Art is an experiment in perspective and space movement. See *ibid.*, p. 162.

113. These Mexicans have impressed American artists by their direct, dynamic presentation of ideas, as in Orozco's "Prometheus" frescoes at Pomona College. In Los Angeles, Alfredo Ramos Martínez, founder of Mexico's first open-air free art school, lived and painted for several years. See Arthur Millier, "New Developments in Southern California Painting," *Am. M. Art,* 27 (May, 1934), 247. For other examples of Mexican influence, see Larkin, pp. 356, 423.

114. See Schmeckebier, p. 179. This critic points out that after early creative periods each artist (Orozco, Siqueiros, Charlot) has gone his own way. *Ibid.*, pp. 156–7. For a recent estimate of painting in Mexico see Virginia Stewart, *45 Contemporary American Artists* ([Stanford, Calif., 1951]).

115. American Federation of Arts, *Painters and Sculptors of Modern America* (New York, T. Y. Crowell Co., 1942), p. 61. The italics in the quotation are mine.

116. The work of Doris Rosenthal is an excellent example of the increasing influence of Mexico upon our young painters. See Shoolman and Slotkin, p. 687.

117. See American Federation of Arts, p. 36.

118. *Ibid.*

119. See *ibid.*, p. 94.

120. See A. F. Jaccaci, "The Father of Modern Illustration, Daniel Vierge Urrabieta," *Cent., 46* (June, 1893), 186–203.

121. José María Bernardo Mariano Fortuny was the leader of the modern Spanish school. See Prescott, pp. 491–502.

122. Jaccaci. Vierge simplified in order to bring out the important features of his subject. In his character was, perhaps, more Moor than Spaniard. See *ibid.*, p. 201.

123. *Pen Drawings and Pen Draughtsmen, Their Work and Their Methods* (London, 1889), p. 40. See also Hispanic Society of America, *Handbook, Museum and Library Collections* (New York, Printed by Order of the Trustees, 1938), pp. 39–40.

124. Fortuny's influence was widespread, affecting, for example, the technique of Edwin A. Abbey. Indeed, it may be said that Fortuny revolutionized this phase of art in Spain and developed a school which was instrumental in making American illustration what it is. See Mrs. E. R. Pennell, "A Survey of Spanish Art," p. 412. Fortuny was strongly influenced by French and Italian art.

125. See C. H. Caffin, "Robert Frederick Blum," *Int. Studio, 21* (Dec., 1903), clxxviii.

126. Stephen Ferris' son, Jean Léon Gérôme Ferris, became a historical painter. Like his father, he studied the work of Fortuny.

127. See Robert J. Wickenden in *DAB, 2,* 396.

128. Frank Weitenkamp, *American Graphic Art,* new ed., rev. and enl. (New York, Macmillan Co., 1924), p. 195.

129. *The Alhambra by Washington Irving with an Introduction by Elizabeth Robins Pennell Illustrated with Drawings of the Places Mentioned by Joseph Pennell* (London, 1896); and *Castilian Days by John Hay with Illustrations by Joseph Pennell* (Boston, 1903).

130. Joseph Pennell, *The Adventures of an Illustrator Mostly in Following His Authors in America & Europe* (Boston, Little, Brown & Co., 1925), p. 57.

131. Bryant, pp. 226–7; Caffin, *Story of American Painting,* p. 371.

132. For example, in his illustrations for Carleton Beals' *Mexican Maze* (Philadelphia [1931]). For comment on Miguel Covarrubias and other Mexican illustrators, see Helm, pp. 182–97.

133. The American dealer, whose fascinating story does not warrant much space in this book, has had great influence in increasing interest in Spanish art. He has had, so Europeans believe, his own peculiar traits. From the sharp merchant-trader abroad or in New York he has sometimes developed into the executive of a powerful firm, who could aid in the purchase (1905) of an El Greco for the Metropolitan Museum for $37,500, thus arousing the anger of foreign buyers. From *The American Art Annual* I have compiled an illuminating record of prices paid in this country for Spanish paintings. This list indicates that the number of Spanish paintings sold has never been so large as those of the French and English painters. This conclusion is not surprising, and it is less important than the increasingly high prices paid for Spanish masterpieces. A few random facts are submitted to indicate the general trend of interest. In 1898–99 eight out of a total of twenty-seven Spanish paintings were sold for prices in four figures. At this time a Zamacois went for $7,600 and a Fortuny for $7,700. The third highest bid was for Murillo's *Magdalene* at $4,550. Thirty-one Spanish paintings were sold in 1914–15 at prices ranging

from $50 for a *Martyrdom of St. Andrew* by an unknown artist to $1,100 for El Greco's *The Napkin of Veronica*. Prices were high in 1929–30. In this period more than forty Spanish paintings were sold. Among these were Goya's *The Guardsman* ($4,700); Velázquez' *King Philip IV of Spain* ($6,100); El Greco's *The Virgin and St. Anne* ($9,500); and the same artist's *St. Peter* ($15,000). Goya's *La Maitresse de Goya* fetched $21,000. These data, which may be supplemented from the following references, suggest in no uncertain terms the constant desire to acquire Spanish works of art. See *The American Art Annual*, *2*, 51–76; *5*, 47–108; *10*, 23–74; *12*, 269–303; *17*, 280–341; *22*, 312–79; *27*, 426–89; *32*, 484–503; *36*, 373–435.

134. See Dunlap, *3*, 270. Robert Gilmor, of Baltimore, drew up a list of pictures which contained "A fine Head of a Monk; formerly Mr. Meade's.— *Velasquez.*" *Ibid.,* p. 274.

135. See Brimo, p. 18. See also H. W. Foote, *John Smibert, Painter; with a Descriptive Catalogue of Portraits* (Cambridge, Harvard University Press, 1950), p. 52.

136. In a letter to Henry Pelham, New York, Sept. 29, 1771, J. S. Copley refers to a visit to William Allen, chief justice of Pennsylvania, and describes his collection of paintings. See *Letters and Papers of John Singleton Copley and Henry Pelham, 1739–1776*, Mass. Hist. Soc. Coll., *71* ([Boston] 1914), 163–4. In a letter to his mother [n. p.], Nov. 18, 1774, Pelham mentions receiving an "introduction to Governor Penn and his Collection of Paintings, which is very great and Elegant." *Ibid.,* p. 272.

137. W. E. Curtis, p. 419.

138. In 1826 Thomas Sully visited the Bonaparte Collection and in 1830 the Abrahams Collection and commented on their Velázquezes and Murillos. See Dunlap, *3*, 277–80. As an instance of these early methods in forming collections, in 1847 an old sea captain brought to America the portrait called *The Almsgiver*, a work in the tenebrose manner. See Reginald Poland, "The Almsgiver, Painted in the Style of Velasquez's First Period," *Art in Am., 6* (Feb., 1918), 102–8.

139. See Henry Johnson, *Descriptive Catalogue of the Bowdoin College Art Collections* (Brunswick, Me., 1895), p. 41; and F. J. Mather Jr., "Drawings by Old Masters at Bowdoin College," *Art in Am., 1* (Oct., 1913), 244–53.

140. Meade, a Philadelphia merchant whose family was engaged in the West India trade, lived in Spain from 1804 to 1817 and there formed the nucleus of his collection.

141. See John Sartain, *The Reminiscences of a Very Old Man* (New York, D. Appleton & Co., 1899), pp. 167–8. This picture, purchased from Meade, was destroyed in 1844 in the burning of the Academy of Fine Arts in Philadelphia.

142. During the middle years of the nineteenth century collectors were primarily interested in the realistic productions of the Parisian school or those of Düsseldorf. See Brimo, p. 48.

143. American collectors were aided by economic conditions in Europe which made necessary the sale of masterpieces. See Hans Tietze, *Masterpieces of European Painting in America* (New York, Oxford University Press [1939]), p. 12. Of more than three hundred paintings selected by Tietze, twenty-eight

were by Spanish painters, among them Bermejo, El Greco, Velázquez, Zurbarán, Murillo, and Goya.

144. See Cortissoz, pp. 442–8.

145. For the Spanish paintings in the various collections, see these volumes. In *Noteworthy Paintings in American Private Collections*, ed. John La Farge and A. F. Jaccaci (New York, 1907), only one Spanish painting is described: Velázquez' portrait of Philip IV in the possession of Mrs. Jack Gardner. See, however, the later L. M. Bryant, *What Pictures To See in America* (New York, J. Lane Co., 1915), pp. 23–7, 126–7; and Earl Shinn, *The Art Treasures of America, Being the Choicest Works of Art in the Public and Private Collections of North America* (Philadelphia [1886]). See also A. L. Mayer, "Notes on Spanish Pictures in American Collections," *Art in Am., 3* (Oct., 1915), 309–20. In 1916 a critic observed that since the American interest in old masterpieces was steadily increasing it was strange that more collectors were not specializing in the Spanish school. M. T. Jackson, "Portrait of a Girl by Velasquez," *Art in Am., 4* (Feb., 1916), 119. See also Brimo and W. W. S. Cook, "Spanish and French Paintings in the Lehman Collection," *Art Bul., 7* (Dec., 1924), 51–70.

146. Even now there are in the United States hardly more than a dozen Zurbaráns. See M. S. Soria, "Zurbaran, Right and Wrong," *Art in Am., 32* (July, 1944), 126–41.

147. See Morris Carter, *Isabella Stewart Gardner and Fenway Court* (Boston, Houghton Mifflin & Co. [1925]), pp. 107, 111, 233, 240–1. The so-called "Spanish Cloister," with its Moorish arches, forms the background for Sargent's *El Jaleo*.

148. See R. H. Lamborn, *Mexican Painting and Painters* (New York, 1891). This little-known but exciting book, printed in a limited edition, is a precious record of the attitude in the United States at this time toward painting in Mexico. It begins: "The great historians of art apparently have maintained a 'conspiracy of silence' regarding the artists of New Spain. The Alps, the Apennines, and the Pyrenees have been diligently searched in all their recesses for names wherewith to lengthen already unduly swollen lists, while Mexico's more than a hundred recorded painters, a number of whom have left us pictures of great excellence, are utterly ignored or passed with the merest mention." See p. 21. See, in particular, the list on pp. 71–6: "Paintings Illustrating the Mexican Branch of the Spanish School. The Work of Artists in New Spain during the Seventeenth and Eighteenth Centuries."

149. Brimo, p. 72.

150. Eighteen years later the academy owned a Fortuny and six paintings with Spanish subjects. See its *Descriptive Catalogue of the Permanent Collections of Works of Art on Exhibition in the Galleries*, 2d ed. (Philadelphia, 1894).

151. An exhibition at this institution from June 9 to September 10, 1939, contained nine Spanish items, including Ribera, Velázquez, El Greco, and Goya. See Boston, Museum of Fine Arts, *Art in New England* (Cambridge, Mass., 1939), Nos. 59, 60, 61, 62, 107, 110, 135, 136, 274.

152. See D. C. Preyer, *The Art of the Metropolitan Museum of New York* (Boston, L. C. Page & Co., 1909), pp. 188–201. For an account of the Velázquezes,

see H. R. Wehle, "A Great Velazquez," *Met. Mus. Bul.,* N. S., *1* (Nov., 1942), 117–22. For the Murillos, which are not numerous in American galleries, see Louise Burroughs, "A Painting of the Virgin and Child by Murillo," *ibid.* (May, 1943), 261–5. See also W. E. Howe, *A History of the Metropolitan Museum of Art* (New York, 1913–46).

153. Bryant, *What Pictures To See in America.* It must be remembered that American interest in the old masters is relatively recent. When James J. Jarves brought his collection to America in 1860, the only other was that of Thomas Jefferson Bryan. The Morgan, Altman, and Frick collections were all assembled after 1900. See Michael Friedsam, *The Significance of Art in America* (New York [1924]). Several old inventories list private collections of the Dutch little masters. See Esther Singleton, *Social New York under the Georges, 1714–1776* (New York, D. Appleton & Co., 1902), p. 87.

154. Cortissoz, p. 18.

155. Among the ardent collectors of Picasso is Earl Horter. Dr. Albert Barnes of Philadelphia owns a superb collection of Cézannes, Seurats, Renoirs, Picassos, etc., but he has excluded the public because these paintings suffered so many insults. See American Federation of Arts, p. 6.

156. Henry Clay Frick's first purchase was Luis Jiménez Aranda's *In the Louvre.* In 1895 he acquired Martín Rico's *Fisherman's House, Venice,* in 1904 Murillo's *Portrait of the Artist,* and in 1905 his first El Greco, *Portrait of a Cardinal.* This last proved to be the earliest Spanish picture which he thought worthy of including in the final collection. For the Spanish works in the collection, see the *Catalogue of the Henry C. Frick Collection of Paintings* (New York [Gilliss Press], 1908); and G. B. M. Harvey, *Henry Clay Frick, the Man* (New York, C. Scribner's Sons, 1928), pp. 331–43.

157. *The Hispanic Society of America* (New York, 1904), p. 15.

158. See *Catalogue of Paintings (14th and 15th Centuries) in the Collection of the Hispanic Society of America by Elizabeth du Gué Trapier* (New York, 1930). Besides the Sargents and other paintings in debt to the old Spanish masters, the society owns fine landscapes, such as those by Childe Hassam, of Toledo, Seville, and Ronda. Oil paintings by Ernest Lawson, Max Kuehne, and William J. Potter portray Spanish towns and countrysides. Kuehne, who was often in Spain, has in the society collection thirty-one oils of Granada, Segovia, and Sepúlveda. Here are Potter's paintings of Mallorca. In addition, we find sketches of the Pórtico de la Gloria, Santiago Cathedral, by William Sanger, and fourteen water colors of Spain by Florence Robinson, and two of Salamanca and Burgos by Carroll Bill. See *Handbook,* p. 52. In addition, there are numerous etchings, pen or pencil drawings, and illustrations of all kinds. See *ibid.,* pp. 52–3.

159. For example, at the sixth annual exhibition of the Pennsylvania Academy of the Fine Arts, in May, 1817, *The Roman Daughter* by Murillo was the only Spanish work among the 271 items. Other early exhibitions, as described in the catalogues, occurred in the years 1823, 1850, 1852, 1854, and 1856. The catalogues of the Boston Athenæum between 1827 and 1873 indicate the showing of an occasional Spanish picture: Ribera, Murillo, Velázquez, etc. Paintings on Spanish subjects were exhibited as early as 1827. See Swan, pp.

86–7, 187, 199, 214, 219, 223, 229, 233, 253, 254, 255, 256, 261, 266, 267, 280, 281, 282. See also A. H. Everett, "Exhibition of Pictures at the Athenæum Gallery," *NAR, 21* (Oct., 1830), 309–37.

160. About 140 Spanish items were exhibited, some on loan from Spain. For the paintings, which included work by Murillo, Velázquez, and Ribera, see R. S. Fletcher, *The Centennial Exhibition of 1876* (Philadelphia, 1876), *1*, 18–21, 107, 108–9. A few paintings from Mexico, Argentina, and Brazil were included. See also U. S. Centennial Commission, *Official Catalogue*, 2d and rev. ed. (Philadelphia, 1876), *2*, 125–33.

161. See Hispanic Society of America, *Handbook*, pp. 42–6. See also W. E. B. Starkweather, "Joaquín Sorolla, the Man and His work," Hispanic Society of America, *Eight Essays on Joaquin Sorolla y Bastida* (New York, The Society, 1909), *2*, 27. See also Cadwallader Washburn, "Sorolla, a Great Spanish Painter of To-Day," *Outlook, 71* (May 3, 1902), 19–26. William Merritt Chase thought the Sorolla exhibition so important that he took his entire class at the Pennsylvania Academy of the Fine Arts to New York to see it. *Philadelphia Inquirer*, Feb. 28, 1909. The total attendance at the exhibition was 160,000. For other accounts of this exhibition see "Sorolla y Bastida," *Nation, 88* (Feb. 11, 1909), 151; New York *World*, Feb. 13, 1909; *Cincinnati Times-Star*, Feb. 27, 1909. See also "Appreciations of the Press" in *Eight Essays on Joaquin Sorolla, 2*, 135–372. Sorolla is still well known in this country, but in late years his popularity and influence have lessened appreciably.

162. *Cincinnati Times-Star*, Feb. 27, 1909, quoted in *ibid., 2*, 309.

163. *Catalogue of Paintings by Ignacio Zuloaga Exhibited by the Hispanic Society of America, March 21 to April 11, 1909* (New York, 1909). Under different auspices, there were other exhibitions of Zuloaga in 1916–17 and 1925.

164. See Bryson Burroughs, "Spanish Paintings from El Greco to Goya," *Met. Mus. Bul., 23* (Feb., 1928), 39–44. See also Howe, *2*, 131. See also the account of the Brooklyn exhibition of 1935 in Philippa Gerry, "Spanish Painting at Brooklyn," *Am. M. Art, 28* (Nov., 1935), 671–5. This exhibition showed five Goyas, four Velázquezes, four Riberas, and sixteen El Grecos. It is impossible even to list the innumerable exhibitions of the twentieth century which dealt with Spanish painting. Recent ones include those at the Schaeffer Galleries and the Virginia Museum of Fine Arts in February, 1953.

165. See "Accessions and Notes," *Met. Mus. Bul., 23* (May, 1928), 136.

166. See "Spain's Old Masters," *Lit. Digest, 96*, No. 11 (March 17, 1928), 24–5.

167. Mather, *Estimates in Art*, p. 239.

168. J. C. Van Dyke, *American Painting and Its Tradition* (New York, C. Scribner's Sons, 1919), p. 197.

169. Roof, pp. 96–7.

170. *Ibid.*, pp. 168–9.

171. Chase's private collection of about six hundred paintings included works of many Spanish artists, among them Villegas, El Greco, Ribera, Fortuny, and Sorolla. See *ibid.*, p. 300.

172. *Ibid.*, pp. 168–9.

173. *Ibid.*, p. 276.

174. *Ibid.*, p. 280.

175. Eakins admired, besides Velázquez, Ribera (and Rembrandt) and, among the moderns, Gérôme.

176. Goodrich, p. 28.

177. *Ibid.,* p. 30.

178. *Ibid.,* p. 45.

179. See Alan Burroughs, *Limners and Likenesses* (Cambridge, Harvard University Press, 1936), p. 199.

180. See La Follette, p. 188. For the works painted by Eakins in Spain, see Goodrich, p. 162.

181. See Bryant, *What Pictures to See in America,* p. 89.

182. See Neuhaus, p. 194. See also Caffin, *Story of American Painting,* pp. 288–9; and Morris Davidson, *Understanding Modern Art* (New York, Coward-McCann, Inc. [1931]), pp. 170–1.

183. See Mather, *The American Spirit in Art,* p. 70.

184. Quoted in E. H. Wuerpel, "Whistler—the Man," *Am. M. Art,* 27 (May, 1934), 252. One of Whistler's sketches which reveals his interest in the Spanish character is his *Portrait of Sarasate.* This touching picture of the Spanish violinist was exhibited in New York at about the time Whistler died (1903). See Bryant, pp. 94–5.

185. For a discussion of Whistler's debt to Velázquez, see Royal Cortissoz, *Art and Common Sense* (New York, C. Scribner's Sons, 1913), pp. 84, 184–5, 197–8.

186. To balance this history of Sargent's Spanish interests, see the important article, J. P. Leeper, "John Singer Sargent. A Revaluation," *Mag. Art,* 44 (Jan., 1951), 11–15. See also Larkin, p. 303; and in particular, Roger Fry, *Transformations, Critical and Speculative Essays on Art* (London, Chatto & Windus, 1926), pp. 125–35. "Sargent was to him nothing but a brilliant journalist whose work had no artistic value and would have no more permanent interest than the work of an expert photographer." Virginia Woolf, *Roger Fry. A Biography* (London, Hogarth Press, 1940), p. 111.

187. James, p. 101.

188. Downes, p. 10.

189. *Ibid.*

190. See, for example, the discussion in Cortissoz, *Art and Common Sense,* p. 236. In this we are asked to compare the brilliance of Carmencita's costume with the "melting, bloomlike beauty of a dress worn by one of the Infantas in the Prado. The clear *timbre* of the older colorists, resonant and haunting, has always struck me as lying outside the scope of Sargent's art."

191. See James, pp. 98–103. For descriptions of these paintings, see Downes, pp. 124, 125–6, 128–9. Some critics have praised *Don Antonio the Englishman* as a tribute to Velázquez' masterpieces in the Prado. See Hispanic Society of America, *Handbook,* p. 52.

192. Six of the twelve illustrations for Alma Strettell's *Spanish & Italian Folk-Songs* (London, 1887) were by Sargent.

193. Cortissoz, *Art and Common Sense,* pp. 227–8.

194. James, p. 103.

195. *Ibid.*

196. Charteris, p. 113.

197. Allan Marquand and A. L. Frothingham Jr.'s *A Text-Book of the History of Sculpture*, new ed., rev. (New York [1921]) allots in its chapter on Renaissance sculpture in Europe only about one page to Spanish sculpture. Influenced by both the classical tradition and French art, Spanish sculpture was often a kind of embroidered and ornamented classicism, with characteristics not always attractive to American sculptors. Americans do not seem to have studied a certain type of realistic Catalonian sculpture. For an account of Spanish sculpture, see Kineton Parkes, *The Art of Carved Sculpture* (London, 1931), *1*, 212–30.

198. E.g., chap. xv, "An Æsthetic Company."

199. See Mather, *The American Spirit in Art*, p. 178.

200. *Ibid.*, p. 183.

201. See *William Rimmer, 1816–1879, Whitney Museum of American Art, New York, November 5–27, 1946* ([New York, 1946]).

202. 5th Ser., *12* (Dec., 1821), 499.

203. See L. E. Hinkle, "Some Things We Owe to Spain," *Hisp.*, *8* (Feb., 1925), 19.

204. See U. S. Centennial Commission, *2*, 125–33.

205. See A. L. Mayer, "Some Late Spanish Romanesque Sculpture," *Art in Am.*, *14* (Feb., 1926), 56–9.

206. See Howe, *2*, 214. For other Spanish sculpture in the Metropolitan Museum, see Joseph Breck, *Catalogue of Romanesque, Gothic, and Renaissance Sculpture* (New York, 1913), pp. 95–103.

207. See *Painting and Sculpture in the Museum of Modern Art*, pp. 267, 278. Again the proportions seem to hold if this gallery is typical of others in the United States: Spanish sculpture is subordinate to the French, German, or Italian. One particularly interesting sculptured subject is Jo Davidson's *Portrait of La Pasionaria*. See *ibid.*, p. 260.

208. *Spanish Travels*, p. 65.

209. See Epiphanius Wilson, "Some Examples of Spanish Wood-Carving," *Cosmopol.*, *30* (Dec., 1900), 169–75.

210. See M. A. Wilder with Edgar Breitenbach, *Santos, the Religious Folk Art of New Mexico* ([Colorado Springs, Colo.] Taylor Museum [1943]), pp. 13–15 and, in particular, the sixty-four plates. "Shrines at humble hearthsides and little chapel altars in New Mexico still hold Santos, exquisite and ancient, often blackened by the smoke of devotional candles lit by unnumbered generations . . . They constitute a powerful, primitive form of Christian art that sprang from New World soil, and flourished probably before Plymouth Rock and before Jamestown." See Sheldon Cheney and Martha Candler, "Santos, an Enigma of American Native Art," *Parnassus*, *7*, No. 4 (May, 1935), 22–4.

211. American music did not omit the inexhaustible subject of Columbus. For the Centennial in Philadelphia Dudley Buck composed the music for the *Centennial Meditation of Columbus* and, in addition, a cantata, *The Voyage of Columbus*, for a libretto in six scenes based on Irving's biography of the explorer. See J. T. Howard, *Our American Music*, 3d ed. (New York, T. Y. Crowell Co. [1946]), pp. 593–4. Buck composed also *The Legend of Don Munio*, a metrical version of Irving's *The Alhambra*, for a small orchestra

and chorus. For standard operas, often performed in America, with scenes in Spain, see J. M. Chapple, *Vivid Spain* (Boston, Chapple Publishing Co., Ltd., 1926), pp. 173–4.

212. Harl McDonald's symphony, *The Santa Fe Trail* (1934), reflects in its second movement the life of the Spanish settlements. See Gilbert Chase, *The Music of Spain* (New York, W. W. Norton & Co. [1941]), p. 303. This valuable book contains a chapter on Spanish music in America. See *ibid.*, pp. 160, 174, 175, 189, 212–14, 312. See the review of this book by H. G. Doyle in *Hisp.*, 25 (Dec., 1942), 505–8. The Negro composer, William Grant Sill, is the author of a symphony called *Old California*, performed by the New York Philharmonic Symphony Orchestra on Jan. 5, 1944.

213. See L. C. Elson, *The History of American Music*, rev. ed. (New York, Macmillan Co., 1915), p. 99. See *New-York Evening Post*, Nov. 30, 1825; *New York Mirror*, Dec. 3, 1825; and *New-York Literary Gazette*, Dec. 17, 1825. See Julius Mattfield, *A Hundred Years of Grand Opera in New York, 1825–1925* (New York, New York Public Library, 1927), pp. 13–23. For other Spanish operas, see *ibid.*, p. 560. See also Chase, pp. 210–13. This troupe, not considered first rate in London, surpassed at this time any similar organization in the United States. Between Nov. 29, 1825, and Sept. 30, 1826, the company gave seventy-nine performances. See also David Ewen, *Music Comes to America* (New York, T. Y. Crowell Co. [1942]), pp. 53–4.

214. See *Revista de estudios hispánicos*, 2 (enero–marzo, 1929), 91. See also T. A. Brown, *A History of the New York Stage from Its First Performance in 1732 to 1901* (New York, Dodd, Mead & Co., 1903), *3*, 92, 180. Raquel Meller was presented at the Empire Theatre in New York on April 14, 1926. During a four-week engagement this Spanish *diseuse* sang about twelve or fifteen songs at each performance. See Burns Mantle, *The Best Plays of 1925–26* (New York, 1926), pp. 6–7, 584. On April 3, 1911, Madame Tetrazzini was very successful with her Spanish song, *Carceleras,* for Ruperto Chapí's zarzuela, *Las hijas de Zebedeo.* See Carl Van Vechten, *The Music of Spain* (London, K. Paul, Trench, Trubner & Co., 1920), p. 92.

215. On January 15, 1918, the Schola Cantorum under Kurt Schindler gave a concert in which the program offered songs in the repertoire of Orféo Catalá, a choral society founded by Amadeo Vives. See *ibid.*, p. 71. The zarzuela is one of the most distinctive of Spanish musical art forms. Invented in the seventeenth century, it is, the Spanish say, the mother of *opéra bouffe* although other critics have linked it with the *ballet de cour*. With the early zarzuelas are associated the names of Lope de Vega and Calderón. Zarzuelas were performed in New York in 1916, 1917, and 1918. See *ibid.*, pp. 72–5.

216. Reginald De Koven wrote an opera called *Don Quixote*. See Elson, p. 237. Albert Stoessel composed his *Hispania Suite* (see Howard, p. 483) and Carl McKinley his *Masquerade (ibid.*, p. 497). Before 1908 Oscar Hammerstein had produced two operas concerned with Spain: Moszkowski's *Boabdil* and Beethoven's *Fidelio*. See Van Vechten, pp. 7–9. The teacher of Edward Alexander MacDowell was the fiery Teresa Carreño, the famous Venezuelan pianist, to whom he dedicated his second piano concerto. She introduced his *First Suite* and the better-known *Second Suite*. MacDowell dedicated the scherzo of his *Concerto in D Minor* to Teresa Carreño. See Marta Milinowski,

Teresa Carreño (New Haven, Yale University Press, 1940), p. 173. Another of MacDowell's teachers was the Colombian pianist, Juan Buitrago. See Eugenio Pereira Salas, *Notes on the History of Music Exchange between the Americas* (Washington, D. C., Pan American Union [1943]), p. 9. The bandmaster John Philip Sousa was the son of a political refugee from Spain. Among others who settled in the United States were Gonzalo Núñez and Julio C. Arteaga from Puerto Rico and the Mexican song writer, María Grever. See *ibid.*, p. 8, and Howard, p. 567. Isaac Albéniz, the composer and pianist, came to the United States in the seventies, Enrique Granados y Campiña, another pianist, in 1915–16. Isidora Martínez King, the Chilean soprano, was here in 1887, Carlos Hucke, the Chilean pianist, in 1892, José White, the violinist and composer, in 1876. In 1920 Joaquín Valverde's *The Land of Joy* was produced in New York by a Spanish company, which introduced La Argentina—and so on.

217. See Chase, p. 152. An account of this piano playing occurs in Miguel Raux Deledicque, *Albéniz, su vida inquieta y ardorosa* ([Buenos Aires], Ediciones Peuser [1950]), p. 142: "Cuántas veces, en España y también en Cuba, se le había ocurrido, para divertir a sus amigos, tañer el piano, de espaldas al instrumento y cruzados los brazos por detrás!"

218. For accounts of these and other musicians, see Richard Aldrich, *Concert Life in New York, 1902–1923* (New York, G. P. Putnam's Sons [1941]), pp. 56–7. See also pp. 248–9, 253–4, 348–9, 494–5. See Chase, pp. 160, 205, 217, 220, etc. See D. A. Paine, "Is Spanish Practical?," *Hisp., 15* (May, 1932), 274, etc. Enrique Granados y Campiña died at sea in 1916 when his ship was torpedoed in the English Channel. For an excellent study of this musician see J. R. Longland, "Granados and the Opera *Goyesca*," *Notes Hispanic, 5* (1945), 95–112.

219. Irving to Mrs. Sarah Storrow, Madrid, March 16, 1844 (Y.).

220. See Nina Sturgis, "Traditional Music of the Spanish Pyrenees," *Scrib., 14* (June, 1877), 237–41. The author of the article transcribed these songs in St. Jean de Luz in the summer of 1871.

221. Gustave Michaud, "The Popular Songs of Spain," *Bookm., 14* (Oct., 1901), 162–7.

222. *Ibid.*, p. 166.

223. See *ibid.*, p. 162.

224. See Luisa Espinel, *Canciones de mi padre, Spanish Folksongs from Southern Arizona* (Tucson, 1946); Eleanor Hague, *Early Spanish-California Folk-Songs* (New York [1922]); C. F. Lummis, *Spanish Songs of Old California* (Los Angeles [1923]); M. R. Van Stone, *Spanish Folk Songs of New Mexico* (Chicago [1926]).

225. Under Francisco Martínez y Torrens this troupe made several tours of the United States. See Pereira Salas, p. 8. In 1850 Señor Marty sent another capable opera company to New York. See Elson, p. 107.

226. See Pereira Salas, p. 6. *A Tus Ojos* and *Las Habaneras* were among the popularized melodies which he introduced to the North American public. Gottschalk was at least partly responsible for the success in the United States of Teresa Carreño. See L. M. Gottschalk, *Notes of a Pianist* (London, 1881), pp. 54, 59, 62, 64, 67–9, 71–5. See also Chase, p. 302.

227. During the years from 1924 to 1939 ninety-three concerts were given

and 108 musicians were presented. See Pereira Salas, pp. 17, 30–3. For an account of the growth of Latin-American musical programs in the United States, see E. R. Hutton, "Popular Interest in the Study of Spanish and Portuguese" in Doyle, *Handbook on the Teaching of Spanish and Portuguese*, p. 11. Among the composers after 1900 who were aware of the music of Latin America were Charles Martin Loeffer, Paul Bowles (*Pastorela,* 1941), John A. Carpenter (*The Birthday of the Infanta,* 1919), Aaron Copland (*El Salón México*), and Emerson Whithorne. See Chase, pp. 303–4.

228. By Henry Kimball Hadley. See Howard, p. 373.

229. On January 30, 1891, a ball was given at the Madison Square Garden Amphitheatre in honor of Carmencita. See T. A. Brown, *3,* 90.

230. The influence of Spanish dancing has been definite, and on several levels of taste. We think of Fanny Elssler, who toured the United States in 1840 and who inspired Longfellow in the creation of his character, Preciosa, in *The Spanish Student.* In contrast, there was, in 1934, Vicente Escudero with his "talking Castanets." One link with literature was Gertrude Stein's study during her two years in Spain of the connection between certain Spanish rhythms and her own use of words. See Van Vechten, p. 43. Harl McDonald's *Rumba Symphony* appeared in 1935. See Chase, p. 303.

231. Actually, the origins were much earlier, notably in the Cathedral of Santo Domingo (and probably others) about 1525. See E. W. Palm, *Rodrigo de Liendo, arquitecto en la Española,* Publicaciones de la Universidad de Santo Domingo, Vol. *28* (Ciudad Trujillo, 1944).

232. See G. H. Edgell, *The American Architecture of To-Day* (New York, C. Scribner's Sons, 1928), p. 306.

233. See T. F. Hamlin, *The American Spirit in Architecture* (New Haven, Yale University Press, 1926), p. 319.

234. See, for example, the descriptions of the Custom House in *The Scarlet Letter* or of "the old Pyncheon house" in *The House of the Seven Gables.*

235. For a description of the "Camúlos Rancho," really a "casa de campo," formerly the "Rancho San Francisco," the original of Señora Moreno's home in *Ramona,* and for comment on the actual places and persons in this novel, see Newcomb, *The Old Mission Churches and Historic Houses of California,* pp. 344–7.

236. It is possible to see in Mexican architecture a revolt against the "strictly Spanish," to find in it a new "Spanish-Mexican vernacular," possessing a kind of "barbaric splendor." See Newcomb, p. 99. The importance of the Indian craftsman was considerable, even if the precise nature of his work is sometimes difficult to define. See Alfred Neumeyer, "The Indian Contribution to Architectural Decoration in Spanish Colonial America," *Art. Bul.,* 20 (June, 1948), 104–21. "Without the Indian craftsman this style would never have appeared on American soil, but it is expressive more of a universal process than of a specific feature of Indian art . . . While the history of styles developed after its own inner laws in Europe, in America it remained more static just as any folk art remains static. It sank down to the deeper layers of the populace and created the folk art of Latin America . . . Gradually the art of the Indians became transformed into an Hispanic-Indian folk art." *Ibid.,* p. 121.

237. For dates and places of particular missions in California, Texas, New

Mexico, and Arizona, see Prent Duell, "A Complete List of the Missions in the Southwest" in his *Mission Architecture As Exemplified in San Xavier Del Bac* (Tucson, Arizona Archaeological and Historical Society, 1919), pp. 125–33. See also T. E. Sanford, *The Architecture of the Southwest, Indian, Spanish, American* (New York, W. W. Norton & Co. [1950]), Pts. III, IV, and V.

238. See Edgell, p. 26. For an excellent general account of the influences in Florida, the Southwest, and California, see H. S. Morrison, *Early American Architecture from the First Colonial Settlements to the National Period* (New York, Oxford University Press, 1952), chaps. vi–vii. In California the missions began at Loreto in 1697. Under the Jesuits the system finally extended as far north as Santa Maria. In 1768 the era of the Franciscans began, followed in 1772 by that of the Dominicans. For a detailed study of this phase, see Peveril Meigs 3d, *The Dominican Mission Frontier of Lower California,* Calif. Univ. Pub. Geog., Vol. 7 (Berkeley, Calif., 1935).

239. See Hamlin, p. 327.

240. Rexford Newcomb, *Spanish-Colonial Architecture in the United States* (New York, J. J. Augustin [1937]), p. 36.

241. By 1915 there were excellent examples in Washington and other eastern cities. See Marrion Wilcox, "Certain Phases of Spanish Colonial Architecture," *Arch. Rec., 37* (June, 1915), 535.

242. See Rexford Newcomb, "The Architecture of the Spanish Renaissance in California," *Art and Archaeol., 5* (Feb., 1917), 119.

243. See Hamlin, p. 166. As in painting, the exposition of 1876 introduced a new self-confidence in architecture.

244. See *ibid.,* p. 22.

245. See William Harbeson, "Mediaeval Philadelphia," *PMHB, 67* (July, 1943), 235–6.

246. In the revivals at the turn of the century there were various imitations of the Giralda in Florida and California. One of the most interesting examples was the clock tower on the Ferry Building on Market Street in San Francisco.

247. See H. C. Chatfield-Taylor, "Seville, the Fair," *Cosmopol., 21* (May, 1896), 4.

248. See Washington Irving, *The Life and Voyages of Christopher Columbus,* Irving's Works, Geoffrey Crayon Edition ([New York, 1888–93]), *10, 360.*

249. See Frances Trollope, *Domestic Manners of the Americans,* ed. Donald Smalley (New York, A. A. Knopf, 1949), pp. xl–xliv.

250. E.g., Richardson visited Spain in 1882. See H. R. Hitchcock Jr., *The Architecture of H. H. Richardson and His Times* (New York, Museum of Modern Art, 1936), p. 247.

251. Evidence of Richardson's visit to Spain appeared in the Albany Cathedral and the Pittsburgh jail! See *ibid.,* pp. 247 and 139–40. See also T. E. Tallmadge, *The Story of Architecture in America* (New York, W. W. Norton & Co. [1927]), p. 173; and Edgell, p. 37.

252. Possibly the first work on Spanish architecture printed in this country was a collection of loose plates published by George H. Polley and Co. in 1889 called *Spanish Architecture and Ornament.* See also J. A. Gade, *Cathedrals of Spain* (Boston, 1911). This book was based on G. E. Street's *Some Account of Gothic Architecture in Spain* (London, 1865), according to a reviewer in *NAR,*

194 (Aug., 1911), 313. G. G. King's *Way of Saint James* (New York, 1920), a wonderful blend of learning and insight, was followed by her posthumous *Heart of Spain*, ed. Agnes Mongan (Cambridge, Mass., 1941). This book was a record of a journey in 1926. Miss King published in 1914 an edition of Street's work, in which she attempted to report all the changes that had occurred since the original edition and to comment on whatever new facts scholarship had brought to light.

253. The present cathedral was announced by decree on October 8, 1536. For dates and other facts see Manuel Toussaint, *Catedral de México*, Colección Anáhuac de arte mexicano, 2 (México [1948]), 1–4. For superb illustrations, see the monumental monograph by the same author, *La Catedral de México y el sagrario metropolitano; su historia, su tesoro, su arte* (México, 1948).

254. See T. E. Sanford, *The Story of Architecture in Mexico* (New York, W. W. Norton & Co. [1947]), p. 218.

255. For authoritative accounts of the buildings of Santa Fe, see George Kubler, *The Religious Architecture of New Mexico in the Colonial Period and Since the American Occupation* (Colorado Springs, Taylor Museum, 1940), pp. 79–81, 100–2, 124–5, 147–8. See also Sanford, *Architecture of the Southwest*, pp. 90–5.

256. See Carey McWilliams, *North from Mexico* (Philadelphia, J. B. Lippincott Co., 1949), pp. 19–28.

257. Tallmadge, pp. 124–6. For a discussion of the relations of the baroque and the Churrigueresque, see Bernard Bevan, *History of Spanish Architecture* (London, B. T. Batsford, Ltd. [1938]), pp. 158–66. See also the exposition and the magnificent illustrations in the six-volume work of Gerardo Murillo, Manuel Toussaint, and others, *Iglesias de México* (México, 1924–27), *3*, "Tipos ultra-barrocos, Valle de México."

258. See the analysis of ultrabaroque by R. C. Taylor, "Francisco Hurtado and His School," *Art Bul., 32* (March, 1950), 25–61. "The neoclassical detractors of the Baroque joyfully seized upon this unusual polysyllabic name and from it coined the name *churrigueresque* to stigmatize the style they so heartily detested. The result is that today the whole style bears his name." *Ibid.*, p. 29.

259. See Tallmadge, pp. 124–5.

260. See *ibid.*

261. For discussion of the place of the Indian in relation to Spanish culture, see George Kubler, *Mexican Architecture of the Sixteenth Century* (New Haven, Yale University Press, 1948), especially chap. viii and Conclusion.

262. For recent discoveries of Franciscan architecture and painting, see R. G. Montgomery and others, *Franciscan Awatovi, the Excavation and Conjectural Reconstruction of a 17th-Century Spanish Mission Establishment* (Cambridge, Mass., 1949).

263. E.g., see Newcomb, *The Old Mission Churches*, pp. 234, 284, 298.

264. See E. O. Christensen, *The Index of American Design* (New York, Macmillan Co., 1950), pp. 28–9.

265. See Ruth Laughlin, *Caballeros* (Caldwell, Id., Caxton Printers, Ltd., 1945), p. 264.

266. See *ibid.*, p. 265.

267. *Ibid.*, pp. 266–7.

268. In 1945 there were some fifty weavers in Santa Fe, and in Chimayo a guild of weavers was at work. See *ibid.*, p. 258.

269. The use of wool was a Spanish contribution. Drawn-work was the occupation of gentlewomen. Examples are still found on lace-trimmed altar cloths and priests' surplices. "Savanillas" were homespun tapestries embroidered in wool and given on special anniversaries as altar hangings. See *ibid.*, pp. 261–3. For examples of baskets, stirrups, chairs, chests, etc., see Christensen, pp. 28–40.

270. Laughlin, pp. 250–2.

271. *Ibid.*, pp. 246–7.

272. *Ibid.*, pp. 247–8.

273. *Ibid.*, pp. 248–9.

274. See Hamlin, p. 22.

275. See Sanford, *Architecture of the Southwest*, p. 141. See also E. L. Hewett and R. G. Fisher, "Sanctuaries That Survived" in their *Mission Monuments of New Mexico* ([Albuquerque] University of New Mexico Press, 1943), pp. 103–34.

276. See Hamlin, p. 23.

277. *Ibid.*, p. 24. See, in particular, Duell, *Mission Architecture*.

278. See *Ramona*, chap. ii, for the descriptions of these American "pedlers," "traders," "American thieves," "hated Americans." In California as late as 1890 some of the American pioneer's contempt for everything connected with the defunct Spanish civilization still persisted, in the ignorance of even the vestiges of Spanish culture, such as mills, ditch-fences, "zanjas," cemeteries, homesteads, and other buildings. See C. H. Shinn, "Spanish Pioneer Houses of California," *Mag. Am. Hist.*, *33* (May, 1890), 353–60.

279. See *Old Santa Fe. Guide to the City and Vicinity, and to the Museum of New Mexico* ([Santa Fe], 1946), pp. 9–17. See also Sanford, *Architecture of the Southwest*, p. 91.

280. *Ibid.*, pp. 239–40.

281. Since 1910 there has been a "staunch regard for these fine old structures and a real desire to make them . . . the inspiration of new architectural work, both private and public." Newcomb, *Spanish-Colonial Architecture,* p. 36.

282. See *ibid.*, p. 37.

283. See Edgell, p. 217. For a description of Highland Park City Hall in Dallas, Tex., see *ibid.*, pp. 238–9. This style was well adapted for museums, as in the Fine Arts Building, Balboa Park, San Diego. See *ibid.*, pp. 252, 254.

284. See La Follette, pp. 278–9

285. See Hamlin, p. 221.

286. See *ibid.*, p. 233.

287. See *ibid.*

288. See H. R. Fairclough, "Classical Architecture of the Panama-Pacific Exposition," *Art and Archaeol.*, *3* (Jan., 1916), 5–19.

289. Some of our critics were lyrical in their praise of this "brave and laughing modernistic fantasy." See Hamlin, p. 221.

290. See Edgell, p. 61.

291. For a description of these Spanish buildings, see *ibid.*, pp. 64–6, and Hamlin, p. 235. The California building deserved study. Its dome was in

debt to the church at Taxco, its tower to structures in Cordova and Seville. See E. L. Hewett, "Ancient America at the Panama-California Exposition," *Art and Archaeol.*, 2 (Nov., 1915), 69, 71. The bridge is said to have been modeled after the great Alcántara Bridge at Toledo. C. M. Price, "The Panama-California Exposition, San Diego, California," *Arch. Rec.*, 37 (March, 1915), 244. See also Eugen Neuhaus, *The San Diego Garden Fair* (San Francisco [1916]), pp. 29–32.

292. The purpose of the exposition was to create a "Spanish city of flower-grown white surfaces, reflecting the sunlight and the history and the romance of Southern California." Price, p. 242. This article describes in detail the Spanish buildings.

293. R. S. Requa, *Inside Lights on the Building of San Diego's Exposition, 1935* ([San Diego, 1937]), p. 26.

294. See *Bertram Grosvenor Goodhue—Architect*, ed. C. H. Whitaker (New York, American Institute of Architects, 1925), p. 14.

295. See *ibid.*, p. 38. For suggestive lists of books on Spanish architecture which Goodhue studied, see *ibid.*, p. 15. He collaborated with Sylvester Baxter in writing *Spanish-Colonial Architecture of Mexico*. See Price, p. 240.

296. See American Institute of Architects, *The Journal*, 7 (April, Sept., 1924), 276, 404–5.

297. In 1905 Goodhue designed Trinity Church in Havana in the manner of Churriguera, with evident delight in outdoing the previous masters of this style. See Tallmadge, p. 260.

298. See C. H. Walker in *Bertram Grosvenor Goodhue*, p. 38.

299. See *ibid.*, pp. 257, 259–63.

300. See T. F. Hamlin, "What Makes It American?," *Pencil Points*, 20 (Dec., 1939), 767. Presumably it was these abuses of style which prompted one writer to describe the Spanish or Mexican fashion as "a deplorable architectural influence throughout the region." See McWilliams, p. 73. See also I. F. Morrow, "Spanish," *Arch. Rec.*, 74 (Oct., 1928), 345.

301. Quoted by McWilliams, p. 73.

302. Charles Rollo Peters (1862–1928) loved to make paintings of these ancient buildings. In a sense he shared the Spanish revivals in both painting and architecture. See Neuhaus, *The History & Ideals of American Art*, p. 243.

303. Newcomb, *Spanish-Colonial Architecture*, p. 37. For the Spanish revival in Florida, see the 184 large plates in *Florida Architecture of Addison Mizner* (New York [1928]).

304. See *Am. Arch.*, 129 (Jan. 5, 1926), 78. John Carrère and Thomas Hastings encouraged a return to the Spanish traditions. See Fiske Kimball, *American Architecture* (Indianapolis, Bobbs-Merrill Co. [1928]), p. 129.

305. See Edgell, pp. 106–9. This book describes other residences in Florida in the Spanish-American style. See also Kimball, pp. 206–7.

306. See Newcomb, *Spanish-Colonial Architecture*, p. 37.

307. It must be remembered that a series of fires destroyed large parts of eighteenth-century New Orleans. See Tallmadge, p. 132.

308. *Ibid.*, pp. 131–9.

309. See the description of this building in *"Griego-Romano* Type of Herrara [sic] and the Spanish Classicists," Tallmadge, p. 133.

431

310. Newcomb, *Spanish-Colonial Architecture,* p. 37.

311. See Duell, *Mission Architecture,* pp. 2, 38, 126–7 (list of Texas missions). Mexican life, as in the market on Saturday evenings in San Antonio, is still a distinct influence. In this city are houses in the mission style and also in that of the Greek revival.

312. See Hamlin, *American Spirit in Architecture,* p. 23. See also C. M. Brooks Jr., *Texas Missions, Their Romance and Architecture* (Dallas, 1936), and J. S. Hildrup, *The Missions of California and the Old Southwest* (Chicago, 1909), pp. 91–5.

313. Hamlin, p. 24.

314. See Newcomb, *Spanish-Colonial Architecture,* pp. 37–8.

315. See Laughlin, chap. v, "Pueblo-Spanish Architecture," and chap. vi, "Old Castles in Spain," pp. 119–61. "The Indians gave it sculptured mass, plastic lines and indented doorways. The Spanish added the nave and transept in the form of the cross in their churches and the fortress compound in their one-storied palaces." See p. 124.

316. Nina Otero, *Old Spain in Our Southwest* (New York, Harcourt, Brace & Co. [1936]), p. 64.

317. See Newcomb, *Spanish-Colonial Architecture,* p. 38. Examples of the new are the Museum of New Mexico or the Laboratory of Anthropology. The architecture of this region, though it attracts tourists, is freer than Florida or California from the cheapening pressures of the real-estate and moving-picture industries. See *ibid.*

318. For an account of Willa Cather's residence in New Mexico, see Pearce, *The Beloved House,* p. 176. Her first stay was in 1913. See above, p. 244.

319. The other building is the Church of San Miguel. See Sanford, *Architecture of the Southwest,* pp. 93–4.

320. See Writers' Program, New Mexico, *New Mexico. A Guide to the Colorful State* (Albuquerque, University of New Mexico Press, 1945), pp. 198–9. See also E. L. Hewett and W. L. Mauzy, *Landmarks of New Mexico* ([Albuquerque], University of New Mexico Press [1940]), p. 22; and for many illustrations, *Art and Archaeol.,* 7 (Jan. and Feb., 1918).

321. See Laughlin, p. 143.

322. See *ibid.,* p. 147.

323. See *ibid.,* pp. 148–9.

324. See *ibid.,* p. 149.

325. See *ibid.,* p. 157.

326. See *ibid.,* pp. 159–60.

327. Examples of the true Arizona manner are not numerous. One instance is the remodeled Cathedral of Saint Augustine at Tucson. See Newcomb, *Spanish-Colonial Architecture,* p. 38. For a discussion of Arizona styles, see Writer's Program, Arizona, *Arizona. A State Guide* (New York, Hastings House, 1940), pp. 141–6. In this book are described San Xavier del Bac and San José de Tumacácori; the University of Arizona, the Methodist Church, and the Pioneer Hotel (Tucson); and Trinity Episcopal Church (Phoenix).

328. San Juan Capistrano is architecturally advanced but lacking in Christian symbolism. "According to local tradition," its master mason was an Aztec! Santa Barbara is notable for its stations of the cross and its paintings. Carmel

has a doorway at once Moorish, Gothic, and plateresque Renaissance. See Tallmadge, pp. 128–9.

329. Much modern Spanish architecture has been undistinguished. There were the popular "Monterey" buildings, whose character had been determined by the Pacific winds, the hot days, and the available materials. See Hamlin, "What Makes It American?," pp. 768–70. See also the description of "simple forms" and "a modern Hispanic architecture" in Newcomb, *Spanish-Colonial Architecture*, pp. 38–9.

330. See *ibid.*

331. The house of Herbert Coppell (designed by Goodhue); Thomas H. Ince's "Dias Dorados" at Beverley Hills; W. T. Jefferson's home at Pasadena. These are some of the examples cited by G. H. Edgell, pp. 103–6. See also Hamlin, *American Spirit in Architecture*, pp. 270–1, 335; and Porter Garnett, *Stately Homes of California* (Boston, 1915), pp. 21–9, 45–61.

332. See the description of the Los Angeles Biltmore, with its ornate lobby in the Spanish style, in Edgell, p. 340, and of the Van Nuys building in the same city, *ibid.*, p. 311. This hotel might be compared with the Franciscan in Albuquerque, which is in the pueblo style on a large scale. See *ibid.*, p. 340.

333. Hamlin, *American Spirit in Architecture*, p. 320.

334. See *ibid.*, p. 244.

335. See G. E. Hale, "The National Academy of Sciences," *Bertram Grosvenor Goodhue*, p. 46.

336. See "The Bells of San Gabriel," *Poems of Charles Warren Stoddard*, ed. Ina Coolbrith (New York, J. Lane Co., 1917), pp. 21–4.